Basic Accounting

Concepts, Principles, and Procedures

Second Edition

Volume 1

Building the Conceptual Foundation

Basic Accounting

Concepts, Principles, and Procedures
Second Edition

Volume 1

Building the Conceptual Foundation

Gregory Mostyn
Mission College

Worthy & James Publishing

Before you buy or use this book, you should understand . . .

Disclaimer: If you decide to use this book, then you agree and understand that this book is designed to provide you only general educational instruction and support in basic accounting principles. This book should be used with the understanding that the author, publisher, and contributors do not solicit herein, and are not providing, accounting, financial, tax, legal, or any other kind of professional services. If professional services are needed, competent professional advice should be sought and obtained from other sources and other parties. Although every effort has been made to make this book as relevant, useful, and accurate as possible up to the date of printing, the book may contain errors and omissions. Moreover, the author and publisher make no guarantees or warranties, express or implied, and shall have neither liability nor responsibility, even if advised of such possibility, for any loss or damage either caused or alleged to be caused, directly or indirectly, by the use of this book.

Except for actual companies whose real identity is made clear within the context of the text, all characters, organizations, and entities in this book are completely fictional, and any resemblance to actual persons, organizations, or entities, past or present, is purely coincidental.

Cataloging-in-Publication Data
Mostyn, Gregory R.
Basic accounting. Volume 1, Building the conceptual foundation / Gregory Mostyn.
p. cm.
Includes index.
"Concepts, principles, and procedures."
LCCN 2006940449
ISBN-13: 978-0-9914231-0-1
ISBN-10: 0-9914231-0-0
Previous edition cataloged as follows:
1. Accounting. I. Title.

HF5636.M67 2007 657'.042
QBI07-600006

Worthy & James Publishing
P.O. Box 360215
Milpitas, CA 95036
www.worthyjames.com

Suggestions, questions, comments, criticism? E-mail us: inquiry@worthyjames.com

To my parents, Bob and Melita, who by word and deed
have taught me the value of lifelong learning

And

Daisy, who has always been exactly right about
the importance of long walks in the park

BRIEF Contents

SECTION VII FINANCIAL STATEMENT ANALYSIS

SECTION VIII PARTNERSHIPS

Contents

Preface

Basic Accounting Concepts, Principles, and Procedures provides a new pedagogical approach for introductory accounting. The content does not begin with a focus on the accounting profession and introductory accounting procedures. Instead, the text first explains the basic concepts and structure of a business to create a meaningful context for the accounting concepts that follow. The conversational, relaxed approach is built on a research-based instructional design that improves comprehension and retention, and minimizes stress. The system's special design becomes immediately apparent by viewing the appearance of the material.

As any experienced accounting instructor can relate, accounting knowledge is very much a building-block architecture. Accounting skills rest on the foundation of critical basic concepts. Instructors know that introductory accounting students who miss the early concepts seldom successfully complete a course. ***Basic Accounting Concepts, Principles, and Procedures***, particularly Volume 1, is specifically designed to address this weakness in traditional texts, in which *early foundation concepts receive no greater emphasis than later content.* These two volumes provide the reader with guidance that strongly reinforces key foundation concepts, particularly those that beginning students often find most difficult. Volume 1, for example, places great emphasis on building a clear understanding of transaction analysis. In Volume 2, each type of adjusting entry is reinforced in a separate appendix to the adjusting entries learning goal. This approach provides special emphasis for key concepts as well as for difficult concepts and is applied to all topics. In our experience, this builds the confidence that assures future progress and creates curiosity about the value (and shortcomings) of accounting. At the same time, the flexibility of the design allows readers to move quickly through the parts of the material with which they are comfortable.

Particularly in Volume 2, Applying Principles and Procedures, the reader will also benefit from real-world practical help. Some examples are: what to do if a bank reconciliation will not balance, how to handle partial payments, a checklist for an accounting software purchase, and how to identify the hidden costs of accounting software.

Basic Accounting Concepts, Principles, and Procedures is a complete self-study package. The two volumes contain full coverage of the traditional first accounting principles course plus a complete first-course coverage of corporate accounting and financial statements analysis. The importance of ethics in business and accounting is reinforced by exposition as well as by articles and questions, including Internet exercises.

The disk included with each volume contains detailed solutions to learning goal questions and problems, a complete basic math review with problems and solutions, and templates that provide an unlimited supply of various types of accounting paper, worksheets, journals, and ledgers.

About the Author

Greg Mostyn is an accounting instructor at Mission College, Santa Clara, California. He is a member of the American Accounting Association and American Institute of Certified Public Accountants. He has served as accounting department chairman and has extensive experience in accounting curriculum design and course development. He has authored several books and published articles in the areas of learning theory and its application to accounting instruction, textbook use, and accounting education research.

Acknowledgments

No book can ever be written alone. I wish to especially acknowledge the following individuals for their excellent suggestions, useful criticism, and creative ideas. They have fixed mistakes and generously shared their wisdom in more ways than I can describe.

William Bernacchi, CPA, MBA
William E. Bjork, JD, CPA, MBA
Randy Castello, CPA, MBA
Jennifer Chadwick, CPA, EA, MBA
Betty Paine Christopher, CMA, CFP, EA, MBA
George Dorrance, CPA, MBA
Magdy Farag, Ph.D., MBA
Richard Hobbs, MA
John Hui, CPA, MPA
Ching-Lih Jan, Ph.D., MAS, MBA
John Koeplin, Ph.D., CPA, MA, MBA
Christopher Kwak, CPA, MBA
Shellie Mueller, MBA
Jose Nava, CPA, MBA
Ernestine Porter, CPA, MBA
Howard Randall, CPA (retired), MBA
Diana Smith, CPA, MBA
Teresa Thompson, CPA, MBA
James Van Tassel, Ph.D., MBA
Guoli Zhang, MA, MS

Cover Design: David Ruppe, Impact Publications
Interior Design: Mark Ong
Typesetting: MPS Limited

Cover Images

Skyline: Stockbyte/Getty Images
Basketball Players: Jim Cummins/Taxi/Getty Images
Office: Stockbyte/Getty Images
Golden Gate Bridge: Andrew Gunners/Digital Vision/Getty Images
Market: David Buffington/Photodisc/Getty Images

How to Use This Book

MANY RESOURCES FOR YOU	
Enhanced or standard	You can begin your study of accounting with a special **enhanced** introduction or a **standard** introduction. See the next page.
"Overviews" and "quick reviews"	■ Each *section* has an overview to direct you to the parts of the book that are most important for you. Be sure to read each section "overview" when you come to it. ■ Each *learning goal* has a short overview of the content of the goal. Read this overview before you begin. Then, after you study a learning goal, read the "quick review" and "vocabulary."
Answers to questions and problems	All the learning goal questions and problems in this book (except for Internet exercises and instructor-assigned problems) have detailed solutions. These solutions are in the computer disk that is located on the inside back cover of this book. **Solutions are also available at www.worthyjames.com**
Cumulative tests	This book includes cumulative tests with answers after each test. Each test also has a **Help Table.** After you check the answers, use the **Help Table** to specifically identify your strong and weak knowledge areas. Use this for review.
Accounting paper	The disk at the back of the book contains a complete selection of all types of accounting paper that you can use for the solution of any problem type in the book. You can print out an unlimited supply of accounting paper by using the disk. **Accounting paper is also available at www.worthyjames.com**
Complete basic math review	The disk at the back of the book also contains a comprehensive, step-by-step math review beginning at the most basic level. The review contains many types of problems, all with solutions. The review continues on the disk for Volume 2 with fractions, ratios, and basic algebra.

Enhanced Introduction or Standard Introduction?

How to Begin This Book

Two Ways To Begin

This book provides you two ways to begin your study of accounting. You can begin with a very gradual and detailed introduction beginnning on page 3 (Learning Goals 1–9). Instead of this, you can begin with the standard type of introduction beginning on page 217 with learning goal 10.

If you are using this book for a class, your instructor will assign what is best for the content of your class. Be sure to ask your instructor if you have any questions or want advice.

The introduction and early material of a first accounting class are very important. This is because the rest of your accounting study depends upon a clear understanding of the early concepts.

Using The Enhanced Introduction

The enhanced introduction in this book introduces you to essential business and accounting concepts in a simple, step-by-step process. You may want to use the enhanced introduction if:

- you prefer to study the information more slowly, in smaller amounts
- you prefer more practice that is in smaller steps
- you want a more detailed explanation of concepts

If you use the enhanced introduction you should allow more study time. If you can, also allow yourself time to review the material in the standard introduction after you complete the enhanced introduction.

Using The Standard Introduction

The standard introduction allows you to begin more quickly. It contains the same accounting concepts as the enhanced introduction but in a more condensed presentation, and does not review basic business concepts. You may want the standard introduction if:

- your time is limited
- you are in a class that usually begins with this type of introduction
- you want to study more quickly than with the enhanced introduction.

YOU CAN USE BOTH!

- If you are beginning with the **standard introduction** you can select parts of the enhanced introduction to give you extra review or explanation.
- Alternatively, you can begin with the **enhanced introduction** and then decide to move to the standard introduction when you feel ready or as a review.

How to Study Accounting

Overview

Acquire a Balanced Understanding

Accounting is a system of activities that analyzes, processes, and communicates and interprets financial information about a business or other entity. If you wish to acquire a clear understanding of this system, you will need to spend some time studying three important areas of accounting knowledge:

- how a business operates
- analyzing and processing business data
- communicating and interpreting financial reports

Each of these areas is very important in its own right and should not be underestimated. For example, an understanding of:

- "how a business operates" is needed by accountants, business owners, managers, management consultants, operations specialists, investors, and lenders.
- "analyzing and processing business data" is needed in bookkeeping, auditing, and information system use (or design), especially in new "intranet" systems that integrate all kinds of accounting and other information.
- "communicating and interpreting financial reports" is important for accountants and managers. Interpreting financial reports is also very important for business owners, investors, bankers, voters, union members, and everyone and anyone with a financial or social interest in business and the economy.

At some point in your future career, you might become a specialist or be involved in work that is related to any of the three areas just mentioned. However, because all of these areas interact with and affect each other and because you cannot be entirely sure where your career will take you, it is wise to be sure that you acquire some working knowledge in each area. This book and other good introductory accounting textbooks introduce you to each of these areas in a balanced and careful way.

Study Techniques for Students

Overview

The following suggestions are study tips that really work. Each additional one that you are able to consistently use is "money in the bank" toward success in your accounting study.

Study Techniques for Students, *continued*

Consistent Study in Small Amounts

This is probably the *most important and powerful technique* of all. For a great many people, it is also the most difficult to apply. Many people often put off a task until a large block of time becomes available. This is very inefficient, for the following reasons:

- Large blocks of time do not frequently become available.
- You can learn only a limited amount before you become tired.
- You will not have frequent repetition, which is essential.

Rule: Use any small amount of time and **give yourself permission to stop after doing only one or two small things.** You can do more, but always make it acceptable to stop after a small period of time **because you will use another small period of time soon.** You will be surprised at how this method of using many small time periods eases anxiety and increases your cumulative output.

Join or Form a Study Group

Controlled research studies have demonstrated that students who belong to a study group perform significantly better in class than those students who are not in study groups. Whether the group is small or large, meet regularly. It will make you feel much better.

Know What You Don't Know

Always be very aware of what you don't understand. As you are reading (or listening), be aware of *exactly where* the confusion or uncertainty begins. Make a note, so you can develop a list of "confusion points." Then you can focus on these particular items that you know will give you trouble.

Do Not Miss Any Classes

Even if you have the most boring, record-setting, dullest teacher in the history of education, keep going to class. You will pick up important class content by just being aware of the subjects that the teacher likes to emphasize: this alone will give you clues for exams. More likely though, you will also pick up important explanations that will save you a great deal of study time.

Ask, Ask, ASK!

You have probably heard this a million times: "Never be afraid to ask questions." We are always anxious about looking foolish or ignorant, but remember this: you are putting in your valuable time, effort, and money on this subject! Your teacher *owes you* the best and most patient explanation possible, or he or she is not doing the best job possible.

If a teacher acts impatient or rushed, maybe that person is just busy at the moment. Politely suggest another time, but be persistent. (Persistence is always a good habit to develop anyway.)

continued ▶

Examination Strategy

- Do *not* begin to work on the first question immediately.
- *Do* scan the test. If the test has individual problems, find a problem that:
    - you know how to solve, AND
    - is worth a lot of points.

Work these kinds of problems **first!** By doing this, you know that you are getting the most points as fast as possible. This will *relax* you and give you *confidence*. This way you will perform and think better when you do the other problems.

Mistakes Are Not a Disaster!

Sad but true, we often learn the most by making mistakes. (In a class, the best idea is to make most of your mistakes on homework, where they will hurt you the least.) However, even the occasional bad exam score can serve as good motivation. Mistakes and failure can almost always serve as guides to success, but you must be smart enough to see that this is how things work in the world.

Before You Begin . . .

'Read "How to Use This Book" on page xvii.'

SECTION I

What Is a Business?

OVERVIEW

What this section does	This section begins the enhanced step-by-step introduction to accounting, beginning with the fundamental features of a business: ▪ purpose ▪ how a business operates ▪ basic financial structure ▪ economic entities ▪ ownership types
Use this section if . . .	. . . you are unfamiliar with *any* of the features above and you want the enhanced introduction (see prior page xviii).
Do not use this section if . . .	. . . you want the standard introduction (page 217).

LEARNING GOALS

"Welcome to the territory of business!"

LEARNING GOAL 1

Explain What a Business Is and What It Does

Welcome

Speak the Language of Business . . .

Welcome! Thank you for selecting me as your guide in this part of your journey through the territory of business and commerce. To prosper in this territory and to enjoy your journey, you will need to learn the languages of the region. The most important language to learn is called "accounting."

When educated people in this region want to describe a business or explain what has happened to it, they often use the language of accounting. When you use this book, you will be carefully and thoroughly trained in the fundamentals of this language.

. . . But First Learn What a Business Is

A common dilemma for beginning accounting students is the double burden of struggling to learn accounting while at the same time being expected to understand what a "business" is—the thing that the accounting is trying to describe. The student is expected to learn what a business is by having to learn the language that describes it. This would be like me telling you, in a new language, all the details about some beautiful tree even though you are not exactly sure what a tree is.

I suggest that we try something more interesting and fun. Instead of beginning right away with the details of accounting, let's first take a little time to understand what a business is and how it operates. After that, accounting discussions will make more sense to you.

If you decide to extend your study of accounting, you will later learn that, with small modifications, accounting can also be used to describe non-business activities, such as governments and charities. However, business is where accounting is used the most.

Important

You are beginning the enhanced introduction to this book's content. Be sure to read prior page xviii before you begin your reading.

In Learning Goal 1, you will find:

Identify a Business

Business Characteristics

Definition: A Business

A "business" is an organization with the primary goal of accumulating wealth by creating valuable new resources and selling them to customers.

Note: Valuable resources have a dollar value, so they are also called ***economic resources.***

Examples of businesses . . .	Desired resource created . . .
An automobile manufacturer	Automobiles
An automobile dealer	A selection of automobiles to buy
A veterinarian	Medical services for animals
An accounting firm	Accounting and tax services
A movie theater	Entertainment
A bakery	Delicious bread and desserts

Business Characteristics, *continued*

Not a Business

- A public university (primary purpose is not accumulating wealth)
- A charitable organization (primary purpose is not accumulating wealth)
- A city government (primary goal is public service, not accumulating wealth)

Important Difference

Government or nonprofit organizations (such as charities) do carry on business-like activities such as detailed record-keeping, paying bills, incurring expenses, commercial transactions, and so on. However, because the primary goal of these organizations is not the accumulation of wealth, none of them is called a "business."

The Two Kinds of Resources

Overview

Only two kinds of resources can be created: property and services.

Property and Services

A business creates and sells valuable resources that people want. Only two possible kinds of resources can be created and sold:

- ***Property:*** Any resource that can be *owned*. Property generally (but not always) has a dollar value. Examples are a computer, a book, or a car.
- ***Services:*** The *use of* labor or the *use of* someone else's property. Services generally (but not always) have a dollar value. Examples are repairing a truck, delivering a pizza, giving financial advice, teaching a class, renting out a copy machine, or renting out an apartment.

Synonym

Property and services are often referred to as "goods and services."

Classifying a Business

Classify by Type of Resource Created

- A *service business* creates services. Examples of services are repairs, communication, legal advice, entertainment, and health care.
- A *merchandising business* offers a convenient selection of merchandise to customers. Merchandising businesses do not make products. Examples of merchandising businesses are a grocery store, a bookstore, a clothing store, and an automobile dealer.
- A *manufacturing business* creates new property. Examples are an automobile manufacturer, a food manufacturer, and a computer manufacturer.

Combined Types

It is not unusual for one business to combine activities. Examples are an automobile dealer (a merchandiser) that may also do repairs (services), or a bakery (a manufacturer) that may also sell to the public (a merchandiser).

Business Operations

What Is Wealth?

Overview

Because the primary goal of a business is to accumulate wealth, it is important to understand exactly what "wealth" means in business language.

Wealth Defined

Wealth is property that has a dollar value.

The Idea of Wealth

"Wealth" refers to the *dollar value* characteristic of property. If the property is in the form of money, its value is easy to know, and it can be used to buy things and pay debts. Other property that has value, but that is not money, can be sold or exchanged for money (example: selling equipment).

Although most property is also physically useful (like equipment), the concept of wealth ignores this utility and focuses only on the dollar value.

Wealth is important because its value can be used to acquire any other resource.

"I'm bored. Let's go into business!"

What Is Wealth, *continued*

Wealth Examples

- Money
- Equipment that you could sell for $500
- ***Account receivable*** (the *legal right* to collect money from a customer)
- Shares of stock that you could sell
- Clothing for sale in a store
- Land that is worth $100,000
- A car that you can sell for $5,000
- A calculator that you can sell for $5
- Office supplies worth $900

Note: All of these examples have dollar value *and* can be owned.

Not Wealth

This item . . .	is not wealth because . . .
Old broken equipment that no one wants	it has no value.
Shares of stock in a bankrupt business	it has no value.
Food that is spoiled and dangerous	it has no value.
The services of an employee	a service cannot be owned (because it is immediately consumed).
The telephone service you receive	a service cannot be owned (because it is immediately consumed).
The financial advice that you receive from an accountant	a service cannot be owned (because it is immediately consumed)..
The rental of a computer	a service cannot be owned (because it is immediately consumed).

Property and Services Compared

The table below helps you compare property and services, and indicates whether or not they can be called wealth.

Resource	Useful?	Can it have dollar value?	Can it be wealth?
Services	Yes	Yes	No, because it cannot be owned.
Property	Yes	Yes	Yes, because it can be owned.

Coming Up Next . . .

Exactly *how* does a business operate so that it can accumulate wealth?

Check Your Understanding

Write the completed sentences on a separate piece of paper. The answers are below.

A business is an organization that creates and sells new resources and that has the primary goal of accumulating · · · · · · · ·. This is property that has a dollar · · · · · · · ·.

Only two kinds of resources can be created and sold. They are · · · · · · · · and · · · · · · · ·. Only · · · · · · · · can be wealth because it can be owned.

Answers

A business is an organization that creates and sells new resources and that has the primary goal of accumulating wealth. This is property that has a dollar value.

Only two kinds of resources can be created and sold. They are property and services. Only property can be wealth because it can be owned.

How a Business Accumulates Wealth

Overview

A business accumulates wealth by creating and selling goods or services (resources) that people (customers) need. Because these resources have value, the business is paid other valuable property by the customers. A business creates value!

Examples

The table below shows you some examples of how a business creates resources and accumulates wealth.

A business does this:	so it created the valuable resource of . . .	and the business accumulates wealth because . . .
performs computer repairs for $300	computer repairs (service)	the customer pays $300 cash for the value of the repairs received
shows a movie	entertainment (service)	the customers pay for the value of the tickets and to be entertained
makes and sells 1,000 loaves of fresh bread	loaves of bread (property)	it receives money for the value of the bread
makes and sells 100 new computers for $200,000	computers (property)	the customers pay $200,000 cash for the value of the computers
operates a grocery store that sells 1,000 loaves of bread and other foods	providing a selection of bread and other foods (service)	the customers pay the store for the value of the food and the service provided

How a Business Creates a New Resource

Overview

Now you know that a business creates and sells new resources, but that does not explain *how* a business creates the new resources. The discussion coming up tells you how that is done.

Resources Are Used Up

A business creates valuable new resources by using up other valuable resources. In other words, a business creates new property and services by using up other property and services.

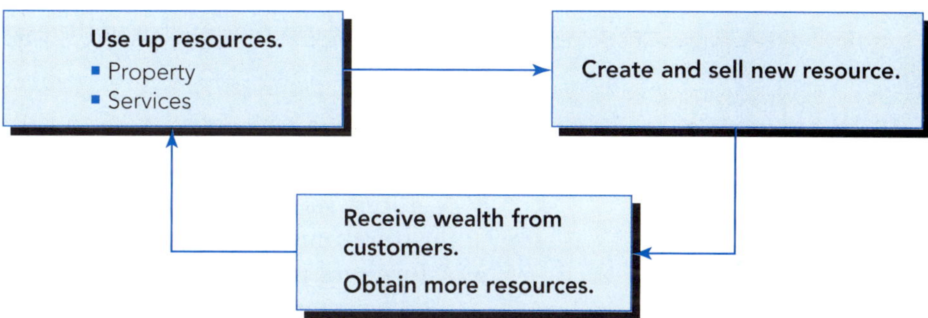

In the table below, notice that the only two kinds of resources used up are property and services, in order to create new and different property or services.

Business action:	The resource created is . . .	and examples of resources used up by the business are . . .
Richland Bakery makes and sells 1,000 loaves of fresh bread.	1,000 loaves of bread, a resource, which did not exist until it was produced,	the flour, water, and other ingredients of the bread dough; employee and manager labor; the equipment wear and tear.
Brookhaven grocery store sells the bread to shoppers.	the service of providing access to a selection of different breads,	employee and manager labor; electricity for light, heat, and power; the bread that the store had to purchase in order to sell.
El Paso Company manufactures 100 new computers.	a computer, which did not exist until it was manufactured,	employee and manager labor; metal and plastic components in the computer; the air and water of the city where the business is located.
Your local theater group presents Shakespeare's "Hamlet."	the service of entertainment,	the rental of the theater; the use of actors' labor; the wear and tear on the costumes.

continued ▶

How a Business Creates a New Resource, *continued*

Business Term: Expenses

People in business have a name for the dollar amount of a resource consumed in the operations that create a new resource. The *dollar cost* of any resource used up in the process of creating a new resource is called an ***expense.***

> *Note:* "Used up" or "consumed" means not replaced by any other resource.

It does not make any difference what kind of resource is consumed. Services, supplies, equipment, merchandise, or any other kind of resource can be used up to create a new resource. Whatever the cost of the resource consumed, that is the amount of the expense.

Examples of Expenses

- $100 of office supplies used up is called "Office Supplies Expense."
- $2,000 value of employees' services is called "Wages Expense."
- A grocery store buys bread for a cost of $500. When the bread is sold to the store's customers, the store has $500 "Cost of Sales Expense."
- A furniture maker uses wood, nails, and fabric to make chairs. When the chairs are sold, the cost of these materials are "Cost of Sales Expense."
- The value of advertising services is called "Advertising Expense."

Not Expenses

- A business uses up $10,000 to pay off a bank loan. This is not an expense because paying a debt is not part of the process of creating a new resource for customers.
- A business gives up $100 cash to buy $100 of supplies. This is not an expense because one resource is simply replacing another (supplies for cash). Total value of resources remains the same.

How Much Value Is Created?

Overview

The entire purpose of using up resources is to create a new resource *that is valuable.* A business does not want to create something that has little or no value because no one will buy it. A business tries hard to create as much value as it can for every dollar of resources used up.

How Much Value Is Created? *continued*

Added Value

The total dollar value of a new resource that a business creates is called the ***added value***. The process of incurring expenses to create a new valuable resource is sometimes called *adding value.*

The table below shows you some examples of added value and the expenses that create it.

The resource created:	so the added value is . . .	and value was added by incurring expenses such as . . .
Blinn Bakery makes *muffins* that can be sold for $1 each,	$1 each,	Wages Expense, Supplies Expense, and Cost of Sales Expense.
Blinn Bakery makes *walnut muffins* that can be sold for $1.25 each,	$1.25 each,	walnuts, which increased expense, but also increased the added value by $.25 per muffin.
Laredo Plumbing Service does *plumbing repairs* and charges the customer $375 for the job,	$375 for the job,	Labor Expense and Parts Expense.
Computers are manufactured by San Antonio Company. A computer can be sold for $1,000,	$1,000 each,	Labor Expense, Utility Expense, Rent Expense, Supplies Expense, and Cost of Sales Expense.
Kilgore Nursery offers *a selection* of young pine trees for $20 each,	$20 each,	Utilities Expense, Fertilizer Expense, and Labor Expense.

Warning to Businesses!

Expenses Do Not Always Add Value

As you have seen in the examples, a business consumes resources because it is trying to create added value. Unfortunately, while producing a new resource, businesses often consume resources that actually create very little or even no value. These expenses are wasted because little or no value is added. The customer will not pay for the amount of these expenses as part of the price of the resource created. A successful business eliminates as much of this nonvalue-added resource consumption as possible.

continued ▶

How Much Value Is Created? *continued*

Examples of NO Value Added

The resource created:	The business has this expense:	and the expense does not add value because . . .
Jones Company manufactures and sells a computer.	$10,000 for *storing the computers* before they are sold,	customers do not want to pay more just because the company made too many computers and had to pay for storage.
Jones Company manufactures and sells a computer.	the company president *uses the company airplane* to fly his dog back and forth between New York and Los Angeles,	the cost of these flights, and wear and tear on the airplane, do not make the computers more useful or valuable to customers. Using the company airplane in this way will not add value, even though it makes the dog happy.
Jones Company manufactures and sells a computer.	$25,000 *labor time* required to repair manufacturing mistakes,	customers do not want to pay for the cost of fixing new merchandise. Customers want a product that works properly the first time.

"Really? And just how much value do you add with that stupid flag?"

How Much Value Is Created? *continued*

Added Value Is Difficult to Predict

In reality, the amount of added value that a business creates is only an educated guess until the resource is actually sold. A business can never be completely sure of the total added value until it sells what it has created. It is the customer who finally determines the actual added value by purchasing the resource and paying for it.

Regardless of how carefully a business designs or sells the resource it creates, "value" is still just a feeling in the mind of the customer—a feeling that can change at any time. Moreover, customers are different, and some customers perceive value differently than others.

Here are some interesting examples of how added value can be unpredictable:

If a company . . .	**then we would guess that the added value will be . . .**	**because . . .**
uses higher quality parts in the toasters it makes,	probably greater than before	many people want improved reliability and quality and will pay more for it.
offers Christmas tree ornaments for sale on December 1 for $25 each,	$25 each	customers are willing to pay this amount because they are excited about Christmas and want new ornaments.
offers the same Christmas ornaments on February 1 for $25 each,	probably a lot less than $25 each	people are not so excited about Christmas anymore. Changing the time of the year reduced the total amount of added value.
angers potential customers because it damages the environment,	anywhere from a little less to a lot less than before	people become so angry that they refuse to purchase the company products. (This actually happens. For example, customers boycotted tuna products until tuna sellers agreed to stop killing dolphins in tuna nets.)
pays for a big advertising promotion for a product, although not changing the product in any way,	probably greater	even though the product itself has not changed, it may have improved in the *minds* of the customers! Resources used for repeated advertising can add significant value, even if a product is actually unchanged.

continued ▶

How Much Value Is Created? *continued*

The Value Chain

Every business has a value chain. The ***value chain*** is the sequence of all the activities that consume resources for the purpose of adding value. Together, all the expenses in the value chain result in the total cost of all resources consumed.

> *Note:* The term "value chain" may be a little misleading because, as we know now, all resources consumed do not always add value.

Example of Value Chain

Bad Apple Cider Company has to pay for fertilizer, water, and labor to maintain the apple trees. Then it pays for processing the apples into cider. After that, it pays for the cost of distributing and selling the cider. During all of these operations, the business also pays for the cost of management.

Question for the owner: Do all parts of this value chain add significant value?

Check Your Understanding

Write the completed sentences on a separate piece of paper. The answers are below.

A business accumulates wealth by creating and selling new resources. New resources can only be created when a business uses up other · · · · · · · ·. The business term for the dollar cost of resources used up for this purpose is · · · · · · · ·.

The dollar value of the new resources that a business creates is called · · · · · · · · · · · · · · · ·. This is usually (easy/difficult) · · · · · · · · to precisely predict. As a general rule, (all/not all) · · · · · · · · expenses will add significant value.

Answers

A business accumulates wealth by creating and selling new resources. New resources can only be created when a business uses up other resources. The business term for the dollar cost of resources used up for this purpose is expense.

The dollar value of the new resources that a business creates is called added value. This is usually difficult to precisely predict. As a general rule, not all expenses will add significant value.

Confirming the Value Created

Overview

You know that added value is difficult to predict. The point at which a business finally knows exactly how much total value has been created is when a sale is made to a customer.

Confirming the Value Created, *continued*

Business Term: Revenue

When a business actually makes a sale to a customer, the true total of added value is confirmed. Businesspeople have a special name for the "confirmed" added value: revenue. ***Revenue*** is the dollar value of a sale. It is the amount the customer pays for the resource created.

Example #1 of Revenue

Blinn Bakery incurs expenses and makes 100 muffins that can be sold for $1 each. So far, the company has sold 70 muffins for a total of $70.

- The total amount of added value that the company believes has been created is $100 because 100 muffins normally sell for that amount.
- The total revenue is $70 because this is the actual dollar value of sales up to now. The company has received $70 from customers. This means that $70 of added value has been confirmed so far.

Example #2 of Revenue

Vancouver Company makes glazed clay pots for gardens. The company incurs expenses to make 20 blue pots and offers the pots for sale at $10 each, based on past experience. So the added value of the 20 pots *appears to be* $200.

- The company sells 10 of the clay pots, so it has $100 of revenue. This confirms the added value of 10 clay pots as $100.
- However, the company is unable to sell the remaining 10 clay pots and must reduce the price to $8 per pot. At this price, all the remaining pots are sold. The company has $80 of revenue for the remaining 10 pots, thus confirming their added value.

The total revenue of $180 for all 20 pots confirms that their real added value is actually $180. (The company has received $180 in wealth from customers.)

Example #3 of Revenue

Artie, the golf pro, owns the golf shop next to the municipal golf course. Artie offers golf lessons for $100 per hour. Artie sold 20 hours of golf instruction this month. Artie says, "The business earned $2,000 of instruction revenue." This means that the business wealth increased by $2,000 because the business created and sold $2,000 of added value in the form of golf instruction.

Not Revenue

- Burnaby Company collected $10,000 from a bank loan. This money is not revenue because it does not come from making a sale. It must be repaid.
- The owner of Surrey Company invests $10,000 in his business. This money is not revenue because it does not come from making a sale.

continued ▶

Confirming the Value Created, *continued*

Do Not Confuse Revenue with Wealth

"Revenue" refers to the dollar amount of a sale. Making a sale is one particular source of wealth.

"Wealth" is the dollar value of the *property* that is received from the sale. This property could be anything—cash, accounts receivable, gold, supplies, land—although, in reality, wealth from making a sale is almost always in the form of cash or accounts receivable.

Success or Failure?

Two Requirements for Success

To be successful, a business must do two things:

- It must create value.
- It must be sure that the cost of the resources consumed are less than the value created.

The owners and managers of businesses must determine which combination of resources adds the most value. This is not easy to do because, as we have seen, the amount of value added is only an estimate until whatever is created is actually sold. Then, the managers must also be sure that resources consumed do not exceed the total value added.

Example of Combining Resources

Bad Apple Cider Company makes and sells apple cider. The company makes 200 gallons of apple cider that the managers estimate can be sold for $10 per gallon, an added value of $2,000. When the cider is actually sold, the company has $2,000 of revenue, confirming the amount of value created and wealth received from customers.

The owners of Bad Apple Cider Company say, "We have earned $2,000 of cider revenue." The owners must also figure out precisely what combination of resources can create the most added value at the lowest cost. Is it some combination of the types of apples used to make the cider? How about the method of processing? The quality of the apples? The convenience of the store? The selection of ciders in the store? The time of year? . . . Business is tricky.

Success: Net Income

If a business creates and sells more value than the cost of the resources consumed, it will be successful. This means that revenues are greater than expenses. When *revenues are greater than expenses,* the business has a *profit.* People in business call this ***net income.*** Net income makes the wealth of a business increase and the business grows.

Success or Failure, *continued*

Failure: Net Loss

If *revenues are less than expenses,* the business has a loss. This is called a ***net loss.*** Net loss is bad because the business is using up a greater value of resources than it is receiving from customers. Wealth is decreasing. There are two possible reasons for this:

- The expenses (resources used up) cannot add enough total value.
- The business is not charging enough for the actual value that it is creating.

These are reasons why businesses lose money and go out of business.

Example #1: Net Income

Swell Computer Manufacturing Company charges $2,500 per computer, and the company makes and sells 100 computers. The cost of the resources consumed (expenses) is $1,500 per computer. So, the business has total revenue of $250,000 and total expenses of $150,000. This is a net income of $100,000. Even though some of the $150,000 expenses might not add value, other expenses created enough value to result in a net income.

Example #2: Net Loss

At the end of the year, Jiffy Tax Services has $300,000 of revenue for all the tax returns that it prepared. Expenses were $400,000. Jiffy has a net loss of $100,000. There are two possible reasons:

- The expenses do not add enough total value. The business must change the way it uses resources or go out of business. This means:
  - Use the resources more efficiently so total expenses are less.
  - Use the resources in a different way so greater value is created.
- The business is not charging enough for the actual value that it is creating. In this case, the business should increase what it charges customers.

Sometimes the word "revenue" is confused with "net income" (profit). Revenue is the total amount of the sales price. Net income is what is left over after subtracting expenses from the revenue.

Ethics in Business and Accounting

In this introduction we are developing an understanding of business operations and structure. We will then see how these are reported by the use of accounting. This is technical knowledge. However, even at this early point in our study we also need to understand that technical knowledge alone is not sufficient to provide reliable financial reporting. Technical knowledge must be combined with an understanding of ethical standards. As we continue further in this book, we will have discussion, examples, and exercises that help explain the importance of ethical standards in business conduct and the effects on financial reporting.

QUICK REVIEW

- A business is an organization that has the primary goal of accumulating wealth by creating and selling new and valuable (economic) resources.
- There are only two economic resources: property and services.
- "Wealth" is property that has value.
- A business creates a valuable new resource by consuming other resources. The total value of the new resource is called the "added value." The cost of a resource consumed to add value is called an "expense."
- Unfortunately, not all expenses add value, and final added value is difficult to predict.
- "Revenue" is what the new resource actually sells for. Revenue confirms the actual added value.
- In a successful business, revenues exceed expenses. In an unsuccessful business, revenues are less than expenses.

VOCABULARY

Account receivable: the legal right to collect an amount owed by a customer (page 7)

Added value: the value created when a new resource is created (page 11)

Economic resource: a resource that can be valued or measured in dollars (page 4)

Expense: the cost of a resource used up in the process of creating a new resource (page 10)

Net income: when revenues are greater than expenses (page 16)

Net loss: when expenses are greater than revenues (page 17)

Property: any resource that can be owned (page 5)

Revenue: the dollar value of a sale—what a customer pays (page 15)

Services: the use of labor or the use of someone's property (page 5)

Value chain: the sequence of activities that consumes resources for the purpose of adding value (page 14)

PRACTICE Learning Goal 1

Solutions are in the disk at the back of the book and at: www.worthyjames.com

Learning Goal 1 is about defining and identifying a business. Use these questions and problems to practice what you have learned about a business.

Multiple Choice

Select the best answer.

1. A business is
   a. an easy way to get rich.
   b. an organization that has the purpose of accumulating wealth.
   c. an organization that always adds value.
   d. an activity that provides little or no benefit to society.
2. The way a business operates is by
   a. borrowing and obtaining investments.
   b. using up resources.
   c. avoiding all risk.
   d. using up resources to create and sell new resources.
3. When a business creates a new resource that customers will want, the business is sai
   a. adding value.
   b. making sales.
   c. doing market research.
   d. advertising.
4. "Bad Apple Cider Company had $200 of revenue." This statement refers to
   a. cash, in the amount of $200.
   b. an increase in business wealth in the amount of $200, caused by making a sale.
   c. a profit of $200.
   d. all of the above.
5. To add value, a business always has to
   a. make a profit.
   b. consume resources.
   c. make a sale.
   d. both (b) and (c).
6. Expenses
   a. will always add significant value.
   b. may add little or no value.
   c. require a nonvalue-added activity.
   d. none of the above.
7. Added value results from any expense that
   a. is not excessive.
   b. is cost effective.
   c. makes the final product more valuable or useful to customers.
   d. uses up resources.
8. The actual amount of revenue (total added value) is always determined
   a. by business management.
   b. by the productivity of the employees.
   c. by how much the customers decide to pay for the resource created.
   d. by a predetermined mathematical calculation for each product.
9. A business knows that it has net income when
   a. revenues are greater than expenses.
   b. expenses are greater than revenues.
   c. it is still able to repay its loans.
   d. it is certain that it is adding value.

PRACTICE Learning Goal 1, continued

Solutions are in the disk at the back of the book and at: www.worthyjames.com

10. Which of the following expenses probably do not add any value?

a. The $500 cost of the utilities to air-condition an accounting office.
b. The $15,000 cost of the employee wages in the computer assembly operation.
c. The $2,000 cost of the cookie dough that was spoiled in the bakery refrigerator.
d. The $750 cost of the janitorial service.

Reinforcement Problems

LG 1-1. How is value being added? For each of the following situations, write a short and clear explanation of how the business is adding value.

a. A restaurant prepares a meal.

b. A bank advertises its new services and low loan rates.

c. An automobile manufacturer crash-tests the new models.

d. A doctor studies new surgical techniques.

LG 1-2. Determine the amount of added value. In each situation below, give your advice about what you think the final value will be.

a. Thinking that they have created the greatest new product since sliced bread, executives at Great Products Company produce liver-flavored toothpaste. Each tube costs $1.50 to produce, and this cannot be changed. The management wants to sell the product for $2 per tube. The managers have heard about added value, and they want you—a consultant—to tell them if their proposed selling price is a good estimate of the added value of their product.

b. Management at Green Bay Company is thinking about spending $100,000 to install on-site exercise and child-care facilities for its employees. However, to pay for this, the company will have to cancel the purchase of four new delivery trucks. Management wants to maximize added value and is not sure how their decision will affect the added value of the products. Write a brief response to the managers.

LG 1-3. Learning Goal 1 Cumulative Review. Jerry Berg recently graduated from veterinary school and received his license to practice veterinary medicine. A few months ago, he opened a veterinary clinic. The clinic provides medical care for animals and also sells pet-care merchandise that customers frequently need. Last month, the clinic billed customers a total of $38,500 for medical care services. At the beginning of the month, the merchandise was marked up to a total selling price of $2,500. However, for various reasons, the merchandise sold for only $2,200. $10,000 of the cash received from customers was used to purchase new equipment.

To operate the clinic, Dr. Berg employs a medical staff of five people. Employee wages last month totaled $21,200. The clinic also pays $2,000 per month for rent and $450 for utilities. The cost of the merchandise was $2,000. Repair services for equipment that was damaged by a poorly trained employee cost $1,100. Supplies were an additional $800. The clinic advertises its services in local magazines and papers at a cost of $400 per month. Finally, accounting and management services are $750 per month.

PRACTICE Learning Goal 1, continued

Solutions are in the disk at the back of the book and at: www.worthyjames.com

LG 1-3, *continued*

Answer the following questions about the clinic.

a. Would you classify this business as service, merchandising, or manufacturing?

b. How does this business add value? What kind of new resource is being created?

c. What was the actual added value as determined by the revenue? Was this different in any way from what was expected?

d. What kinds of resources does this clinic use up in order to add value?

e. Describe the value chain for this business. What was the total expense in the value chain?

f. Did all expenses in the value chain add significant value?

g. As a business, was the clinic successful or unsuccessful for the month? How much did the wealth of the business change?

LG 1-4. Challenging questions

a. **Accounts receivable as property.** In this learning goal, we said that wealth is property; that is, something that the business owns that has money value. How does an account receivable qualify as property? Or should we just say that it is the same as cash?

b. **Exchanges.** In this learning goal, we said that a business accumulates wealth by creating and selling things that people need, and then the business in turn receives other valuable property from its customers. Suppose that two companies exchange services with each other. Although services are valuable resources, we know that services cannot be owned. Can an exchange of services qualify as part of the process of accumulating wealth?

Your Questions?

It is *very* important to be aware of what you need to understand better. What do you need to understand better about this learning goal? On a separate piece of paper, write the questions that you want to discuss with your classmates, instructor, or supervisor. Try to be very specific about what is bothering you, such as explanations that you do not fully understand.

Do You Like a Good Story?

It Might Help You to Remember Better

Sometimes people remember information better when the information is part of an interesting story. The story that begins on the next page tells about how humanity first discovered what a business really is. The story has adventure, mystery, and romance—all for your enjoyment! So, if you think a story might help you remember better, or if you just want to have some fun, go ahead . . . the adventures of Darius await you.

Technical Content

This part of the story contains the following technical content:

- The basic financial structure of any business
- The definition of "asset"
- Asset valuation basics
- Claims on assets
- Using the accounting equation

You Can Skip the Story

If you prefer to study the technical content listed above more quickly, you can skip the story and go directly to page 33, where the current presentation and practice continue.

AN HISTORICAL FABLE

The Wealth of Darius

Part I

How Darius Came to Be a Merchant

Long, long ago, when civilization was just beginning, when the world was fresh, and when the Greek people believed that gods lived far above the clouds on the heights of great Mount Olympus, there lived a youth named Darius. What happened to Darius changed the world forever.

Darius was the child of a poor family, with many brothers and sisters, but he was lucky. The gods had given Darius the gifts of the artist. Everyone in the village admired the child for his fine drawing and painting. His skill surprised everyone, for none of his brothers or sisters nor his mother or father had ever shown the slightest of such talents.

Darius grew into a dark-haired and athletic young man, and he became an apprentice to a painter who painted wall designs and frescoes, and sometimes pottery for wealthy collectors. Darius had such exceptional talent that it was not long until he became more skilled than his master, a friendly man named Ammon.

One day Ammon came to Darius and said, "Young man, it is time for you to be on your own. There is nothing more that I can teach you now. Your beautiful designs, bright colors, and expert painting show the world that you are already better than the master. I am getting old, and it is time for me to enjoy the rest of my life without the worries of business."

Ammon continued. "You have such great talents, Darius. I would be honored if you would buy my shop from me and carry on the name of this honorable business. I will sell it to you for 7,000 gold coins, even though I might be able to get more."

When he heard Ammon say these things, Darius' heart rose and then fell. Darius had very little money. He had no chance to buy the business.

But Ammon continued. "I know that you are still a poor apprentice. I will wait seven years, and then you can pay me for the business. By that time, I think you will be a rich and famous painter. In the meantime, I only ask that you allow me to work for you as your employee for two gold coins per week so that I may have some income. I also ask two additional gold coins per week for allowing you to have the seven years to pay me."

Darius' eyes filled with tears of gratitude. He and Ammon signed an agreement according to Ammon's terms. Poor but talented young Darius was now the owner of his own business. He soon earned the admiration of all who saw and purchased his beautiful and original paintings and designs.

Darius' Troubles

Darius worked very, very hard to prove to Ammon that he could succeed. However, Darius was worried, and every day he prayed to the gods on Mount Olympus to help him.

Darius had the talents of an artist, not a businessperson. So, when Darius began to be responsible for the business, he soon felt confused and frightened. He did not dare ask Ammon for too much advice because he did not want to worry and trouble the old man. Besides, Darius was sure that neither Ammon nor any other merchant would have the answer to his most frightening worry of all.

What worried Darius most of all was that he did not know a way to determine what kind of condition the business was in. How does one know if a business is successful or unsuccessful? Even if there were many customers, would there be enough money to pay back the debt to Ammon? A few times, Darius asked other merchants how they would know if a business was successful, but he always received different answers from different people.

One merchant answered, "Well, that is easy! The more gold you have, the more successful you are." Another merchant said, "Success is when the business does not have debts." Still another said, "Many customers means success." Darius just became more confused than before.

At first, Darius sometimes wondered whether he was more prosperous because he owned a business. But after a while, he stopped thinking about his own prosperity because all he thought about was paying Ammon. Even worse, Darius then remembered the other people to whom the business owed money: Aulis, the merchant who sold paint and glaze; and Hela, the merchant who supplied the paper, ink, and drawing tools Darius used for designs.

Darius tried to think: "Let me see . . . the business has some gold now. The business owes money to Aulis and Hela and will have to pay Ammon four gold coins per week. But there is still some paint that I bought last month, and the prince Cronos has not yet paid for the large wall painting that was finished last week, and there are brushes and drawing tools, and . . . aaahh! How does all that tell me if the business is any better or worse than when I bought it? How do I know if I will ever be able to pay Ammon? I will be shamed in front of the world. I am sorry Ammon, sorry, *sorry*!"

When Darius returned to his house that evening and lay down to sleep, the worry demons whispered and giggled in his ears the entire night, and he never closed his eyes.

The Gods Intervene

The mysterious and immortal gods, who can observe all that mortal humans do, had been watching Darius. The gods reposed in the garden of eternity on Mount Olympus and debated what they should do with Darius. The god Hermes (pronounced *HER-meez*) was especially interested. Hermes wore winged sandals and was the god of commerce and the marketplace. Of all the gods, Hermes was the cleverest and most cunning, and he was forever causing discord and arguments among the other gods.

"I think it is time for humans to learn a secret of commerce from us," Hermes said. "These foolish mortals pretend to do business, they buy and they sell, they count their worthless little coins, and still they have almost no idea of what a business is or what they are doing. Let us give them new knowledge."

"Yes," said Apollo, the god of music, truth, and light. "It is time to give humanity a secret. After all, we already make the dull little beasts suffer enough with our games."

"What! Give them a secret of the gods? Never!" said Artemis, the goddess of hunting and of all wild things. "What a waste it would be. They would never know what to do with a secret of ours, and this fool Darius only knows how to paint pictures."

"Well," rumbled Hades (pronounced *HAY-deez*), the god of the dead and the world below, who had heard the discussion and appeared from his lands under the earth, "it will do them no good when they come to spend their time with me," at which Hades and Artemis laughed heartily, while Apollo frowned.

Hermes had started another argument and felt pleased with himself. Now he was ready for his next trick. "So," he said, "if none of the gods themselves can decide, let us wager that Darius can decide for us! I will test this mortal, and if he passes my test, I will reward him with a secret of the gods that will end his worries. If he fails my test, then Artemis may turn him into a wild pig to be hunted anytime she wishes."

"Yes, excellent!" they roared, Artemis shouting the loudest.

Hermes was happy with himself again. He had tricked the gods into gambling one of their secrets on the test of a human which, as we all know, no one can ever be sure about.

A Strange Event

Darius felt exhausted, confused, and full of worry when he left his house the next morning. He walked down the road to a small favorite lake, where he planned to bathe and regain his energy after a night with no sleep. He had been walking for perhaps ten minutes when he observed a dark form next to the road. As he approached the object, Darius began to notice a foul odor coming from the shape. To his surprise, the form was a filthy old beggar woman, disgustingly soiled and infested with lice.

The woman screeched, "I am hungry! I have no place to stay. Give me food and a place to stay! I am too tired to walk. Carry me to a place to rest!" Darius was already burdened with his own worries and concerns. He did not want another problem, so he walked away from the repellent woman. After a few steps, however, he thought, "Her problems are just as important to her as mine are to me. Who knows? If I fail in my business, as seems likely now, someday I may be nearly the outcast she is today."

With that thought he turned, picked up the disgusting woman, and carried her back to his house. He gave her bread, what meat he had left, heated some water for her bath, and told her to rest as long as she wished. As Darius prepared to leave his house the second time, a brilliant light filled the room, momentarily blinding him. As he regained his vision, he saw the old woman disappear. A large, powerful-looking man wearing winged sandals replaced her at the center of the light.

"You have passed," proclaimed the figure. Darius also heard the sounds of laughter and angry voices, but he could not see anyone else in the room. In that moment, he knew that he was in the presence of a god. Darius threw himself to the floor, trembling.

"Yes," said Hermes, who had disguised himself as the foul old woman, "you may be full of your own concerns, but you did not abandon someone even more hopeless than yourself, poor mortal." With that, the imposing god threw back his head, his thundering laughter filling the room, and pronounced, "You have defeated the gods!"

The huge, brilliant figure spoke again. "And now, Darius, as the god of commerce, I reward you with a secret of the gods that will end your present confusion. I thereby bring you peace of mind, for now. Rise up and listen, so that I may give you the secret of knowing the condition of your business at any time you wish."

As Darius slowly rose, the god continued. "Listen carefully to what I tell you now, mortal. The true picture of a business is simply this: wealth and claims on the wealth. That is all.

"At any time you choose, you may determine the condition of your business. First, determine the wealth of the business. Business wealth means any valuable things that belong only to the business. These things are called 'assets.' Assets are the business wealth. They are also used by the business to operate.

"Next, determine the claims on the assets. There are no more than two kinds of claims. The owner, of course, has a claim on the assets. But if there are business debts, which are the claims of creditors, then the creditors have first claim. Whatever value of all assets exceeds the claims of the creditors, then this excess may be claimed by you, the owner."

Finishing, the god said, "Here is how to remember what I have told you today: First, determine the value of all the assets. Next, determine the claims on the assets—the creditors and the owner. The total claims always equal the total assets . . . but the creditors have first claim.

"Remember this well, mortal, for it is the essence of every business. I expect you to understand this. I will visit you again in one year, when I will decide if you have learned to properly use the gift of knowledge that I have given to you."

With that, the god and the bright light disappeared in a shower of arching golden sparkles, leaving Darius dazzled and speechless. There was a roll of parchment paper on the wooden table in the center of the room. Written on the paper in gold print were the words:

Darius Tries Out the Secret

When he recovered his senses, Darius looked at the words on the paper and felt happier than he had felt since he had bought the business. He thought, "No longer will I operate my business in darkness! I will learn to use this at once!" Excitedly, Darius grabbed the paper and raced toward town, passing the place where he had met the old woman, and ran the entire distance to his shop.

Ignoring everyone else in the shop, Darius flew straight to his table in the back, where he did his planning and drawing. Slowly he took a deep breath, found a piece of paper to write on, and began to think.

"Let me see," he thought, "first I determine the wealth of the business. The name for this is assets. Hermes himself told me that an asset is anything with value that belongs to the business. So, what assets does my business have?"

Slowly and carefully, Darius began to list the assets belonging to the business, along with their values:

Gold *$2,500*
Receivable from Prince Cronos..................... *500*
Painting equipment...............................

As he was about to write down a number for the painting equipment, Darius began to hesitate. "What is the value of this equipment? I think I could sell it for $3,000 because Thrice, that bandit, offered me only $1,500 for it last week. Everyone knows that he never offers more than half." Still hesitating, Darius thought, "Yet, I cannot be certain until I actually sell it."

Then Darius had an excellent idea. "I know! I will use the cost that I paid for the equipment when I bought it. At least this is a number of which I can be completely certain. Only when I actually sell the equipment will I find out if it has some other value. This is acceptable."

And so, using this rule, he continued writing:

Painting equipment................ *2,700* *(my cost)*
Painting supplies .... *1,900* *(my cost)*
Other supplies........................ *300* *(my cost)*
Other assets .... *800* *(my cost)*

These were all the assets that he could see. He tried to think if there were any other assets that might belong to the business. "The building!" he thought. But then he remembered that the building was actually owned by Amar, the landlord, and Darius paid Amar $25 in gold each month to use the building. So, the building really belonged to Amar.

Then Darius thought about Ammon. "Is Ammon an asset?" he wondered. Ammon was still a very valuable employee, but did he actually belong to the business like the equipment and supplies?

What Do You Think?

If you could help Darius answer this question before he decides what to do, how would you advise him? Should Ammon be considered a business asset? Write your answer on a separate piece of paper.

After giving the problem much thought, Darius remembered that Hermes said that an asset must not only have value, but that it must also belong only to the business. So Darius decided that he could not include Ammon, because Ammon did not belong to the business like a table or a chair.

Darius then added up the assets and wrote the total on a piece of paper:

Total assets: $8,700

This was beginning to make sense! Under his breath, he thanked the gods one more time. Anxiously, Darius now began to write down the total business debts:

Owing to Ammon.................... $7,000
Owing to Aulis 400
Owing to Hela.......................... 600

He could not think of any more debts, except he wondered if Ammon's future wages were a business debt. Also, Darius owed his neighbor one gold coin for some meat he bought when he prepared dinner for his family last week. He stopped writing and thought hard about these two items.

What Do You Think?

If you could help Darius answer this question before he decides what to do, how would you advise him? Are Ammon's future wages a business debt right now? How about the money that Darius owes to his neighbor? Write your answer on a separate piece of paper.

Darius thought for a long time. He slowly began to realize that Ammon's wages could not be a debt if Ammon had not yet done the work. The business did not owe money for things that it had not yet received, and so it did not owe Ammon for work that was not yet done.

As to the one gold coin owing for the meat—well, that was a debt, all right, but it was not a business debt. It was Darius' personal debt because he was the one who had received the meat. Again, the business itself had not received anything, and so it did not owe anything.

Darius then added up the total business debts: $8,000.

Darius looked again at the words on the paper Hermes had left for him. He remembered that Hermes said that the owner's claim on the business wealth was whatever value of assets exceeded what was owed to the creditors.

The Owner's Claim

Darius realized that now all he needed to do was simply make the totals on each side be equal. To do this, he needed to determine if the assets' value exceeded the creditors' claims. This excess would be the amount of owner's claim, if there was any. Darius started writing down the total assets and total creditors' claims. He already knew the total assets and creditors' claims, so he only had to fill in . . .

Assets	=	*Creditors' Claims*	+	*Owner's Claim*
$8,700		*$8,000*		________

Before Darius could write more, he realized what was happening and his heart leaped into his throat. He held his breath. Electricity flashed down his spine. He stood up and sat down. He stood up and sat down again. And again. Then he jumped into the air and shouted out, "Oh yes, by the gods, I am worthy!" People in the shop stopped and looked at him.

What made Darius so deliriously happy was what the calculation showed: The condition of his business was such that the business had enough wealth ($8,700) to pay *all* the $8,000 of debts (including Ammon!) and still have $700 which Darius could claim for himself as owner. He had not failed as a business owner!

Finally, when his heart was beating more slowly, Darius sat down again and finished writing the calculation:

Assets	=	*Creditors' Claims*	+	*Owner's Claim*
$8,700		*$8,000*		*$700*

Darius was an artist, so he drew a picture of the condition of his business, because he knew this would help him to remember it better. His picture looked like this:

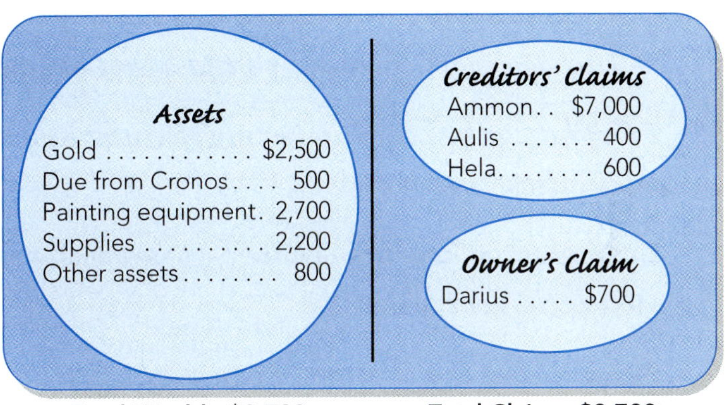

Assets
Gold $2,500
Due from Cronos 500
Painting equipment. 2,700
Supplies 2,200
Other assets 800
Creditors' Claims
Ammon. . $7,000
Aulis 400
Hela. 600
Owner's Claim
Darius $700

Total Wealth: $8,700 Total Claims: $8,700

It was all as clear as day to him. Darius realized that now he had the power at any time to clearly see the picture of his business. This made him remember what Hermes had said: "The picture of a business is simply wealth and claims on that wealth."

How Darius Used His Knowledge

At first, Darius was so excited about his newfound power that he wanted to calculate the condition of his business almost every day. However, because the condition changed so little from one day to the next, he began the habit of calculating the condition at the end of each month. When he did this, Darius could clearly see the change in the condition of the business every month.

He discovered that the total wealth—that is, the total of the assets—often changed. Sometimes the total of the assets increased a little and sometimes a lot, and sometimes it even decreased. Not only did the total amount of the assets change, but Darius discovered that the individual assets also changed. For example, sometimes the business had more gold or less gold than before, or more supplies or less supplies than before, and so on.

Also, the total amount owing to the creditors sometimes changed. Sometimes the business owed more to creditors than before and sometimes less. Darius watched the debts carefully.

Darius felt so good that he found a piece of paper and made a list of all the wonderful things that the calculation had made possible:

What I can see now but I could not see before:

- *I now see that the condition of my business is made up of assets and an equal amount of claims on those assets:*
  - *Assets are wealth (and are also used by the business).*
  - *The two types of claims on the assets are the creditors' and the owner's.*
- *I can know the condition of my business any time I want to by calculating these values.*
- *I can observe how the condition of my business is changing by doing the calculation every month.*
- *By watching the changes, I can make better decisions.*

Because of the success of the business, Darius was able to withdraw a little more money from the business for himself. His greatest enjoyment was to share his money and have dinners and parties for his mother and father and brothers and sisters, who had always been poor.

As the seasons passed, Darius continued on in this way. He worked hard, calculated the condition of his business, and was good to his family and friends.

But Darius had forgotten something important: Hermes' promise. It was now exactly a year since Hermes had promised to return.

To be continued . . .

LEARNING GOAL 2

Define and Identify Assets

Overview

Introduction

In business, the word for property is "assets." Assets (especially the right kind) make a business wealthy, successful, and powerful.

However, before we begin discussing business assets, we will do a quick review of all resources—property and services—just to make sure that these basic ideas are clear.

In Learning Goal 2, you will find:

A Review of Resources

Resources in a Business

Resources Consumed to Add Value

A business consumes resources for the purpose of creating and selling more valuable resources. This is often called "adding value."

Only Two Kinds of Resources

On the planet Earth, only two kinds of resources can be bought and sold: property and services. These resources are also called "goods and services."

- ***Property*** is any resource that can be owned.
- ***Services*** are the use of labor or the use of someone else's property.

Note: Because they can be bought and sold at some money amount, goods and services are sometimes called "economic" resources.

A Business Creates Both Kinds

A business can add value by producing either property or services, or both.

Example

Your business makes and sells fresh bread. The business has created bread, a valuable resource that can be owned. Your business also delivers the bread to restaurants and charges for this service. The delivery service is another valuable resource that customers want. However, the delivery service—although valuable—is not something that can be owned (because services are immediately used up).

Which Resource Is Most Important?

Both property and services are essential to any business, because both are needed to make a business operate. For example, a bread company needs ovens (property) and oven repairs (services) to operate.

However, in addition to being a useful resource, another feature of property makes it more important than services: property is also wealth.

The Dual Nature of Property

Property as Resource and Wealth

Property Provides Two Benefits

Most property has a dual nature that allows it to be used in two ways. First, property can be consumed as a *useful resource* in the adding-value process. Secondly, property is also *wealth.*

Property as a Useful Resource

A business obtains benefits by *consuming* property. In the examples below, each property item provides benefits as the item is used up or worn out in the adding-value process of operations.

Property	Benefits
Computer equipment	Calculations, projections, document preparation
Book	Knowledge
Insurance policy	Protection from losses
Truck	Delivery and transportation
Coffee supplies	Nourishment

Property as Wealth

Wealth is property that has a dollar value. Because wealth is property, wealth can be owned and kept for future use. This makes it extremely useful for obtaining other resources.

Wealth (property)	which has value because . . .
Computer equipment	it could be sold for cash (used to obtain other resources).
Book	it could be sold for cash (used to obtain another resource).
. . . and so on, for all the other property listed above.	

Exceptions

Some property has only monetary value. This kind of property is not a resource that is physically consumed in the adding-value process. Money is the best example of this kind of property. Another example is accounts receivable. These items are strictly wealth.

The Two Essential Characteristics of Assets

Overview

Introduction

People spend a lot of time thinking about assets. It probably has been that way from the time that two cavemen argued about who was entitled to sleep on the bearskin. Assets seem to appease deep psychological needs for security, power, and pleasure.

Human beings are amazing in how many ways they can think of for creating different assets and exchanging them back and forth. Common examples of business assets can be simple things like cash, office supplies, automobiles, or land. Sometimes assets can be strange and unusual things, like a "capitalized lease" or a "financial market derivative." (Whoever thought up those things?) You will learn more about assets as you progress in your study of accounting and business.

Assets: The Everyday Meaning and the Business Meaning

Everyday Assets

It is important to distinguish the everyday meaning of the word "asset" from the business meaning. In everyday language, we usually use the word "asset" to mean anything useful or beneficial, such as:

- Cash (because you can buy things with it)
- A car (because it provides transportation)
- A computer (because you can use it to do calculations)
- An education (because it will help you get a good job)
- Beauty (because it helps you meet people and get invited to parties)
- A sense of humor (because it helps you make friends)

Assets: The Everyday Meaning and the Business Meaning, *continued*

"Assets, sir. Everywhere you look!"

Business Assets

In business, the general idea of ***asset*** is similar to the everyday meaning—something useful or beneficial. However, for business purposes, *general beneficial qualities are not enough.* An asset must be property, and the property must have the following two specific qualities to qualify as an asset:

- The property must provide future economic benefits to a business.
- The property must be owned by a business as a result of a past event.

continued 

Assets: The Everyday Meaning and the Business Meaning, *continued*

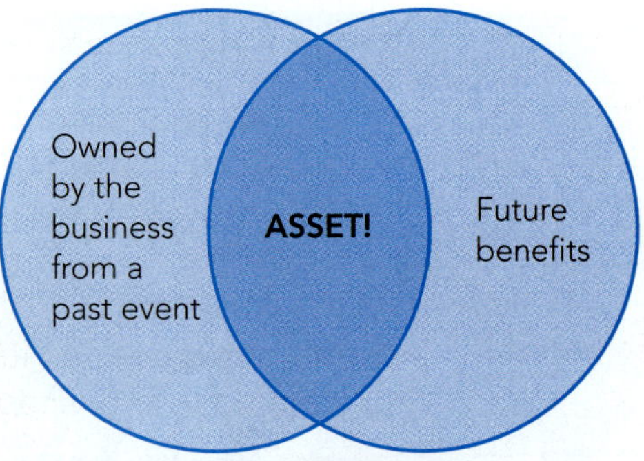

You can visualize the necessary qualities of an asset as two circles. An asset is described only in the space where the circles intersect.

The "Future Benefit" Characteristic

Future Benefit (Property Is Useful)

A future benefit of an asset is whatever benefit or advantage an asset will bring to a business at any time in the future. The benefit can be either physical use of the asset or its cash value.

The asset must benefit the business in some way in the future, whether the benefit is five minutes in the future, five years in the future, or any other future time. Past benefits are gone. Only future benefits can help a business.

Note: Sometimes these future benefits are called ***service potential***.

Examples of Future Benefits (Service Potential)

	For a business to . . .	Using the asset releases benefits
Cash	. . . get a different asset, it might exchange its cash for a computer. . . . operate and grow, it might exchange its cash for employee services. . . . pay a debt, it might use its cash to pay a bank loan.	By exchanging its cash for assets or services or by using its cash to pay debts, a business can . . . 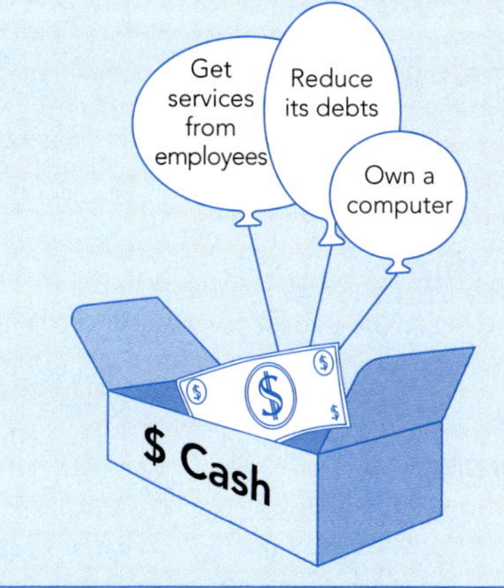
Noncash: Computer	. . . operate and grow, it might consume its computer by using it to: ▪ record revenues and expenses ▪ create marketing documents ▪ e-mail bills to customers *Analogy:* driving a car wears it out and therefore uses it up. Similarly, using office equipment wears it out.	As it uses up or wears out its computer, a business can . . . 
Noncash: Supplies	. . . operate and grow, it might use up or consume its office supplies to: ▪ write letters to customers and vendors ▪ make copies of documents ▪ prepare bills for customers	By using up or consuming its supplies, a business can . . . 

The "Owned by the Business as a Result of a Past Event" Characteristic

Ownership from a Past Event

- ***Ownership:*** As a characteristic of an asset, "ownership" means complete control over all uses of property, provided that the uses are legal. Having this control means that a business has the legal right to receive any and all benefits from the property, including use in operations, selling, exchanging, and disposing in any manner.
- ***Past event:*** This means a completed transaction; in other words, the event has already taken place at some time in the past.

Examples of Ownership

- A business buys a computer to use in its operations.
- A business creates an account receivable by a sale to a customer.

Not Ownership

- A business rents a computer from another company. (Renting is not ownership. *Note:* Renting is also called ***leasing.***)
- A business pays employees who work for the business. (People are not property.)

Examples of a Past Event

- Last month a business bought a computer.
- Yesterday a business made a sale to a customer.

Not a Past Event

- A business creates a budget that includes buying a new computer. (A budget is a plan, but the new computer has not yet been purchased.)
- A very good customer tells us that he will make a purchase tomorrow. (This is only an intention; the sale has not actually happened yet.)

More Benefits of "Past Event"

By requiring "past event" to be a characteristic of an asset, two important benefits happen. First, the past event provides *objective evidence*. Second, *historical cost* is identified.

Objective evidence refers to documents that prove the amount of cost as well as when and where the asset was acquired. Examples of objective evidence are documents such as invoices, receipts, and canceled checks.

Historical cost refers to the asset value used in the past event. This provides a reliable method of determining the dollar-value amount of the asset. Even though an item qualifies as an asset, a dollar value is still necessary to record it.

Is an asset the same thing as revenue? No. Revenue is the dollar value of a sale. A business receives that value in the form of assets – usually cash or accounts receivable.

More Examples of Assets and Their Characteristics

Cash

Cash is the most useful of all assets. Its dollar value is clear, and it provides the most kinds of possible future benefits. This is because cash can easily be used to obtain any other kind of resource—whether property or services—or to pay debts.

"Cash is the most useful of all assets."

Non-Cash Assets

Non-cash assets are any assets other than cash. Non-cash assets have a money value and also are frequently used physically or consumed as part of the business operations.

Non-Cash Examples

- Accounts receivable: the legal right to collect money from customers
- Office supplies: small items that are quickly used up in the office such as pens, pencils, paper, computer disks, and coffee for employees
- Office equipment: long-lasting equipment that is used in the office such as desks, file cabinets, computers, and copy machines
- Automobiles
- Land
- Prepaid services: advance payments such as prepaid insurance and prepaid rent

Monetary Assets

Some assets have only money value. These assets are not physically used or consumed as part of the value-adding operations of a business. Common examples of monetary assets are cash and accounts receivable. Notes receivable, a more formal right to collect money, is also a monetary asset.

continued ▶

More Examples of Assets and Their Characteristics, *continued*

Not Assets

- ***Employees:*** Although employees are a valuable resource, people are not property, and *they do not belong to the business.*
- ***Rented truck:*** Although the truck is useful to the business that uses it, the truck *does not belong to that business.* It is an asset of the business that actually owns it and rents it to other businesses. (Renting is a service.)
- ***Broken calculator:*** If the calculator is broken and cannot be repaired, it will never function and will not provide future benefits (no service potential). It will not work and cannot be sold, so it will give *no future benefits.*
- ***Repair service:*** *Services cannot be owned* because they are immediately consumed. Services are never assets.
- ***Good credit:*** The good credit does belong to the business, is very important, and surely will provide future benefits. However, *it was not acquired from an identifiable past event,* and no dollar value can be identified.

QUICK REVIEW

- Only two kinds of economic resources are available to a business:
  - services, which are useful in the operations, and
  - property, which is both useful *and* is wealth.
- A business property is called an "asset."
- To qualify as an asset, the property resource must meet two requirements:
  - It must provide future benefits.
  - It must belong to the business as the result of a past event.
- A business has both cash (monetary) and non-cash assets.

VOCABULARY

Asset: business property The property must: 1. Provide future benefits 2. Be owned by the business as the result of a past event. (page 37)

Historical cost principle: the requirement that transactions be recorded at actual cost (page 40)

Leasing: renting property (page 40)

Objective evidence: proof provided by a past transaction (page 40)

Service potential: the future benefits that any asset provides (page 38)

PRACTICE Learning Goal 2

Solutions are in the disk at the back of the book and at: www.worthyjames.com

Learning Goal 2 is about defining and identifying assets in a business. Use these questions and problems to practice what you have learned about assets.

Reinforcement Problems

LG 2-1. Characteristics of an asset. This exercise will help you remember and understand the correct definition of the word "asset." Write the completed sentences on a separate piece of paper.

An asset is · · · · · · · · that is · · · · · · · · by a business. Every asset must be able to provide a future · · · · · · · · to the business to which it belongs. The asset must be · · · · · · · · by the business as a result of a · · · · · · · · event.

On a separate page, write a short, clear answer to each of the following questions:

LG 2-2. What is the everyday, nontechnical meaning of the word "asset"?

LG 2-3. Name the two essential qualities of an asset for business purposes.

LG 2-4. Make up an example of an asset. Using a bicycle as your subject, create your own example that compares the bicycle used as an everyday asset (meaning a non-business asset) to the bicycle used as a business asset. (*Tip:* when writing the example, think of the essential qualities of a business asset. An everyday asset will be missing some or all of those essential qualities. A business asset will have all of them.)

LG 2-5. Identify assets and non-assets. Use a blank sheet of paper to complete the table. Identify what items are assets and what items are not. If an item is *not* an asset, identify the *missing* quality. Use the first two items as examples.

Business item	It is . . .		*Missing* quality	
	an asset	not an asset	Future benefits	Owned as a result of a past event
a. The supervisors of a business		✓		✓
b. Office supplies	✓			

PRACTICE Learning Goal 2, continued

Solutions are in the disk at the back of the book and at: www.worthyjames.com

LG 2-5, *continued*

Business item	It is . . .		*Missing* quality	
	an asset	not an asset	Future benefits	Owned as a result of a past event
c. Cash in the checking account	(Reminder: Use a separate sheet of paper to complete the table.)			
d. The legal right to collect $500 that customers owe the business				
e. The new airport to be built next year, five miles from your business				
f. A 12-year-old computer that is no longer functional				
g. An expensive French impressionist painting purchased to hang in the lobby of your office				
h. A building that your company rents from Multnomah Company				
i. A prepaid $700 fire insurance policy				
j. The business owner's master's degree				
k. The computer that your business rents and uses to produce marketing brochures				
l. A promise by a good customer to buy $10,000 of merchandise from your business				
m. The $5,000 increase in value of the French painting your business bought six years ago.				
n. A mission statement explaining company goals that managers prepared				
o. The employees of a business				
p. A budgeted amount to buy office equipment				
q. Money that your business owes to vendors				

LG 2-6. **Asset Value.** This learning goal talks about recording assets at some value. Where does asset value come from? What is the source of asset value where recording an asset?

PRACTICE Learning Goal 2, continued

Solutions are in the disk at the back of the book and at: www.worthyjames.com

LG 2-7. Identify the type of resource. On a separate piece of paper, identify each resource item in the table below as property or service by placing a mark in the correct box. The first item has been done for you as an example.

Item	Property	Service
a. The aircraft of a commercial airline company	✓	
b. A medical examination by your doctor	(Reminder: Use a separate sheet of paper to complete the table.)	
c. The medical equipment in the doctor's office		
d. The gasoline in your car		
e. The cash in a savings account		
f. The classroom lecture from your accounting instructor		
g. The rental of a computer to a business that does not own one		
h. A six-month fire insurance policy paid in advance		

LG 2-8. Challenging questions

a. Suppose that your business owns an old machine. The machine is no longer functional and cannot be repaired. However, the machine can still be sold for salvage value of $250. Would you still call the machine an asset for accounting purposes?
b. Suppose that the machine is still functional and useful in the business operations and helps create cash flow into the business. However, it has no market value and cannot be sold for any amount. Would you still call the machine an asset for accounting purposes?
c. Suppose that the machine cannot be sold at any price and is also no longer useful to the business. However, the machine is still functional. Is it still an asset to the business?
d. Could an item be acquired at a zero dollar value and still be an asset?

Instructor-Assigned Problems

If you are using this book in a class, these review problems may be assigned by your instructor for homework, group assignments, class work, or other activities. Only your instructor has the solutions.

IA2-1. Identify assets and non-assets. On a piece of paper, draw a table like the one below. Identify which items are assets and which items are not by entering a checkmark. If an item is not an asset, identify the missing quality.

Business Item	Asset	Not an Asset	Future Benefits	Owned as a Result of a Past Event
a. A computer that was purchased last year				
b. A computer that is being leased from another company				
c. A computer that was purchased last year but is no longer functional and cannot be repaired				
d. The legal right to collect money from customers				
e. A promise by a good customer to purchase merchandise tomorrow				

PRACTICE Learning Goal 2, continued

IA2-1, *continued*

Business Item	Asset	Not an Asset	Future Benefits	Owned as a Result of a Past Event
f. Office supplies				
g. Airline tickets that our company paid for in advance, but that have not been used yet				
h. Cash in the company savings account				
i. Employees of our business				
j. An amount in the company budget to purchase office supplies				
k. A bill from the telephone company for telephone service				
l. An appraisal report that indicates an increase in the value of land owned by the company				
m. A major improvement in the road in front of our store				
n. Computer repair and maintenance services we paid for				
o. Merchandise inventory that your company will sell to customers				
p. Office furniture that our company owns that we are renting to another company				
q. A new roof for a building				

INTERNET EXERCISES

Develop a business startup checklist. Do an Internet search for "small business startup" and "small business."

a. Use the links you locate to develop a **checklist** for a person who wants to begin a new business. Look for a link to the Small Business Administration (*www.sba.gov*). Many states have general checklists and state-specific checklists for new businesses. So check state government home pages. For example, the state of Idaho Department of Commerce provides a checklist called "Starting a Business in Idaho" at *http://business.idaho.gov/startingabusiness.aspx*. The Small Business Administration provides useful advice (sba.gov). (Use bookmark/favorites to save the locations in an "Accounting References" folder.)
b. What important training and/or resources does the checklist indicate that you had not anticipated? Explain why you feel they are important.
c. What do you think are the most important items in your checklist? Why?
d. Did you have search results that were primarily advertising that you excluded from your checklist? Give three examples.

Your Questions?

It is *very* important to be aware of what you need to understand better. What do you need to understand better about this learning goal? On a separate piece of paper, write the questions that you want to discuss with your classmates, instructor, or supervisor. Try to be very specific about what is bothering you, such as explanations that you do not fully understand.

LEARNING GOAL 3

Define and Identify the Two Claims on Assets

Overview

Introduction

In the previous learning goal, you learned how to identify business assets. In this learning goal, you will learn who gets to claim these assets and why . . . and it is not always just the owner!

Rules for Claims on Assets

- There is always at *least* one kind of claim on business assets—the owner's.
- There are never more than two possible claims—the owner's and the creditors'.

"Equity" Means a Claim

Equity, as used in business, means the legal right to claim the value of assets. Another way of expressing the same idea is to say that equity means a legal claim on the business wealth.

In Learning Goal 3, you will find:

The Owner's Claim and the Creditors' Claims

The Owner's Claim and the Creditors' Claims

Owner's Equity and Creditors' Equity Defined

Two Possible Kinds of Equity

There are two kinds of legal claims on assets:

- The owner's equity
- The creditors' equity

Definition of Owner's Equity

Owner's equity is the owner's legal claim on the value of business assets. This is the most basic claim on the assets. There is always an owner's equity for every business.

Other terms used for owner's equity are ***net worth*** and ***net assets***.

Example of Owner's Equity

Ramos Enterprises has a $10,000 value of various kinds of assets, consisting of cash, accounts receivable, supplies, equipment, and so on. Andy Ramos (the owner) has the legal right to claim the entire $10,000 value of the business assets for himself if there are no business debts to pay.

Definition of Creditors' Equity (Liability)

Creditors' equity is a legal claim on the value of business assets by a creditor. This kind of claim is usually called a ***liability***. Liability simply means a debt of the business.

Examples of Liabilities

- An unpaid bank loan (the bank is the creditor)
- Amounts owing to suppliers (for items purchased on credit)
- Wages owing to employees (who are creditors until they are paid)
- An unpaid telephone bill (the telephone company is the creditor)

What Is the Amount of a Liability?

The amount of a liability is the unpaid value of the resources provided. When a business fully pays a creditor, the liability disappears.

Owner's Equity and Creditors' Equity Defined, *continued*

Examples: Not Liabilities

- A company purchases various items of office supplies and pays cash. The seller is fully paid, so no liability exists.
- A contract is signed for $5,000 of accounting services to be received next month. No resources (services) have yet been provided, so no liability exists.
- Totally defective supplies are received from a seller. No acceptable resources (supplies) have yet been provided, so there is no liability to the seller.

Check Your Understanding

Write the completed sentences on a separate piece of paper.

.... is the owner's claim on the value of the business assets. Other terms that mean the same are .... and .... The word .... is used to describe the total creditors' equity claim on assets. If a business purchased $900 of supplies and paid $500 to the seller, a liability of $ .... would exist. The creditors' claims have (higher/lower) .... priority than the owner's claim.

Answers

Owner's equity is the owner's claim on the value of the business assets. Other terms that mean the same are net worth and net assets. The word liabilities is used to describe the total creditors' equity claim on assets. If a business purchased $900 of supplies and paid $500 to the seller, a liability of $400 would exist. The creditors' claims have higher priority than the owner's claim.

Why the Two Claims Exist

Overview of the Two Claims

Directly or indirectly, the owner and the creditors provide all the resources to a company, both assets and services.

- *The owner* invests his/her own assets into a business. The owner also invests services—time and energy—and by doing this creates a business operation that adds value and obtains wealth from customers.
- *Creditors* directly supply both assets and services to a business.

Why Owner's Equity Exists

The owner's equity claim exists because the business belongs to the owner.

continued 

Why the Two Claims Exist, *continued*

Why Creditors' Equity Exists

The creditors' equity (liabilities) exists because the creditors provided goods and services resources to the business that the business has not yet paid for.

When . . .	and . . .	then . . .
resources are provided by someone other than the owner	the resources are not immediately paid for,	a liability is created (creditor's equity).

Claims Are Usually on the Total Assets

The liability claims and owner's equity claim are normally against the entire dollar value of all assets, up to the amount of the claim, and not against the value of any specific asset.

Exception: Sometimes a creditor's claim may be "secured" by a particular asset. This means that a creditor has the right to seize and sell a particular asset to pay a debt, if the debt is not paid on time. The particular asset is said to be ***security*** for the debt.

TIP

A supplier of goods or services is sometimes called a ***vendor***. "Vendor" means the same as "seller."

Compare the Claims

The Most Important Difference

Owner's equity claim and the liability claim are different in several ways, which are listed for you in the comparison table on page 52. However, the *most important difference* is that they do not have the same priority for payment.

Liabilities Have First Priority

Liabilities have first priority over owner's equity. This means that if a business does not have enough assets to pay both the creditors and the owner, then the creditors must be paid first.

If all liabilities are fully paid, any remaining asset value can be claimed by the owner.

Compare the Claims, *continued*

Examples of Liability Priority

- Tishomingo Enterprises has a $10,000 bank loan coming due this week. The owner must make sure there is sufficient asset value to pay the loan before considering how much asset value might be available for himself.
- Wilmington Company has $90,000 of assets and $50,000 of liabilities. The company decides to cease operations and go out of business. Therefore, all company debts are now due and payable. The owner must wait and make sure that all the debts are fully paid before he can claim any of the asset value for himself.

Owner's Equity Is Residual

Whenever there are liabilities, the owner's equity is the amount of asset value that would be left over if all the liabilities were fully paid. Therefore, the owner's equity is always a residual amount. The formula is:

Assets – Liabilities = Owner's Equity

Example of Owner's Equity Residual

The accounting records of Georgetown Company show $52,000 of total assets and $35,000 of various liabilities. To calculate the amount of the owner's equity, calculate the value of assets that would be left over if the business were to pay off all its liabilities: $52,000 – $35,000 = $17,000 owner's equity.

Sometimes when a business is liquidated (sold), the assets will sell for more or less than what is shown in the accounting records. That will make the liquidating owner's equity be more or less than what was recorded.

continued ►

"It says: 'There are no more than two kinds of claims on assets.'"

Compare the Claims, *continued*

Liabilities Compared to Owner's Equity

This table compares the three important characteristics of liabilities and owner's equity.

Compare . . .	Liabilities . . .	Owner's Equity . . .
priority of payment	always have first priority	is second priority
when it must be paid	▪ the day a debt becomes due, according to its terms, or ▪ when the business terminates	has no requirement to be paid at a particular time—it is a residual
intended risk	none, because the creditor expects to be fully paid	resources that are invested can be lost

Sometimes the word "liability" is confused with the word "expense." We discuss expenses in Learning Goal 6. "Liability" only means a debt.

Check Your Understanding

Write the completed sentences on a separate piece of paper. The answers are below.

There are two kinds of claims on the assets of a business. The owner's claim is called ········ ········ and the creditor claims are called ········. Directly or indirectly, the owner and the creditors together provide all the ········ to a company, both assets and services.

The (owner's equity/liabilities) ········ always has (have) legal priority for payment. Claims are usually against (total assets/a particular asset) ········.

Answers

There are two kinds of claims on the assets of a business. The owner's claim is called owner's equity and the creditor claims are called liabilities. Directly or indirectly, the owner and the creditors together provide all the resources to a company, both assets and services.

The liabilities always have legal priority for payment. Claims are usually against total assets.

Management of a Business Changes the Owner's Equity

Good Management

Regardless of whether an owner manages a business or employs other people to manage it, management can be good or bad. Good management will cause the business assets to grow because the managers will operate the business so it will create and sell more value than the value of resources it uses up. When assets increase this way, owner's equity also increases.

Bad Management

Bad management will cause the business to use up more resource value than the value that is created and sold. This will cause assets to decrease as more resources flow out than come in. When assets decrease this way, owner's equity decreases.

Example Using Equation

Good: Assets $\uparrow$ = Liabilities + Owner's Equity $\uparrow$

Bad: Assets $\downarrow$ = Liabilities + Owner's Equity $\downarrow$

QUICK REVIEW

- There are only two possible types of claims on business assets:
  - creditors' claims, which are called liabilities.
  - owner's claim, which is called owner's equity.
- The owner's equity exists because the owner owns the business and provided assets and services to the business. The creditors' claim exists because the creditors provided assets and services which have not been paid for.
- The claims do not have equal rights; the creditor always has priority. This means:
  - Debts must be paid when they are due.
  - Debts have first claim if a business is liquidated.
- Liabilities are normally against the entire total dollar value of the assets.
- The most important cause of change in the owner's equity is the manner in which a business is managed.

VOCABULARY

Equity: a claim on asset value (page 47)

Liability: a debt; a creditor's claim on assets (page 48)

Net assets: a synonym for owner's equity (page 48)

Net worth: a synonym for owner's equity (page 48)

Owner's equity: an owner's claim on assets (page 48)

Security: the particular asset or assets a creditor can claim for nonpayment of a debt (page 50)

Vendor: any seller of goods or services (page 50)

PRACTICE Learning Goal 3

Solutions are in the disk at the back of the book and at: www.worthyjames.com

Learning Goal 3 is about identifying the claims on assets. Use these questions and problems to practice what you have learned about a business.

Reinforcement Problems

LG 3-1. What creates and changes claims on assets? Claims on the wealth of a business (the assets) result from only two providers of resources.

a. Who are these two providers of resources? What do they provide?

b. Why do they have claims on the wealth of a business?

c. Why isn't the owner's claim equal to the value of whatever assets the owner invested minus the value of whatever the owner has withdrawn?

d. Do the owner's services have a fixed dollar value, like wages of an employee?

LG 3-2. Explain changes in equities.

a. A supplier sells merchandise to a business for $800 on credit. Does the supplier have a claim on the assets? How much?

b. A computer repair service charges a business $500 on credit for repairs made. Does the repair service have a claim on the assets? How much? If the business later pays $100 of the liability, does the claim change?

c. An owner invests $5,000 in his small video store. Does this affect the owner's claim on the assets? By how much?

d. The owner of a video store invests 500 hours of his time managing the store. He thinks his time is worth $30 per hour. Does this affect the owner's claim on assets? By how much?

LG 3-3. On a separate piece of paper, write a short, clear definition of "owner's equity."

LG 3-4. On a separate piece of paper, write a short, clear definition of "liabilities" and give three examples.

PRACTICE Learning Goal 3, continued

Solutions are in the disk at the back of the book and at: www.worthyjames.com

LG 3-5. YOU be the teacher! While I was writing this book, a student made the following suggestion about how to describe the meaning of equities. He said:

> "Why not just say that equities are a claim against assets because the equities are the source of those assets? So, you could look at equities as *simply direct sources of assets and also as claims on assets.* That's all there is to it!"

I appreciated his good suggestion, but why is he not quite complete in his description of equity claims? How do I answer him? (*Hint:* Is there more than one kind of resource that a business has to pay for?)

LG 3-6. Explain the priority of liabilities. "The creditors' liability claims always have priority over the owner's claim." Does this mean that an owner cannot withdraw money from his business until he pays off all the debts first?

LG 3-7. Identify the kind of claim. For each separate item described, indicate if it is a creditors' equity claim or an owner's equity claim. Use a blank sheet of paper to complete the table.

Description of Equity Characteristic	Creditors' Equity	Owner's Equity
a. It always has the first claim on assets.	**(Reminder: Use a separate sheet of paper to complete the table.)**	
b. It is increased by the owner's hard work and risk-taking.		
c. It is usually called "liabilities."		
d. It is known as a "residual" claim on assets.		
e. They are the debts of the business.		
f. It is increased when the owner invests in his/her business.		
g. It is created when someone other than the owner provides assets or services to the business that are not immediately paid for.		
h. Together they always add up to the total amount of assets.		

Your Questions?

It is *very* important to be aware of what you need to understand better. What do you need to understand better about this learning goal? On a separate piece of paper, write the questions that you want to discuss with your classmates, instructor, or supervisor. Try to be very specific about what is bothering you, such as explanations that you do not fully understand.

LEARNING GOAL 4

Use the Accounting Equation to Show the Condition

Overview

The Most Basic Question

The most fundamental and basic question about any business is: "What is the condition *right now*?" Every business owner and every investor will ask this question hundreds of times during the life of a business.

What "Condition" Means

The "condition" of a business as used in this book means the total value of the assets and the total claims on the assets, at any specified point in time. This simply means the wealth and the claims on the wealth.

Synonym

Another word used to refer to the condition of a business is *position.*

Purpose of This Learning Goal

In this learning goal, we will study how the condition of a business can always be expressed by the accounting equation. Then we will practice using the equation to show condition.

You will also learn a way to visually picture the condition of a business.

In Learning Goal 4, you will find:

The Financial Condition of a Business

The Financial Condition of a Business

The Accounting Equation

The Final Result of Business Activities

The daily operations of a business can be quite complex, involving marketing, finance, production, research and development, and a complex flow of resources into and out of the business. **But the final result of all these activities always shows up like this simple picture:**

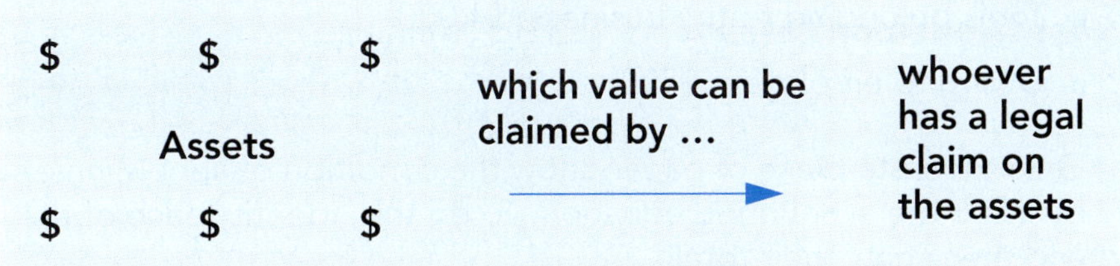

This is the fundamental condition of any business.

Assets and the claims on assets are the essential elements of the condition of any business entity. That is why we have taken such a long time to talk about them. No matter how complex the business operations might be, the result of all the activities can still be expressed like this simple picture.

The Accounting Equation

Instead of drawing a picture, we can use the accounting equation as a clear and powerful way to describe the condition of a business:

$$\text{Assets} = \text{Liabilities} + \text{Owner's Equity}$$

or

$$A = L + OE$$

This means that the total dollar value of the assets is claimed by no more than two providers of resources: the creditors and owner. This is a very powerful idea and it applies to any business. In fact, it even applies to charities, governments, or you and me! We all have assets and claims on the assets.

Rearranging the Equation

The equation can also be rearranged to show:

- Liabilities: $A - OE = L$
- Owner's equity: $A - L = OE$

Check Your Understanding

Last month, your aunt Minnie opened up an appliance repair business. She is thinking about applying for a loan and wants to know how to show the bank the financial condition of her business at the end of the first month. At the end of the month, she provides you with the following information from her business records:

- Cash in the bank: $7,500
- Debts to suppliers: $2,000
- Office supplies on hand: $300
- Car belonging to the business: $10,000
- Tools belonging to the business: $4,000
- Owing to employee: $500

On a separate piece of paper, show the condition of aunt Minnie's business at the end of the month by using the accounting equation. To do this, identify each of the individual asset and equity items and then show their totals.

What do you think about the financial condition of aunt Minnie's business?
Do you think the business looks strong or weak now? Using the accounting equation, what would you say to explain to aunt Minnie what would make her business be stronger or weaker?

Answers

Assets	=	Liabilities	+	Owner's Equity
$21,800		$2,500		$19,300
($7,500 cash + $300 supplies + $10,000 car + $4,000 tools)		($2,000 debts to suppliers + $500 owing to employee)		(assets of $21,800 less the liabilities of $2,500)

The business looks strong now. Creditors have only a $2,500 claim on $21,800 of assets. (This is only 11.5% of assets needed to pay debts.) Stronger or weaker? If the *liabilities were lower* or the *assets were greater*, the business would be stronger because more wealth would be available for operations. The reverse situation would make the business weaker. Owners and managers spend a lot of time worrying about this!

Visualizing the Condition

Most People Are Visual Learners

Most people learn a lot by remembering mental pictures. Using a picture in your head is called "visualizing." If I were to say the word "car," the first thing you probably would think of is a picture of some kind of car. This is a very good way to remember and understand.

Visualize the Condition of a Business

For many people, it is helpful to visualize the condition of a business in addition to using the accounting equation of A = L + OE.

Suppose for a moment that I give you a "magic" camera. You can point this magic camera at any business and the camera will give you an accurate picture of the condition of the business in its most basic form. The picture would always come out like this:

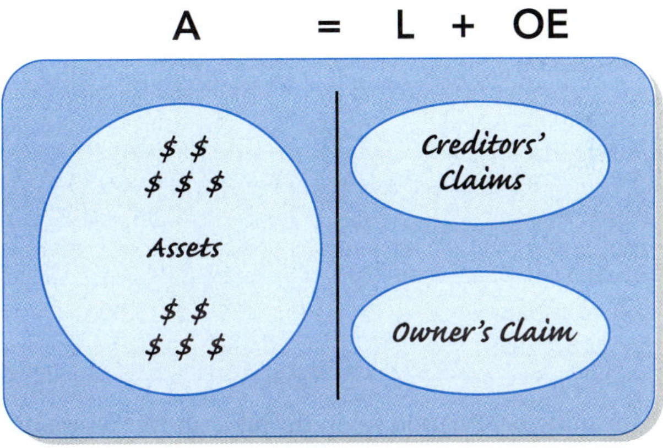

Continue to Visualize . . .

Soon, we will spend a lot of time watching how business events can cause changes in the three parts of the picture, but remember that the financial condition of every business can always be visualized like this picture.

Any change or business event you might encounter in an accounting book (or in "real life") can always be understood by visualizing how it affects the three basic parts of the business condition. Try to keep this picture in mind as you study the rest of the book.

PRACTICE Learning Goal 4

Solutions are in the disk at the back of the book and at: www.worthyjames.com

Learning Goal 4 is about using the accounting equation. Use these questions and problems to practice what you have learned.

Reinforcement Problems

LG 4-1. Make the equation balance. In the table below, calculate the missing amounts in the accounting equation.

	Total Assets =	Total Liabilities +	Owner's Equity
a. Mohawk Company (June 30, 2018)	$251,000	$200,000	?
b. Nez Perce Company (December 31, 2018)	?	$18,500	$22,200
c. Lakota Company (October 31, 2017)	$50,000	?	$35,000
d. Modoc Company (March 31, 2017)	?	$45,000	$180,000
e. Cherokee Company (April 30, 2018)	$200,000	$251,000	?
f. Seminole Company (December 31, 2018)	$815,000	?	$645,000

What is the meaning of situation (e) in the table above? Is situation (e) actually possible?

LG 4-2. Identify specific items in the accounting equation. Use a blank sheet of paper to complete the table. In the space to the right of each item, indicate if the item is an asset (A), a liability (L), owner's equity (OE), or none of the above (none).

Item	A, L, or OE
a. Money owed to a supplier	(Reminder: Use a separate sheet of paper to complete the table.)
b. Cash	
c. Office supplies	
d. Money owed to the bank for a loan	
e. The amount of assets that would go to the owner after the all creditors are paid	
f. A signed contract requiring us to provide services next month	
g. A computer	
h. Computer software	
i. A bill from the telephone company for this month's service	

PRACTICE Learning Goal 4, continued

Solutions are in the disk at the back of the book and at: www.worthyjames.com

LG 4-2, *continued*

Item	A, L, or OE
j. Land	
k. An employee	
l. An office building our company is renting	
m. Money owed to us by our customers	

LG 4-3. What does the accounting equation explain? Someone in another business class who has never studied accounting wants to know if it is true that the accounting equation somehow "explains any business." Write a brief, but complete, answer to this person here:

LG 4-4. A practical application. The Schuylkill River Rowing and Sailing School has a bank loan. The bank requires that total liabilities including the loan (which is $80,000) can never be more than 40% of the company's assets. What is the minimum amount of assets that the company must maintain if there are no other debts? What is the minimum amount of owner's equity?

INTERNET EXERCISES

What is the difference? What are the differences among the following professions?

- Certified public accountant auditor
- Certified fraud examiner
- Forensic accountant

a. Briefly describe the main activities and the type of work described by these titles. To help with your research, you can use the following Internet websites. (Use bookmark/favorites to save the locations of links you use in an "Accounting References" folder.)

- www.startheregoplaces.com
- www.aicpa.org (follow the links for: students, landing a job, career path)
- www.acfe.com
- www.forensicaccounting.com

b. If you are interested in protecting the environment, how could being a CPA help you in your goals?

Your Questions?

It is *very* important to be aware of what you need to understand better. What do you need to understand better about this learning goal? On a separate piece of paper, write the questions that you want to discuss with your classmates, instructor, or supervisor. Try to be very specific about what is bothering you, such as explanations that you do not fully understand.

LEARNING GOAL 5

Define "Entity" and Identify Different Types

Overview

Introduction

In the prior learning goal, you learned how to calculate the basic financial condition of a business. In this learning goal, you will see that to calculate a condition, something else must be done first: an "entity" must be identified. Unless this is done, it is impossible to calculate the condition of a business.

In Learning Goal 5, you will find:

Economic Entities

The Economic Entity Explained

Definition of an Entity

An ***economic entity*** is any activity for which the financial condition or financial information is to be reported separately. An economic entity is also called an ***entity***.

Examples of Economic Entities

- A candy store business is an economic entity. A hardware store business is a different economic entity. Another candy store is a different entity.
- The owner of a business and the business that she owns are two separate economic entities.
- A charity is an economic entity.

The more specific the entity, the more detailed the financial information can be.

- A large company is an economic entity. However, the management of the company wants more detailed information about the operations of the company. The company is therefore divided into different divisions, and financial records of business activity will be kept for each division. Each division is an entity. If each division is divided into departments and financial records are kept for each department, then each department is an entity.
- A government is an economic entity. Each department within the government is also an entity, if the department must report its operations separately.

Not Economic Entities

- Your Wednesday night chess group is not an economic entity because the group is a social entity and not an economic one. There is no intention of preparing financial reports concerning the group.
- You own three businesses and you do not keep separate records for any of the individual business activities. The individual operations are not economic entities because there is no way to identify their separate activities. It is impossible to report their financial information individually. Only the combination of the three activities is an economic entity. This combined information is not very useful.

The Economic Entity Assumption

Assumption

The ***economic entity assumption*** states that it must be possible to correctly identify an economic entity for which accounting is to be done.

A Priority Requirement

The economic entity assumption is the most fundamental requirement in accounting.

Why Is It Important?

If there is no identifiable entity, then accounting will be impossible.

Before you can calculate financial condition or report financial activities, you must identify the entity for which you are doing the calculating and reporting. If no entity can be identified, no reporting can be done. If the operations of different entities are all mixed up like scrambled eggs, then financial reporting will be all mixed up like scrambled eggs.

Example

You own a video rental store, an ice cream store, and a real estate sales office. You do not identify them as separate entities, and you make no effort to keep separate records of the business activities.

> *Result:* You will not be able to determine the condition of any of the businesses or analyze the operations of each business.

How to Identify an Economic Entity

Follow these Steps

Step	Action	
1	Identify an activity.	
2	**IF** someone needs to make financial decisions concerning this activity . . .	**THEN** go to Step 3. Otherwise, this is not a economic entity.
3	Maintain separate financial records concerning only this activity.	

How to Identify an Economic Entity, *continued*

Examples of Separate Record-Keeping

When an economic entity is identified, the entity must keep separate records of its financial activities, apart from any other entity. This is the only way to accurately identify the true financial condition of an entity.

- Dave's dry cleaning business has $275,000 in various assets such as cash, supplies, and equipment, as well as business debts. Dave personally owns another $190,000 in various assets that are not part of the business. Dave wants to make financial decisions about the operations of the business and about his own personal affairs, so he must keep completely separate records for the business and for himself. These records will show assets, claims on assets, income, expenses, and so on.
- Eduardo owns a yogurt shop and a motorcycle repair shop. Therefore, he must keep separate records for three entities: the yogurt business, the motorcycle repair business, and himself.
- Diana owns a beauty salon business and uses only one credit card for purchases of beauty supplies and cash advances. She uses some of the purchases and cash in her beauty salon business; the rest of the beauty supplies and cash she uses personally. Without a tremendous amount of reconstruction and analysis, Diana will *not* know:
  - how much credit card debt is personal and how much is business.
  - how much cash and beauty supplies were used in the business and how much were personal. (Where did the cash and supplies go?)

Check Your Understanding

Write the completed sentences on a separate piece of paper. The answers are below.

The ········ assumption means that each economic ········ can be ········. After this is done, separate ········ must be maintained. An airline company (is/is not) ········ an economic entity, and each individual ticket agent for the airline (is/is not) ········ an economic entity of the airline.

You are tutoring accounting. A student asks you this: "Why keep a separate checking account for my business? If I own the business, then I own the cash in the business. So why not just keep that cash with my personal cash all in one account?"

Answers

The entity assumption means that each economic entity can be identified. After this is done, separate records must be maintained. An airline company is an economic entity, and each individual ticket agent for the airline is not an economic entity of the airline.

The issue is not just that all the cash belongs to her. The issue is knowing how to account for it. Otherwise, she will manage her business poorly.

Can the student identify exactly where all the cash came from—how much from business activities and how much from personal activities? The student probably will not know how much cash is business cash and how much comes from personal activities, such as investments, loans, gifts, or another job. If she says, "I keep a record of all the deposits and checks," then she has the potential to reconstruct separate records for each entity, but it will be a very slow and difficult process.

The Proprietorship, *continued*

"Economic Entity" Compared to "Legal Entity"

As you know, every business must be identified as a separate *economic* entity. "Economic" refers to identifying financial activity for record-keeping purposes. This is done so the operations are correctly identified and the financial condition is properly reported.

However, legal rights and responsibilities are also a part of being in business. These legal rights and responsibilities must always connect to some particular person. A ***legal entity*** is a person with legal rights and responsibilities.

For a business, a legal entity can be different from an economic entity. A perfect example of how these two entities can be different for a single business is the proprietorship. A proprietorship is a separate *economic* entity from its owner and other businesses. The owner keeps separate records for the business and himself or herself.

But *legally*, there is no distinction between the owner and the business! It is the owner who has the ultimate obligation to pay the business debts and who legally owns the business assets. There is **one** *legal* entity—the person who is the owner. However, for financial record-keeping, there are **two** *economic* entities: the business and the owner.

Example 1

Al owns a flower shop proprietorship that has $75,000 of assets, including a $35,000 delivery van. Even if the van is used only by the business, Al's name is on the state motor vehicle department records that show he owns the van. If Al permanently withdraws the van asset from the business operations and uses the van personally, the van still belongs to the same legal entity—Al.

However, for the purpose of identifying financial assets and claims on assets, the van has moved from one economic entity (the business) to a different economic entity (Al).

Example 2

Al's flower shop has $50,000 of liabilities. Suppose the business cannot sell its assets for enough money to pay these business debts. Al, the owner of the business, is *personally* responsible to pay the business debts with his own personal assets. The personal obligation to pay business debts is called ***personal liability***. Even though the business is a separate economic entity for record-keeping purposes, the *legal* entity, Al, has the ultimate obligation to pay the debts.

The Proprietorship, *continued*

Example 3

If Al works in the business and pays himself cash from the business, this is not an expense of the business even though Al calls it a "salary." Like all the other proprietorship assets, the cash is already owned by Al. Even though Al might be taking the money out of the business bank account, he is simply paying himself what he already owns. It is just a withdrawal of an asset by the owner.

The Partnership

Definition

A ***partnership*** is a business that is owned by two or more people acting together as partners.

Attributes of a Partnership

The following table describes the important attributes of a partnership.

Partnership Attribute	Description
Number of owners	Two or more, acting together as partners
Who manages it?	The partners
How difficult to start?	Technically, as easy as a proprietorship. Only a verbal agreement is legally required, but this is very unwise. For practical purposes, partnerships can be extremely tricky to form properly. A written partnership agreement should be used, along with the help of a lawyer and an accountant experienced in partnerships.
How common is it?	Less common than proprietorships and corporations.
Type of business	Any kind of business can be a partnership. Usually partnerships are businesses that require more investment than a proprietorship.

continued ▶

The Partnership, *continued*

General vs. Limited Partnership

The kind of partnership we are discussing is called a ***general partnership***.

Like a proprietorship, the partners in a general partnership have personal liability for partnership debts.

A different kind of partnership is a ***limited partnership***. These are special partnerships in which certain partners do not have personal liability; however, these partners cannot manage the business.

The Corporation

Definition

A ***corporation*** is a business that is *one* combined legal *and* economic entity given "life" by the laws of the state in which the corporation was formed.

General Features of a Corporation

- The document that creates a corporation is called a ***charter***.
- The charter creates the corporation as a legal "person." The corporation is *both* a combined legal and economic entity, and the owners of a corporation do *not* have personal liability or ownership of the business assets.
- The ownership of a corporation is divided into many small shares, called ***common stock***. Anyone can buy shares of the stock, so it is possible that the stock may be owned by just one or many thousands of people. These people are called ***stockholders*** or ***shareholders***. Large corporations obtain millions of dollars of investment money because there can be many stockholders. Corporations are the largest type of business.
- A corporation has an unlimited life.
- A corporation is the most complex of all businesses to form and operate.

Section VI provides more details about corporations and corporate accounting.

The Limited Liability Company (LLC)

Definition

A ***limited liability company*** (also called an LLC) is a legal business entity that has features of both a partnership and a corporation. It is often the preferred form of legal organization by small to moderate-sized businesses. The key advantages of an LLC are that: 1. It provides the owner(s) limited liability, similar to a corporation. 2. If there is more than one owner, an LLC can flexibly allocate its taxable income and cash withdrawals to each owner using different methods, similar to a partnership. Alternatively, an LLC can elect to pay tax as a single corporate entity.

Other features:

- An LLC is easier to form than a corporation. The document that creates an LLC is called an "operating agreement". Owners are often referred to as "members". Usually an attorney is required.
- Generally an LLC can acquire more investment capital than a partnership or proprietorship because of the attractiveness of limited liability.
- An LLC can specify either a limited life or a continuous life.

The Same Basic Principles for All Business Types

All Entities Use the Same Principles

Regardless of the type of entity, the same principles determine the financial condition of the business. The business classification does not alter these principles.

Example

Bill Smith owns a proprietorship but changes it to a partnership by signing a partnership agreement with Louise and Dave. The basic principles of business condition are exactly the same. The only difference is that the ownership claim is divided among three people, which is more time-consuming to analyze.

Later on, if the partners agree to make the business a corporation, the basic accounting principles will still be exactly the same, even though there might be many stockholders. Now the ownership claim is called "stockholders' equity." Even though there may be certain special stockholder equity transactions, that is only a refinement of the basic principles, which still apply.

Visual Picture of Condition for the Three Basic Types

The pictures below show the condition of the business as a proprietorship, partnership, and corporation. The idea of assets and claims on assets is unchanged. In all cases, the accounting equation is still A = L + OE. The only difference is how the owner's equity is described.

A Proprietorship

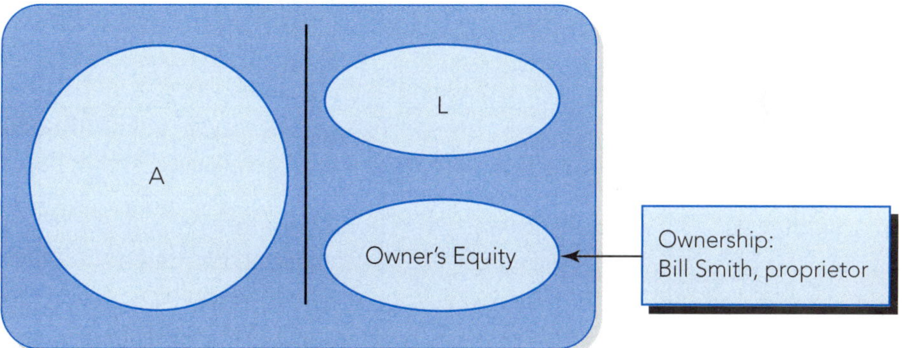

A Partnership

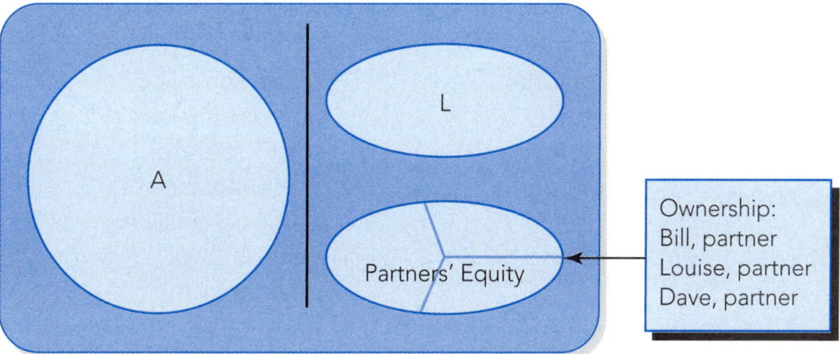

continued ►

The Same Basic Principles for All Business Types, *continued*

A Corporation

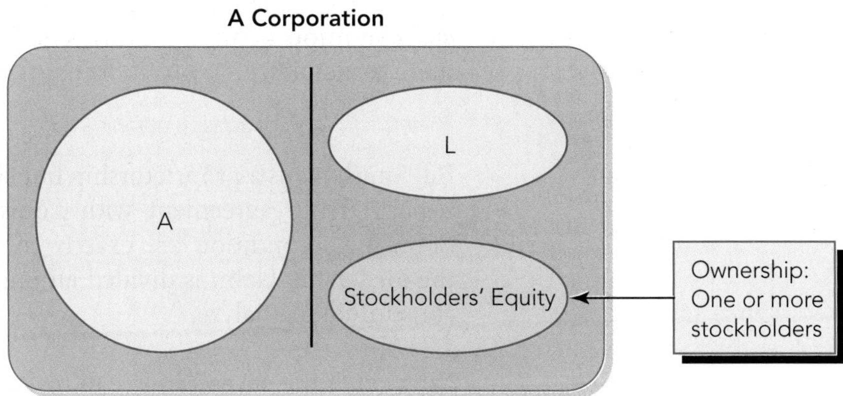

Overview of Organization Features

Feature	*Proprietorship*	*Partnership*	*Corporation*
Ownership	1 owner	2 or more partners	1 or more stockholders
Owner personal liability?	Yes	Yes (unless a limited partnership)	No
Life	Limited (to termination or life of owner)	Limited (fixed period or same partner group)	Unlimited
Separate records kept?	Yes	Yes	Yes
Same accounting rules?	Yes	Yes	Yes
Main advantages	▪ Easy to start ▪ One person controls the business ▪ Simple records	▪ Greater resources than a proprietorship ▪ Greater flexibility in allocating profits and losses to owners than a corporation	▪ No personal liability (with limited exceptions) ▪ Potentially greater resources ▪ Often easier ownership transfer
Main disadvantages	▪ Personal liability ▪ Limited resources	▪ More complex and expensive to start, operate, and manage ▪ Personal liability ▪ Potential for partner conflict is high	▪ Most complex and expensive to start, operate, and manage ▪ Corporate income is taxed twice: on the profits and on the dividends (special elections can eliminate double taxation for small corporations)

QUICK REVIEW

- An economic entity is any activity or operation for which financial condition or financial information is to be reported.
- The economic entity assumption means that it must be possible to correctly identify an economic entity for which accounting is to be done.
- Once an entity is identified, separate financial records must be maintained for that entity.
- It is necessary to distinguish between economic entities and legal entities.
- Business entities are commonly classified by the nature of their ownership:
  - proprietorship (one owner)
  - partnership (two or more owners acting as partners)
  - corporation (one or more stockholders)

VOCABULARY

Charter: the legal document that creates a corporation (page 70)

Common stock: ownership shares of a corporation (page 70)

Corporation: a business that is a combined legal and economic entity and is owned by one or more individuals as stockholders (page 70)

Economic entity: any activity or operation for which the financial condition or financial information is to be reported (page 63)

Economic entity assumption: assumption that it is possible to identify an individual economic entity for which financial reporting is to be done (page 64)

Entity: another term for economic entity (page 63)

General partnership: a partnership where all partners have personal liability and full management authority (page 70)

Legal entity: the entity that has legal ownership of assets and legal responsibility for debts (page 68)

Limited liability company: a form of legal organization that provides advantages of both a corporation and a partnership. (page 70)

Limited partnership: a partnership in which certain partners do not have personal liability (page 70)

Partnership: a business with two or more owners acting as partners (page 69)

Personal liability: being personally responsible to make good all business debts (page 68)

Proprietorship: a noncorporate business that is owned by one person (page 67)

Shareholder: another word for stockholder (page 70)

Stockholder: an owner of stock of a corporation (page 70)

PRACTICE Learning Goal 5

Solutions are in the disk at the back of the book and at: www.worthyjames.com

Learning Goal 5 is about defining the meaning of "entity" and identifying different types of entities. Use these questions and problems to practice what you have learned about entities.

Multiple Choice

Select the best answer.

1. A general partnership
   a. is not an economic entity.
   b. is not a legal entity.
   c. cannot be created by only a verbal agreement.
   d. all of the above.
2. A proprietorship
   a. is not a separate economic entity from the owner.
   b. is difficult and time-consuming to start.
   c. cannot be easily managed by the owner.
   d. is the most common form of business organization in the United States.
3. The economic entity assumption means that
   a. separate recording-keeping is important.
   b. it must be possible to correctly identify a particular financial activity.
   c. if an entity cannot be identified, accounting cannot be done.
   d. all of the above.
4. Which of the following is *not* an economic entity?
   a. a bowling club
   b. a stockholder
   c. the marketing department of a corporation
   d. a group of accountants who meet every Wednesday night just to go bowling
5. Which of the following is a combined economic entity *and* a legal entity?
   a. the De Anza Partnership Company
   b. the West Valley Corporation
   c. the Mission Proprietorship
   d. none of the above.
6. The owners of a corporation are usually called
   a. stockholders.
   b. partners.
   c. proprietors.
   d. investors.
7. For which of the following would "A = L + OE" *not* apply?
   a. Proprietorship
   b. Partnership
   c. Corporation
   d. none of the above
8. You have a business that manufactures gasoline tanks for cars. Which form of entity would you select for your business?
   a. Proprietorship
   b. Partnership
   c. Corporation
   d. none of the above

PRACTICE Learning Goal 5, continued

Solutions are in the disk at the back of the book and at: www.worthyjames.com

Reinforcement Problems

LG 5-1. What are the characteristics of the entity? Write the correct answer on a separate piece of paper.

a. How many owners form a proprietorship?

b. What document brings a corporation into existence?

c. What is the length of life of a partnership?

d. What entity is most difficult to form?

e. What entity is technically easy to form but for practical purposes has many potential complications?

f. What entity is a legal "person" that incurs liability separate from the owners of the entity?

g. The owners of what business are called "stockholders" or "shareholders"?

h. As an owner, you will have personal liability if you form what type of entity?

i. What is the most common form of business?

j. What form of business is easiest to create?

k. What are the three biggest advantages of a corporation?

l. How many owners form a partnership?

m. How many owners form a corporation?

n. What is the length of life of a corporation?

o. What are the main disadvantages of a proprietorship?

p. The owner of a proprietorship writes herself a check from the business bank account. What is this payment called?

q. What indicates ownership in a corporation?

r. What is the type of entity that potentially can obtain the most money from investors?

r. What is the type of entity that potentially can obtain the most money from investors?

s. What form of business organization is often selected by small business owners because it combines advantages of both a corporation and partnership?

SECTION

Transactions—Analyzing and Visualizing

OVERVIEW

What this section does	This section shows you how to analyze and see the effects of transactions so you can understand how they change the condition of a business.
Use this section if. . .	. . . you do not fully understand how transactions affect a business, . . . you want more practice analyzing transactions before recording transactions and using debits and credits.
Do not use this section if. . .	. . . you already know how to analyze the effects of transactions. You can proceed to recording transactions in Learning Goals 11 and 22.

LEARNING GOALS

Do You Like a Good Story?

It Might Help You to Remember Better

Sometimes people remember information better when the information is part of an interesting story. The story that continues on the next page is the second part of a three-part adventure, mystery, and romance story. If you have not read the first part of the story, you can return to the beginning on page 23 to find out how it all began—or you can start here. So, if you think a story might help you remember better, or if you just want to have some fun, go ahead! The adventures of Darius continue.

Technical Content

This part of the story contains the following technical content:

- Identifying transactions
- How to analyze the effects of transactions
- Revenues and expenses explained
- Identifying all changes in owner's equity

You Can Skip the Story

If you prefer to study the technical content listed above more quickly, you can skip the story and go directly to page 94, where the current presentation and practice continue.

The Wealth of Darius

Part II

It happened when Darius least expected it. Early in the morning, just after sunrise, Darius was walking in the marketplace toward the vegetable seller's stall when he felt a hand on his arm.

A cackling voice called to him, "Come here, young man!"

He turned instantly and saw the old woman, dressed in black, grasping his sleeve. It was the same woman he had helped a year ago. She pulled his sleeve and her voice rattled, "You come with me."

Remembering her and what she had become, Darius felt the strength drain from his body. He fought to keep his legs from folding. In a moment, the old woman pulled Darius out of the market and around a corner. Darius was at once blinded by a flash of intense white light. For an instant, he felt himself being lifted off his feet by a strong wind, and then he remembered nothing.

When Darius awoke, he was standing in his shop. The large, dazzling Hermes loomed before him. They were alone. "Well?" Hermes boomed. "I promised you that I would return in exactly one year, and here I am!"

Darius threw himself down and whispered into the floor, "I have used what you have given me, and I have given it much thought. I am grateful beyond words! I thank you daily!"

"Up, mortal!" the god ordered. A force snapped Darius back into a standing position. "Yes, I know," Hermes continued, "and I am pleased that you say you have given this valuable gift much thought. Tell me what you have thought about it."

Darius tried hard to think clearly. Then with relief he remembered that he had made a list of all the things that the formula, which he had received from the god, had made possible. He found the paper and timidly handed it to Hermes. In a shaky voice, Darius said, "I have given much thought to the correct value to use for the assets when I calculated the condition of my business."

"You did well to use the price that you paid for the assets," Hermes responded.

"I gave much thought to what assets and debts to use in the calculation. I have never included assets or debts that did not belong to the business."

"You did well again," the voice rumbled.

"Each time I prepared the calculation, I carefully watched the changes in the total assets and the changes in the total debts. Sometimes this helped me make better decisions about when to buy more assets and how much debt I would allow the business to have."

Hermes looked down at Darius and spoke. "You have done correct things, but I expected no less from you. After all, you have received a great gift, have you not?"

"Yes, a very great gift." Darius bowed his head.

"Very well, then. You spoke of changes in the condition of your business. How do you explain those changes?"

Darius began to tremble because he had nothing else to say. His mind raced. What had he overlooked?

"You have nothing else to tell me or to ask me after an entire year?" The force of Hermes' voice was now vibrating the tools lying on the table. "You have no other questions about the changes in your business?"

As if he were a forest animal caught in a bright light, poor Darius was so paralyzed that he could only stare, transfixed by the sparkling brilliance around Hermes. Darius could no longer think.

Hermes softened his voice. "Darius, you have calculated the condition of your business. You learned to use the special formula A = L + OE to see the wealth and claims on wealth. That is good. But isn't there something else that you need to know each time you use the formula?"

Silence.

"Mortal, you try my patience!" The tools bounced off the table. "Very well, the gods will teach you!"

In a white blaze, Hermes was gone. Darius remained frozen, staring into the space Hermes had just occupied. In the distance, like a faraway echo, Darius heard, ". . . gods will teach you . . . gods will teach you. . . ."

What Darius Forgot

Another perfect day warmed the fields of blooming clover on the distant heights of Mount Olympus. Gentle zephyrs puffed and nudged the sweet blossoms and borrowed their fragrance to bring to the gods, who relaxed among a grove of oak trees in a grand garden.

"So, Hermes," said Artemis, goddess of hunting and all wild things, "tell us about your visit to that mortal Darius."

"He demonstrates that mortals remain flawlessly impaired."

"Yes," replied Artemis, "in their own way, they are as perfect as we are."

Aphrodite (pronounced *afro-DYE-tee*), the goddess of love and beauty, asked, "He is such a handsome young man. What did you find deficient in him, Hermes?" She lifted a silver cup of ambrosia to her lips.

"What I find deficient," replied Hermes, "is that Darius faithfully calculates the condition of his business, yet he does not bother to ask himself *why the condition changes!* He watches the changes but does nothing to discover the reasons. He does not appreciate my gift! After all I did for him!"

"Really. They are such simple beings," said Athena, the goddess of wisdom and courage.

"And worst of all, worst of all," Hermes continued, "is that he has done nothing to explain the reasons why his owner's claim on the wealth has changed. What could be more important to a merchant or a businessperson than explaining why the owner's claim on the business wealth has increased or decreased?"

Apollo, god of truth and music, had been listening the whole time and added, "I would think that explaining all the changes in his claim on the business wealth would be the first thing an owner would always do. It would be the first thing the owner would want to understand. After all, if an owner can explain the reasons why his claim on the wealth has changed, then he can begin to control the causes of the change! He is thereby sure to improve his claim."

"Exactly," replied Hermes. "You describe it perfectly, Apollo."

"Perhaps he has become too satisfied," Apollo said. "After all, his owner's claim has only been increasing. Why should he trouble himself to find out?"

"Yes," Hermes said. "So far, he has not had a good reason to learn what causes the changes in his business—especially the changes in the owner's claim. I believe it is time for me to give him a reason to learn. I will ask Aphrodite to help me."

"What are you going to do?" all the others asked at once, as they turned to look at Aphrodite.

"Oh, nothing really," smiled Hermes. "I will simply give him reasons to want to know."

Hermes' First Trick on Darius

After the second visit from Hermes, Darius tried to go about his business as if nothing had happened, and for a while nothing at all was different.

He watched his business grow. He was grateful and thanked the gods. Darius now prayed to the gods even more frequently, but in his heart he was not sure if he wanted his prayers answered or not.

He worked hard. He carefully observed the calculation each week, and observed the changes in the amounts of assets and claims on assets. What more could the gods want?

One day, Darius had been working in the back of his shop and did not notice the increasing buzz of conversation and gossip in the front. Then Ammon's daughter, Dana, who now sometimes worked in the shop, said, "Darius! Can you believe it? What are you going to do?"

"Do about what?" Darius asked.

Dana smiled gently at him. Darius was always too intent on his work to notice that Ammon's attractive daughter never smiled in the same way for anyone else. "Look across the street, Darius."

As Darius looked out the front of his shop, he saw that the shop directly across from him did not look the same. It had been a sandal maker's shop, but the sandal maker was gone. To Darius' great amazement, paintings of every size were displayed in front of the shop.

Another painter had moved into the shop directly across from Darius' painting business! The new painter's name was Somnus. He had traveled many miles from his old town to settle in Darius' village and open a new shop. Somnus later told people that he moved because of a powerful dream that he had. In that dream, he heard the god Hermes telling him to move. Then, in the dream, he had seen Darius' village.

Darius soon discovered that Somnus was an artist of great experience and talent. He was about the same age as Darius but, unlike Darius, Somnus was a businessman. Somnus always spent extra time with customers or gave them small gifts. He would tell each customer what great artistic understanding the customer had.

Because there was another painter right across the street, Darius noticed that customers did not buy paintings from his shop quite so quickly as before. Even regular customers did not always choose to have Darius design a fresco or wall painting anymore. Now they would always speak to Somnus before deciding.

Darius began to notice something else happening when he did his monthly calculation. The assets of the business no longer seemed to be increasing so quickly, and the owner's claim hardly changed at all.

After two months, something happened that Darius had never seen before: slowly at first, then faster, his owner's claim began to decrease. As the business lost its wealth, the owner's claim began to diminish. Darius did not understand the reasons for this, and so he could only watch helplessly as the business began to dissolve like a small piece of candy.

Unexpected Help from a Friend

Month after month, Darius watched as his owner's claim decreased. Finally, at the end of a year, to Darius' dismay, the calculation showed:

Assets	=	Creditors' Claims	+	Owner's Claim
$14,700		$7,700		$7,000

The creditors' claims were now again greater than the owner's claim—something Darius had promised to never let happen again.

While Somnus continued to create new wall designs and find new customers, Darius watched his own business sink further. At the end of the next month, his calculation showed:

Assets	=	Creditors' Claims	+	Owner's Claim
$10,400		$7,700		$2,700

To Darius, the causes of the changes seemed unknowable and beyond his control. Darius had no idea what to do!

Darius tried to find some comfort with friends. He still gave his dinners for neighbors, especially the poorest ones. On the evening of the same day that he had done his last calculation, Darius prepared a large birthday dinner for Ammon and his family.

Darius was unable to enjoy the party. He smiled and wished Ammon a happy birthday, but each time he spoke with Ammon the old worries returned. At a quiet moment, after the toasts were finished, Ammon's daughter, Dana, approached Darius and looked into his eyes.

"Darius, I know you. I watch you every day in the shop. Something is troubling you. What is wrong?"

Darius began to say that everything was fine and deny that he was worried, but instead he found himself saying, "Dana, you are a clever girl. I have seen how well you bargain with the other merchants. If you can keep a secret, I will show you something tomorrow at the shop. If you have any of your clever ideas, now is the time that I can use them."

The next day, Darius showed Dana the formula he had received from Hermes and how to calculate the condition of a business. At first, Dana was amazed at how this worked, but then she began to frown. "Darius, lately your owner's claim has been decreasing rapidly. It has gone from $7,000 to $2,700 in only one month. Soon you will not be able to claim any of the wealth of the business. It will all go to the creditors!"

"Now you know why I am worried," he said. "I have no idea what is making my owner's claim decrease in such a way."

Dana looked at him for a long time and said, "Darius, you are a wonderful artist. That is what you do best. I will go home tonight and think more about the condition of your business. Together we can think of something." She smiled in the way that she saved just for Darius.

Early the next morning, when Dana entered the shop she went to Darius at his table and said, "I have an idea. We will carefully observe every business event that might affect the condition of your business. Then we will see which ones affect your owner's claim. We can use the good picture that you drew, with the three circles, to visualize the condition."

Darius looked at her with admiration and, for the first time, noticed her beautiful smile.

Transactions: Why the Picture Changes

For the next week, Darius and Dana watched as many business events as they could. To analyze an event, they wrote a description and drew a picture of the change in the condition of the business. Inside the circles, they showed only the particular item that was affected by the change. They analyzed the circles one at a time by asking three specific questions.

The first event they observed was when the business used five gold coins to purchase some paint supplies.

First: Did any *assets* change? Yes (Gold decreased by $5 and paint increased by $5; one asset was given up for another asset.)

Second: Did any *creditors' claims* change? No (Debts were not affected.)

Third: Did the *owner's claim* change? No (The owner's claim was not affected because the total assets are the same and the total debts are the same.)

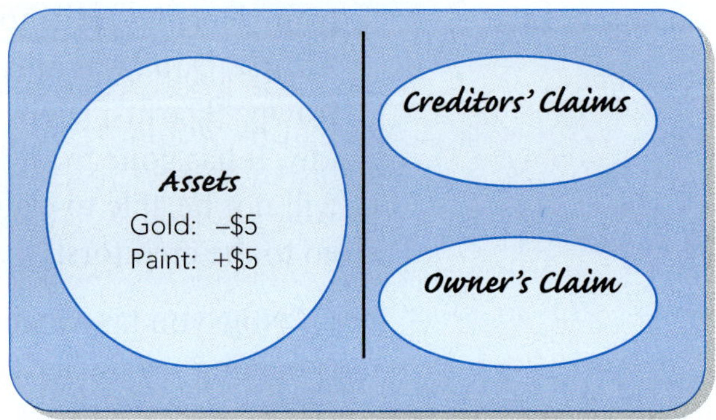

The picture showed them that there were more supplies than before—and less gold—but that was the only change in the condition of the business. None of the claims seemed to be affected at all by this event. Exchanging one asset for another asset only affected the assets.

In the next event that they observed, the business used $20 to pay Hela, a creditor.

Again, Darius and Dana wrote a description of what happened. Then they drew a picture of the business, showing the changes. One at a time, they analyzed each circle:

First: Did any *assets* change? Yes (Gold decreased by $20, and this change reduced total wealth to $10,380.)

Second: Did any *creditors' claims* change? Yes (The creditors' claims also decreased, so the total claims on wealth decreased to $10,380.)

Third: Did the *owner's claim* change? No. Although paying a debt reduced assets, it also reduced a creditor's claim on the assets. Thus, the owner's claim stayed the same. So Darius and Dana saw that paying a debt only had an effect on the creditors' claims but not on the claim of the owner.

Pay $20 debt owing to Hela

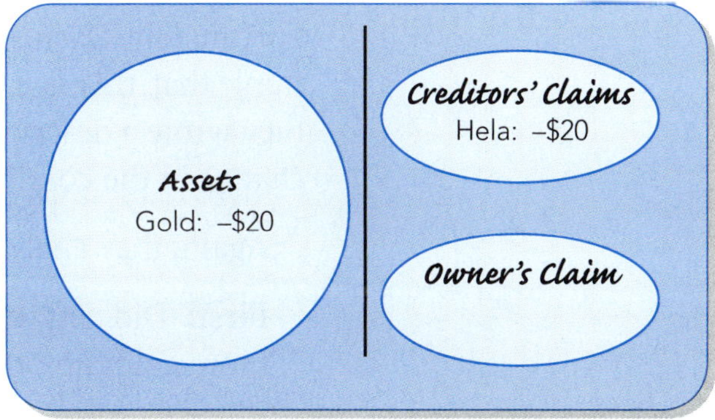

Total Wealth: $10,380 **Total Claims: $10,380**

The next event occurred when Aulis visited the shop to tell Darius that he would be raising the price of many of the paints, beginning next month. When Aulis left, Darius and Dana talked about what happened. They decided that although this was a business event, it did not yet affect the financial condition of the business. The information did not change any part of the picture.

Darius and Dana continued watching the events. They even gave the events a special name. Any event that changed the picture of the condition of the business they called a "transaction."

What Do You Think?

Darius and Dana are developing a procedure to find out how each transaction makes a change in the condition of the business. What are the three questions they ask in the procedure?

1. **Assets:** Did the transaction cause any assets to change?
2. **Creditors' claims:** Did the transaction cause any creditors' claims (liabilities) to change?
3. **Owner's claim:** Did the transaction cause the owner's claim (owner's equity) to change?

In the meantime, Darius watched as Somnus continued to attract even more customers. Two days later, in a moment of desperation, Darius decided to take all of his savings and invest them in the business. The business would then have money to purchase some special and rare paint colors. Darius went home and took $250—his entire savings—from a secret hiding place. He went back to town and placed the $250 in a metal box under the floor in his shop. The money now belonged to the business. With this new money, the business would buy the special paints and, therefore, might take some customers back from Somnus.

Transactions That Affect the Owner's Claim

Fortunately, Darius told Dana what he had done. She said, "Darius, I think that this is a transaction, and an important one." As before, they wrote a description of the transaction, and drew a picture of the change in the condition.

Again, they analyzed the circles one at a time:

First: Did any *assets* change? Yes (The business now has $250 more gold; no other asset is affected.)

Second: Did any *creditors' claims* change? No (The asset did not come from a creditor.)

Third: Did the *owner's claim* change? Yes! (The gold came entirely from the owner. This must be an increase in the owner's claim!)

Darius invests $250 in his business

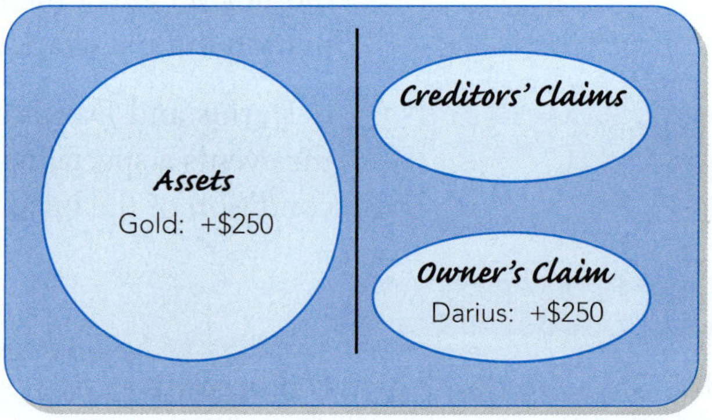

Total Wealth: $10,630 Total Claims: $10,630

Sure enough, when they drew the picture of the business, they could see the increase in assets and the increase in the owner's claim. Dana and Darius had discovered the first transaction that affected the owner's claim: the owner's investment in the business.

Then Dana began to think some more. "If an owner's investment increases the owner's claim, then would an owner's withdrawal of assets decrease it?" She asked, "Darius, did you withdraw gold from the business this month to pay any of your own personal debts?"

"Yes," he said. "This month I obtained the money to pay for your father's birthday party by withdrawing $80 from the business."

"Let us draw a picture of an owner's withdrawal of $80," Dana said. Before completing the picture, they analyzed each circle, one at a time, as they did before:

First: Did any *assets* change? Yes (Gold decreased by $80; the wealth is reduced to $10,550.)

Second: Did the *creditors' claims* change? No (No debt was paid or changed.)

Third: Did the *owner's claim* change? Yes! (The owner's claim is only the excess of the assets over the debts. If the total assets decrease and the debts (creditors' claims) do not change, then the owner's claim must decrease.)

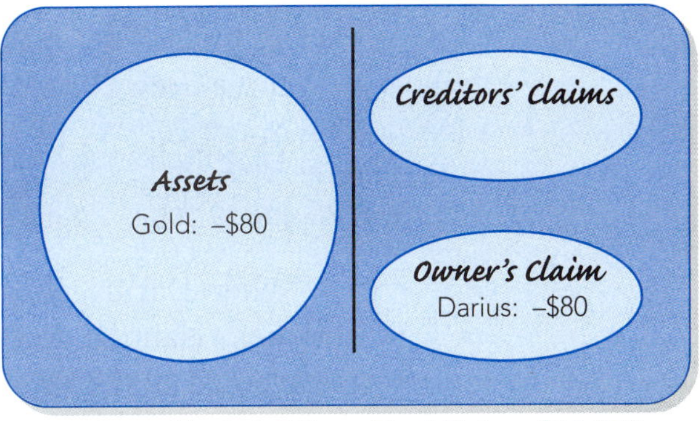

Together they made their second discovery: when an owner withdraws assets, the decrease in assets also decreases the owner's claim. Now they had found two causes for changes in the owner's claim: investments and withdrawals. They hoped that these changes would explain the entire change in the owner's claim.

They would be disappointed. They had not yet discovered two more important changes to the owner's claim.

At the End of the Month

When Darius prepared the calculation of the condition at the end of the current month, to his shock he saw the condition was even worse than before:

Assets	=	Creditors' Claims	+	Owner's Claim
$9,300		$7,400		$1,900

This time, Darius drew two pictures: a picture of the condition at the end of the prior month and a picture of the condition at the end of the current month. These pictures showed the total assets and the total claims after all the transactions were completed for each month.

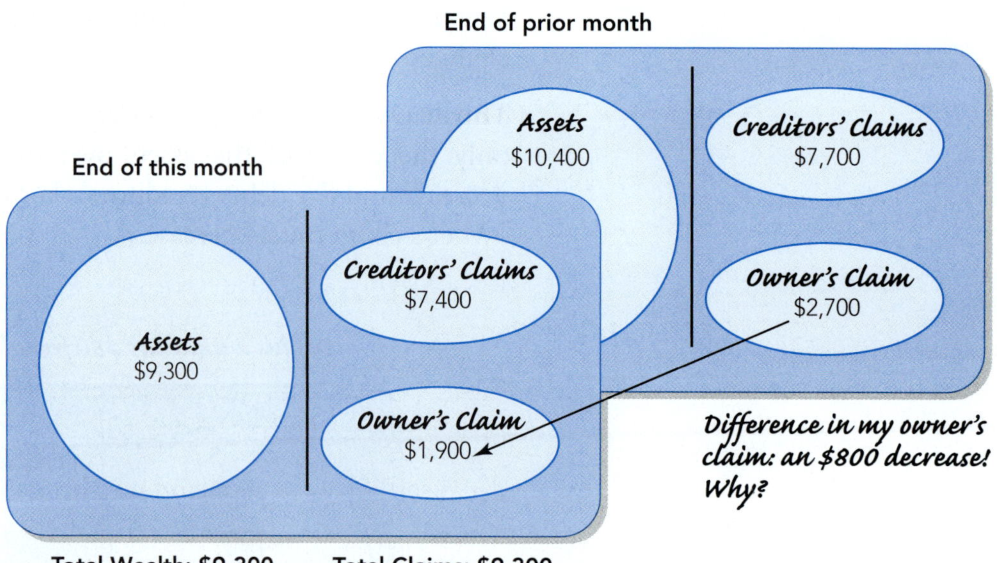

When Darius showed this to Dana, she looked concerned. "Your owner's claim is down another $800, Darius, and we still have not explained all the reasons why."

Then they wrote down how much of the change in the owner's claim they had been able to explain so far:

Owner's investment:	+	*$250*
Owner's withdrawal:	−	*80*
Net change identified:	+	*170*

"Well, we certainly have more work to do," Dana said. "The total change in the owner's claim was a *decrease* of $800. So far, we have only identified the part of the change that is an *increase* of $170. There must be $970 of some other decrease hidden somewhere. We are still far from a complete answer! And at this rate of decrease, Darius, you will only have a few more months to operate your business."

What Do You Think?

What are the two causes of the changes in the owner's claim that Darius and Dana have discovered so far? They have not yet discovered two more causes of change in the owner's claim. Any guesses?

Changes in owner's claim identified so far:
1. An investment by the owner, which increases the owner's claim
2. A withdrawal of assets by the owner, which decreases the owner's claim

The Other Transactions That Affect the Owner's Claim

Darius made a suggestion. "I have an idea. Because I have no more money left to invest, there will be no increases in my owner's claim. Next week, I will not withdraw any gold or other assets from the business, so there will be no changes caused by withdrawals. . . ."

Dana finished his thought. ". . . so any change in your owner's claim will have to be caused by whatever is missing. Correct?"

"Yes, and this time, we will watch every transaction until we find what is missing," Darius answered.

Because they were alert and watching every transaction, it did not take much time to find something interesting. The next afternoon, a customer came into the shop, and Darius painted a small portrait of her. When she left, she paid Darius $25. Both Darius and Dana immediately saw that assets had increased by $25.

As before, they wrote a description of the transaction and drew a picture showing how the condition changed:

First: Did *assets* change? Yes (Gold increased by $25, and this increased total assets to $9,325.)

Second: Did the *creditors' claims* change? No (Creditors were not involved; we did not borrow $25.)

Third: . . .

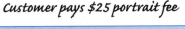

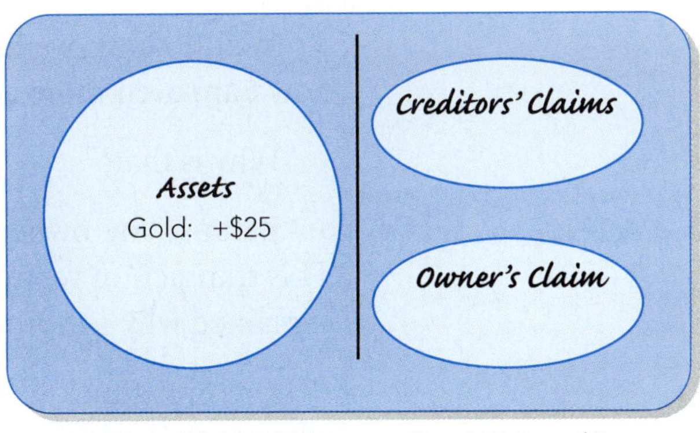

"What do you think, Darius?" Dana asked. "What is the only thing left?"

Darius' eyes opened wide. "I think I understand! The owner operates the business and takes the risks. Therefore, the owner claims any increase in wealth that the business gets from customers. The assets increase because of the efforts of the owner, so the owner's claim also increases."

Dana said, "Yes, I agree. Fees do increase assets. So fees cause an increase in the owner's claim. I think we should give this kind of increase in the owner's claim a special name to show that it comes from making sales to customers."

Dana chose the word "revenue," which is derived from a word meaning "to return, or to come back home after being away." She finished drawing the picture:

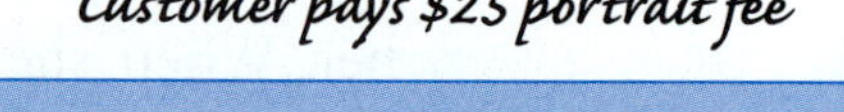

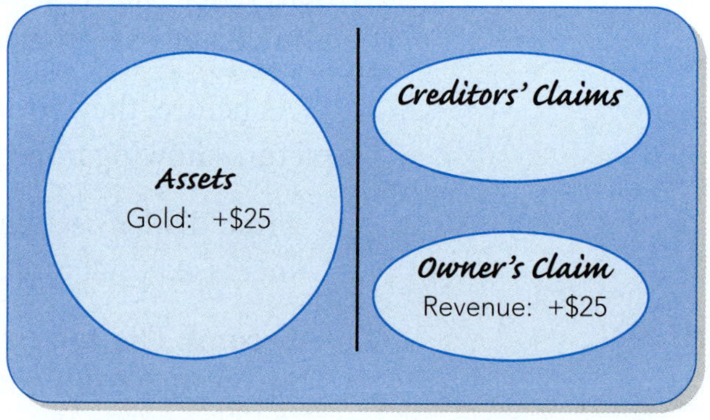

Total Wealth: $9,325 Total Claims: $9,325

Dana could see that Darius was thinking about something. "What is it?" she asked.

"Well, I think we are correct in what we just did," he said, "but now I am even more confused than I was before."

"Why is that?"

"Because my owner's claim has been decreasing, not increasing! This transaction we just found is an increase! So we still have not yet explained why my owner's claim has been decreasing so quickly."

Dana was quick to respond. "Darius, I thought about this before when I watched you working. I think the answer has to do with what we have just seen. Tell me, do you think that customers give you money just because they want to be generous?"

"Of course not," he said. "I have to provide them with something they want—something valuable."

"Yes," she continued, "and are you able to do that at no cost to yourself? Do the gods just give you your supplies free?"

"No, no. What are you saying? I buy supplies and tools, I pay employees, I use up paints and glazes, I use up candles and incense in the shop, I use up gold, I . . ." He stopped.

"Now do you see what I am saying?" she asked.

"Well . . . ," he said, "I have to use up assets to operate the business. When assets are used up in my operations so I can create something to sell, there are less assets than before. My owner's claim is less!"

He continued, "So the 'operations' is almost like a race. Operations increase the owner's claim when I make a sale but decrease the owner's claim when assets are used up."

Dana said, "I can look at your operations and see two examples of using up assets right now. First, how much paint did you use up for the portrait you just painted?"

"I am not exactly sure. I can guess it would be about $10."

"So, let us draw a diagram of that and see if it changed your owner's claim and the condition of your business."

Use up $10 of paint and glaze to operate

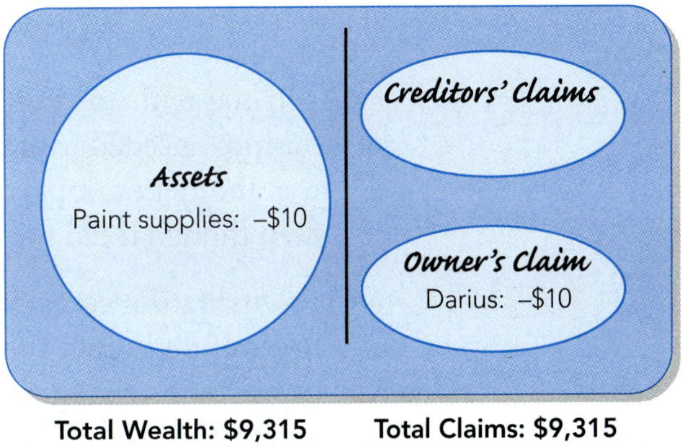

Assets
Paint supplies: –$10

Creditors' Claims

Owner's Claim
Darius: –$10

Total Wealth: $9,315 **Total Claims: $9,315**

Darius and Dana thought in the same slow, careful way as before:

"I know that $10 of the asset supplies was used up," Darius reasoned. "There was no reduction in creditors' claims. Therefore, using up assets as part of business operations must cause a decrease to my owner's claim."

Dana said, "It is very clear to me now. Because of its operations, the business will receive the value of what it creates. That was $25: the fee you charged the customer. This increases the owner's claim."

She continued, "At the same time, to create something of value, the operations also consume assets: the $10 of paint supplies used up. This decreases the owner's claim."

Dana chose the word "expense" to mean the value of the assets used up that helps to create revenue.

Just to be sure, they looked at another example of an expense. That morning, Darius had paid the rent to Opheron, the landlord. The monthly rent was $250 which Darius always paid on time. In this case, the asset used up was gold:

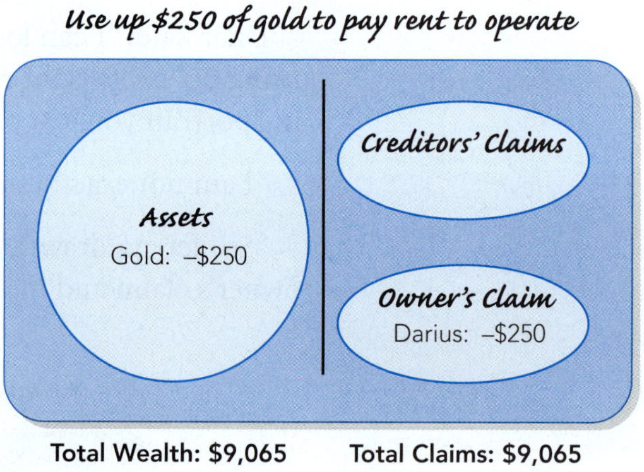

Use up $250 of gold to pay rent to operate

Assets
Gold: –$250

Creditors' Claims

Owner's Claim
Darius: –$250

Total Wealth: $9,065 **Total Claims: $9,065**

If the rent was not paid, there would be no shop to work in. The business needed a shop to operate and create value. So, paying rent was another example of using up assets as part of business operations, even though it did not involve a job for some particular customer.

During the remainder of the week, Dana and Darius continued to carefully watch the transactions. They drew pictures of how the transactions changed the condition of the business. Except for operations, they were not able to discover anything else that increased or decreased the owner's claim. At the end of the week, they decided that business operations were the cause for the rest of the change in the owner's claim.

After thinking about the operations for several days, Darius asked, "Dana, do you think the business is using up assets in operations faster than it is receiving them from customers?"

"Yes, I think that is your problem," Dana suggested. "That would cause your owner's claim to decrease."

"But how can I be sure?"

"Darius, I do not know for certain. All I can suggest is that every day you keep a record of all the transactions. Then you can identify which ones are affecting your owner's claim the most. Whatever you find, you need to begin making changes soon."

"By the gods, that would be a great amount of effort! And I have never tried such a thing."

From far above, Hermes smiled as he watched the two mortals and thought to himself, "If Darius—poor mortal—thinks that business is difficult now, he has much to learn! I will soon favor him with a much bigger surprise."

Hermes' second trick would be of surpassing quality.

To be continued . . .

What Do You Think?

Darius and Dana spent much time searching for all the causes of change in the owner's claim (owner's equity). They discovered four kinds of events that affect the owner's claim—two cause increases and two cause decreases. Do you remember what the four kinds of transactions are?

The two increases: Owner's investment and revenue
The two decreases: Owner's withdrawals and expenses
Revenues and expenses are caused by business operations.

LEARNING GOAL 6

Analyze Individual Transactions

Overview

Introduction

In this learning goal, we will begin the most basic analysis of *changes* in the condition of a business. After some practice looking at changes, you will begin to see something pretty amazing: most of the events that change the condition of a business fall into typical patterns. Learning to analyze these patterns will give you a lot of confidence in your ability to understand the transactions of any business.

Fundamental Principle

Because the condition of any business has only three basic parts, the effect of any change should be analyzed according to how it affects these three basic parts: A = L + OE. This is the essential idea for this learning goal.

"Double-entry" Accounting

Using an equation approach to analyze and record transactions is called ***double-entry*** accounting. Double-entry accounting has two basic requirements:

- Analyze every change by how it affects the three parts of the equation.
- The equation must always stay in balance.

Reminder: Because we are forced to keep the equation in balance, every transaction always creates *at least two changes* within the equation. This is the only way to keep the equation in balance. That is why the method is called "double-entry"—at least two changes with every transaction.

What Is "Single-entry"?

Single-entry accounting is a simple, very old-fashioned system in which some items in the accounting equation are recorded, but there is no concept of describing a business by using an equation to describe all the items.

For example, if you keep a record of the balance of your checking account and all the deposits and checks, but you do not keep a record of how the deposits and checks affected any other items in the accounting equation, you are doing single-entry accounting.

In Learning Goal 6, you will find:

Introduction to Transactions

Transactions That Always Involve Assets

Expenses and Revenues in More Detail

Nonasset Transactions: Liabilities and Owner's Equity

Nonasset Transactions: Other

The Six Basic Patterns of Transactions

Introduction to Transactions

What Is a Transaction?

Definition

A ***transaction*** is any event that causes a change in the accounting equation.

"Well, boys, I'd say a 'transaction' is any event that causes a change in the accounting equation."

Examples of a Transaction

- Owner investment
- Paying a debt
- Borrowing money
- Selling to a customer
- Using up supplies
- Buying more supplies

Not a Transaction

- Signing a contract (because the accounting equation is not affected)
- The bank offering to loan money (because nothing has happened yet)
- A proposed law affecting business (because nothing has changed yet)

Note: Some accountants make a technical distinction between the words "transaction" and "event." However, what really matters is knowing if the equation is affected.

Overview of Transactions

Four Ways to Classify

Transactions can be generally classified by the type of event that causes them:

- External
- Internal
- Exchange
- Non-exchange

External and Internal Events

External events are transactions that take place between an entity (for example, a business) and some other entity. Internal events occur only within an entity.

Exchange and Non-exchange Transactions

Exchange transactions are always external. Exchange transactions result from events in which separate entities give or receive something of value between each other. Non-exchange transactions are events in which an entity gives up or receives something with nothing in return.

Examples

The table below shows examples of general classification of transactions.

	Exchange	Non-exchange
External	▪ Buy equipment ▪ Borrow money ▪ Pay a bill ▪ Perform services ▪ Sell a product ▪ Use services ▪ Collect from a customer ▪ Trade assets	▪ Owner investment ▪ Owner withdrawal ▪ Fire or other casualty loss ▪ Theft of property ▪ Give or receive a gift
Internal		▪ Consume supplies ▪ Wear out equipment ▪ Use materials to put into a product

continued ▶

Overview of Transactions, *continued*

Coming Up . . .

Coming up now are some examples of transactions that always involve assets. These are the most common kinds of transactions. For each example you will see the three steps of analysis. Under the three steps you will see the visualization using the accounting equation *and* the illustration. We will label each illustration as a "snapshot" of the event.

Go slowly and let yourself absorb each example at a comfortable pace, being careful and methodical. You do not have to rush because the analysis will become easier and easier as you practice.

Note: Also watch for events that do not qualify as accounting transactions.

Watch out for the owner's personal transactions. The owner's personal transactions are never part of the business activity and are never recorded by the business. (Example: The owner buys a computer for use at home.)

Check Your Understanding

Write your answers on a blank piece of paper.

1. Briefly and accurately define the word "transaction."
2. Write an overview that explains the main types of transactions.
3. What does "double-entry" mean?

Answers

1. A transaction is any event that causes a change in the accounting equation.
2. Transactions can be generally classified by the events that cause them. In this way, transactions are classified as external, internal, exchange, and non-exchange. External transactions occur between two or more entities. Internal transactions occur within a single entity. Exchange transactions are external transactions in which each entity gives and receives something. Non-exchange transactions are external transactions in which an entity gives or receives something with nothing in return.
3. "Double-entry" means keeping the accounting equation in balance. Keeping the accounting equation in balance requires that at least two items within the equation elements must change with each transaction. This is the only way the accounting equation can remain in balance. For example, if a business borrows $1,000, the assets increase and so do the liabilities. Or, if a business uses $100 of cash to purchase supplies, cash decreases by $100 and supplies increase by $100.

Transactions That Always Involve Assets

Examples of Analysis and Patterns

The Three Analysis Steps

To analyze the effect of any event on a business, always ask these three questions:

Step 1: Are *assets* affected?
Step 2: Are *liabilities* affected?
Step 3: Is *owner's equity* affected?

Visualize: Two Useful Methods

As part of the analysis, it is very helpful to visualize the effects of transactions on a business. Students often find two visualizing methods helpful when they are first learning how to analyze the effects of transactions:

Method 1: Use the accounting equation. The best way to do this is to write the equation and use up or down arrows to help you see the effects on the equation. Example: Suppose the owner invests $100,000 cash in a new business. Using the equation, you can visualize this as:

$$\begin{array}{ccccc} A\uparrow & = & L & + & OE\uparrow \\ 100{,}000 & & & & 100{,}000 \end{array}$$

Method 2: Take an imaginary picture (a "snapshot") of the business, showing the changes. Using the same example, you would see:

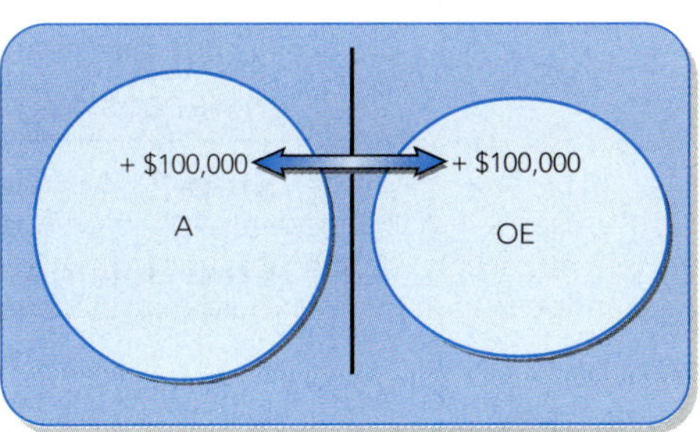

Use Either Method—We Will Show Both

It does not make any difference which method you prefer. Some people prefer to use the equation, and other people prefer the illustration.

To help you decide which method works best for you, we will show both methods in each of the examples that follow.

continued ►

Examples of Analysis and Patterns, *continued*

Analysis	Effect on Condition
Step 1: Are *assets* affected? Yes (Cash goes up by $100,000.)	↑A = L + OE
Step 2: Are *liabilities* affected? No (No debt is involved.)	
Step 3: Is *owner's equity* affected? Yes (Owner's equity increases by $100,000.)	↑A = L + ↑OE

A↑ = L + OE↑
100,000 100,000

Snapshot #1

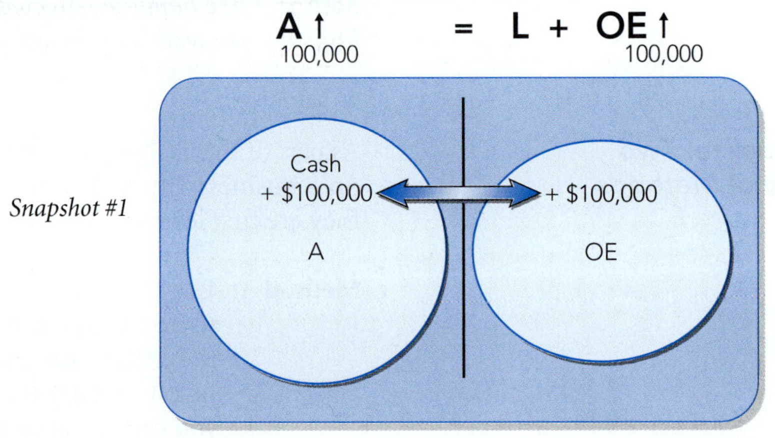

Use Cash to Purchase an Asset

The business buys $500 of computer software for cash. One asset is given up (Cash) for another asset (Computer Software), so total assets do not change.

Analysis	Effect on Condition
Step 1: Are *assets* affected? Yes (Cash decreases by $500; software increases $500.)	↓↑A = L + OE
Step 2: Are *liabilities* affected? No	
Step 3: Is *owner's equity* affected? No	

A↑ ↓ = L + OE
500 500

Snapshot #2

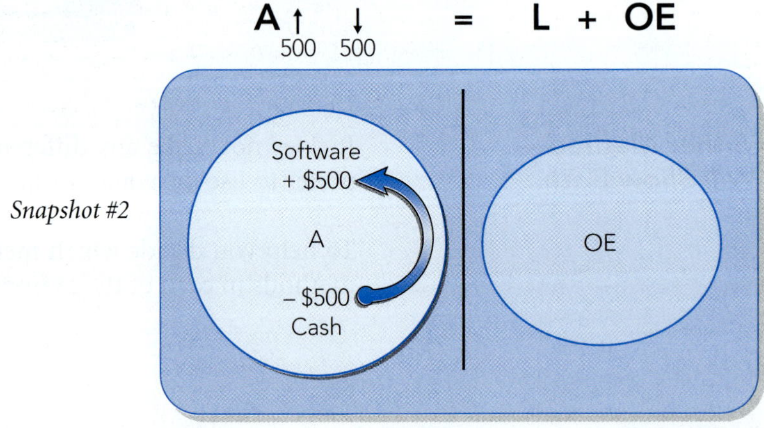

Examples of Analysis and Patterns, *continued*

Purchase Asset on Credit

The business buys $50,000 of testing equipment "on account." Total asset value increases, but now there is a creditor's claim because the equipment is not paid for.

Analysis	Effect on Condition
Step 1: Are *assets* affected? Yes (Equipment increases by $50,000.)	↑A = L + OE
Step 2: Are *liabilities* affected? Yes (Accounts Payable increases by $50,000.)	↑A = ↑L + OE
Step 3: Is *owner's equity* affected? No	

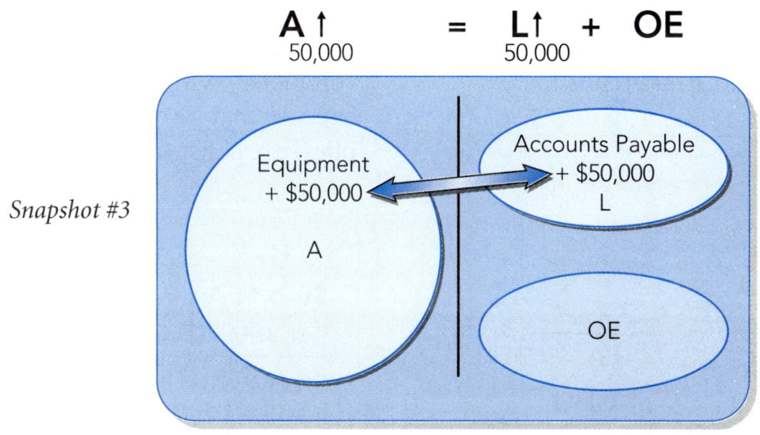

Snapshot #3

Borrow Money

The business borrows $25,000 from a bank. Total assets increase, but so do creditors' claims.

Analysis	Effect on Condition
Step 1: Are *assets* affected? Yes (Cash increases by $25,000.)	↑A = L + OE
Step 2: Are *liabilities* affected? Yes (Loan Payable increases by $25,000.)	↑A = ↑L + OE
Step 3: Is *owner's equity* affected? No	

continued ►

Examples of Analysis and Patterns, *continued*

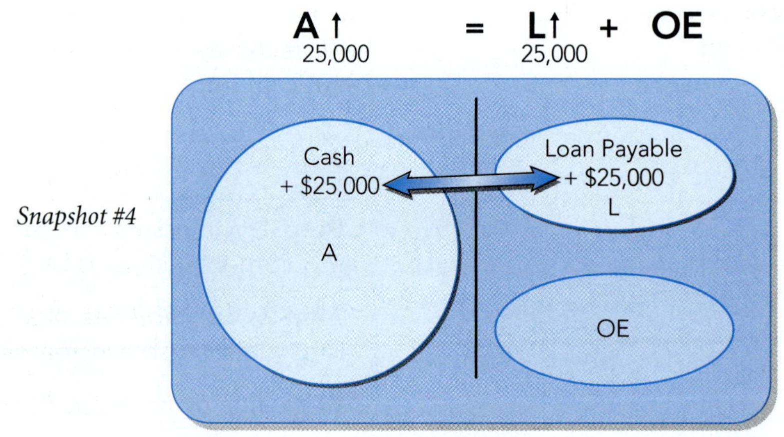

Snapshot #4

Use Up an Asset in the Operations

The business uses up $275 of supplies during operations. This event is completely within the business, so it is an *internal* transaction. This is an expense that decreases owner's equity because resources (in this case, supplies) are consumed in the process of operations to produce revenue.

Analysis	Effect on Condition
Step 1: Are *assets* affected? Yes (Supplies decrease by $275.)	↓A = L + OE
Step 2: *Are liabilities* affected? No (Nothing happens with creditors.)	
Step 3: Is *owner's equity* affected? Yes (Owner's equity decreases by $275.)	↓A = L + ↓OE

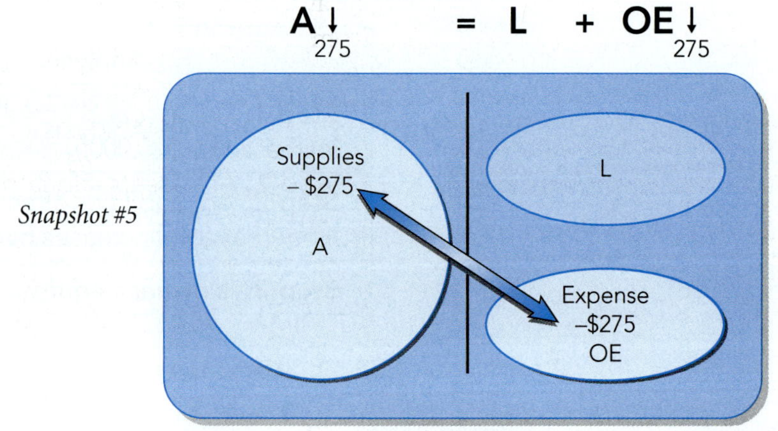

Snapshot #5

Examples of Analysis and Patterns, *continued*

Payment of a Liability

The business uses $500 cash to pay some of the liability from the equipment purchase on account. The creditor (the supplier) is the *external* party to the transaction. Assets are used to reduce creditor claims.

Analysis	Effect on Condition
Step 1: Are *assets* affected? Yes (Cash decreases by $500.)	↓A = L + OE
Step 2: Are *liabilities* affected? Yes (Account Payable decreases by $500.)	↓A = ↓L + OE
Step 3: Is *owner's equity* affected? No	

Snapshot #6

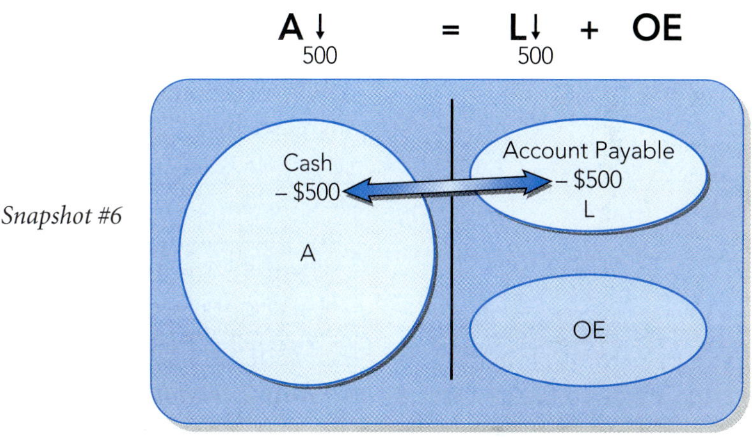

Perform Services for Customers

The business completes a diagnostic job for a customer and receives $2,500 cash. Providing services is revenue. It increases owner's equity because the new asset (Cash) was earned by the business. It did not come from creditors.

Analysis	Effect on Condition
Step 1: Are *assets* affected? Yes (Cash increases by $2,500.)	↑A = L + OE
Step 2: Are *liabilities* affected? No	
Step 3: Is *owner's equity* affected? Yes (Owner's equity increases by $2,500.)	↑A = L + ↑OE

continued ▶

Examples of Analysis and Patterns, *continued*

Snapshot #7

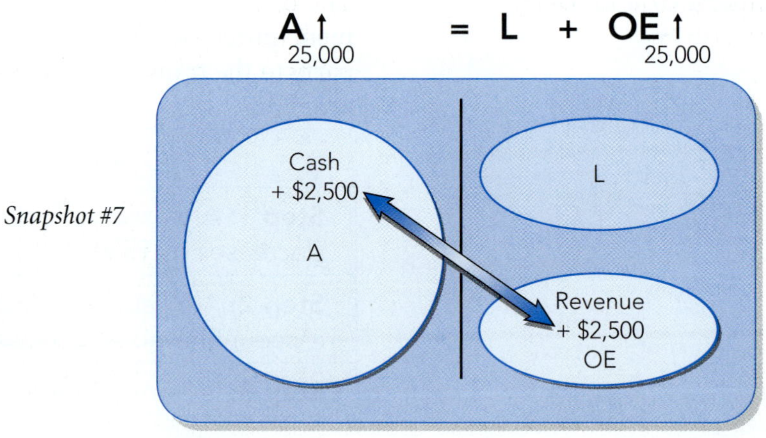

Sale on Account

The company performs $1,200 of diagnostic services. The company sends a bill to the customer for the amount of services. Accounts Receivable increases by $1,200 and owner's equity increases by the same amount.

Analysis	Effect on Condition
Step 1: Are *assets* affected? Yes (Accounts Receivable increases by $1,200.)	↑A = L + OE
Step 2: Are *liabilities* affected? No	
Step 3: Is *owner's equity* affected? Yes (Owner's equity increases by $1,200.)	↑A = L + ↑OE

Snapshot #8

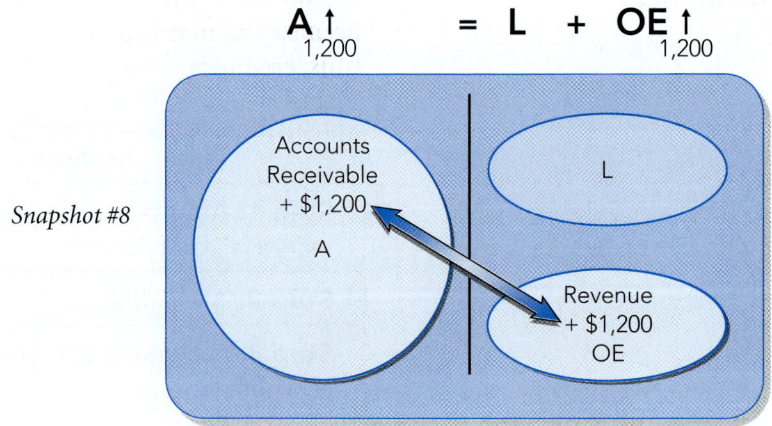

Note: It is not necessary to receive cash when the revenue is earned. Any asset can be received (such as accounts receivable).

Examples of Analysis and Patterns, *continued*

Collect an Account Receivable

The company collects $1,500 cash from a customer's account receivable. Cash increases and Accounts Receivable decreases the same amount. Total assets do not change—they simply shift as one asset increases and the other decreases.

Analysis	Effect on Condition
Step 1: Are *assets* affected? Yes (Cash increases by $1,500 and Accounts Receivable decreases by $1,500.)	A ↑ ↓ = L + OE
Step 2: Are *liabilities* affected? No	
Step 3: Is *owner's equity* affected? No	

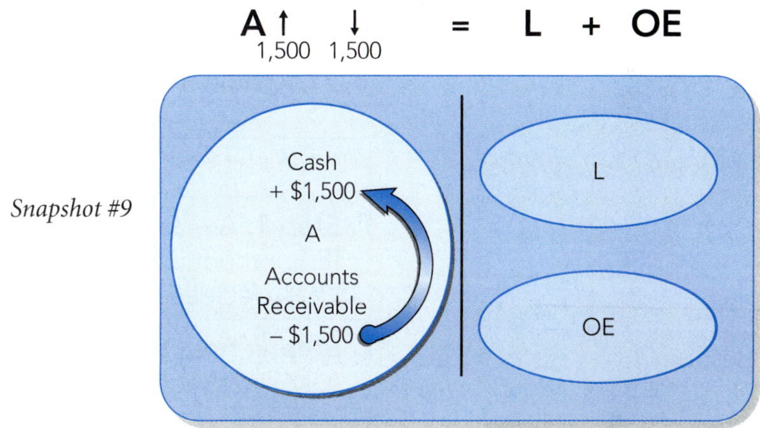

Snapshot #9

Expense: Cash is Used to Pay for Services

The business uses up $150 cash to pay the telephone company for telephone service as soon as the bill is received (so liabilities are not affected). This is an expense that decreases owner's equity. Owner's equity decreases because cash decreases to pay for the resource (telephone service) consumed to help create revenue.

Analysis	Effect on Condition
Step 1: Are *assets* affected? Yes (Cash decreases by $150.)	↓ A = L + OE
Step 2: Are *liabilities* affected? No	
Step 3: Is *owner's equity* affected? Yes (Owner's equity decreases by $150.)	↓ A = L + ↓ OE

continued ►

Examples of Analysis and Patterns, *continued*

Snapshot #10

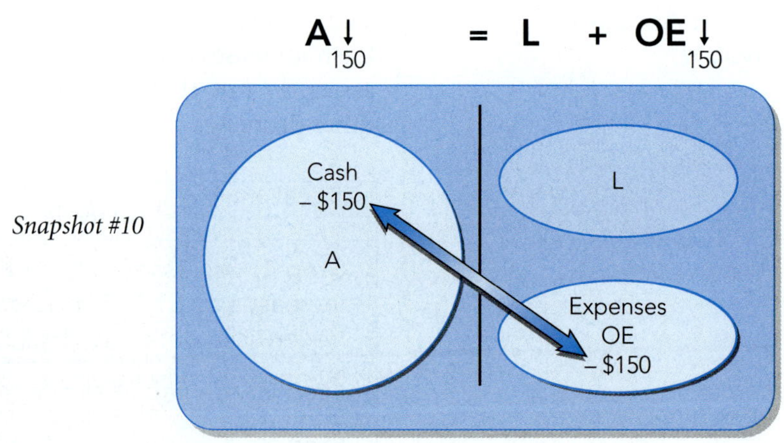

Use Cash and a Note Payable to Purchase Equipment

The company buys $9,000 of equipment by paying $2,000 cash and signing a note payable for the balance of the price. (*Result:* Total assets increase by $7,000 and total liabilities increase by $7,000.)

Analysis	Effect on Condition
Step 1: Are *assets* affected? Yes (Equipment increases by $9,000 and Cash decreases by $2,000.)	A↑↓ = L + OE
Step 2: Are *liabilities* affected? Yes (Liabilities increase by $7,000.)	A↑↓ = ↑L + OE
Step 3: Is *owner's equity* affected? No	

Snapshot #11

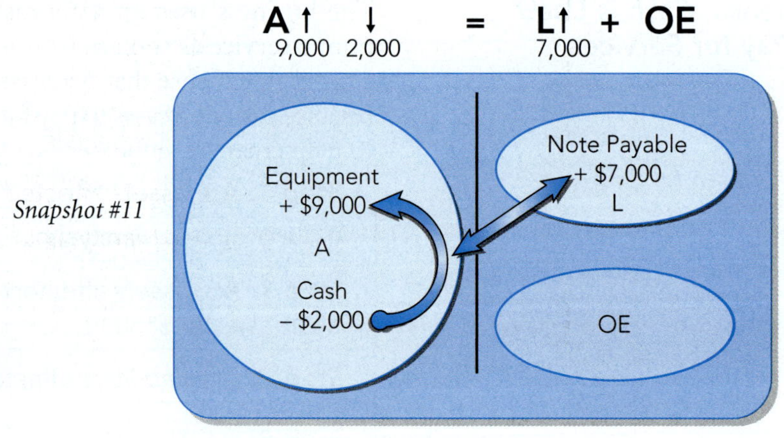

Examples of Analysis and Patterns, *continued*

Casualty Loss: Fire Destroys Assets

A fire destroys $10,000 of uninsured office equipment. The fire is the *external* agent of change in this non-exchange transaction. Owner's equity decreases because the owner of a business always assumes the risk of losses.

Analysis	Effect on Condition
Step 1: Are *assets* affected? Yes (Equipment decreases by $10,000.)	↓A = L + OE
Step 2: Are *liabilities* affected? No	
Step 3: *Is owner's equity* affected? Yes (Owner's equity decreases by $10,000.)	↓A = L + ↓OE

Snapshot #12

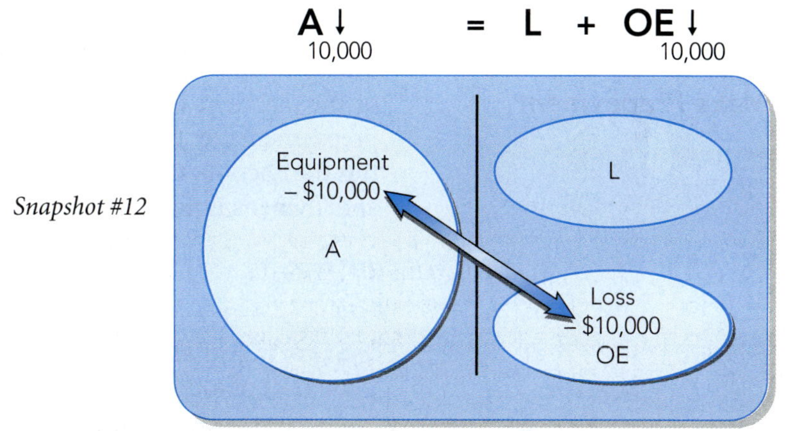

Unrecordable Event

The business signs a new contract with the employee labor union. This is a legal event. No economic event will happen until the employees are actually paid. There is no change to the condition of the business.

Analysis	Effect on Condition
Step 1: Are *assets* affected? No	
Step 2: Are *liabilities* affected? No	
Step 3: Is *owner's equity* affected? No	

continued ▶

Examples of Analysis and Patterns, *continued*

Snapshot #13

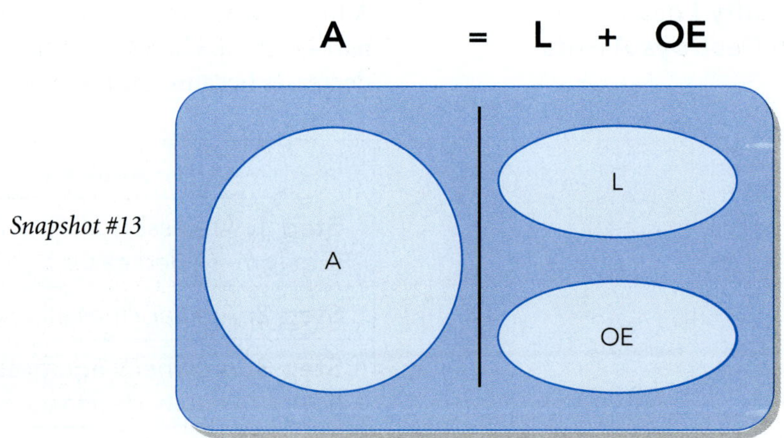

Use Cash to Pay Expense and Make Prepayment

The company makes a $4,000 payment to the landlord for office rent. $1,000 of the payment is for the current month's rent. The remaining $3,000 is a prepayment for the next three months' rent. (Three items are affected by this transaction: Cash decreases by $4,000, Prepaid Rent increases by $3,000, and Owner's Equity decreases by $1,000 because of the rent expense.)

Analysis	Effect on Condition
Step 1: Are *assets* affected? Yes (Prepaid Rent increases by $3,000 and Cash decreases by $4,000.)	A ↑ ↓ = L + OE
Step 2: Are *liabilities* affected? No	
Step 3: Is *owner's equity* affected? Yes (Owner's equity decreases $1,000 because of the expense.)	A ↑ ↓ = L + OE ↓

Snapshot #14

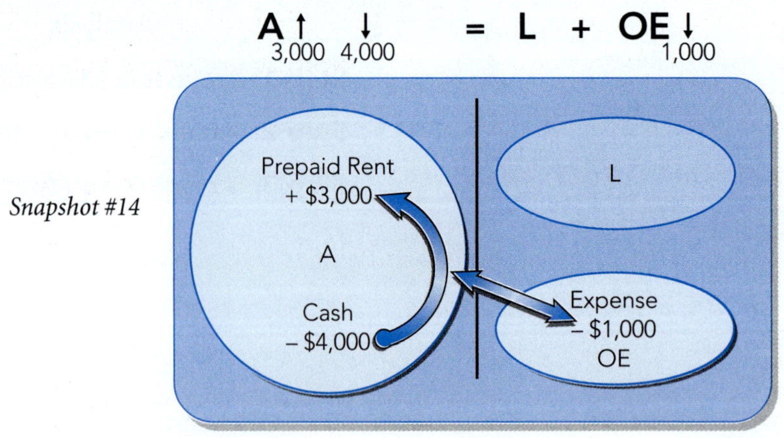

Examples of Analysis and Patterns, *continued*

Owner Withdraws Assets from a Business

The owner of the business needs some cash for personal expenses, so she withdraws $2,000 cash from her business. Assets are reduced and not used to pay creditors, so owner's equity is the claim that decreases.

Analysis	Effect on Condition
Step 1: Are *assets* affected? Yes (Cash decreases by $2,000.)	↓A = L + OE
Step 2: Are *liabilities* affected? No	
Step 3: Is *owner's equity* affected? Yes (Owner's equity decreases by $2,000.)	↓A = L + ↓OE

Snapshot #15

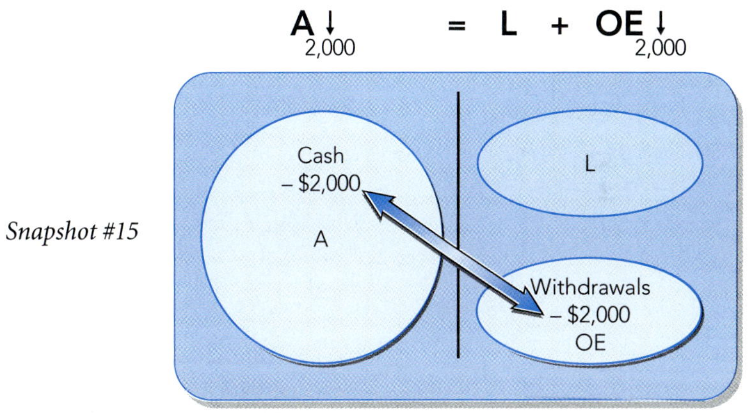

Owner's Personal Expenditure

The owner spends the $2,000 she withdrew from the business on the purchase of furniture for her home. This is not a transaction of the business, so the condition of the business is not affected.

Analysis	Effect on Condition
Step 1: Are *assets* affected? No	
Step 2: Are *liabilities* affected? No	
Step 3: Is *owner's equity* affected? No	

Snapshot #16

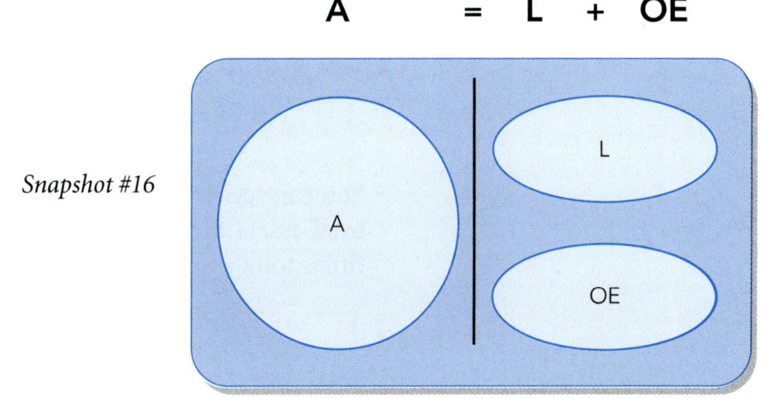

continued ▶

Examples of Analysis and Patterns, *continued*

Summary: Three Types of Asset Transactions

If you take a moment to review all the transactions that you have just analyzed, you will notice that every recordable transaction always involved an asset in some way. All of these transactions can be classified into three possible types of asset transactions (or combinations of the three):

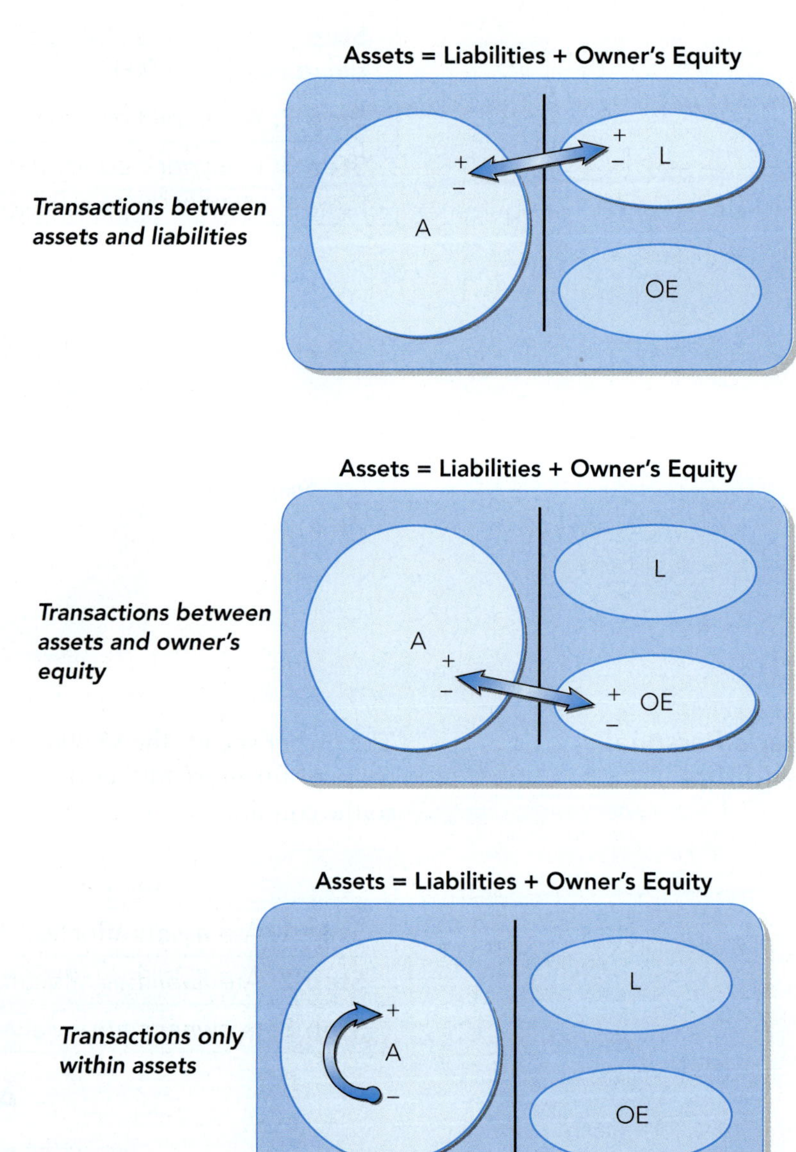

You can see that so far every transaction has involved an asset. Sometimes total assets did not change, sometimes total assets decreased, and sometimes total assets increased.

Check Your Understanding

For each of the transactions given to you, write the change in the accounting equation and draw a diagram that illustrates the change in the condition of the business.

1. A purchase of $800 of supplies for cash
2. A $1,000 loan payment
3. A purchase of $200 of supplies on credit
4. Using up $300 of supplies in operations
5. A $700 sale to a customer on credit
6. Purchase $5,000 of equipment by paying $1,000 cash and signing a $4,000 note payable

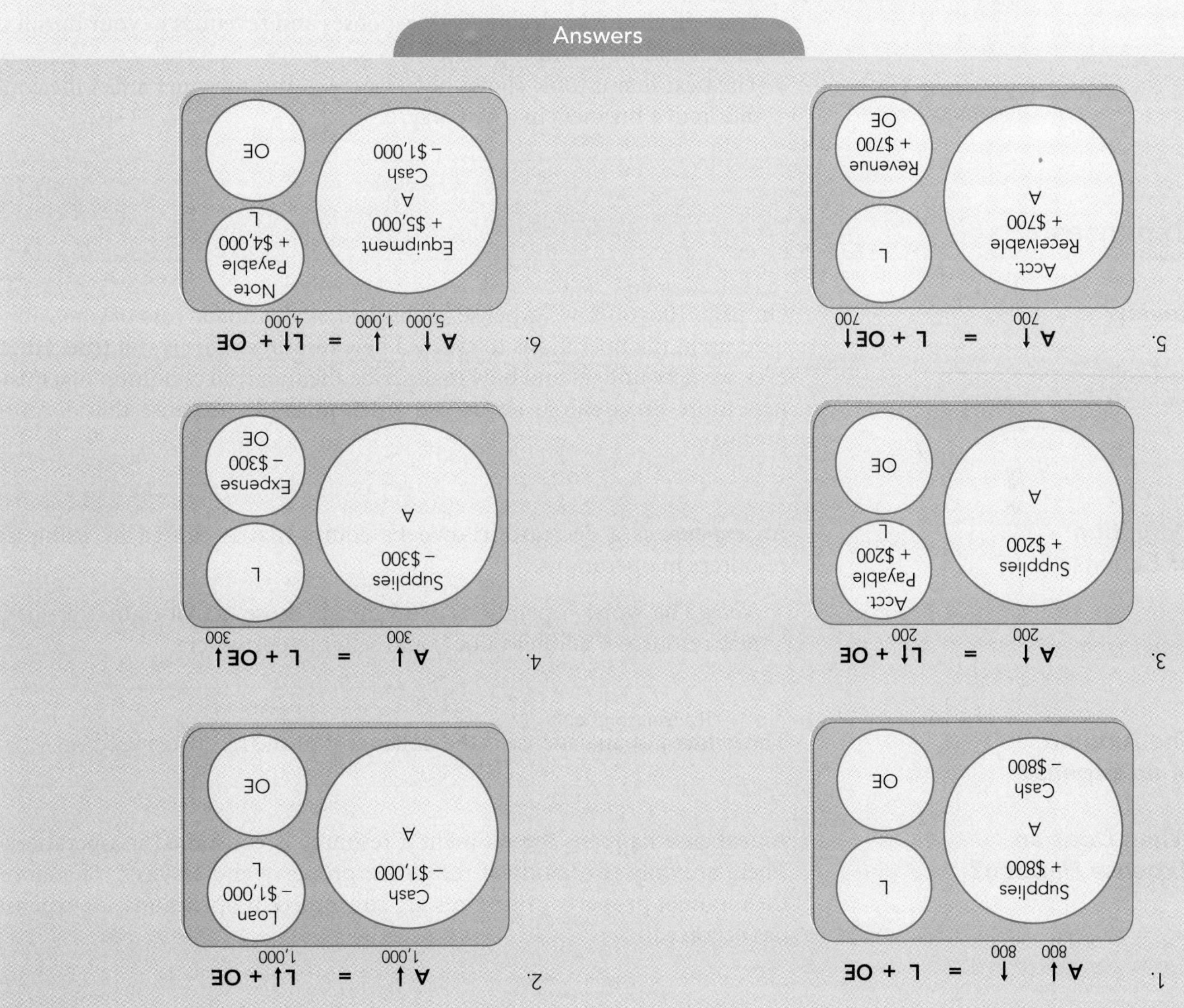

Expenses and Revenues in More Detail

Overview

The Need for Precision

One of the most common errors that students make in basic accounting is the misinterpretation of the words "expense" and "revenue." It is vital that you have a clear understanding of these words for the following reasons:

- Expenses and revenues are the most powerful force of change on any business.
- You will always be dealing with expenses and revenues in your business classes and/or business practice.
- The next major topic shows how expenses and revenues affect the condition of a business in a new way.

Expenses

Review

On page 10, you saw "expense" described as the dollar cost of a resource used up in the operations to create a new resource. This is still true. However, we now understand how to describe the financial condition of a business more precisely, so let us use a definition for expense that is more precise.

Definition of Expense

An ***expense*** is a decrease in owner's equity that is caused by using up resources in operations.

> *Note:* The word "operations" still means those activities that create a new resource ("adding value") and sell it to customers.

The Amount of an Expense

The *amount* of an expense is the dollar cost of the resources used up.

When Does an Expense Happen?

An expense happens the moment a resource is consumed in operations. There are only two kinds of resources: property and services. Therefore, the moment property or services are consumed in operations, an expense has occurred.

Expenses, *continued*

Using up Resources Always Decreases Assets

A business operates by consuming property resources and services resources. Using up these two resources always causes assets to decrease. Assets decrease like this in two possible ways:

- *Noncash asset used up:* Often, an asset itself is the resource (property) that is consumed in the operations. When the noncash asset is consumed, total assets decrease. (Examples: Using up supplies or wearing out equipment.)
- *Cash used up:* The asset cash is used to pay for services consumed in the operations. When the services resource is consumed, total assets decrease because cash is used to pay for the services. (Examples: Paying employees for their services or paying the telephone company for telephone service or paying rent.)

Examples of Expenses

The table below shows some expenses. In each case, a property or services resource is consumed in operations. This causes total assets to decrease and also decreases the owner's equity.

Description	Amount of expense	What resource consumed?	What asset decreased?
Waterville Company used up supplies costing $400. The supplies would have cost $475 to replace.	$400	Supplies (property)	Supplies (The asset is also the resource consumed.)
Augusta Company received a telephone bill for $200 and immediately paid it.	$200	Telephone services	Cash (to pay for telephone services)
Bangor Enterprises completely wore out a machine that had cost $5,000.	$5,000	Machine (property)	Machine (The asset is also the resource consumed.)
Portland Company paid $7,500 for employee wages in the current month's production.	$7,500	Employee services	Cash (to pay for employee services)

continued ▶

Expenses, *continued*

Not Expenses

All of the following transactions or items do not involve an expense. The missing quality is indicated to the right.

Transaction or Item	Missing Quality
A liability is paid.	Assets decrease, but liabilities (debts) decrease the same amount, so owner's equity is not affected.
Cash is used to purchase supplies.	Owner's equity is not affected. There is no decrease in resources—one asset is given up but another is obtained.
An uninsured fire loss destroys equipment.	The resources are not consumed as part of *operations*. (A "loss" is an incidental decrease in owner's equity caused by casualty, theft, or other incidental event.)

Why Does an Expense Make Owner's Equity Decrease?

When assets decrease as a result of the business operations, the owner's equity decreases. The accounting equation clarifies how the owner's claim decreases:

When assets decrease, we know that part of the change in the condition of the business will show up like this: $\downarrow A = L + OE$

To keep the equation in balance, what else must happen? *Owner's equity* also decreases: $\downarrow A = L + \downarrow OE$

(The creditors are not going to let *their* claim be decreased!)

More Examples of Expenses

This expense . . .	would be called . . .
Consuming office supplies	Office Supplies expense
Wearing out equipment	Depreciation expense
Consuming gasoline	Fuel expense

This expense . . .	would be called . . .
Consuming repair services	Repairs expense
Consuming advertising services	Advertising expense
Using city services	Property Tax expense

Note: Each business decides what name to use for an expense, so there is always some variation in the exact names that are used.

Expenses, *continued*

TIP

Remember that "expense" means a *change*—a decrease—in the owner's equity. When you think of expense, think of a *negative change in owner's equity*. If something similar confuses you, always test it for this feature:

You must see a **decrease** in the owner's equity resulting from **operations.**

Decrease in Assets Can be Delayed

So far, in all the transactions that involve an expense, an asset immediately decreases when a resource is consumed. (See Snapshot #5 on page 102 and Snapshot #10 on page 106.) So an asset and the owner's equity both decrease.

However, if a service is the resource that is being consumed, it is often possible to delay payment. This is because service providers often allow 30 to 60 days (sometimes more) to pay a bill.

If payment is delayed, this will delay the need to decrease assets (cash). In the next major topic, we will see what this transaction looks like. If you want to study this right now, you can turn to page 120. Otherwise, let us next define the meaning of "revenue."

Check Your Understanding

Write the completed sentences on a separate piece of paper. The answers are on page 116.

An expense is a(n) (increase/decrease) ········ in ········ ········, caused by using up ········ in ········. The amount of the expense is the dollar ········ of the resources used up. Using up resources will always cause total ········ to decrease. This decrease (may/may not) ········ be delayed until later, when a payment is made.

None of the items listed below are expenses. Explain why each item is **not** an expense.

- Payment of a debt
- A flood that destroys a warehouse
- Using up cash to pay for supplies

Answers

An expense is a decrease in owner's equity, caused by using up resources in operations. The amount of the expense is the dollar cost of the resources used up. Using up resources will always cause total assets to decrease. This decrease may be delayed until later, when a payment is made.

- A debt payment is not an expense because owner's equity is not affected. It is the creditor's equity that is being reduced.
- A casualty like a flood does reduce owner's equity, but this does not happen as part of the operations process. It is an incidental loss.
- Using cash to pay for supplies is not an expense because there is no overall using up of resources, so owner's equity does not decrease. One asset (cash) is simply exchanged for another (supplies).

Revenues

Review

On page 15, you saw "revenue" described as the dollar value of a sale. However, we now understand how to describe the financial condition of a business more precisely, so let us use a definition for revenue that is also more precise.

Definition of Revenue

A ***revenue*** is an increase in owner's equity that is caused by a sale of goods or services.

The Amount of a Revenue

The *amount* of a revenue is the dollar amount that the customer agreed to pay for the goods or services provided.

When Does a Revenue Happen?

Generally, a revenue happens the moment that a customer receives the goods or services that were asked for.

Note: At that time, the revenue is said to be "earned."

A Revenue Increases Assets

When a business makes a sale to a customer, assets increase. This is because the business receives valuable property from the customer. Usually the kind of assets that a business receives are:

- Cash
- Accounts receivable (a legal right to collect money)

Note: Rarely, a business might receive some other kind of valuable resource, but this is quite unusual. I know of an attorney who was once paid in gold nuggets—mostly as a joke.

Revenues, *continued*

Examples of Revenue

The table below shows various examples of revenue and how each one conforms to the characteristics just described.

Description	Amount of revenue	What was sold?	What asset is increased?
Hutchinson Company provided $1,000 of advertising services and was paid immediately.	$1,000	Advertising (services)	Cash
Butler County Enterprises sold $25,000 of farm equipment to a customer on credit.	$25,000	Equipment (property)	Accounts Receivable
Casper Editing Company provided $10,000 of book editing services "on account."	$10,000	Editing (services)	Accounts Receivable
Sheridan Pizza Company sold $300 of pizza and was paid in cash.	$300	Pizza (property)	Cash

Not Revenue

All of the following transactions or items do not involve a revenue. The missing quality is indicated to the right.

Transaction or Item	Missing Quality
Cash is received from a loan.	Owner's equity is not affected because there is no sale. The money must be paid back to the creditor, so only the creditors' equity is affected *(liability increase)*.
Cash is collected from a customer's account receivable from a prior sale.	Owner's equity is not affected because the cash receipt is not from a sale. The sale happened previously. *There is only an increase in one asset (cash) and a decrease in another (accounts receivable).*
A company wins a $100,000 lawsuit and collects the cash.	Although owner's equity increases, it does not happen because of a sale. *(This is called a "gain," which is an incidental increase in owner's equity.)*

continued ▶

Revenues, *continued*

Why Does Revenue Increase Owner's Equity?

When sales are made by a business, it means that the business receives assets from customers, so total assets increase. The owner can claim this increase in assets. (The owner is certainly not going to let the creditors claim the new asset value!) The accounting equation can clarify how the owner's claim increases.

If total assets increase, then we know that part of the change in the condition of the business will show up like this: $\uparrow$ A = L + OE

So, to keep the equation in balance, what else must happen? *Owner's equity* also increases: $\uparrow$ A = L + $\uparrow$ OE

The word "revenue" is sometimes confused with the words "account receivable." An account receivable is an asset that is recorded because of earning revenue. "Revenue" is a description of an increase in owner's equity caused by a sale.

Assets Can Also Increase Before the Revenue Is Earned!

So far in our discussion of the transactions that involve a revenue, an asset is immediately increased at the moment revenue happens (see Snapshots #7 and #8 on page 104).

However, sometimes a customer pays a business in advance, before the goods or services are provided. When this happens, the assets of a company increase before the sale actually occurs. In the next major topic, you will see what this transaction looks like.

Remember that "revenue" means a *change*—an increase—in the owner's equity. When you think of revenue, think of a *positive change in owner's equity* caused by operations—making a sale. If something similar confuses you, always test it for this feature:

You must see an **increase** in the owner's equity resulting from **a sale** of services or product.

Review: Avoid These Mistakes with Expenses and Revenues

Revenue Does NOT Always Mean Receiving Cash

- Cash can come from loans and other sources such as owner investments. These have nothing to do with revenues.
- Revenue can cause *any* asset to increase (for example, accounts receivable). Usually, however, cash or accounts receivable are the assets that increase.

Review: Avoid These Mistakes with Expenses and Revenues, *continued*

Expense Does NOT Always Mean Paying Cash

- Cash can be paid for many different reasons that have nothing to do with expenses, such as paying back a loan.
- An expense can cause almost any asset to be used up, such as supplies. Using up supplies is an example of an expense *without cash being used.*

"Revenue" and "Expense" are Explanations, Not Things

Revenues and expenses are not "things" like assets.

The words "revenue" and "expense" are simply *explanations* for events that cause certain kinds of *changes in owner's equity*... changes caused by operations.

Check Your Understanding

Write the completed sentences on a separate piece of paper. The answers are below.

A revenue is a(n) (increase/decrease) ········ in ········ ········, caused by making a sale to a customer. The amount of the revenue is the dollar amount of the ········. A revenue will always cause total ········ to increase. This increase (may/may not) ········ be received in cash before the revenue is actually earned.

None of the items listed below are revenues. Explain why each item is **not** a revenue.

- Receipt of cash from a loan
- Winning a lawsuit
- Collecting cash from accounts receivable

Answers

A revenue is an increase in owner's equity, caused by making a sale to a customer. The amount of the revenue is the dollar amount of the sale. A revenue will always cause total assets to increase. This increase may be received in cash before the revenue is actually earned.

- Receiving cash from a loan is not a revenue because there is no sale to a customer, so owner's equity is not affected. Only the creditor's equity increases.
- Winning a lawsuit is not a revenue because there is no sale to a customer. (Winning a lawsuit would be a "gain," an incidental, nonoperational increase in owner's equity.)
- Collecting cash from accounts receivable is not revenue because there is no sale. (The sale has already happened at some previous time.) This is simply increasing cash and reducing accounts receivable—a change in assets.

Nonasset Transactions: Liabilities and Owner's Equity

Overview

Introduction

Previously, all the individual transactions that we analyzed involved assets. Asset-related transactions are probably the most common types, so that is why we have looked at them first. However, another frequent kind of transaction is the kind that happens between liabilities and owner's equity. We will study those transactions here.

The Two Types

Transactions between liabilities and owner's equity can happen in two directions. In the illustration below, you can see that in one situation, owner's equity decreases and liabilities increase. In the other situation, liabilities decrease and owner's equity increases. We will look at each of these situations separately.

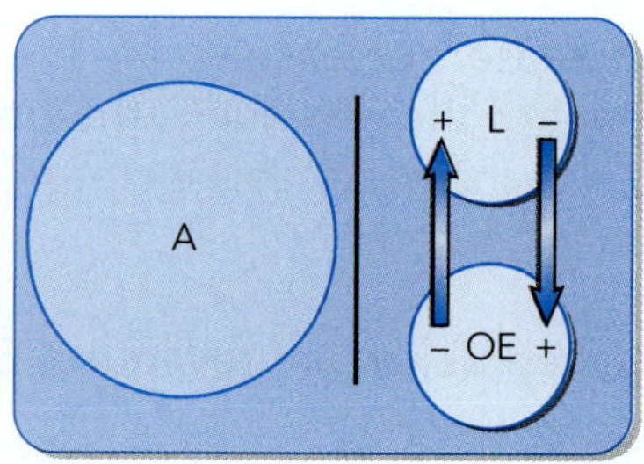

Expenses That Increase Liabilities

A Delayed Decrease in Assets

In the prior discussion about expenses on page 113, you read that an expense always causes assets to decrease. Often, assets decrease at the same time the expense happens. That is what you have studied up to now.

However, when a business has an expense because of services that were consumed, the company can often choose to pay later. Typically, a provider of services allows 30 to 90 days for payment. Thus, there is a *delayed decrease in assets*, even though the expense has occurred when the resource (the service) was consumed.

Expenses That Increase Liabilities, *continued*

Examples

- In March, Glendale Company receives a $500 utility bill for electrical services consumed during March. The company does not pay the bill until April; therefore, assets (cash) do not decrease until April, even though the expense was in March.
- Tsaile Corporation used $2,500 of computer programming services in October. The company did not pay the bill until November 15; therefore, assets (cash) do not decrease until November 15, even though the expense was in October.
- The last day of the December payroll for Tucson Company is December 31. However, the company does not actually pay the employees until January 3; therefore, assets (cash) do not decrease until January 3, even though the expense was in December.

How an Expense Can Create a Liability

Whenever a business consumes a service and decides to pay for it later, liabilities increase because of the amount owed.

A new liability—a creditor's claim—is recorded against the value of the company assets. The liability is a legal obligation. Although total assets have not decreased yet, some assets (cash) are now as good as gone. In the three examples above, each company has a liability until the cash is paid.

The accounting equation will show an increase in liabilities: A = ↑ L + OE

What must happen to keep the equation in balance if the assets have not yet decreased? A decrease in *owner's equity:* A = ↑ L + ↓ OE

The owner has given up some of her claim on assets to the creditor.

When Does the Business Condition Change?

Condition changes at the time the expense occurs. This is when the service resource is consumed. A picture of the change looks like this:

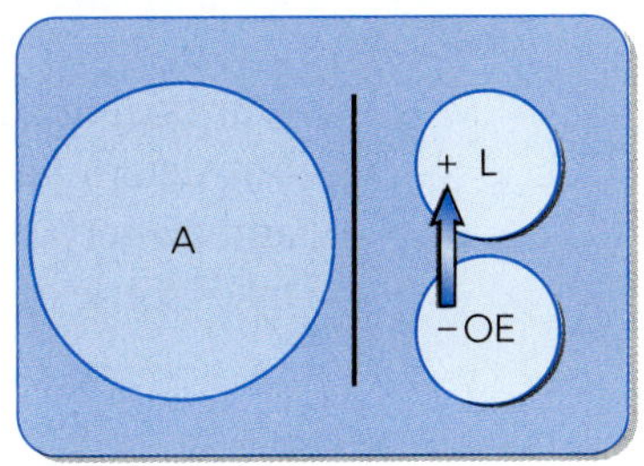

continued ▶

Expenses That Increase Liabilities, *continued*

When do the Assets Actually Decrease?

When the debt is paid a short time later, the assets will decrease. You can use the accounting equation to show this: ↓ A = ↓ L + OE

Notice that now owner's equity is not affected. Why? Because there is no expense. The expense happened before, when the resource was consumed. That was when the company decided to delay payment, so liabilities increased. Later, assets must be used to pay the new liability.

Summary

The following table shows the stages of the condition of a company as these transactions happen:

Stage	Event	Accounting Equation
1	Business incurs an expense but delays payment.	A = ↑ L + ↓ OE
2	Business pays the creditor who provided the service. Assets decrease when debt is paid.	↓ A = ↓ L + OE

Final Result

The final result is:

- Assets have decreased.
- Owner's equity has decreased.
- The liability is gone—it was created and then paid.

More Examples

Starting on page 100, you saw 16 "snapshots" illustrating transactions. We continue here with examples of expenses that increase liabilities, beginning with Snapshot #17.

Stage 1: Bill Received, But Not Paid Immediately

Our business receives a $120 bill from the telephone company on July 10, but delays payment. Because the bill is not paid, liabilities now increase and owner's equity decreases because the creditor (the telephone company) takes some of the owner's claim on assets.

Expenses That Increase Liabilities, *continued*

Analysis	Effect on Condition
Step 1: Are *assets* affected? No (Assets are not used to pay the bill.)	
Step 2: Are *liabilities* affected? Yes (Accounts Payable increase by $120.)	A = ↑ L + OE
Step 3: Is *owner's equity* affected? Yes (Owner's equity decreases by $120.)	A = ↑ L + ↓ OE

Snapshot #17

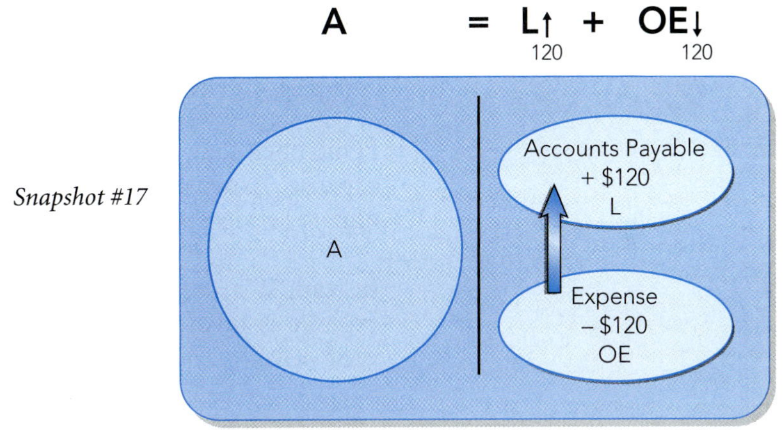

Stage 2: The Liability is Paid

The business in the example above pays the $120 telephone bill on August 2. As assets decrease, the creditor's claim also decreases. Owner's equity is unaffected by the payment to creditors.

Analysis	Effect on Condition
Step 1: Are *assets* affected? Yes (Assets decrease by $120.)	↓ A = L + OE
Step 2: Are *liabilities* affected? Yes (Accounts Payable decrease by $120.)	↓ A = ↓ L + OE
Step 3: Is *owner's equity* affected? No	

continued ▶

Expenses That Increase Liabilities, *continued*

Snapshot #18

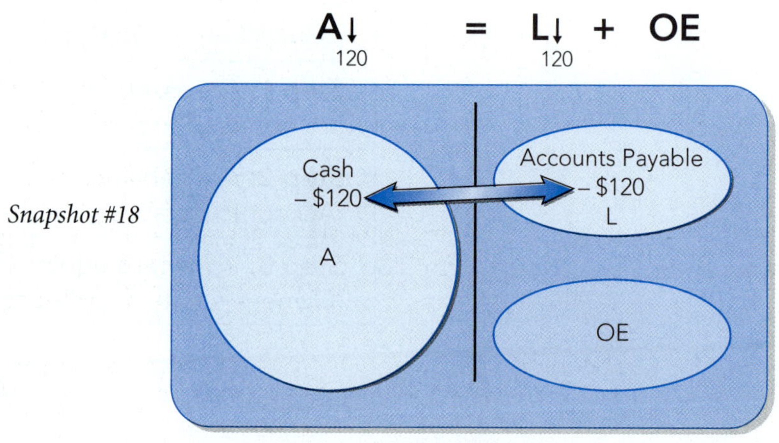

Caution!

Remember that not every increase in a liability happens because of an expense. Expenses and liabilities usually occur together when there are unpaid services consumed in operations.

Instead, if a company borrows money or buys supplies on credit, no expense is involved. Can you use the equation (or draw the picture) to verify this?

Analysis	Effect on Condition
Step 1: Are *assets* affected? Yes (Cash or Supplies increase.)	↑A = L + OE
Step 2: Are *liabilities* affected? Yes (They increase.)	↑A = ↑L + OE
Step 3: Is *owner's equity* affected? No (no expense)	

Caution! Don't Confuse "Liability" and "Expense"

Beginning students often confuse the word "liability" with the word "expense." I am not exactly sure why this happens; perhaps they both seem like negative or bad kinds of things or because they sometimes occur together.

An expense can happen with or without a liability, and a liability can happen with or without an expense. The fact that they sometimes occur in the same transaction does not mean that they are the same thing.

A liability is not an expense, and an expense is not a liability. (*Suggestion:* Go to the glossary at the back of the book and review the definitions of "expense" and "liability.")

"He thinks a 'liability' is the same thing as an 'expense.'"

Check Your Understanding

Write the completed sentences on a separate piece of paper. The answers are on page 126.

An asset is not always used up at the same time an expense occurs. Sometimes, there is a ········ decrease in assets. Instead of decreasing assets, ········ are increased. This usually happens when a (property/service) ········ resource is consumed and not immediately ········.

Use up and/or down arrows (↑ ↓) in the accounting equation to show these transactions:

- Beebe Company used $5,000 of accounting services in June, but did not pay for them.
- In July, Beebe Company paid the amount owing for the accounting services.

Answers

An asset is not always used up at the same time an expense occurs. Sometimes, there is a delayed decrease in assets. Instead of decreasing assets, liabilities are increased. This usually happens when a service resource is consumed and not immediately paid.

- A = ↑L + ↓OE
- ↓A = ↓L + OE

Revenues That Decrease Liabilities

Assets Increase in Advance

On page 116, you read that a revenue always causes assets to increase. Frequently, assets increase at the same time a revenue is earned. That is what you have studied up to now.

However, sometimes a business receives an advance payment from a customer *before* goods or services are provided to the customer. When this happens, the business has increased its assets *before the revenue is earned.*

Examples

- Louisville Corporation receives a $2,000 advance payment from a customer one month before the merchandise is sold.
- Bowling Green Legal Services requires a $1,000 advance payment from a client before they begin doing the legal work.

The Advance Receipt Creates a Liability

Suppose that Blarney Advertising Company receives an advance payment of $800 from a customer in October. The advertising service will begin in November. Assets increase by $800 when payment is received in October. However, no revenue is recorded. Why? Because no services have been provided yet!

Because Blarney Advertising Company received cash and has not yet performed services, *the company has a liability.* Until the services are provided, the company is obligated to return the money.

At this point, the accounting equation will show this: ↑A = ↑L + OE

$800 $800

Revenues That Decrease Liabilities, *continued*

Earning the Revenue Decreases the Liability

When Blarney Advertising Company provides the advertising service in November, it has earned the revenue. At this point, the liability will disappear because the service has been provided. Now owner's equity increases. The customer's claim on the cash payment has now shifted to the owner because the business provided the service.

The accounting equation will now show this: A = ↓ L + ↑ OE
$800 $800

Name of the Liability

The name of the liability created by receiving an advance payment from a customer is ***unearned revenue***. It is also sometimes called ***deferred revenue***.

Summary

The following table shows the stages of the condition of a company as these transactions happen:

Stage	Event	Accounting Equation
1	Company receives advance payment.	↑ A = ↑ L + OE
2	Company provides service or product and earns the revenue.	A = ↓ L + ↑ OE

Final Result

The final result for Blarney Advertising Company is that cash increased by $800 and owner's equity increased by $800. The liability is gone.

Note: If the company had not performed the services, it would have to return the money. Both cash and liabilities would decrease by $800.

More Examples

Each of the following examples show how the condition of a business changes for businesses that receive advance payments from customers.

continued ▶

Revenues That Decrease Liabilities, *continued*

Stage 1: Company Receives Advance Payment

White-Knuckle Airlines receives $550 for a standard ticket. The flight will be in two weeks. The customer is a creditor until the flight is provided. Notice that the airline cannot yet record an increase in owner's equity because the service has not been provided.

Analysis	Effect on Condition
Step 1: Are *assets* affected? Yes (Cash increases by $550.)	↑A = L + OE
Step 2: Are *liabilities* affected? Yes (Liabilities increase by $550.)	↑A = ↑L + OE
Step 3: Is *owner's equity* affected? No	

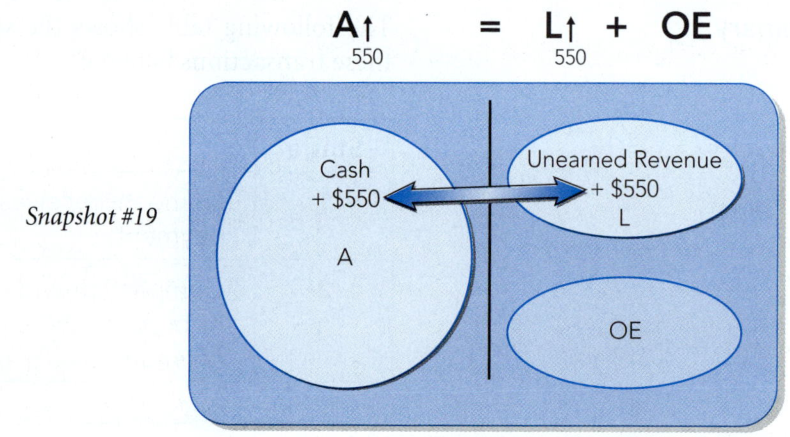

Snapshot #19

Stage 2: Revenue Is Earned

Two weeks later, the customer uses the ticket and takes the flight. The service is provided to the customer, so the liability is gone and revenue is earned.

Analysis	Effect on Condition
Step 1: Are *assets* affected? No	
Step 2: Are *liabilities* affected? Yes (Liabilities decrease by $550.)	A = ↓L + OE
Step 3: Is *owner's equity* affected? Yes (Owner's equity increases by $550.)	A = ↓L + ↑OE

Revenues That Decrease Liabilities, *continued*

Snapshot #20

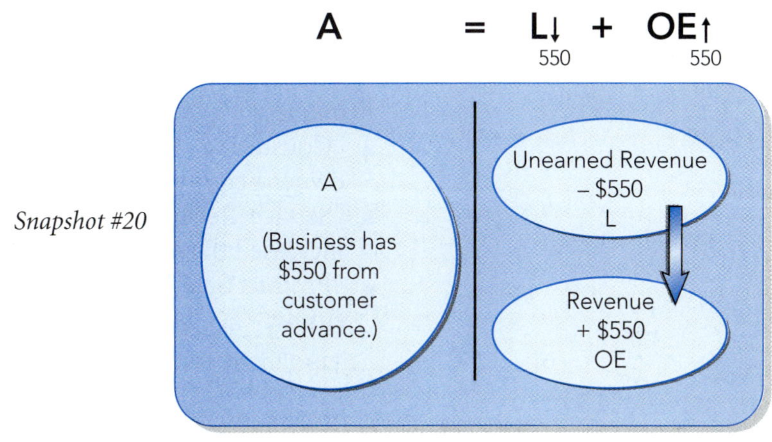

Stage 2: Different Example

Last month, a lawyer received a $2,000 advance (called a "retainer") from a client. The lawyer now performs the services and earns the revenue.

Analysis	Effect on Condition
Step 1: Are *assets* affected? No	
Step 2: Are *liabilities* affected? Yes (Liabilities decrease by $2,000.)	A = ↓ L + OE
Step 3: Is *owner's equity* affected? Yes (Owner's equity increases by $2,000.)	A = ↓ L + ↑ OE

Snapshot #21

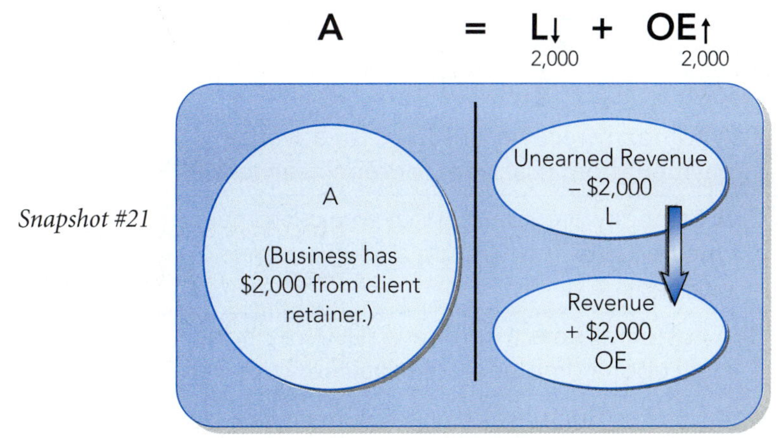

continued ►

Revenues That Decrease Liabilities, *continued*

Naming Revenues

To give decision makers detailed information, each company identifies a revenue by the type of sale that is made.

Examples:

- "Consulting Fees" means that consulting revenues increased the owner's equity.
- "Service Revenue" means that some kind of service activity revenue increased the owner's equity.
- "Product Sales" means that sales of merchandise increased the owner's equity.

Check Your Understanding

Write the completed sentences on a separate piece of paper. The answers are on page 131.

Sometimes a business receives an advance payment from a customer. This creates (a/an) ········. When the business later provides the service or product to the customer, revenue is earned and the ········ will (increase/decrease) ········.

Comparing revenue types. The table below shows various transactions. For each transaction, place a mark in the correct box to show if the transaction is a revenue with an immediate increase in assets, a revenue with a decrease in liabilities, or is not a revenue.

Transaction	A revenue with a:		Not a Revenue
	Immediate Increase in Assets	Decrease in Liabilities	
1. A company receives a $300 cash advance payment from customer for repair services.	**(Reminder: Use a separate sheet of paper to complete the table.)**		
2. A company provides service to a customer who had previously made a $300 advance payment.			
3. A customer pays a company $300 immediately upon completion of repair services.			
4. A business increases its cash when it borrows $4,000 from a bank.			
5. An accountant prepares a tax return and sends a bill to his client.			

Answers

Sometimes a business receives an advance payment from a customer. This creates a liability. When the business later provides the service or product to the customer, revenue is earned and the liability will decrease.

Transaction	A revenue with a: Immediate Increase in Assets	Decrease in Liabilities	Not a Revenue
1. A company receives a $300 cash advance payment from customer for repair services.			✓
2. A company provides service to a customer who had previously made a $300 advance payment.		✓	
3. A customer pays a company $300 immediately upon completion of repair services.	✓ (Cash)		
4. A business increases its cash when it borrows $4,000 from a bank.			✓
5. An accountant prepares a tax return and sends a bill to his client.	✓ (Accounts Receivable)		

"How could I forget! A revenue can either increase an asset or decrease a liability."

Nonasset Transactions: Other

Overview

Well Done!

You have already covered the most frequently occurring transactions in a business! Most business transactions you see fall into one or a combination of these basic categories that you have studied.

The Last Two Types

The only basic types of transactions that remain are the following:

- Transactions only within the liabilities
- Transactions only within the owner's equity

These transactions happen much less frequently than the others, so we will not spend much time on them.

Transactions Within Liabilities

Why They Happen

These transactions happen when a company replaces old debts with new debts. For example, if a loan is coming due, a company can go to a new bank and obtain a new loan that pays off and replaces the old loan.

The accounting equation would show: A = ↓↑ L + OE

Picture Example

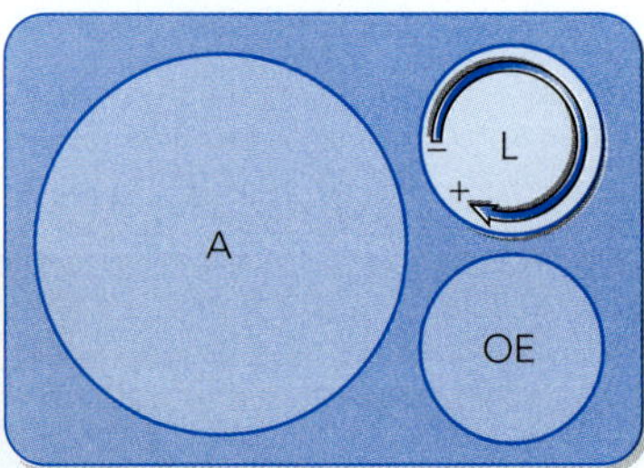

Transactions Within Owner's Equity

Why They Happen

These types of transactions involve reorganizing the owner's equity accounts. The most important kind is called "closing the books," which is discussed in Volume 2 of this series. The other transactions of this type involve certain partnership and corporation transactions. Corporate stockholders' equity transactions are discussed in Learning Goals 28–30.

The accounting equation will show: A = L + ↓↑ OE

Picture Example

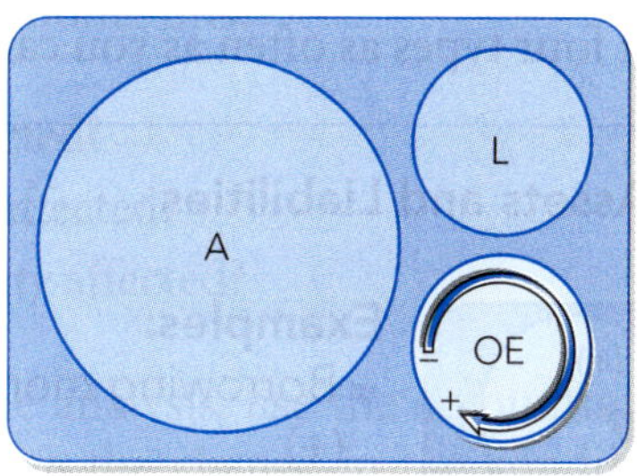

The Six Basic Patterns of Transactions

A Summary of All Transaction Patterns

Now You Have Seen Them All

Congratulations! Now you know all the basic types of transactions that can happen to a business. Although there are thousands of possible different transactions that can occur, they all fall within six patterns as to how they change the condition of a business. You have now seen all six patterns. The last two types you will not see very often, so it is the first four that you need to practice the most. These are:

Type 1: Transactions between assets and liabilities
Type 2: Transactions between assets and owner's equity
Type 3: Transactions within assets
Type 4: Transactions between liabilities and owner's equity

continued ►

PRACTICE Learning Goal 6

Solutions are in the disk at the back of the book and at: www.worthyjames.com

Learning Goal 6 is about analyzing individual transactions. Use these questions and problems to practice what you have learned about analyzing individual transactions.

Multiple Choice

Select the best answer.

1. Which of these transactions would increase an asset and increase a liability?
   a. an owner's investment into a business
   b. borrowing money by signing a note payable
   c. purchasing supplies for cash
   d. performing services for a customer on account
2. Which of these transactions would increase an asset and decrease an asset?
   a. collecting an account receivable
   b. purchasing supplies for cash
   c. purchasing supplies on account
   d. both a and b
3. Which of these transactions would decrease an asset and decrease a liability?
   a. an owner's withdrawal of assets
   b. borrowing money by signing a note payable
   c. purchasing supplies on account
   d. paying a debt
4. Earning revenue by performing services on account would
   a. increase total assets and decrease total liabilities.
   b. decrease total assets and decrease total liabilities.
   c. increase total assets and increase owner's equity.
   d. decrease total assets and decrease owner's equity.
5. If San Jose Circuits Company bought $10,000 of equipment by paying $3,000 cash and signing a note payable for the balance, then
   a. total assets decrease and total liabilities increase.
   b. one asset increases and one liability increases.
   c. one asset increases, one asset decreases, and one liability increases.
   d. none of the above.
6. If $500 of supplies were used up in business operations, then
   a. total assets decrease and total liabilities increase.
   b. total assets increase and total liabilities decrease.
   c. total assets decrease and owner's equity decreases.
   d. total assets decrease and owner's equity increases.
7. The payment of an account payable would
   a. decrease total assets and increase total liabilities.
   b. increase total assets and increase total liabilities.
   c. decrease total assets and decrease total liabilities.
   d. not change total assets, total liabilities, or owner's equity.
8. Collection of an account receivable would
   a. increase total assets and increase owner's equity.
   b. increase total assets and increase total liabilities.
   c. decrease total assets and decrease total liabilities.
   d. not affect total assets or owner's equity.

PRACTICE Learning Goal 6, continued

Solutions are in the disk at the back of the book and at: www.worthyjames.com

Reinforcement Problems

LG 6-1. Give examples based on the information. Give at least one example of a transaction that would cause the following changes to happen. Also identify any change described that cannot happen.

a. Assets increase and liabilities increase.

b. One asset decreases while another asset increases.

c. Owner's equity decreases and assets decrease.

d. Assets decrease and liabilities increase.

e. Owner's equity decreases and liabilities increase.

f. Assets decrease and liabilities decrease.

g. Liabilities decrease and owner's equity increases.

LG 6-2. Using the three steps to analyze a transaction. Use a blank sheet of paper to complete the table. In the table below, columns 1, 2, and 3 are for the three steps to use in analyzing each transaction. If any step results in a change in the condition of a business, write in the amount of the change with a ↑ to indicate an increase or a ↓ to indicate a decrease. Use the first item as an example.

	A =	L +	OE
Transaction	**Step 1: Are assets affected?**	**Step 2: Are liabilities affected?**	**Step 3: Is owner's equity affected?**
a. The owner of Ellisville Enterprises invests $10,000 in his business.	↑ $10,000	No	↑ $10,000
b. Senatobia Company borrowed $5,000.	**(Reminder: Use a separate sheet of paper to complete the table.)**		
c. Youngstown Service Company earned $1,000 of revenue that had already been prepaid by a customer last month.			
d. Canton Corporation used $5,000 of cash to purchase supplies.			
e. Brownsville Company provided $2,500 of consulting services to a customer on credit.			
f. Harlingen Partnership received a telephone bill and paid it at once.			
g. Chula Vista Corporation used $2,500 of consulting services and did not pay for them immediately.			
h. Redding Company purchased $10,000 of equipment by paying $2,000 cash and borrowing $8,000.			
i. Shasta Company collects $1,000 owed by a customer on account.			

PRACTICE Learning Goal 6, continued

Solutions are in the disk at the back of the book and at: www.worthyjames.com

LG 6-3, *continued*

g.

Business Photograph	Explanation
A = L + OE L A (+) ⟷ (+) OE	(Assume that this happens as part of business operations.)

h.

Business Photograph	Explanation
A = L + OE L A (+) ⟷ (+) OE	(Assume that this transaction is not part of business operations.)

i.

Business Photograph	Explanation
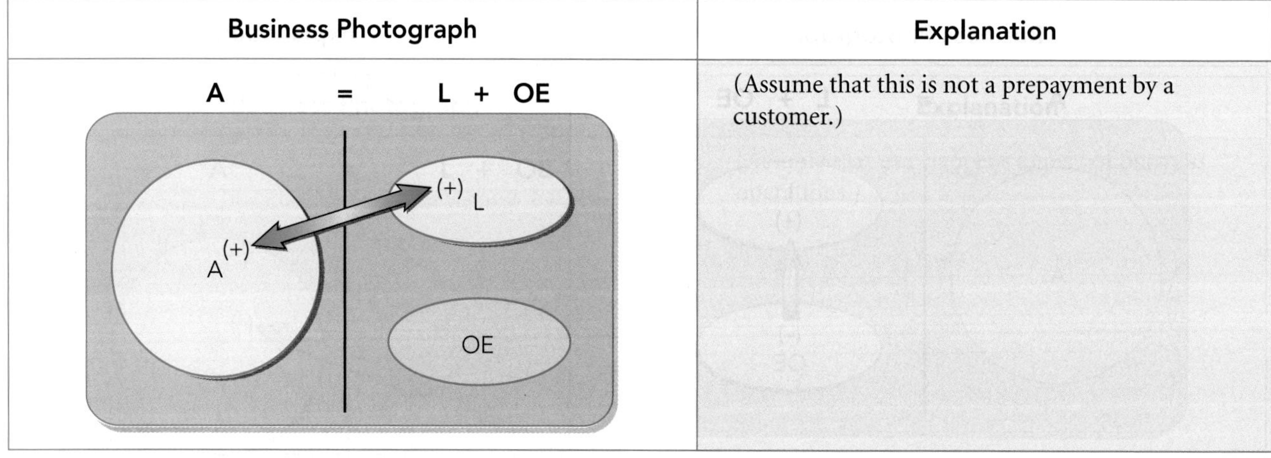	(Assume that this is not a prepayment by a customer.)

PRACTICE — Learning Goal 6, continued

Solutions are in the disk at the back of the book and at: www.worthyjames.com

LG 6-3, *continued*

j.

Business Photograph	Explanation
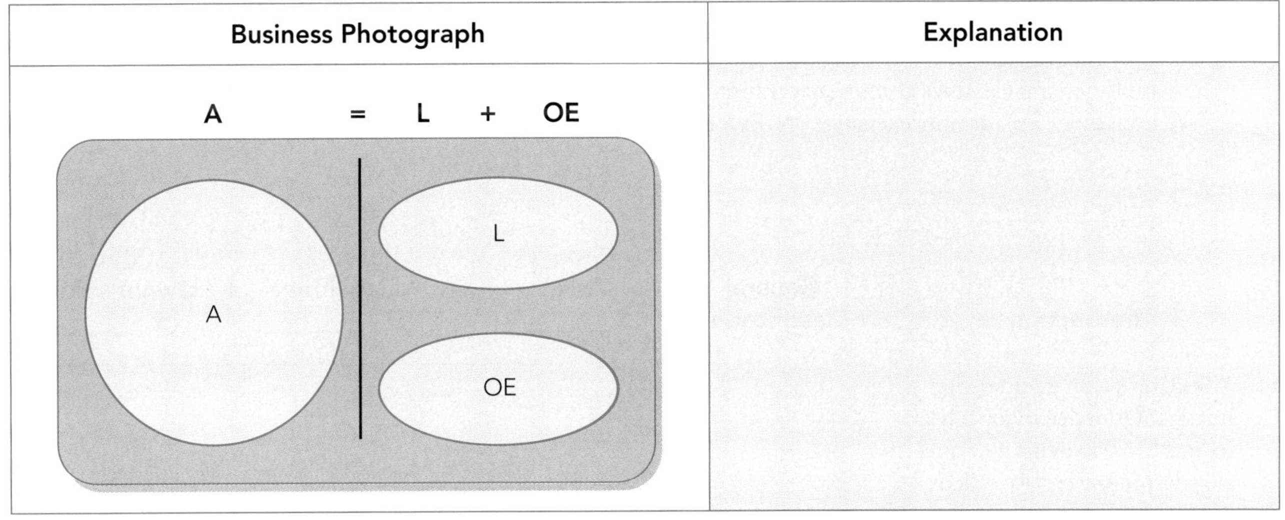	

LG 6-4. What could have made the equation change? Each situation below changes the prior balances and shows new balances in the three elements of the accounting equation. Assuming that just one transaction caused each new balance, on a separate piece of paper, write a brief, accurate explanation of what possible kind of business transaction it could be. There is at least one business transaction for each situation. The solution to the first situation is shown as an example.

	BALANCES					EXPLANATION
	Assets	=	*Liabilities*	+	*Owner's Equity*	
	$5,000				**$5,000**	**Beginning Balances**
a.	$12,000		$7,000		$5,000	a. Business borrowed $7,000 or purchased $7,000 of assets on credit or received an advance of $7,000 from a customer.
b.	$17,000		$7,000		$10,000	**(Reminder: Use a separate sheet of paper to complete the table.)**
c.	$11,000		$1,000		$10,000	
d.	$11,000		–0–		$11,000	
e.	$8,000		–0–		$8,000	
f.	$8,000		–0–		$8,000	
g.	$8,000		$4,000		$4,000	

PRACTICE Learning Goal 6, continued

Solutions are in the disk at the back of the book and at: www.worthyjames.com

LG 6-5. A comprehensive review for identifying and analyzing individual transactions. Print out copies of this problem from the disk at the back of the book (so you can use this problem again). The following problem consists of different transactions. Complete the visualization box by drawing the circles, and indicating plus or minus, as needed, to show what assets or equities are affected by the transaction. Above the box, show the dollar *changes* in the accounting equation. Then apply general classification to each transaction by type of event as internal (Int), external (Ext), exchange (Ex), or non-exchange (N-Ex). Here is an example for the first transaction:

Example:

Transaction	General Classification	(Step 1) Assets $ ______	=	(Step 2) Liabilities $ ______	+	(Step 3) Owner's Equity $ ______
a. Mike Craven, an ex-firefighter but an interior decorator at heart, invests $15,000 in his new interior decorating service called "Hot Spots."	___					

Solution:

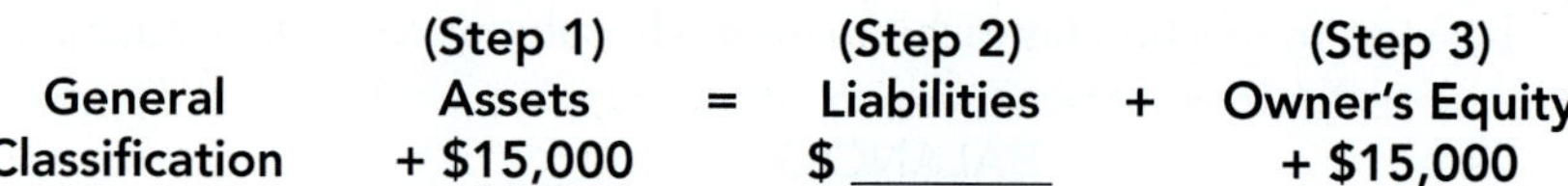

General Classification	(Step 1) Assets + $15,000	=	(Step 2) Liabilities $ ______	+	(Step 3) Owner's Equity + $15,000

Ext, N-Ex

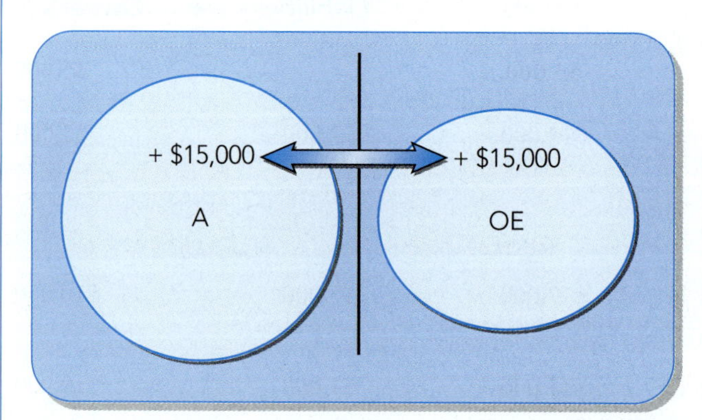

PRACTICE

Learning Goal 6, continued

Solutions are in the disk at the back of the book and at: www.worthyjames.com

LG 6-5, *continued*

Transaction	General Classification	(Step 1) Assets $ ______	=	(Step 2) Liabilities $ ______	+	(Step 3) Owner's Equity $ ______
b. The company purchases $1,000 of supplies for cash.	___					

Transaction	General Classification	(Step 1) Assets $ ______	=	(Step 2) Liabilities $ ______	+	(Step 3) Owner's Equity $ ______
c. The company purchases another $1,000 of supplies, but this time on credit.	___					

Transaction	General Classification	(Step 1) Assets $ ______	=	(Step 2) Liabilities $ ______	+	(Step 3) Owner's Equity $ ______
d. A large bank pays $5,000 to Hot Spots for decorating consulting services for its new corporate offices.	___					

PRACTICE Learning Goal 6, continued

Solutions are in the disk at the back of the book and at: www.worthyjames.com

LG 6-5, *continued*

Transaction	General Classification	(Step 1) Assets $ _______	=	(Step 2) Liabilities $ _______	+	(Step 3) Owner's Equity $ _______
e. The company pays the office help $1,200 in wages.	___					

Transaction	General Classification	(Step 1) Assets $ _______	=	(Step 2) Liabilities $ _______	+	(Step 3) Owner's Equity $ _______
f. The business pays $750 of the amount owing for the supplies.	___					

Transaction	General Classification	(Step 1) Assets $ _______	=	(Step 2) Liabilities $ _______	+	(Step 3) Owner's Equity $ _______
g. The company uses up $250 of supplies.	___					

PRACTICE

Learning Goal 6, continued

Solutions are in the disk at the back of the book and at: www.worthyjames.com

LG 6-5, *continued*

Transaction	General Classification	(Step 1) Assets $ ______	=	(Step 2) Liabilities $ ______	+	(Step 3) Owner's Equity $ ______
h. The company receives a telephone bill showing $150 of telephone services. The bill is not paid immediately.	___					

Transaction	General Classification	(Step 1) Assets $ ______	=	(Step 2) Liabilities $ ______	+	(Step 3) Owner's Equity $ ______
i. The company signs a contract with a new client. The client advances Hot Spots $1,200 before any services are performed.	___					

Transaction	General Classification	(Step 1) Assets $ ______	=	(Step 2) Liabilities $ ______	+	(Step 3) Owner's Equity $ ______
j. Hot Spots fully performs all the work that was required according to the terms of the contract in the previous transaction.	___					

PRACTICE Learning Goal 6, continued

Solutions are in the disk at the back of the book and at: www.worthyjames.com

LG 6-8, *continued*

Transaction	A	= L	+ OE
a. The owner invested $5,000 in her business.	C+		I+
b. Paid a repair bill immediately upon receipt.	**(Reminder: Use a separate sheet of paper to complete the table.)**		
c. Purchased supplies but did not pay the bill immediately.			
d. Purchase equipment for $10,000 by making a cash payment of $4,000 and signing a note payable.			
e. Received an advance payment from a customer.			
f. Received an advertising services bill but did not pay it immediately.			
g. Borrowed money from the bank and signed a note payable.			
h. Paid the employee wages.			
i. Performed consulting services and billed the client who will pay later.			
j. Received payment from the client for the amount owed one month later.			
k. The owner withdraws $1,500 cash from the business.			
l. Performed consulting services and collected the amount in full from the client upon completion of the job.			

Instructor-Assigned Problems

If you are using this book in a class, these review problems may be assigned by your instructor for homework, group assignments, class work, or other activities. Only your instructor has the solutions.

IA6-1. Jamestown Company experienced the events described below. As demonstrated in Learning Goal 6, analyze each event by:

- drawing an illustration of the effect of the event on the business, and
- using the accounting equation with amounts and arrows to indicate the effect.

a. The owner, Donald Alworth, invested $25,000 cash in the business. (example on pages 99 to 100)
b. The company purchased $500 of office supplies on account.
c. The business borrowed $10,000 from the local bank.
d. The company purchased $8,000 of office furniture by paying $2,500 cash and signing a note payable for the balance.
e. The company provided $800 of services to a client, who paid in cash.
f. The company received a $150 telephone bill, which was not paid immediately.
g. The company used up $200 of office supplies.
h. The company paid the amount owing for the office supplies in (b) above.
i. Donald Alworth withdrew $1,000 cash from the business for his personal use.
j. The bank notified the company that it has $15,000 additional credit available to borrow at any time.

PRACTICE Learning Goal 6, continued

IA6-1, *continued*

k. The company provided $2,000 of services to a client. The client did not pay immediately.
l. The business received a $1,100 advance payment from a customer for future services.
m. The business paid $6,000 for rent. $2,000 of this amount is for the current month rent expense, the remainder is an advance payment for rent for the next two months.
n. The company made a loan payment to the bank in the amount of $400. $300 of this amount is for interest expense, and the balance is for a payment on the amount owing on the loan.
o. The client in (k) above paid half of the amount owed to the business.
p. The company paid $2,000 wages to an employee.
q. A water leak destroyed $1,500 of computer equipment.
r. The company provided the services to the client in (l) above.
s. The company paid the amount owing in (f) above.
t. The company received the $600 monthly bill from an Internet service provider. It was not paid immediately.
u. The company provided $1,000 of services to a client who paid $250 cash and will pay the balance next month.

IA6-2. Trenton Enterprises experienced the events described below. Analyze each event by:

- drawing an illustration of the effect of the event on the business, and
- using the accounting equation with amounts and arrows to indicate the effect.

a. The owner, Janice Valentino, invested $20,000 cash in the business. (example on pages 99 to 100)
b. The company purchased $11,000 of computer equipment by paying $5,000 cash and signing a note payable.
c. The company received a $250 cleaning bill, which was not paid immediately.
d. The company paid $1,200 for airline tickets, but they will not be used until next month.
e. The company purchased $975 of office supplies on account.
f. The business borrowed $15,000 from the local bank.
g. The company provided $450 of services to a client, who paid in cash.
h. The company used up $125 of office supplies.
i. Janice Valentino withdrew $2,200 cash from the business for her personal use.
j. The bank notified the company that it has $25,000 additional credit available to borrow at any time.
k. The company paid the amount owing for the office supplies in (e) above.
l. The business received a $900 advance payment from a customer for future services.
m. The business paid $4,000 for insurance. $1,000 of this amount is for the current month insurance expense, the remainder is a prepayment for insurance for the next three months.
n. The company provided $3,100 of services to a client. The client did not pay immediately.
o. The company received the $400 monthly bill from an Internet service provider. It was not paid immediately.
p. The company made a loan payment to the bank in the amount of $700. $550 of this amount is for interest expense, and the balance is for a payment on the amount owing on the loan.
q. The client in (n) above paid half of the amount owed to the business.
r. An electrical fire destroyed $2,000 of office furniture.
s. The company provided the services to the client in (l) above.
t. The company paid the amount owing in (o) above.
u. The company provided $1,200 of services to a client who paid $700 cash and will pay the balance next month.

LEARNING GOAL 7

Identify Common Assets and Liabilities

Overview

Introduction

We have defined the concept of assets, liabilities, and owner's equity. You also know how together they all describe the condition of any economic entity. Now you are ready to learn about some specific kinds of assets and liabilities that show up frequently in most businesses.

Asset Types

Definitions and Examples

The table below defines common kinds of assets and gives examples.

Kind of Asset	Examples
Cash: Money	▪ Currency that a business has on hand ▪ Checking and savings accounts that can be withdrawn on demand
Supplies: Materials that are frequently required for the daily operations of a business and are used up relatively quickly	▪ Office supplies (paper, copier toner, computer diskettes) ▪ Cleaning supplies (soap, disinfectant) ▪ Automotive supplies (oil, belts, hoses)
Accounts receivable: A legal right to collect money, usually as the result of a sale and usually collectible in less than 90 days (the opposite of accounts payable)	▪ A sale is made to a customer "on account." The customer accepts the service or merchandise and therefore the seller has the right to require payment according to the credit terms of the sale.

Asset Types, *continued*

Kind of Asset	Examples
Notes receivable: A stronger legal right to collect money as the result of a borrower signing a *written promise* to pay, called a "promissory note." It normally involves receiving interest (the opposite of notes payable).	▪ Money is loaned to a borrower. The borrower signs a formal written promise to repay according to specified terms. ▪ A sale is made, and the seller requires the buyer to sign a promissory note.
Comment: Receivables that are created ***by sales to customers***—either accounts receivable ***or*** notes receivable—are said to be "on account" and are called ***trade receivables.***	
Interest receivable: The amount of interest that is earned and not yet received on a note receivable. Interest receivable is always recorded separately from the note receivable.	▪ The borrower must make regular payments to pay off the amount of a loan AND pay interest on the loan.
Prepaid expense: An advance payment ***paid*** to a provider for services ***before*** the services are received (usually for services to be received in a year or less)	▪ The next 12 months of fire insurance is paid in advance (Prepaid Insurance). ▪ The next three months of rent is paid in advance (Prepaid Rent). ▪ Sometimes supplies are also referred to as a prepaid expense.
Inventory: The goods that a merchant has in stock for the purpose of selling to customers	▪ Golf clubs in a sporting goods store ▪ Meat in a grocery store ▪ Video camera in an electronics store
Furniture, fixtures, and equipment: Long-lived (more than a year) non-real estate assets used in operations	▪ A computer ▪ A truck ▪ A desk
Comment: The key difference between supplies and equipment is that supplies are used up quickly (in a year or less) whereas equipment is used up over a longer period of time. For example, "office supplies" (such as paper, pencils, computer disks, and binders) are used up relatively quickly, whereas "office equipment" (such as furniture, filing cabinets, and computers) provide their benefits over a period of years.	

continued ▶

Asset Types, *continued*

Kind of Asset	Examples
Real estate: Land, buildings, and improvements to land.	▪ Land ▪ Building ▪ Parking lot
Intangible assets: Assets that have no physical substance—you cannot touch them! Intangible assets are usually legal rights.	▪ Patent ▪ Trademark ▪ Franchise right—you can't open a MacDonald's hamburger operation without permission from the company. This permission is called a **franchise,** which gives you the legal right to operate someone else's business (in this case, MacDonald's) in a certain location.

Liability Types

Definitions and Examples

The table below defines common kinds of liabilities and gives examples.

Kind of Liability	Examples
Accounts payable: A legal obligation to pay money, usually as the result of a purchase and usually requiring payment in less than 90 days (the opposite of accounts receivable).	▪ $50 of supplies are purchased and not paid for immediately. A bill is received from the seller. An account payable of $500 is owed to the seller. ▪ A $200 bill is received from the telephone company. $200 is the account payable to the telephone company.
Comment: Accounts payable are promises to pay made using the general credit of a business, are often referred to as made "on open account," and are called ***trade payables.***	

Liability Types, *continued*

Kind of Liability	Examples
Notes payable: A stronger obligation to pay money as the result of a borrower signing a *written promise* to pay, called a "promissory note." It normally requires the payment of interest (the opposite of notes receivable).	▪ Money is loaned to a borrower. The borrower signs a formal written promise to repay according to specified terms. ▪ A sale is made and the seller requires the buyer to sign a promissory note.
Interest payable: The amount of interest that is due and unpaid on a note payable. It is always recorded separately from the amount of the note payable.	▪ The borrower must make regular payments to pay off the amount of a loan ***and*** pay interest on the loan.
Unearned revenue: An advance payment *received* from a customer *before* goods or services are provided to that customer (usually for goods or services to be provided in a year or less).	▪ An insurance company receives an advance payment for 12 months of fire insurance. ▪ A landlord receives an advance payment for the next three months of office rent.
Comment about comparing unearned revenue and prepaid expense: Unearned revenue is a liability that is created because a business *receives cash* before a service or product is provided to the customer. Prepaid expense is an asset that is created because a business *pays cash* before a service or product is received.	

continued ▶

Liability Types, *continued*

Unearned revenue is *always* a liability. Unearned revenue is *always* a liability; it is *never* a revenue. Remember that any time you see the word "revenue" with the word "unearned" in front of it, it's a liability.

A creditor does not own the asset. Sometimes people think that a creditor's claim on assets is the same as the creditor actually owning the assets. This is not accurate. Remember that one part of the definition of an asset requires that it belong to a business. For example, even though a car is security for a bank loan, the car is still a business asset—not a bank asset—and the business can use the car however it wishes without asking the bank for permission. The business still owns the car, as long as it makes all the payments on the loan.

"Unearned revenues are . . . LIABILITIES!"

PRACTICE Learning Goal 7

Solutions are in the disk at the back of the book and at: www.worthyjames.com

Learning Goal 7 is about defining and identifying common assets and liabilities. Use these questions and problems to practice what you have learned.

Reinforcement Problems

LG 7-1. Can you identify the assets and liabilities? On a separate piece of paper, write the name of the item.

a. A formal written promise by someone else to pay cash to our business
b. Amounts owing suppliers or service providers, usually due in 30–90 days
c. Items needed for the daily operation of a business and consumed in a year or less
d. Money that is collectible in addition to a note receivable
e. Currency on hand, plus amounts in checking and savings accounts
f. A formal written promise by our business to pay someone else
g. Amounts owed to us by our customers, usually due in 30–90 days
h. Money that is owed because of item (f), above, but is not yet paid
i. A payment to a provider of services or goods before they are received
j. The receipt of a prepayment from a customer before providing goods or services to that customer

LG 7-2. Explain the difference. Briefly and accurately explain the difference between an account receivable, a note receivable, and interest receivable:

LG 7-3. Explain the difference. Briefly and accurately explain the difference between office supplies and office equipment:

Your Questions?

It is *very* important to be aware of what you need to understand better. What do you need to understand better about this learning goal? On a separate piece of paper, write the questions that you want to discuss with your classmates, instructor, or supervisor. Try to be very specific about what is bothering you, such as explanations that you do not fully understand.

Do You Like a Good Story?

It Might Help You to Remember Better

Often people remember information better when the information is part of an interesting story. The story that continues on the next page is the third part of a three-part adventure, mystery, and romance story. If you have not read the first two parts of the story, you will probably want to go back to the beginning on page 23 or the second part which begins on page 78. If you think a story might help you remember better, or if you just want to have some fun, go ahead! The adventures of Darius continue.

Technical Content

This part of the story contains the following technical content:

- Identifying all changes in owner's equity
- Summary statement: statement of owner's equity
- Identifying the operational changes in owner's equity
- Summary statement: income statement
- Business decision making: use the income statement to analyze operations

You Can Skip the Story

If you prefer to study the technical content listed above more quickly, you can skip the story and go directly to page 187, where the current presentation and practice continue.

The Wealth of Darius

Part III

Hermes' Second Trick

It was morning on the day of rest, and Darius was walking to Dana's house. He carried a basket of white roses and blue wildflowers that he had picked for her. Darius had decided that no matter what happened with his business, it was time to show Dana that he valued her special friendship. He smiled when he thought about seeing her again.

Hermes, however, had a surprise for Darius that day. Hermes had decided that Darius needed to fall in love, but not with Dana. To his regret, the god did not possess the power to make this happen by himself. Instead, Hermes persuaded Aphrodite, the goddess of love and beauty, to help him make things happen in the way he wanted.

Aphrodite had a son named Cupid who could make people fall in love. Cupid was not a small baby with wings as we often see depicted, but rather a beautiful youth, a young man who himself yearned to be loved by a mortal woman. However, Cupid lived with a terrible curse. Cupid could never allow himself to be seen by any mortal. So great was Cupid's beauty that all who gazed upon him would become hypnotized by desire and lose the power to love, or to think, or even to live. Because of his beauty, Cupid forever lived without the love he wanted.

Even so, Cupid had the power to make others fall in love. He had a bow that shot invisible magic arrows. Cupid would wait until someone was looking at another person. At that moment, Cupid would shoot one of his arrows. Whoever was hit by one of Cupid's arrows would fall desperately, madly, hopelessly, and completely in love with the person he or she was gazing upon at that moment.

Cupid waited until he saw Darius walking on the road to the village. Cupid watched as Darius passed by a wealthy local trader walking with his family. As Darius went by, he happened to see the trader's oldest daughter. She was a tall, graceful, black-haired woman named Lamia. In the next second, Darius felt himself overcome by admiration, love, and desire for this woman whom he had never seen before. Darius rushed up to her, introduced himself, and told her that she was the most beautiful woman he had ever seen. Then he anxiously asked her father for permission to visit the next day. Because Lamia was already past the age at which a woman was usually married, her father readily agreed to the visit.

Darius, who normally worked very hard, foolishly forgot his important business problems. He forgot that he was going to see Dana. Instead, Darius withdrew precious money from the business to buy rare eastern perfumes and silks as gifts for Lamia.

The next day Darius, holding the same flowers that he had intended for Dana, knocked on the door of Lamia's house and was shown into the main room to wait for her. As Darius walked into the room, he stopped in amazement. There, standing in the room and coldly staring back at him, was Somnus, who was also holding gifts and flowers.

The Test Is Revealed

Perhaps you have decided by now that it is best to never try to guess what the gods will do. That would be a wise decision, particularly with Hermes. The trickster Hermes had persuaded Aphrodite to ask her son Cupid to make Somnus fall in love with the same woman as Darius. Somnus, while he was in the market, also received one of Cupid's arrows.

Lamia, smiling a devious smile, entered the room with her father. If Darius and Somnus had not been so dumbstruck in their complete admiration of her, they would now have understood why no man had yet asked her to be his wife. Her devious greed soon became apparent as she spoke:

> "Darius and Somnus, I am honored that you both seem to feel such strong love and admiration for me. Unfortunately, I cannot choose between you. My father and I have decided that it would be best to have a contest. Because you are both merchants and my family is a merchant family, we will have a contest of merchants. I will agree to marry the man who can demonstrate that he is the most successful.
>
> The contest will be this: at the end of each month for six months, you will both visit me and my father to report the amount of your business wealth and debts. At the end of the six months, we will see which business could pay off all its debts and have the most wealth left over. The owner of that business will be the winner. You may not invest any money in your business. You must do this strictly by operating the business.

> One last requirement: the loser of this contest will agree to give up his entire business to my father. If you do not have the courage to agree to this, you cannot be in the contest, and you will never have my hand in marriage. . . ."

Of course, if Darius had been in his right mind he would never have agreed to such a ridiculous contest. Certainly, Lamia and her father wanted nothing more than to obtain the businesses of both men. In truth, Lamia cared little about any man and, like her father, was excited only by wealth and power. She would do what was necessary to obtain them.

Darius saw none of this, and as he and Somnus signed the document agreeing to the terms of the contest, Somnus turned and growled, "Darius, you are a boy trying to do a man's job." Lamia and her father smiled at this, but Darius did not see them. He was too much in love with Lamia to notice.

Darius Sees What the Contest Is Really About

Everyone in town thought Darius and Somnus were possibly the two greatest fools in the history of civilization, which even then was quite a while. There was much ridicule and laughter behind the backs of the two passionate competitors.

Darius was considered to be the greater of the two fools. Most people knew how much Dana cared for Darius. They knew that she was a sweet, intelligent, and faithful woman. This meant that Darius, instead of losing only his business, could lose both of the most valuable prizes in his life.

Lamia had said that the winner would be the man whose business could pay off all its debts and have the most wealth remaining. That sounded familiar to Darius. Then, he remembered that the owner's claim was how much the value of assets exceeded the amount of the debts.

Darius then realized that this was really a contest about which man could increase his owner's claim the fastest! "Oh, by the gods," he thought, "this is the same problem that I was trying to fix before!" Darius decided to go to Dana, the only person he trusted to help him.

Dana, with great difficulty, continued to work in the shop during the last two days, although she and Darius had not spoken. So strong was the power of Cupid's arrow on Darius, and so great was Darius' desire to win, that after work that day Darius asked Dana to help him.

He did not consider her pain when she learned what he had done. He did not consider how the laughter in the town made her feel. He did not consider that she looked pale or that her eyes were red with dark circles under them. The same Darius, who had always been so generous to others, could now only think of himself . . . such is the power of Cupid's arrows.

Darius said, "Dana, when we spoke last week, you said it would be necessary to identify how each transaction changes the picture of the business. You said it would be necessary to identify which of the changes affected the owner's claim, and to keep a record of these items."

"Yes."

"Dana, I am not sure I can identify all the transactions that affect the owner's claim. Also, I do not know how to keep a record of all of them. It is very important to me now that I increase my owner's claim as fast as possible."

Dana looked down and waited a long time before she quietly spoke. To Darius, it seemed as if Dana was having difficulty speaking. Then she said, "I am sorry, Darius, but I do not feel well. Please forgive me, but I would rather not discuss this matter again with you."

Darius Creates a Plan

Darius, in his heart, knew that Dana was a good person and that she had been good to him. He did not ask her anything more or try to speak to her again except for routine matters of the shop. But he had an idea: he remembered that fees from customers increase the owner's claim. Why not try to increase the fees by making more sales to more customers? Also, Darius thought it would be much easier to only keep a record of sales transactions rather than all the transactions.

Darius had several ideas for increasing sales. He decided to purchase brighter and more long-lasting paints. He would purchase some new and unusual colors and paint more pottery. This was more costly but he would have more customers. He would hire another employee to help him with the complicated designs of large wall paintings. Yes, making more sales to customers was the key!

The day of the first month's comparison with Somnus approached, and Darius was hopeful.

After the first month passed, Darius completed his record of the fees earned. He was very proud of his work. It showed each type of fee and looked like this:

Revenue	*Month 1*
Portrait fees	$ 500
Wall and fresco fees	900
Pottery fees	400
Total fees earned	$1,800

The following day, Darius would meet with Lamia and her father. This was the day that Darius and Somnus were going to show their progress after the first month. Darius felt the excitement of seeing Lamia again, and he felt especially good because his fees had been increasing. Darius excitedly began to prepare the statement of condition of his business.

Darius calculated the condition of his business and could not believe what he saw. He calculated the condition a second time. Then he compared the statement of condition at the end of last month to the statement of condition he had just completed. This is what Darius saw:

End of this month		
Assets =	Creditors' Claims +	Owner's Claim
$8,800 =	$7,500	$1,300

End of last month		
Assets =	Creditors' Claims +	Owner's Claim
$9,300 =	$7,400	$1,900

Darius sat in amazement. What had happened? How could his owner's claim have decreased by another $600? He went to bed that night with one hope—that Somnus had a worse month.

The next day, Darius was disappointed. As they were instructed, Darius and Somnus each presented a statement of the wealth and debts of their businesses. Somnus began to smile when he saw that he was winning.

Darius	
Total Wealth	$8,800
Gold	300
Due from customers	1,450
Supplies	1,700
Equipment	5,350
Total Debts	$7,500

Somnus	
Total Wealth	$25,300
Gold	4,300
Due from customers	950
Supplies	4,700
Equipment	15,350
Total Debts	$7,400

Darius tried to keep his wits. He noticed that neither Somnus nor Lamia nor Lamia's father knew how to calculate the condition of a business in the way that Darius knew how. They simply compared the wealth and the debts. When Darius saw this, he remembered something that he had learned from Hermes.

Immediately, Darius pointed out that Somnus had included his personal clothing and household furniture as part of the equipment of the business. Lamia and her father had to agree that this was incorrect. They reduced Somnus' business assets by the amount of the items that were personal. Somnus clenched his fists and glared at Darius.

Then Darius showed that Somnus had also included his shop as part of the equipment. Somnus, like Darius, rented his shop, so the shop did not belong to Somnus' business. After this was subtracted, the wealth of the two businesses was almost equal. Lamia and her father smiled at Somnus' rage. They really did not care who won. They knew that both businesses would soon be under their control.

The Second Month

Darius knew he had been lucky this time. Somnus would be more careful the next time. Darius tried harder than before for more fees. He and his assistant worked longer, used better paints, and painted better pottery. At the end of the second month, Darius calculated the total fees, and saw they were $940 greater than the first month:

Revenue	*Month 1*	*Month 2*
Portrait fees	$ 500	$ 840
Wall and fresco fees	900	1,100
Pottery fees	400	800
Total fees earned	$1,800	$2,740

Darius felt momentary relief, but when he prepared his statement of condition, this is what he saw:

End of Month 2		
Assets =	Creditors' Claims +	Owner's Claim
$8,500 =	$7,250	$1,250

The owner's claim and the assets had decreased again. The owner's claim was $50 less than the first month of the contest. At the two-month comparison, Darius watched Somnus smile with glee when the comparisons were made. Somnus did not make the same mistakes that he had made the last time.

Darius looked closely. Although Somnus did not think about calculating an owner's claim, Darius mentally calculated Somnus' owner's claim by subtracting $3,500 from $12,900. Somnus had a claim of $9,400. Then Darius anxiously looked back at his own claim again—only $1,250!

Darius	
Total Wealth	$8,500
Gold	250
Due from customers	350
Supplies	2,550
Equipment	5,350
Total Debts	$7,250

Somnus	
Total Wealth	$12,900
Gold	4,100
Due from customers	1,100
Supplies	2,150
Equipment	5,550
Total Debts	$3,500

When he returned to his shop, Darius knew that he had been much too confident in his plan. It was not working. The problem was that he had not yet fully explained the operational change in his owner's claim. He had not done what Dana had suggested when they worked together.

Darius had not bothered to keep a record of the assets used up in operations. Because it was easier, he had only been recording the operational increases caused by the fees. Only four months to go!

To get control, Darius knew now that he also needed to identify the decreases caused by operations. Darius was not sure that he could identify all the operational decreases, but now he had to try. He had no choice.

The Third Month

Darius discovered that keeping a record of all the operational decreases in his owner's claim was a great amount of extra work. There were so many of them! Even the name "assets used up in operations" was too long and too difficult to say. He started using the name "expenses" because assets were being expended . . . that is, used up.

To keep a record of expenses, Darius worked hard and his days were long. It was not easy to know exactly when there was an expense. It was clear to Darius when the business used up paints or canvas—that was an expense. (It helped to create value.) It was clear to him that when the business used up gold to pay an employee—that was an expense. It was less clear when he paid the rent, but then he remembered he could not do his work for customers without a shop to work in. So, paying the rent was an expense.

Paying the creditors puzzled Darius. After much thought, he decided that paying debts was not an expense, because this was only benefiting the creditors, not the customers. Paying debts did not use up assets as part of the process of creating something valuable for customers. The purpose of paying debts was to reduce a creditor's claim. With practice, Darius became better at identifying expenses.

At the end of the third month, Darius summarized the fees and the expenses with a new table:

Revenue	*Month 2*	*Month 3*
Portrait fees	$ 840	$ 850
Wall and fresco fees	1,100	1,500
Pottery fees	800	1,900
Total fees earned	$2,740	4,250
Expenses		4,500
Operational decrease in owner's claim		$ – 250

Darius now began to sense what was wrong. When he looked at the results of Month 3, he could see that his owner's claim was decreasing mostly because of operations. The operations used up assets as expenses faster than the operations received assets (the fees earned) from customers. For Month 3, operations used up $250 more in the value of the assets than was received from customers, which reduced the wealth of the business and the owner's claim.

Then Darius calculated the condition of his business and compared it to the condition at the end of last month. *Worse!* His owner's claim was down again!

End of Month 3		
Assets =	Creditors' Claims +	Owner's Claim
$9,050 =	$8,100	$950

End of Month 2		
Assets =	Creditors' Claims +	Owner's Claim
$8,500 =	$7,250	$1,250

Darius again looked at the owner's claim. The difference between $950 and $1,250 was a $300 decrease, not $250. Why the extra $50 decrease?

Darius felt his neck tighten and his head ache. He sensed that he could not try much harder. He already had worked very, very hard. He had kept a record of all sales. He had kept a record of all expenses. All this plus doing all his usual painting and design work! "Perhaps I am just too stupid to compete against Somnus," he thought. A feeling of sadness overcame him as he remembered all his wonderful dreams of a life together with beautiful and graceful Lamia.

On the next day, the meeting confirmed his fears. Again, Somnus was further ahead. Somnus' business had even paid off all its debts! Somnus loudly suggested that Darius quit the contest so he would not embarrass himself anymore. Lamia laughed and seemed not to notice Darius at all.

Darius	
Total Wealth	$9,050
Gold	100
Due from customers	1,550
Supplies	2,050
Equipment	5,350
Total Debts	$8,100

Somnus	
Total Wealth	$14,900
Gold	4,000
Due from customers	1,200
Supplies	2,700
Equipment	7,000
Total Debts	$0

The Fourth Month

Darius did not go to the shop the next day. Instead, he walked in the meadows around his house. He began to think about the real possibility of losing his business.

Darius did not go to work for the next two days. On the fourth day, when he returned to his shop, he had not shaved. Darius did not work on any new designs, and he did not do the thing that he loved the most—his painting.

Darius gave up recording the sales and the expenses. Although Darius had always liked to talk with his employees and customers, he seldom spoke now. For more than a week, he did no painting. He did nothing. Customers became angry waiting for their work. Two creditors, Aulis and Hela, came to Darius and told him that they were tired of waiting to be paid. They would not supply any more materials unless the business paid them more quickly.

All the employees, of course, observed this. Among them, Dana worried the most. Darius' foolish behavior had not stopped Dana from caring about what happened to him. Even though she had given up all hope for Darius' love, her noble character would not let him continue to suffer.

One day, she came to him in the shop and said, "Darius, I have not seen you do much painting lately. Are you thinking about new designs?"

"No," he said, "I am finished with that and I am finished with painting."

"Why is that?"

"Because I have discovered that I am probably too stupid to be any good at what I am trying to do. I think that my painting is poor and my ideas are poor. Even if I were a good painter, I am unable to be a businessman. It has taken me all this time to finally understand how operations decreased my owner's claim, and now I am too stupid to do anything more with this knowledge."

This shocked Dana. Darius had been a wonderful artist ever since he was a small child, and he loved painting more than anything in life. She decided to be bold. "Darius, I know all about this contest with Somnus. Everyone knows that one of you will lose his business." Darius opened his eyes wide when he heard her say this.

"I understand how taken you are with Lamia. But I know you well, Darius. There is something that you love even more than Lamia, and that is the joy you feel when you paint. Are you willing to give up painting because of her? Is her approval that important to you? Is she going to take your life away?" Darius stared at her with his mouth open.

"As for being stupid . . . well, Darius, do you not realize what you have just done? By identifying the fees earned and the expenses, you have explained all the operational changes to your owner's claim! This is powerful knowledge. Use it to change whatever is wrong! You are acting ridiculous, Darius. I will not watch you give up everything. Would you like me to help?"

"Help?" Darius mumbled. "Me? Now?"

"Darius," Dana said, putting her hand on his shoulder, "it is time to take what you have learned and really use it. We will figure out a way to make your owner's claim grow and then you can beat Somnus. But first help me put all this information together so we can understand what has happened." With Dana's encouragement, Darius began to think about his business again.

Over the next several hours, Dana and Darius designed a statement that explained all the changes in the owner's claim that they had found. (Their creation was so good that a similar statement is still used today.)

As a starting point, they wrote down the beginning and ending balances of the owner's claim for Month 3. This is what it looked like:

Statement of All Changes in Owner's Claim for Month 3	
Prior balance, end of **Month 2**	$1,250
Current balance, end of **Month 3**	$ 950

Total decrease is $300!

Next, they prepared the statement showing the operational changes in the owner's claim because of fees and expenses. This was similar to what Darius had already prepared.

Statement of Operational Changes for Month 3	
Fees Earned	
Portraits	$ 850
Walls and frescoes	1,500
Pottery	1,900
Total fees earned	4,250
Total Expenses	4,500
Operational decrease	($250)

Then, in the statement of owner's claim, they entered the $250 operational decrease. Dana used brackets ( ) to show a minus amount, because it was easier to see than a minus sign of "–". Next, Dana wrote a "?" to show that a change was still unidentified.

Statement of All Changes in Owner's Claim for Month 3	
Prior balance, end of **Month 2**	$1,250
Less: Operational decrease	(250)
???	?
Current balance, end of **Month 3**	$950

Statement of Operational Changes for Month 3	
Fees Earned	
Portraits	$ 850
Walls and frescoes	1,500
Pottery	1,900
Total fees earned	4,250
Total Expenses	4,500
Operational decrease	($250)

Finally, Dana asked if there were any changes caused by investments and withdrawals. Darius had made no investments, but remembered that he had taken out $50 in withdrawals. This was the missing $50 dollar decrease! This completed all the changes in the owner's claim!

Statement of All Changes in Owner's Claim for Month 3	
Prior balance, end of **Month 2**	$1,250
Add: Owner's investments	–0–
Less: Operational decrease	(250)
Less: Owner's withdrawals	(50)
Current balance, end of **Month 3**	$950

Statement of Operational Changes for Month 3	
Fees Earned	
Portraits	$ 850
Walls and frescoes	1,500
Pottery	1,900
Total fees earned	4,250
Total Expenses	4,500
Operational decrease	($250)

The Mystery Is Solved

When they had finished, Dana clapped her hands. "Darius, look at what we have done! We have completely explained the entire change in your owner's claim with these two beautiful statements! The $300 decrease in your owner's claim was caused by just two kinds of increases and two kinds of decreases! Your investments and the fees from customers are the two increases. Withdrawals and expenses are the two decreases. The fees and expenses are from operations. We have solved the mystery!"

"This must be what Hermes had wanted," Darius said.

"Now comes the matter of beating Somnus," Dana answered. "Darius, I think I see what you need to do and it is rather important."

"What is that?" he asked.

"The expenses," she said. "Your troubles, I think, are caused by the operational decrease in your owner's claim. The expenses seem to be reducing your owner's claim faster than the fees from customers are increasing it."

"Yes, I think I understand that now."

"Good. But Darius, you have not yet detailed all the expenses as you have done with the fees. If you knew how much each of the individual expenses were, you could make decisions about changing or reducing them. I think we need to start keeping a record of *each kind* of expense. I can help you do this."

This is how Darius and Dana began keeping detailed records of the business operations. They began with the sales and expenses from the beginning of Month 4, and they continued recording for the remainder of the month. For Month 4, they had a much more detailed explanation of the operational change in the owner's claim. It looked like this:

Revenue	*Month 3*	*Month 4*
Portrait fees	$ 850	$ 1,200
Wall and fresco fees	1,500	2,750
Pottery fees	1,900	3,450
Total fees earned	4,250	7,400
Expenses	4,500	
Portrait materials and supplies		200
Walls/frescoes materials and supplies		1,250
Pottery materials and supplies		6,450
Rent		250
Other expenses		100
Operational decrease in owner's claim	$ (250)	$ (850)

The size of the decrease shocked Darius. He prepared the statement of condition at the end of Month 4. He could not believe what he saw.

End of Month 4		
Assets =	Creditors' Claims +	Owner's Claim
$8,250 =	$8,200	$50

Next, he prepared the statement that explained all the changes in his owner's claim.

Statement of All Changes in Owner's Claim for Month 4	
Prior balance, end of **Month 3**	$950
Less: Operational decrease	(850)
Less: Withdrawals	(50)
Current balance, end of **Month 4**	$50

Statement of Operational Changes for Month 4	
Fees Earned	
Portraits	$1,200
Walls and frescoes	2,750
Pottery	3,450
Total fees earned	7,400
Expenses	
Portrait materials/supplies	200
Walls/frescoes materials/supplies	1,250
Pottery materials/supplies	6,450
Rent	250
Other expenses	100
Total expenses	8,250
Operational decrease	($850)

As usual, Darius had not made any investments, so they omitted the line for investments.

"By the gods, I have only $50 of owner's claim left! I am practically finished!"

"No, you are not," Dana replied. "I think that now is your best opportunity. Tomorrow I will show you why I believe this, after you finish your meeting with Somnus and Lamia. Stay strong, Darius."

When Darius presented his wealth and debts at the end of the fourth month, he endured even more humiliation than usual. Somnus asked, "Darius, why do you not stop the contest to avoid further humiliation? You can leave town quietly." Both Somnus and Lamia burst into laughter when they saw Darius' presentation of wealth and debts. Darius remained silent as he clenched his jaw.

What Do You Think?

- What amount caused an increase in owner's claim? Where do you find it?
- What two amounts caused a decrease in owner's claim? Where do you find them?
- What business or financial advice would you offer to Darius now?

Total revenues of $7,400 caused the increase in owner's claim. It is on the Statement of Operational Changes. (An owner's investment would also have increased owner's claim, but Darius did not do this.)

Expenses of $8,250 decreased the owner's claim. Expenses are on the Statement of Operational Changes. A withdrawal of $50 also decreased the owner's claim. This is shown separately on the Statement of All Changes in Owner's Claim because it is not part of operations.

The Fifth Month—Important Business Decisions

Darius returned from the monthly meeting more angry and upset than usual. Dana immediately said, "All right, Darius, now is our time."

"I am ready to try anything," he said. "What was the opportunity that you spoke of yesterday?"

"Darius, you now have something very special—something that neither Somnus nor anyone else understands. You possess detailed information that tells you all the reasons why operations have decreased your owner's claim. To increase your claim, all you need to do now is use this information so you can make decisions that change the way you operate. Are you ready?"

"For anything."

"Good. I am certain that the answers you need are hiding in the two parts of operations—expenses and fees. There is one question for each part. First, the expenses: look closely at the total amount of each expense. Is the expense justified for the amount of value it creates? Second, the fees: are you charging the right price for each kind of work that you do?"

"I will need some time to think," he replied.

"Then think about these questions carefully tonight. We will discuss this again tomorrow."

Darius stayed in his shop that night. He lit many candles to keep his shop bright, and then thought intently about the two questions. One at a time, he thought about each expense that he saw on the statement of operations. For each expense, he asked himself, "*Is the expense justified* by the amount of value—that is, the fees—it helps my business get?"

The expenses of the pottery work amazed him, and as he began to think more about it, Darius realized that the special paints and glazes for pottery were always the most expensive supplies. Also, the waste was significant because pottery often baked improperly in the ovens and had to be thrown away.

The second question was, "Am I charging the right price for each kind of work?" For months, Darius had charged less than Somnus for everything: the portraits, the walls and frescoes, and the pottery. Darius hoped that selling for less would attract more customers, but this did not seem to attract many new customers, except for pottery painting.

After giving all of this much thought, Darius then made three business decisions:

First, he decided to increase some of his prices. He would charge the same as Somnus for walls and frescoes. Also, Darius decided to double his prices for portraits because they took so much time, and because he was a much better portrait painter than Somnus.

Second, Darius decided that he would try to reduce the cost of the wall and fresco designs.

Darius enjoyed his third decision most of all. Except for a few special customers, Darius decided to completely stop all the pottery painting!

Why? Darius realized that it would be impossible for pottery painting to be profitable. The pottery painting was slow and much more costly than he had ever realized. What was worse, he could never raise prices for pottery painting! Most customers refused to pay very much for the pottery painting because eventually pottery breaks and needs to be replaced. Except for a small number of wealthy customers, painting pottery would always cause large losses.

When he looked at the statement of operational changes for Month 4, Darius saw that pottery painting was the single biggest cause of his problems with the business. The pottery expenses of $6,450 were much greater than the pottery fees of $3,450. The pottery expenses simply could never create enough value!

The Perfect Trick

Then Darius had a wonderful idea, a trick that was worthy of Hermes himself! Darius decided to tell everyone that he was giving up pottery painting because Somnus was so much better. If the plan worked, then arrogant Somnus would eagerly take all of Darius' old pottery customers. In this way, Somnus would soon have all the same pottery expenses and begin to destroy his own business.

Darius realized that Somnus did not understand about the complete calculation of the condition of a business. He certainly had no idea about calculating the operational changes in the owner's claim. So, it would be a long, long time—if ever—before Somnus would find out what was wrong. The perfect trick!

On the next morning, when Darius and Dana discussed the decisions about increasing prices and trying to reduce the cost of wall and fresco designs, she agreed. She had reached those conclusions herself. And when Dana heard Darius' reasons for letting Somnus take over all the pottery painting in the village, she bubbled with excitement. "Why Darius, you are as clever as Hermes himself!" and she laughed so long that she had to sit on a bench as tears streamed from her eyes. Darius could not restrain his own smile.

On the second day of the fifth month of the contest, Darius raised his prices. He began telling most of his customers that he would no longer paint pottery for them because Somnus was too good. Somnus fell right into the trap. Soon he was working long hours for all his new pottery customers. He had to buy new equipment and hire an extra employee.

Darius could hardly wait until the end of the month.

It had started out as a difficult month, but it seemed to become easier to pay the creditors as the month progressed. Darius had high hopes as the time came to calculate the monthly statement of condition. Before he did this, Darius summarized his fees and expenses and compared them to Month 4.

Revenue	*Month 4*	*Month 5*
Portrait fees	$ 1,200	$ 2,200
Wall and fresco fees	2,750	3,250
Pottery fees	3,450	–0–
Total fees earned	7,400	5,450
Expenses		
Portrait materials and supplies	200	250
Walls/frescoes materials and supplies	1,250	1,150
Pottery materials and supplies	6,450	–0–
Rent	250	250
Other expenses	100	100
Operational change in owner's claim	$ (850)	$ 3,700

When Darius saw the results of Month 5, satisfaction filled him like nourishment to a starving man. The operations had increased owner's equity by $3,700! The plan was beginning to work.

Next, he prepared the three necessary statements: the basic statement of condition and the two statements explaining the changes in the owner's claim.

End of Month 5		
Assets =	Creditors' Claims +	Owner's Claim
$10,850 =	$7,200	$3,650

Statement of All Changes in Owner's Claim for Month 5	
Prior balance, end of **Month 4**	$50
Add: Investments	–0–
Add: Operational decrease	3,700
Less: Withdrawals	(100)
Current balance, end of **Month 5**	$3,650

Statement of Operational Changes in Owner's Claim for Month 5	
Fees Earned	
Portraits	$2,200
Walls and frescoes	3,250
Pottery	–0–
Total fees earned	5,450
Expenses	
Portrait materials/supplies	250
Walls/frescoes materials/supplies	1,150
Pottery materials/supplies	–0–
Rent	250
Other expenses	100
Total expenses	1,750
Operational increase	$3,700

In the meeting at the end of the fifth month, Darius watched a different Somnus review wealth and debts for Lamia and her father. Somnus' assets had decreased and his debts had increased.

Darius	
Total Wealth	$10,850
Gold	1,900
Due from customers	1,550
Supplies	2,050
Equipment	5,350
Total Debts	$7,200

Somnus	
Total Wealth	$13,500
Gold	2,750
Due from customers	1,200
Supplies	2,550
Equipment	7,000
Total Debts	$3,900

Somnus kept staring at the paper and taking quick little breaths, which made him stammer. "Do not wor . . . wor . . . worry, Lamia, it is jus . . . jus . . . just . . . one mm . . . mm . . . month."

It was true that Somnus still had more wealth and fewer debts than Darius. It was also true that if this had been the last month of the contest, Somnus would win, because after paying all his debts Somnus would have $9,600 of wealth left over. Darius only had an owner's claim of $3,650. However, there was still one more month to go, and Darius was catching up.

The Final Month

As the sixth month began, Darius felt his determination surge like a rising river. Now he could chuckle to himself as he saw Somnus toiling at his shop every day, seldom resting, trying to complete all of his pottery painting work. Moreover, because Somnus now spent so much time on pottery painting, he began to lose some wall and fresco painting customers to Darius. Darius' decision now looked even better than before.

Dana also noticed the difference. Darius had both higher prices and new wall painting customers. Meanwhile Somnus, by painting so much pottery, was sinking into a hole that he was digging for himself. Dana felt that Darius had a chance to win when Lamia made the last comparison.

Dana was happy that Darius had a chance to save his business and that he was painting again. Every day she prayed for him to win. But Dana also knew that if Darius won, she would soon be out of his life. Lamia would see to that. The moment that Lamia selected Darius, Lamia would throw Dana out. Dana promised herself that no matter what, she would always be a friend to Darius; she would always give Darius the best advice that she knew. Her special smile would always belong to him.

The last day of Month 6 arrived. Darius calculated the fees and expenses for the sixth month and compared them to Month 5.

Revenue	*Month 5*	*Month 6*
Portrait fees	$2,200	$2,100
Wall and fresco fees	3,250	3,400
Pottery fees	–0–	–0–
Total fees earned	5,450	5,500
Expenses		
Portrait materials and supplies	250	300
Walls/frescoes materials and supplies	1,150	600
Pottery materials and supplies	–0–	–0–
Rent	250	250
Other expenses	100	50
Operational increase in owner's claim	$3,700	$4,300

Nervously, Darius calculated the condition of his owner's claim:

End of Month 6		
Assets =	Creditors' Claims +	Owner's Claim
$14,900 =	$7,000	$7,900

Darius and Dana again prepared the statements explaining the changes in the owner's claim. However, what Darius really worried about now was the final balance of his owner's claim. It was the end of the six months and Darius' balance was $7,900. At the end of the previous month, Somnus had shown $9,600. Darius could only hope that the pottery losses were enough to bring Somnus down below $7,900.

That night, Darius slept restlessly, tossing and turning. He dreamed of Ammon, and Darius felt his old fears of losing the business. He dreamed of the old woman dressed in black and of the frightening visits by Hermes. He dreamed about his friends, the birthdays, and the wonderful feasts and good times. He dreamed about the beautiful Lamia and her father. In his dream they became great spiders, and he could hear their spider fangs clicking together and their spider feet brushing the ground as they hungrily approached him . . . and he awoke with a scream.

The day's first light illuminated the silver dew on every tree and flower and soon changed the silver into millions of glowing rainbow drops. As the minutes brightened, birds began sharing their melodies in a joyful chorus that proclaimed the fresh day. Darius made his final decision.

He bathed and ate a small breakfast. He picked up the paper on which he had written the business wealth and debts for Lamia and her father to examine and put it into his pocket.

He went directly to Dana's house. Ammon answered the door, and Darius said, "Ammon, I apologize if I am too early this morning. However, may I speak to your daughter?"

"Yes, Darius, one moment."

In a few minutes, Dana appeared. Darius looked at her directly and then said, "Dana, as you know, I am meeting with Lamia, her father, and Somnus this morning. I would like you to be there with me."

She stared at him. "Darius, you love Lamia. How can you ask me to do this?"

"Dana, trust me and be my friend one last time, please."

She was a true friend and, despite her uncertainty, she left with Darius. In another moment, Darius and Dana were walking on the road together. In less than an hour, they arrived at the home of Lamia and her father. Somnus arrived at almost the same time. Sullen and dark, he glared at them and said, "Now Darius, it is at last time for you to see who is the better man. It is time for you to disappear."

They were shown into the house, where Lamia and her father were waiting, smiling. Lamia's eyebrows arched and her eyes showed surprise when she saw Dana.

"Well, Dana, this is truly an unexpected pleasure. Did you come here to say good-bye?" Lamia and her father smiled hungrily. Lamia continued, "This is the moment, dear Darius and dear Somnus, I know you both have eagerly awaited. Now show me the statements you have prepared, and the winner will be my husband."

Darius handed his statement to Lamia. Somnus turned and glowered at Darius, to which Darius responded with a smile and a wink. Choking down his fury, Somnus shoved his statement into Lamia's outstretched hand.

"Gentlemen, gentlemen," she said, "let us now see which one of you shall enjoy the blessings of my companionship for the rest of your life." With that, she placed the two statements on a table so all could see:

Darius	
Total Wealth	$14,900
Gold	4,550
Due from customers	3,500
Supplies	1,500
Equipment	5,350
Total Debts	$7,000

Somnus	
Total Wealth	$15,500
Gold	1,100
Due from customers	2,700
Supplies	3,800
Equipment	7,900
Total Debts	$7,800

Lamia seemed to hesitate and consulted with her father. She turned and faced the three people in front of her. "Somnus, if we subtract the debts from the wealth, your business would have $7,700 of wealth remaining if it were to pay off all its debts today. Darius, I am surprised to say that your business would have $7,900 of wealth remaining if it were to do the same. Darius, you appear to be the winner."

Shaking, Somnus snarled, "Fraud!"

"No," Darius said, "you may check and verify everything, as I am sure Lamia will do."

Lamia now ignored Somnus and smiled directly at Darius. "Oh Darius, you are much the better man. You know, I never once doubted you. You have truly won my heart and you will at last be my husband." Then Lamia turned to a servant and said, "Show Dana the door. It is time for her to leave."

At the same moment, Somnus exploded into a rage, shrieking, "Fraud, fraud, you are a *fraud!*" Madly shaking, raving, Somnus screamed, "I . . . YOU . . . I challenge you, Darius, to a duel! . . . to the death . . . *the death!* . . . now, at this instant!"

Quick as cats, two of Lamia's servants were upon Somnus and forced him into a chair. After several minutes, Somnus began to calm and Darius spoke.

"First, Somnus, I regretfully decline your offer of a duel. It is not my intention to demonstrate your unworthiness twice in one day, and at the cost of your life."

Then Darius turned to Lamia. "Lamia, I have indeed won the contest. Regrettably, I must inform you that I decline your offer as well. You will not be my wife. However, as the winner, I will choose to keep my business for myself. I suggest that you and Somnus will be excellent for each other."

Darius reached over to Dana, and brought her nearest hand to his lips. "As for me, I have already won my prize, long before today."

Epilogue

And so that is what happened when the gods decided to let humankind learn about the condition of a business. Darius came to realize that despite all his troubles, he had received two wonderful gifts for which he always thanked the gods.

The first great gift was the ability to explain the condition of a business and why the condition changes, especially the change in the owner's claim. Darius, always generous, decided to share this knowledge with other merchants—yes, even with Somnus, who years later came to hold Darius in high esteem as his one true friend.

Darius told the other merchants that three statements are necessary: the first one, the basic statement of condition, is like a picture drawn at a point in time. The other two statements explain change, so they show what happened over a period of time. Darius made a list:

STATEMENT OF CONDITION

- *a picture of the business at any point in time*

STATEMENT OF CHANGES IN OWNER'S CLAIM

- *summarizes all the changes in the owner's claim*

STATEMENT OF OPERATIONAL CHANGES IN OWNER'S CLAIM

- *explains in detail the changes in the owner's claim caused by operations. These have the most powerful effect on the owner's claim*

Darius, always the artist, drew a diagram as an example for the other merchants to show them the three kinds of statements. In the diagram, Darius showed the condition of his business at the end of Month 3, Month 4, and Month 5 of the contest. Then he drew the two statements that showed change, explaining the changes in the owner's claim for Months 4 and 5.

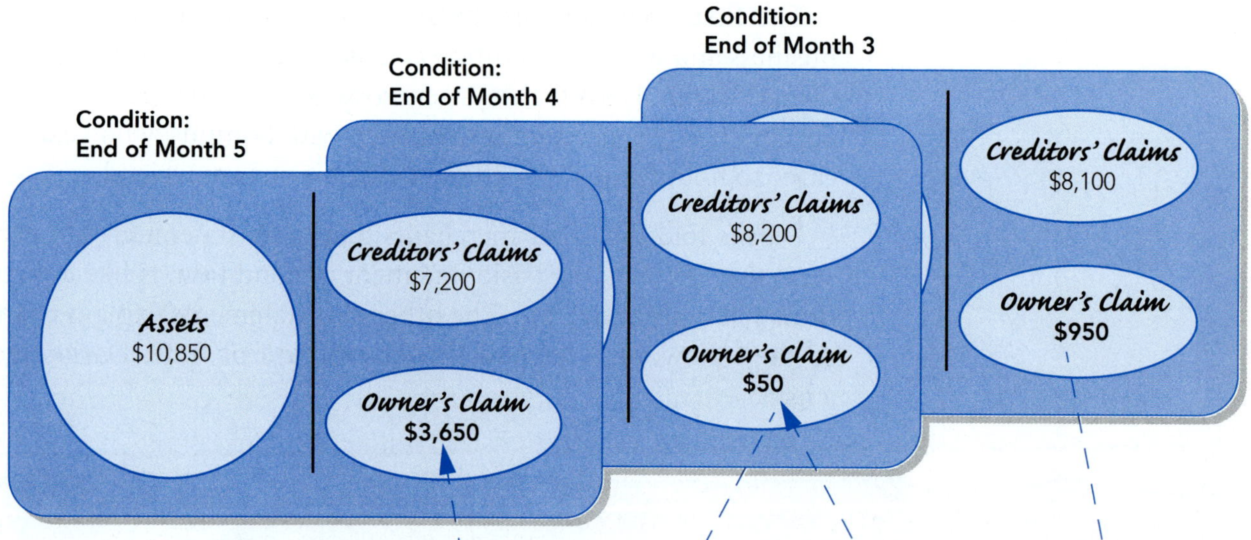

Month 5 Statement of Changes in the Owner's Claim	
Beginning balance	$ **50**
Add: Investments	–0–
Less: Withdrawals	(100)
Operational increase	3,700
Ending balance	**$3,650**

Month 4 Statement of Changes in the Owner's Claim	
Beginning balance	$ **950**
Add: Investments	–0–
Less: Withdrawals	(50)
Operational decrease	(850)
Ending balance	**$ 50**

Month 5 Operational Changes in the Owner's Claim	
Fees earned	$5,450
Expenses	
Portrait supplies	$ 250
Wall/fresco supplies	1,150
Rent	250
Other	100
Total expenses	1,750
Operational increase	$3,700

Month 4 Operational Changes in the Owner's Claim	
Fees earned	$7,400
Expenses	
Portrait supplies	$ 200
Wall/fresco supplies	1,250
Pottery supplies	6,450
Rent	250
Other	100
Total expenses	8,250
Operational decrease	$(850)

This knowledge has been passed from generation to generation throughout history, and to this very day, the condition of a business is still shown in the same way! Moreover, people in business today still use two statements to show the four changes to their owner's claim in the same way, except that now the two statements are called the "statement of owner's equity" and the "income statement."

The second great gift was even more valuable. Darius learned the real meaning of love, a power that turned out to be stronger than Cupid's arrows. Darius also shared this gift with all the people that he met, and of course with Dana, his wife. Unfortunately, this gift has been more difficult for humankind to understand. However, 2,500 years later, a famous poet and writer who understood all about accepting people as they are, wrote these timeless words so everyone could remember:

> *The quality of mercy is not strained,*
> *It falls as gentle as the rain.*

"And what happened to Hermes?" you're asking. He decided not to reveal any more secrets to Darius. Instead, Hermes became involved in other amusements and diversions, such as creating the false science of alchemy (a belief that any metal could be turned into gold), which wasted many lives. On a later whim, he caused the famous Dutch tulip speculation, which resulted in the great panic of 1636.

Then, 2,970 years after our story, Hermes, in a moment of diabolical merriment, decided that it was now time to reveal the statement of cash flows to humankind. A frantic businessman desperately needed to explain all the changes in his cash balance . . . well, I suppose that is a story we should save for another day.

What Do You Think?

- Darius had special business knowledge that Somnus did not have. As a result of this knowledge, what was the most important thing that Darius could do better than Somnus? Why did this matter?

- Darius had a special advantage because he prepared business data so he could use it effectively. How did Darius prepare the data?

- Darius was able to make better *decisions*. These decisions improved the way Darius operated his business. This would not have been possible without improved information.
- The special way Darius had to learn to prepare business data consisted of two things:
  - Once he learned how to analyze transactions, he kept a cumulative record of all the transactions.
  - He then prepared ***statements that summarized*** the cumulative record. These summaries were the statements that (1) showed the condition of the business and (2) analyzed the changes in the owner's claim. These are the essentials of the financial statements that we will study in Section IV.

LEARNING GOAL 8

Explain the Four Basic Changes in Owner's Equity

Overview

Introduction

Because there are several different reasons for the changes in owner's equity, students who are just beginning their study of business and accounting sometimes forget or become confused by some of these changes. Owner's equity is so important—it is the owner's claim on business wealth—that its essential features are summarized for you in this learning goal.

There are four basic changes in owner's equity.

In Learning Goal 8, you will find:

The Features of Owner's Equity

Essential Features of Owner's Equity

It Is a Secondary Claim on Asset Value

Owner's equity is the owner's claim on the value of the business assets. However, when you are the owner, your owner's claim is secondary to the claim of the creditors. The owner's claim is calculated like this:

Assets – Liabilities = Owner's Equity

The Name to Use in a Specific Business

For any business (except a corporation), the owner's equity is identified by the word "capital" and the owner's name. For each individual business, the name of the owner of that business is written before the word "capital" to show whose claim it is.

Example

If your name is John Elton, then the owner's equity for your particular business would be called "John Elton, Capital."

Synonyms

Owner's equity is sometimes called ***net worth*** or ***net assets.***

"What do you mean . . . 'My claim is secondary'?"

The Changes in Owner's Equity

All the Changes in Owner's Equity

The Causes of Change

There are actually six causes for increase or decrease in the owner's equity:

Cause	Increase or Decrease	Example
OWNER'S DIRECT ACTIONS		
▪ ***Investments***	Increase	You invest $5,000 of your own cash into your business.
▪ ***Withdrawals***	Decrease	You remove $5,000 cash from your business and use it personally.
OPERATIONAL CHANGES		
▪ ***Revenues***	Increase	The business sells $500 of services to a client.
▪ ***Expenses***	Decrease	The business uses up $100 of supplies.
OTHER CHANGES INCIDENTAL TO BEING IN BUSINESS		
▪ ***Gains***	Increase	The business sold some old equipment for $2,000 more than it cost.
▪ ***Losses***	Decrease	A fire burned down the warehouse.

The First Four Changes

The first four items—*investments, withdrawals, revenues,* and *expenses*—are by far the most important. These occur regularly in every business. These are the changes you will continue to study in this book.

The Last Two Changes

The last two items—*gains* and *losses*—are incidental occurrences that happen much less often than revenues and expenses. However, they have the same effect on owner's equity as revenues and expenses. For this reason, gains and losses will not be part of this discussion of owner's equity. Gains and losses are discussed again in the learning goals about corporations and in Volume 2.

continued ▶

All the Changes in Owner's Equity, *continued*

Illustration

The four basic causes of change in the owner's capital balance is illustrated below for an imaginary business in the years 2015 to 2017.

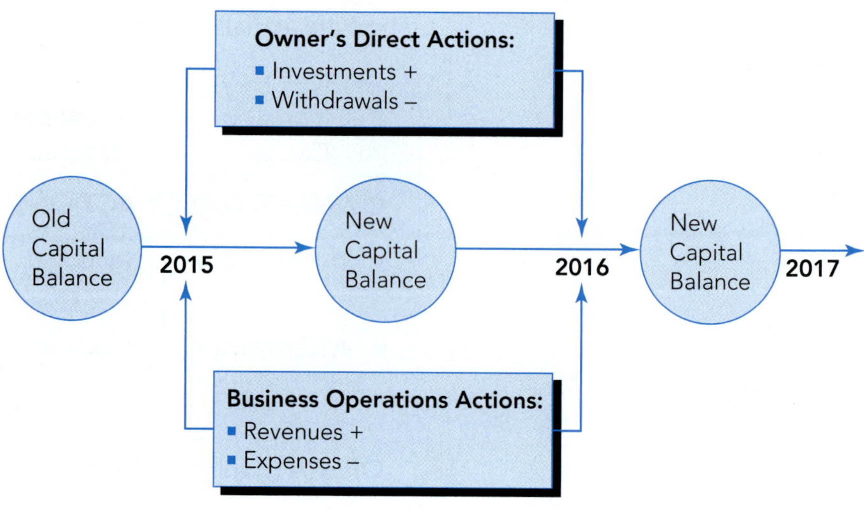

The Four Basic Changes

Owner's Investment

An owner's investment always causes an *increase* in owner's equity (also called owner's capital) because the owner contributes cash or other personal wealth into the business. These items become assets of the business, so this causes the total assets in the business to increase. As a result, the owner's equity increases. Using the equation:

$$A \uparrow = L + OE \uparrow$$

Note: Rarely, an owner may pay the debts of the business with his or her own personal funds. This is an owner investment that makes liabilities decrease instead of assets increase.

Owner's Withdrawals

Withdrawals (also called *drawing*) is a *decrease* in the owner's equity caused by the owner's withdrawal of cash or other assets out of the business for personal use. This causes the total assets to decrease, so the owner's claim decreases. Using the equation:

$$A \downarrow = L + OE \downarrow$$

The Four Basic Changes, *continued*

Revenue

Revenue is an *increase* in the owner's equity that results from making a sale of goods or services. The amount of the revenue is whatever the customer pays for the product or service. Owner's equity increases because the sale always causes either assets to increase or liabilities to decrease. Using the equation:

$A\uparrow = L \quad + OE\uparrow$	Example: A business makes a \$500 sale on account. Accounts receivable increase \$500 and revenue increases \$500.
or	
$A \quad = L\downarrow + OE\uparrow$	Example: Last month a customer made a \$300 advance payment, recorded as unearned revenue. This month the services are provided, decreasing unearned revenue (a liability) \$300, and increasing revenue \$300.

Expense

An expense is a *decrease* in the owner's equity caused by the business operations consuming resources. The amount of the expense is the cost of the asset or services consumed. The owner's equity decreases because an expense always causes either assets to decrease or liabilities to increase. Using the equation:

$A\downarrow = L \quad + OE\downarrow$	Example: \$750 of supplies are used. Supplies decrease and supplies expense increases (a reduction in owner's equity) \$750.
or	
$A \quad = L\uparrow + OE\downarrow$	Example: A \$200 bill is received for telephone service and is not immediately paid. This increases a liability (accounts payable) and decreases owner's equity. The decrease in owner's equity is recorded as "telephone expense".

Summary of the Four Basic Changes

The table below summarizes the features of the four basic changes:

Increases or Decreases	Owner's Direct Actions	Operational Activity	Effect on Assets and Liabilities
Increases in owner's equity	Owner investments	Revenues	Assets ↑ **or** liabilities ↓
Decreases in owner's equity	Owner withdrawals	Expenses	Assets ↓ **or** liabilities ↑

Changes in a Corporation

For a corporation, the changes are practically identical, except that owners' investments in a corporation are called "paid-in capital" (or "contributed capital") and withdrawals are called dividends. (See Part VI, Learning Goals 28–31 for more detailed discussions of corporations.)

QUICK REVIEW

- For any business (except a corporation), use the owner's name followed by the word "capital" to describe the ownership claim.
- There are four basic changes in owner's equity:
  - *Changes caused by operations:* revenues and expenses
  - *Changes caused by the owner directly:* investments and withdrawals
- Revenues and investments are increases.
- Expenses and withdrawals are decreases.

VOCABULARY

Net assets: another name for owner's equity (page 188)

Net worth: another name for owner's equity (page 188)

Withdrawals: a decrease in the owner's capital caused by the owner's withdrawal of cash or other assets out of the business for personal use (page 190)

Do You Want More Examples?

Most problems in this book have detailed solutions. To use them as additional examples, do this: 1) Select the type of problem you want 2) Open the solution on your computer or mobile device screen (from the disc or worthyjames.com) 3) Read one item at a time and look at its answer. Take notes if needed. 4) Close the solution and work as much of the problem as you can. 5) Repeat as needed.

PRACTICE Learning Goal 8

Solutions are in the disk at the back of the book and at: www.worthyjames.com

Learning Goal 8 is about explaining the four basic causes of change in the owner's equity. Use these questions and problems to practice what you have learned.

Reinforcement Problems

LG 8-1. Is it an expense? Is the transaction of *paying a liability* an expense? Give a brief, accurate answer in the space below.

LG 8-2. A review of different items. Use this question to review all the specific kinds of assets, liabilities, and owner's equity items. On a separate piece of paper (so you can practice the problem again without seeing answers), place the correct letter next to each number.

a. Cash	h. Unearned revenue
b. Supplies	i. Revenue
c. Accounts receivable	j. Equipment
d. Note receivable	k. Withdrawal
e. Prepaid expense	l. Owner investment
f. Account payable	m. Expense
g. Note payable	n. Dividends

1. An increase in owner's equity caused by either an increase in assets or a decrease in liabilities as a result of performing services or selling products is called ········.
2. Items such as paper, computer disks, binders, staples, solvents, and paper towels are called ········.
3. An asset created when a sale is made to a customer "on account" (that is, no cash is received at the time of sale) is ········.
4. A liability that is created on the books of the seller when a customer prepays before the service or product is provided to the customer is called ········.
5. An asset that is created for the lender when a formal written promise to pay a certain amount is signed is called (a/an) ········.
6. A liability that is created for the payor when a formal written promise to pay a certain amount is prepared and signed is called (a/an) ········.
7. The owner transferring personal assets into a business is called ········.
8. A decrease in owner's equity caused by a decrease in assets or an increase in liabilities resulting from the process of operating the business is (a/an) ········.
9. An obligation to pay money (normally in 30–90 days) to a supplier is (a/an) ········.
10. Currency that a business has on hand and the amounts in the checking and savings accounts that can be withdrawn on demand is called ········.
11. A short-term asset created when a business pays for goods or services before it receives them or uses them up is (a/an) ········.
12. The owner's withdrawal of assets from the business for his or her personal use is called (a/an) ········.

PRACTICE Learning Goal 8, continued

Solutions are in the disk at the back of the book and at: www.worthyjames.com

LG 8-3. **Practice with revenues affecting assets and liabilities.** Revenues always increase the owner's equity. The revenue transaction either causes an increase in assets or a decrease in liabilities. The purpose of this exercise is to have you identify whether a revenue is causing an increase in assets or a decrease in liabilities. (Just for fun, we've also included some examples that are not revenues. This is to remind you that not *all* increases in assets or decreases in liabilities are caused by revenues!)

Use a blank sheet of paper to complete the table. For each item, also draw an arrow indicating which part of the accounting equation is increasing and/or decreasing. Use the first two transactions as examples.

Transaction	Assets increased or liabilities decreased?	Revenue?	Why is it a revenue or not a revenue?	A	=	L	+	OE
a. An accountant performs $2,000 of accounting services and is paid in cash.	Yes (The asset Cash increases.)	Yes	Assets increase because services are performed for a customer, so it is a revenue transaction.	↑				↑
b. The accountant borrows $2,000 from her bank.	Yes (The asset Cash increases.)	No	Assets increase because of a loan, so it is not a revenue transaction.	↑		↑		
c. An accountant receives a $2,000 cash advance from a client as a prepayment for future services.	(Reminder: Use a separate sheet of paper to complete the table.)							
d. The accountant fully performs all the services for the client who prepaid her in (c) above.								
e. The accountant invests an additional $5,000 in her business.								
f. In September, the accountant performs $2,500 of services "on account."								

PRACTICE — Learning Goal 8, continued

Solutions are in the disk at the back of the book and at: www.worthyjames.com

LG 8-3, *continued*

Transaction	Assets increased or liabilities decreased?	Revenue?	Why is it a revenue or not a revenue?	A	=	L	+	OE
g. The accountant collects $2,000 cash from the accounts receivable.								
h. A magazine publisher mails magazines to its subscribers who prepaid subscriptions.								
i. A computer consultant is paid $1,000 immediately after finishing a job.								

LG 8-4. **Why isn't it a revenue?** A revenue increases assets or decrease liabilities. All of the following transactions either increase assets or decrease liabilities, but *none* of them are revenues. What critical attribute are they all missing that causes them *not* to be revenues?

- A business receives a $1,000 cash advance from a customer. (The asset Cash increases.)
- Supplies are purchased on account. (The asset Supplies increases.)
- Cash is collected from accounts receivable. (The asset Cash increases.)
- Accounts payable are paid. (The liability Accounts Payable decreases.)
- Owner invests $10,000 in the business. (The asset Cash increases.)

LG 8-5. **Why isn't it an expense?** An expense decreases assets or increases liabilities. All the following transactions either decrease assets or increase liabilities, but *none* of them are expenses. What critical attribute are they all missing that causes them *not* to be expenses?

- The owner withdraws $1,000 cash from the business. (The asset Cash decreases.)
- The business pays off a $200 account payable. (The asset Cash decreases.)
- The business borrows $10,000 from a bank. (The liability Notes Payable increases.)
- The business purchases $500 of supplies for cash. (The asset Cash decreases.)
- The business buys supplies on credit. (The liability Accounts Payable increases.)

LG 8-6. **Practice with expenses affecting assets or liabilities.** Expenses always decrease the owner's capital, and this can involve either a decrease in assets or an increase in liabilities. The purpose of this exercise is to have you identify whether an expense is causing a decrease in assets or an increase in liabilities. (For more fun, some of these items are *not* expenses.)

PRACTICE Learning Goal 8, continued

Solutions are in the disk at the back of the book and at: www.worthyjames.com

LG 8-6, *continued*

Use a blank sheet of paper to complete the table. For each item, also draw an arrow indicating which part of the accounting equation is increasing and/or decreasing. Use the first two transactions as examples.

Transaction	Assets decreased or liabilities increased?	Expense?	Why is it an expense or not an expense?	A	=	L	+	OE
a. The business pays off a loan of $10,000.	Yes (The asset Cash decreases.)	No	Only creditors' equity is affected, not the owner's.	↓		↓		
b. $1,500 of supplies are used up.	Yes (The asset Supplies is used up.)	Yes	A direct using up of resources in operations.	↓				↓
c. A business pays off an account payable of $1,500.	**(Reminder: Use a separate sheet of paper to complete the table.)**							
d. A business pays employees $1,500 in wages as soon as they are earned.								
e. A business receives a $750 repair bill for this month's computer repair services. The bill is not paid immediately.								
f. The owner pays himself a "salary" and withdraws $1,000 in cash.								
g. A business pays this month's telephone bill of $300 as soon as it is received.								
h. A business owes its employees $15,000 in wages but will not pay them until next Monday.								
i. Next Monday, the business pays the wages to the employees.								

PRACTICE Learning Goal 8, continued

Solutions are in the disk at the back of the book and at: www.worthyjames.com

LG 8-7. Sometimes liabilities and expenses go together and sometimes they don't. Use a blank sheet of paper to complete the table. The purpose of this exercise is to help remind you that when liabilities are created, it sometimes involves an expense and sometimes not. What matters is *why* the liability is being created. From the description of the transaction, indicate if there is an expense and the reason for your answer. Use the first transaction as an example.

Transaction	Expense?	Liabilities increased?	Did event happen as part of revenue-earning operations?
a. The business borrows $10,000 and records a liability to Fifth National Bank.	No	Yes (The liability Notes Payable increases.)	No (Borrowing money is not part of revenue-earning operations.)
b. The business owes its employees $8,500 for this week's wages and records it as a new liability by classifying it as Wages Payable.	**(Reminder: Use a separate sheet of paper to complete the table.)**		
c. The business receives a bill for this month's utilities.			
d. The business receives a bill for this month's accounting services.			
e. The business purchases $700 of supplies "on account."			
f. The $700 of supplies is consumed.			
g. The business purchases $4,000 of equipment on account.			
h. The business receives a $1,000 bill for this month's computer repair services.			
i. The business receives a $500 prepayment from a customer for services to be performed next month.			

PRACTICE **Learning Goal 8, continued**

Solutions are in the disk at the back of the book and at: www.worthyjames.com

LG 8-8. Practice with the four kinds of changes to owner's equity. Use a blank sheet of paper to complete the table. Revenues and expenses and investments and withdrawals are the four basic kinds of changes in owner's equity, and they are always accompanied by changes in either the assets or the liabilities. In the following exercise, *all the transactions affect owner's equity.* In each transaction, indicate the type of change to owner's equity that is occurring, if the change is an increase or decrease, if an asset or a liability is affected, and whether that is an increase or decrease. Use the first transaction as an example.

Transaction affecting owner's equity	Type of change to owner's equity	Owner's equity increase or decrease?	Asset or liability affected?	Asset or liability increase or decrease?
a. An accountant prepares a tax return and collects $500 from a client.	Revenue	Increase	Asset (Cash)	Increase
b. An owner invests $10,000 cash in her business.	**(Reminder: Use a separate sheet of paper to complete the table.)**			
c. Office supplies are used up.				
d. A business receives a bill for consulting services payable on account.				
e. The same accountant as in (a) above prepares another tax return for $400 and sends the bill to the client.				
f. A real estate company receives and pays its current bill for advertising.				
g. A law firm receives its current bill from the telephone company but doesn't immediately pay it.				
h. An owner withdraws $500 worth of supplies from his business.				
i. An airline company provides a flight to a customer who purchased the ticket three months ago.				
j. The accountant receives a $950 bill for computer repair services for this month.				
k. An owner pays a debt of his business by writing a check on his personal checking account (not a good business practice).				

PRACTICE

Learning Goal 8, continued

Solutions are in the disk at the back of the book and at: www.worthyjames.com

LG 8-9. Practice with transactions that don't affect owner's equity. For each of the five transactions below, on a separate piece of paper (so you can practice the problem again without seeing answers), briefly and accurately explain the reason why they *don't* affect owner's equity.

a. Supplies are purchased on account.

b. A business receives a prepayment from a customer before services are provided.

c. A business pays an account payable.

d. A business borrows money.

e. A business collects cash from an account receivable.

Your Questions?

It is *very* important to be aware of what you need to understand better. What do you need to understand better about this learning goal? On a separate piece of paper, write the questions that you want to discuss with your classmates, instructor, or supervisor. Try to be very specific about what is bothering you, such as explanations that you do not fully understand.

LEARNING GOAL 9

Analyze the Cumulative Effect of Transactions

Overview

Introduction

Until now, we have carefully analyzed the effect of each *individual* transaction on the condition of a business. In this learning goal, we use the accounting equation to analyze the ***cumulative effect*** of many transactions. One simple but useful way to do this is to calculate the total change in assets, liabilities, and owner's equity balances. Doing this gives a basic overview of what has happened to a business over a period of time.

There are many ways to summarize and analyze the cumulative effects of transactions. It is a very important subject. You will return to it again in Section IV on page 273 when you study how financial statements are specialized summaries of the cumulative effects of transactions.

"Cumulative Effect" Defined

The "cumulative" effect of transactions means whatever total change in assets, liabilities, and owner's equity occurs over some period of time and what balances result from these transactions.

Examples

- On January 1, the beginning balance of total assets was $100,000 and on December 31, the ending balance was $90,000. The total assets decreased by $10,000.
- If the beginning balance of owner's equity on October 1 is $35,500 and the owner's equity increased by $4,000, then the ending balance on October 31 is $39,500.
- If the ending balance of liabilities on June 30 was $20,000 and liabilities increased by $5,000 during June, then the beginning balance on June 1 must have been $15,000.

Use the Accounting Equation for the Analysis

It is most useful to analyze changes on all the parts that make up the condition of a company. For this reason, cumulative changes are usually expressed in the format of the accounting equation.

Overview, *continued*

Example

If total liabilities of De Kalb Company last month increased by $50,000 and total owner's equity decreased by $12,000, what was the change in the total assets? Using the accounting equation:

Assets	=	**Liabilities**	+	**Owner's Equity**
?		+ $50,000		– $12,000

Notice that the equation now shows *changes* rather than balances. We can still use the equation, but now it will show changes. Because the right side increased by a total of $38,000 (+50,000 – 12,000), the left side will increase by the same amount. Assets must have increased by $38,000.

Note: Read the "Introduction to Algebra and Equations" section in the disk at the back of the book if you need practice with simple equations.

How to Solve "Cumulative Effect" Problems

Procedure

The following table shows how to use the accounting equation to solve "cumulative effect" problems.

IF the problem is about . . .	**THEN use . . .**
only calculating a ***change***, and not a beginning or ending balance,	Format #1 (see below)
calculating a beginning or ending balance that involves cumulative changes,	Format #2 (see below)

Format #1

	A	**=**	**L**	**+**	**OE**
Cumulative change					

Format #2

	A	**=**	**L**	**+**	**OE**
Beginning balance					
Cumulative change					
Ending balance					

continued ▶

How to Solve "Cumulative Effect" Problems, *continued*

Examples of Format #1

Long Beach Luggage Company assets increased by $40,000, and owner's equity increased by $10,000. How much did liabilities change?

Solution: This problem only asks how much liabilities changed. It provides no information about beginning or ending balances (use Format #1).

	A	= L	+ OE
Cumulative change	+ $40,000	?	+ $10,000

Calculation: The left side changed by $40,000 so the right side must change by the same total. The increase in liabilities is: $40,000 – $10,000 = $30,000.

Suppose the facts are the same for the Long Beach Luggage Company except that the owner's equity *decreased* by $10,000.

	A	= L	+ OE
Cumulative change	+ $40,000	?	– $10,000

Calculation: The left side changed by $40,000 so the right side must change by the same total. The increase in liabilities is: $40,000 + $10,000 = $50,000.

How to Solve "Cumulative Effect" Problems, *continued*

Examples of Format #2

The Pyare Square Cleaning Service had assets of $100,000 and liabilities of $70,000. If assets decreased by $12,000 and liabilities decreased by $20,000, what is the new balance of owner's equity?

Solution: This problem has information about beginning and ending balances, and also wants to know an ending balance (use Format #2).

	A	= L	+ OE
Beginning balance	$100,000	$70,000	?
Cumulative change	–$12,000	–$20,000	?
Ending balance			?

First: Calculate the beginning balance of OE:
$100,000 – $70,000 = $30,000

Second: Calculate the cumulative change in OE:
– $12,000 – (–$20,000) = $8,000

Third: Calculate the ending balance of OE:
$30,000 + $8,000 = $38,000

The completed table looks like this:

	A	= L	+ OE
Beginning balance	$100,000	$70,000	**$30,000**
Cumulative change	– $12,000	– $20,000	**$8,000**
Ending balance			**$38,000**

Notice that you can check your answer by filling in all the remaining blank spaces. Then verify that the equation still balances.

PRACTICE Learning Goal 9

Solutions are in the disk at the back of the book and at: www.worthyjames.com

Learning Goal 9 is about calculating the cumulative effect of transactions on the condition of a business. Use these questions and problems to practice what you have learned.

Reinforcement Problems

LG 9-1. The assets of Vermont Street Surf Shop increase by $5,000 and liabilities increase by $15,000. What is the change in owner's equity? Try to evaluate what has happened to the company.

LG 9-2. The owner's equity of Gainesville Internet Services Shoppe increased by $20,000 and liabilities increased by $20,000. What is the change in total assets? Try to evaluate what has happened to the company.

LG 9-3. Diablo Valley Consulting Enterprises had liabilities decrease by $9,000 and owner's equity increase by $25,000. What is the change in total assets? Try to evaluate what has happened to the company.

LG 9-4. On December 31, 2018, Athens Computer Services had assets of $95,000 and liabilities of $25,000. During the year, assets increased by $12,000 and liabilities decreased by $15,000. What was the balance of owner's equity on January 1, 2018? Try to evaluate what happened to the company during the year.

LG 9-5. On June 1, Bucks County Enterprises had total assets of $90,000 and total owner's equity of $75,000. If assets increased by $12,000 and owner's equity decreased by $10,000, what are the total liabilities on June 30? Try to evaluate what happened to the company during June.

LG 9-6. On January 1, Thieu Nguyen's company had total assets of $400,000 and total liabilities of $300,000. For each of the following *separate* situations, calculate the missing amount at December 31 year-end for his company:

a. If total assets increased by $25,000 and owner's equity increased by $25,000, what are the liabilities?

b. If total assets increased by $25,000 and total liabilities increased by $20,000, what is the owner's equity?

c. If total liabilities decreased by $25,000 and owner's equity increased by $20,000, what are the total assets?

d. If total assets increased by $25,000 and total liabilities decreased by $20,000, what is the owner's equity?

e. If total assets increased by $45,000 and owner's equity increased by $55,000, what are the total liabilities?

PRACTICE **Learning Goal 9, continued**

Solutions are in the disk at the back of the book and at: www.worthyjames.com

LG 9-7. During the year, Indianapolis Company's assets increased by $51,000 to a December 31 year-end balance of $644,000. The year-end balance of owner's equity was $406,000. The net income for the year was $119,000, and the owner had withdrawn $50,000 without making any investments. What was the January 1 amount of liabilities?

LG 9-8. On July 1, the assets of Bloomington Enterprises were $305,000 and liabilities were $96,000. During the quarter, net income was $18,000, and the owner withdrew $72,000 and made no investments. If liabilities decreased $41,000 during the quarter, what was the amount of assets on September 30?

LG 9-9. During September, the owner of Terre Haute Company invested $19,000 in the business and withdrew $6,000. The net loss during September was $11,000. The liabilities on September 30 were $320,000 and exceeded assets by $79,000. What was the balance of owner's equity on September 1?

LG 9-10. The owner's equity of Gary Enterprises on December 31 was $598,000, which was $303,000 greater than the liabilities, which had decreased by $27,000 during the year. Also during the year, the company had a net loss of $87,000, the owner investments were $101,000, and the withdrawals were $51,000. What were the total assets on January 1?

LG 9-11. For the month of April, Lafayette Company reported a net income of $19,000. The owner investments were $28,000, the withdrawals were $9,000, and assets decreased by $7,000. What was the change in the liabilities during April?

PRACTICE Learning Goal 9, continued

Instructor-Assigned Problems

If you are using this book in a class, these review problems may be assigned by your instructor for homework, group assignments, class work, or other activities. Only your instructor has the solutions.

IA9-1. Calculate the cumulative effect of transactions. Calculate the answer to each item.

a. The liabilities of Pittsburgh Company decreased by $19,000 and the assets increased by $5,000. What was the change in owner's equity?
b. On December 31 year-end, the owner's equity of Altoona Enterprises was $128,000 and the assets were $204,000. During the year, liabilities decreased by $45,000 and assets decreased by $12,000. What was the owner's equity on January 1?
c. During the current year, the liabilities of Reading Company increased by $21,000 to $236,000. At the same time, the owner's equity increased by $11,000 to $498,000. What was the amount of the assets at the beginning of the year?
d. On June 1, the assets of Allentown Partnership totaled $488,000, and on June 30, the assets were $509,000. If the liabilities had increased by $42,000, what was the change in the owner's equity?
e. The owner's equity of Harrisburg Company on January 1 was $246,000 and total liabilities were $135,000. During the year, total liabilities increased by $29,000 and owner's equity decreased by $35,000. What was the amount of total assets on December 31?
f. Philadelphia Partnership's liabilities increased by $20,000 and owner's equity increased by $14,000. What was the change in total assets during September?
g. During the year, Chester Company's assets decreased by $137,000 to a year-end balance of $800,000. The year-end balance of owner's equity was $510,000. The net income for the year was $199,000, and the owner had withdrawn $50,000 without making any investments. What was the amount of liabilities on January 1?
h. On July 1, the assets of Erie Enterprises were $335,000 and liabilities were $106,000. During the quarter, net income was $15,000, and the owner withdrew $80,000 and made no investments. If liabilities decreased $35,000 during the quarter, what was the amount of assets on September 30?
i. During October, the owner of Cincinnati Enterprises invested $15,000 in the business and withdrew $4,000. The net loss during October was $5,000. The liabilities on October 31 were $315,000 and exceeded assets by $85,000. What was the balance of owner's equity on October 1?
j. The owner's equity of Dayton Company on December 31 was $636,000, which was $490,000 greater than the liabilities, which had increased by $50,000 during the year. Also during the year, the company had a net loss of $77,000, the owner investments were $100,000, and the withdrawals were $44,000. What were the total assets on January 1?
k. For the month of April, Akron Company reported net income of $12,000. The owner investments were $21,000, the withdrawals were $7,000, and assets increased by $15,000. What was the change in liabilities during April?
l. On January 1, the Youngstown Partnership had assets of $281,000 and owner's equity of $103,000. During the year, assets decreased by $147,000 and liabilities increased by $152,000. What was the amount of liabilities on December 31?
m. On November 1, the net amount of assets minus liabilities of Canton Company was $160,000. During November, the net amount increased by $10,000. What was the balance of owner's equity on November 30?

PRACTICE Learning Goal 9, continued

IA9-2. Calculate the cumulative effect of transactions. Calculate the answer to each item.

a. On May 1, the assets of Manhattan Company totaled $376,000, and on May 31 the assets were $471,000. If the liabilities had decreased by $39,000, what was the change in the owner's equity?

b. On February 1, the net amount of assets minus liabilities of Long Island Property Company was $140,000. During February the net amount increased by $17,000. What was the balance of owner's equity on February 28?

c. On December 31 year-end, the owner's equity of Syracuse Enterprises was $131,000 and the assets were $219,000. During the year, liabilities decreased by $27,000 and assets decreased by $14,000. What was the owner's equity on January 1?

d. During the current year, the liabilities of Buffalo Partnership increased by $4,000 to $226,000. At the same time, the owner's equity increased by $15,000 to $588,000. What was the amount of the assets at the beginning of the year?

e. The owner's equity of Rochester Company on January 1 was $216,000 and total liabilities were $325,000. During the year, total liabilities increased by $9,000 and owner's equity decreased by $75,000. What was the amount of total assets on December 31?

f. On August 1, the assets of Staten Island Enterprises were $425,000 and liabilities were $101,000. During the quarter, net income was $24,000, and the owner withdrew $83,000 and made no investments. If liabilities decreased $32,000 during the quarter, what was the amount of assets on August 31?

g. During September, Albany Partnership's liabilities increased by $38,000 and owner's equity decreased by $15,000. What was the change in total assets during September?

h. The liabilities of Trenton Company decreased by $14,000 and the assets increased by $11,000. What was the change in owner's equity?

i. For the month of October, Newark Company reported net income of $18,000. The owner investments were $24,000, the withdrawals were $25,000, and assets increased by $4,000. What was the change in the liabilities during October?

j. During January, the owner of Jersey City Enterprises invested $37,000 in the business and withdrew $3,000. The net loss during January was $7,000. The liabilities on January 31 were $327,000 and exceeded assets by $78,000. What was the balance of owner's equity on January 1?

k. On September 1, the Paterson Partnership reported assets of $263,000 and owner's equity of $109,000. During the year, assets decreased by $157,000 and liabilities increased by $162,000. What was the amount of liabilities on September 30?

l. The owner's equity of Atlantic City Proprietorship on December 31 was $536,000, which was $291,000 greater than the liabilities, which had increased by $44,000 during the year. Also during the year, the company had a net loss of $72,000, the owner investments were $96,000, and the withdrawals were $39,000. What were the total assets on January 1?

m. During the year ended December 31, Montclair Company's assets decreased by $145,000 to a year-end balance of $800,000. The year-end balance of owner's equity was $515,000. The net income for the year was $186,000, and the owner had withdrawn $62,000 without making any investments. What was the January 1 amount of liabilities?

PRACTICE Learning Goal 9, continued

Your Questions?

It is *very* important to be aware of what you need to understand better. What do you need to understand better about this learning goal? On a separate piece of paper, write the questions that you want to discuss with your classmates, instructor, or supervisor. Try to be very specific about what is bothering you, such as explanations that you do not fully understand.

CUMULATIVE VOCABULARY REVIEW

This is a vocabulary review for Learning Goals 1 through 8. On a separate piece of paper, match each description with the term that it describes. The answer for each term is in the right column. (*Suggestion:* Cover the answers in the right column as you test your vocabulary.)

Term	Description	Answers
1. Accounts payable	a. A system of accounting that always maintains the equality of assets and claims on assets	1e
2. Accounting equation	b. The removal of business assets for personal use by the owner	2s
3. Net income	c. A business with one owner (not a corporation)	3t
4. Asset	d. A seller of goods or services	4l
5. Vendor	e. Short-term debts to suppliers of goods and services	5d
6. Equity	f. An advance payment from a customer	6q
7. Personal liability	g. Revenue earned from a loan but not yet received	7p
8. Bookkeeping	h. The owner's claim on the asset value in a business	8o
9. Partnership	i. The term for a particular owner's claim on assets	9r
10. Double-entry accounting	j. Increase in owner's equity as a result of making a sale	10a
11. Leasing	k. A debt	11u
12. Owner's capital, such as "Bill Jones, Capital"	l. A future economic benefit that is owned or controlled by the business as a result of measurable past events	12i
13. Liability	m. A payment of an expense in advance	13k
14. Expense	n. Another name for owner's equity	14v
15. Revenue	o. The part of the accounting process that is primarily concerned with recording transactions	15j
16. Drawing	p. The condition of personal assets being subject to creditors' claims for business debts	16b
17. Owner's equity	q. A general term meaning a claim on asset value	17h
18. Notes receivable	r. A business that is not a corporation and that is owned by two or more people	18y
19. Interest receivable	s. A = L + OE	19g
20. Unearned revenue	t. When revenues are greater than expenses	20f
21. Paid-in capital	u. The act of renting property	21x
22. Accounts receivable	v. The decrease in owner's equity caused by using up resources in operations	22w
23. Add value	w. Money owed to a business by its customers	23z
24. Prepaid expense	x. The stockholders' investment in a corporation	24m
25. Proprietorship	y. Money receivable recorded by a written promise	25c
26. Net worth or net assets	z. Use resources to create something valuable people will want	26n

CUMULATIVE TEST Learning Goals 1–9

Time Limit: 55 minutes

Instructions

*On a separate piece of paper, enter the best answer to each question. Do **not** look back in the book when taking the test. (If you need to do this, you are not ready.) After you finish the test, refer to the answers and circle the number of each question that you missed. Then go to the **Help Table** (on page 215) to identify your strong and weak knowledge areas by individual learning goal.*

Multiple Choice

Select the best answer.

1. An asset
   a. is a future economic benefit.
   b. always must belong to and be controlled by a business.
   c. ownership cannot be contingent upon future events.
   d. all of the above.
2. How many categories of claims on the total assets of business can there be?
   a. one (just for the owner)
   b. two (the owner and the creditors)
   c. three (the owner, the creditors, and the investors)
   d. more than three in any combination
3. Which of the following is a correct presentation of the accounting equation?
   a. A = L + OE c. A – OE = L
   b. A – L – OE = 0 d. all of the above
4. The only business type in which the owner(s) do (does) not have personal liability for business debts is a
   a. general partnership. c. proprietorship.
   b. corporation. d. any of the above.
5. A business is
   a. an organized group of activities that uses up resources.
   b. an organized group of activities that creates and sells resources.
   c. organized with the intention of making the owner richer.
   d. all the above.
6. If $50,000 of land is purchased by paying $30,000 cash and signing a $20,000 note payable for the remainder,
   a. total owner's equity increases c. total assets decrease.
   b. total assets increase. d. total owner's equity decreases.
7. Money that is owed to suppliers and service providers, but not yet paid, is called
   a. accounts payable. c. notes payable.
   b. unearned revenue. d. accounts receivable.
8. The two changes that are increases in the owner's equity are
   a. owner investments and withdrawals. c. owner investments and revenues.
   b. expenses and revenues. d. withdrawals and expenses.
9. A revenue is
   a. a sale of a service or product causing an increase in owner's equity.
   b. an increase in business cash.
   c. any increase in owner's equity.
   d. any combination of an increase in assets and/or decrease in liabilities.

CUMULATIVE TEST Learning Goals 1–9, continued

10. Money that is advanced to a business by a customer before services are performed is called
a. accounts payable. c. notes payable.
b. unearned revenue. d. interest payable.

11. The following event (transaction) takes place for Santa Clara Company: liabilities decrease by $1,000. Therefore,
a. owner's equity will decrease by $1,000.
b. total assets could decrease by $1,000 or owner's equity could decrease by $1,000.
c. total assets could increase by $1,000 or owner's equity could decrease by $1,000.
d. total assets could decrease by $1,000 or owner's equity could increase by $1,000.

12. Butte Dry Cleaners spends $50,000 to renovate its lobby and storefront.
a. This will probably add more than $50,000 value to its services.
b. Exactly $50,000 of value will be added.
c. It is difficult to say how much value is added until revenues are added up.
d. This cannot add value.

13. Which of the following probably does not add value?
a. throwing away parts damaged in production
b. consuming resources in order to create economic resources
c. spending money for janitorial services
d. spending money on advertising

14. The accounting equation describes
a. the condition of a business over a period of time.
b. the condition of a business at one point in time.
c. the condition of any economic entity at one point in time.
d. none of the above.

15. If a business incurs an expense, then the owner's equity decreases because the expense
a. caused either liabilities to increase or assets to decrease.
b. caused either assets to increase or liabilities to increase.
c. caused either assets to decrease or liabilities to decrease.
d. caused both assets and liabilities to decrease.

16. Which of the following is not an asset?
a. a sculpture purchased for the front office
b. a prepayment of rent for three months
c. the owner's equity
d. a 15-year-old company truck that is occasionally used for deliveries

17. Select the one item that is an asset.
a. accounts receivable
b. company employees
c. suggestions by employees that will increase efficiency
d. the owner's capital

18. Yorrick's bookstore is going out of business. Who has first claim on the assets?
a. the creditors c. both creditors and owner equally
b. the owner d. both creditors and owner proportionately

19. At the start of the month, Travis Company has total debt of $10,000 and Travis Patterson, Capital is $40,000. During the month, total assets increased by $10,000 and total liabilities increased by $3,000. What is the balance of owner's equity at the end of the month?
a. $40,000 c. $47,000
b. $50,000 d. $37,000

CUMULATIVE TEST SOLUTIONS Learning Goals 1–9

Multiple Choice

1. d **2.** b **3.** d These are just variations of the same equation. **4.** b **5.** d

6. b Total assets increase because a $50,000 asset (land) is received and a $30,000 asset (cash) is given up.

7. a **8.** c **9.** a **10.** b

11. d It will probably help to visualize this by drawing the diagram of a business with the circles or by using the accounting equation with up and down arrows. **12.** c **13.** a

14. c The accounting equation applies to any economic entity or unit (business, government, nonprofit, etc.). **15.** a Visualize by drawing a diagram or by using the equation with up and down arrows. **16.** c The owner's equity is a claim on assets. **17.** a **18.** a

19. c (Figures in bold are calculated.)

	Assets	=	Liabilities	+	Owner's Equity
Beginning Balance	**$50,000**		$10,000		$40,000
Change	+ 10,000		+ 3,000		
Ending Balance	**60,000**		**13,000**		**47,000**

20. c (A proprietorship is always a separate financial and economic entity, even though it is not a separate legal entity.)

21. d Assets increased by $10,000. (Figures in bold are calculated.)

	Assets	=	Liabilities	+	Owner's Equity
Beginning Balance	**$80,000**		$40,000		$40,000
Change	**+ 10,000**				
Ending Balance	**90,000**		40,000		50,000

22. a **23.** a Payment of debt never affects owner's equity, only creditor's equity.

24. d Remember, an "entity" can be any business, a division of a business, an individual, or any other economic operation or unit for which financial reporting is wanted.

25. c (Figures in bold are calculated.)

	Assets	=	Liabilities	+	Owner's Equity
Beginning Balance	**$65,000**		**$33,000**		**$32,000**
Change	+ 5,000				– 10,000
Ending Balance	70,000				22,000

26. d (Visualize with a circle diagram of condition or use the accounting equation with arrows.)

27. b **28.** b **29.** c

30. c An increase in value is always a subjective estimate and is not considered to be measurable. There is no objective evidence such as a sale that confirms value. For now, it's a matter of opinion.

31. b Of course, it is also called owner's equity.

32. d Total equities of $168,000 minus the known assets of $151,000 = $17,000 of equipment.

33. d One asset (accounts receivable) is given up in exchange for another asset (cash) of equal amount.

34. c (Figures in bold are calculated.)

	Assets	=	Liabilities	+	Owner's Equity
Beginning Balance	**$75,000**		$25,000		$50,000
Change	+ 20,000		+ 15,000		
Ending Balance	**95,000**		**40,000**		**55,000**

35. b (Draw the diagram of a business with the circles or use the accounting equation with up and down arrows.) **36.** c Equipment increases, cash decreases, and notes payable increases. (Visualize using the diagram or accounting equation.) **37.** c (A = L + OE, therefore A = 37,000 + 22,000)

HELP TABLE — Identify Your Strengths and Weaknesses

The questions in this test cover the nine learning goals of Sections I and II. After you have circled the number of each question that you missed, look at the table below.

Go to the first learning goal category in the table: "Explain What a Business Is and What It Does." The second column in the table shows which questions on the test covered this learning goal. Look on the test to see if you circled numbers 5, 12, or 13. How many did you miss? Write this number in the "How Many Missed?" column. Repeat this process for each of the remaining learning goal categories in the table.

If you *miss* ***two*** *or more questions* for any learning goal, you are too weak in that learning goal and you need to *review*. The last column shows you where to read and practice so you can improve your score.

Some learning goal categories have more questions because you need to be especially well prepared in these areas. More questions means your performance must be better.

Learning Goal	Questions	How many missed?	Material begins on . . .
SECTION I			
1. Explain What a Business Is and What It Does	5, 12, 13		page 3
2. Define and Identify Assets	1, 16, 17, 30		page 33
3. Define and Identify the Two Claims on Assets	2, 18, 29, 31		page 47
4. Use the Accounting Equation to Show the Condition	3, 14, 32, 37		page 56
5. Define "Entity" and Identify Different Types	4, 20, 22, 24		page 62
SECTION II			
6. Analyze Individual Transactions	6, 11, 23, 26, 33, 35, 36		page 94
7. Identify Common Assets and Liabilities	7, 10, 27		page 152
8. Explain the Four Basic Changes in Owner's Equity	8, 9, 15, 28		page 187
9. Analyze the Cumulative Effect of Transactions	19, 21, 25, 34		page 200

SECTION III

Transactions—Basic Recording Concepts

OVERVIEW

What this section does	This section begins the standard introduction to basic accounting. For the enhanced introduction, see page 1. This Section III explains what an accounting system is and gives you practice that makes it easier to record transactions without using confusing terminology.
Use this section if . . .	. . . you want an introduction to fundamental accounting concepts. . . . you want special practice that will make it easier for you to understand and use debits and credits when recording transactions in Learning Goal 22.
Do not use this section if. . .	. . . you already understand how to analyze transactions, and you now feel ready to learn about debits and credits in a real accounting system (see Learning Goal 22).

LEARNING GOALS

LEARNING GOAL 10

Accounting: The Big Picture

In Learning Goal 10, you will find:

Accounting Defined

Accounting

Definition of "Accounting"

Accounting is a system of activities that analyzes, processes, communicates, and interprets financial data about a business or other entity. The objective of accounting is to provide financial information that is useful for decision making.

Examples

- The information system used by a college to record tuition receipts and operating expenses
- The work done by the people in the accounting department of a business to record transactions and prepare financial statements
- The system used by a church to record contributions and expenditures
- A manufacturing company recording and analyzing product costs

The Accounting Process

Three-Stage Process

Overview

An accounting system functions by a process of sequential steps. The process begins each time an event can potentially affect the financial condition of a business. If an event does affect the financial condition, the financial information from that event continues through each stage in the process that you see illustrated below.

Process Illustrated

The illustration below shows the sequential stages of the accounting system as a process. The process begins with the analysis of a business event (Stage 1). This analysis identifies any event that is a transaction. If the event qualifies as a transaction, the data concerning that event will also pass through Stage 2 and Stage 3.

The Accounting Cycle

The steps that make up the accounting process are often referred to as the "accounting cycle." As you progress through this book and the first part of Volume 2, you will learn more detailed procedures of the accounting cycle.

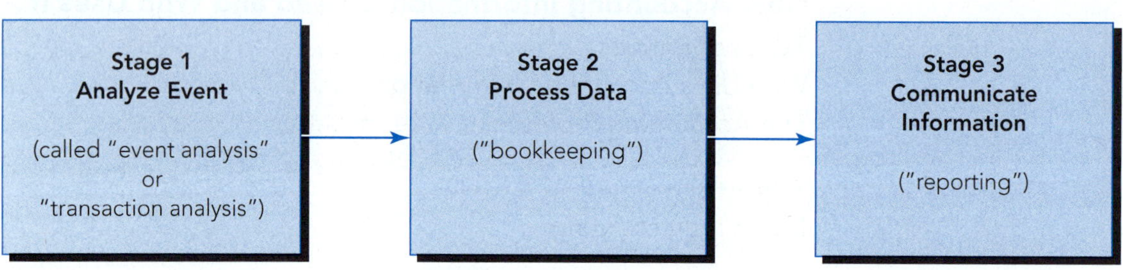

What Happens

- Test the event: Is there a change in financial condition?
- Identify:
  - Classification
  - Valuation
  - Timing
- If yes, go to stage 2. If no, stop.

What Happens

- Record transactions if:
  - Reliable data
  - Relevant data
- Summarize results.

What Happens

- Prepare financial reports and interpret them.

Stage 1: Analyze the Event (Transaction Analysis)

Overview

Analyzing an event is called *event analysis* or *transaction analysis*. Whatever you prefer to call it, to analyze an event for accounting purposes means to evaluate what has happened to see if the financial condition has been changed in some way. **Any possible change in financial condition must be identified three ways: By classification, by value, and by time (date) of occurrence.**

We will begin to study the classification and valuation of transactions in the next learning goal. (As well, the enhanced introduction provides additional event analysis practice in Learning Goal 6.)

Classification

Classification means identifying *what specific parts* of financial condition are increased or decreased because of an event: assets, liabilities, or owner's equity (page 223). To do proper classification you need to: (1) understand the definition of these items so you can identify them, and (2) carefully think about an event so that you can determine which of the items are affected, and how they are affected.

Valuation ("Measurement")

Valuation means determining the correct dollar values (economic values) to use. Valuation is also called ***measurement***.

Valuation is important and sometimes quite controversial—accountants do not always agree on the correct values for many kinds of items!

We will return to this topic in Learning Goal 18 and again in Volume 2, but right now the **two essential points** you need to remember about valuation are:

1. Valuation means determining what dollar values should be used to record changes in financial condition.
2. Valuation is determined in two phases. First, an original transaction value is recorded when a transaction occurs. The value of an item when it is first recorded is usually clear and is available from documents.

   Second, there are some situations that require the initial recorded value be changed to a different value. This most often happens at a later date, when circumstances or an event have caused a significant loss of value. In volume 2, we discuss in detail when and how some of these important valuation changes are made.

continued ▶

Stage 1: Analyze the Event (Transaction Analysis), *continued*

Valuation Example

- **Initial value:** On June 12, our business purchased merchandise inventory. The billing document shows an amount of $5,000. This is the value used to record the transaction.
- **Value change:** By December 31, the selling price of the inventory has decreased to $3,000. For this kind of asset, accounting rules require that the value be reduced to $3,000 in the accounting records.

Timing

Timing means identifying the correct date on which an event causes a change in financial condition. As you will see in this volume and especially in the next volume, event timing is especially important for correctly determining the net income or net loss for a business.

Why Event Analysis Is So Important

Correct event analysis is extremely important! This cannot be overemphasized. If event analysis is incorrect, everything else—especially the financial reports, which many people depend on—will be incorrect. The resulting decisions based on those reports will be flawed, misleading, and potentially damaging. It is important for you to begin thinking about **cla**ssification, **va**luation, and **ti**ming whenever you think about transactions. (Think: "Mr. **Clavati**" to help you remember.) If analyzed incorrectly, these three elements can create confusion, and they can also be misused for financial manipulation and fraud.

Proper classification, valuation, and timing make up the heart of good accounting.

Stage 2: Process Data

Overview

After the event is analyzed and identified as a transaction that affects the financial condition, the transaction data must be processed. The processing stage is usually referred to as ***bookkeeping***. Bookkeeping consists primarily of recording and summarizing functions. The next learning goal introduces you to some of these procedures as you learn how to analyze events.

Recording

Recording means formally entering the transaction data into the accounting books and records. Recording is also referred to as ***recognition.*** Recording (recognition) places the transaction data into the accounting system consistent with the results of the analysis from Stage 1.

Stage 2: Process Data, *continued*

Two requirements must be met for recording to take place:

- The recorded data must be *reliable*. This means that the transaction data can be verified as authentic and that the data is unbiased.
- The data must be *relevant*. This means that the data will provide information that is useful and significant—it is not irrelevant or immaterial. Reliable and relevant data will ultimately result in reliable and relevant information in financial reports.

Summarizing

Summarizing means accumulating and organizing data in ways that make the recorded data more understandable and useful. Proper summarizing makes it possible to present and analyze data in financial reports. Summarizing also makes it possible for management to accurately use the data when dealing with customers, vendors, and other parties. When summarization happens, the data can be transformed into useful and usable *information*.

Stage 3: Communicate Information

Overview

The entire accounting process takes place with the ultimate goal of creating and presenting useful financial information about a business or other entity.

Financial Reports

Useful financial information is most often presented in the form of financial reports. Usually, at least four types of financial reports are prepared. You will begin to learn how to identify and prepare these reports beginning in Learning Goal 12. In practice, these reports also contain footnotes, charts, graphs, tables, and other analysis to help the users of the reports.

Example of All Stages

The Event

On May 19, Ohlone Company purchases $250 of office supplies on credit.

Analyze Event

- Classification: Does the event affect the financial condition of the business? Yes, Office Supplies, and business debts both increase.
- Valuation: Office supplies increases and debts increase. The dollar value is given as $250. We are given this amount as the exchange value of the event. Thus, the amount is clear and there are no other values to consider.
- Timing: The date of the event (the purchase) is May 19.

continued ▶

Example of All Stages, *continued*

Conclusion: This event is a transaction because the event causes changes in financial condition that we can classify, that are measurable in dollar value, and that happen at an identifiable date. The classification, valuation, and timing show us how to properly record the transaction.

Process Data

- Recording: The data from the transaction (accounts, values, date) are verified as reliable and relevant by examining documentation. The data are then recorded into the accounting books and records of Ohlone Company.
- Summarizing: At regular intervals, the data from this transaction with other accumulated data from other transactions are totaled and reorganized using bookkeeping methods.

Communicate Information

Ohlone Company prepares monthly financial reports. Reports are prepared in specific ways that communicate the condition of the company as of the end of May and that explain the operations during May. The summarized data in the books and records of the company is the source of most of the information presented on the financial reports.

The Accounting Equation: How to Show Basic Financial Condition

What Financial Condition Is and What It Means

Overview: What is "Financial Condition"?

Previously we said that every change in financial condition must be analyzed for classification, valuation, and timing. What is "financial condition", exactly? The essential financial condition of any economic entity is described by the ***accounting equation***. All financial accounting is based on this equation. To begin, we will apply the accounting equation to a proprietorship (one owner) business, although with small changes the accounting equation is also used for any other type of business, such as a corporation or partnership.

Accounting Equation

The accounting equation ("financial condition") for a proprietorship is:

Assets = Liabilities + Owner's Equity

Or, more simply: A = L + OE

What Financial Condition Is and What It Means, *continued*

The Parts of the Equation

- ***Assets:*** Assets are economic resources owned by a business or other entity. For an item to qualify as a business asset it must be property that is: 1) already owned by a business and that: 2) will provide a future benefit to the business, near-term or long-term. Assets generally have value, and therefore represent the wealth of a business.
- ***Liabilities:*** Liabilities are the debts that are owed to creditors. They are the creditor's claims on the asset value. Creditors always have first claim on asset value.
- ***Owner's equity:*** Owner's equity is the owner's claim on the value of the assets. It is a residual claim, which means that owner's equity is the amount of business wealth that the owner can claim after all the creditors are paid, if the business were to be sold or liquidated. Owner's equity is also called ***net worth***.

What the Equation Means

A = L + OE means that there are two possible claims on the wealth of a business. The first claim is the creditors' and the second claim is the owner's. Example: The total assets of James Wilson Company are $450,000. Total liabilities are $200,000. Therefore the remaining owner's equity is $250,000.

Assets		Liabilities		Owner's Equity
$450,000	=	$200,000	+	$250,000

What is the owner's equity if assets are $700,000?

Assets		Liabilities		Owner's Equity
$700,000	=	$200,000	+	?

Solution: $700,000 – $200,00 = $500,000 owner's equity

Common Types of Assets and Liabilities

Assets

The most familiar assets are cash, supplies, equipment, and land. Other common asset types are:

- ***Account receivable:*** A legal right to collect money, usually created as the result of a sale to a customer. A bill is sent to the customer, who promises to pay later. Payment is generally required in 30 to 60 days.
- ***Note receivable:*** A stronger legal right to collect money as the result of a borrower signing a written promise to pay, called a "promissory note".
- ***Interest receivable:*** The amount of interest that has been earned on a note receivable (or other investment) but not yet received in cash.
- ***Prepaid expense:*** An advance payment made to a provider of goods or services before they are provided. Common examples are prepaid insurance, prepaid rent, and prepaid travel, such as airline tickets.
- ***Merchandise inventory:*** The goods that a merchant has in stock for the purpose of selling to customers.

continued ▶

Common Types of Assets and Liabilities, *continued*

Liabilities

There are many different kinds of liabilities. A liability name often is followed by the word "payable" to indicate that it is a liability.

- ***Account payable:*** A legal obligation to pay money, usually created as the result of a purchase of goods or services. Payment is generally required in 30 to 60 days. The opposite of account receivable.
- ***Note payable:*** The opposite of note receivable. A note payable is the legal obligation to pay money as the result of signing a promissory note.
- ***Unearned revenue:*** An advance payment received from a custombler before goods or services have been provided to the customer. The advance payment creates an obligation to return the money until goods or services are provided.

The Elements of Owner's Equity

Owner's Equity

Owner's equity is sub-divided into parts so that someone who analyzes a financial report is able to see both the current changes in the owner's equity as well the total balance of owner's equity. The parts of owner's equity are:

- ***Revenue:*** An increase in owner's equity caused by making a sale of goods or services. The dollar amount of a sale causes an increase in owner's equity referred to as "revenue".
- ***Expense:*** A decrease in owner's equity caused by using up resources to operate a business, so it can create revenue. The dollar amount of a resource used up causes a decrease in owner's equity referred to as "expense".
- ***Withdrawal (Drawing):*** A decrease in owner's equity caused by the owner removing cash or other assets from a businesses for personal use. The dollar amount of the asset removed is the owner's equity decrease.
- ***Capital:*** A term used for the total owner's equity of a particular business using the owner's name, such as "Bill Smith, Capital". Capital is the combined total of the three separately recorded changes (revenue, expense, and withdrawals) plus owner investments, which are recorded as direct increases in capital, rather than being recorded separately.

Owner's Equity Example

On June 3, Bill Smith started a business by investing $10,000. Because it is a new business, the June 3 "Bill Smith, Capital" is zero. However, this now increases to $10,000 because of the owner's investment.

During the month of June the three separately recorded changes were: $5,000 of revenues (owner's equity increase), $3,500 of expenses (owner's equity decrease), and Bill Smith withdrew $700 for personal use (owner's equity decrease). Bill uses this information to analyze the results of operations.

The Elements of Owner's Equity, *continued*

If Bill wishes to know total owner's equity for his business at the end of the current period on June 30, he combines the $10,000 "Bill Smith, Capital" balance with the other three current period changes in owner's equity (revenue, expense, and withdrawal). The combined total is $10,800. The total owner's equity on June 30 is therefore $10,800 and for this particular business is called "Bill Smith, Capital".

So, how many types of changes in owner's equity did we see in Bill Smith's business? Four: two increases and two decreases — owner investment (increase), revenue (increase), expense (decrease), and owner withdrawal (decrease).

The Equation Always Stays in Balance

In order for the accounting equation to remain in balance, every increase or decrease in owner's equity also occurs with a change in the assets or liabilities. Therefore, the accounting equation always remains in balance. In the next learning goal, we will practice analyzing transactions and recording changes to the three parts of the accounting equation, so we can see how this happens.

How Accounting Information is Used and Who Uses It

Types of Entities

Overview

Many different individuals and organizations require financial information that is useful to them. The organizations are frequently referred to as "economic entities". Accounting provides the necessary financial information for an entity. In fact, accounting cannot be applied unless a specific economic entity is identified that needs the accounting information. Different types of economic entities are described below.

Definition: Economic Entity

An ***economic entity*** is any unit or organization with an activity for which the financial condition or financial information of that activity that must be reported separately.

continued ►

Types of Entities, *continued*

Examples: Business Economic Entities

- ***Proprietorship:*** A business activity that is owned by a single individual, and that is not a corporation.
- ***Partnership:*** A business activity that is owned by two or more owners, acting as partners. There are different types of partnerships.
- ***Corporation:*** A activity that is organized and given "life" as an individual legal entity, separate from its owners, under the laws of the state in which it is created. Corporation owners are called ***stockholders*** or ***shareholders*** because their ownership percentage is determined by how many shares of corporate stock they own. There are different types of corporations, including both profit and non-profit. The largest business organizations are corporations, primarily because of the ability to issue stock and to protect stockholders from business debts and obligations.
- ***Limited Liability Company (LLC):*** An activity that combines certain legal and tax advantages of partnerships and corporations. There can be one or more owners (called either members or partners) in an LLC. As with corporations, an LLC can be either profit or non-profit.

Other Economic Entities

As indicated above, in order for accounting to be used, an entity must be identified first. The more specific the entity, the more specific and detailed the accounting information. For example, a large corporation may have different divisions. Each division is an economic entity. Each division may have multiple departments. Each department can be an entity. If you own your own proprietorship, your business is one economic entity and you are a separate economic entity. A charitable organization is an entity. What all of these examples have in common is that they require financial information and that information is specific to an activity.

Who Uses Accounting Information

Overview

Accounting information is summarized in financial statement reports that explain different aspects of the financial condition of an entity. The most common financial reports are those prepared for businesses. The people and organizations that use these financial reports are often called stakeholders. A ***stakeholder*** is a person or organization that needs to use accounting information reported by an entity because that person or organization has an interest in the entity. The accounting information is usually necessary in order to make a decision regarding the entity.

Examples of How Accounting Information is Used

There are many different kinds of stakeholders with different information requirements. Here are a few common examples of how stakeholders use accounting information:

Manage a business. Most importantly, financial information is used by owners and managers for the purpose of managing a business. Financial information is used to analyze the need for changes in business operation (called "feedback" information) and to do future planning. (Learning Goal 32 in this book discusses various methods for analyzing financial information.)

Who Uses Accounting Information, *continued*

Make an investment. Accounting information is used before purchasing a business, entering a partnership, or buying stock in a corporation for an investment or retirement planning.
Make a loan. A bank will always use accounting information to analyze the financial condition of a company before approving a loan. A supplier of materials or products needs accounting information to analyze the financial condition of buyer before giving a buyer credit to make purchases.
Purchase a product. Before making a purchase that will require future technical support, maintenance, or product updates, a buyer will use accounting information to evaluate the financial condition of the seller.
Develop a new product, start, or expand a business. A business requires accounting information in order to analyze possible financial outcomes of new product development or business expansion.
Analyze tax reporting. Government taxing authorities carefully analyze income reporting in order to verify compliance with tax laws. This tax reporting uses accounting information with which both a reporting business and the taxing authority must be familiar.
Change jobs or negotiate with an employer. Employees changing jobs will want to ensure that the new employer is in sound financial condition and will be able to continue the employment relationship. Unions or employee organizations negotiating for improved pay or benefits will need to accurately understand the real financial condition of an employer before beginning negotiations. Accounting information can be a source of this understanding.

The Accounting Profession

Overview

Accountants are professional individuals who are academically trained and who are able to correctly apply the theory and the procedures to properly complete the entire accounting process. Because of their training, accountants are essential and indispensable people who implement the accounting process. Some accountants with advanced training obtain professional licenses.

Accountants with Special Certification

A ***certified public accountant*** (CPA) is a person who has passed a rigorous state examination to obtain a professional license to practice public accounting. CPAs have many financial skills; however, only a CPA can audit the financial statements of a company and express an opinion as to the fairness of the statements. CPAs are required to maintain a high level of independence and integrity. These qualities, in addition to the professional training, mean that CPAs perform essential roles in the accounting process. The main types of work in public accounting are:

- Auditing: CPAs who perform auditing services examine the books and records of a company and express a professional opinion as to the fairness of the company's financial statements.

continued ▶

The Accounting Profession, *continued*

- Taxation: CPAs who specialize in taxation prepare tax returns and offer tax planning advice. These accountants also represent clients when they are being examined by taxing authorities such as the Internal Revenue Service. As well, CPAs also work for taxing authorities.
- Consulting services: This type of work is often called *management consulting*. It generally consists of designing accounting and other types of information systems but may also involve other specialized types of work.

A ***certified management accountant*** (CMA) is a person who analyzes the accounting process of a single company, with an emphasis on analyzing the procedures and operations. This is often called *managerial accounting*. A qualifying examination is required to obtain the CMA designation, and CMAs are also expected to maintain a high level of integrity. Areas of managerial accounting include:

- Accounting information system analysis
- Product cost analysis
- Budgeting
- General internal accounting and recording functions
- Internal auditing

The Importance of Ethics

Ethics in Accounting

Overview

Ethical behavior is an essential part of every action in the accounting process that we are discussing. The entire process would become completely meaningless if it consisted only of the application of technical knowledge, without the ultimate goal of providing honest and reliable financial information. Many people and organizations depend heavily on reliable financial information in many important ways. To meet the needs of these people and organizations and to ensure the integrity of the accounting process, accountants have a special ethical responsibility.

The Ethical Attitude

Ethics is the soul of good accounting. Ethical conduct means doing the right thing. Sometimes choices are clear because of existing rules or laws. At other times, choices can be dificult and complicated because it may not be exactly clear what is the right choice among various alternatives. However, in the end, the foundation of ethical conduct is always the same—the consistent *attitude* of always trying to do what one believes to be honest and right. The ethical attitude should be developed and matured by consistent ethics education.

Ethics in Accounting, *continued*

Important Ethical Standards

Professional accounting organizations have developed codes of conduct that members are expected to follow. Examples of these organizations are the American Institute of Certified Public Accountants (AICPA) and the Institute of Management Accountants (IMA).

Here are some important ethical standards from the AICPA code of conduct:

- **Integrity:** Basic honesty, never violating the trust of others
- **Objectivity:** Being impartial and fair to all parties
- **Independence:** Avoiding all relationships that impair objectivity
- **Due Care:** Properly applying all the necessary knowledge and skills

Guideline

The following table presents a guideline for ethical decision making when no clear rules, codes, or laws are available.

Step	Action
1	Recognize the moral issue of a potentially wrongful act that can result in loss, injury, or damage.
2	Review all the facts, including who is potentially involved.
3	List the alternative decisions.
4	Evaluate the possible outcomes of each alternative. ▪ What decision does the most good and/or least harm? ▪ Will everyone be treated fairly, regardless of the decision that is made?
5	Make a decision.
6	Thoughtfully appraise the results of your decision.

The Ethical Dilemma

The following examples illustrate the application of ethical guidelines and an ***ethical dilemma***. An ethical dilemma is a situation in which an ethical decision must be made between alternative choices, but no choice will likely provide a fully satisfactory ethical outcome.

Example

Thi Ngo, an accountant for Santa Clara Consulting Corporation, discovers that $20,000 of revenue was incorrectly recorded as consulting revenue. In fact, it was rental revenue from leasing some extra office space that the corporation had available for one year. Her supervisor tells Thi not to worry—there will be no effect on the net income of the company and the company does not want to worry investors with accounting technicalities. Thi knows that the revenue is not classified correctly but does not want to anger her supervisor and is uncertain about what to do.

- **Moral Issue:** Consulting is the main operation of the company, not renting, and overstating consulting revenue could mislead people into believing that the business is more successful than it really is. People could make investment or employment decisions that might cause them to lose money or damage their careers if the business is actually less successful than it appears to be.

continued ▶

Ethics in Accounting, *continued*

- **Review of Facts:** (a) $20,000 of rental revenue is incorrectly recorded as consulting revenue. (b) The affected parties are investors, lenders, suppliers, employees, corporate officers, and the responsible staff in the accounting department.
- **Alternatives:** (a) Do nothing. (b) Discuss again with the supervisor emphasizing the implications of the ethical issue. (c) Discuss with a higher authority within the company. (d) Make an anonymous report to top management, the auditors, or the board of directors. (e) Resign.
- **Possible Outcomes:** Doing nothing at a minimum establishes a pattern of unethical behavior. Worse outcomes are loss of business reputation and financial losses and job losses of stakeholders who relied on the information. Another discussion might annoy the supervisor but also might possibly help resolve the issue. A discussion with a higher authority may also help resolve the issue, although it would anger the supervisor even more, with possible consequences to Thi. Resigning immediately would mean loss of Thi's job without having attempted to solve the problem, although it would clearly avoid participation in an unethical action.
- **Decision:** The choice is not easy or obvious. Thi decides that the fair alternative that does the most good with the least harm is to first try another discussion with her supervisor, emphasizing the importance of the issue to the company and the investors. If the supervisor fails to act, Thi decides that she will look for a job with another company, while informing higher authorities within Santa Clara Corporation of the problem (as well as the auditors).

Example

John Dobbs, the chief financial officer of Empire Company, has been very successful in all of his duties with the company. He has risen to the position of chief financial officer, and he is often considered to be a possible future candidate for the position of president of the company. John frequently accompanies the company president and other top managers on business trips. On these trips, John sees the company president spend hundreds and sometimes thousands of dollars on lavish or personal expenses such as very expensive hotels, luxury travel, personal sightseeing, and gifts for his wife and friends. John also knows that the company president records these items as business expenses and that he is reimbursed by company for all the expenditures.

- **Moral Issue:** The president is using his position of authority to defraud the company by submitting false expense reports.
- **Review of Facts:** The company is spending thousands of dollars on expenditures that have nothing to do with its operations and that are personal expenditures of the president. These expenditures can be documented or accurately estimated.
- **Alternatives:** (a) Do nothing. (b) Discuss his concerns with the president emphasizing the implications of the ethical issue. (c) Make an anonymous report to the auditors or the board of directors. (d) Resign.

Ethics in Accounting, *continued*

- **Possible Outcomes:** Doing nothing means that the company will continue to be defrauded. Furthermore, the president is in a position of authority, and other managers may begin to imitate his actions. This could further weaken the company ethics and begin to create a widespread attitude resulting in actions (such as financial statement fraud) that can ultimately lead to dangerous consequences. On the other hand, John knows that his job is at risk if he openly reports this situation. John does not believe that he should resign because of the unethical actions of the president.
- **Decision:** John decides that the least damaging and most ethical action is to anonymously report the situation to the company's auditors and the board of directors. He will then watch to see if the situation improves.

A Continuing Concern

Ethical behavior is always an ongoing concern in accounting. Lapses in the ethical behavior of just a few people can damage the good reputations of many people. Unethical behavior of a few can ultimately lead to the destruction of entire companies (for example, Arthur Andersen Company—formerly the largest CPA firm worldwide, and Enron, formerly the large energy company).

SEC Required Disclosures

Ethical standards are enhanced by legally required disclosures. The SEC (Securities and Exchange Commission) requires that all publicly traded companies submit the following disclosure documents according to SEC guidelines. These documents are publicly available and viewable online at the SEC website.

- 10K: Annual financial report.
- 10Q: Quarterly financial report
- 8K: Report on significant events at the time they occur.
- Proxy statement: Required disclosure to stockholders in advance of the annual stockholders' meeting. Includes executive compensation and directors' backgrounds.
- S-1: Detailed company and financial disclosures prior to registering stock for sale to the public.

Check Your Understanding

Write the completed sentences on a separate piece of paper.

Accounting is a three-stage process that provides financial information to decision makers who need this information. The first stage in the process is to .... to identify transactions that cause changes in the accounting equation. In this stage, any change in the equation must be identified three ways. These three ways are ...., ..., and .... ("Mr. Clavati").

The second stage in the process requires you to .... This means to first .... provided that the data is .... and relevant. The second procedure in this stage requires you to ...., which is done by applying various bookkeeping methods.

The final stage in the process is to ...., which is usually done by preparing financial reports.

All of the stages above are essentially meaningless if they are manipulated or become unreliable. Therefore, the highest .... attitude is required of accountants.

Answers

Accounting is a three-stage process that provides financial information to decision makers who need this information. The first stage in the process is to analyze events to identify transactions that cause changes in the accounting equation. In this stage, any change in the equation must be identified three ways. These three ways are classification, valuation, and timing ("Mr. Clavati").

The second stage in the process requires you to process data. This means to first record transactions provided that the data is reliable and relevant. The second procedure in this stage requires you to summarize data, which is done by applying various bookkeeping methods.

The final stage in the process is to communicate information, which is usually done by preparing financial reports.

All of the stages above are essentially meaningless if they are manipulated or become unreliable. Therefore, the highest ethical attitude is required of accountants.

QUICK REVIEW

- Accounting is a three-stage process consisting of event analysis (classification, valuation, and timing), processing data, and communicating information.
- The accounting process is implemented by accountants, people who are academically and professionally trained in theory and procedure. Accountants with special certification are CPAs and CMAs.
- High ethical standards are essential to accounting. These standards include integrity, objectivity, independence, and due care.
- Assets provide future benefits and also represent the wealth of a business, while liabilities are debts.
- The essential financial condition of any economic entity is described by the accounting equation, which is: Assets = Liabilities + Owner's Equity. This can also be written as A = L + OE.
- Owner's equity is subdivided into four parts: revenue, expense, owner withdrawals, and capital.
- Accounting can only be applied after an economic entity is identified. Common organizations that are economic entities are proprietorships, partnerships, corporations, and limited liability companies.

VOCABULARY

Accounting: a system of activities that has the objective of providing financial information that is useful for decision-making (page 217)

Accounting equation: Asset = Liabilities + Owner's Equity (page 222)

Account payable: a legal obligation to pay money, usually created as the result of purchase of goods or services. (page 224)

Account receivable: a legal right to collect money, usually created as the result of a sale to a customer. (page 223)

Asset: economic resource that is owned by a business and that will provide a future benefit. Assets also represent the wealth of a business. (page 223)

Bookkeeping: another name for the processing functions in the accounting process (page 220)

Capital: A term used for the total owner's equity of a particular business. (page 224)

Corporation: an activity that is organized and given "life" as an individual legal entity, separate from its owners, under the laws of the state in which it is created (page 226)

Ethical Dilemma: A situation in which an ethical decision must be made between alternative choices, but no choice will likely provide a fully satisfactory ethical outcome. (page 229)

Expense: a decreaes in owner's equity caused by consuming resources for the purpose of operating a business to make sales. (page 224)

Interest receivable: the amount of interest that has been earned on a note receivable but not yet received. (page 223)

Liabilities: debts(page 223)

Limited liability company: an activity that combines certain legal and tax advantages of partnerships and corporations. (page 226)

Measurement: another name for the valuation step in the accounting process (page 219)

Merchandise inventory: the goods that a merchant has in stock for sale to customers. (page 223)

Net worth: another term for owner's equity. (page 223)

Note payable: the legal obligation to pay money as the result of signing a promissory note. (page 224)

Note receivable: a legal right to collect money as the result of a borrower signing a promissory note. (page 223)

Owner's equity: owner's claim on the business wealth, after the creditors are paid. (page 223)

Partnership: a business activity that is owned by two or more owner's acting as partners. (page 226)

Prepaid expense: an advance made to a provider of goods or services before they are provided. (page 223)

Proprietorship: a business activity that is owned by a single individual, and that is not a corporation (page 226)

Recognition: recording a transaction (page 220)

Revenue: an increase in owner's equity caused by making a sale of goods or services (page 224)

Stakeholders: people and organizations that use accounting information of an entity because they have an interest in the entity (page 226)

Unearned revenue: a liability that results from an advance payment received from a customer before goods or services are provided. (page 224)

Withdrawal (drawing): a decrease in owner's equity caused by the owner removing cash or other assets from a business for personal use. (page 224)

"It's up to you now Miller. The only thing that can save us is an accounting breakthrough."

PRACTICE Learning Goal 10

Solutions are in the disk at the back of the book and at: www.worthyjames.com

Learning Goal 10 explains the accounting process. Use these questions to practice what you have just read. Select the best answer to each question.

Multiple Choice

Select the best answer.

1. Stage 3 of the accounting process, "communicate information" includes
   a. preparing and interpreting financial reports.
   b. recording transactions.
   c. analyzing the event.
   d. all of the above.
2. The people and organizations that use accounting information are often called
   a. internal users.
   b. external users.
   c. creditors.
   d. stakeholders.
3. For stage 1, "analyze the event," we have previously learned to analyze an event in three steps by asking: "Are assets affected? Are liabilities affected? Is owner's equity affected?" Now we refine our event analysis by analyzing these three essential elements of each step:
   a. classification, valuation, application
   b. classification, valuation, timing
   c. interpretation, valuation, summarization
   d. confirmation, recordation, recognition
4. The question "What items in the accounting equation are affected?" refers to analyzing which element of an event?
   a. classification
   b. valuation
   c. recognition
   d. interpretation
5. The question "What is the dollar amount of change in the items affected?" refers to analyzing which element of an event?
   a. classification
   b. valuation
   c. recognition
   d. interpretation
6. The question "When did the event happen?" refers to analyzing which element of an event?
   a. classification
   b. valuation
   c. timing
   d. interpretation

PRACTICE Learning Goal 10, continued

Solutions are in the disk at the back of the book and at: www.worthyjames.com

7. Event analysis is extremely important to the accounting process because
   a. incorrect event analysis will ultimately result in incorrect and misleading financial reports.
   b. the decision making based on the financial reports could be flawed, useless, or potentially damaging.
   c. both a and b.
   d. none of the above.
8. Stage 2 of the accounting process, "process data," includes
   a. recording transactions.
   b. summarizing the data.
   c. preparing financial statements.
   d. both a and b.
9. The most fundamental requirement for ethical behavior is
   a. attitude.
   b. independence.
   c. technical skills.
   d. consistency.
10. Basic honesty, never violating the trust of others, is which AICPA ethical standard?
    a. due care
    b. integrity
    c. independence
    d. objectivity
11. Being impartial and fair to all parties is which AICPA ethical standard?
    a. due care
    b. integrity
    c. independence
    d. objectivity
12. The first step in the ethical decision-making guideline is to
    a. review all the facts, including who is potentially involved.
    b. review possible outcomes that will do the most good, the least harm, and treat all parties fairly and impartially.
    c. recognize the moral issue of a potentially wrongful act.
    d. make a decision.

Reinforcement Problems

LG 10-1. Identify the type of business. The left column of the table describes a type of business organization. In the right column, enter the type of business being described.

Description	Type of Organization
1. A business with one owner, and that does not issue shares of stock.	
2. A business with one or more owners and that does issue shares of stock.	
3. A type of business with one or more owners that combines certain legal and tax advantages of a partnership and a corporation.	
4. A business with two more owners that act together as partners.	
5. A corporation that is organization for charitable purposes.	

PRACTICE Learning Goal 10, continued

Solutions are in the disk at the back of the book and at: www.worthyjames.com

LG 10-2. **Identify the item.** The left column of the table describes items that are part of the accounting equation as a specific kind of asset, liability, or owner's equity for your company. In the right column, identify the item. If the item is a change in owner's equity, identify it as a revenue, owner investment, expense, or withdrawal.

Description	Item
1. A six-month advance payment to an insurance company.	
2. The legal right to collect money from a bill sent to a customer	
3. Using advertising services, and owner's equity decreases	
4. Providing consulting services to a client, and owner's equity increases	
5. Owner makes a deposit to the business bank account from her own personal funds	
6. An advance payment received from a customer before services are provided.	
7. On December 31, the total amount of owner's equity for a business owned by Mary Yee.	
8. The legal obligation to pay money as a result of signing a formal promise to pay a specific amount on a certain date.	
9. Mark Andersen, the owner, wrote himself a check on the business checking account.	
10. The legal obligation to pay money as pay money as a result fo receiving a bill from a supplier.	
11. The combined total of a beginning capital balance with current period revenues, expenses, and owner drawing.	
12. Consuming resources in order to operate the business and make sales.	

LG 10-3. **Make the equation balance.** In the table below, calculate the missing amounts in the accounting equation.

	Total Assets =	Total Liabilities +	Owner's Equity
a. Mohawk Company	$251,000	$200,000	?
b. Nez Perce Company	?	$18,500	$22,200
c. Lakota Company	$50,000	?	$35,000
d. Modoc Company	?	$45,000	$180,000
e. Cherokee Company	$200,000	$251,000	?
f. Seminole Company	$815,000	?	$645,000

What is the meaning of situation (e) in the table above? Is situation (e) actually possible?

PRACTICE **Learning Goal 10, continued**

Solutions are in the disk at the back of the book and at: www.worthyjames.com

LG 10-4. Practice event analysis. Use a blank sheet of paper to complete the table. For each event on the following table, analyze the event to determine if it is a recordable transaction. If the event is a recordable transaction, enter the date that the transaction should be recognized in the T (timing) column. Write the name of the items affected in the C (classification) columns and the values to record in the V (valuation) columns. Also put a "+" in the V column if assets, liabilities, or owner's equity are increased and a "( )" around any value that is a decrease. Use the first item as an example.

Event		Assets Affected?		Liabilities Affected?		Owner's Equity Affected?	
	T	C	V	C	V	C	V
a. On April 30, a count of supplies shows $400 of supplies used up.	April 30	Supplies	(400)			Supplies Expense	(400)
b. The owner invested $5,000 in his business on May 7.	(Reminder: Use a separate sheet of paper to complete the table.)						
c. $500 was collected from accounts receivable on October 12.							
d. On June 1, received $2,700 from a tenant for 3 months office rent beginning on June 1.							
e. On December 31, purchased $1,900 of supplies and will pay later.							
f. Provided $750 services to customer on December 31. Customer will pay later.							
g. On August 3, purchased $9,500 of equipment by paying $3,000 cash and signing a 2-month note payable.							
h. On January 5, received $300 bill from the telephone company for *telephone services up to December 31.*							
i. The owner wrote a $2,500 check to himself from the business checking account on November 23.							
j. It is now June 30, the end of the first month after item d above.							
k. On October 3, borrowed $6,500 on a new long-term note and used the money to pay off the note in item g.							

PRACTICE Learning Goal 10, continued

Solutions are in the disk at the back of the book and at: www.worthyjames.com

LG 10-5. Practice classification, valuation, and timing. The table below contains a series of independent events. On a separate piece of paper, identify the classification, valuation, and timing for each event to determine if the event is a transaction and should therefore be recorded. Record revenues and expenses as increases and decreases to owner's equity. For classification of items, you can use ↑ for increase and ↓ for decrease. Identify any events that are not recordable transactions. Use the first item as an example.

Event	Classification	Valuation	Timing
a. On March 11, the owner invested $10,000 cash and $2,000 of supplies in her business.	Cash ↑ Supplies ↑ Owner's Equity ↑	$10,000 $ 2,000 $12,000	March 11
b. On December 31, a business counts the supplies inventory and determines that the amount of supplies have decreased by $900 during the last quarter. Financial statements are quarterly.	**(Reminder: Use a separate sheet of paper to complete the table.)**		
c. On September 4, a business performs $3,000 of services and sends the bill to the customer. No cash is received.			
d. On November 12, a business pays $5,000 cash to buy some computer equipment. The invoice is not received until November 23.			
e. On May 3, a commercial trade school receives a donation of 20 computers. Although the school can use the computers, it would be difficult to sell them because they are obsolete.			
f. On January 23, the local bank calls and offers to loan our business $25,000 no later than 7 days from today.			
g. A computer that had cost $1,500 suddenly stops functioning on June 23. It is not worth repairing.			
h. On October 27, $50,000 of merchandise inventory is destroyed by a fire.			
i. On November 23, a business hires a new employee at a salary of $80,000 per year.			
j. On July 16, the owner of business withdraws $5,000 cash from the business.			
k. On August 9, our business used a consulting service and incurred $2,000 of consulting expense. A bill arrived, but we will pay it later.			

PRACTICE

Learning Goal 10, continued

Solutions are in the disk at the back of the book and at: www.worthyjames.com

LG 10-6. ***Review of owner's capital*** The table below shows the various elements of the capital for a business owned by Mary Jones. Complete the missing item in the table for the month of May in each different situation.

	Mary Jones, Capital, May 1, 2017	Revenue	Investments	Expense	Withdrawals	Mary Jones, Capital, May 31, 2017
#1	$100,000	$23,000	$ -0-	$19,000	$1,000	?
#2	207,000	84,000	20,000	120,000	-0-	?
#3	45,000	26,000	14,000	21,000	5,000	?
#4	125,000	?	3,000	44,000	1,000	$135,000
#5	139,000	55,000	-0-	?	3,000	130,000
#6	?	138,000	5,000	112,000	2,000	495,000

LG 10-7. We used the name "Mr. Clavati" as a memory tool to help remember something very important. What are we making sure that we remember?

INTERNET EXERCISES

Ethics—analyze cases. Go to the Waterloo University Centre for Accounting Ethics (at https://uwaterloo.ca/centre-for-accounting-ethics/) and select two level 1 cases and two level 2 cases that interest you. (Use bookmark/favorites to save the location in an Accounting References folder.)

a. Read each case, then write down the name of the case and apply the ethics discussion and guidelines in this learning goal to analyze the case.
b. Make a decision or take a position. Write a paragraph to explain how you reached your decision or position.
c. Arthur Andersen Company, a large and respected CPA firm worldwide, no longer exists due to ethical issues. Do an online search. What happened to Arthur Andersen Company?

PRACTICE Learning Goal 10, continued

Solutions are in the disk at the back of the book and at: www.worthyjames.com

Your Questions?

It is *very* important to be aware of what you need to understand better. What do you need to understand better about this learning goal? On a separate piece of paper, write the questions that you want to discuss with your classmates, instructor, or supervisor. Try to be very specific about what is bothering you, such as explanations that you do not fully understand.

LEARNING GOAL 11 Begin to Record

Concepts: Begin to Record

Get a Job!

Because you have progressed this far, I have decided that it is time for you to get a job. I want you to meet a friend of mine. His name is Jack "Flash" Davis, a professional guitar player who performs in his own band called "Flash." To supplement his performance income, Jack is opening a small guitar school in June, where he will give guitar lessons at all levels from beginner to master class. He needs accounting help, and I have recommended you to be the accountant for his guitar school.

To help you get started, I suggest that you keep a permanent record of all the increases and decreases for each item in the accounting equation. One possible way to do this is by using a column for each separate asset, liability, and owner's equity item. The increases and decreases are then shown in each column with a "+" or a "–." Using some imaginary transactions, such an approach would look like what you see below.

Assets = Liabilities + Owner's Equity

Transaction	Cash	Accounts Receivable	Supplies	Accounts Payable	Jack Davis, Capital
Owner's investment of cash	(+) $10,000				(+) $10,000
Purchase supplies	(–) 500		(+) 500		
Balance	9,500		500		10,000
Earned revenue "on account"		(+) 750			(+) 750
Balance	9,500	750	500		10,750
Collect receivable	(+) 750	(–) 750			
Balance	10,250	–0–	500		10,750
Withdraw cash	(–) 1,000				(–) 1,000
Balance	9,250		500		9,750
Use up supplies			(–) 100		(–) 100
Balance	9,250		400		9,650

. . . and so on, with each new transaction being added to or subtracted from the applicable columns, such that the equation always remains in balance.

Separate Columns for Increases and Decreases

One Column for Increase and One Column for Decrease

A better way to record the changes in each of the equation items is to have separate increase columns and decrease columns for each item. The advantage of this method is that all the increases and decreases are easier to locate. What's more, this is the method that is used in practice and that you will learn later when studying accounts and debits and credits. Using the same transactions, the recording would look like the illustration below.

	Assets						= Liabilities		+ Owner's Equity	
Transaction	Cash		Accounts Receivable		Supplies		Accounts Payable		Jack Davis, Capital	
	Increase	Decrease	Increase	Decrease	Increase	Decrease	Decrease	Increase	Decrease	Increase
Owner's investment of cash	$10,000									$10,000
Purchase supplies		500			500					
Balance	9,500				500					10,000
Earned revenue "on account"			750							750
Balance	9,500		750		500					10,750
Collect receivable	750			750						
Balance	10,250		–0–		500					10,750
Withdraw cash		1,000							1,000	
Balance	9,250				500					9,750
Use up supplies						100			100	
Balance	9,250				400					9,650

Same Balances as Before

We get exactly the same balances as before, except that now all the increases and decreases are easier to locate. We will use the two-column approach here so that you can get used to it. In this way, the increases and decreases for each item are split out into separate columns.

Use Accounting Customs

The custom in accounting is that "increase" columns for items on the left side of the equation (assets) are always placed to the left of each item name, and that "increase" columns for items on the right side of the equation are always placed to the right of each item name.

How to Analyze the Event

When analyzing each event follow these three steps:

Step1: Are assets affected?

Step2: Are liabilities affected?

Step3: Is owner's equity affected? (which part?)

continued ►

Separate Columns for Increases and Decreases, *continued*

Here are the transactions for June, the first month of business (recorded on both pages):

A. **Owner investment.** Jack deposits $12,000 cash from personal funds into a business checking account. →

Assets: $12,000 =

Cash

Increase	Decrease
$12,000	

B. **Equipment purchased for cash.** The business purchases some sound amplifiers and digital electronic equipment for $5,500 cash. (Notice that total assets don't change.) →

Assets: $12,000 =

Cash

	Increase	Decrease
A	$12,000	
B		$5,500
Balance	$6,500	

Equipment

Increase	Decrease
$5,500	
$5,500	

C. **Purchase supplies on credit.** The business purchases $200 of office supplies "on account." Notice that total assets increase by $200, but so do creditors' claims (Accounts Payable). →

Assets: $12,200 =

Cash

	Increase	Decrease
A	$12,000	
B		$5,500
C		
Balance	$6,500	

Supplies

Increase	Decrease
$200	
$200	

Equipment

Increase	Decrease
$5,500	
$5,500	

Notice that the custom is to always place balances on the "increase" side for each item because an increase means a positive number. Because the natural balance of any item is always a positive number, it makes sense to put a balance on the increase—the positive—side. For example, after two transactions, Cash has a balance of $6,500. Of course, this $6,500 balance is a positive number, so we place it on the positive side.

Separate Columns for Increases and Decreases, *continued*

Step 1. Assets: Cash increases Step 2. Liabilities: No change Step 3. Owner's equity: Capital increases

Liabilities + Owner's Equity: $12,000

Owner's Equity

Jack Davis, Capital		Operational Change in Owner's Equity	
Decrease	Increase	Expense	Revenue
	$12,000		

Step 1. Assets: Cash decreases, equipment increases Step 2. Liabilities: No change Step 3. Owner's equity: No Change

Liabilities + Owner's Equity: $12,000

Owner's Equity

Jack Davis, Capital		Operational Change in Owner's Equity	
Decrease	Increase	Expense	Revenue
A	$12,000		
B			
Balance	$12,000		

Step 1. Assets: Supplies increase Step 2. Liabilities: Accounts payable increases Step 3. Owner's equity: No Change

Liabilities + Owner's Equity: $12,200

Accounts Payable

Decrease	Increase
A	
B	
C	$200
Balance	$200

Owner's Equity

Jack Davis, Capital		Operational Change in Owner's Equity	
Decrease	Increase	Expense	Revenue
	$12,000		
	$12,000		

Be sure that you are following the analysis: step 1, step 2, step3, above.

continued ►

Separate Columns for Increases and Decreases, *continued*

D. **Revenue earned.** Jack teaches a beginners' class and receives $350 in cash from his students. (Notice that the revenue is an operational increase in owner's equity.)

Assets: $12,550 =

	Cash		Supplies		Equipment	
	Increase	Decrease	Increase	Decrease	Increase	Decrease
A	$12,000					
B		$5,500			$5,500	
C			$200			
D	**$350**					
Balance	$6,850		$200		$5,500	

E. **Revenue earned.** Jack teaches a blues weekend master class at the university and receives $2,000 on account, plus $500 in cash. (Notice that three items are affected with this transaction.)

Assets: $15,050 =

	Cash		Accounts Receivable		Supplies		Equipment	
	Increase	Decrease	Increase	Decrease	Increase	Decrease	Increase	Decrease
A	$12,000							
B		$5,500					$5,500	
C					$200			
D	$350							
E	**$500**		**$2,000**					
Balance	$7,350		$2,000		$200		$5,500	

You are in Jack's office and the door suddenly opens. Jack walks in with an angry look on his face. "Can you explain this to me?" he asks, his face red and upset. "I have only been in this business a few weeks and already I have lost almost $5,000!" You ask him how he found that out. "I invested $12,000 of my hard-earned money, and now the bank statement shows that I only have $7,350 left. That's how I know! That's almost a $5,000 loss in just a few weeks! You're the accountant. How did I have this loss and what happened to my money?" What do you think you should say to Jack?

Separate Columns for Increases and Decreases, *continued*

Step 1. Assets: Cash increases Step 2. Liabilities: No effect Step 3. Owner's equity: Increases from revenue

Liabilities + Owner's Equity: $12,550

Accounts Payable

	Decrease	Increase
A		
B		
C		$200
D		
		$200

Owner's Equity

Jack Davis, Capital		Operational Change in Owner's Equity	
Decrease	Increase	Expense	Revenue
	$12,000		
			$350
	$12,000		**$350**

Step 1. Assets: Cash increases and accounts receivable increases
Step 2. Liabilities: No change
Step 3. Owner's equity: Increases from revenue

Liabilities + Owner's Equity: $15,050

Accounts Payable

	Decrease	Increase
A		
B		
C		$200
D		
E		
		$200

Owner's Equity

Jack Davis, Capital		Operational Change in Owner's Equity	
Decrease	Increase	Expense	Revenue
	$12,000		
			$350
			$2,500
	$12,000		**$2,850**

TIP

What is the total owners equity? It is $12,000 + $2,850 = $14,850.

continued ▶

Separate Columns for Increases and Decreases, *continued*

First, you're silent for a moment, reflecting on Jack's questions. Then you open the lower desk drawer and pull out the manila folder that contains the accounting papers you have been using to record the changes in Jack's business. You see that Jack is right about the cash; your records do show a balance of $7,350.

The first thing that you say is, "OK, I've got all the data right here for you. Let's look at the cash." You show Jack that there have been four cash transactions: (Item A) a $12,000 increase from his investment; (Item B) a $5,500 decrease spent on equipment; (Item D) a $350 increase from the revenue for the beginner's class that he taught; and (Item E) a $500 increase from the master blues class revenue.

Jack says, "Well, OK, at least I can see what has happened to the cash, but how could I have had a loss so quickly?"

"Jack," you say, "I have some good news for you. You do not have a loss. You actually have net income—you know, a profit."

"How's that?"

You say, "How much did you invest?"

He answers, "$12,000."

"Jack, look at these records. They show that you have $15,050 in assets: $7,350 in cash, $2,000 in an accounts receivable, $200 in supplies, and $5,500 in equipment. If you subtract the $200 you owe on the account payable, that leaves you with $14,850 in owner's equity—you know, assets that you could claim. That's $2,850 more than you invested!"

Jack is quiet for a little while and then you hear him say, "Ah . . . aaaaah, I think I see! When I have a profit or loss, that doesn't necessarily mean that it will all be just in cash. I have to count everything!"

You smile politely.

Check Your Understanding

Write the completed sentences on a separate piece of paper. The answers are below.

For any item that normally appears on the left side of the equation, the custom in accounting is to place the "increase" column to the (left/right) · · · · · · · · of the name of that item. For any item that normally appears on the right side of the equation, the custom is to place the "increase" column to the (left/right) · · · · · · · · of the name of that item. A decrease column is then simply opposite from the · · · · · · · · column.

Because balances are positive amounts, balances are shown in the · · · · · · · · column of each item.

Answers

For any item that normally appears on the left side of the equation, the custom in accounting is to place the "increase" column to the left of the name of that item. For any item that normally appears on the right side of the equation, the custom is to place the "increase" column to the right of the name of that item. A decrease column is then simply opposite from the increase column.

Because balances are positive amounts, balances are shown in the increase column of each item.

continued ▶

"When I count my wealth, it isn't always just in cash. I have to count everything."

Separate Columns for Increases and Decreases, *continued*

F. **Expenses incurred on credit.** The school receives a utility bill for $100 and a telephone bill for $70 that are not paid immediately.

Assets: $15,050 =

	Cash		Accounts Receivable		Supplies		Equipment	
	Increase	Decrease	Increase	Decrease	Increase	Decrease	Increase	Decrease
A	$12,000							
B		$5,500					$5,500	
C					$200			
D	$350							
E	$500		$2,000					
F								
Balance	$7,350		$2,000		$200		$5,500	

G. **Payment of a liability.** The school pays the $200 account payable owing on the supplies. (Notice that paying a liability affects the creditors' claim but not the owner's.)

Assets: $14,850 =

	Cash		Accounts Receivable		Supplies		Equipment	
	Increase	Decrease	Increase	Decrease	Increase	Decrease	Increase	Decrease
A	$12,000							
B		$5,500					$5,500	
C					$200			
D	$350							
E	$500		$2,000					
F								
G		$200						
Balance	$7,150		$2,000		$200		$5,500	

Separate Columns for Increases and Decreases, *continued*

Step 1. Assets: No change

Step 2. Liabilities: Accounts payable increases

Step 3. Owner's equity: Decreases from expense

Liabilities + Owner's Equity: $15,050

	Accounts Payable		Owner's Equity			
			Jack Davis, Capital		Operational Change in Owner's Equity	
	Decrease	Increase	Decrease	Increase	Expense	Revenue
A				$12,000		
B						
C		$200				
D						$350
E						$2,500
F		**$170**			**$170**	
		$370		**$12,000**	**$170**	**$2,850**

Step 1. Assets: Cash decreases

Step 2. Liabilities: Accounts payable decreases

Step 3. Owner's equity: No change

Liabilities + Owner's Equity: $14,850

	Accounts Payable		Owner's Equity			
			Jack Davis, Capital		Operational Change in Owner's Equity	
	Decrease	Increase	Decrease	Increase	Expense	Revenue
A				$12,000		
B						
C		$200				
D						$350
E						$2,500
F		$170			$170	
G	**$200**					
		$170		**$12,000**	**$170**	**$2,850**

continued ▶

Separate Columns for Increases and Decreases, *continued*

H. **Incur expense from consuming an asset.** You check the supplies cabinet to find that only $50 of supplies remain ($150 has been used).

Assets: $14,700 =

	Cash		Accounts Receivable		Supplies		Equipment	
	Increase	Decrease	Increase	Decrease	Increase	Decrease	Increase	Decrease
A	$12,000							
B		$5,500					$5,500	
C					$200			
D	$350							
E	$500		$2,000					
F								
G		$200						
H						$150		
Balance	$7,150		$2,000		$50		$5,500	

I. **Incur expense from consuming service.** The school pays $800 for rent expense for the month.

Assets: $13,900 =

	Cash		Accounts Receivable		Supplies		Equipment	
	Increase	Decrease	Increase	Decrease	Increase	Decrease	Increase	Decrease
A	$12,000							
B		$5,500					$5,500	
C					$200			
D	$350							
E	$500		$2,000					
F								
G		$200						
H						$150		
I		$800						
Balance	$6,350		$2,000		$50		$5,500	

Separate Columns for Increases and Decreases, *continued*

One day, you meet Jack walking into your office. He is in a great mood because Flash has just signed for a three-week gig to play in a big Los Angeles club. Jack happily pulls a $15,000 check from his pocket and asks you to deposit it for him in the business checking account. What's your comment? (See next page for answer)

Liabilities + Owner's Equity: $14,700

	Accounts Payable		Owner's Equity			
			Jack Davis, Capital		Operational Change in Owner's Equity	
	Decrease	Increase	Decrease	Increase	Expense	Revenue
A				$12,000		
B						
C		$200				
D						$350
E						$2,500
F		$170			$170	
G	$200					
H					**$150**	
		$170		**$12,000**	**$320**	**$2,850**

Step 1. Assets: Cash decreases Step 2. Liabilities: No change Step 3. Owner's equity: Decrease from expense

Liabilities + Owner's Equity: $13,900

	Accounts Payable		Owner's Equity			
			Jack Davis, Capital		Operational Change in Owner's Equity	
	Decrease	Increase	Decrease	Increase	Expense	Revenue
A				$12,000		
B						
C		$200				
D						$350
E						$2,500
F		$170			$170	
G	$200					
H					$150	
I					**$800**	
		$170		**$12,000**	**$1,120**	**$2,850**

continued ►

Separate Columns for Increases and Decreases, *continued*

You say, "Well, look—it's probably a lot better if you just hold the check until you can deposit it in your own personal account." Jack looks at you in a funny way, but says nothing, so you continue. "You see, Flash is a separate business—it's your band—and is not part of the guitar school. There is something in accounting called the 'entity assumption'... well, never mind, Jack. Just remember not to mix up the income between the guitar school and the band, OK?"

J. **Collecting accounts receivable.** The school collects $750 of the open account receivable from the university. (Total assets don't change; neither do liabilities or owner's equity.)

Assets: $13,900 =

	Cash		Accounts Receivable		Supplies		Equipment	
	Increase	Decrease	Increase	Decrease	Increase	Decrease	Increase	Decrease
A	$12,000							
B		$5,500					$5,500	
C					$200			
D	$350							
E	$500		$2,000					
F								
G		$200						
H						$150		
I		$800						
J	**$750**			**$750**				
Balance	$7,100		$1,250		$50		$5,500	

Collection of an account receivable (transaction J) does not create revenue! It is just a shift from one asset (accounts receivable) to another (cash). The revenue was created previously (transaction E) when the sale was made.

Separate Columns for Increases and Decreases, *continued*

Step 1. Assets: Cash increases and accounts receivable decreases

Step 2. Liabilities: No change

Step 3. Owner's equity: No change

Liabilities + Owner's Equity: $13,900

	Accounts Payable		Owner's Equity			
			Jack Davis, Capital		Operational Change in Owner's Equity	
	Decrease	Increase	Decrease	Increase	Expense	Revenue
A				$12,000		
B						
C		$200				
D						$350
E						$2,500
F		$170			$170	
G	$200					
H					$150	
I					$800	
J						
		$170		**$12,000**	**$1,120**	**$2,850**

Have you noticed how the accounting equation always balances after every transaction? At this point, total assets are $13,900 and total liabilities plus owner's equity is also $13,900.

What is the total owner's equity? It is $12,000 (initial balance) – $1,120 (expenses) + $2,850 (revenues) = $13,730

continued ►

Separate Columns for Increases and Decreases, *continued*

K. **Jack withdraws $1,000 cash** out of the business for his own personal use. He calls it a "salary." (Notice that if Jack "pays" himself a "salary," it's still really just a withdrawal—a capital reduction—not an expense of the business, no matter what he wants to call it.)

Assets: $12,900 =

	Cash		Accounts Receivable		Supplies		Equipment	
	Increase	Decrease	Increase	Decrease	Increase	Decrease	Increase	Decrease
A	$12,000							
B		$5,500					$5,500	
C					$200			
D	$350							
E	$500		$2,000					
F								
G		$200						
H						$150		
I		$800						
J	$750			$750				
K		$1,000						
Balance	$6,100		$1,250		$50		$5,500	

When an owner withdraws cash (or other assets) from a business, this is a recordable business event. However, when the owner uses the cash for personal purposes, this is not a business event and is not recorded on the business books. The owner and the business are separate economic entities.

Separate Columns for Increases and Decreases, *continued*

Step 1. Assets: Cash decreases.
Step 2. Liabilities: No change
Step 3. Owner's equity: Decreases from owner withdrawal.

Liabilities + Owner's Equity: $12,900

	Accounts Payable		Owner's Equity: Jack Davis, Capital		Owner's Equity: Withdrawal	Owner's Equity: Operational Change in Owner's Equity	
	Decrease	Increase	Decrease	Increase	Decrease	Expense	Revenue
A				$12,000			
B							
C		$200					
D							$350
E							$2,500
F		$170				$170	
G	$200						
H						$150	
I						$800	
J							
K					**$1,000**		
		$170		**$12,000**	**$1,000**	**$1,120**	**$2,850**

continued ►

Separate Columns for Increases and Decreases, *continued*

L. **Unearned revenue.** A student's parent pays an advance to the school in the amount of $250 cash for six weeks of lessons. (Receiving a customer advance payment creates a liability called "unearned revenue." No service has been provided yet, so there is an obligation to return the money until the revenue is actually earned.)

Assets: $13,150 =

	Cash		Accounts Receivable		Supplies		Equipment	
	Increase	Decrease	Increase	Decrease	Increase	Decrease	Increase	Decrease
A	$12,000							
B		$5,500					$5,500	
C					$200			
D	$350							
E	$500		$2,000					
F								
G		$200						
H						$150		
I		$800						
J	$750			$750				
K		$1,000						
L	$250							
Balance	$6,350		$1,250		$50		$5,500	

Separate Columns for Increases and Decreases, *continued*

Step 1. Assets: Cash increases

Step 2. Liabilities: Unearned revenue increases

Step 3. Owner's equity: No change

Liabilities + Owner's Equity: $13,150

	Accounts Payable		Unearned Revenue		Owner's equity: Jack Davis, Capital		Owner's equity: Withdrawal	Owner's equity: Operational Change in Owner's Equity	
	Decrease	Increase	Decrease	Increase	Decrease	Increase	Decrease	Expense	Revenue
A						$12,000			
B									
C		$200							
D									$350
E									$2,500
F		$170						$170	
G	$200								
H								$150	
I								$800	
J									
K							$1,000		
L				**$250**					
		$170		**$250**		**$12,000**	**$1,000**	**$1,120**	**$2,850**

If you feel that you want an additional review of the three steps for event analysis, Learning Goal 6 provides more detailed practice.

continued ▶

Separate Columns for Increases and Decreases, *continued*

M. **Unearned revenue is earned.** Jack gives a $50 lesson to the student whose parents previously advanced the $250 for lessons. (Notice that when the revenue is earned, the liability is reduced. By performing $50 worth of services, Jack removed $50 of the liability and increased his own claim on the assets by $50.)

Assets: $13,150 =

	Cash		Accounts Receivable		Supplies		Equipment	
	Increase	Decrease	Increase	Decrease	Increase	Decrease	Increase	Decrease
A	$12,000							
B		$5,500					$5,500	
C					$200			
D	$350							
E	$500		$2,000					
F								
G		$200						
H						$150		
I		$800						
J	$750			$750				
K		$1,000						
L	$250							
M								
Balance	$6,350		$1,250		$50		$5,500	

Separate Columns for Increases and Decreases, *continued*

Summary

What the Processing Has Accomplished So Far

- You have recorded all transactions in an organized way.
- You now have a permanent record of:
  - the individual transactions.
  - the current balance of each item in the accounting equation.

By separately identifying the operational changes, we can now see that the business operations increased the owner's equity, and therefore the owner's wealth, by $2,900 – $1,120 = $1,780. This means that the business was profitable—it has a "net income" of $1,780. Total owner's equity is $12,000 (initial balance) – $1,000 (withdrawal) + $1,780 (net income) = $12,780. The business might also call this combined total "Jack Davis, Capital", $12,780, as of the **end of the period.**

Liabilities + Owner's Equity: $13,150

	Accounts Payable		Unearned Revenue		Owner's equity: Jack Davis, Capital		Withdrawal	Operational Change in Owner's Equity	
	Decrease	Increase	Decrease	Increase	Decrease	Increase	Decrease	Expense	Revenue
A						$12,000			
B									
C		$200							
D									$350
E									$2,500
F		$170						$170	
G	$200								
H								$150	
I								$800	
J									
K							$1,000		
L				$250					
M			$50						$50
		$170		$200		$12,000	$1,000	$1,120	$2,900

"An Ethical Issue"

The day after you meet Jack in the parking lot with his $15,000 check, he walks into your office and says, "You know, now that things are going well, I have a loan application here that I'm working on to see if we can get some additional funds to expand our teaching facilities. The bank wants to see the financial statements of the business, and I need to show the best situation possible on the loan application. I want to make sure that we get that loan. I have an idea that I want you to use on the financial statements.

"When we get paid for lessons in advance, you have been showing the money we receive as a liability called 'unearned revenue.' This does not show up as revenue until later, when the lesson is given. I don't like this! After all, sooner or later we are going to give the lessons and earn the revenue anyway.

"I want you to show these receipts as revenue as soon as we get the money. I do not want you to show it as a liability. We will have a big advance coming in soon and this is a really good way to show a big increase in our profits right away."

He looks you straight in the eye and says, "You know, this bank loan is going to be very important to both of us ... to both of our jobs ... do you understand what I mean?"

How do you respond to Jack? Is his proposal ethical?

Jack is assuming that accounting rules can be changed to satisfy his own purposes and that he can force you to do what he wants. He is asking you to change an accounting method that you know is correct to one that is incorrect—for the sole purpose of misleading the bank by making the business look more profitable.

Only one safe and ethical course of action is open to you. First, you need to explain to Jack that you are obligated to follow a set of accounting principles. One of those principles requires that revenue can only be shown after it is fully earned and not before. The purpose of this is to provide reliable financial statements that do not make the business seem more profitable than it really is. You should also tell Jack that he will be much better off in the long run if the banker learns that the business financial statements are always accurate and that Jack is an ethical and trusted customer of the bank.

Right now, Jack is not acting in an ethical way either to the bank or to you. By insisting that you do as he wishes, Jack puts you in a no-win situation because he is implying that if you don't cooperate, he will fire you. On the other hand, if you do cooperate, you put your own reputation and career at risk.

If Jack completely refuses to listen to you, you have no alternative but to respectfully and politely quit. As an accountant, your ethical conduct must set a standard for others. The financial statements you prepare must be reliable because so many people depend upon them. However difficult leaving may seem at the time, it is far better than developing a relationship in which Jack knows that he can always manipulate you. In a situation like this, your career and life will inevitably suffer as his demands become greater and greater every month.

This situation should be viewed as one of the occasional causes of job turnover in a field in which ethical requirements are unusually high.

PRACTICE Learning Goal 11

Solutions are in the disk at the back of the book and at: www.worthyjames.com

Learning Goal 11 is about beginning to record transactions. Use these questions and problems to practice what you have learned.

Reinforcement Problems

LG 11-1. In this learning goal, we analyzed transactions in three steps by asking three questions. Step 1: are assets affected? Step 2: are liabilities affected? Step 3: is owner's equity affected? For each transaction, complete the table below by entering a "Yes" or "No". If you enter a "Yes", include the name of the item affected and an up ↑ or down ↓ to show the effect. Remember that the accounting equation always must balance. Use the first transaction as an example.

	A =	L +	OE
	Step 1: assets affected?	**Step 2:** liabilities affected?	**Step 3:** owner's equity affected?
a. James Garcia invested $10,000 cash in his business.	Yes. Cash ↑	No	Yes. OE ↑ (Capital ↑)
b. The business purchased $300 of supplies on account.			
c. Performed services and received cash of $500.			
d. Paid office salaries $2,500.			
e. Performed services on account, $700.			
f. The business received bills that were not immediately paid: utilities, $200; advertising $900; accounting services, $500.			
g. Paid accounts payable, $750.			
h. Received an advance payment from a customer, $1,000.			
i. Collected accounts receivable, $900.			
j. Purchased supplies for cash $200.			
k. The owner withdrew $1,000 for personal use.			
l. The business purchased $10,000 of equipment by paying $6,000 cash and signing a note payable for the balance of $4,000.			

PRACTICE Learning Goal 11, continued

Solutions are in the disk at the back of the book and at: www.worthyjames.com

LG 11-2. Record transactions. Anne Wilson began operating a home decorating consulting business on May 1.

a. On a separate piece of paper, using the column recording format from Learning Goal 11, record the business transactions listed below, and show the correct final balances. Identify revenues,expenses, and withdrawals next to the column for owner's equity.(You can also make copies of the transaction recording paper template in the disk at the back of the book.)
b. Determine the amount of net income or net loss for the period.

a. Anne opened a business bank account and deposited $25,000 from her personal savings.
b. Purchased supplies on account for $950.
c. Paid part of the account payable in the amount of $500.
d. Received an advance payment from a client, $1,000.
e. Performed consulting services for a corporate client, and billed the client $3,000.
f. Paid $1,800 for the monthly rent.
g. Received bills for the following expenses, which were not immediately paid: utilities expense, $225; advertising, $1400; computer services $1,100.
h. Performed all of the services for the client in 'd', above.
i. Paid office salary, $2,500
j. Received a payment of $1,500 from the client in 'e', above.
k. Anne Wilson withdrew $1,000 for personal use.

LG 11-3. Record transactions. Timothy Hsu began operating a tennis racket repair business on October 1.

a. On a separate piece of paper, using the column recording format from Learning Goal 11, record business transactions listed below, and show the correct final balances. Identify revenues, expenses, and withdrawals next to the column for owner's equity.(You can also make copies of the transaction recording paper template in the disk at the back of the book.)
b. Calculate the amount of net income or net loss for the period.

a. Tim opened a business bank account and deposited $12,000 from his personal savings.
b. Purchased supplies on account for $750.
c. Paid part of the account payable in the amount of $300.
d. Purchased $5,000 of equipment by paying $3,000 cash and signing a note payable for the $2,000 balance.
e. Performed repair services for a customer, and billed the customer $350.
f. Performed repair services for a customer and received $250 cash.
g. Received bills for the following expenses, which were not immediately paid: utilities expense, $370; advertising, $500; accounting services $420.
h. Paid current month's rent, $700.
i. The customer in 'e' above paid $300 on the amount owed.
j. Made repairs for a tennis club and billed the club $2,300.
k. The owner, Timothy Hsu, withdrew $$800 for personal use.
l. Timothy counted the remaining supplies and determined that $300 of supplies remained; therefore, $450 of supplies had been used.

PRACTICE Learning Goal 11, continued

Solutions are in the disk at the back of the book and at: www.worthyjames.com

LG 11-4. Record transactions. You are the accountant for Sugar Éclair's Gym and Aerobics Club. On a separate piece of paper, using the column recording format from Learning Goal 11, record the following September transactions, and total the columns. Identify revenues andexpenses in columns next to the column for owner's equity; however, the owner prefers that you record withdrawals as direct reductions to the capital account. Beginning balances as of September 1 are given below. (You can also make copies of the transaction recording paper template in the disk at the back of the book.)

Beginning balances:

Cash	$10,300	Gym Equipment	$25,000
Accounts Receivable	$ 4,100	Accounts Payable	$ 200
Gym Supplies	$ 620	Sugar Éclair, Capital	$39,820

September transactions

a.	$100 of supplies are purchased for cash
b.	The club collects $2,000 cash from accounts receivable
c.	The club prepays a nine-month fire insurance policy for $1,500.
d.	Member dues of $5,300 cash for the current month are collected.
e.	The club sends out bills of $2,900 to other members for the current month.
f.	The club receives and immediately pays the utilities bill $550.
g.	The club receives but does not pay the telephone bill of $185.
h.	$200 of the accounts payable are paid.
i.	The club borrows $50,000 from the 5th National Bank and signs a 15-year note.
j.	Cash of $590 is received a businessthat prepays a conference room rental fee.
k.	The owner, Sugar Éclair, withdraws $2,000 for personal living expenses.
l.	The club purchased $500 of supplies and $1,000 of equipment on credit.
m.	Air conditioning repairs of $900 are required. The bill will be paid later.
n.	Sugar spends the $2,000 she withdrew for new furniture for her home.

What are the total revenues for September? ____________________
What are the total expenses for September? ____________________
What is the net income or net loss for September? ________________

PRACTICE **Learning Goal 11, continued**

Solutions are in the disk at the back of the book and at: www.worthyjames.com

LG 11-5. You be the teacher—identify some common exam mistakes. The transactions below were all recorded incorrectly by students taking mid-term examinations. The accounting equation at the right of each transaction item shows how the transactions were recorded in the accounting equation.

a. For each item, use the three steps presented in this learning goal to analyze the transaction.
b. Explain why the recording shown is incorrect.
c. Correctly record the transaction in the accounting equation (so you can show it to the student).

Item	Incorrect Recording in Equation
a. $8,000 of equipment is purchased by paying $2,000 cash and promising to pay the balance in 90 days.	↓A = ↑L + OE 2,000 6,000
b. A business collected $900 owing from a customer for a sale made on account three months ago.	↑A = L + ↑OE 900 900 (revenue)
c. A business paid $2,000 to purchase some office supplies.	↓A = L + ↓OE 2,000 2,000 (expense)
d. This month, a business pays a $750 account payable that was recorded last month.	↓A = L + ↓OE 750 750 (expense)
e. A $200 bill is received from the telephone company but will not be paid until later.	Not recorded
f. A customer makes an advance payment of $500 for services that will be provided sometime later.	↑A = L + ↑OE 500 500 (revenue)

LG 11-6. Record transactions.

a. On a separate piece of paper, using the column recording format from Learning Goal 11, record the following transactions for Computer Training Services Company, and total the columns. However, the book keeper for this company asks you to record all the changes for owner's equity directly in the owner's capital decrease and increase columns rather than in separate columns. She wants to see the final balance of owner's equity as one number in Edgar Mendoza, capital. (You can make copies of the transaction recording paper template from the disk at the back of the book.)

b. Calculate the net income or loss of the business.

(1) Edgar Mendoza invested $15,000 cash to begin his new business, Computer Training Services.
(2) The business paid $1,200 to purchase office equipment.
(3) The business used $210 cash to purchase some supplies.
(4) The business received an advance payment of $3,300 from a corporate customer.
(5) The business paid $1,100 rent expense for the office.
(6) The business provided $800 of training services to a client who paid in cash.
(7) The business received a $750 bill for legal services that was not immediately paid. (Legal service is the resource consumed.)
(8) The business purchased an additional $250 of supplies on account.
(9) The business used $120 of supplies. (Supplies are the resources consumed.)
(10) The business provided $1,500 of training service on account.
(11) Edgar Mendoza withdrew $900 from the business for his personal use.
(12) The business paid the legal bill (7) in full.
(13) The business received a $550 advertising bill that was not immediately paid. (Advertising service is the resource consumed.)
(14) The business provided $1,650 of training service. The client paid $1,000 cash and will pay the balance later.
(15) The client in transaction (10) above paid the account balance in full.

PRACTICE **Learning Goal 11, continued**

Solutions are in the disk at the back of the book and at: www.worthyjames.com

(16) The business provided $2,000 of services to client in (4) above who made the advance payment.
(17) The business collected $250 from a customer on account.
(18) The business paid the advertising bill (13) in full.

LG 11-7. On a separate sheet of paper, use the information for items a through p, below, to record which specific items increase or decrease as a result of each event. Write in the name of the item affected in the "increase" or "decrease" columns below. Use the first item as an example.

	Assets		= Liabilities		+ Owner's Equity	
	Increase	Decrease	Decrease	Increase	Decrease	Increase
a. A business collects $1,000 of accounts receivable from a customer.	Cash	Accts. Rec.				
b. A business pays a bill to a vendor.	(Reminder: Use a separate sheet of paper to complete the table.)					
c. A business purchases supplies on account.						
d. A business makes a sale on account.						
e. A business uses up some supplies.						
f. A business buys a $5,000 computer, pays $1,000 cash, and signs a note.						
g. A business receives an advance payment from a customer.						
h. The owner removes some cash and supplies from her business.						
i. A business prepays rent for three months in the amount of $1,500.						
j. The owner buys a new car for herself.						
k. A business pays the wages to its employees.						
l. One month has passed since the rent was prepaid in item i, above.						
m. A business receives a bill from the telephone company.						
n. The business performs services for the customer who prepaid in item g, above.						
o. A business that incurred a liability pays the liability.						
p. A customer pays a business for an amount owed.						

PRACTICE Learning Goal 11, continued

Solutions are in the disk at the back of the book and at: www.worthyjames.com

Instructor-Assigned Problems

If you are using this book in a class, these review problems may be assigned by your instructor for homework, group assignments, class work, or other activities. Only your instructor has the solutions.

IA11-1. Record transactions. Susan Monahan opened a civil engineering consulting business in her home office on June 1.

a. On a separate piece of paper, using the column recording format from Learning Goal 11, record the business transactions listed below, and show the correct final balances. Identify revenues,expenses, and withdrawals next to the column for owner's equity.(You can also make copies of the transaction recording paper template in the disk at the back of the book.)
b. Calculate the amount of net income or net loss for the period.

a. Susan opened a business bank account and deposited $20,000 from her personal savings.
b. Prepaid $600 for a one-year business insurance policy.
c. Performed consulting services for a corporate client, and billed the client $5,000.
d. Purchased supplies on account for$800.
e. Paid part of the account payable in the amount of $300.
f. Received an advance payment from a client, $1,500.
g. Paid office salary, $3,900
h. Performed $1,000 of the services for the client in 'f', above.
i. Received bills for the following expenses, which were not immediately paid: utilities expense, $340; computer services $400; Internet services $900.
j. Received a payment of $3,500 from the client in 'c', above.
k. Susan Monahan withdrew $1,200 for personal use.
l. A count of supplies at month-end indicates a balance of $200; therefore, $600 has been used.

IA11-2. Record transactions. James Tanaka started Internet Design Services on February 1.

a. On a separate piece of paper, using the column recording format from Learning Goal 11, record the business transactions listed below, and show the correct final balances. Identify revenues,expenses, and withdrawals next to the column for owner's equity.(You can also make copies of the transaction recording paper template in the disk at the back of the book.)
b. Calculate the amount of net income or net loss for the period.

a. James opened a business bank account and deposited $10,000 from his personal savings.
b. Paid rent for the current month in the amount of $1,500.
c. Purchased supplies on account for $500.
d. Purchased computer equipment for $12,000 by paying $5,000 cash and signing a note payable for the remainder of $7,000.
e. Performed $700 of the services for a client who immediately paid with a check.
f. Performed Website Design services for a corporate client, and billed the client $5,000.
g. Received bills for the following expensesthat were not immediately paid: utilities expense, $340; advertising expense, $1,100; painting services $650.
h. Paid accounts payable in the amount of $1,290.
i. Received a payment of $3,000 from the client in 'f', above.
j. James Tanaka withdrew $1,200 for personal use.
k. James used the $1,200 to purchase a computer for his own use.
l. A count of supplies at month-end indicates a balance of $350; therefore, $150 has been used.

PRACTICE Learning Goal 11, continued

Solutions are in the disk at the back of the book and at: www.worthyjames.com

IA11-3.

a. Using the column recording format from Learning Goal 11, record the following transactions and total the columns. Identify revenues and expenses and withdrawals next to the column for capital. (Transection recording paper for this format is available from the disk at the back of this book.)
b. Calculate the net income or loss of the business.

(1) David Aldrich invested $15,000 cash to begin his new business, Aldrich Internet Consulting.
(2) The business used $300 cash to purchase some supplies.
(3) The business paid $3,000 to purchase office equipment.
(4) The business purchased an additional $400 of supplies on account.
(5) The business received an advance payment of $2,700 from a client for future services.
(6) The business used $150 of supplies.
(7) The business provided $1,200 of consulting services to a client who immediately paid in cash.
(8) The business paid $1,900 rent expense for the office.
(9) The business provided $2,500 of consulting service on account.
(10) David Aldrich withdrew $1,000 from the business for his personal use.
(11) The business received a $650 telephone bill that was not immediately paid.
(12) The business provided $900 of consulting service. The client paid $700 cash and will pay the balance later.
(13) The client in transaction (9) above paid the account balance in full.
(14) The business provided $850 of services to client in (5) above who made the advance payment.
(15) The business used $100 of supplies.
(16) The business received a $750 bill for legal services that was not immediately paid.
(17) The business paid the telephone bill (11) in full.

IA11-4.

a. Using the column recording format from Learning Goal 11, record the following transactions and total the columns. However, the book keeper asks you to record all owner's equity changes directly in the owner's capital decrease and increase columns. (Transection recording paper for this format is available from the disk at the back of this book.)
b. Calculate the net income or loss of the business.

(1) Jennifer Chang invested $42,000 cash to begin her new business, Chang Book Design Services.
(2) The business paid $3,000 to purchase $2,500 of computer equipment and $500 of supplies.
(3) The business purchased an additional $340 of supplies on account.
(4) The business received an advance payment of $4,000 from a client for future design services.
(5) The business used $270 of supplies.
(6) The business provided $1,900 of consulting service on account.
(7) The business provided $3,100 of consulting services to a client who immediately paid in cash.
(8) The business paid $2,400 rent expense for the office.
(9) Jennifer Chang withdrew $2,500 from the business for her personal use.
(10) The business received a $1,590 advertising bill that was not immediately paid.
(11) The business provided $2,100 of design services. The client paid $400 cash and will pay the balance later.
(12) The business received a call from a publisher confirming the intention to contract for $3,500 of design services.
(13) The client in transaction (6) above paid the account balance in full.
(14) The business provided $2,700 of services to client in (4) above who made the advance payment.
(15) The business received a $600 bill for accounting services, which was not immediately paid.
(16) The business received a $980 bill for Internet advertising services that was not immediately paid.
(17) The business paid the advertising bill (10) in full.

PRACTICE

Learning Goal 11, continued

Solutions are in the disk at the back of the book and at: www.worthyjames.com

INTERNET EXERCISES

Ethics—analyze cases. Go to the Santa Clara University Markkula Center for Applied Ethics (at https://www.scu.edu/markkula). Select Ethics Resources and three cases that interest you. (Use bookmark/favorites to save the location in an Accounting References folder.)

a. Read each case, then write down the name of the case and apply the ethics discussion and guidelines in Learning Goal 10 to analyze the case.
b. Make a decision or take a position. Write a paragraph to explain how you reached your decision or position.

Your Questions?

It is *very* important to be aware of what you need to understand better. What do you need to understand better about this learning goal? On a separate piece of paper, write the questions that you want to discuss with your classmates, instructor, or supervisor. Try to be very specific about what is bothering you, such as explanations that you do not fully understand.

SECTION IV

The Essential Financial Statements

OVERVIEW

What this section does	This section explains the four essential financial statements, and shows you how they are prepared. The section also explains the conceptual framework of accounting.
Use this section if. . .	. . . you want to understand the purpose of the balance sheet, income statement, statement of owner's equity, and statement of cash flows. . . . you want to learn how to prepare all of these statements, except for the statement of cash flows, and you want to learn how they are all connected.
Do not use this section if. . .	. . . you already understand the meaning of the financial statements and how to prepare them, or . . . you have studied Section III, and now you want to study debits and credits (see Section V starting on page 384).

LEARNING GOALS

LEARNING GOAL 12

Describe the Financial Statements

Review and Preview

Review

In the prior learning goal, you practiced Stages 1 and 2 of the accounting process: you analyzed events and, if the events qualified as transactions, you recorded them.

In This Learning Goal . . .

This learning goal introduces you to Stage 3 in the accounting process: communicating what has happened to a business. Communication in accounting is done by summarizing the recorded events into financial statements.

In Learning Goal 12, you will find:

Financial Statements and What They Do

Financial Statements Are Summaries

What Are Financial Statements?

Financial statements are well-organized summaries of all the transactions that have already been recorded.

What Financial Statements Do

Because financial statements are well-organized summaries, they can *communicate* important financial information about a business to the people and organizations (the stakeholders) who make decisions concerning the business. This clarified overview would be impossible by only looking at individual transactions one at a time.

The Types of Financial Statements

Four General-Purpose Financial Statements

Four general-purpose financial statements are normally prepared to provide information to stakeholders:

- The balance sheet (explains the basic statement of financial condition)
- The income statement (explains certain changes in the balance sheet)
- The statement of owner's equity (explains certain changes in the balance sheet)
- The statement of cash flows (explains certain changes in the balance sheet)

These statements are called "general purpose" because they are prepared for general use by any ***stakeholder***—an owner, a manager, an investor, a lender, or anyone else.

Note: An individual financial statement is sometimes called a "report."

continued ▶

"So . . . tell me all about financial statements."

The Types of Financial Statements, *continued*

Special-Purpose Financial Statements

Accountants can also prepare special-purpose reports. These reports usually focus on the business operations in great detail, such as analysis of costs and profitability of services and products. They are intended only for owners and managers for use within a business. This kind of work is called ***managerial accounting***.

The Annual Report

Large companies present the four general-purpose reports at the end of each year's operations in a single document called the ***annual report***.

Features of the Annual Report

Frequency

Annual.

Financial Statements

The four general-purpose financial statements are in the annual report: balance sheet, income statement, statement of owner's equity, and statement of cash flows.

Full Disclosure

Annual reports must contain very detailed footnotes, graphs, charts, and tables that explain the numbers in the financial statements.

The importance of full and understandable disclosure cannot be overemphasized, as was dramatically revealed as the 21st century began with the surprise bankruptcies of very large companies such as Enron, WorldCom, and Global Crossing. Because their financial statements gave the impression that the companies were all viable "going concerns," the bankruptcies surprised many stakeholders and resulted in large financial losses, numerous fraud allegations, and the subsequent collapse of a major accounting firm, Arthur Andersen Company.

These events revealed the weaknesses in the existing disclosure rules. In 2002, as a result, the United States Congress created the ***Public Company Accounting Oversight Board***, also called the PCAOB. The PCAOB now independently supervises the full-disclosure and auditing standards that accountants must apply to large corporations that have publicly-treded stock.

Example of Failure to Disclose

Using complex accounting methods, Enron Corporation created numerous partnerships with other parties. However, Enron never disclosed the business purpose of these transactions (often there was none—only to hide losses or remove debt) or that a share of property sale gains would go to senior Enron officers. Stakeholders lost aproximately 70 billion dollars when Enron later collapsed.

Features of the Annual Report, *continued*

Audited

The financial statements in the annual report are audited by Certified Public Accountants, so the financial statements must conform to generally accepted accounting principles. (This is not true of unaudited interim reports.)

MD & A

Annual reports also contain management's opinion about the past and future performance of the company. This is called "management discussion and analysis" or simply ***MD & A***. The MD & A must include an explanation of liquidity (cash position), sources of capital invested in or loaned to the company, and the operating results. The MD & A must also discuss the management's opinion about the future performance of the company.

The Qualities of Information

How Good Is Information in the Financial Statements?

It Must Be Useful!

If you want to use a financial report to make a financial decision next week, do you want the report to contain numbers that are only guesses? Do you want information about the cost of eggs in Boston in 1909? Do you want information that was calculated using one method one month and a different method the next month? Of course not—none of this would be useful to you. The highest authority in accounting, the Financial Accounting Standards Board, has stated that the most important quality of the information on financial statements is that it must be *useful*.

Various Qualities Required

If you study more advanced accounting, you will discover a surprising number of separate qualities that are needed to make financial information useful. The most essential of these important qualities are shown below.

PRACTICE Learning Goal 12

Solutions are in the disk at the back of the book and at: www.worthyjames.com

Learning Goal 12 describes the four general-purpose financial statements. Use these questions to practice what you have just read. Select the best answer to each question.

Multiple Choice

Select the best answer.

1. The most fundamental requirement for accounting information is that it
   a. must be accurate.
   b. must be useful.
   c. is prepared at least annually.
   d. is relevant.
2. Financial statement information that can be verified and is free of material error describes the information quality of
   a. relevance.
   b. comparability.
   c. reliability.
   d. consistency.
3. Information that is important enough to make a difference in a decision if it is not available describes the quality of
   a. relevance.
   b. comparability.
   c. reliability.
   d. consistency.
4. Due to the collapse of major corporations such as Enron, WorldCom, and Global Crossing, the United States Congress in 2002 created the · · · · · · · ·, which independently supervises the full-disclosure and auditing standards that must be used by CPA firms when auditing large (publicly traded) companies.
   a. Securities and Exchange Commission (SEC)
   b. American Auditing Board
   c. Public Company Accounting Oversight Board (PCAOB)
   d. Chartered Accountants Oversight Board
5. MD & A is a required management presentation that is always part of a(n)
   a. income statement.
   b. balance sheet.
   c. tax return.
   d. annual report.
6. Which of the following is *not* a feature of an annual report?
   a. balance sheet, income statement, statement of owner's (or stockholders') equity, and statement of cash flows that have been audited
   b. MD & A
   c. tax return
   d. footnotes, graphs, and tables
7. The kind of accounting that focuses on the detailed internal information needs of a company is
   a. managerial accounting.
   b. internal auditing.
   c. tax accounting.
   d. fund accounting.

PRACTICE Learning Goal 12, continued

Solutions are in the disk at the back of the book and at: www.worthyjames.com

8. Which of the following is considered to be a "general purpose" financial statement?
   a. balance sheet
   b. income statement
   c. statement of cash flows
   d. all of the above
9. Information on financial statements that is determined by using the same accounting methods and procedures each reporting period has the quality of
   a. consistency.
   b. reliability.
   c. relevance.
   d. comparability.
10. If you are looking at the financial statements of several companies which you are analyzing for the purpose of making an investment, an additional quality of information on the financial statements that is important to you is
    a. consistency.
    b. reliability.
    c. relevance.
    d. comparability.
11. If the management of a company knows that a large bank loan is coming due and will require full payment in the near future, the requirement that this information be made available as part of the financial statements is called
    a. consistency.
    b. full disclosure.
    c. relevance.
    d. reliability.
12. Full financial statements disclosure consists primarily of
    a. charts and graphs.
    b. footnotes.
    c. tables.
    d. all of the above.

INTERNET EXERCISES

Finding and analyzing websites of CPA firms. Do an Internet search and locate ten to fifteen CPA firms in your local area. (Suggestion: Try 'CPA firms' followed by name of a city as one source.) Use bookmark/favorites to save the web links in an "Accounting References" folder.).

a. What services are most frequently offered? Which are the most unusual?
b. Can you find descriptions of these services at the firms' websites? If so, briefly describe the services for each firm, naming the firm.
c. Which services would be most useful to an individual, a small business, and a large business?

Your Questions?

It is *very* important to be aware of what you need to understand better. What do you need to understand better about this learning goal? On a separate piece of paper, write the questions that you want to discuss with your classmates, instructor, or supervisor. Try to be very specific about what is bothering you, such as explanations that you do not fully understand.

LEARNING GOAL 13

Identify and Prepare an Income Statement

In Learning Goal 13, you will find:

What It Is and the Four Steps to Prepare It

Overview

Preparation Sequence

When all the financial statements are being prepared, the income statement is normally prepared first. This and the next three learning goals explain each of the financial statements in the order in which they are normally prepared: income statement (Learning Goal 13), statement of owner's equity (Learning Goal 14), balance sheet (Learning Goal 15), and statement of cash flows (Learning Goal 16).

Introduction

What the Income Statement Shows

The ***income statement*** shows the change in owner's equity that was caused by the business operations. *Remember:* "Operations" means the process of creating and selling desired resources.

The Income Statement Formula

The basic formula for the income statement is: R – E = NI (or NL), where:

- R means total revenues.
- E means total expenses.
- NI and NL mean net income and net loss.

Reason for the Income Statement

Revenues and expenses are the *most powerful* force of change on the condition of the business.

All the efforts that go into operating the business show up in the amount of revenues and expenses. Revenues and expenses are of great interest to all users of financial statements. Financial statement users want to identify and analyze the individual amounts of revenues and expenses. To provide this detail, the types of revenues and expenses are identified individually on a separate statement—the income statement.

Do you remember *exactly* what the word revenue means and what the word 'expense' means? Many people often misunderstand these words. See if you can define these two words now. The answers are on page 285. (Don't look first!)

Features of the Income Statement

Time Period

Unlike the balance sheet, the income statement is for a *period of time*.

Why a Period of Time?

The date of an income statement shows a period of time because the income statement shows change, and *change happens over time*. This could be a month, a quarter, a year, etc. Notice in the example below for Jack's Guitar School that the date is "for the *month ended* June 30, 2017." Therefore, this is the operational change in owner's equity that happened during June.

Individual Sections

The basic income statement has one section for revenues and another section for expenses.

Synonyms

Other names for the income statement are:

- ***Statement of earnings***
- ***Operating statement/statement of operations***
- ***Profit and loss statement***
- **P & L statement**

Note: The financial statements shown in this learning goal are introductory examples. Larger and more complex examples are presented in Volume 2 and in the discussion of corporations later in this book.

continued ▶

Features of the Income Statement, *continued*

Example

Jack's Guitar School Income Statement For the Month Ended June 30, 2017		
Revenues		
Instruction fees		$2,900
Expenses		
Rent expense	$800	
Supplies expense	150	
Utilities expense	100	
Telephone expense	70	
Total expenses		1,120
Net income		$1,780

Source of the Numbers

The numbers for this income statement come from the totals of the revenue and expense transactions that are recorded for Jack's Guitar School (see pages 260–261).

Check Your Understanding

Write the completed sentences on a separate piece of paper. The answers are below.

The date of an income statement is for a ········ of ········ because the income statement shows ········. This is different than a balance sheet, which shows the condition of the business at a ········ in time.

What the income statement explains is the ········ ········ in owner's equity. This is caused by ········ and ········.

Answers

The date of an income statement is for a period of time because the income statement shows change. This is different than a balance sheet, which shows the condition of the business at a point in time.

What the income statement explains is the operational change in owner's equity. This is caused by revenues and expenses.

Four Steps in Preparing an Income Statement

Summary of Steps

The following pages show you how to prepare an income statement in four basic steps. Here is a summary of the steps:

1. Write the title.
2. List the revenues (type and amount).
3. List the expenses (type and amount).
4. Calculate and enter net income (or loss) and enter it on the statement.

STEP 1	
Action	**Rule**
Write the title.	The title is always prepared in the following order: 1. Name of company 2. Name of statement 3. Time period

Example

Jack's Guitar School
Income Statement
For the Month Ended June 30, 2008

STEP 2	
Action	**Rule**
List the revenues (type and amount).	■ If there are separate types of revenues, the total of each type is always shown. ■ If there are more than one type, show the largest total first. ■ The total of revenues is shown above the expenses.

continued ▶

Four Steps in Preparing an Income Statement, *continued*

STEP 3	
Action	**Rule**
List the expenses (type and amount).	▪ If there are separate types of expenses, the total of each type is always shown (examples are wages expense, supplies expense, etc.). ▪ The total of expenses is shown below the revenues.

Note: Expenses can be listed in different ways, but we will put the *largest expenses first*. Listing expenses this way makes it easy to quickly see the expenses that reduced the net income the most.

Example of Steps 2 and 3

Jack's Guitar School
Income Statement
For the Month Ended June 30, 2017

Revenues		
Instruction fees		$2,900
Expenses		
Rent expense	$800	
Supplies expense	150	
Utilities expense	100	
Telephone expense	70	
Total expenses		1,120

STEP 4	
Action	**Rule**
Calculate and enter net income (or loss).	▪ ***Net income*** or ***net loss*** is always calculated by subtracting total expenses from total revenues. (The completed statement is on page 282.)

Rule for Dollar Signs

A dollar sign ($) is placed next to the top number in any column of numbers. A dollar sign is also placed next to the final total—the number above the double line.

Answers

'Revenue' is an increase in owner's equity that results from making a sale. Owner's equity increases because the sale will either cause assets to increase or liabilities to decrease. Remember: 'revenue' is not a thing (like an asset or liability); it is an **explanation** for an increase in owner's equity.

'Expense' is a decrease in owner's equity caused by using up resources in operations (the adding – value process). Owner's equity decreases because an expense will either cause assets to decrease or liabilities to increase. Expense is not a thing (like an asset or liability); it is an **explanation** for a decrease in owner's equity.

QUICK REVIEW

The income statement			
Also called: ▪ Operating statement ▪ P & L statement ▪ Profit and loss statement ▪ Statement of earnings ▪ Statement of operations			
explains . . .			
the *operational* changes in *owner's equity*			
and contains . . .			
▪ Revenues ▪ Expenses			

VOCABULARY

Income statement: a report that explains the operational changes in owner's equity for a specific period of time (page 282)

Net income: when revenues exceed expenses (page 284)

Net loss: when expenses exceed revenues (page 284)

Operating statement: another name for the income statement (page 281)

P & L statement: another name for the income statement (page 281)

Profit and loss statement: another name for the income statement (page 281)

Statement of earnings: another name for the income statement (page 281)

Statement of operations: another name for the income statement (page 281)

PRACTICE Learning Goal 13

Solutions are in the disk at the back of the book and at: www.worthyjames.com

Learning Goal 13 concerns the identification and preparation of the income statement. Use these three problems to practice the material you just read.

Reinforcement Problems

LG 13-1. Prepare an income statement. On July 1, 2017, David Running-Elk begins his new orthopedic medical practice with an investment of $37,000, which he has obtained from his friends and relatives. As of the end of the first month of operation, the bookkeeper has determined the balances for the items below. On a separate sheet of paper, use the correct items to prepare an income statement for David Running-Elk, M.D., for the month of July.

Accounts Payable	$ 1,100	Rent Expense	$ 1,500	Note Payable	$ 9,000
Unearned Revenue	$ 500	Drawings	$ 1,000	Accounts Receivable	$ 3,100
Supplies	$ 700	Fees Earned	$ 4,250	Interest Expense	$ 300
Cash	$ 8,500	Equipment	$35,000	Prepaid Insurance	$ 750
Wages Expense	$ 850	Utilities Expense	$ 150		

LG 13-2. Missing information—prepare an income statement. An analysis of the owner's equity of the De Anza Operating Company shows the following items for the year ended December 31, 2017.

Rent Expense	$12,000	Supplies Expense	?	Owner Withdrawals	$5,000
Service Revenue Earned	?	Wages Expense	$7,500	Utilities Expense	$2,000
Advertising Expense	$3,000				

Other information: The net income for the year was $10,000. On January 1, the company had $3,000 of supplies and on December 31, the company had $5,000 of supplies. During the year, the company purchased $4,000 of supplies.

Required: On a separate sheet of paper, prepare an income statement for the De Anza Operating Company. Show calculations separately and in good form.

LG 13-3. Business operations. You know that the income statement explains the effect of business operations on the owner's equity. Operations affect the owner's equity because of two transaction types. What are the two types of transactions?

a.

b.

Your Questions?

It is *very* important to be aware of what you need to understand better. What do you need to understand better about this learning goal? On a separate piece of paper, write the questions that you want to discuss with your classmates, instructor, or supervisor. Try to be very specific about what is bothering you, such as explanations that you do not fully understand.

LEARNING GOAL 14 Identify and Prepare a Statement of Owner's Equity

Review

What It Shows

The ***statement of owner's equity*** explains *all* the changes in owner's equity for a specific period of time. The statement of owner's equity combines the *operational* change in owner's equity from the income statement *with the rest of the changes* in owner's equity. The rest of the changes are:

1. Owner's investments
2. Owner's withdrawals

The Owner's Equity Statement Formula

The formula for the statement of owner's equity consists of three parts: beginning balance + (current changes) = ending balance.

Three possible current changes are:

1. Net income or net loss (+/–)
2. Owner's investment (+)
3. Owner's withdrawals (–)

Net Income Combines Two Effects

Question: We previously said that four transaction types can affect owner's equity: revenues, expenses, investments, and withdrawals. Why do we see only three current changes on the statement of owner's equity?

Answer: Two of the changes—revenues and expenses—are combined into one number—net income (or net loss)—from the income statement.

In Learning Goal 14, you will find:

What It Is and the Four Steps to Prepare It

What It Is and the Four Steps to Prepare It

Features of the Statement of Owner's Equity

Date

Like the income statement, the statement of owner's equity is for a *period of time* because it is a statement that shows change.

Same Final Balance as Shown on the Balance Sheet

The final balance on the statement of owner's equity is the same balance of owner's equity as on the balance sheet (which we discuss in the next learning goal). The statement of owner's equity is simply itemizing the current changes to arrive at the final balance of owner's equity.

Synonym

The statement of owner's equity is sometimes called the ***capital statement***.

Example

Note: Beginning balance is zero because this is a new business.

Jack's Guitar School
Statement of Owner's Equity
For the Month Ended June 30, 2017

Jack Davis, Capital, June 1	$ 0
Add: Owner investment	12,000
Net income	1,780
	13,780
Less: Drawings	1,000
Jack Davis, Capital, June 30	$12,780

Notice that for reporting purposes, we are now combining all the elements of equity into one amount of $12,780 and calling it "Jack Davis, Capital".

Check Your Understanding

Write the completed sentences on a separate piece of paper. The answers are below.

The statement of owner's equity is for a ········ of time and summarizes ········ the changes in owner's equity. The statement has three parts: (1) the ········ balance of owner's equity, (2) the ········ ········, and (3) the ········ balance. The ending balance of owner's equity must be the same number as the owner's equity that appears on the ········ ········.

Answers

The statement of owner's equity is for a period of time and summarizes all the changes in owner's equity. The statement has three parts: (1) the beginning balance of owner's equity, (2) the current changes, and (3) the ending balance. The ending balance of owner's equity must be the same number as the owner's equity that appears on the balance sheet.

Four Steps in Preparing the Statement of Owner's Equity

Summary of Steps

The following pages show you how to prepare a statement of owner's equity in four basic steps. Here is a summary of the steps:

1. Write the title.
2. Enter the beginning balance (with description).
3. Enter the current changes (with descriptions).
4. Calculate the ending balance (with description) and verify it.

STEP 1	
Action	**Rule**
Write the title.	The title is always prepared in the following order: 1. Name of company 2. Name of statement 3. Time period

continued ▶

Four Steps in Preparing the Statement of Owner's Equity, *continued*

Example

Jack's Guitar School
Statement of Owner's Equity
For the Month Ended June 30, 2017

STEP 2	
Action	**Rule**
Enter the beginning balance (with description).	The beginning balance is always: ▪ The ending balance from the *prior* statement of owner's equity or balance sheet, or . . . ▪ For a new business, the beginning balance of owner's equity is zero.

STEP 3	
Action	**Rule**
Enter the current changes (with descriptions).	The possible current changes are: ▪ Net income (or loss) from the income statement ▪ Owner investments ▪ Owner withdrawals

Four Steps in Preparing the Statement of Owner's Equity, *continued*

Example

The beginning balance and current changes for Jack's Guitar School are shown below.

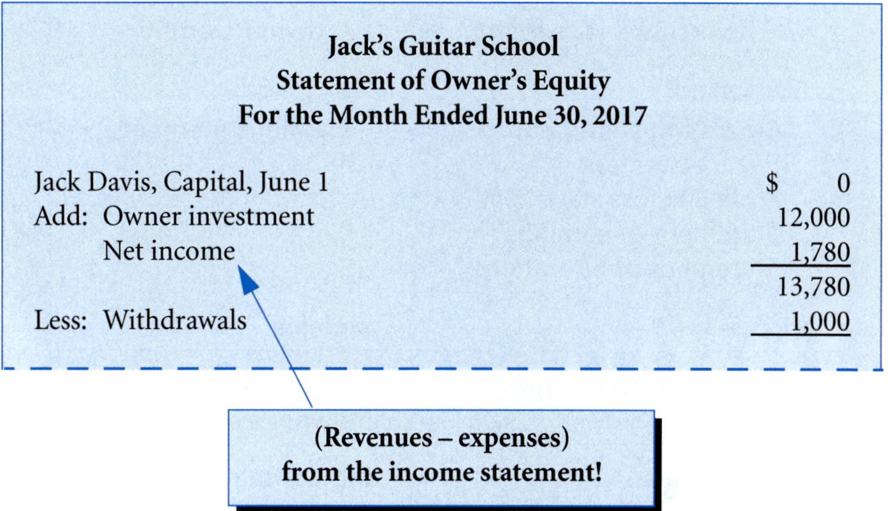

Jack's Guitar School
Statement of Owner's Equity
For the Month Ended June 30, 2017

Jack Davis, Capital, June 1	$ 0
Add: Owner investment	12,000
Net income	1,780
	13,780
Less: Withdrawals	1,000

STEP 4	
Action	**Rule**
Calculate the ending balance (with description) and verify it.	▪ The ending balance is calculated by adding/subtracting the three possible current changes to the beginning balance. ▪ The ending balance is verified by checking that it is the same amount as the owner's equity showing on the balance sheet.

Example

An example of the completed statement of owner's equity for Jack's Guitar School is on page 288.

QUICK REVIEW

(Prepare first) The income statement	(Prepare second) The statement of owner's equity		
Also called: ▪ Operating statement ▪ P & L statement ▪ Profit and loss statement ▪ Statement of earnings ▪ Statement of operations	Also called: ▪ Capital statement		
explains . . .	**explains . . .**		
The *operational* changes in *owner's equity*	*All* the changes in *owner's equity*		
and contains . . .	**and contains . . .**		
▪ Revenues ▪ Expenses	▪ Net income (loss) ▪ Investments ▪ Withdrawals		

VOCABULARY

Capital statement: another name for the statement of owner's equity (page 288)

Statement of owner's equity: the financial statement that explains all the changes in owner's equity (page 287)

PRACTICE Learning Goal 14

Solutions are in the disk at the back of the book and at: www.worthyjames.com

Learning Goal 14 concerns the identification and preparation of the statement of owner's equity. Use these two problems to practice the material you just read.

Reinforcement Problems

LG 14-1. Prepare a statement of owner's equity. On July 1, 2017, David Running-Elk began his new orthopedic medical practice with an investment of $37,000, which he has obtained from his friends and relatives. As of the end of the first month of operation, the bookkeeper has determined the balances for the items below. On a separate sheet of paper, use the correct items to prepare a statement of owner's equity for David Running-Elk, M.D., for the month of July. Remember that you can use the information on the income statement that you already prepared in the Practice for Learning Goal 13 (see page 286, Reinforcement Problem LG 13-1).

Accounts Payable	$ 1,100	Fees Earned	$ 4,250
Unearned Revenue	$ 500	Equipment	$35,000
Supplies	$ 700	Utilities Expense	$ 150
Cash	$ 8,500	Note Payable	$ 9,000
Wages Expense	$ 850	Accounts Receivable	$ 3,100
Rent Expense	$ 1,500	Interest Expense	$ 300
Withdrawals (Drawing)	$ 1,000	Prepaid Insurance	$ 750

LG 14-2. Missing information—prepare a statement of owner's equity. Lucy Palangian, the owner of West Valley Company, wants you (her assistant) to prepare a statement of owner's equity and to determine the net income or loss for the year ended December 31, 2017. Unfortunately, there is no detailed information that shows individual revenue or expense transactions.

Luckily, Ms. Palangian does remember that she invested $15,000 in the business this year and withdrew $5,300 for personal expenses. The balance of owner's equity on January 1, 2017 was $3,800. On December 31, total assets are $41,000 and total liabilities are $37,000.

Required: On a separate sheet of paper, prepare a statement of owner's equity. Then tell the owner the net income or loss for the year. Show any calculations clearly and in good form.

Your Questions?

It is *very* important to be aware of what you need to understand better. What do you need to understand better about this learning goal? On a separate piece of paper, write the questions that you want to discuss with your classmates, instructor, or supervisor. Try to be very specific about what is bothering you, such as explanations that you do not fully understand.

LEARNING GOAL 15

Identify and Prepare a Balance Sheet

In Learning Goal 15, you will find:

What It Is and the Four Steps to Prepare It

Features of the Balance Sheet

What It Shows

The ***balance sheet*** is like a flash picture—it shows assets and claims on assets at a moment in time. In other words, a balance sheet shows the business wealth and claims on the wealth at a point in time. Notice that in the example on page 295 for Jack's Guitar School, the date is a point in time—June 30—meaning at the end of the business day on June 30. The date is not for a period of time, like "the month of June."

It Balances

The total claims on assets equal the total assets. In the example, the total assets are $13,150. The creditors' claims of $370 + the owner's claim of $12,780 = $13,150.

Individual Sections

The assets, liabilities, and owner's equity are each presented in their own sections, and the total is calculated for each section.

Format: Report Form and Account Form

The side-by-side presentation of assets and equities in the example is called the ***account form*** of the balance sheet. Sometimes the form of the balance sheet varies slightly, with all assets shown at the top of the report and the liabilities and owner's equity shown below the assets. Such a format is called the ***report form***.

Features of the Balance Sheet, *continued*

Synonym

The balance sheet is sometimes called the ***statement of position*** or the ***statement of condition***.

Source of the Information

The asset and liability amounts come from the ending balances of the individual accounting equation items for Jack's Guitar School (see pages 260 and 261). The owner's equity is the ending balance that was calculated in the statement of owner's equity.

See it as a photograph. Try to remember the balance sheet as a "flash photograph" of the business at a moment in time.

Example: Completed Balance Sheet (Account Form)

Jack's Guitar School
Balance Sheet
June 30, 2017

Assets		**Liabilities**	
Cash	$6,350	Accounts payable	$ 170
Accounts receivable	1,250	Unearned revenues	200
Supplies	50	Total liabilities	370
Equipment	5,500		
		Owner's Equity	
		Jack Davis, Capital	12,780
Total assets	$13,150	Total liabilities and owner's equity	$13,150

This must also be the ending balance on the statement of owner's equity (page 288).

continued ▶

Four Steps in Preparing a Balance Sheet, *continued*

STEP 3	
Action	**Rule**
Enter the owner's equity and verify it.	▪ Use the ending balance on the statement of owner's equity to find the amount of owner's equity. ▪ Owner's equity must be labeled by writing the owner's name followed by the word "capital." ▪ Owner's equity is *verified* by subtracting total liabilities from total assets.

STEP 4	
Action	**Rule**
Total the liabilities and owner's equity and compare to asset total.	▪ The total of the liabilities and the owner's equity is always shown. It must be equal to the total assets.

Example

The completed balance sheet for Jack's Guitar School is on page 295. Notice that total assets of $13,150 minus total liabilities of $370 verify owner's equity of $12,780.

Rule for Dollar Signs ($)

A dollar sign ($) is placed next to the top number in any column of numbers. A dollar sign is also placed next to the final total—the number above the double line.

> *Note:* Some preparers of financial statements omit dollar signs entirely because they believe that it is understood that all amounts are in U.S. dollars. (Do not do this without checking with your instructor or supervisor.)

QUICK REVIEW

(Prepare first) The income statement	(Prepare second) The statement of owner's equity	(Prepare third) The balance sheet	
Also called: ▪ Operating statement ▪ P & L statement ▪ Profit and loss statement ▪ Statement of earnings ▪ Statement of operations	Also called: ▪ Capital statement	Also called: ▪ Statement of position ▪ Statement of condition	
explains . . .	**explains . . .**	**shows . . .**	
The *operational* changes in *owner's equity*	*All* the changes in *owner's equity*	The condition of a business at a point in time	
and contains . . .	**and contains . . .**	**and contains . . .**	
▪ Revenues ▪ Expenses	▪ Net income (loss) ▪ Investments ▪ Withdrawals	▪ Assets ▪ Liabilities ▪ Owner's equity	

VOCABULARY

Account form: a balance sheet format in which assets are placed on the left side of page, and liabilities and owner's equity are placed on the right side (page 294)

Balance sheet: a report that shows the assets and claims on assets as of a specific date (page 294)

Liquidity: how quickly an asset can be turned into cash (page 297)

Report form: a balance sheet format in which assets are placed at the top of a page and liabilities and owner's equity are placed below the assets (page 294)

Statement of condition: another name for the balance sheet (page 295)

Statement of position: another name for the balance sheet (page 295)

PRACTICE Learning Goal 15

Solutions are in the disk at the back of the book and at: www.worthyjames.com

Learning Goal 15 concerns the identification and preparation of the balance sheet. Use these two problems to practice the material you just read.

Reinforcement Problems

LG 15-1. Prepare a balance sheet. On July 1, 2017, David Running-Elk began his new orthopedic medical practice with an investment of $37,000, which he has obtained from his friends and relatives. As of the end of the first month of operation, the bookkeeper has determined the balances for the items below. On a separate sheet of paper, use the correct items to prepare an account form balance sheet for David Running-Elk, M.D., as of July 31. Remember that you can use the information from the financial statement you prepared for this company in the Practice section for Learning Goal 14 (see page 293, Reinforcement Problem LG 14-1).

Accounts Payable	$ 1,100	Fees Earned	$ 4,250
Unearned Revenue	$ 500	Equipment	$35,000
Supplies	$ 700	Utilities Expense	$ 150
Cash	$ 8,500	Note Payable	$ 9,000
Wages Expense	$ 850	Accounts Receivable	$ 3,100
Rent Expense	$ 1,500	Interest Expense	$ 300
Drawings	$ 1,000	Prepaid Insurance	$ 750

LG 15-2. Missing information—prepare a balance sheet. The Fulton Avenue Company shows all the April 30, 2017 balance sheet data as follows:

Cash:	$25,000	Accounts Receivable:	$?	Don Chen, Capital:	?
Supplies:	$?	Accounts Payable:	$12,000	Equipment:	$10,000

Other information: On the March 31 balance sheet, the balance of supplies was $1,000. During April, Fulton Avenue Company purchased $7,000 of supplies and used $4,000 of supplies. On April 30, the total liabilities and owner's equity are $41,000.

Required: On a separate sheet of paper, prepare the Fulton Avenue Company balance sheet as of April 30. Show any calculations clearly and in good form.

LEARNING GOAL 16

Identify the Statement of Cash Flows

Overview

Why It Is Important

Like a plant without water, a business will soon die without enough cash. Owners and managers always want to know exactly why business cash is increasing or decreasing.

In this section we learn the basics of how to identify and use a statement of cash flows. Details on the preparation of the statement is a more advanced subject that we discuss in Volume 2.

What It Does

The ***statement of cash flows*** is a report that explains the change in a company's cash balance during a specific period of time—the same period of time that corresponds to the income statement and the statement of owner's equity. The change that is explained is the difference between the total cash balance on one balance sheet and the total cash balance appearing on the next balance sheet.

Three Types of Change in Cash

The change in the cash balance is explained by categorizing the cash transactions into three possible categories. Each category is a major activity in which there can be inflows or outflows of cash. The three categories are:

1. Operating activities
2. Investing activities
3. Financing activities

Operating Activities

Definition

Operating activities are the inflows and outflows of cash that are caused by regular business operations, or by short-term investment trading.

Examples

- Cash paid to employees
- Cash paid to vendors for materials and services used in operations
- Cash received from customers
- Cash received from interest earned
- Cash paid for interest expense

Nonexamples of Operating Activities

See the examples for investing and financing activities on page 302.

Investing Activities

Definition

Investing activities are the inflows and outflows of cash that are caused by acquiring and disposing of assets that are generally long-term in nature, or are owned as investments, unless the purpose of the investments is short-term trading.

Examples

- Cash paid to buy equipment
- Cash paid to invest in stock of another company
- Cash paid to make a loan
- Cash paid to buy computers
- Cash received from selling equipment
- Cash received from selling an investment
- Cash received from collecting a loan.

Nonexamples of Investing Activities

See the examples for operating and financing activities.

Financing Activities

Definition

Financing activities are the inflows and outflows of cash that are caused by borrowing and by the investments and withdrawals of the owner(s).

Examples

- Cash received from borrowing money
- Cash received from the owner(s) or stockholders investment
- Cash paid to a repay a loan
- Cash paid to an owner or stockholders

Note: Notice the difference between being a lender and a borrower. Borrowing and paying back is a financing activity, while lending and collecting is an investing activity (above).

Nonexamples of Financing Activities

See the examples for operating and investing activities.

Operating activities are the most important source of cash flow because these activities result from recurring business operations. Operating activities indicate the ability of a business to generate cash from ongoing future efforts. Unethical management sometimes tries to record investing and financing transactions as operating activities.

Example of a Statement of Cash Flows

The Net Cash Flow

The statement of cash flows for Jack's Guitar School is shown below. The ***net cash flow*** (the net change in cash) for June was a net increase of $6,350.

The Ending Cash Balance Ties to the Balance Sheet

Because this is a new business, the beginning cash balance was zero, so the ending cash balance is also $6,350. If you look again at the June 30 balance sheet on page 295, you will see that *this balance exactly corresponds to the amount of cash showing on the balance sheet.*

Example

What you see below is a simple statement of cash flows.

Jack's Guitar School
Statement of Cash Flows
For the Month Ended June 30, 2017

Cash flows from **operating** activities:		
Receipts:		
Cash collections from customers		$ 1,850
Payments:		
Cash payments for expenses and to vendors		(1,000)
Net cash provided by operating activities		850
Cash flows from **investing** activities:		
Purchase of equipment		(5,500)
Cash flows from **financing** activities:		
Investment by owner	$12,000	
Withdrawal by owner	(1,000)	
Net cash provided by financing activities		11,000
Net increase in cash		6,350
Cash balance June 1		–0–
Cash balance June 30		$ 6,350

Note: Another popular format for the statement of cash flows calculates cash flows from operating activities using a more indirect procedure, beginning with net income. It gives exactly the same results.

You can see an example of this format in the financial analysis Learning Goal 32, on page 686.

PRACTICE Learning Goal 16, continued

Solutions are in the disk at the back of the book and at: www.worthyjames.com

LG16-2. Simple preparation of a statement of cash flows.

Using the statement of cash flows on page 303 as your model format and using your knowledge of the three different types of cash activities, create a November statement of cash flows for Murphys Company using the summary totals shown below. (Note: some items may not be applicable!) The November 1 beginning cash balance was $12,300.

	Item
a.	Collection of accounts receivable: $24,900
b.	Payment of accounts payable for various operating expenses: $18,300
c.	Loaning money to a customer for a purchase: $12,000
d.	Paying interest on a loan: $1,500
e.	Owner invests $25,000 in the business
f.	Collecting interest on a loan: $700
g.	Borrowing $15,000 on a long-term loan from a bank
h.	Buying equipment and paying $10,000 cash
i.	Selling equipment for $1,000 cash
j.	Sales on account of $7,500
k.	Customer in "c" above pays back $6,000 of the loan
l.	Owner withdraws $5,000 cash
m.	Owner withdraws supplies worth $400
n.	Utility bill in the amount of $220 is recorded but not paid.

LG16-3. Challenging question. Explain the following:

1. Why is net income different from cash flow from operating activities? (See illustrations on pages 282 and 303 for Jack's Guitar School.)
2. Which is more important information: net income or cash flow from operating activities?

PRACTICE Learning Goal 16, continued

Solutions are in the disk at the back of the book and at: www.worthyjames.com

INTERNET EXERCISES

Credit Protection

Lending and financial information. For useful (although never guaranteed) lending and financial information go to the following Internet sites. (Use bookmark/favorites to save the locations of links you use in an "Accounting References" folder.)

a. Go to www.bankrate.com.
   (1) Do a search for "Small Business." List three links that you think would be most useful to a small business. Why did you select these links?
   (2) Find the link that explains credit scores, and click the link to calculate your FICO credit score. (Your FICO score is used by lenders to evaluate a loan application. The score affects your ability to obtain credit and the interest rate you will be charged.) Calculate your FICO score.
   (3) Scan some other categories of interest to you. How might they be useful either personally or for a small business?

b. Go to www.moneycafe.com. (Use bookmark/favorites to save the locations of links you use in an "Accounting References" folder.) Compare the information on this site to the one above. What similarities and differences do you see in the sites? If you needed credit, interest, or lending information, what are the advantages of using *both* sites?

c. What is the Fair Credit Reporting Act (FCRA)? How does it protect you, and what rights does it give you? What is a security freeze on your credit file, and how does it protect you? (Suggestion: View the Equifax and Consumers' Union home pages for a quick summary of key rights.)

d. For general U.S. financial and economic data, go to the St. Louis Federal Reserve Bank site at http://research.stlouisfed.org/fred2/ (FRED). Scan several links that interest you, and then return to the home page to get an overview of the available links.
   (1) Using this site, determine the last daily quote for the bank prime rate. What is the bank prime rate? Where do you think this quote comes from? (Suggestion: Go back to bankrate.com and search the site for "prime rate definition.")

Your Questions?

It is *very* important to be aware of what you need to understand better. What do you need to understand better about this learning goal? Use this space to write the questions that you want to discuss with your classmates, instructor, or supervisor. Try to be very specific about what is bothering you, such as explanations that you do not fully understand.

LEARNING GOAL 17

Compare, Contrast, and Connect All the Financial Statements

In Learning Goal 17, you will find:

Comparing the Four Financial Statements

Review

Four Statements

There are four general-purpose financial statements:

- Income statement
- Statement of owner's equity
- Balance sheet
- Statement of cash flows

The Four General-Purpose Financial Statements

One Condition Statement and Three Change Statements Compared

The table below compares the features and functions of the condition statement (balance sheet) and the three change statements.

The Condition Statement is . . .	The Change Statements are . . .		
The balance sheet	*The income statement*	*The statement of owner's equity*	*The statement of cash flows*
Also called: ■ Statement of position ■ Statement of condition	Also called: ■ Operating statement ■ P & L statement ■ Profit and loss statement ■ Statement of earnings ■ Statement of operations	Also called: ■ Capital statement ■ Statement of stock-holders' equity (corporation)	Also called: ■ Cash flows statement ■ Statement of changes in cash position
shows . . .	*explains . . .*	*explains . . .*	*explains . . .*
Wealth and claims on wealth at a point in time	The *operational* changes in *owner's equity*	*All* the changes in *owner's equity*	All the changes in the cash balance
and contains . . .	*and contains . . .*	*and contains . . .*	*and contains . . .*
■ Assets (wealth) ■ Liabilities (claim) ■ Owner's equity (claim)	■ Revenues ■ Expenses	■ Net income (– loss) ■ Investments ■ Withdrawals	■ Operating activities ■ Investing activities ■ Financing activities
and is structured . . .	*and is structured . . .*	*and is structured . . .*	*and is structured . . .*
A = L + OE	R – E = Net Income (or Loss)	Beginning balance + net income (loss) + investments – drawings = ending balance	Beginning balance + operating activities + investing activities + financing activities = ending balance

What Are the Connections Between the Statements?

Each Balance Sheet Is Linked to the Next One

As you can see in the table above, each change statement explains changes in certain key parts of the balance sheet—the owner's equity and the cash balances. You could say that the change statements form "links" between one balance sheet and the next.

continued ►

What Are the Connections Between the Statements? *continued*

Example: Two Balance Sheets

Suppose that you prepared the balance sheet for a company as of June 30 and later prepared another balance sheet for that company as of July 31:

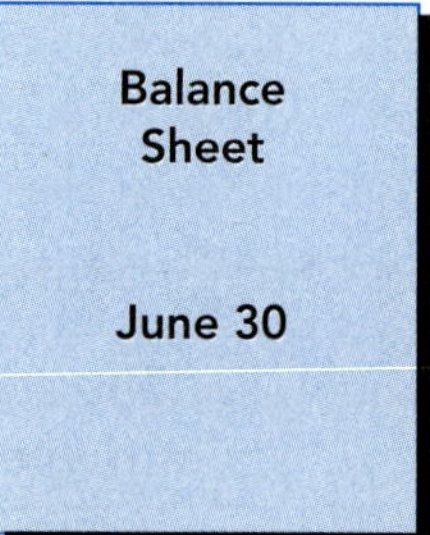

Balance
Sheet
July 31

Explain the Changes in the Owner's Equity and Cash

- You want to explain why the owner's equity is different on the July 31 balance sheet than on the June 30 balance sheet.
- You also want to explain why the cash balance on the July 31 balance sheet is different than on the June 30 balance sheet. How can the changes in these items be explained? By preparing the statements that show change: the income statement, statement of owner's equity, and statement of cash flows.

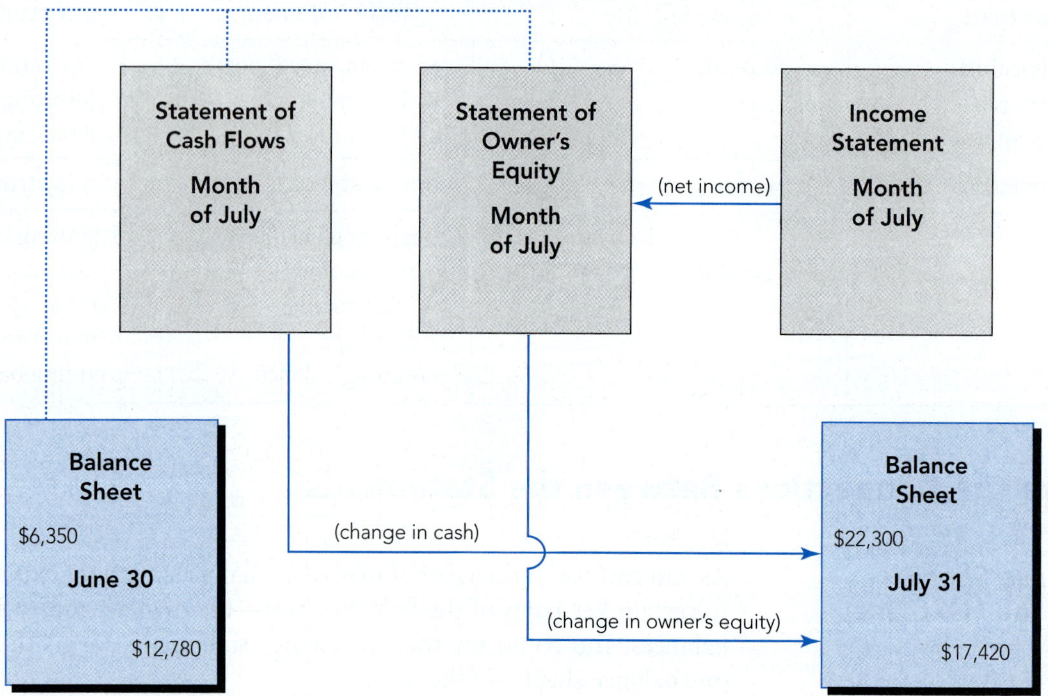

What Are the Connections Between the Statements? *continued*

Prior Balance Sheet Provides the Beginning Balances For Cash and Owner's Equity

The line from the June 30 balance sheet to the statement of cash flows and to the statement of owner's equity means the following:

- The beginning cash balance of $6,350 on the statement of cash flows, before any July transactions, comes from the June 30 balance sheet.
- The beginning owner's equity balance of $12,780 on the statement of owner's equity, before any July transactions, also comes from the June 30 balance sheet.

Current Period Transactions Complete the Links

The link to the July 31 balance sheet by each change statement is completed like this:

- All the current period July transactions that affect cash are summarized on the statement of cash flows, which explains the ending cash balance on the July 31 balance sheet of $22,300.
- All the current period July transactions that affect owner's equity are summarized on the statement of owner's equity and the income statement. Together they explain the July 31 owner's equity on the balance sheet of $17,420.

The ending balances showing on the statement of cash flows and on the statement of owner's equity correspond exactly to the same balances on the July 31 balance sheet. The statement of cash flows and the statement of owner's equity now link the June 30 and the July 31 balance sheet balances of cash and owner's equity.

Articulation

Whenever any change statement is connected to another financial statement, this connection is called "articulation."

Examples of the Connections

Jack's Guitar School July Results

Imagine that you have also recorded the July transactions and prepared the July financial statements for Jack's Guitar School, for which you followed the June transactions in Learning Goal 11. Without actually looking at any specific July transactions, assume that an overview of the results is what you see on page 316, with the cash and owner's equity balances shown to you.

continued ▶

Examples of the Connections, *continued*

Prior Balance Sheet June 30				(July changes) Transactions	Current Balance Sheet July 31			
	Assets		Liabilities			Assets		Liabilities
Cash	$6,350	*xxx*	$$$$	*Cash* $15,950 →	*Cash*	$22,300	*xxx*	$$$$
xxx	$$$$	*xxx*	$$$$		*xxx*	$$$$	*xxx*	$$$$
xxx	$$$$	*xxx*	$$$$		*xxx*	$$$$	*xxx*	$$$$
xxx	$$$$	*Owner's Equity*	$12,780	O.E. $4,640 →	*xxx*	$$$$	*Owner's Equity*	$17,420
Totals	**$13,150**		**$13,150**			**$32,520**		**$32,520**

July Changes

You can see that the July transactions are the reasons for changes in the balance sheet amounts. The new balance sheet as of July 31 is clearly different than the previous one. Specifically, we are most interested in the changes in cash and owner's equity.

The cash balance has changed from $6,350 on June 30 to $22,300 on July 31. The owner's equity balance has changed from $12,780 on June 30 to $17,420 on July 31.

Page 318 shows an illustration of the July 31 balance sheet, along with the three change statements *that explain the changes* in cash and owner's equity balances *during July*. These change statements are the "links" between the June 30 and July 31 balance sheet totals of cash and owner's equity.

Examples of Cash Transactions Connecting Balance Sheet and Statement of Cash Flows

Suppose that during July:

- The business spent $500 cash to purchase supplies. This transaction reduced the cash balance on the balance sheet and was a use of cash in the "Operating activities" explanation on the July statement of cash flows.
- The business spent $4,200 to buy equipment. This transaction reduced the cash balance on the balance sheet, and was a use of cash in "Investing activities" on the July statement of cash flows.
- The business collected $800 from a customer. This increased cash on the balance sheet (and decreased accounts receivable). This increase in cash is shown as a source of cash from "Operating activities" on the statement of cash flows.

Examples of the Connections, *continued*

Examples of Transactions Connecting Balance Sheet and Statement of Owner's Equity and Income Statement

Suppose that during July:

- The business sold $1,500 of teaching services to a customer on account. This transaction increased accounts receivable on the balance sheet and is explained on the July income statement as "Revenue," which increased owner's equity.
- The business used up $200 of supplies in the operations. This transaction decreased the asset supplies and is explained on the July income statement as "Expense," which decreased owner's equity.
- The total revenues exceeded the total expenses by $2,940. This net income was the overall increase to owner's equity from operations and is detailed on the July income statement. The net amount also appears on the July statement of owner's equity.

Cash Flow and Owner's Equity

Sometimes a transaction may affect both cash and owner's equity.

Examples:

- An owner's cash investment will increase both cash and owner's equity on the balance sheet. Therefore, the transaction will be explained on both the statement of owner's equity and the statement of cash flows.
- Paying cash for an expense item is a decrease to cash on the balance sheet. It is also an expense which reduces net income and owner's equity.

To Summarize

The essential idea here is to remember that financial statements are linked to each other, and that a transaction can affect more than one financial statement.

In particular, remember that one balance sheet is linked to the next balance sheet by the following statements that explain the key changes: income statement, statement of owner's equity, and statement of cash flows.

continued ▶

Examples of the Connections, *continued*

July Statement of Cash Flows

(The July Changes in Cash)

Operating activities:		
Collection from customers		$33,000
Less: Operating Expenditures		(14,550)
Net cash from operating activities		$18,450
Investing activities:		
Purchase of equipment		(4,200)
Financing activities:		
Owner investments less drawing		1,700
Net change in cash		15,950
Beginning cash balance	**July 1, 2017**	6,350
Ending cash balance	**July 31, 2017**	**$22,300**

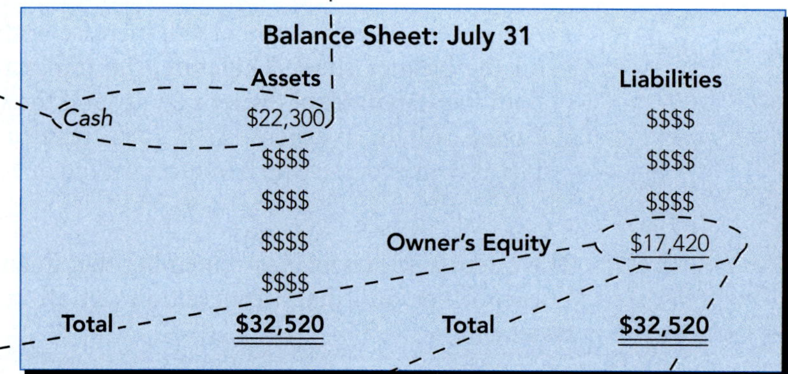

Balance Sheet: July 31

Assets		Liabilities	
Cash	$22,300		$$$$
	$$$$		$$$$
	$$$$		$$$$
	$$$$	**Owner's Equity**	$17,420
	$$$$		
Total	**$32,520**	**Total**	**$32,520**

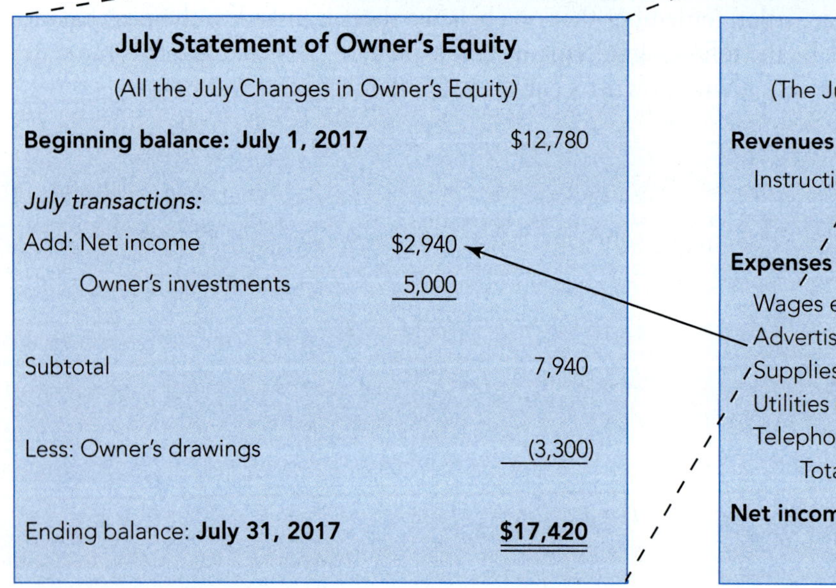

July Statement of Owner's Equity

(All the July Changes in Owner's Equity)

Beginning balance: July 1, 2017		$12,780
July transactions:		
Add: Net income	$2,940	
Owner's investments	5,000	
Subtotal		7,940
Less: Owner's drawings		(3,300)
Ending balance: **July 31, 2017**		**$17,420**

July Income Statement

(The July Operational Changes in Owner's Equity)

Revenues		
Instruction fees		$27,390
Expenses		
Wages expense	$12,100	
Advertising expense	11,730	
Supplies expense	300	
Utilities expense	200	
Telephone expense	120	
Total expense		24,450
Net income		**$2,940**

Check Your Understanding

Write the completed sentences on a separate piece of paper.

1. The statement that shows the financial condition (wealth and claims on wealth) at a point in time is called the ·········· ··········. Three change statements explain the changes in owner's equity and cash between two balance sheets. The first change statement explains the change in owner's equity caused by operations. This statement is called the ·········· ··········. The net result of this statement flows into the ········· ········· ········· ·········, which explains all the changes in ········· ··········. The final statement change statement is the statement of ········· ·········, which explains the changes in the ········· balance.

2. **Show how transactions affect the financial statements**
   a. Place the dollar amount of each transaction in the correct location(s) in the table below to show how each financial statement is affected by each transaction. To show negative amounts on the balance sheet, statement of owner's equity, and statement of cash flows, place amounts in parentheses ( ).
   b. Use the balance sheet asset and liability column totals to verify the correct final balance of owner's equity. Enter an amount in the balance sheet owner's equity column only as a total after you compute the final balance from the columns for the statement of owner's equity (item 14).
   c. Total the income statement columns to verify the amount of net income.
   d. Total the statement of cash flow columns to calculate the net change in the cash balance.

      (1) The owner invests $25,000 in his new business.
      (2) A $300 electric bill arrives and is paid.
      (3) The business performs $3,500 of services for a client, and client will pay later.
      (4) A client makes an advance payment of $2,000.
      (5) An advertising bill for $900 arrives and will be paid later.
      (6) $1,450 of supplies are purchased, and the bill will be paid later.
      (7) The business performs the services for the client who made the advance payment.
      (8) The owner withdraws $1,500 cash.
      (9) The business collects $2,000 from accounts receivable.
      (10) $300 of supplies are used.
      (11) Employee wages for this month are $2,900. Employees will be paid next week.
      (12) The employee wages in (11) are paid.
      (13) At the end of the period the net income is determined to be $1,100
      (14) The final balance of owner's equity is calculated from the statement of owner's equity, and this amount is placed on the balance sheet.

continued ▶

Detailed Examples of Owner's Equity Connections, *continued*

Revenue Reduces Unearned Revenue

The final revenue transaction for the day involves a document delivery for a customer that already prepaid for delivery services. The delivery fee is $500. Because the customer had already paid, there is Unearned Revenue liability on the balance sheet, which now decreases. On the balance sheet, this liability decrease is not connected with any other asset or liability, so the owner's equity (U.B., Capital) increases by $500 to $21,500.

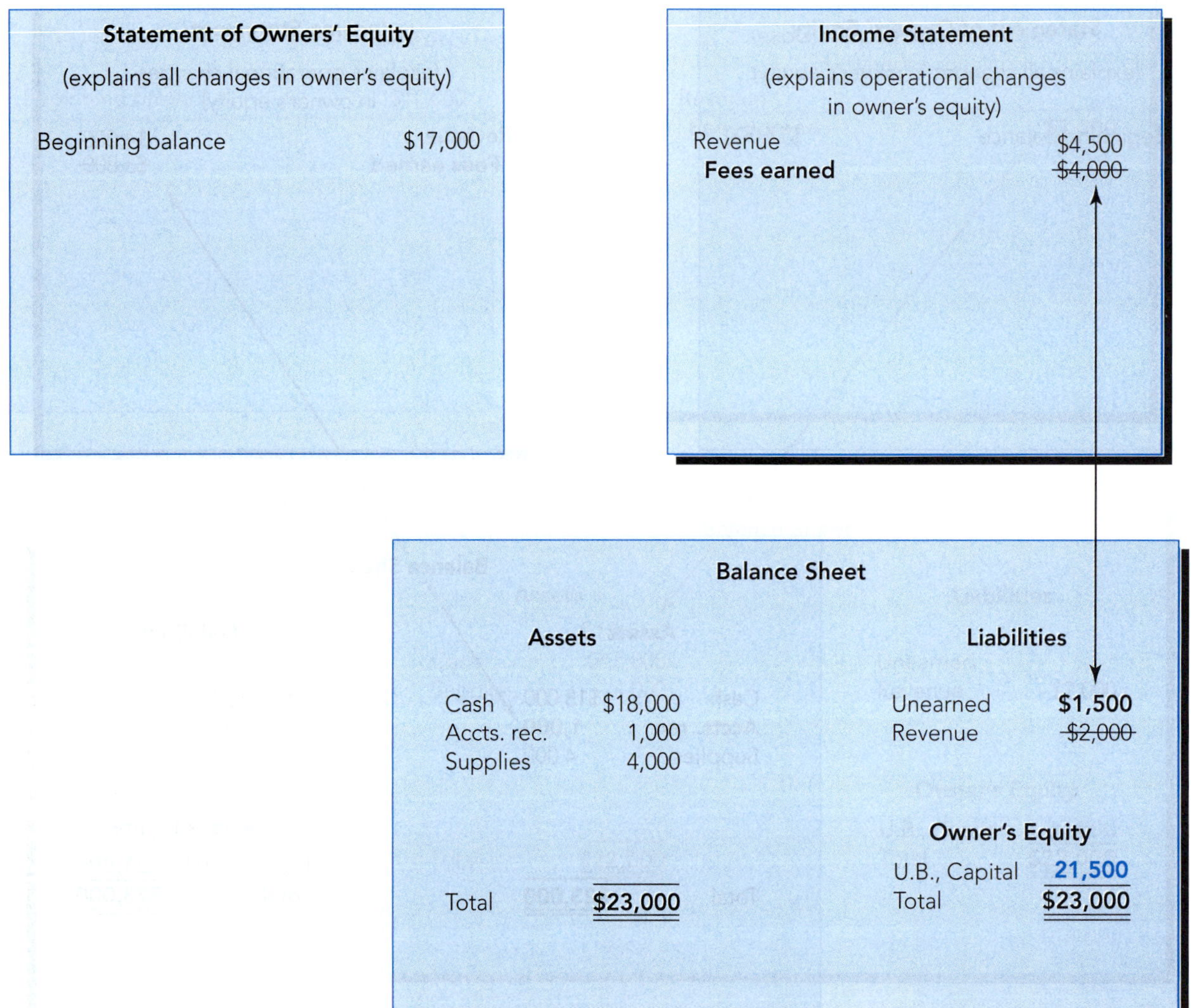

Using the Equation

The equation would show the changes as:

$$A = \downarrow L + \uparrow OE$$

Detailed Examples of Owner's Equity Connections, *continued*

Expense Decreases Cash

The first expense transaction of the day is a $2,000 cash payment to the landlord for the office rent. This is an operational transaction that appears as Rent Expense on the income statement and also causes cash to decrease. On the balance sheet, this asset decrease is not connected with any other asset or liability, so the owner's equity also decreases by $2,000 to $19,500.

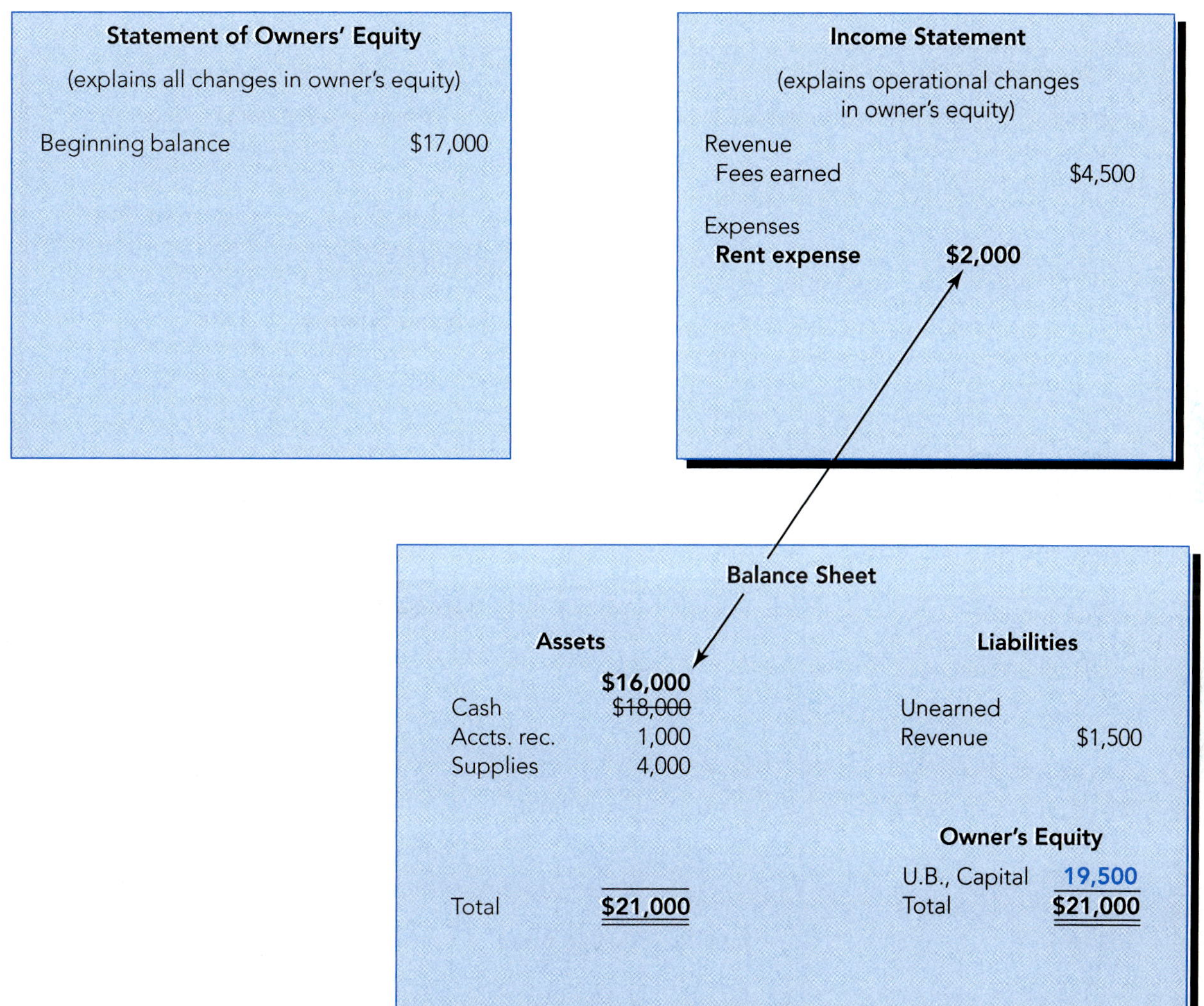

Using the Equation

The equation would show the changes as:

$$\downarrow A = L + \downarrow OE$$

continued ▶

Detailed Examples of Owner's Equity Connections, *continued*

Expense Decreases Other Assets

The next expense of the day for Uncle Billy's Courier Service happens when the business uses up $1,000 of the office supplies to prepare some packages for delivery. The decrease in Supplies is an operational transaction that appears as Supplies Expense on the income statement. On the balance sheet, this asset decrease is not connected with any other asset or liability, so the owner's equity also decreases by $1,000 to $18,500.

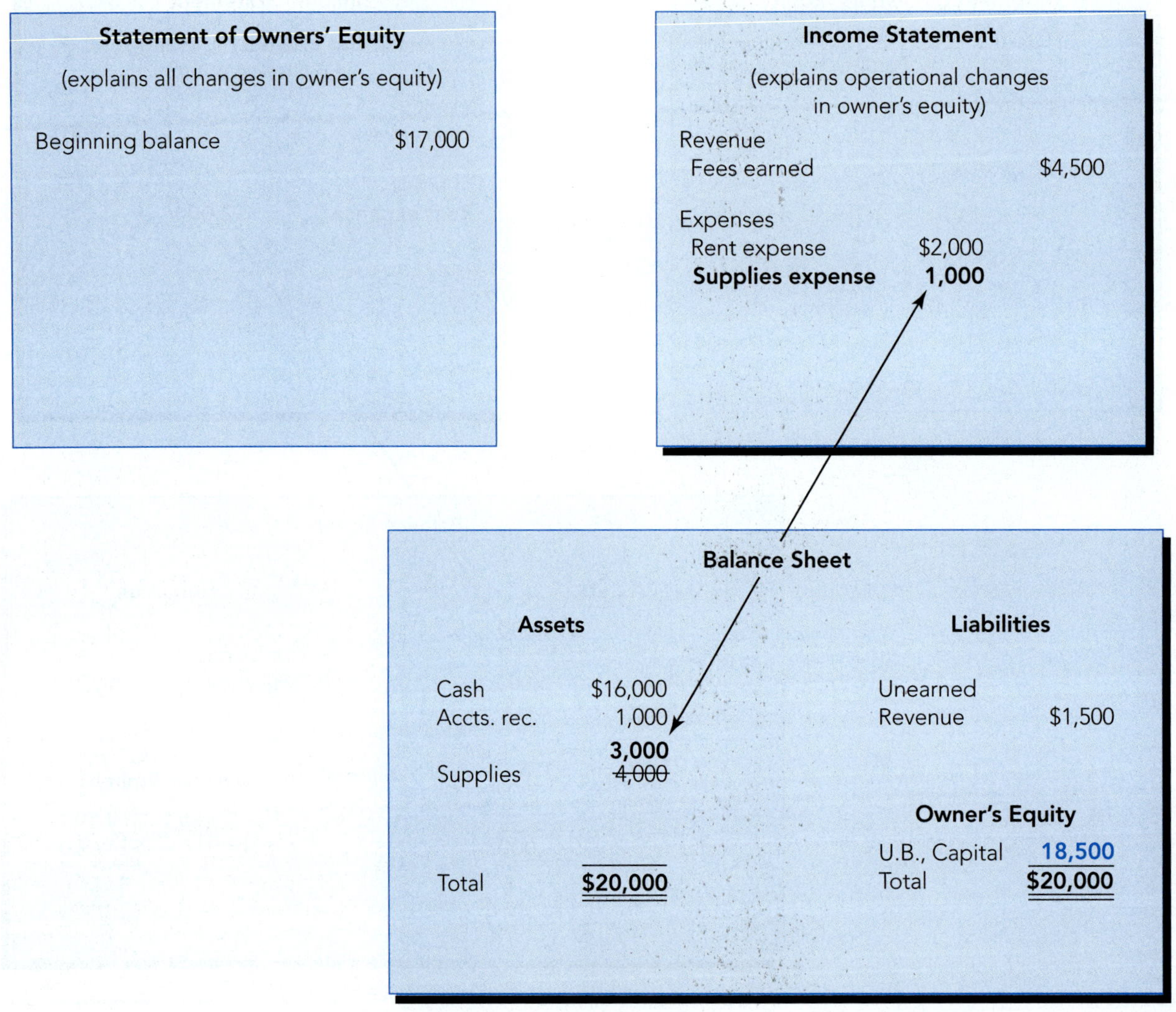

Using the Equation

The equation would show the changes as:

$$\downarrow A = L + \downarrow OE$$

Detailed Examples of Owner's Equity Connections, *continued*

Expense Increases Accounts Payable

The final expense of the day occurs when the business uses a consulting firm to help improve efficiency after the business had a problem with a delivery. The consulting firm sends a bill for $2,000 that will be paid next week. This is an expense on the income statement, which also causes accounts Payable to increase. On the balance sheet, this liability increase is not connected with any other asset or liability, so owner's equity also decreases by $2,000 to $16,500.

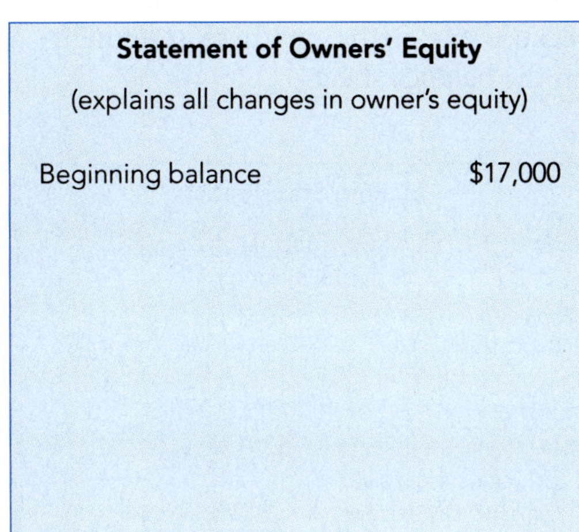

Statement of Owners' Equity

(explains all changes in owner's equity)

Beginning balance	$17,000

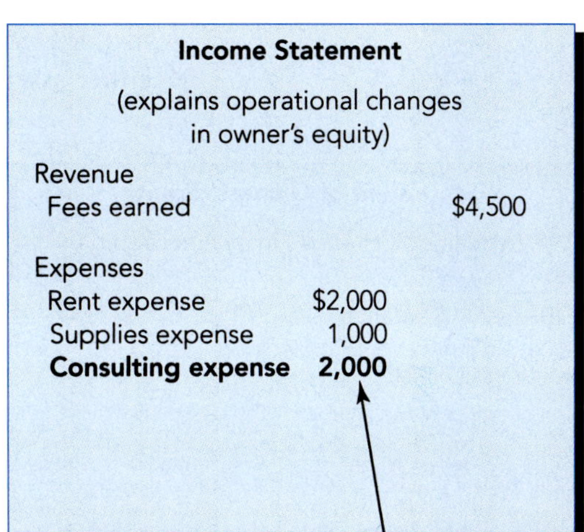

Income Statement

(explains operational changes in owner's equity)

Revenue		
Fees earned		$4,500
Expenses		
Rent expense	$2,000	
Supplies expense	1,000	
Consulting expense	**2,000**	

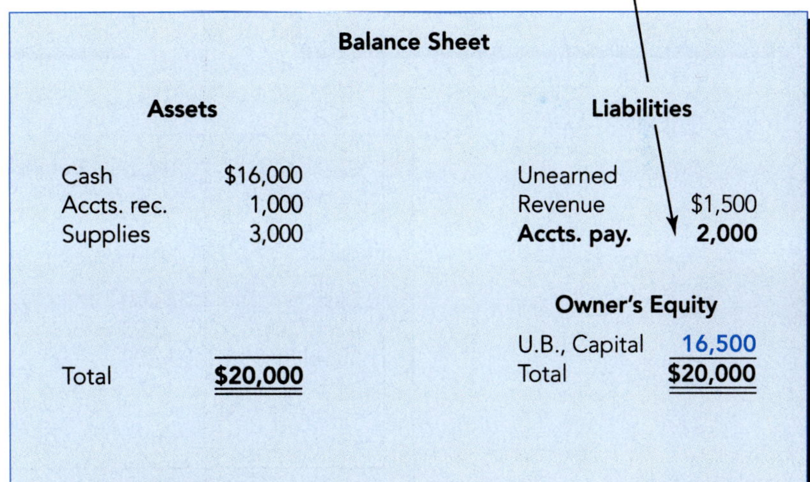

Balance Sheet

Assets		Liabilities	
Cash	$16,000	Unearned Revenue	$1,500
Accts. rec.	1,000	**Accts. pay.**	**2,000**
Supplies	3,000		
		Owner's Equity	
		U.B., Capital	16,500
Total	**$20,000**	Total	**$20,000**

Using the Equation

The equation would show the changes as:

$$A = \uparrow L + \downarrow OE$$

continued ▶

Detailed Examples of Owner's Equity Connections, *continued*

Final Result

The final result of all the income statement (operational) transactions is a $500 net loss that is also recorded on the statement of owner's equity. It shows the reduction in owner's equity to a balance of $16,500. This can be verified on the balance sheet by subtracting total liabilities of $3,500 from total assets of $20,000.

On the balance sheet, you can see how the $16,500 of owner's equity, U.B. Capital, has been explained by the income statement and statement of owner's equity. This is because the items on these statements affected either assets or liabilities on the balance sheet.

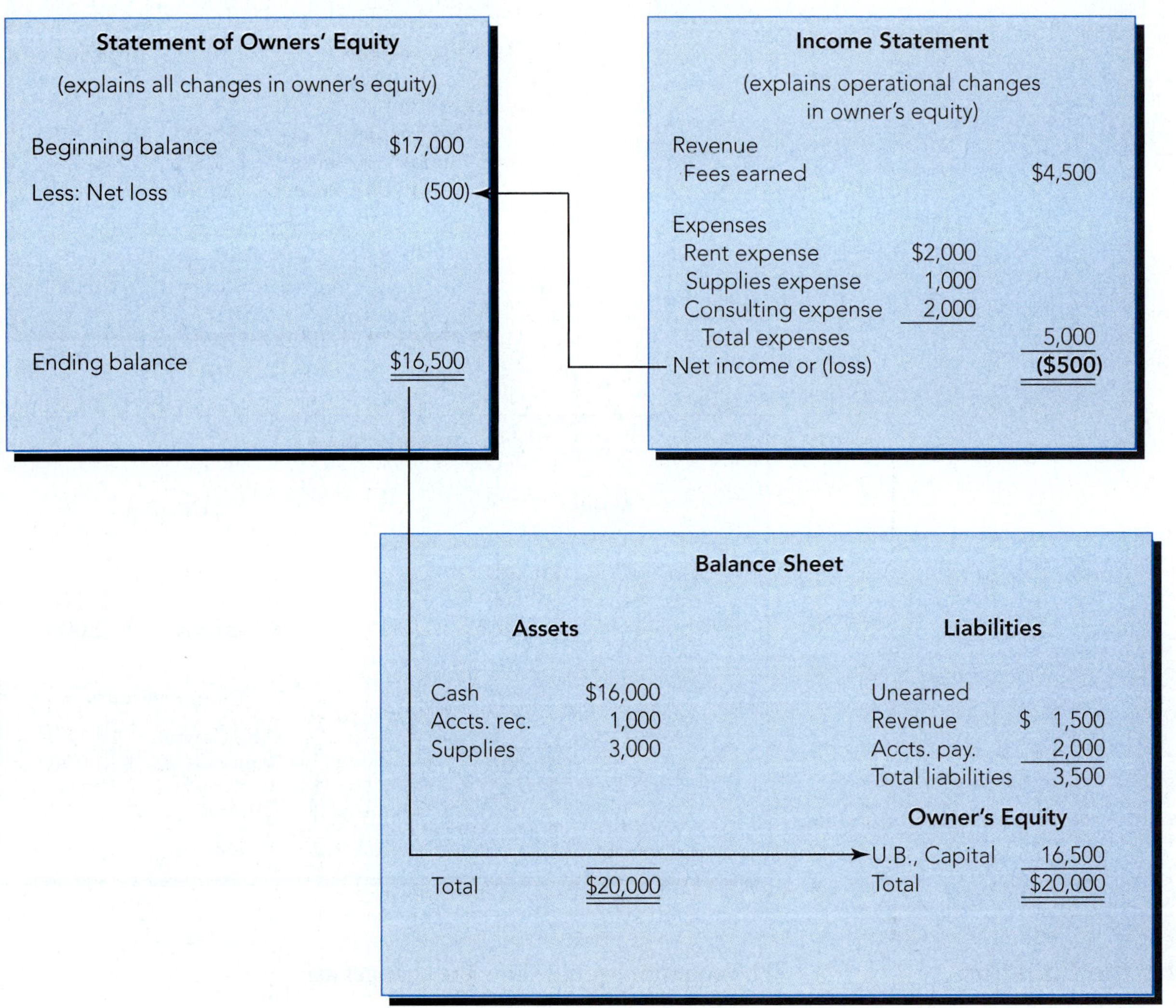

Detailed Examples of Owner's Equity Connections, *continued*

Balance Sheet Effects of Statement of Owner's Equity Items

These last two transactions are specific to the statement of owner's equity: the owner's investments and withdrawals. These transactions directly affect both the statement of owner's equity and the balance sheet, but they do not affect the income statement. The typical balance sheet effects are:

- **Investments increase owner's equity and . . .**
  - Increase cash
  - Increase other assets
- **Withdrawals decrease owner's equity and . . .**
  - Decrease cash
  - Decrease other assets

  Note: Investments and withdrawals can also affect liabilities. For example, an owner could pay business debts with her own personal cash. This is an owner's investment that decreases liabilities and increases owner's equity. However, because these are not typical transactions, we do not illustrate them here.

continued 

Detailed Examples of Owner's Equity Connections, *continued*

Owner's Investment Increases Cash

Returning to Uncle Billy's Courier Service, suppose that on the morning of December 23, Uncle Billy made a $5,000 cash investment into the business. This increases cash on the balance sheet and is also shown as a statement of owner's equity item. On the balance sheet owner's equity increases to $21,500.

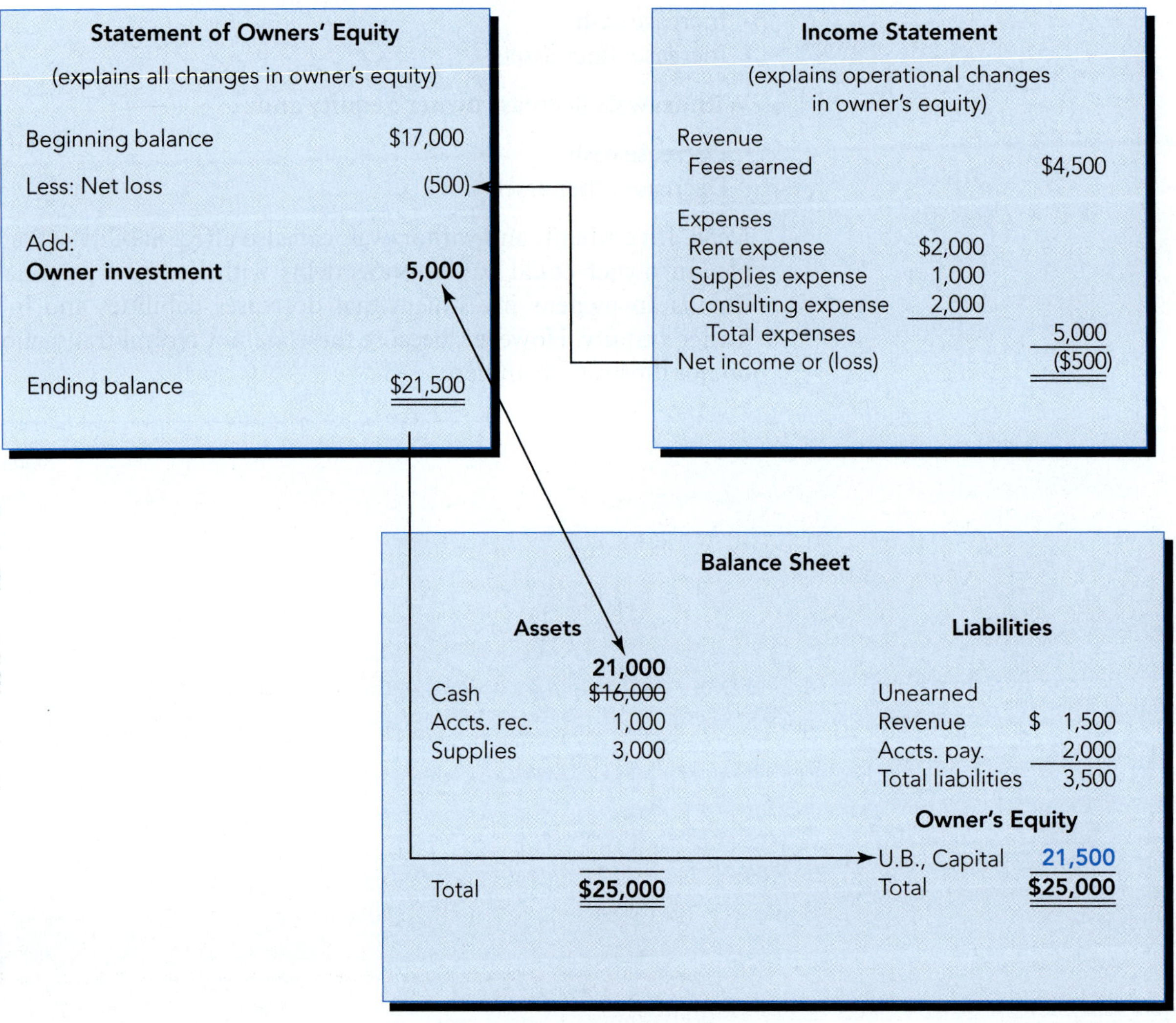

Statement of Owners' Equity
(explains all changes in owner's equity)
Beginning balance $17,000
Less: Net loss (500)
Add:
Owner investment 5,000
Ending balance $21,500
Income Statement
(explains operational changes in owner's equity)
Revenue
Fees earned $4,500
Expenses
Rent expense $2,000
Supplies expense 1,000
Consulting expense 2,000
Total expenses 5,000
Net income or (loss) ($500)
Balance Sheet
Assets
Cash 21,000 $16,000
Accts. rec. 1,000
Supplies 3,000
Total $25,000
Liabilities
Unearned Revenue $ 1,500
Accts. pay. 2,000
Total liabilities 3,500
Owner's Equity
U.B., Capital 21,500
Total $25,000

Using the Equation

The equation would show the changes as:

$$\uparrow A = L + \uparrow OE$$

Detailed Examples of Owner's Equity Connections, *continued*

Owner's Withdrawal Decreases Cash

Finally, suppose that in the afternoon (quite a busy day), Uncle Billy decides that he needs $1,000 for personal reasons and withdraws the money from his business. On the balance sheet, this reduces cash and causes a decrease in the owner's equity, U.B., Capital.

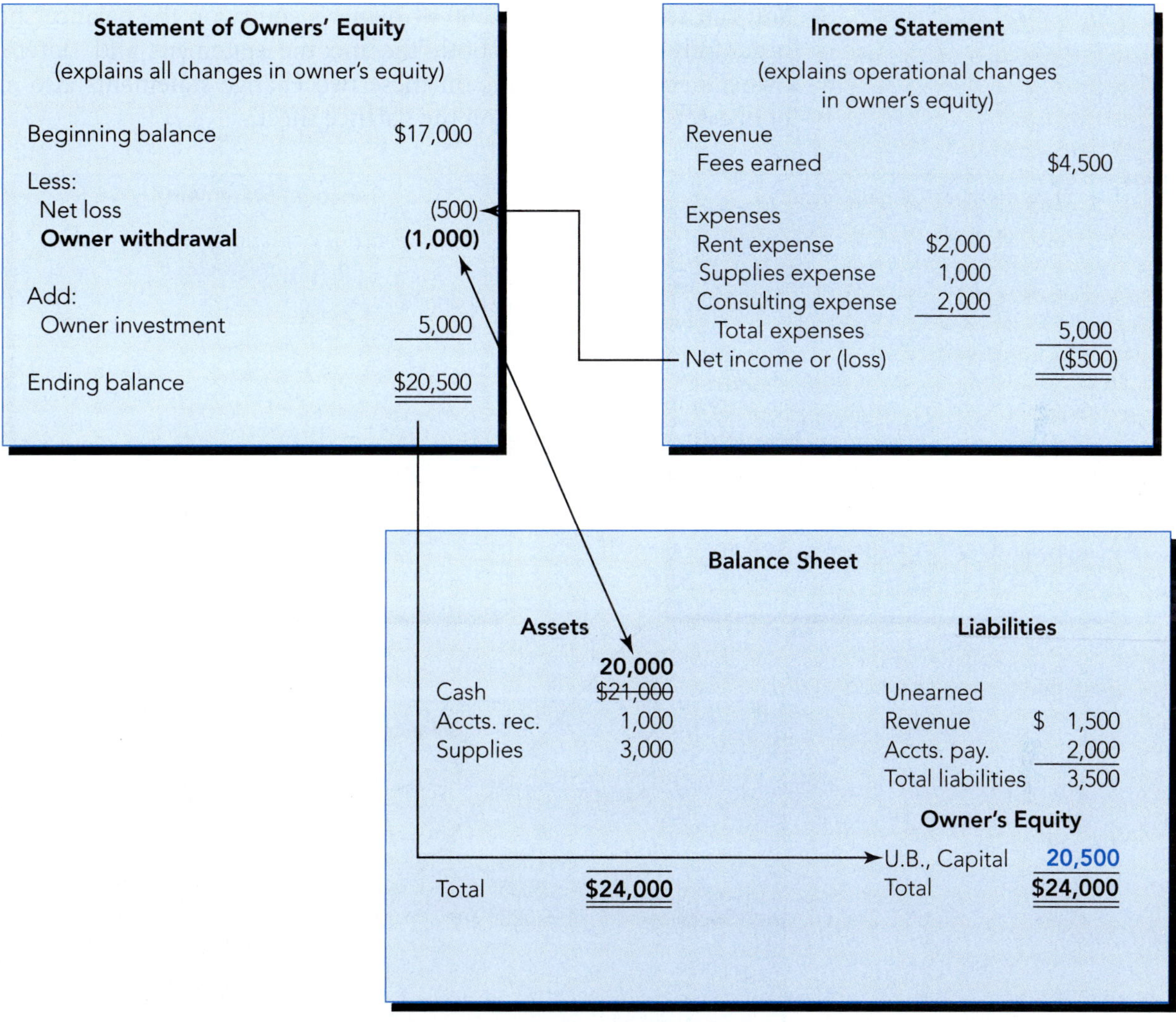

Using the Equation

The equation would show the changes as:

$$\downarrow A = L + \downarrow OE$$

continued ►

Detailed Examples of Owner's Equity Connections, *continued*

Final Result

The result of the owner's investment and withdrawal actions is a $4,000 net increase in owner's equity to a final balance of $20,500. You can verify this on the balance sheet by subtracting the total liabilities of $3,500 from the total assets of $24,000.

You can see how the $20,500 of owner's equity on the balance sheet has been fully explained by both the income statement and statement of owner's equity. The items on these two change statements also affected both assets and liabilities on the balance sheet.

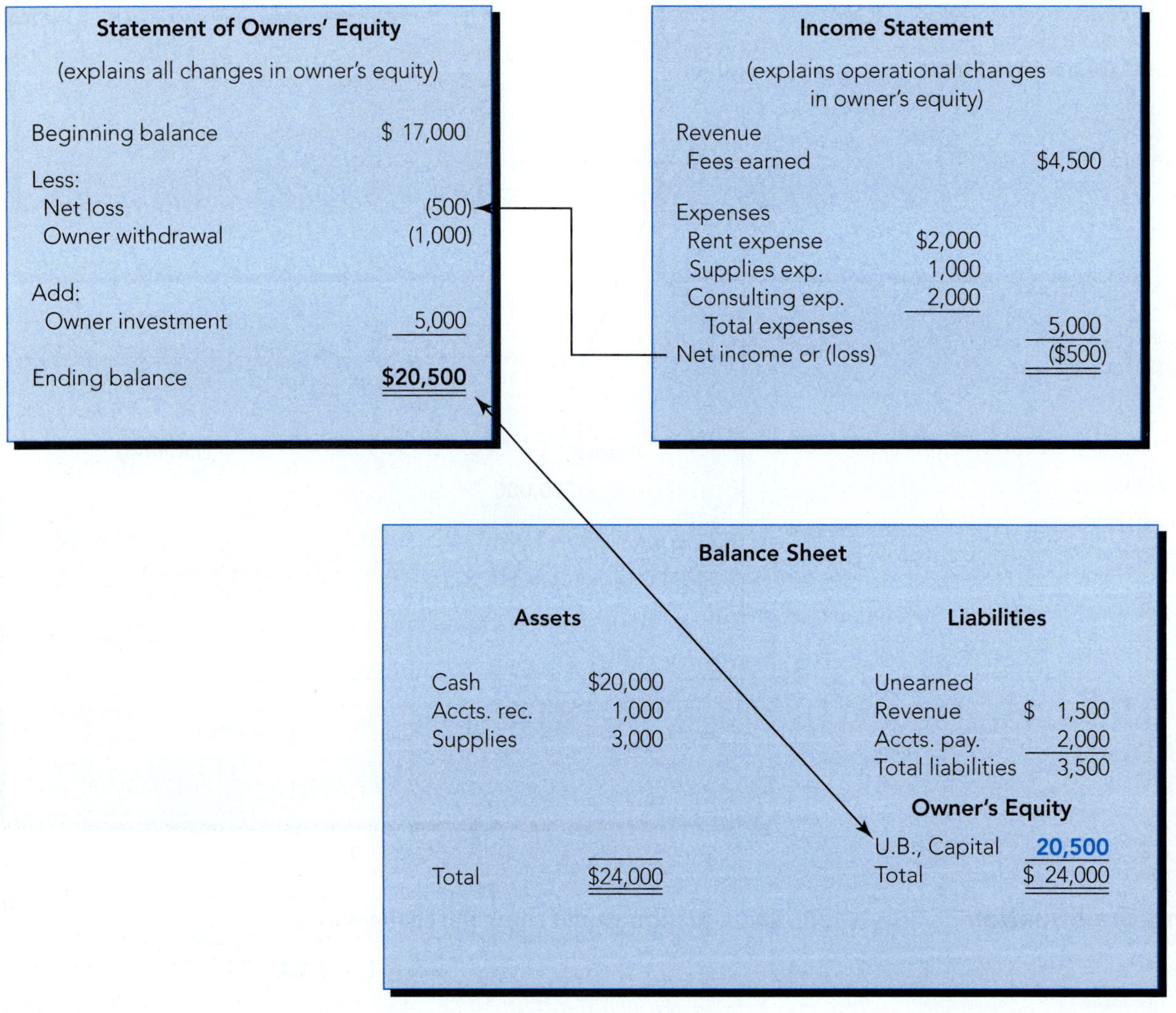

Detailed Examples of Owner's Equity Connections, *continued*

Summary

What you have seen are accurate, but simplified, examples of how individual owner's equity transactions connect three financial statements. But keep in mind that in "real life":

- Individual transaction data are never entered directly onto financial statements, as we did here. Instead, the data are first recorded and classified in special accounting records over a period of time. Then the data are summarized, and the summary totals are placed on the financial statements. In the next section, you will begin to do this for yourself.
- Financial statements are never prepared "moment by moment" for each individual transaction as we did here. This would be impossible and totally unnecessary (actually, crazy). Financial statements are normally prepared at useful intervals such as monthly, quarterly, or annually.

However, you would be perfectly correct to say that the summary totals used on financial statements consist of many individual transactions, and some of them are owner's equity transactions that form connections between the statements, as you have seen here.

Analyze, Don't Just Memorize

Occasionally students ask this question: "Will you please just draw a picture of an income statement, statement of owner's equity, and balance sheet and then draw lines to show all the kinds of transactions that create links between the statements? Then we can memorize how all the items connect the statements."

I would love to do that. However, a really complete and accurate picture would be very confusing. There are so many different potential transactions connecting these statements that the picture would have lines going everywhere. It would look like a spaghetti dinner!

A much better idea is this:

1. *Learn the relationships between the statements*. This is what we have just finished doing. The illustration on page 334 and the table on the next page summarize these relationships.
2. *Learn to analyze each transaction.* This is what we did in Learning Goal 11. If you can analyze a transaction, you will be much clearer about its effects on the financial statements. You will not have to do much memorizing.

continued ▶

Detailed Examples of Owner's Equity Connections, *continued*

Summary Table

The following table summarizes how owner's equity transactions shown on the income statement and statement of owner's equity affect the balance sheet.

<table>
<tr><th colspan="2">Change Statement</th><th colspan="2">Balance Sheet</th></tr>
<tr><th>Income Statement</th><th>Statement of Owner's Equity</th><th>Effect</th><th>Example</th></tr>
<tr><td colspan="4">OWNER'S EQUITY IS INCREASED</td></tr>
<tr><td rowspan="2">Revenue</td><td rowspan="2">Owner Investment</td><td>Assets ↑
or</td><td>▪ Cash or A/R received when services are performed. (Revenue)
▪ Owner invests cash in the business. (Owner investment)</td></tr>
<tr><td>Liabilities ↓</td><td>▪ Unearned revenue decreases when services are performed. (Revenue)
▪ Owner personally pays business debts. (Owner investment)</td></tr>
<tr><td colspan="4">OWNER'S EQUITY IS DECREASED</td></tr>
<tr><td rowspan="2">Expense</td><td rowspan="2">Owner Withdrawal</td><td>Assets ↓
or</td><td>▪ Cash is used to pay for repairs when completed. (Expense)
▪ Supplies are used up. (Expense)
▪ Owner takes cash from the business. (Owner withdrawal)</td></tr>
<tr><td>Liabilities ↑</td><td>▪ Repairs are done but will be paid later. (Expense)
▪ Business incurs debt, but owner keeps the money. (Withdrawal—rare)</td></tr>
</table>

Could Other Change Statements be Created?

Sure! In addition to only explaining the changes in owner's equity (income statement and statement of owner's equity) and cash (statement of cash flows), you could design a statement to explain the changes in any other balance sheet item, such as Accounts Receivable, Inventory, Notes Payable, and so on. In fact, many companies keep informal internal records analyzing the changes in many balance sheet items (for example, Accounts Receivable and Inventory). However, these records are not prepared as formal financial statements because of time, cost, and other considerations.

Detailed Examples of Owner's Equity Connections, *continued*

Which statement should you prepare first? It is best to prepare the financial statements in the following order:

1. *Income statement*—because net income is used in the statement of owner's equity
2. *Statement of owner's equity*—because the ending balance of owner's equity is the owner's equity on the balance sheet
3. *Balance sheet*—because balance sheets are needed to prepare the statement of cash flows
4. *Statement of cash flows*

QUICK REVIEW

- There are four general-purpose financial statements:
  - Income statement
  - Statement of owner's equity
  - Balance sheet
  - Statement of cash flows
- The balance sheet is a statement of condition at a point in time. The other statements are all "change" statements. They summarize the kinds of transactions that caused changes in either the cash balance or the owner's equity balance on the balance sheet.
- Because the change statements explain the differences between two balance sheets, the change statements can be viewed as the "links" between one balance sheet and the next.
- The connection between a change statement and any other financial statement is called "articulation."
- The kinds of transactions that create connections from a prior capital balance to the next capital balance are:
  - Revenues
  - Expenses
  - Investments
  - Withdrawals

PRACTICE Learning Goal 17

Solutions are in the disk at the back of the book and at: www.worthyjames.com

Learning Goal 17 is about comparing, contrasting, and connecting financial statements. Use these questions and problems to practice what you have learned.

Multiple Choice

Select the best answer.

1. If revenue of $1,000 is earned and received in cash, then
   a. assets will increase and revenue will appear on the statement of owner's equity.
   b. assets will decrease and revenue will appear on the statement of owner's equity.
   c. assets will decrease and expense will appear on the statement of owner's equity.
   d. assets will increase and revenue will appear on the income statement.
2. If the owner withdraws $1,000 in cash, then
   a. assets will decrease and expense will appear on the statement of owner's equity.
   b. assets will decrease and revenue will appear on the statement of owner's equity.
   c. assets will decrease and drawing will appear on the statement of owner's equity.
   d. assets will decrease and drawing will appear on the income statement.
3. An income statement
   a. details all the changes in owner's equity.
   b. shows total assets, liabilities, and owner's equity.
   c. shows the revenues and expenses at a specific date.
   d. none of the above.
4. If a telephone expense of $500 appears on the income statement, then
   a. assets have decreased and expenses will appear on the statement of owner's equity.
   b. either assets have increased and/or liabilities have decreased.
   c. either assets have decreased and/or liabilities have increased.
   d. none of the above.
5. If Service Fees Earned of $10,000 appears on the income statement, then
   a. assets have increased and expenses will decrease on the income statement.
   b. either assets have increased and/or liabilities have decreased.
   c. either assets have decreased and/or liabilities have increased.
   d. none of the above.
6. Four kinds of transactions affect owner's equity, but the statement of owner's equity only shows three change items: (1) net income/(loss); (2) owner's investments; and (3) owner's drawings. This is because
   a. owner's drawings need to be considered as an expense.
   b. owner's investments are never counted as a change.
   c. showing four changes would be an overstatement.
   d. the revenues and expenses are combined into one number.
7. If accounts receivable have increased by $1,500, then most likely
   a. the owner has invested in the business.
   b. revenue has been earned.
   c. expenses have been incurred.
   d. none of the above.

PRACTICE **Learning Goal 17, continued**

Solutions are in the disk at the back of the book and at: www.worthyjames.com

8. One balance sheet prepared on March 31 is linked by the other financial statements to the next balance sheet prepared on April 30 because
   a. the statement of cash flows for April explains the difference between the two cash balances.
   b. revenues and expenses on the April income statement affect the owner's equity on the balance sheet.
   c. the drawings and owner investments on the April statement of owner's equity affect the owner's equity on the balance sheet.
   d. all of the above.
9. The Mikado Tea Shop income statement for the month of October shows a net loss of $14,000. There were no withdrawals or investments. Which of the following is *not* true?
   a. The statement of owner's equity will show a decrease item of $14,000.
   b. Total assets on the balance sheet have decreased and/or total liabilities have increased.
   c. Expenses have exceeded revenues.
   d. The change in the cash balance can be determined from this information.
10. The statement of cash flows is primarily
    a. a statement of condition.
    b. a statement of equity.
    c. a statement of change.
    d. none of the above.
11. The three types of activities that change the cash balance are
    a. operating, investing, and withdrawing.
    b. operating, recording, and financing.
    c. operating, investing, and financing.
    d. none of the above.
12. You are interested in investing in a company. Which financial statement(s) would you use to analyze the profitability of the company?
    a. statement of owner's equity or statement of cash flows
    b. statement of owner's equity and income statement
    c. income statement
    d. balance sheet
13. You are a supplier of auto parts. Kansas City Company wants to make a large purchase from you on account, with payment in 30 days. Which financial statement(s) would you use to find out how much debt Kansas City Company already has coming due in the near future and how much available cash it has?
    a. statement of cash flows
    b. statement of owner's equity and income statement
    c. income statement
    d. balance sheet
14. Financial statements are usually prepared in the following order:
    a. balance sheet, income statement, statement of cash flows, owner's equity statement
    b. income statement, balance sheet, statement of cash flows, owner's equity statement
    c. income statement, owner's equity statement, balance sheet, statement of cash flows
    d. The order varies among accountants.

PRACTICE Learning Goal 17, continued

Solutions are in the disk at the back of the book and at: www.worthyjames.com

15. On an income statement, the net loss is $7,000 and total expenses are $50,000. Total revenue
    a. is $43,000.
    b. is $57,000.
    c. is greater than $57,000.
    d. cannot be determined with this information.
16. On the statement of owner's equity for Pettigrew Company, the ending balance of owner's equity is $90,000, the net loss was $10,000, owner's drawings were $12,000, and the owner's investment was $5,000. What is the beginning balance of owner's equity?
    a. $107,000
    b. $100,000
    c. $73,000
    d. none of the above
17. During the month of October, total assets of Macon Company increased by $50,000 and total liabilities increased by $30,000. If the owner had invested $5,000 but did not withdraw anything, the income statement will show
    a. a net income of $15,000.
    b. a net income of $20,000.
    c. a net loss of $20,000.
    d. a net income of $80,000.
18. A balance sheet is often called a(n)
    a. statement of cash flows.
    b. P & L statement.
    c. statement of position.
    d. operating statement.
19. The financial statements that show change in a business are
    a. the balance sheet, the income statement, and the statement of owner's equity.
    b. the balance sheet, the income statement, and the statement of cash flows.
    c. the income statement, statement of owner's equity, and the statement of cash flows.
    d. the income statement and the balance sheet.
20. Which financial statement is similar to a "flash photograph" of a business?
    a. the balance sheet
    b. the income statement
    c. the statement of cash flows
    d. the statement of owner's equity

Discussion Questions and Brief Exercises for Learning Goals 12–17

1. What is the correct format for writing a title to a financial statement?

2. Explain how the date should be written for each of these financial statements: income statement, statement of owner's equity, and balance sheet. Give examples for the year that ends on December 31, 2017.

3. What are the two categories of items that appear on an income statement? Explain what they mean.

PRACTICE Learning Goal 17, continued

Solutions are in the disk at the back of the book and at: www.worthyjames.com

4. What are the three categories of items that appear on a balance sheet? Explain what they mean.

5. What is the purpose of an income statement? What does it explain?

6. What is the purpose of a statement of owner's equity? What does it explain?

7. What is the purpose of a balance sheet? What does it explain?

8. What is the purpose of a statement of cash flows? What does it explain?

9. Your study group partner Rasheed Marshall is preparing for an exam in another accounting class. He wants to make sure that he understands how the income statement, statement of owner's equity, and balance sheet relate to each other, and if some of the numbers on one statement appear on other statements. What would you say to him in the study group?

10. Fall River Consulting Services Company finished a job for a client, who paid the company $5,000 as soon as the job was completed. What are the two effects on the income statement, the two effects on the statement of owner's equity, and the two effects on the balance sheet?

11. Lowell Internet Services Company used up $900 of supplies in its operations during the month of June. What are the two effects on the income statement, the two effects on the statement of owner's equity, and the two effects on the balance sheet?

12. On September 30, month-end, the owner's equity on the balance sheet of Worcester Company was $250,000. The statement of owner's equity showed a September 1 balance of $259,000. The owner withdrew $15,000 cash during the month but made no investments. What is the net income that should appear on the income statement?

13. Which of the following would be a "change statement"? Which would be a "condition statement"? (1) balance sheet, (2) income statement, (3) statement of cash flows, (4) or statement of owner's equity.

14. Identify four important qualities of information on financial statements. Which two are most important?

PRACTICE Learning Goal 17, continued

Solutions are in the disk at the back of the book and at: www.worthyjames.com

Reinforcement Problems

LG 17-1. Which statement is it on? Use a blank sheet of paper to complete the table. The following table shows items that occur in the four financial statements. Place a "✓" in the correct space to identify which financial statement the item appears on. The financial statements are for the month ending May 31 and the condition as of May 31 of the Bill Jones Company. Use the first item as an example.

Item	Balance Sheet	Income Statement	Statement of Owner's Equity	Statement of Cash Flows
Office Supplies	✓			
Service Revenue	**(Reminder: Use a separate sheet of paper to complete the table.)**			
Accounts Payable				
Net Loss				
Withdrawals (Drawing)				
Financing Activities				
Bill Jones, Capital—May 31				
Wages Expense				
Net Income				
Accounts Receivable				
Operating Activities				
Investing Activities				
Rent Expense				
Bill Jones, Capital—May 1				
Unearned Revenue				
Wages Payable				
Cash				
Prepaid Rent Expense				

PRACTICE Learning Goal 17, continued

Solutions are in the disk at the back of the book and at: www.worthyjames.com

LG 17-2. Prepare financial statements. Using the financial information below for the Capistrano Company, prepare an income statement and statement of owner's equity in good form for the year ended December 31, 2017 and an account form balance sheet in good form as of December 31, 2017. The owner, John Hood, withdrew $20,000 of cash during the year.

Wages expense	$112,300	Capital, January 1	$316,490
Owner investments	5,500	Unearned revenue	27,500
Cash	114,310	Travel expense	2,600
Prepaid rentexpense	2,000	Accounts receivable	9,450
Service revenue	275,450	Utilities expense	880
Office equipment	98,500	Notes payable	50,000
Land	310,500	Rent expense	24,000
Accounts payable	19,600		

LG 17-3. Review: Identify which transactions affect owner's equity. Use a separate sheet of paper to complete the table. In the table below, indicate whether each transaction increases owner's equity (**+**), decreases owner's equity (**–**), or has no effect on owner's equity (**NE**). Use the first transaction as an example.

Transaction	Effect
a. The owner invests $7,500 in his business.	+
b. The business earns service revenue and receives $500 cash.	**(Reminder: Use a separate sheet of paper to complete the table.)**
c. The business buys $100 of office supplies on account.	
d. The business buys $2,000 of equipment for cash.	
e. The business pays rent expense of $1,500.	
f. The business earns service revenue for $1,000 on account (accounts receivable).	
g. The business pays the $100 account payable for the purchases of supplies.	
h. The owner withdraws $200 cash.	
i. The business collects $1,000 cash from the account receivable.	

PRACTICE **Learning Goal 17, continued**

Solutions are in the disk at the back of the book and at: www.worthyjames.com

LG 17-4. Explain the effects of transactions on financial statements.

a. Place the dollar amount of each transaction in the correct location(s) in the table on page 345 to show how each financial statement will be affected by each transaction. To show negative amounts on the balance sheet, statement of owner's equity, and statement of cash flows, place amounts in parentheses ( ).
b. Total the balance sheet asset and liability columns to verify the correct final balance of owner's equity. Use the owner's equity column in the balance sheet only after you compute the final balance from the statement of owner's equity (item 16).
c. Total the income statement columns to verify the amount of net income.
d. Total the statement of cash flow columns to calculate the net change in the cash balance.

Suggestion: You may want to practice this problem more than once. Make a copy of the table on page 345 or use the blank worksheet template in the disk at the back of the book.

Transactions:

(1) The owner invests $40,000 cash in her new business.
(2) $1,800 of supplies were purchased and the bill will be paid later.
(3) The business paid $1,100 for a one-year insurance policy.
(4) The business performed $3,300 of services for a client on account.
(5) A client makes an advance payment of $2,850.
(6) The business performed $1,650 of services for a client, and the client paid cash.
(7) The business received a $700 bill for repairs expense. The bill will be paid later.
(8) A $200 bill for telephone expense is received and is paid immediately.
(9) $820 of supplies are used up.
(10) The owner withdraws $2,100 cash.
(11) The business collects $1,700 from customers on account.
(12) The business performed services and earned 40% of the advance payment received in (5).
(13) The repair bill in (7) is paid.
(14) Employee wages for the month are $3,100 and are not paid immediately.
(15) At the end of the period, the net income is determined to be $1,270.
(16) The final balance of owner's equity is calculated from the statement of owner's equity, and this amount is placed on the balance sheet.

PRACTICE Learning Goal 17, continued

Solutions are in the disk at the back of the book and at: www.worthyjames.com

LG 17-4, *continued*

	Balance Sheet			Income Statement		Statement of Owner's Equity		Statement of Cash Flows	
	Asset	Liability	Owner's Equity	Revenue	Expense	Net Income/ Investment	(Net Loss/ Withdrawal)	Source of Cash	(Use of Cash)
(1)									
(2)									
(3)									
(4)									
(5)									
(6)									
(7)									
(8)									
(9)									
(10)									
(11)									
(12)									
(13)									
(14)									
(15)									
(16)									

PRACTICE **Learning Goal 17, continued**

Solutions are in the disk at the back of the book and at: www.worthyjames.com

LG 17-5. You be the teacher—grade the financial statements! You have just given a weekly quiz and asked the students to prepare financial statements for the month of November 2017. Here is a paper from one of your students who has just taken the quiz. Each mistake is minus one point. The three statements together are worth 30 points. Grade the exam. What score would you give? (Mistakes are from actual exams.)

Moorpark Repair Services
Balance Sheet
November 30, 2017

Assets		**Debts**	
Cash	$10,540	Accounts payable	$ 2,000
Equipment	$15,440	Wages payable	$540
Supplies	$95	Total	$ 2,540
Accounts receivable	$1,050		
		Owner's Equity	
		Diane Smith, Capitol	$24,485
Total	$27,385	Total liabilities and owner's equity	$27,385

Moorpark Repair Services
Income Statement
November 30, 2017

Revenues		
Service revenues	$44,200	
Unearned revenues	3,500	
Total revenues		47,700
Expenses		
Wages expense	$24,100	
Rent expense	4,950	
Prepaid expenses	4,100	
Telephone expenses	290	
Total expenses		33,440
Profit		$14,260

Moorpark Repair Services
Statement of Owner's Equity
For the Period Ending November 30, 2017

Diane Smith, Capital, November 1		$ 6,325
Add: Owner investment	$ 5,000	
Net income	14,620	
		19,620
Less: Withdrawals		1,000
Diane Smith, Capital, November 30		$24,945

PRACTICE Learning Goal 17, continued

Solutions are in the disk at the back of the book and at: www.worthyjames.com

LG 17-6. Calculate missing financial statement balances using information from other financial statements. For each of the four separate businesses below, calculate the missing amounts for 2017 on a separate piece of paper.

	Mheta Tarsal Medical School	Lynne Guinni Cooking College	Pop Flies Baseball Clinic	Manuel Dexterity Acting Academy
JANUARY 1, 2017				
Assets	$ 75,000	$100,000	g. ________	$120,000
Liabilities	$ 15,000	$ 20,000	$ 15,000	j. ________
Owner's Equity	a. ________	d. ________	h. ________	k. ________
DECEMBER 31, 2017				
Assets	$120,000	$112,000	$ 51,000	l. ________
Liabilities	$ 40,000	e. ________	$ 1,000	$ 50,000
Owner's Equity	b. ________	f. ________	i. ________	$ 22,000
CHANGE IN OWNER'S EQUITY DURING 2017				
Owner Investment	c. ________	$ 12,000	$ –0–	$ 10,000
Revenues	$ 52,000	$ 82,000	$ 49,000	$ 98,000
Expenses	$ 35,000	$ 71,000	$ 22,000	$178,000
Withdrawals	$ 5,000	$ 3,000	$ 8,000	$ –0–

LG 17-7. Prepare financial statements. Using the information below for the Wendy Monahan Real Estate Company, prepare an income statement and statement of owner's equity for the year ended December 31, 20XX, and a report form balance sheet as of December 31, 20XX.

Computer Equipment	$9,000	Service Revenue	$221,800
Unearned Revenue	3,200	Wages Payable	7,500
Office Furniture	5,750	Rent Expense	24,000
Notes Payable	25,000	Prepaid Insurance	3,660
Insurance Expense	780	Wages Expense	108,000
Land	185,200	Wendy Monahan, Withdrawals	55,000
Accounts Payable	24,220	Interest Expense	2,100
Office Supplies	2,000	Accounts Receivable	47,500
Cash	37,100	Telephone Expense	2,450
Travel Expense	650		
Wendy Monahan Capital, January 1	183,470	During the year the owner made an $18,000 investment in the business.	

PRACTICE   Learning Goal 17, continued

Solutions are in the disk at the back of the book and at: www.worthyjames.com

LG 17-8. Prepare financial statements—use them for a decision. Robert Jimenez started his real estate sales business on January 1, 2017 with an investment of $10,000. At year-end on December 31, 2017, Robert gives you a listing of the assets and liabilities as well as the revenues and expenses for the year. Robert withdrew $17,000 during the year. On a separate piece of paper, prepare an income statement and statement of owner's equity for the year ended December 31, 2017, and a balance sheet as of December 31, 2017 in good form.

Robert wants to take the financial statements to his bank to apply for a business loan, but he isn't sure what the loan officer will think of them. Based on the information in the financial statements, do you think that Robert's business will be able to borrow money? How much do you think you would lend Robert if you were the banker?

Cash	$38,000	Unearned Fees Revenue	$3,800
Notes Payable	10,000	Travel Expense	2,050
Accounts Receivable	12,000	Accounts Payable	1,150
Fees Earned	84,000	Utilities Expense	1,000
Prepaid Insurance Expense	2,500	Insurance Expense	3,000
Rent Expense	18,400	Equipment	15,000

LG 17-9. Prepare financial statements and determine missing item on the statement of owner's equity. Listed below are amounts of various financial statement items for the Sanderson Ecology Services Company. From the amounts listed, prepare an income statement and a statement of owner's equity for the year ended December 31, 2017 and a balance sheet as of year-end. Dave Sanderson opened the firm with an investment of $250,000 on January 1. He cannot remember the amount of his drawings. Please tell him.

Service Fees	$122,500	Cash	$199,300
Wages Expense	104,300	Accounts Receivable	43,080
Rent Expense	16,500	Supplies	3,800
Utilities Expense	1,400	Office Equipment	25,600
Supplies Expense	750	Prepaid Insurance	1,500
Advertising Expense	3,300	Accounts Payable	23,750
Travel Expense	8,150	Unearned Service Fees	12,300

PRACTICE Learning Goal 17, continued

Solutions are in the disk at the back of the book and at: www.worthyjames.com

LG 17-10. Calculate missing information and determine the owner's equity. When the Traverse City Company had a fire in its office, some of the information on its December 31, 2016 and December 31, 2017 balance sheets was destroyed. The bookkeeper summarized all the information like this:

December 31, 2016	
Cash	$25,000
Accounts Receivable	$12,000
Supplies	$4,000
Equipment	$40,000
Accounts Payable	$5,000
J. Dunfield, Capital	?

December 31, 2017	
Cash	$39,000
Accounts Receivable	?
Supplies	$5,000
Equipment	$41,000
Accounts Payable	$20,000
J. Dunfield, Capital	?

The income statements were destroyed, but the owner remembered that the net income for 2016 was $15,000, and for 2017 was $17,000. There were no other changes to owner's equity. The owner hopes that you can fill in the missing information. Can you help the owner?

LG 17-11. Classification, valuation, and timing. (See Learning Goal 10 if you wish to review this topic). In Learning Goal 10, we emphasized the importance of correctly analyzing the classification, valuation, and timing of every event that affects the accounting equation. Apply your knowledge by answering the following questions:

a. For Uncle Billy's Courier Service, refer to the supplies transaction on page 328 and the completed financial statements on page 334.
   (1) How was correct classification important in this transaction? How would the financial statements have been affected if either item in the transaction had not been classified correctly? List some possible misclassifications.
   (2) Suppose that a valuation error had been made and that the amount of supplies used had been mistakenly valued as $3,000. How would the financial statements have been affected?
   (3) What would have happened to the financial statements if the supplies had been intentionally reported as being used in January instead of when they were actually used in December? Is this primarily an issue of classification, valuation, or timing?

b. Refer to the owner's investment transaction on page 332 and the completed financial statements on page 334. Assume that the investment transaction had intentionally been recorded as $15,000 of Fees Earned. What would the effect be on the financial statements? Which element(s) is (are) involved: classification, valuation, or timing?

PRACTICE Learning Goal 17, continued

Instructor-Assigned Problems

If you are using this book in a class, these review problems may be assigned by your instructor for homework, group assignments, class work, or other activities. Only your instructor has the solutions.

IA17-1. Connect transactions to financial statements

a. Place the dollar amount of each transaction in the correct location(s) in the table on page 352 to show how each financial statement would be affected by each transaction. To show negative amounts on the balance sheet, statement of owner's equity, and statement of cash flows, place amounts in parentheses ( ).
b. Use the balance sheet asset and liability column totals to verify the correct final balance of owner's equity. Enter an amount in the balance sheet owner's equity column only as a total after you compute the final balance from the columns for the statement of owner's equity. (item 16).
c. Total the income statement columns to verify the amount of net income.
d. Total the statement of cash flow columns to calculate the net change in the cash balance.

To complete the problem, first make a copy of the table on page 352 or print out a blank worksheet from the disk at the back of the book.

Transactions:

(1) $500 of supplies are used up.
(2) The business collected $2,100 from customers on account.
(3) The business performed $5,000 of services for a client on account.
(4) The owner invested $20,000 in the business.
(5) $750 of supplies are purchased, and the bill will be paid later.
(6) A client made an advance payment of $2,600.
(7) The business received a 1,500 bill for accounting services. The bill will be paid later.
(8) The owner withdrew $3,000 cash.
(9) The business performed services and earned 20% of the advance payment received in (6) above.
(10) The business performed $1,650 of services for a client and the client paid cash.
(11) A $200 bill for telephone expense is received and is paid immediately.
(12) The accounting bill in (7) is paid.
(13) The business purchased $5,000 of computer equipment by paying $1,000 cash and signing a note payable.
(14) Employee wages for the month are $3,100 and are paid.
(15) At the end of the period, the net income is determined to be $1,870.
(16) The final balance of owner's equity is calculated from the statement of owner's equity, and this amount is placed on the balance sheet.

PRACTICE **Learning Goal 17, continued**

IA17-2. Connect transactions to financial statements

a. Place the dollar amount of each transaction in the correct location(s) in the table on page 352 to show how each financial statement would be affected by each transaction. To show negative amounts on the balance sheet, statement of owner's equity, and statement of cash flows, place amounts in parentheses ( ).
b. Use the balance sheet asset and liability column totals to verify the correct final balance of owner's equity. Enter an amount in the balance sheet owner's equity column only as a total after you compute the final balance from the columns for the statement of owner's equity. (item 16).
c. Total the income statement columns to verify the amount of net income.
d. Total the statement of cash flow columns to calculate the net change in the cash balance.

To complete the problem, first make a copy of the table on page 352, or print out a blank worksheet from the disk at the back of the book.

Transactions:

(1) The business collected $3,500 from customers on account.
(2) The owner invested $25,000 in the business.
(3) The business performed $3,400 of services for a client on account.
(4) $700 of supplies are used up.
(5) $900 of supplies are purchased, and the bill will be paid later.
(6) The business received a $5,700 bill for legal expense. The bill will be paid later.
(7) A client made an advance payment of $4,000.
(8) The owner withdrew $4,500 cash.
(9) The business performed services and earned 50% of the advance payment received in (7) above.
(10) A $380 bill for telephone expense is received and is paid immediately.
(11) The legal bill in (6) is paid.
(12) The business performed $1,650 of services for a client, and the client paid $1,000 cash.
(13) The business purchased $38,000 of automotive equipment by paying $15,000 cash and signing a note payable.
(14) Employee wages for the month are $5,800 and are not immediately paid.
(15) At the end of the period, the net loss is determined to be $5,530.
(16) The final balance of owner's equity is calculated from the statement of owner's equity, and this amount is placed on the balance sheet.

PRACTICE Learning Goal 17, continued

	Statement of Cash Flows Activity Type	$ Effect on Cash Flow
a.		
b.		
c.		
d.		
e.		
f.		
g.		
h.		
i.		
j.		
k.		
l.		
m.		
n.		
o.		

IA17-6. Simple preparation of a statement of cash flows. Using the statement of cash flows on page 305 as your model format and using your knowledge of the three different types of cash activities, create a May statement of cash flows in good form for San Andreas Company using the summary totals shown below. (Note: some items may not be applicable!) The May 1 beginning cash balance was $29,500.

	Item
a.	Owner invests $10,000 in the business
b.	Payment of accounts payable for various operating expenses: $15,100
c.	Collection of accounts receivable: $31,200
d.	Loaning money to a customer for a purchase: $22,000
e.	Paying interest on a loan:$1,900
f.	Sales on account of $10,500
g.	Collecting interest on a loan: $200
h.	Borrowing $20,000 on a long-term loan from a bank
i.	Buying equipment and paying $20,000 cash
j.	Selling equipment for $2,900 cash
k.	Utility bill in the amount of $500 is recorded but not paid.
l.	Customer in "d" above pays back $5,000 of the loan
m.	Owner withdraws $17,500 cash
n.	Owner withdraws supplies worth $1,000
o.	Cash sales to customers $2,200

PRACTICE

Learning Goal 17, continued

Locating and viewing annual reports. Select three well-known companies. Perform an Internet search to find how many internet (online) sources you can locate that will provide you with *free* annual reports of these companies. Actually view the information to be sure they are the complete annual reports including financial statements, MD & A, and footnotes—not just summaries of selected information. Be sure to include the company websites in your search. Identify the sources that you found. (Use bookmark/favorites to save the locations in an "Accounting References" folder.)

Your Questions?

It is *very* important to be aware of what you need to understand better. What do you need to understand better about this learning goal? On a separate piece of paper, write the questions that you want to discuss with your classmates, instructor, or supervisor. Try to be very specific about what is bothering you, such as explanations that you do not fully understand.

LEARNING GOAL 18

Describe the Conceptual Framework of Accounting

Overview

Purpose of This Learning Goal

The purpose of this learning goal is to give you an overview, or "big picture," of the basic theory and principles of financial accounting. This will give you an understanding of why things are done the way they are in accounting.

In Learning Goal 18, you will find:

The Conceptual Framework and Its Components

Components of the Operating Guidelines

Five Important Broad GAAP Rules

Important Accounting Organizations

The Conceptual Framework and Its Components

The Conceptual Framework of Accounting

Definition of Conceptual Framework

The ***conceptual framework*** of accounting is the organized reasoning that explains the basic nature of accounting. The framework justifies why things are done in certain ways and gives guidance to accountants.

Examples of Conceptual Frameworks

To perform any activity well, it is always necessary to set a precise goal. After that is done, you must understand the basic operation and conditions of the activity. Finally, with experience, you develop rules and principles to follow.

Examples

Here are some examples of "conceptual frameworks" for everyday activities:

Activity	Set Goal(s)	Understand the Activity	Develop Rules and Principles
Kick a soccer ball	▪ Score a goal	▪ Force and spin on ball ▪ Angles of kicking ▪ Effect of other players ▪ Weather conditions	▪ Attempt goal when . . . ▪ Pass the ball when . . .
Mow a lawn	▪ Short grass ▪ Healthy lawn ▪ Attractive lawn	▪ How mowers work ▪ How lawns grow ▪ Different types of grass ▪ What people like to see	▪ Set mower at certain height . . . ▪ Do not mow when wet . . .
Study accounting	▪ Grade of "A" ▪ Prepare for job	▪ The way I learn things ▪ How much time I need ▪ Asking questions ▪ Priorities	▪ Write notes when . . . ▪ Study schedule of . . . ▪ Write questions when . . .

continued ▶

The Conceptual Framework of Accounting, *continued*

The Accounting Conceptual Framework

The accounting conceptual framework has the same basic parts:

Set goal(s)
- "Objectives of financial reporting"

Understand the activity
- "Qualitative characteristics"
- "Elements of financial statements"

Develop rules and principles (GAAP)
- "Operating guidelines"

Objectives of Financial Reporting

Three Objectives

What is accounting trying to do? The objectives are shown below. However, the first objective is by far the most important and all-inclusive. The objectives of financial accounting are to provide information that:

- is useful in making financial decisions.
- explains cash flows.
- identifies assets, claims on assets, and the causes of changes in them.

Qualitative Characteristics

Overview

Accounting creates financial information. This information has many different features, or "qualities." This subject is mostly beyond the scope of this book; however, two very important qualities of accounting information are discussed below. This topic is also discussed in Learning Goal 12.

Two Key Qualitative Characteristics

- *Reliability:* Reliable information is dependable and can be verified.
- *Relevance:* Relevant information is useful.

There are also other important characteristics, such as consistency and comparability (see Learning Goal 12), but the two mentioned above are the most important. In more advanced classes, you will study the various qualitative characteristics of financial information.

Elements of Financial Statements

Definition

Elements of financial statements are the items that appear on the financial statements.

Why They Are Important

You have already learned many of these elements. The elements of financial statements are important because if people do not understand them, the financial statements are unusable.

Examples

- *Balance sheet elements:* assets, liabilities, and owner's equity
- *Income statement elements:* revenues and expenses

Operating Guidelines

Definition

Operating guidelines are the rules, assumptions, and limitations that accountants must use for guidance when deciding how to do something.

Various (and Confusing) Names Used

The operating guidelines consist of three basic parts: GAAP, modifying constraints, and assumptions. Unfortunately, the guidelines are frequently referred to by different names by different people. This can be really confusing.

For example, sometimes the word "concepts" is used to mean all of the different individual parts of operating guidelines. At other times, "concepts" is used to refer to basic assumptions. Sometimes the words "concepts" and "principles" are used interchangeably. Even though the ideas are consistent, the words can be very confusing.

Our Labels

We will use the most common labels here. However, if you are reading another accounting book and find a different name, don't panic. Just take a moment to compare it to what you see below, and it will be clear.

Some simple, accurate, and easy-to-use definitions of the three operating guidelines are described below.

Principles

"Principles" are rules or methods to be followed when doing accounting work. Principles say: "how to . . . ." In accounting, these are called ***Generally Accepted Accounting Principles,*** or just simply ***GAAP*** (pronounced *gap*).

continued ▶

Operating Guidelines, *continued*

Underlying Assumptions

"Underlying assumptions" are the basic conditions that must exist for the principles to be applied.

Constraints

"Constraints" are limitations on the way in which principles are used, so that improper or ridiculous outcomes do not result even when the correct principles are applied.

Components of the Operating Guidelines

GAAP (Generally Accepted Accounting Principles)

What Is GAAP?

In the United States, GAAP is a set of rules and standards that guide accountants as to when and how to properly record transactions and how to prepare proper financial statements. GAAP is not like unchanging laws of physics. GAAP is designed to meet the needs of society. GAAP is always evolving as the economic environment changes. Also, GAAP only refers to rules of accounting in the United States. Different countries have different rules for different purposes.

Broad GAAP

There are a few broad GAAP principles that provide general guidance and that apply to all types of transactions. These are fundamental accounting rules. These are like general traffic laws. Some of these are discussed below.

Specific GAAP

Specific GAAP rules offer specific direction for important kinds of specific situations. As you continue your study of accounting and learn how to record specific types of transactions, you will be learning specific GAAP rules.

Examples of some specific GAAP rules are:

- How uncollectible accounts receivable should be recorded
- Acceptable methods for calculating inventory cost
- How interest should be calculated on certain kinds of debt

GAAP (Generally Accepted Accounting Principles), *continued*

GAAP Is Not Perfect

Just as with other kinds of rules, GAAP is not perfect. GAAP is often subject to interpretation. Estimates are frequently required. The application of different methods is allowed, which can make comparability difficult to achieve. Furthermore in many situations GAAP can be subject to manipulation in such a way as to show more favorable results, while not technically violating any authoritative rules. This is called ***earnings management***. However, despite these various shortcomings, GAAP is essential to financial reporting. In this learning goal, we learn important basic GAAP.

Where Does GAAP Come From?

GAAP developed from various sources. Early GAAP developed from various accepted financial and business practices, tradition, and experience. As this occurred, the American accounting profession also created a series of authoritative organizations that organized, clarified, and modified existing accounting practices into official accounting standards. These organizations also continually researched and developed new authoritative standards. Today, these standards are called ***Statements of Financial Accounting Standards,*** or ***"SFAS"***. Currently, the organization responsible for developing SFAS pronouncements is called the ***Financial Accounting Standards Board,*** or ***"FASB".***

Over the years, a large volume of authoritative literature became available, such as the official SFAS pronouncements, plus other sources such as SFAS interpretations, technical bulletins, practice bulletins, emerging issues recommendations, and Securities and Exchange Commission rules.

In order to manage these many sources and to clarify authoritative ranking, all of the relevant literature was organized into one authoritative reference called the ***Accounting Standards Codification (ASC),*** which became effective in 2009. The ASC is therefore the source of American accounting standards; in other words, it is the source of authoritative GAAP for American non-governmental entities. The ASC is regularly updated as new standards and guidelines are developed. An update is called an "ASU" (Accounting Standards Update).

There are some circumstances in which GAAP in the ASC do not apply. For example, the ASC does not apply to governmental entities, which follow a different set of standards. Second, there are circumstances in which simplified or specialized rules are followed, called "special purpose frameworks". Finally, the ASC does not apply to non-GAAP reporting. Advanced accounting classes discuss these topics.

Underlying Assumptions

Basic Conditions

Underlying assumptions are the most basic conditions that *must exist* before GAAP can be applied. If these conditions do not exist, accounting as we know it cannot be used. Underlying assumptions are the "foundation" of the operating guidelines.

The essential underlying assumptions are defined in the illustration on page 363. (Underlying assumptions are sometimes called "concepts.")

Modifying Constraints

They Constrain Results

Modifying constraints are rules that are used to make sure that GAAP rules are applied sensibly—not in some arbitrary way that would result in ridiculous distinctions or foolish outcomes.

- **Materiality:** Strict adherence to GAAP is not required for items not important enough to make a difference to a decision maker.
- **Conservatism:** When two alternatives equally satisfy GAAP requirements, select the least favorable alternative.
- **Cost/benefit:** The cost of providing specific information should not exceed the benefits to those who use it.

Example

The GAAP matching principle requires expenses to be recorded when resources are used up to produce revenues.

Suppose that Mega Corporation purchased a $20 wastebasket that would last about 10 years. Literally and technically, GAAP would require the business to allocate the cost as an expense of $2 per year for 10 years.

The modifying constraint of *materiality* would say: "Are you kidding? This item is so small (not material) that you can record the entire $20 as an expense at the time the wastebasket is purchased."

"Overstate" and "Understate". Are you familiar with these terms? To "overstate" means to show a number that is too high. To "understate" means to show a number that is too low. For example, if you prepared an income statement that showed revenue as $80,000 when the correct revenue was $75,000 you would have overstated revenue by $5,000.

Illustration of the Conceptual Framework of Accounting

Overview of All Elements

This illustration gives you an overview of the conceptual framework of accounting. Notice how operating guidelines work together to achieve reliable and relevant financial statements useful for decision making.

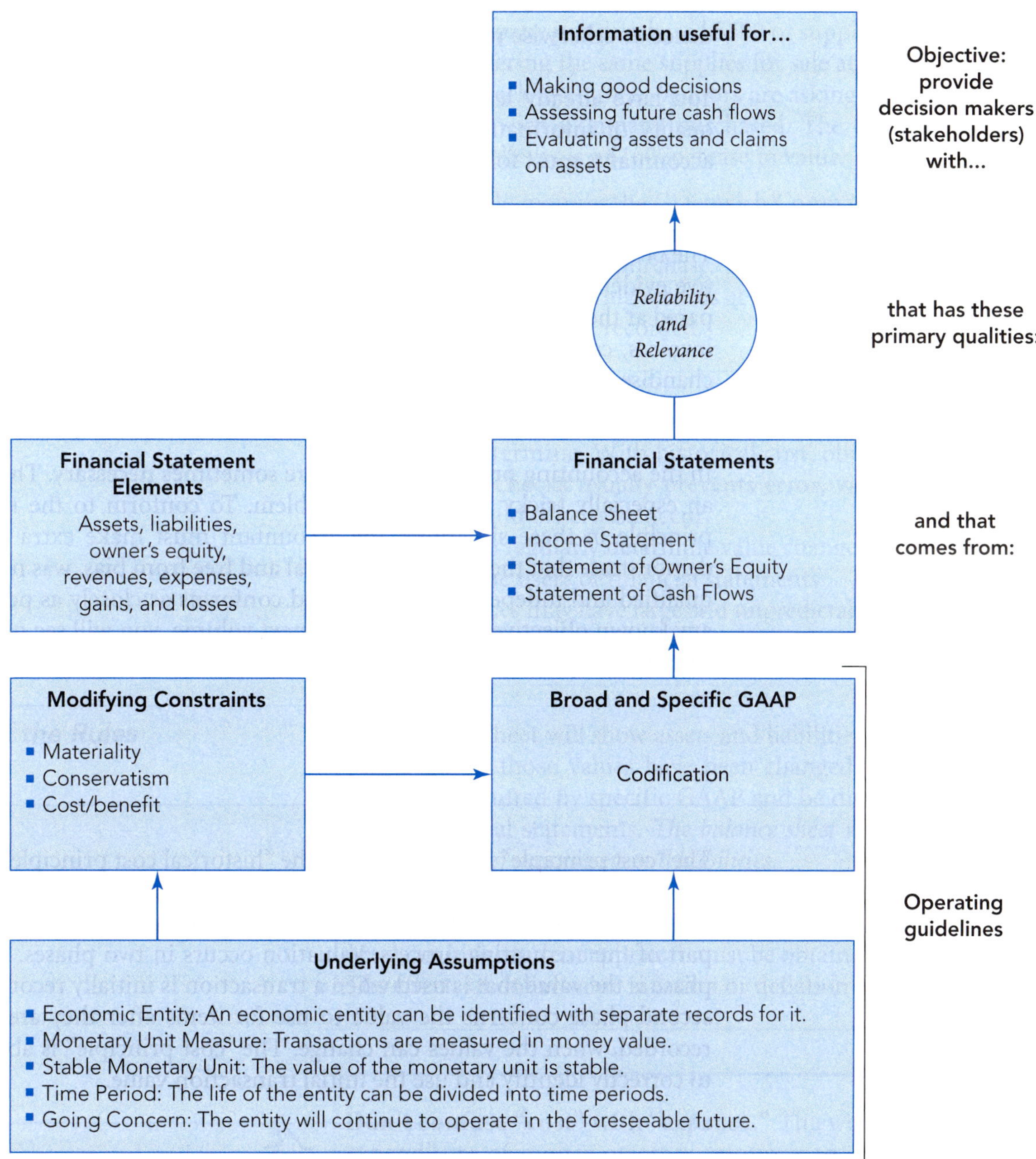

Cost Principle, *continued*

Terminology Confusion

The phrase "historical cost" implies that a value is determined by purchasing something. Although most assets are obtained by purchase, there are numerous exceptions. Examples of exceptions are owner investments, donated property, accounts receivable that result from sales, and notes receivable that result from loaning money or making sales. Therefore, it is more useful to think of the phrase "historical cost" as really meaning "original transaction value," which is a more accurate description.

Liabilities Too?

Yes, historical cost applies to liabilities as well as assets. The idea is the same: The "historical cost" of a liability is the original transaction value of the debt when the transaction occurred.

Revenue Recognition Principle

Rule

The revenue recognition principle (also called the "revenue principle") requires that accountants record revenue only *when it is earned.*

When Is Revenue Earned?

Revenue is earned from the sale of services or products when all three of the following conditions are satisfied:

- The seller has delivered the service or product that the customer wanted.
- The sale price can be clearly determined.
- The buyer can reasonably be expected to pay. Receiving cash is not necessary to record revenue.

Why the Principle Is Important

The revenue recognition principle is particularly important because many businesses are often eager to prematurely record revenue to show a higher net income. The revenue recognition principle is the accountant's guideline when confronting these situations. The principle provides guidance on how and when to properly record revenue.

We will return to this topic in greater depth in Volume 2 when we discuss methods of applying the revenue recognition principle in practice.

Does receiving cash mean that revenue has been earned? Is it necessary to receive cash to record revenue? In correct accounting, CASH HAS NO CONNECTION FOR WHEN TO RECORD REVENUE. The customer could pay in advance, at the time the service or product is delivered, or could pay later.

The Matching Principle

What Is "Matching"?

Revenues happen because a business is willing to incur expenses. It is important to be sure that related expenses are recorded in the same period as the revenues that the expenses helped to create. "Matching" means reporting expenses in the same period as their related revenues and subtracting the expenses from those revenues. When expenses are correctly matched against revenue, the correct net income is the result.

Rule

Record expenses in the same accounting period as the revenues that the expenses helped to create.

We will return to this topic in greater depth in Volume 2 when we discuss methods for applying the matching principle in practice.

Why the Principle Is Important

The matching principle is essential to correctly determine each period's net income. For example, to put a November expense on a December income statement would cause both the November and December reported income to be incorrect.

Using the revenue and matching principles together is called "accrual accounting".

The Full Disclosure Principle

What Is Full Disclosure?

Full disclosure means including all information that is relevant to assure a full understanding of financial statements by their users.

Rule

When financial statements are prepared, additional relevant information must also be presented to assure a full understanding of the statements.

How Is It Done?

To satisfy the full disclosure principle, accountants use footnotes (very important!), tables, charts, graphs, and carefully group items on financial statements. These additional disclosures more fully explain the meaning of the statements beyond the numbers that are presented on them.

Examples

A great many types of disclosure items are either required by GAAP or are otherwise important. Examples of disclosures are: Changes in important accounting procedures, details about accounting methods used, asset value changes, significant sources of revenue, and the terms of loans.

Important Accounting Organizations

Financial Accounting Standards Board (FASB)

Overview

The FASB is a private organization that has the primary responsibility for developing accounting principles and standards. As previously stated, these principles and standards are generally referred to as "GAAP" (Generally Accepted Accounting Principles) and apply to companies that do financial reporting in the United States.

Further Information

- Authority: The FASB is the most important American organization for developing accounting principles and standards in the United States. The FASB derives its authority from the Security and Exchange Commission. The FASB also derives authority from the fact that state licensing boards accept its pronouncements as highest authority.
- Official pronouncements: An official pronouncement of the FASB is called a "Statement of Financial Accounting Standards," or SFAS.

Securities and Exchange Commission (SEC)

Overview

The SEC is a federal government agency that is part of the United States Treasury Department. The SEC is responsible for developing laws and enforcing federal securities laws that protect investors. A primary function is investigation and enforcement. Civil sanctions can result in fines and loss of employment as corporate officers and securities dealers and indirectly, as accountants. The SEC also works closely with law enforcement in criminal investigations which may result in imprisonment.

Authority to Regulate

The SEC is a federal government agency established by federal law. The SEC has the authority to regulate companies that issue publicly traded securities (stocks and bonds) as well as the companies that sell the securities.

Authority to Develop Accounting Principles

In general, the SEC has allowed the FASB to be the primary authoritative source for developing accounting principles and procedures. Nevertheless, sometimes the SEC does not accept FASB pronouncements and requires the FASB to make changes. The SEC also encourages the FASB to develop new standards on important topics.

American Institute of Certified Public Accountants (AICPA)

Overview

The AICPA is the national professional organization of Certified Public Accountants.

Functions

- Auditing rules: The AICPA develops and oversees authoritative auditing standards and procedures for audits of entities that do not have publicly traded stock. (The Public Company Accounting Oversight Board (PCAOB) has this authority for companies that have publicly traded stock. The PCAOB is a private sector non-profit organization that reports to the SEC. It was created following the collapse of large corporations such as Enron and WorldCom in the early 2000's.)
- Ethics rules: The AICPA performs the important function of developing and enforcing the rules of professional ethics for certified public accountants.
- Education: The AICPA maintains an extensive program of continuing professional education. This program helps practicing certified public accountants maintain high levels of skill and meet state continuing education licensing requirements. The AICPA also designs the uniform CPA examination.
- Audit and Accounting Guides: The AICPA issues audit and accounting guides for audit practioners. Additionally, the AICPA issues other practice guides and "how to" advice that conform to authoritative standards.

IFRS and IASB

International Accounting Rules (IFRS)

As previously mentioned, GAAP refers only to American accounting principles. Authoritative GAAP is the required standard for American financial reporting. However, many other countries conform, in varying degrees, to a different set of rules that are international accounting standards. These are called ***international financial reporting standards,*** or more commonly, ***"IFRS".*** The authoritative source of these standards is called the International Accounting Standards Board, or IASB.

Although there are many basic similarities between GAAP and IFRS, there are also many differences. The Financial Accounting Standards Board and the International Accounting Standards Board have worked for a number of years to reduce these differences and to converge the standards as much as possible. The ultimate goal is to create a single set of worldwide authoritative accounting standards. Whether or not this outcome is really possible at the present time remains highly uncertain, because accounting rules are expressions of the societies and cultures that create those rules.

QUICK REVIEW

- The conceptual framework of accounting is the organized reasoning that explains the basic nature of accounting.
- The conceptual framework consists of:
  - objectives of financial reporting
  - qualitative characteristics
  - financial statements and their elements
  - operating guidelines
- GAAP (Generally Accepted Accounting Principles) are the rules that accountants must follow.
- GAAP comes from several sources, but the most important authority is the FASB (Financial Accounting Standards Board).
- In addition to GAAP, the other two parts of the operating guidelines are assumptions and constraints.
- Important American accounting organizations are Financial Accounting Standards Board (FASB), the Securities and Exchange Commission (SEC), and the American Institute of Certified Public Accountants (AICPA).

VOCABULARY

Accounting Standards Codification: The authoritative source for GAAP. (page 361)

Conceptual framework: the organized reasoning that explains the basic nature of accounting (page 357)

Earnings management: the manipulation of GAAP for the purpose of intentionally showing favorable results or desired outcomes, while avoiding a technical violation of GAAP rules. (page 361)

Elements of financial statements: the basic components of financial statements (page 359)

Financial Accounting Standards Board (FASB): the highest standard-setting authority in American accounting (page 368)

Generally Accepted Accounting Principles (GAAP): the rules and methods that accountants must follow (page 360)

International Financial Reporting Standards (IFRS): authoritative accounting rules that apply to countries outside of the United States. (page 369)

Operating guidelines: the principles, constraints, and assumptions part of the conceptual framework that gives guidance to accountants (page 359)

Statements of Financial Accounting Standards (SFAS): the official pronouncements of the Financial Accounting Standards Board (page 361)

PRACTICE Learning Goal 18

Solutions are in the disk at the back of the book and at: www.worthyjames.com

Learning Goal 18 is about the conceptual framework of accounting. Use these questions and problems to practice what you have learned.

Multiple Choice

Select the best answer.

1. GAAP refers to
   a. all of accounting theory that is called "generally accepted accounting principles."
   b. basic conditions that must be satisfied for accounting to function correctly.
   c. "generally accepted auditing procedures."
   d. rules or standards that must be followed by accountants when they perform their work, called "generally accepted accounting principles."
2. Which of the following creates new GAAP?
   a. general industry practice over time
   b. the Internal Revenue Service
   c. the FASB
   d. Emerging Issues Task Force (EITF)
3. When determining the total current value of a business, the information can be found on
   a. the balance sheet.
   b. the income statement.
   c. the statement of owner's equity.
   d. none of the above.
4. It is a good idea to use the balance sheet to
   a. determine the current value of the assets.
   b. determine the reasons for the change in the cash balance.
   c. identify the historical costs of assets and the claims against them.
   d. determine the current net income or net loss.
5. Which of the following is true?
   a. Historical cost is reliable but is not a good indicator of value.
   b. Historical cost is reliable and is a good indicator of value.
   c. Historical cost is not reliable and is not a good indicator of value.
   d. Historical cost misstates expenses on the income statement.
6. The purpose of the matching principle is
   a. to make sure that revenues are matched against the correct expenses of a period.
   b. to make sure that assets are matched against the liability claims on them.
   c. to make sure that expenses are matched against the revenues they helped to create.
   d. none of the above.
7. In July, an architect prepares drawings for a new patio and charges the client $750. The client pays the architect in August. Using the correct method of revenue recognition,
   a. the revenue should be recorded in July because that is when it was earned.
   b. the revenue should be recorded in August because that is when it was paid.
   c. the revenue is recorded in either July or August because it was earned in July and cash received in August.
   d. the revenue should not be recorded until the expenses related to it are recognized.
8. The historical cost principle
   a. requires that all transactions be recorded at original cost.
   b. requires that assets be reported on the balance sheet at original cost, unless a specific GAAP rule requires otherwise.
   c. both (a) and (b).
   d. none of the above.

PRACTICE Learning Goal 18, continued

Solutions are in the disk at the back of the book and at: www.worthyjames.com

9. Paseo Rancho Castilla Company owns several stores that all together cost $800,000. A buyer calls the company and offers $1,000,000 for the three stores. The company hires an appraiser who says the stores are worth $1,300,000. Based on this information, the company
   a. should make no changes to its balance sheet.
   b. should change the assets to $1,300,000.
   c. should change the assets to $1,000,000.
   d. none of the above.
10. Which of the following qualitative characteristics are most essential to financial statements?
    a. relevance
    b. reliability
    c. both (a) and (b)
    d. none of the above
11. "Underlying Assumptions" refers to
    a. the specific GAAP rules that accountants use in their daily practice of accounting.
    b. limitations in the way GAAP is properly applied.
    c. the annual decisions by the FASB.
    d. the conditions that must exist in any enterprise if GAAP accounting is to be applied.
12. An American company and a French company both show approximately $1,000,000 of net income.
    a. The true increase in the owners' wealth would be the same for both companies.
    b. The net income of the French company is probably incorrect.
    c. The net income of the French company probably cannot be measured according to GAAP rules.
    d. GAAP rules probably apply to both companies.
13. A cost is
    a. the amount of money spent on something.
    b. the amount of resources given up to acquire something.
    c. an expense.
    d. a decrease in owner's equity.
14. FASB refers to
    a. the Financial Assets Securities Board.
    b. the Financial Accounting Standards Board.
    c. the Financial Auditing Standards Board.
    d. none of the above.
15. An example of a stakeholder would be
    a. the owner.
    b. the customer.
    c. the financial analyst.
    d. all of the above.
16. "Operating guidelines" refers to
    a. broad GAAP and specific GAAP.
    b. assumptions, constraints, and GAAP.
    c. when to identify and record expenses.
    d. all of the above.
17. A generally accepted accounting principle is
    a. a standard or rule that guides accountants on how to do something.
    b. a required condition that must exist for accounting to function.
    c. an objective of financial reporting.
    d. a limitation on the way certain rules can be applied.

PRACTICE Learning Goal 18, continued

Solutions are in the disk at the back of the book and at: www.worthyjames.com

18. New Orleans Enterprises buys $10,000 of equipment. The equipment normally sells for $14,000, but New Orleans Company does not record this amount. This is an example of the
- a. matching principle.
- b. going-concern principle.
- c. full disclosure principle.
- d. cost principle.

19. Shreveport Company signed a contract to sell $50,000 of merchandise to a customer. The merchandise has been identified and packaged, and it is ready to ship. The accountant for the company records $50,000 of revenue. This is an error in applying which basic accounting principle?
- a. the revenue recognition principle
- b. the matching principle
- c. the reliability principle
- d. the cost principle

20. Baton Rouge partnership bought some equipment last month. The accountant cannot find an invoice, so she calls the seller. The seller of the equipment tells her that the equipment sold for $25,000. The accountant does not use this information right away. Instead, she locates a canceled check. This is an example of applying which accounting principle?
- a. the revenue recognition principle
- b. the matching principle
- c. the reliability principle
- d. the cost principle

21. The primary reason that the cost principle is used is because it
- a. results in reliable numbers.
- b. keeps the balance sheet at current values.
- c. ensures that net income will be correctly reported.
- d. does not prematurely report income.

22. The primary reason that the matching principle is used is because it
- a. results in reliable numbers.
- b. keeps the balance sheet at current values.
- c. ensures that expenses are recorded in the correct periods.
- d. does not prematurely report income.

Discussion Questions and Brief Exercises for Learning Goal 18

1. What does "GAAP" stand for? What does GAAP refer to?

2. Describe the two general categories of GAAP.

3. Where does GAAP come from?

4. What are the three objectives of financial reporting? Give some examples of how financial reporting meets these objectives.

5. What is the cost principle? Identify the two rules that are applied for this principle. What are the advantages and disadvantages of the cost principle?

6. At what value would you record each of the following transactions?

- Equipment is purchased for $900. The next day the buyer discovers that another dealer is selling the same equipment for $750. A month later the equipment is being sold for $1,200.
- A city donates land to a corporation so it will relocate to the area.

PRACTICE Learning Goal 18, continued

Solutions are in the disk at the back of the book and at: www.worthyjames.com

7. What is the revenue recognition principle? What rule is applied for this principle?

8. In which of the following situations do you think revenue has been earned? Discuss your reasons.

   - You have never met me. While you are on vacation, I paint your house and send you a bill for $5,000.
   - You order some equipment from me. The equipment is ready to be shipped to you. I send you a bill for $10,000.
   - It is December, and my company desperately needs to record more revenue at the end of the year to obtain new investors. I ask you to buy more of my merchandise, but you tell me that you already have more than you need. If you buy the merchandise, I agree to allow you to return as much as you want beginning in January. You agree to buy $25,000 of merchandise.
   - I own an Internet website. You own an Internet website. I sell advertising space on my website to you and you sell advertising space on your site to me for exactly the same amount. We both show more revenue on our income statements.

9. What are the characteristics of reliability and relevance? What do they mean?

10. What are the three elements of the "operating guidelines" of accounting? Describe the elements.

11. What is the full disclosure principle? Why is it important?

12. What are underlying assumptions? Give two examples for accounting.

Your Questions?

It is *very* important to be aware of what you need to understand better. What do you need to understand better about this learning goal? On a separate piece of paper, write the questions that you want to discuss with your classmates, instructor, or supervisor. Try to be very specific about what is bothering you, such as explanations that you do not fully understand.

CUMULATIVE VOCABULARY REVIEW

Match each description with the term that it describes. The answer for each term is in the right column. (*Suggestion:* Cover the answers in the right column as you test your vocabulary.)

Term	Description	Answers
1. GAAP	a. A report, issued annually by publicly held companies, that contains audited financial statements for the current and prior years, as well as a management discussion and analysis of the financial statements.	1p
2. Balance sheet	b. Private organization that conducts accounting research and establishes generally accepted accounting principles.	2h
3. Articulation	c. GAAP, constraints, and underlying assumptions.	3d
4. Revenue recognition principle	d. The connection between the financial statements, such that a change in one statement also causes a related change in another statement.	4j
5. Financing activities	e. A category on the statement of cash flows for transactions involving borrowing and owner's equity.	5e
6. Bookkeeping	f. The financial statement that summarizes the changes in cash over a specific time period.	6s
7. Income statement	g. A GAAP rule that requires that assets be recorded and maintained in the accounting records at their actual (historical) cost.	7k
8. Statement of owner's equity	h. The financial statement that summarizes the amount of assets, liabilities, and owner's equity at a specific date.	8r
9. The accounting process	i. A category on the statement of cash flows for transactions involving investing and long-term assets.	9t
10. Matching principle	j. A GAAP rule that determines when revenues are to be recorded, by requiring that they be recorded in the same time period in which they are earned.	10n
11. Operating activities	k. The financial statement that reports the changes to owner's equity over a specific period of time as a result of revenues and expenses.	11o
12. Underlying assumption	l. Any person or organization that requires financial information about the financial condition or performance of a company.	12q
13. Stakeholder	m. A phrase referring to a transaction in which a promise to pay is given instead of paying cash immediately.	13l
14. FASB	n. A GAAP rule that determines when expenses are to be recorded, by requiring that expenses be recorded in the same time period as the revenues which the expenses had helped to create.	14b
15. Operating guidelines	o. A category on the statement of cash flows for any cash transactions which occur as part of the revenue-earning operations of a business.	15c
16. Investing activities	p. Authoritative rules and standards that accountants must follow, and that are called "Generally Accepted Accounting Principles."	16i
17. Recognize	q. Basic conditions which must exist in order for GAAP accounting to be used.	17u
18. Statement of cash flows	r. The financial statement that summarizes all the changes in owner's equity over a specific time period.	18f
19. Annual report	s. The act of processing or recording accounting information.	19a
20. Historical cost principle	t. Analyze, process, communicate.	20g
21. "On account"	u. Meaning to record in the accounting records.	21m

CUMULATIVE TEST Learning Goals 10–18

Time Limit: 55 minutes

Instructions

*Select the best answer to each question. Do **not** look back in the book when taking the test. (If you need to do this, you are not ready.) After you finish the test, refer to the answers and circle the number of each question that you missed. Then go to the **Help Table** (on page 383) to identify your strong and weak knowledge areas by individual learning goal.*

Multiple Choice

1. The accounting process meets the information needs of stakeholders. A stakeholder is
   a. either an investor or a creditor.
   b. either an owner or a creditor.
   c. any person or organization who needs financial information about a company.
   d. none of the above.
2. The Mission Advertising Agency recorded purchases of $3,000 of art supplies on account. This transaction would have the following effect:
   a. Supplies increase by $3,000 and cash decreases by $3,000.
   b. Cash increases by $3,000 and supplies decreases by $3,000.
   c. Supplies decrease by $3,000 and accounts payable increases by $3,000.
   d. None of the above.
3. Information in financial statements must have these two essential important qualities:
   a. relevance and timeliness
   b. reliability and accuracy
   c. relevance and reliability
   d. ease of use and accuracy
4. If a balance sheet is presented in such a way that the assets are shown at the top of the page and liabilities and owner's equity are shown underneath them,
   a. this would be called the report form.
   b. this would be called the account form.
   c. this would be incorrect.
   d. the balance sheet would not balance.
5. On the income statement of Bridgeport Company, net loss is $10,000 and total expenses are $15,000. Total revenue must have been
   a. $5,000.
   b. $25,000.
   c. $10,000.
   d. some other amount.

CUMULATIVE TEST Learning Goals 10–18, continued

Sue Collette started Salem Graphic Arts Services in January 2016. The comparative balance sheet figures below are for the business as of December 31, 2016 and December 31, 2017. Use these figures to help you answer the multiple choice questions (6) and (7) that follow.

Assets	**2016**	**2017**
Cash	$20,200	$ 7,900
Accounts receivable	7,300	4,300
Supplies	900	250
Office equipment	12,500	12,500
Total assets	$40,900	$ 24,950
Liabilities and owner's capital		
Accounts payable	$ 4,100	$ 2,500
Notes payable	5,000	12,450
Sue Collette, Capital	31,800	10,000
Total liabilities and owner's capital	$40,900	$24,950

6. The statement of cash flows for Salem Graphic Arts Services will show how much net change in cash for 2017?
   a. $20,200 increase in cash   c. $12,300 increase in cash
   b. $21,800 decrease in cash   d. $12,300 decrease in cash
7. If Sue made no investments during 2017 and withdrew $15,000 cash, the statement of owner's equity for Salem Graphics Arts Services will show how much net income or loss for 2017?
   a. $15,950 net income   c. $6,800 net loss
   b. $950 net loss   d. $36,800 net income
8. Which of the following will contain the same item?
   a. the balance sheet and statement of owner's equity
   b. the income statement and statement of owner's equity
   c. the balance sheet and statement of cash flows
   d. all of the above
9. "Generally Accepted Accounting Principles (GAAP)" refers to
   a. the conceptual framework of accounting.
   b. the operating guidelines defined by the FASB.
   c. basic assumptions that must be met by every economic entity.
   d. rules and procedures that accountants must follow when doing their work.
10. A business owner has his business appraised. As a result, he increases the value of the assets by $50,000. This is a violation of which principle?
    a. the matching principle   c. the reliability principle
    b. the cost principle   d. the revenue recognition principle
11. If the Guadalupe Street Design partnership earns fees of $1,500, which of the following is true?
    a. Assets will increase or liabilities will decrease on the balance sheet, and revenues will increase on the income statement.
    b. Assets will decrease or liabilities will increase on the balance sheet, and expenses will increase on the income statement.
    c. Owner withdrawals will increase on the statement of owner's equity.
    d. None of the above.

CUMULATIVE TEST Learning Goals 10–18, continued

12. The Alexandria Company received $75,000 cash when it sold some equipment. On the statement of cash flows, the change in cash would be classified as part of
    a. net income.
    b. investing activities.
    c. financing activities.
    d. operating activities.
13. The owner's capital balance at the end of an accounting period is equal to
    a. net income.
    b. the balance at the beginning of the period plus net income minus withdrawals.
    c. the balance at the beginning of the period plus net income plus investments minus withdrawals.
    d. the balance at the beginning of the period plus net income minus liabilities.
14. The income statement is also called the
    a. operating statement, profit and loss statement, or P & L statement.
    b. position statement or statement of condition.
    c. operating statement, P & L statement, or position statement.
    d. capital statement.
15. The balance sheet shows
    a. assets, expenses, and liabilities.
    b. assets, revenues, and liabilities.
    c. assets, expenses, and owner's equity.
    d. none of the above.
16. If investors are researching a certain large company and need to obtain financial information from audited financial statements that conformed to generally accepted accounting principles, as well as management's discussion and analysis of the statements, they should review
    a. the tax returns of the company before making the investment decision.
    b. the current income statement before making the investment decision.
    c. the annual report before making the investment decision.
    d. *Wall Street Journal* articles before making the investment decision.
17. The recording and processing aspect of the accounting process is called
    a. bookkeeping.
    b. accounting.
    c. GAAP.
    d. transaction analysis.
18. The accountant of Harper Insurance Agency sees that $100 of supplies was used up. How should this be recorded?
    a. Decrease supplies and increase expenses by $100, thereby decreasing Linda Harper, Capital.
    b. Increase supplies and increase expenses by $100, thereby increasing Linda Harper, Capital.
    c. Decrease cash by $100 and increase expenses by $100, thereby decreasing Linda Harper, Capital.
    d. There would be no change to the owner's capital.
19. The final step in the accounting process is
    a. analyzing transactions.
    b. communicating information.
    c. processing transactional information.
    d. auditing financial statements.

CUMULATIVE TEST Learning Goals 10–18, continued

20. Marla and Grace are both taking an accounting class and are practicing recording transactions.

Marla has recorded cash transactions like this:	Cash	Grace has recorded cash transactions like this:	Cash Increase	Cash Decrease
Balance, November 1	?	Balance, November 1	?	
Owner withdrawal	– 1,000	Owner withdrawal		1,000
Collect accounts receivable	+ 2,500	Collect accounts receivable	2,500	
Purchase supplies	– 350	Purchase supplies		350
Service to customer	+ 2,100	Service to customer	2,100	
Balance, November 8	$11,200	Balance, November 8	$11,200	

Because they kept a record of transactions, we can know that the correct November 1 cash balance was

a. $14,450 for Marla and $7,950 for Grace.
b. $14,450 for Marla and $14,450 for Grace.
c. $7,950 for Marla and $7,950 for Grace.
d. $7,950 for Marla and $14,450 for Grace.

21. The bookkeeper of Luzerne Company recorded that $3.77 of pencil erasers had been used up during the last year. The bookkeeper has the receipts. This is an example of information quality that is

a. reliable but not relevant.
b. relevant but not reliable.
c. relevant and reliable.
d. relevant and reliable, but not timely.

22. The balance sheet is based upon the following relationship:

a. Revenues – Expenses = Net Income
b. Beginning balance + (operating, investing, and financing activities) = ending balance
c. Beginning balance + (net income or loss + investments – withdrawals) = ending balance
d. Assets = Liabilities + Owner's Equity

23. Bundsen's Village Coffee Shop has the following balances: Cash $1,000; Meal Revenue $7,000; Utility Expense $850; Wages Expense $2,000; Unearned Revenue $1,500; Prepaid Insurance Expense $700; Rent Expense $2,500; Total liabilities $3,500. The income statement will show net income of

a. $1,950.
b. $3,150.
c. $1,650
d. none of the above.

24. On the statement of owner's equity for Quan Company, the balance of Eric Quan, Capital, on January 1, 2017 is $12,500. On January 31, 2017, it is $10,000. Eric's drawings were $1,000 and his investments were $2,000 during January. Both the statement of owner's equity as well as the income statement show

a. net income of $2,500.
b. net loss of $3,500.
c. net income of $500.
d. net loss of $2,500.

25. The financial statement that explains all the sources of cash and all the uses of cash during any accounting period is the

a. operating statement.
b. statement of position.
c. capital statement.
d. statement of cash flows.

26. If the total assets on the balance sheet of Al's Barber Shop increased by $10,000 at the end of the year, with no change in the total liabilities, and if the barber shop was profitable,

a. the income statement will show net income of $10,000.
b. if there was no drawing, the statement of owner's equity will show an investment of $10,000.
c. if there was no drawing, the income statement and the statement of owner's equity will show some combination of net income and owner's investment, totaling $10,000.
d. none of the above.

Describe Financial Condition, *continued*

Use a Table to Show Changes

However, a more efficient way to show the changes (transactions) is to use the accounting equation to create a table. We use the table to record all the changes in the individual items in the equation. We can create separate columns for all the items in the accounting equation and record the changes directly in the columns. For example, suppose the Nevada Company has recorded all its transactions in this way for the week beginning May 2. You could prepare a table like this:

		Assets			= Liabilities + Owner's Equity	
Week of May 2	**Cash**	**Accounts Receivable**	**Supplies**	**Equipment**	**Note Payable**	**C. Goldman, Capital**
5/2 Balance	17,300	4,500	900	12,000	10,000	24,700
5/4 Collection	+800	–800				
5/5 Revenue		+1,000				+1,000
5/7 Buy supplies	–400		+400			
5/7 Revenue	+2,000					+2,000

On May 8, the Nevada Company recorded the purchase of $5,000 of equipment by paying $1,000 cash and signing a $4,000 note payable. It would look like this:

		Assets			= Liabilities + Owner's Equity	
Week of May 2	**Cash**	**Accounts Receivable**	**Supplies**	**Equipment**	**Note Payable**	**C. Goldman, Capital**
5/2 Balance	17,300	4,500	900	12,000	10,000	24,700
5/4 Collection	+800	–800				
5/5 Revenue		+1,000				+1,000
5/7 Buy supplies	–400		+400			
5/7 Revenue	+2,000					+2,000
5/8 Buy equipment	***–1,000***			***+5,000***	***+4,000***	
5/8 Balance	18,700	4,700	1,300	17,000	14,000	27,700

Describe Financial Condition, *continued*

An Improvement: Separate Columns for Increases and Decreases

Finally, we decided that we could improve this method by using a separate increase and decrease column for each item. Separate increase and decrease columns make it much easier to see all the increases and decreases for each element in the accounting equation. No "+" or "–" signs are required. Also, this is what is actually done in practice and what we practiced in Learning Goal 11.

Because assets are on the left side of the equation, we agree to make left-side columns positive for assets. Because liabilities and owner's equity are on the right side of the equation, we agree to make right-side columns positive for liabilities and owner's equity. This is the usual accounting custom.

If we omit the explanation column to save space, the Nevada Company record of transactions will now look like this (beginning and ending balances are on May 2 and May 8):

	Assets								=	Liabilities + Owner's Equity		
	Cash		*Accounts Receivable*		*Supplies*		*Equipment*		*Note Payable*		*C. Goldman, Capital*	
	Increase	Decrease	Increase	Decrease	Increase	Decrease	Increase	Decrease	Decrease	Increase	Decrease	Increase
5/2	bal. **17,300**		bal. **4,500**		bal. **900**		bal. **12,000**			bal. **10,000**		bal. **24,700**
5/4	800			800								
5/5			1,000									1,000
5/7		400			400							
5/7	2,000											2,000
5/8		1,000					5,000			4,000		
5/8	bal. **18,700**		bal. **4,700**		bal. **1,300**		bal. **17,000**			bal. **14,000**		bal. **27,700**

The Five Data Arrangements

Overview

Transaction Data Are Important

Transaction data are important. The data are the source of all financial information. Transaction data explain and verify changes in the business.

The way data are organized and presented can make a tremendous difference in the efficiency of a business. Therefore, data must be organized to show in the clearest possible way the kind of information that a business will need.

Even when we use computers to electronically process information, the human brain still needs to see the final results presented in a clear, easy-to-use, and well-organized way.

Five Data Arrangements Are Necessary

Accountants, after many years of practice, discovered that transaction data must be arranged in a way that meets five basic information requirements. Look again at the table on page 389 showing the transactions of the Nevada Company. The information is arranged in a way that meets the five requirements presented below.

1. Find a Transaction by Date

Chronological Listing

To easily locate a transaction by date, there must be a *chronological listing of the transactions* as they happened. The earliest transactions are shown first, and the more recent ones follow. From May 2 on, you can follow the sequence of events and easily locate a transaction by date.

Example

Suppose that you want to find all transactions that happened on May 7. Look at the date column on the left side. It is easy to follow it down until you come to May 7 (5/7). It turns out that there were two transactions on May 7. You can now examine the details of each transaction.

2. See All Parts of a Transaction

All Parts Are Easy to See

After you locate a transaction, it is easy to see *all the individual items in each transaction*. This is because all parts of the transaction appear on the same line.

Example

In the May 8 transaction, the company purchased $5,000 of equipment using some cash and borrowing the balance. If you look on the line for May 8, you can easily see all three items that are affected: Cash decreased by $1,000, Equipment increased by $5,000, and Notes Payable increased by $4,000.

3. See if the Equation Stays in Balance

Increases and Decreases in Each Transaction

You can easily prove that each transaction keeps the equation in balance. If you look on any line with a transaction, you can quickly see that the increases and decreases in the equation items keep the equation in balance.

Example

In the May 8 transaction, Cash decreased by $1,000 and Equipment increased by $5,000. This is a net $4,000 increase in total assets. On the right side of the equation for May 8, you can see that the liabilities increased by $4,000. The equation remains in balance.

4. See the Historical Detail of Each Item

A Record of All Increases and Decreases

There is a permanent record of both *the increases and decreases in every item.*

continued ▶

Answers

Transaction data must be arranged in a way that meets five basic information requirements. First, transactions are recorded in chronological order. Second, it must be easy to see all the parts of each transaction. Third, it must be easy to verify that the transaction keeps the accounting equation in balance. Fourth, there must be a permanent historical record of all the increases and decreases of each item. Fifth, it must be easy to find the balance of each item.

Situation	Five Basic Information Arrangements				
	1 Find a transaction by date	*2 See all parts of a transaction*	*3 See if the equation stays in balance*	*4 See the historical detail of each item*	*5 Determine the balance of each item*
1. The owner wants to know how much cash the business has today.					✓
2. A tax auditor wants to know for what purpose a large check was written.	✓	✓			
3. The manager wants to know if the property tax payments were made before December 10 to avoid a late payment penalty.	✓	✓			
4. A customer is disputing the balance we are showing in our account receivable from him.				✓	✓
5. Our business has purchased another business. It is a complex transaction with many changes to the accounting equation.		✓	✓		
6. Before deciding on a loan, the bank wants to know the amount of debt that our business has.					✓
7. The owner wants to know if the May 3 cash deposit was from a revenue or from a customer advance payment.	✓	✓			

LEARNING GOAL 20 Explain the Use of Accounts

Overview

Introduction

At the most basic level, an accounting system is simply a way of recording increases and decreases. Why? Because the financial condition of every business is described by the accounting equation A = L + OE, and there are only two possible ways that the items in the equation can change: either increase or decrease.

The means of keeping a record of all increases and decreases of each item in the accounting equation is the "account." This learning goal explains the account.

In Learning Goal 20, you will find:

The Account and How It Is Used

The Account and How It Is Used

Example

Example of Recording Increases and Decreases

Look again at the last table that we used to record the transactions for the Nevada Company (see page 389). This table uses separate increase and decrease columns for all the items in the accounting equation. For each item, notice that the increase and decrease columns form a "T."

For example, the cash item in the accounting equation of Nevada Company for the week beginning May 2 shows the following entries:

	Cash	
	Increase	**Decrease**
5/2 beginning balance	**17,300**	
	800	400
	2,000	
	______	1,000
5/8 ending balance	**18,700**	

An item can change in only two possible ways—either increase or decrease. By putting an increase column on one side and a decrease column on the other side, a T is formed. All the increases are shown on one side, and the decreases are shown on the other side. The ending balance of 18,700 is calculated by subtracting the total of the decrease side (1,400 on the right side) from the total of the positive (increase) side (20,100 on the left side).

The Account

Definition

Each one of these increase/decrease T arrangements is called an account. An ***account*** is a detailed, historical record that shows all the increases and all the decreases, and balance, of a specific item in the accounting equation.

The Account, *continued*

The T Account

The simplest form of an account is called a ***T account*** (see example on page 396). It shows only the most basic information: name, increases, decreases and balance. (Later on, we will add other useful information and expand the account.)

Entry

Each recording on the left side or right side of an account is called an ***entry***.

Footing

Because an account keeps a record of all increases and all decreases, an account can also show a balance. The balance of an account is called a ***footing***, and to total an account is ***to foot*** it.

Examples

Refer back to the last table for the Nevada Company on page 389.

- Cash, Accounts Receivable, Supplies, and Equipment are asset accounts.
- Note Payable is a liability account.
- C. Goldman, Capital is an owner's equity account.

The Cash account shows four entries: two increases and two decreases. The footing (the balance) of the Cash account on May 8 is $18,700.

Two Information Requirements Are Fulfilled

An account fulfills two of the five information requirements. The two requirements are:

- An account keeps a record of all increases and decreases of a specific item in the accounting equation (the "historical detail").
- An account shows the balance of a specific item in the accounting equation.

continued 

Check Your Understanding

Write the completed sentences on a separate piece of paper. The answers are below.

An account is a detailed historical record of all the · · · · · · · · and all the · · · · · · · · of a specific item in the accounting equation. An account can show the · · · · · · · · of the item at any desired time.

Answers

An account is a detailed historical record of all the increases and all the decreases of a specific item in the accounting equation. An account can show the balance of the item at any desired time.

Rules for Increasing and Decreasing the Accounts

Concept

The essential concept behind all the rules for recording increases and decreases in the accounts is:

- We agree that one side of an account will be the positive side. This is called the ***"normal"*** or ***"natural" side*** of the account, and it is used for increases.
- Therefore, the other side of the account will be the negative side—for recording decreases.

It is actually this simple.

Positive Sides

Over many years, accountants have agreed on the positive sides:

- For accounts in the left side accounting equation (assets), the left side of an account shall be the positive side. ("Left goes with left.")
- For accounts in the right side accounting equation (liabilities and owner's capital), the right side of an account shall be the positive side. ("Right goes with right.")

Rules for Increasing and Decreasing the Accounts, *continued*

Examples

The following illustration and table show you how this rule affects each type of account, when recording changes:

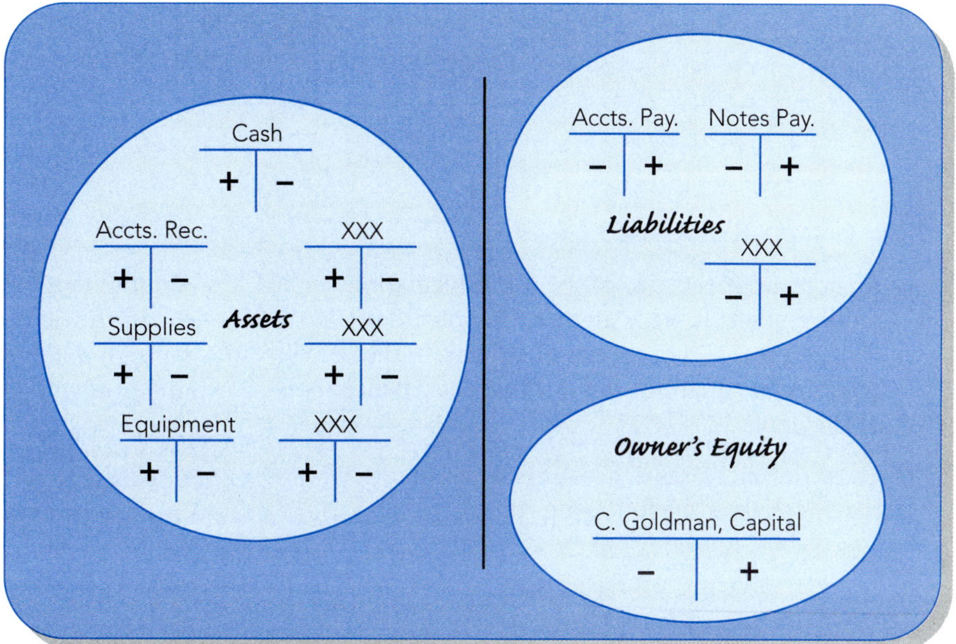

Change	Assets	Liabilities	Owner's Capital
Positive (increase)	Left side	Right side	Right side
Negative (decrease)	Right side	Left side	Left side

Nothing Magic Here!

There is nothing magic or mysterious about this method. We could just as easily agree that the natural positive location should be the top part of an account and decreases should be on the bottom part of an account. To keep a record of increases and decreases that the human brain can see, all we need are two separate locations in each account. Most people find left and right to be easiest, probably because the accounting equation is divided into left and right parts.

continued ▶

Rules for Increasing and Decreasing the Accounts, *continued*

Assets and liabilities cannot be negative. For example, can you imagine negative equipment or negative supplies? Of course not—balances are positive. However, as a shortcut, sometimes accountants will *temporarily* show cash with a negative balance if the cash account is overdrawn, or *temporarily* show accounts receivable with a negative balance because of an overpayment by a customer. Both of these situations are really liabilities, not negative assets.

QUICK REVIEW

- An account meets two of the five information requirements: It keeps an historical record of all the increases and decreases of an item in the accounting equation, and it shows the balance of the item.
- To record increases in accounts, accountants have agreed on the following rules:
  - An item that belongs on the left side of the equation will be increased by a left-side entry.
  - An item that belongs on the right side of the equation will be increased by a right-side entry.
- After we agree on increases, decreases are simply on the opposite side from the increases.

VOCABULARY

Account: a detailed, historical record of all the increases and decreases of a specific item in the accounting equation (page 396)

Entry: the recording of a change in an account; usually refers to recording in ledgers or journals (page 397)

Footing: the balance of an account; the total of a column of numbers (page 397)

"Normal" or "natural" side: the side of an account that records increases (page 398)

T account: the simplest form of an account, in the form of a T, showing name and increases on one side, and decreases on the opposite side (page 397)

To foot: to total an account or a column of numbers (page 397)

PRACTICE Learning Goal 20

Solutions are in the disk at the back of the book and at: www.worthyjames.com

Learning Goal 20 is about learning to use accounts. Use these problems to practice how to record the increases and decreases in accounts.

Reinforcement Problems

LG 20-1. Identify natural positive sides of accounts ("normal" balances). The T accounts below are randomly shown—there is no particular order. Identify the natural positive side of each account by writing a plus sign (+) on the side that is the natural positive side (the "normal" side).

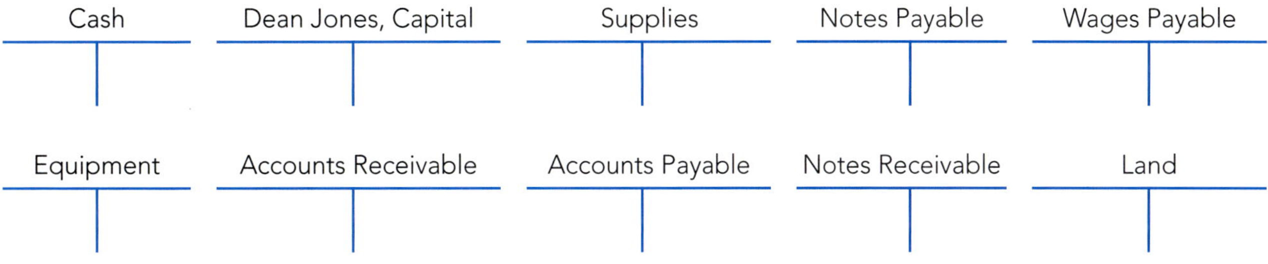

LG 20-2. Explain the meaning and use of the natural positive side. What is the importance of the natural positive side (the "normal" side) of an account? What is the natural positive side used for?

LG 20-3. Identify the changes in the accounts. The accounts shown below have been increased and/or decreased by certain transactions. (If you have difficulty, *remember the natural positive sides* of the accounts you are looking at.)

- Write one sentence that identifies which accounts have increased and which have decreased.
- Write one sentence that accurately describes the transaction.

Example:

Cash		Anna Chan, Capital	
5,000			5,000

- **Increase/decrease:** Cash increases and Anna Chan, Capital increases.
- **Description:** The owner invested $5,000 in her business.

a.

Cash		Accts. Receivable	
750			750

- **Increase/decrease:**
- **Description:**

PRACTICE Learning Goal 20, continued

Solutions are in the disk at the back of the book and at: www.worthyjames.com

LG 20-3, *continued*

b.

- **Increase/decrease:**
- **Description:**

c.

Cash	
	500

Supplies	
500	

- **Increase/decrease:**
- **Description:**

d.

Equipment	
15,000	

Cash	
	5,000

Notes Payable	
	10,000

- **Increase/decrease:**
- **Description:**

e.

Cash	
	300

Accts. Payable	
300	

- **Increase/decrease:**
- **Description:**

f.

- **Increase/decrease:**
- **Description:** (from operations)

PRACTICE Learning Goal 20, continued

Solutions are in the disk at the back of the book and at: www.worthyjames.com

LG 20-3, *continued*

g.

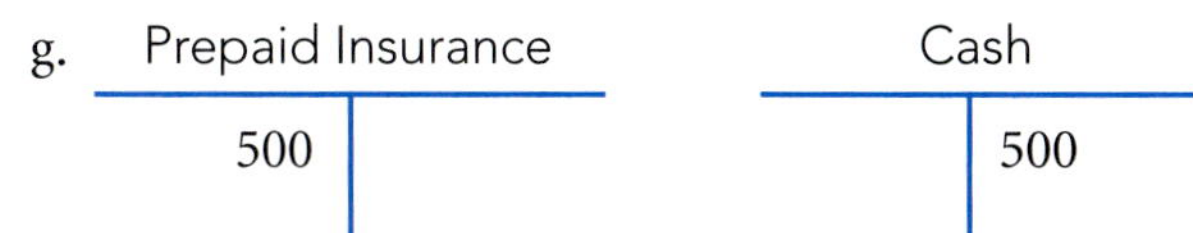

Prepaid Insurance	
500	

Cash	
	500

- **Increase/decrease:**
- **Description:**

h.

Supplies	
	150

Anna Chan, Capital	
150	

- **Increase/decrease:**
- **Description:** (from operations)

i.

Cash	
750	

Unearned Revenue	
	750

- **Increase/decrease:**
- **Description:**

j.

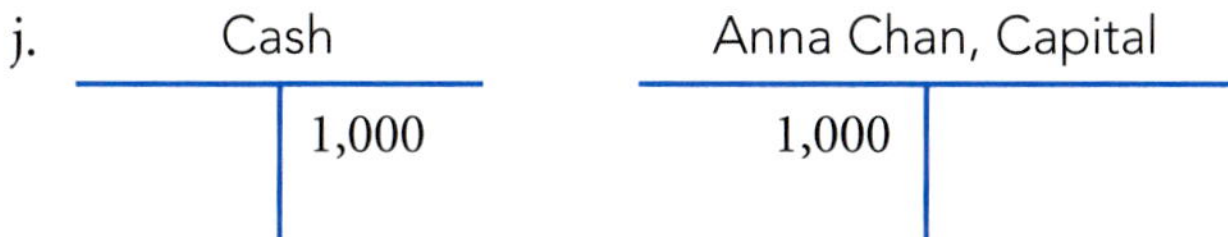

Cash	
	1,000

Anna Chan, Capital	
1,000	

- **Increase/decrease:**
- **Description:** (not from operations)

k.

Accounts Payable	
	750

Anna Chan, Capital	
750	

- **Increase/decrease:**
- **Description:** (from operations)

PRACTICE Learning Goal 20, continued

Solutions are in the disk at the back of the book and at: www.worthyjames.com

LG 20-3, *continued*

1\.

Cash	
500	

Accounts Receivable	
1,500	

Anna Chan, Capital	
	2,000

- **Increase/decrease:**
- **Description:** (from operations)

LG 20-4. Practice recording changes in the accounts. Each question below describes a separate transaction. Blank T accounts are arranged under the accounting equation with each question. For each question, do the following:

- **Analysis:** Identify which accounts increase and/or which accounts decrease.
- **Rules:** Specify what entries on the left or right side of the accounts are required.
- **Entry:** Write the names of the accounts affected above the T accounts, and record the dollar amounts into the accounts. (*Remember:* The entries must keep the equation in balance!)

Suggestion: You may want to practice this problem more than once. Instead of writing answers here, use the T account template to print T accounts from the disk in the back of the book.

Example: San Antonio Company purchases $500 of office supplies for cash.

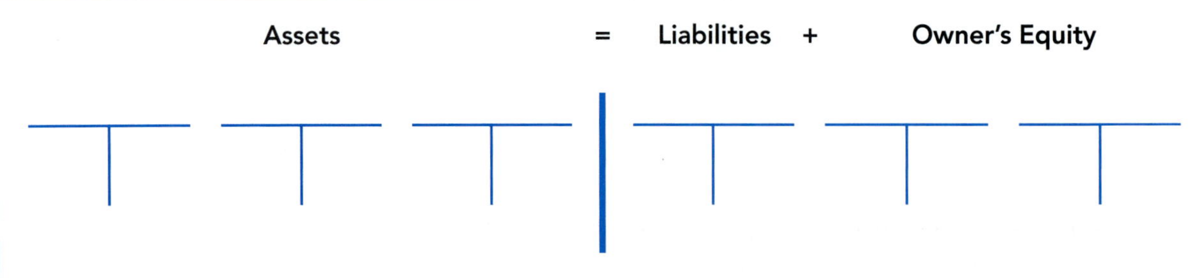

- **Analysis** *(identify which accounts increase and/or which accounts decrease):*
- **Rules** *(specify what entries on the left or right side of the accounts are required):*

PRACTICE Learning Goal 20, continued

Solutions are in the disk at the back of the book and at: www.worthyjames.com

LG 20-4, *continued*

Solution:

Assets = Liabilities + Owner's Equity

Cash: right side 500

Supplies: left side 500

- **Analysis** *(identify which accounts increase and/or which accounts decrease):* The **asset** Cash **decreases** by $500, and the **asset** Supplies **increases** by $500.
- **Rules** *(specify what entries on the left or right side of the accounts are required):* Assets are increased by a left-side entry, so record $500 on the left side of Supplies. Assets are decreased by a right-side entry, so record $500 on the right side of Cash.

a. St. Phillips Company purchases $800 of supplies "on account."

Assets = Liabilities + Owner's Equity

- **Analysis** *(identify which accounts increase and/or which accounts decrease):*
- **Rules** *(specify what entries on the left or right side of the accounts are required):*

b. Bryan Company collects $1,000 from customers "on account."

Assets = Liabilities + Owner's Equity

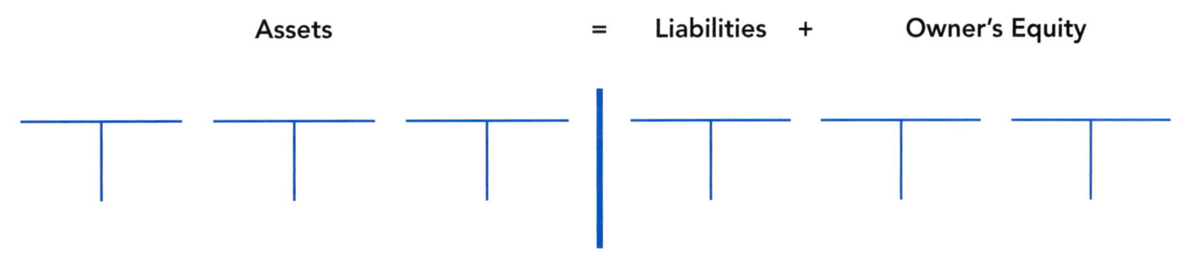

- **Analysis** *(identify which accounts increase and/or which accounts decrease):*
- **Rules** *(specify what entries on the left or right side of the accounts are required):*

PRACTICE Learning Goal 20, continued

Solutions are in the disk at the back of the book and at: www.worthyjames.com

LG 20-4, *continued*

c. Dave Mason, owner of Mountain View Company, invests $10,000 in his business.

Assets	=	Liabilities	+	Owner's Equity

- **Analysis** *(identify which accounts increase and/or which accounts decrease):*
- **Rules** *(specify what entries on the left or right side of the accounts are required):*

d. Richland Company receives a $400 advance payment from a customer.

Assets	=	Liabilities	+	Owner's Equity

- **Analysis** *(identify which accounts increase and/or which accounts decrease):*
- **Rules** *(specify what entries on the left or right side of the accounts are required):*

e. North Harris Company purchased a $5,000 computer by paying $3,000 cash and signing a note payable for the balance.

Assets	=	Liabilities	+	Owner's Equity

- **Analysis** *(identify which accounts increase and/or which accounts decrease):*
- **Rules** *(specify what entries on the left or right side of the accounts are required):*

PRACTICE

Learning Goal 20, continued

Solutions are in the disk at the back of the book and at: www.worthyjames.com

LG 20-4, *continued*

f. San Jacinto Company pays $250 owing to a supplier "on account."

Assets	=	Liabilities	+	Owner's Equity

- **Analysis** *(identify which accounts increase and/or which accounts decrease):*
- **Rules** *(specify what entries on the left or right side of the accounts are required):*

g. Diane Lee, owner of El Paso Company, recorded $750 of revenue "on account."

Assets	=	Liabilities	+	Owner's Equity

- **Analysis** *(identify which accounts increase and/or which accounts decrease):*
- **Rules** *(specify what entries on the left or right side of the accounts are required):*

h. Tarrant Company uses up $100 of supplies during its operations (an expense).

Assets	=	Liabilities	+	Owner's Equity

- **Analysis** *(identify which accounts increase and/or which accounts decrease):*
- **Rules** *(specify what entries on the left or right side of the accounts are required):*

PRACTICE Learning Goal 20, continued

Solutions are in the disk at the back of the book and at: www.worthyjames.com

LG 20-4, *continued*

i. Kingwood Company receives a $500 invoice for repair services. The invoice is not paid immediately (an expense).

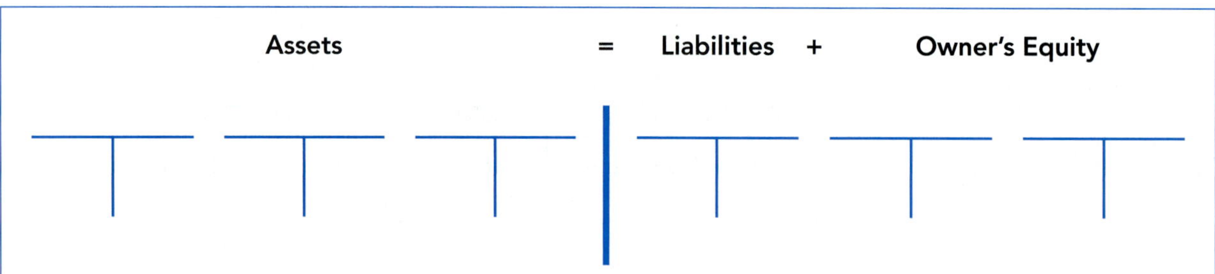

- **Analysis** *(identify which accounts increase and/or which accounts decrease):*
- **Rules** *(specify what entries on the left or right side of the accounts are required):*

j. Grayson Company receives $750 cash upon completion of a job for a customer (a revenue).

Assets = Liabilities + Owner's Equity

- **Analysis** *(identify which accounts increase and/or which accounts decrease):*
- **Rules** *(specify what entries on the left or right side of the accounts are required):*

PRACTICE Learning Goal 20, continued

Solutions are in the disk at the back of the book and at: www.worthyjames.com

LG 20-5. Calculate account balances. Each item below gives information about an account. Draw T accounts and show the entries in each account. Also show the final balance of each account.

Account Beginning Balance	Account Changes
a. Cash: $5,000	Received payment from customer: $1,200. Paid accounts payable: $750. Paid employees: $2,500. Owner investment: $5,000.
b. Accounts Payable: $550	Purchased supplies on account: $500. Received bill from repair service: $3,000. Made payment to supplies vendor: $850.
c. Owner's Capital: $3,500	Owner invested $5,000. Earned $950 revenue. Incurred $350 advertising expense. Owner withdrew $2,000.
d. Owner's Capital: $5,000	Earned $1,000 revenue. Paid $5,000 wages expense. Received a bill for $2,000 utility expense "on account."
e. Supplies: $150	Purchased supplies on account: $500. Used $300 of supplies.
f. Wages Payable: $500	Employees earned $4,000, which has not yet been paid.

LG 20-6. Record transactions into T accounts. Record the transactions shown below into T accounts.

a. Write the accounting equation A = L + OE across the top of a blank sheet of paper, leaving ample space between each part of the equation. (You will have more space if you turn the paper so the long side is horizontal.)
b. Draw some blank T accounts under each part of the equation as in the example below.
c. Record each transaction in the appropriate T account. Write each account's name above the account as needed. Identify the entries of each transaction with the letter of the transaction.
d. After all transactions are recorded, enter the final balance of each T account on the appropriate normal side of the account.

Example:

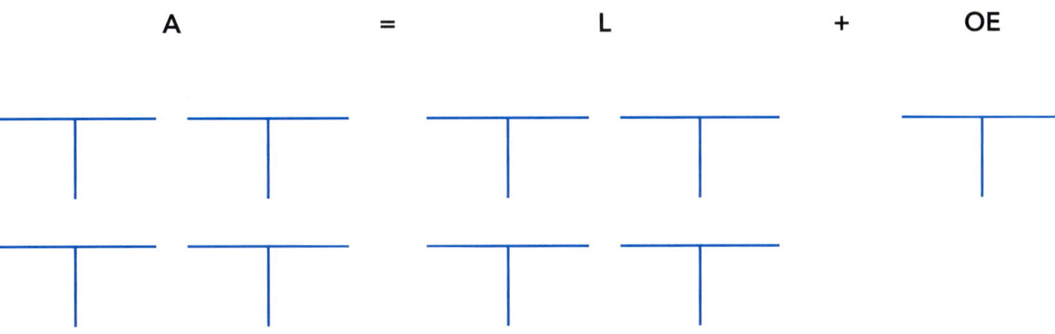

PRACTICE **Learning Goal 20, continued**

Solutions are in the disk at the back of the book and at: www.worthyjames.com

LG 20-6, *continued*

Transactions:

(a) Ron Marcus, the owner of Mountain View Appraisal Company, invested $50,000 in his new business.
(b) The business purchased supplies for $520 on account.
(c) The business purchased office equipment for $7,550 cash.
(d) The business performed consulting services for $1,750 on account.
(e) The business paid the current month's rent, $1,100.
(f) The business received a $2,380 advance payment from a client.
(g) The business received a $125 bill for utility services, which was not paid immediately.
(h) The business performed appraisal services for $2,200 cash.
(i) The business purchased supplies for cash, $295.
(j) The business purchased land for $15,000 by paying $10,000 cash and signing a note payable for the balance.
(k) The business made a $350 payment on account.
(l) The business collected $1,000 from a customer on account.
(m) The business performed $1,500 of services for the client who had made the advance payment.
(n) The owner withdrew $1,400 cash from the business for personal use.

LG 20-7. Analyzing accounts.

After you understand how accounts are used, you can begin to answer questions about why and how accounts have changed. For each of the four situations below, answer the questions about the accounts.

a. The Supplies account of Spokane Enterprises had a normal balance on October 1 of $4,500. The October 31 balance was a normal balance of $3,100, and the income statement shows October Supplies Expense of $5,500. What was the amount of supplies purchased?

b. The Accounts Receivable account of Everett Company shows a normal ending balance of $15,900 on January 31 and a normal January 1 balance of $7,800. If credit sales during the month were $12,500, what is the amount of collections from customers during January?

c. Seattle Service Company had $8,850 of Accounts Payable owing on August 1. During August, the company made $12,000 of payments to creditors and owed $3,300 on August 31. How much did the company purchase on credit during August?

d. Bellevue Corporation shows a February 28 normal cash balance of $75,700. If, during February, the company received $55,200 of cash and paid $81,000 of cash, what was the cash balance on February 1?

PRACTICE

Learning Goal 20, continued

Solutions are in the disk at the back of the book and at: www.worthyjames.com

LG20-8. Financial statements review Using the year-end account balances below, in good form prepare an income statement and statement of owner's equity for the year ending June 30, 2018 and a report form balance sheet as of June 30, 2018 for Wilson Appliance Services Company.

Equipment	$288,100	Unearned revenue	$9,150
Wages expense	293,250	Supplies expense	9,250
Notes payable	125,000	Accounts receivable	15,640
J. Wilson, capital July 1, 2017	291,840	Office expense	1,150
Services Revenue	452,700	Accounts payable	6,390
Prepaid insurance	4,800	Rent expense	42,000
Supplies	32,980	Insurance expense	5,430
Utilities expense	12,180	Cash	?
J. Wilson, Withdrawals	65,000	Wages payable	24,300

IA20-1. Financial statements review Complete problem LG20-8 with the following changed account balances: J. Wilson, capital July 1, 2017: $88,570; Services revenue: $286,120; Wages expense: $241,480; Rent expense: $59,400; Supplies: $19,600; Notes payable: $315,000. The owner also invested $10,000

INTERNET EXERCISES

Reviewing a Board of Accountancy website. Do an Internet search to locate the home page of the Board of Accountancy for the state in which you reside. Save this link into your "Accounting References" folder. (*Note:* State board of accountancy links can also be accessed via the AICPA homepage using the search box and entering "state boards of accountancy." You can also find links at the National Association of State Boards of Accountancy located at nasba.org.)

a. On the state board page, review three links that interest you. Describe the content of the links.
b. What useful consumer information does the site provide?
c. Does the site show the CPA licensing requirements? Using the information, explain one way in which an individual can complete the requirements in your state.
d. Compare your state's Board of Accountancy information to the home pages of three other states. Describe the similarities and differences that you find.

LEARNING GOAL 21 Use the Owner's Capital Accounts

In Learning Goal 21, you will find:

The Parts of Owner's Equity

Overview of Owner's Equity

The Individual Owner's Equity Accounts

In practice, the owner's equity account is subdivided to show the specific kinds of changes that affect owner's equity.

Revenues, expenses, owner drawing, and owner investment are the recurring changes that affect the owner's capital. The first three of these changes—revenues, expenses, and owner drawing—happen frequently and need to be carefully monitored. Therefore, in practice, the owner's capital is subdivided by creating individual accounts for revenues, expenses, and owner drawing.

Rule

Because owner's equity is on the right side of the accounting equation, all increases to owner's equity and the specific accounts that increase owner's equity are recorded on the right side of an account. Decreases are left-side entries.

Overview of Owner's Equity, *continued*

Capital Account Expanded

In the diagram below, the owner's capital is expanded to show the individual owner equity accounts. These separate accounts are a subdivision of the owner's capital. Because investments do not happen frequently and are therefore easy to follow, they are recorded directly into the owner's capital account.

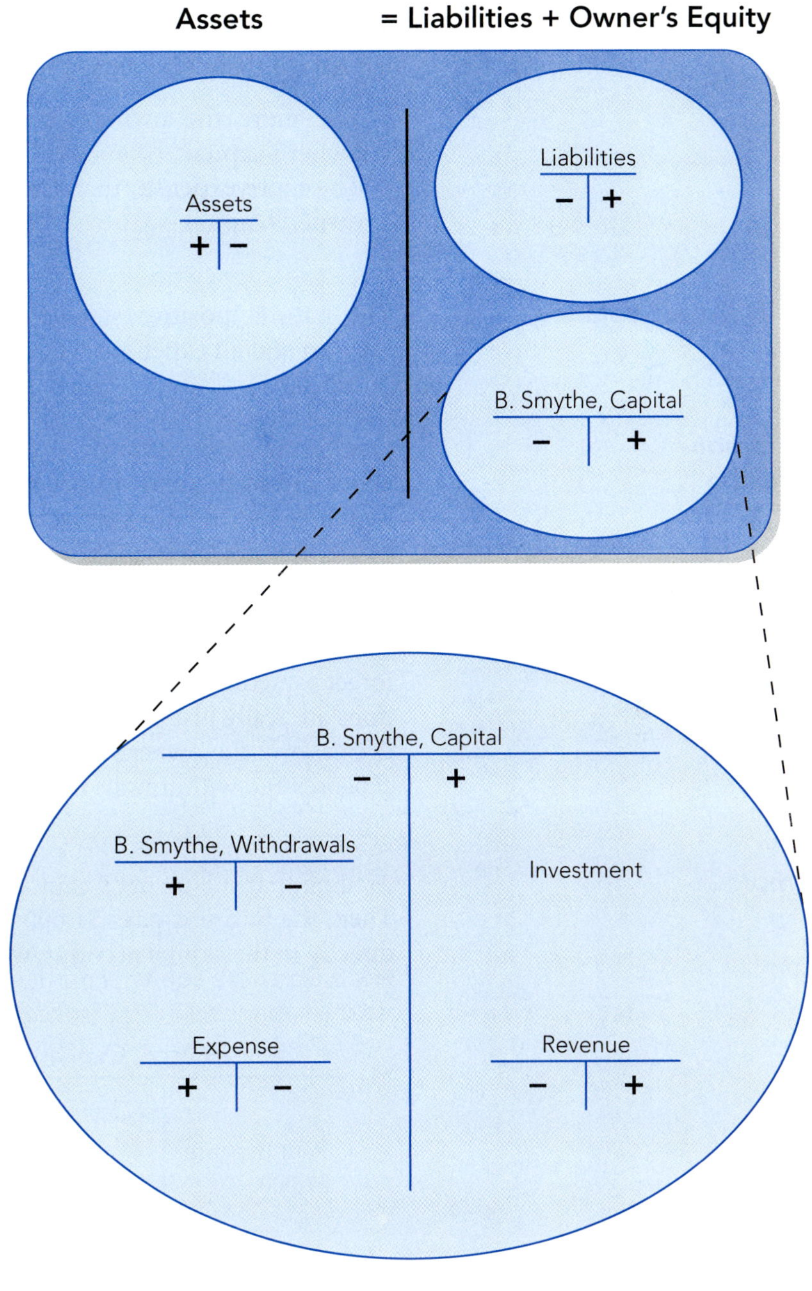

Rules and Examples of Increases and Decreases

Decreasing the Owner's Capital Account

Expenses and Withdrawals

Withdrawals (drawings) and expenses reduce the owner's capital. That is why they are shown as part of the *left side* of the owner's capital account. That is also why increases to drawings and expenses are recorded on the left side of these accounts.

- The more the owner withdraws, the greater the reduction in the owner's capital.
- The more expenses that are recorded, the greater the reduction in the owner's capital.

The "Normal" Balance

The natural positive side (the "normal" balance) of the withdrawals account and all expense accounts is the *left side*.

A Common Confusion

One of the most common confusions for students who are first learning about increasing and decreasing accounts is understanding why expense accounts and the drawing account are increased with left-side entries. In effect, they are asking: "Why is the normal balance of an expense or drawing account on the left side?"

The reason that people temporarily become confused about this is that they forget something important: Expense transactions and withdrawal transactions are really just particular types of decreases in the owner's capital, and decreases in the owner's capital are *always* recorded by left-side entries. So, expenses and withdrawals have to be recorded by left-side entries.

Example

Assume that the owner's capital balance of Watson Company is $25,000. Then, the business pays $1,000 of rent expense. If we record the expense directly in the capital account, we will see:

John Watson, Capital		
	$25,000	Beginning Balance
Rent Expense $1,000		

Decreasing the Owner's Capital Account, *continued*

Why the Owner's Equity Decreased

The owner's capital has decreased by $1,000 because business resources were used up to pay the rent. Or, you could also say: "Rent expense increased by $1,000." No matter how you prefer to describe it, a left-side entry is needed to show the reduction in John Watson, Capital.

Example, continued

Suppose that some time passes, and there are more expense and withdrawal transactions. For now, we will continue to record these transactions as direct decreases in the owner's capital.

John Watson, Capital		
	$25,000	Beginning Balance
Rent Expense $1,000 $1,000		
Repairs Expense $750		
Withdrawals $2,500		
Advertising Expense $3,000		

Example, continued

The owner's capital has now been decreased by transactions that we describe as another $1,000 of rent expense, $750 of repairs expense, $2,500 of withdrawals, and $3,000 of advertising expense. There are now three types of expenses and a withdrawal.

John Watson, Capital is reduced to $16,750. The more left entries we record, the more the owner's capital decreases. At the same time, the total of the expenses and drawing is increasing.

continued ▶

Decreasing the Owner's Capital Account, *continued*

More Transactions . . .

Suppose that more time goes by, and the business has more expenses and withdrawals.

John Watson, Capital		
	$25,000	Beginning Balance
Rent Expense $1,000 $1,000		
Repairs Expense $750 $1,220 $175		
Withdrawals $2,500 $1,000		
Advertising Expense $3,000 $525		

The expenses and withdrawals have now increased to $11,170, and the owner's capital balance is down to $13,830 ($25,000 – $11,170). The more expenses and withdrawals, the more the capital balance decreases. We are recording *increases in negative things*—things that decrease the owner's capital. Each left entry increases the total amount of expense or drawing but, at the same time, it decreases the owner's capital.

Clean Up the Capital Account

The left (decrease) side of the capital account is becoming very messy and crowded, isn't it? This overcrowding is happening with only three types of expenses and a drawing account. In a real business, think what would happen when there are many more expense accounts, each with dozens or hundreds of transactions!

Decreasing the Owner's Capital Account, *continued*

Individual Accounts

You can see that trying to record expenses and withdrawals directly into the owner's capital account becomes messy and difficult due to limited space. The solution to this problem is simply to give each type of decrease in the capital account its own separate account.

Even though the expenses and withdrawals are now recorded in their own individual accounts, we still understand that they are really just particular types of decreases in the owner's capital. We can continue to record their increases with left-side entries, just as if they were still being recorded directly into the capital account.

John Watson, Withdrawals	
2,500	
1,000	

Rent Expense	
1,000	
1,000	

Repairs Expense	
750	
1,220	
175	

Advertising Expense	
3,000	
525	

Reducing a Drawing or Expense Account

You may be wondering when a drawing or expense account would ever be decreased—that is, when an amount would be recorded on the right side. In practice, this is usually the result of some kind of adjustment, correction, or year-end closing. You will study this in Volume 2.

continued ▶

Check Your Understanding

Write the completed sentences on a separate piece of paper. The answers are below.

An expense or withdrawal transaction is always recorded by a · · · · · · · · -side entry. The reason people sometimes become confused about this is they forget that an expense or a withdrawal transaction is really just a particular type of · · · · · · · · in the owner's capital. A decrease in owner's capital is always recorded by a · · · · · · · · -side entry.

However, because of the large number of expense and withdrawal transactions, it (is/is not) · · · · · · · · feasible to record expenses and withdrawals directly in the owner's capital account. Instead, individual expense accounts and a drawing account are used, all of which have · · · · · · · · -side normal balances.

Answers

An expense or withdrawal transaction is always recorded by a left-side entry. The reason people sometimes become confused about this is they forget that an expense or a withdrawal transaction is really just a particular type of decrease in the owner's capital. A decrease in owner's capital is always recorded by a left-side entry.

However, because of the large number of expense and withdrawal transactions, it is not feasible to record expenses and withdrawals directly in the owner's capital account. Instead, individual expense accounts and a drawing account are used, all of which have left-side normal balances.

Increasing the Owner's Capital Account

Introduction

Investments and revenues increase the owner's capital. That is why they are shown on the right side of the owner's capital account.

- The more the owner invests, the greater the increase in the owner's capital.
- The more revenues that are recorded, the greater the increase in the owner's capital.

Increasing the Owner's Capital Account, *continued*

Separate Accounts

As with expenses, because of space limitations, it is not practical to enter all the revenues directly into the owner's capital account. Therefore, a separate account is used to record each type of revenue transaction. For example, service revenue and interest revenue transactions are recorded in two separate revenue accounts.

The "Normal" Balance

Revenue accounts always have normal right-side balances. Increases are always recorded on the right of revenue accounts because revenues are increases in owner's equity, which is increased with a right-side entry.

Decreases in Revenues

You may be wondering when a revenue account would ever be decreased—that is, when an amount would be recorded on the left side. In practice, this is usually the result of some kind of adjustment, correction, or year-end closing. It does not happen very often. You will study this later in Volume 2.

Examples of Owner's Equity Transactions

Introduction

Here are some typical examples of owner's equity transactions using just a few accounts. To remind you that they are really subdivisions of owner's capital, we show the revenue, expense, and drawing accounts under the owner's capital account.

Suppose that on June 5, Jill Hirata decides to start her own business by investing cash. Therefore, the asset Cash increases $10,000 and Jill Hirata, Capital increases $10,000.

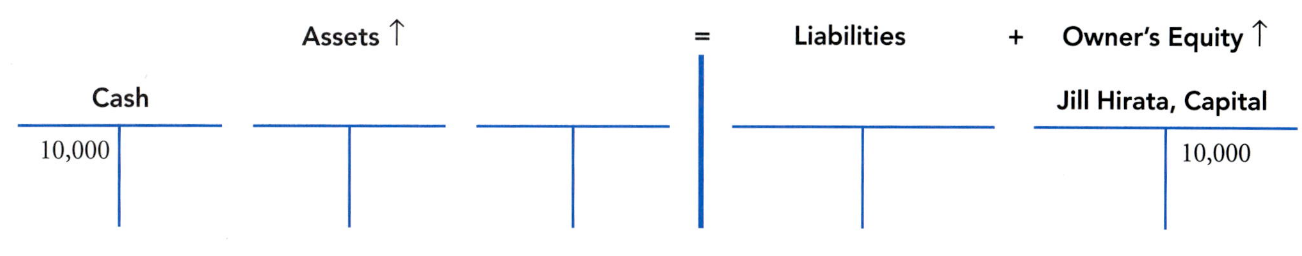

continued ▶

Examples of Owner's Equity Transactions, *continued*

On June 7, the business buys $500 of supplies on account. Therefore, the asset Supplies increases $500 and the liability Accounts Payable increases $500. Owner's capital is not affected.

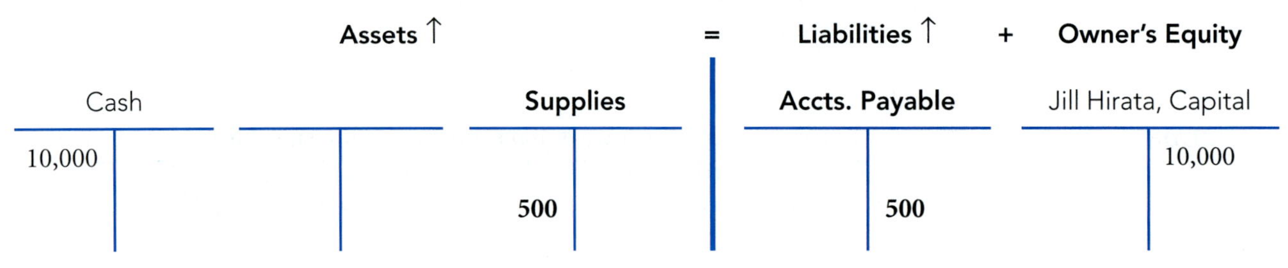

On June 8, the business uses up $100 of supplies. The asset Supplies decreases. The account Supplies Expense increases, thereby decreasing total owner's capital to $9,900.

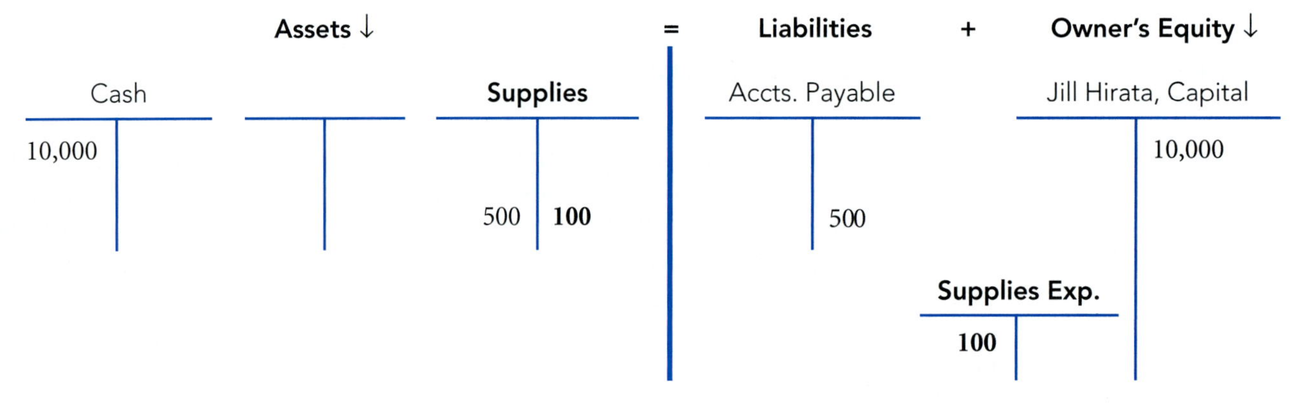

On June 10, the business earns $800 of revenue on account. So, the asset Accounts Receivable increases $800. The revenue account Fees Earned increases by $800, thereby increasing total owner's capital to $10,700.

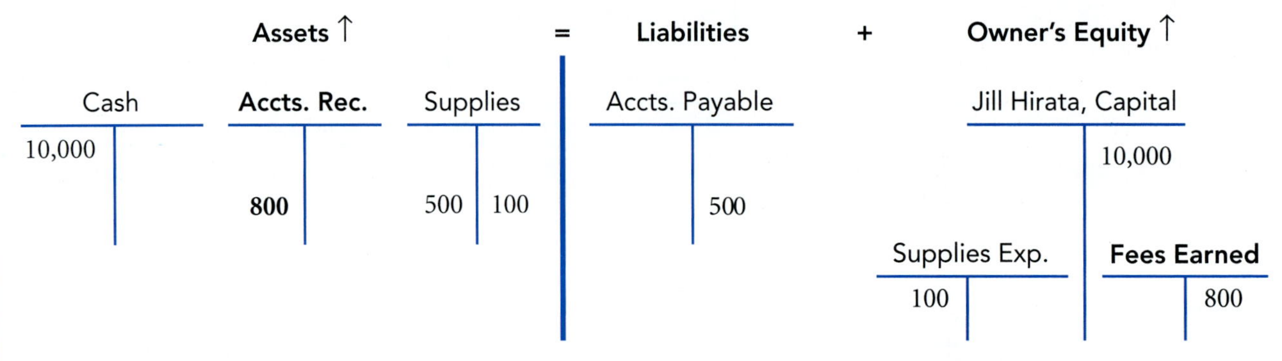

Examples of Owner's Equity Transactions, *continued*

On June 15, the business receives a $300 bill for equipment rental. The bill will be paid early next month, so the liability Accounts Payable increases $300. The expense account Rent Expense increases $300, thereby decreasing total owner's capital to $10,400.

Assets = **Liabilities ↑** + **Owner's Equity ↓**

Account	Debit	Credit
Cash	10,000	
Accts. Rec.	800	
Supplies	500	100
Accts. Payable		500 **300**
Jill Hirata, Capital		10,000
Supplies Exp.	100	
Fees Earned		800
Rent Exp.	**300**	

On June 19, Jill withdraws $250 cash from the business, so the asset Cash decreases $250. The drawing account increases $250, thereby decreasing total owner's capital to $10,150.

Assets ↓ = **Liabilities** + **Owner's Equity ↓**

Account	Debit	Credit
Cash	10,000	**250**
Accts. Rec.	800	
Supplies	500	100
Accts. Payable		500 300
Jill Hirata, Capital		10,000
J. Hirata, Draw.	**250**	
Supplies Exp.	100	
Fees Earned		800
Rent Exp.	300	

QUICK REVIEW

- The owner's capital account is subdivided into three additional types of accounts: revenues, expenses, and owner drawing. There are usually many different types of expenses and several different types of revenues.
- Expenses and drawing are always decreases to the owner's capital. Therefore, the natural positive side of expense and drawing accounts is the left side.
- Revenues are always increases to owner's capital. Therefore, the natural positive side of revenue accounts is the right side.
- Investments are recorded directly into the right side of the owner's capital account.

"Left-side entry to record expenses and drawing, right-side entry to record revenues!"

Do You Want More Examples?

Most problems in this book have detailed solutions. To use them as additional examples, do this: 1) Select the type of problem you want 2) Open the solution on your computer or mobile device screen (from the disc or worthyjames.com) 3) Read one item at a time and look at its answer. Take notes if needed. 4) Close the solution and work as much of the problem as you can. 5) Repeat as needed.

PRACTICE Learning Goal 21

Solutions are in the disk at the back of the book and at: www.worthyjames.com

Learning Goal 21 is about learning the rules for increasing and decreasing the various owner's equity accounts. Use these questions and problems to practice what you have just read.

Discussion Questions and Brief Exercises for Learning Goals 20–21

1. What is an account?

2. What is the normal balance (left or right side) of the accounts?
   a. asset
   b. liability
   c. owner's equity
   d. revenue
   e. expense

3. State the rule for recording increases in accounts. Give three examples.

4. State the rule for recording decreases in accounts. Give three examples.

5. Why does a right side entry decrease an asset *and* increase a liability? When a does a left side entry increase an asset *and* decrease a liability?

6. The beginning balance in a company's Cash account is $7,000. The company then receives $750 cash from a customer, pays $200 cash for office supplies and borrows $2,000. Draw a T account that shows the beginning balance, the increases and decreases in the account, and the ending balance in the account.

7. The beginning balance in an Accounts Payable account is $3,400. The company then purchases $1,500 of supplies on account and pays $2,900 owing to a creditor. Draw a T account that shows the beginning balance, the increases and decreases in the account, and the ending balance in the account.

8. Why are revenues and expenses recorded separately from the owner's capital account?

9. Why are expense increases recorded on the left side of accounts and revenue increases recorded on the right side of accounts?

10. The owner's equity of a business is subdivided into separate accounts. A total of four accounts are used to maintain a record of owner's equity. What are these accounts and what functions do they perform?

11. What are the normal balances of the owner's equity accounts?

12. Debbie Campbell started a new business by investing $10,000. At the end of the first month, the revenue account showed a balance of $2,700, and the various expense account balances totaled $1,800. At the end of the month, the withdrawals account had a balance of $1,000. How much was the owner's equity in the business at the end of the month?

13. The owner's investments in a business are recorded into which account? Is this a left-side entry or a right-side entry? Why?

PRACTICE Learning Goal 21, continued

Solutions are in the disk at the back of the book and at: www.worthyjames.com

Reinforcement Problems

LG 21-1. Explain concepts about owner's capital accounts.

a. Why is the natural positive side ("normal side") of the owner's capital the right side of the account?

b. Why is the owner's capital subdivided into separate accounts for revenue, expense, and drawing, in addition to the owner's capital account?

c. Why is the natural positive side ("normal side") of an expense account or drawing account the left side?

d. The more an expense or drawing account increases, the more the total owner's capital decreases. Why?

e. Why is the natural positive side ("normal side") of a revenue account the right side?

LG 21-2. Negative balance in owner's capital? We know that assets and liabilities cannot really have negative balances, although sometimes assets such as Cash or Accounts Receivable might be temporarily shown with negative balances as a shortcut. However, can the owner's capital account ever have a negative balance? Why?

LG 21-3. Practice using owner's equity accounts. Each of the following statements describes a separate transaction. Below, blank T accounts are arranged under the accounting equation. For each statement, do the following: Using a separate piece of paper, draw the accounts, write the names of the accounts that are affected above the T accounts, and then make entries for the dollar amounts into the accounts. (*Remember:* The entries must keep the equation in balance!)

a. On October 1, David Jefferson invests $15,000 to start a new business called Jefferson Consulting Services.

b. On October 5, the business spends $5,000 cash to purchase $4,000 of computer equipment and $1,000 of office supplies from a vendor.

c. On October 7, the business uses up $500 of supplies in performing a consulting job for a client.

d. On October 20, the business receives a $200 bill from the electric company. The bill will be paid early next month.

e. On October 28, the business completes a consulting job, and the client pays $1,500 cash.

f. On October 31, David Jefferson withdraws $750 cash from his business.

PRACTICE Learning Goal 21, continued

Solutions are in the disk at the back of the book and at: www.worthyjames.com

LG 21-3, *continued*

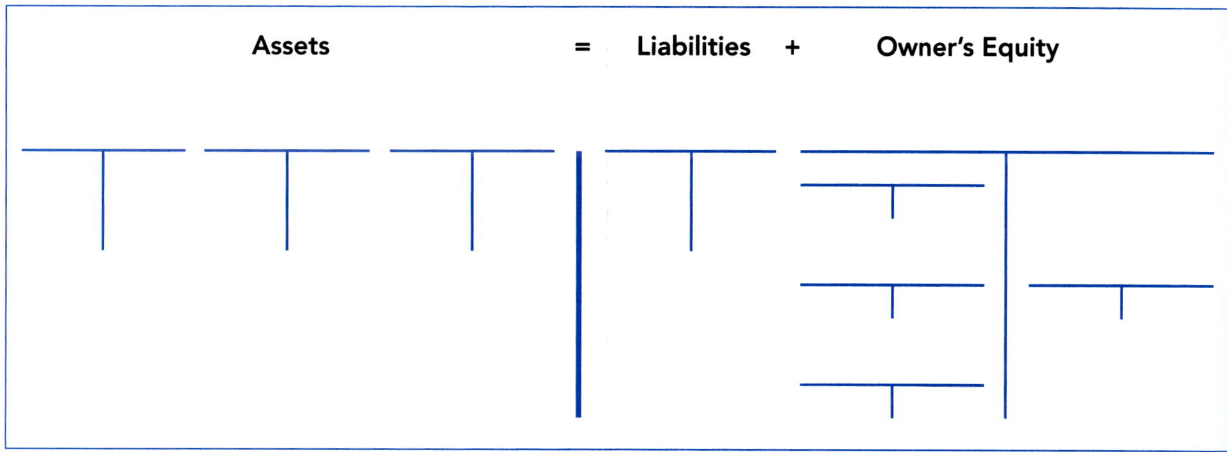

LG 21-4. Practice using owner's equity accounts. Draw the T accounts that you see below on a separate piece of paper. Using the T accounts and the transaction items listed below, enter the increases and decreases in the correct T accounts. Identify each transaction by placing the letter of the transaction next to the entry for the transaction. When you are finished with all the transactions, calculate the account balances and enter them on the correct sides of the accounts. Then calculate the net income or loss of the business.

a. Howard Laguna invested $10,000 in his business.
b. The business paid $2,000 for the current month's rent expense.
c. The business received a bill for advertising in the local paper, $700. The bill was not paid immediately.
d. The business purchased $300 of supplies on account.
e. The business performed services for a client on account, $3,900.
f. The business used $150 of supplies.
g. The business performed services for a client and received $1,500 cash.
h. The business received the utility bill for $90 but did not pay it immediately.
i. The business paid employee wages of $1,600.
j. Howard Laguna withdrew $1,000 cash from the business.

Cash	Accounts Receivable	Supplies	Accounts Payable

PRACTICE **Learning Goal 21, continued**

Solutions are in the disk at the back of the book and at: www.worthyjames.com

LG 21-4, *continued*

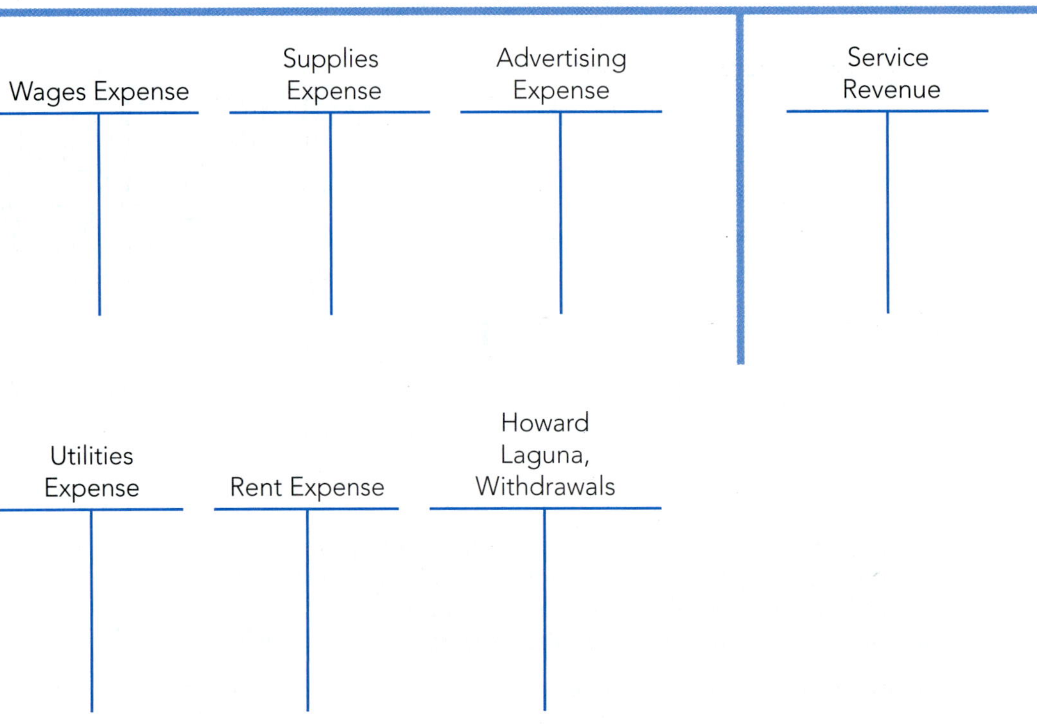

LG 21-5. **Practice using owner's equity accounts.** Draw the T accounts that you see below on a separate piece of paper. Using the T accounts and the transaction items listed below, enter the increases and decreases in the correct T accounts. Identify each transaction by placing the letter of the transaction next to the entry for the transaction. When you are finished with all the transactions, calculate the account balances and enter them on the correct sides of the accounts. Then calculate the net income or loss of the business.

a. Anne Quincy invested $20,000 cash and $500 of supplies in her business.
b. The business paid $3,500 for the current month's advertising expense.
c. The business received an advance payment of $5,000 from a customer.
d. The business performed services for a client on account, $1,300.
e. The business purchased $700 of supplies on account.
f. The business performed services for a client and received $900 cash.
g. The business received a repair service bill of $375 but did not pay it immediately.
h. The business paid employee wages of $3,000.
i. The business used $400 of supplies.
j. The business performed services and earned $3,000 of the unearned revenue.
k. Anne Quincy withdrew $5,000 cash from the business.
l. Received a $500 bill for monthly utilities but did not pay bill immediately.
m. Paid for $300 of additional repairs.

PRACTICE

Learning Goal 21, continued

Solutions are in the disk at the back of the book and at: www.worthyjames.com

LG 21-5, *continued*

Cash

Accounts Receivable

Supplies

Accounts Payable

Unearned Revenue

Anne Quincy, Capital

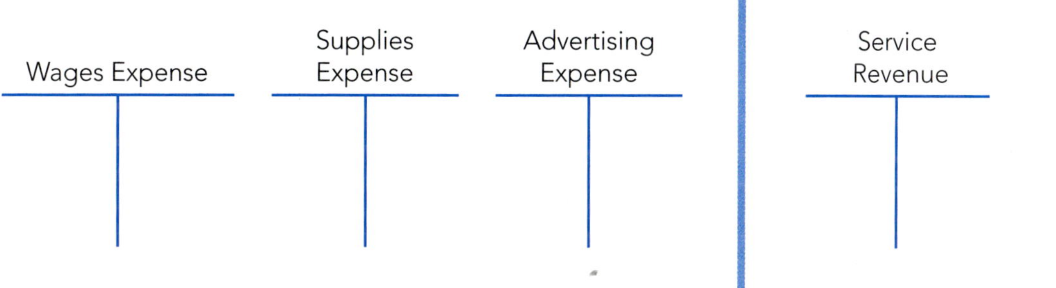

Utilities Expense

Repairs Expense

Anne Quincy Withdrawals

LEARNING GOAL 22

"Debits on the left, credits on the right!"

In Learning Goal 22, you will find:

The Words "Debit" and "Credit"

What Debit and Credit Really Mean

Introduction

Every occupation has its own special terminology. Two of the accounting terms that most people have heard at one time or another are the terms ***debit*** and ***credit***. Even though these words only refer to the left and right sides of an account, there seems to be much confusion and even anxiety about the meaning of these two words.

The truth is really quite simple. Accounting was first developed in Italy during the 1400s. At that time, educated businesspeople spoke Latin. The root word of the Latin term for "left" or "left entry" was "debere" or "debitum". The root word for "right" or "right entry" was "credere" or "creditum". Today, those words have changed into "debit" and "credit" in English, but the meaning is still the same—left and right. The word "debit" is often abbreviated as ***Dr.,*** and the word "credit" is often abbreviated as "***Cr.***"

Rule

- Instead of saying "left side," say "debit."
- Instead of saying "right side," say "credit."

What Debit and Credit Really Mean, *continued*

Do Not Make These Mistakes!

People who should know better (financial writers, TV broadcasters, and even some nonaccounting teachers) often use debit and credit terminology in completely mistaken ways. They think that the words debit and credit mean things like good or bad, or always increase, always decrease, etc. Ignore these people. The words debit and credit *refer only to* **location**—left or right.

The words debit and credit *do not mean* "good" or "bad" or "favorable" or "unfavorable" or "always increase" or "always decrease" or "gain" or "loss" or anything else!

In accounting, debit means "left" and credit means "right." And that is all.

Debit and Credit Rules Applied to All Account Types

Apply Debits and Credits to the Accounts

Introduction

If you have already practiced recording transactions in other learning goals, you will be happy to know that applying debit and credit to accounts does not really involve doing anything different. *All you need to do is remember to say "debit" instead of "left," and "credit" instead of "right." The rules for increasing and decreasing accounts are* **still the same**.

> *Note:* To ***charge*** an account means to debit it. There is no alternative word for credit.

The Recording Rules

As a quick review, the basic recording rules are repeated here:

- **Increases:** Any account that is a *left-side* account in the accounting equation (assets) is increased with a *left-side entry* (debit). Any account that is a *right-side* account in the accounting equation (liabilities and owner's capital) is increased with a *right-side entry* (credit).
- **Decreases:** Learn increases first. Decreases are then recorded on the opposite side from increases. (So, assets are decreased with credits, and liabilities and owner's capital are decreased with debits.)

If you are not completely comfortable with these rules, you can get more practice and review in Learning Goal 11.

continued ▶

Apply Debits and Credits to the Accounts, *continued*

Rules Illustrated

The expanded illustration below shows the rules for recording all transaction types.

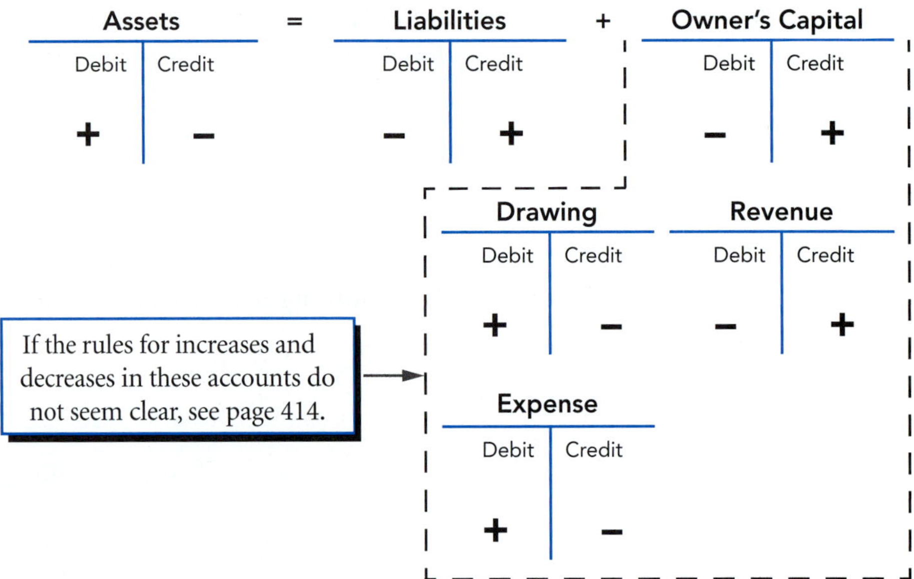

Debit and Credit Rules for the Six Basic Account Types

Summary

The table below shows a summary of the rules for debits and credits for each of the six basic account types in the accounting equation. This is exactly the same information that you see in the illustration above.

	Assets =	Liabilities +		Owner's Equity		
	Assets	**Liabilities**	**Owner's Capital**	**Revenue**	**Expense**	**Drawing**
Debit (left)	Increase (and natural positive balance)	Decrease	Decrease	Decrease	Increase (and natural positive balance)	Increase (and natural positive balance)
Credit (right)	Decrease	Increase (and natural positive balance)	Increase (and natural positive balance)	Increase (and natural positive balance)	Decrease	Decrease

To know if a debit or credit will be an increase or a decrease, **you have to specify the type of account.** Accounts on the left side of the equation (assets) are increased with debits. Accounts on the right side (liabilities and owner's equity) are increased with credits. Decreases are the opposite.

Debit and Credit Rules for the Six Basic Account Types, *continued*

Examples

Philadelphia Company performs $3,000 of consulting services and mails a bill to the client. The bookkeeper debits Accounts Receivable for $3,000 and credits Fees Earned for $3,000.

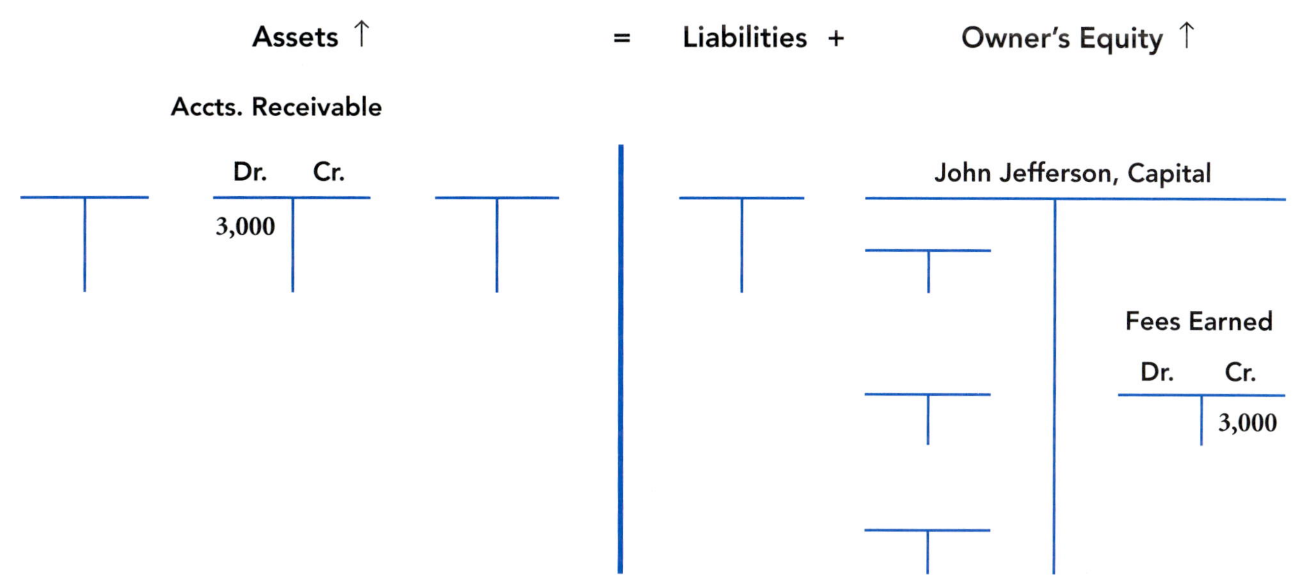

Allegheny Company spends $5,000 cash to purchase $4,000 of computer equipment and $1,000 of office supplies. The bookkeeper records the transaction with a debit to Supplies for $1,000, a debit to Equipment for $4,000, and a credit to Cash for $5,000.

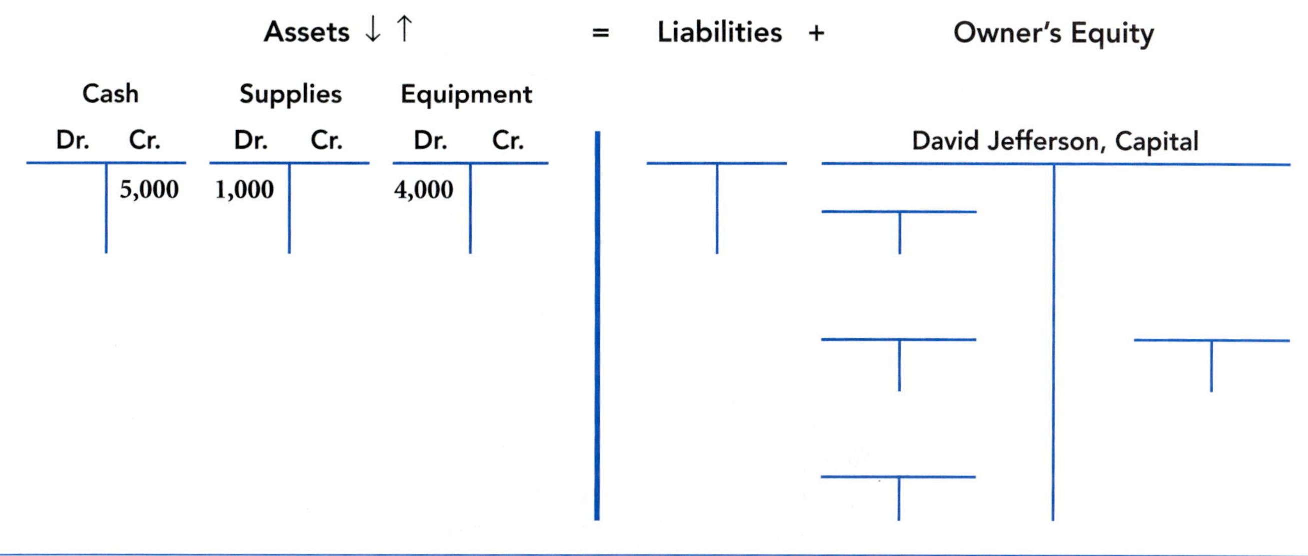

QUICK REVIEW

- The words "debit" and "credit" refer only to location. Debit means left and credit means right. They do not have any other meaning.
- The rules for increasing and decreasing accounts are:
  - Accounts in the left side of the equation are increased with left-side entries, and accounts in the right side of the equation are increased with right-side entries.
  - Remember increases first; then decreases are on the opposite sides.

VOCABULARY

Charge: to debit an account (page 429)

Credit: a right-side entry or the right side of an account (page 428)

Cr.: the abbreviation for the word "credit" (page 428)

Debit: a left-side entry or the left side of an account (page 428)

Dr.: the abbreviation for the word "debit" (page 428)

"They will love it! 'Debit' for left and 'credit' for right!"

PRACTICE Learning Goal 22

Solutions are in the disk at the back of the book and at: www.worthyjames.com

Learning Goal 22 is about using debit and credit terminology when recording transactions. Answer the questions and problems below to practice what you have just read.

Multiple Choice

Select the best answer.

1. Which of the following is *not* true?
   a. Items on the left side of the accounting equation are increased with debits, and items on the right side are increased with credits.
   b. Items on the left side of the accounting equation are decreased with credits, and items on the right side are decreased with debits.
   c. Both sides of the accounting equation are decreased with debits and increased with credits.
   d. Both (a) and (b).
2. The correct meaning of the words "debit" and "credit" is
   a. debit means increase and credit means decrease.
   b. debit means decrease and credit means increase.
   c. they can be interpreted as either "favorable" or "unfavorable" or as "give" and "take," depending on the transaction involved.
   d. none of the above.
3. Albuquerque Company receives a bill for advertising services, which will be paid next week. The company will have to
   a. debit Owner's Capital and credit Cash.
   b. debit Advertising Expense and credit Accounts Payable.
   c. debit Advertising Expense and credit Cash.
   d. wait until payment is made.
4. How are decreases to accounts distinguished from increases?
   a. Decreases are always on the side opposite from the side for increases.
   b. Decreases are always right-side (credit) entries.
   c. Decreases are always left-side (debit) entries.
   d. Decreases are always shown with a minus sign.
5. If the Santa Fe Art Shoppe collected $500 of cash from Accounts Receivable, it would have to
   a. debit Accounts Receivable $500 and credit Cash $500.
   b. debit Cash $500 and credit Accounts Receivable $500.
   c. debit Cash $500 and credit Owner's Equity $500.
   d. none of the above.
6. An account that is increased with a credit is
   a. Cash.
   b. Equipment.
   c. Accounts Payable.
   d. both (a) and (b).
7. The Luna Voc Tour Company purchased $100 of supplies on account. It should
   a. debit Supplies $100 and credit Cash $100.
   b. debit Supplies $100 and credit Owner's Equity $100.
   c. debit Supplies $100 and debit Cash $100.
   d. debit Supplies $100 and credit Accounts Payable $100.
8. Which of the following is *not* true?
   a. Debits increase assets.
   b. Credits decrease assets.
   c. Credits increase liabilities.
   d. Credits decrease liabilities.

PRACTICE

Learning Goal 22, continued

Solutions are in the disk at the back of the book and at: www.worthyjames.com

9. A credit to Accounts Payable is
   a. an increase to Accounts Payable.
   b. a decrease to Accounts Payable.
   c. an unfavorable entry.
   d. both (a) and (c).

10. A credit to Unearned Revenue is
   a. an increase to a revenue.
   b. an increase to a liability.
   c. an increase to an asset.
   d. none of the above.

11. Las Cruces Enterprises shows a Service Revenue account with a credit balance of $44,200. Accounts Payable has a normal balance of $11,000, owner's drawing has a normal balance of $5,000, and expenses total $37,100 normal balance. Las Cruces has
   a. a net loss of $8,900.
   b. a net loss of $3,900.
   c. a net income of $2,100.
   d. a net income of $7,100.

12. Debits record
   a. decreases in liabilities and assets.
   b. decreases in assets and increases in liabilities.
   c. decreases in liabilities and increases in assets.
   d. increases in liabilities and assets.

13. Accounts payable was debited and cash was credited. Which of the following best describes what happened?
   a. The company borrowed cash.
   b. The company used cash to pay accounts payable that was owing.
   c. The company reduced accounts payable by earning income.
   d. The company is owed money for services rendered.

14. Cash is credited and supplies is debited. Which of the following best describes what happened?
   a. The company bought some supplies.
   b. The company used up some supplies.
   c. The company sold some supplies to another business, which owes the cash.
   d. The company sold some supplies and received the cash.

15. Cash is debited and unearned revenue is credited. Which of the following best describes what happened?
   a. The company is owed cash for services rendered to a customer.
   b. The company receives cash for services provided.
   c. The company receives cash for services not yet performed.
   d. None of the above.

16. Cash is debited and accounts receivable is credited. Which of the following best describes what happened?
   a. The company collects cash owing from a customer(s).
   b. The company collects cash prior to rendering services.
   c. The company borrows cash and owes the money to the creditor.
   d. None of the above.

17. Equipment is debited and notes payable is credited. Which of the following best describes what happened?
   a. The company sold equipment and is owed the money by the buyer.
   b. The company purchased equipment for cash.
   c. The owner personally purchased equipment and then contributed it to the company.
   d. None of the above.

PRACTICE

Learning Goal 22, continued

Solutions are in the disk at the back of the book and at: www.worthyjames.com

Reinforcement Problems

LG 22-1. Identify the natural positive side ("Normal Side"). For each of the accounts listed below, indicate if the account has a natural debit or credit balance.

Account
a. Supplies
b. Accounts Payable
c. Service Revenue
d. Cash
e. R. Penland, Drawing
f. R. Penland, Capital
g. Accounts Receivable
h. Rent Expense
i. Prepaid Rent
j. Equipment
k. Unearned Revenue
l. Notes Payable

LG 22-2. Explain how to use debits and credits. For each item below, correctly complete the sentence on a separate piece of paper.

a. Debits are increases when . . .
b. Debits are decreases when . . .
c. Credits are increases when . . .
d. Credits are decreases when . . .

PRACTICE Learning Goal 22, continued

Solutions are in the disk at the back of the book and at: www.worthyjames.com

LG 22-3. The six elements of the accounting equation: Identify the debit and credit rules. On a separate piece of paper, draw a table like the one below. Complete the following table by writing the word "increase" or "decrease" in the spaces in each column of the six elements in the accounting equation. **Write the increases first.** At the bottom of each column, also write "Dr." or "Cr." to identify which side of an account for each element shows the natural positive balance (the "normal balance").

	Assets	Liabilities	Owner's Capital	Revenue	Expense	Drawing
Debit	....	....	....	....	....	....
Credit	....	....	....	....	....	....
Natural Positive Balance?	....	....	....	....	....	....

LG 22-4. You be the teacher—Debits and credits explained. As an accounting teacher, I always get lots of questions when the subject of debits and credits is introduced for the first time. However, this semester I will be away at a conference on the day that we begin the introduction to debits and credits. Instead of canceling class, I am asking you for some help—you be the new teacher today—and answer these (actual) questions from students:

a. "Why doesn't it work so that 'debit' always means increase?"

b. "Why doesn't it work so that 'credit' always means decrease?"

c. "Expenses are part of owner's equity, which is on the opposite side of the equation from assets. So why are assets and expenses both increased with debits?"

d. "How do I figure out how to use debits and credits for increases and decreases?"

LG 22-5. Record debit and credit entries into accounts. In each of the transactions listed below, draw T accounts on a separate piece of paper to record transactions. Before recording each transaction, complete the "analysis" and "apply the rule" sections. The first transaction is presented as an example.

Note: Remember that you can visualize each transaction by either drawing a picture of the condition of the business or by using the accounting equation. Then place T accounts in the picture or under the equation.

PRACTICE

Learning Goal 22, continued

Solutions are in the disk at the back of the book and at: www.worthyjames.com

LG 22-5, *continued*

Example: Annapolis Enterprises pays $550 to purchase office supplies.

Analysis (account type, account name, and increase or decrease):
The *asset Supplies increases* by $550. The *asset Cash decreases* by $550.

Apply the rule (debits and credits):
Assets are decreased with credits: credit Cash $550.
Assets are increased with debits: debit Supplies $550.

Record in T account:

Cash		Supplies	
	550	550	

a. Essex Company receives $1,000 from a customer before the services are provided.

Analysis (account type, account name, and increase or decrease):

Apply the rule (debits and credits):

Record in T account:

b. Montgomery Enterprises receives a $200 electric bill. The bill is not paid immediately.

Analysis (account type, account name, and increase or decrease):

Apply the rule (debits and credits):

Record in T account:

PRACTICE Learning Goal 22, continued

Solutions are in the disk at the back of the book and at: www.worthyjames.com

LG 22-5, *continued*

c. Prince Georges Company finishes consulting services for a client and sends the client a bill for $5,000.

Analysis (account type, account name, and increase or decrease):

Apply the rule (debits and credits):

Record in T account:

d. Cecil Company prepays six months of fire insurance for $2,500.

Analysis (account type, account name, and increase or decrease):

Apply the rule (debits and credits):

Record in T account:

e. James Lafayette, owner of Anchorage Company, invests $9,000 in his business.

Analysis (account type, account name, and increase or decrease):

Apply the rule (debits and credits):

Record in T account:

PRACTICE

Learning Goal 22, continued

Solutions are in the disk at the back of the book and at: www.worthyjames.com

LG 22-5, *continued*

f. Soldotna Company pays a $1,000 account payable.

Analysis (account type, account name, and increase or decrease):

Apply the rule (debits and credits):

Record in T account:

g. Nome Commercial Company purchases $10,000 of equipment, paying $3,000 cash and signing a note payable for the balance.

Analysis (account type, account name, and increase or decrease):

Apply the rule (debits and credits):

Record in T account:

LG 22-6. More practice with debits and credits—Use T accounts to record transactions.
Listed below are the individual transactions from the example of Jack's Guitar School in Learning Goal 11.

- Draw T accounts or print T accounts from the disk at the back of the book. Write the name of each account above the account: Cash, Accounts Receivable, Supplies, Equipment, Accounts Payable, Unearned Revenue, Jack Davis–Drawing, Jack Davis–Capital, Teaching Revenue, Utilities Expense, Telephone Expense, Supplies Expense, Rent Expense
- For each transaction, enter the debits and credits in the accounts.
- Total each of the accounts and enter the account balances in the proper locations.
- After you have finished the exercise and checked the answer, return to Learning Goal 11, page 261 and compare your entries and accounts to the example. Can you see that the basic rule for increasing and decreasing is still the same? The only difference is that now we will call the entries by the names "debit" and "credit." (And we have subdivided the capital account into separate accounts for revenues, expenses, and drawing.)

PRACTICE Learning Goal 22, continued

IA22-1, *continued*

(j) The business received a $2,470 bill for advertising in a business publication. The bill was not paid immediately.
(k) The business purchased new office furniture for $15,000 by paying $5,750 cash and signing a note payable for the balance.
(l) The business made a $400 payment on account.
(m) The business collected $900 from a customer on account.
(n) The business performed $1,900 of services for the client who had made the advance payment.
(o) The business received a $700 bill for other Internet expenses, which was not paid immediately.

IA22-2. Record the transactions shown below into T accounts.

- Write the accounting equation A = L + OE across the top of a blank sheet of paper, leaving ample space between each part of the equation. (You will have more space if you turn the paper so the long side is horizontal.)
- Under each part of the equation, draw as many blank T accounts as you need to record the transactions shown below. Refer to the example shown in the instructions for LG 22-7.
- Record each transaction with debits and credits in the appropriate T accounts. Write each account's name above the account as needed. Identify the entries of each transaction with the letter of the transaction.
- After all transactions are recorded, enter the final balance of each T account on the appropriate normal side of the account.
- Calculate the net income or net loss for the period.

Transactions:

(a) Jackson Green invested $70,000 in his new business, Detroit Printing Services.
(b) The business purchased paper supplies for $5,800 on account.
(c) The business purchased computer equipment for $3,700 cash.
(d) The business purchased $60,000 of printing equipment by paying $40,000 cash and signing a note payable.
(e) The business paid $1,500 for the current month's rent.
(f) The business performed brochure printing services for $3,600 on account.
(g) The business received a $770 bill for printing equipment repairs. The bill was not paid immediately.
(h) The business performed printing services for $11,200 and received $5,000 cash, with the balance owing from the customer.
(i) The business received a $520 bill from the utilities company that was not paid immediately.
(j) The business signed a printing contract and received a $7,500 advance payment from a large client.
(k) The business paid the utility bill in (i) above.
(l) The business collected $900 from a customer on account.
(m) The business received a $1,450 bill for equipment repairs. The bill was paid immediately.
(n) The business performed $3,800 of services for the client who had made the advance payment.
(o) Jackson Green withdrew $2,000 cash from the business for personal use.
(p) A physical count of paper supplies showed that $3,500 of supplies had been used up.

Your Questions?

It is *very* important to be aware of what you need to understand better. What do you need to understand better about this learning goal? On a separate piece of paper, write the questions that you want to discuss with your classmates, instructor, or supervisor. Try to be very specific about what is bothering you, such as explanations that you do not fully understand.

LEARNING GOAL 23 The Ledger

Overview

Introduction

In the prior learning goals, we reviewed different information requirements (Learning Goal 19) and what accounts are and how they are used (Learning Goals 20, 21, & 22.). In this Learning Goal you will learn about how accounts are arranged and identified, and how it is easy to add new accounts.

Our Present Arrangement

So far, we have used a table to record transactions and to meet the five information requirements.

	Assets								=	Liabilities + Owner's Equity			
	Cash		Accounts Receivable		Supplies		Equipment			Note Payable		C. Goldman, Capital	
	Increase	Decrease	Increase	Decrease	Increase	Decrease	Increase	Decrease		Decrease	Increase	Decrease	Increase
5/2	bal. **17,300**		bal. **4,500**		bal. **900**		bal. **12,000**				bal. **10,000**		bal. **24,700**
5/4	800			800									
5/5			1,000										1,000
5/7		400			400								
5/7	2,000												2,000
5/8		1,000					5,000				4,000		
5/8	bal. **18,700**		bal. **4,700**		bal. **1,300**		bal. **17,000**				bal. **14,000**		bal. **27,700**

The Table Is Not Practical

Unfortunately, there is one serious problem in the way we are recording transactions in tables, SPACE! Even though we nicely satisfy all five requirements, we will quickly run out of space for accounts. Because we are placing the accounts across a page, we are limited by the width of a page. Already we will need to show the owner's various capital sub-accounts, and this may include several different revenues and many individual expenses. We will also have additional assets and liabilities. Even if we go across two pages we will never have enough space! However, remain calm . . . you only have to read the next page to find the solution to the problem.

Separate Books for Different Purposes

Two Books: The Journal and the Ledger

To solve the space problem and still satisfy all information requirements, accountants have found that they need to enter the transaction information into *two* separate kinds of records. These records are usually kept in two separate books, called a journal and a ledger. In a computerized system, they are shown as two separate files.

Journal Defined

A ***journal*** is like a daily diary that keeps a list of all the transactions as they happen.

We will discuss the journal in depth in the next learning goal, starting on page 450.

The General Ledger

Ledger Defined

A ***ledger*** is a book that contains individual accounts. The general-purpose kind of ledger that we study here is also called the ***general ledger*** because it contains all the accounts. The accounts in a ledger are sometimes called ***ledger accounts***. A ledger fulfills two information requirements because with a ledger you can see:

- A record of all the increases and decreases in each account
- The balance of each account

The Structure of the Ledger

A ledger solves the space problem by placing each account on its own page. The accounts as individual pages are then placed into the book (the ledger). We can have as many accounts as we want. The book is designed so that the back can be separated and new pages can be added. So, any time we need a new account, we can just add another page! The diagram on the next page illustrates this idea.

The General Ledger, *continued*

Every account has its own page. All the pages are placed together in a book called the ledger.

This makes it possible to keep as many accounts as necessary in one convenient place.

In a computerized system, a computer file is used instead of a book.

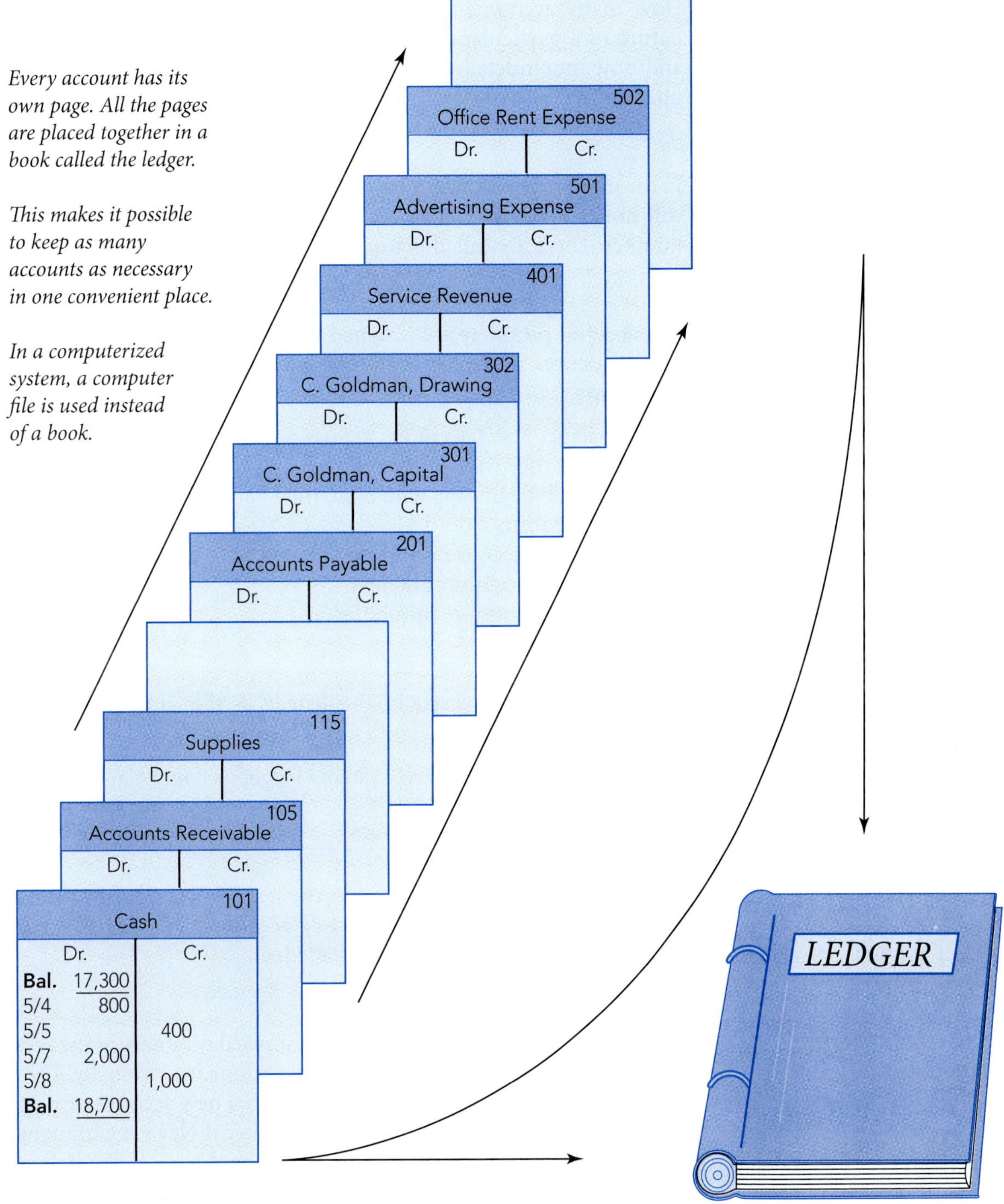

continued ▶

The General Ledger, *continued*

How Many Accounts?

How many accounts a business needs depends upon the size and the nature of a particular business, what kinds of transactions it usually has, and how much detail the owners and managers want to know about the operations.

Account Identification Numbers

In the upper-right corner of each account in the illustration on page 445, you will notice a number. Each account has its own permanent identification number. These are called ***account numbers***.

Rule for Assigning Account Numbers

The account numbers are assigned to accounts in the approximate ordering sequence that the accounts normally appear on the financial statements.

- The balance sheet accounts are assigned the first numbers, in the same order that they will appear on the balance sheet. For example, assets are shown first, beginning with cash, then liabilities, and finally the owner's capital account.
- The drawing account is numbered next.
- The revenue accounts are next.
- Expense accounts are numbered last.

Rule for Placing Accounts in the Ledger

Account pages are placed in the ledger in the same sequence as their account numbers.

Note: In a computerized system, ledger accounts also appear in the same sequence.

The Chart of Accounts

The names of all the accounts and the numbers assigned to them can be found in a listing called the ***chart of accounts***. The chart of accounts is usually located on the first page of a ledger.

Gaps in the Numbering Sequence

You can see that there are large gaps of unused numbers in the sequence of numbers assigned to the accounts. This is done intentionally. The gaps are for numbers that might be needed later when new accounts are added. For example, the number 111 might be used later if Nevada Company wanted to create an account called "Cleaning Supplies."

The General Ledger, *continued*

Example: Chart of Accounts

Although there is no one format for every chart of accounts, here is an example of how the chart of accounts might look for the Nevada Company:

Nevada Company
Chart of Accounts

Asset Accounts: Numbers 101–199

#101	Cash
#105	Accounts Receivable
#115	Supplies
#140	Office Equipment
#160	Building
#170	Land

Liability Accounts: Numbers 201–299

#201	Accounts Payable
#205	Wages Payable
#210	Unearned Revenue

Owner's Capital Accounts: Numbers 301–399

#301	C. Goldman, Capital
#302	C. Goldman, Drawing

Revenue Accounts: Numbers 401–499

#401	Service Revenue
#405	Interest Earned

Expense Accounts: Numbers 501–599

#501	Advertising Expense
#502	Office Rent Expense
#507	Equipment Rent Expense
#510	Wages Expense
#515	Utilities Expense
#520	Supplies Expense
#525	Insurance Expense
#550	Miscellaneous Expense

Can you determine what type of entity a business is (proprietorship, partnership, or corporation) just by looking at the chart of accounts? Yes you can! Simply look at the capital accounts. A proprietorship is what you see above. A partnership shows the names of two or more partners, and a corporation shows the names of capital accounts discussed in Learning Goal 29.

continued ▶

In 'real life' business situations, it is important to give careful thought to designing a chart of accounts. If managers want to know a lot of detail about transactions, more accounts will be created; for example, there might be a separate supplies expense account for each type of supplies used. Also, if a business has various departments or several branch stores, the chart of accounts should show separate account category names and numbers for each department or store.

Finally, when using computerized accounting software, we also have to remember that the software will automatically create financial statements, and these financial statements will typically display accounts in the same sequence and detail that is set up in the chart of accounts. For example, if you wanted to create an income statement category called "General and Administrative Expenses" that shows each of these individual kinds expenses, you would need to create a specific range of individual account numbers just for this category.

QUICK REVIEW

A ledger . . .	
meets these two information requirements . . .	*arranges data by . . .*
▪ keeps a historical record of *all the increases* and *all the decreases* in each account. ▪ shows the *balance* of each account at any time.	▪ accounts, which are all placed in a single book or file. ▪ keeping numbered accounts in numerical sequence.

VOCABULARY

Account numbers: unique identification numbers assigned to accounts (page 446)

Chart of accounts: a listing of account names and identification numbers (page 446)

General ledger: a book or computer file that contains all the ledger accounts (page 444)

Journal: a chronological record of transactions (page 444)

Ledger: a book or computer file that contains accounts (page 444)

Ledger accounts: accounts which are found in a ledger (page 444)

PRACTICE Learning Goal 23

Solutions are in the disk at the back of the book and at: www.worthyjames.com

Learning Goal 23 is about the purpose and function of a ledger. Use these questions to practice what you have just read.

Multiple Choice

Select the best answer.

1. A ledger is
   a. an individual record of increases and decreases of a particular item in the accounting equation.
   b. a book or a file that contains all the accounts of a business.
   c. a chronological record of transaction data.
   d. both (b) and (c).
2. The purpose of a ledger is to
   a. maintain normal balances in accounts.
   b. prove that debits equal credits.
   c. maintain a detailed record of all the increases and decreases and balances in each account.
   d. serve as a source of business transaction documentation.
3. An account number will always be found
   a. in a record of transactions.
   b. on a ledger account.
   c. in the part of the ledger called the "chart of accounts."
   d. both (b) and (c).
4. Which kind of account would you normally expect to see last in a ledger?
   a. Revenues
   b. Liabilities
   c. Assets
   d. Expenses
5. Accounts are usually placed into a ledger in what order?
   a. in the sequence of their account numbers
   b. by size
   c. alphabetically
   d. by type of account
6. If you have only the number of an account, and want to find out the account name, the best plan is to
   a. look through the ledger until you find the account with the correct number.
   b. look in the chart of accounts.
   c. look in the journal.
   d. speak with the accountant who recorded the transactions.
7. Information in the ledger is arranged by
   a. account.
   b. transaction.
   c. size (largest to smallest).
   d. chronological order.
8. A ledger fulfills which of the following information needs?
   a. You can easily see all parts of each transaction and the balance of each account.
   b. You can see that the accounting equation stays in balance with each transaction.
   c. You can see a historical record of the increases and decreases in each account and the account balance.
   d. You can easily see all parts of each transaction and a historical record of each account.

LEARNING GOAL 24

Use a Journal

In Learning Goal 24, you will find:

The Purpose and Structure of a General Journal

Overview

Introduction

A ***journal*** is like a daily transaction diary. A journal is where transaction information is first recorded in an accounting system. This transaction information comes from business documents.

Accountants have discovered that it is actually more efficient to first record the transaction information into a journal. For that reason, the journal is often called the ***book of original entry***. After transaction information is entered into the journal, the same information is then recorded into the ledger accounts.

Both the journal and the ledger contain exactly the same information. However, each book *arranges* the information differently to meet different information needs.

Overview, *continued*

A Journal Meets Three Information Needs

A journal arranges data to meet information needs #1, #2, and #3 (see page 390). With a journal, you can:

- find a transaction by date
- see all the accounts affected by each transaction
- see if the accounting equation stays in balance with each transaction

General Journal

Most businesses have more than one kind of journal. However, we will study the most common kind of journal that all businesses use. This is an all-purpose journal called the ***general journal***. Recording information into a journal is called ***journalizing***.

The Structure of a General Journal

Why the Journal Is Different

Like a ledger, a journal is a book with individual pages. However, the journal is different because it arranges the transaction information differently. In a journal, the journal pages record all of the complete transactions in *the order in which they happen*. This is different from a ledger, which uses each page to record information about only one account.

Example

In the example below, you see the top part of a journal page. On the page are two transactions of the Jill Hirata Company for the week of June 5.

Date	Account	Dr.	Cr.
2017	Cash	10,000	
June 5	Jill Hirata, Capital		10,000
	Owner made investment to start business		
June 7	Supplies	500	
	Accounts Payable		500
	Purchase supplies on account		

Notice that these three information requirements are met:

- Transactions can be located by date because they are recorded chronologically (in order of occurrence).
- You can see each complete transaction.
- All the accounts in each separate transaction are easily identified and it's easy to check if debits equal credits.

Recording Transactions in a General Journal

How Transactions Are Recorded in a General Journal

Using the Example Above . . .

We can use the transaction on the previous page for June 5 to see how an entry should be recorded into a journal.

Rule for Date

Date: The date that is entered is always the date of the transaction, not the date that it is being recorded, which may be later.

Date	Account	Dr.	Cr.
2017 June 5			

Rules for Recording the Debits

- Debits are always recorded first.
- Use the *exact name* of the account that needs to be debited. Do not put something like "cash investment" because there is no account by that name.
- Write the name of the account next to the left margin.
- If there is more than one account to debit, write the name of the next account to be debited on the next line. There is no particular order for entering account names.

Dollar amount: Write the dollar amount being debited into the debit (Dr.) column on the same line as the name of the account. Dollar signs are not used.

Date	Account	Dr.	Cr.
2017 June 5	Cash	10,000	

Where do you find the transaction date? The transaction date can usually be found on the document that verifies the transaction. (An invoice, a check, a receipt, etc.)

How Transactions Are Recorded in a General Journal, *continued*

Rules for Recording the Credits

- Credit entries are recorded after all debits are recorded.
- Use the *exact name* of the account that needs to be credited. Do not put something like "increase in capital" because there is no account by that name.
- It is customary to *indent the name of a credited account,* so it is easy to identify.
- If there is more than one account to credit, write the name of next account to be credited on the next line. There is no particular order for entering account names.

Dollar amount: Write the dollar amount being credited into the credit (Cr.) column on the same line as the name of the account.

Date	Account	Dr.	Cr.
2017			
June 5	Cash	10,000	
	Jill Hirata, Capital		**10,000**

Check Equality

Check to see that the dollar value of debits equals the dollar value of the credits. In this example, it is pretty obvious. In bigger journal entries with multiple debits and credits, however, it is not always so easy to see. If debits do not equal credits, the transaction being recorded will cause the accounting equation to be out of balance.

Equality OK!

Date	Account	Dr.	Cr.
2017			
June 5	Cash	10,000	
	Jill Hirata, Capital		10,000

Explanation Is a Good Idea

Check with your teacher or supervisor to find out if an explanation is required. However, it is usually a good idea to write an explanation. This is especially true in complicated or unusual transactions where you should also *identify the source of the information.* Weeks, months, or years later, when someone asks you for an explanation (like the IRS), you will thank yourself for being so careful.

continued ▶

How Transactions Are Recorded in a General Journal, *continued*

Explanation →

Date	Account	Dr.	Cr.
2017 June 5	Cash Jill Hirata, Capital Owner made investment to start business	10,000	10,000

Skip a Line

Skip a line before you journalize the next transaction. This makes all the individual transactions much easier to identify. Your tired teacher or supervisor will be very grateful.

Check Your Understanding

Write the completed sentences on a separate piece of paper. The answers are below.

The journal is a chronological record of · · · · · · · ·. The journal meets these information requirements: (1) you can locate any transaction by · · · · · · · ·, (2) you can see all the · · · · · · · · in each transaction, and (3) you can see if the accounting equation stays in · · · · · · · ·. The procedure of recording information into the journal is called · · · · · · · ·.

The journal and ledger are different because the journal organizes data by · · · · · · · ·, whereas the ledger organizes data by · · · · · · · ·. Information is always recorded into the journal (before/after) · · · · · · · · the ledger.

Answers

The journal is a chronological record of transactions. The journal meets these information requirements: (1) you can locate any transaction by date, (2) you can see all the accounts in each transaction, and (3) you can see if the accounting equation stays in balance. The procedure of recording information into the journal is called journalizing.

The journal and ledger are different because the journal organizes data by transaction, whereas the ledger organizes data by account. Information is always recorded into the journal before the ledger.

The Best Way to Analyze Transactions and Accounts

Overview: Analyzing Transactions

Two Previous Methods

The ability to correctly analyze a financial event is the foundation of a good understanding of accounting. That is why previously we spent so much time discussing this important question: "How do I analyze events to decide if they are transactions, and—if the events are transactions—how should the transactions be recorded?"

When we first looked at economic events affecting a business, we used illustrations ("snapshots") showing assets and the liability and owner's equity claims on the assets. For example, to show the payment of a $500 Account Payable, we did this:

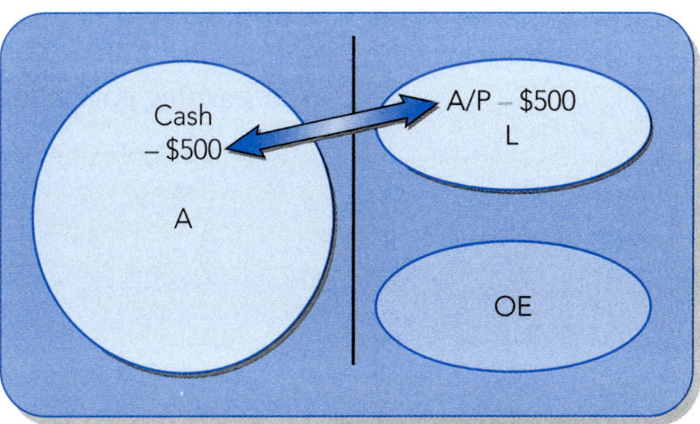

Next, when we learned about the accounting equation, we used it to analyze transactions. For example, the transaction above can be analyzed like this:

A ↓	=	L ↓	+	OE
Cash		A/P		
$500		$500		

Both of these methods are equally correct—using one or the other is simply a matter of preference.

continued ▶

Overview: Analyzing Transactions, *continued*

T Accounts: Use What the Professionals Use

Now that you have learned about T accounts, however, you can use the technique that practicing accountants, bookkeepers, and other financial professionals use to analyze events and transactions. This method is called *T account analysis*. The advantage of this method is that it clearly shows the effects on the accounting equation, *and* it also shows the debits and credits so that you can correctly make journal entries. The method is simply an extension of what you have already learned.

T Account Analysis

Overview

Although a journal is a "book of original entry" (where every transaction is recorded first), many people find it very helpful to use T accounts to *analyze* the classification and valuation of a transaction *before* it is recorded in a journal. This is easy to do by simply writing some T accounts on a blank piece of paper. Using T accounts like this will make all the debits and credits of a transaction easier to see and understand.

This method is especially useful when you are dealing with a complex or unfamiliar transaction. When you finish the T account analysis, simply record the account names and the debits and credits from your analysis into the journal. (The same information is later transferred to the ledger. The next learning goal explains this.)

T Account Analysis, *continued*

Procedure

The table below describes the procedure for analysis using T accounts.

Before you begin, write out the accounting equation on a blank piece of paper.

Step	Action
1	Under the accounting equation, decide which accounts you think will be affected, draw them as T accounts, and label each T account. This is called classification. You can draw arrows to help with Step 2. (See Learning Goal 10 for a review of classification.)
2	For each T account, decide how much it is increasing or decreasing. This is called valuation. (See Learning Goal 10 for a review of valuation.)
3	Using the debit and credit rules (page 428), enter the amounts of the increases and/or decreases in each T account. *Result:* These entries are the same debits and credits that need to be entered in the journal.

Example #1

On April 3, Ferris State Company paid $500 to a vendor on account.

Step 1: Show the T accounts affected (classification).

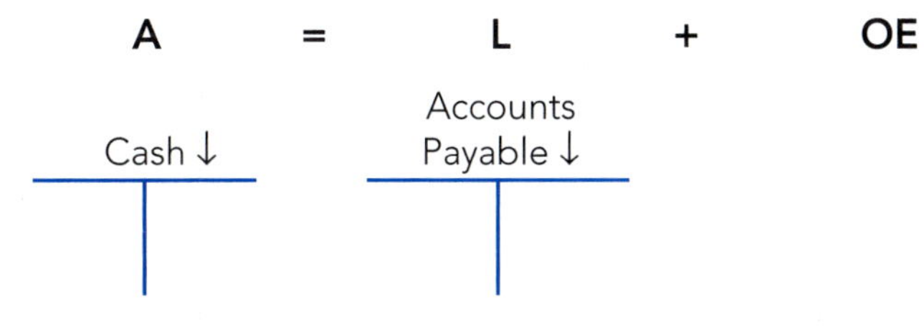

continued ►

T Account Analysis, *continued*

Step 2: Determine the dollar amounts of changes (valuation).

- The asset Cash decreases $500.
- The liability Accounts Payable decreases $500.

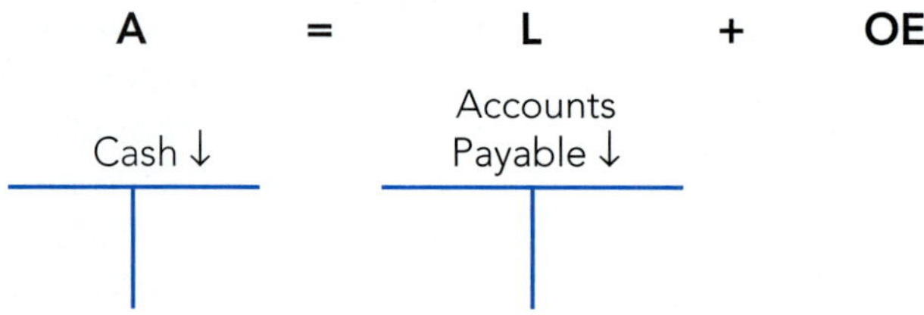

Step 3: Use the debit and credit rules to enter the amounts.

Items on the left side of the equation are decreased with right-side entries (credits). Items on the right side of the equation are decreased with left-side entries (debits). Therefore, credit Cash $500, and debit Accounts Payable $500.

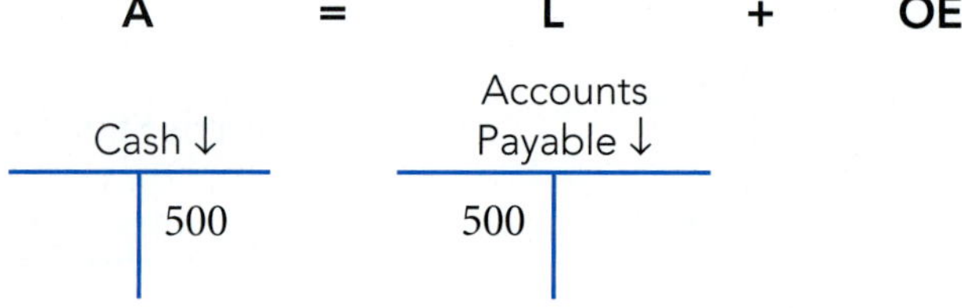

To record this transaction in the general journal, the rule is all debits first and all credits second:

April 3	Accounts Payable	500	
	Cash		500
	Paid vendor on account.		

T Account Analysis, *continued*

Example #2

In a previous period, Humbolt Company received a $900 advance payment from a customer. During the current accounting period, Humbolt performed $750 of services for this customer.

Step 1: Show the T accounts affected (classification).

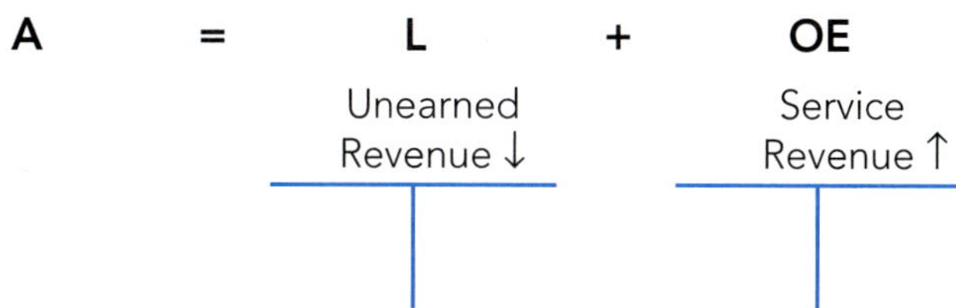

Step 2: Determine the dollar amounts of changes (valuation).

- The liability Unearned Revenue decreases $750.
- Service Revenue increases $750.

A	=	L	+	OE
		Unearned Revenue ↓		Service Revenue ↑

Step 3: Use the debit and credit rules to enter the amounts.

Items on the right side of the equation are decreased with left-side entries (debits). Items on the right side of the equation are increased with right-side entries (credits). Therefore, debit Unearned Revenue $750, and credit Service Revenue $750.

A	=	L	+	OE
		Unearned Revenue ↓		Service Revenue ↑
		750 (debit)		750 (credit)

continued ►

T Account Analysis, *continued*

To record this transaction as a general journal entry, the rule is all debits first and all credits second:

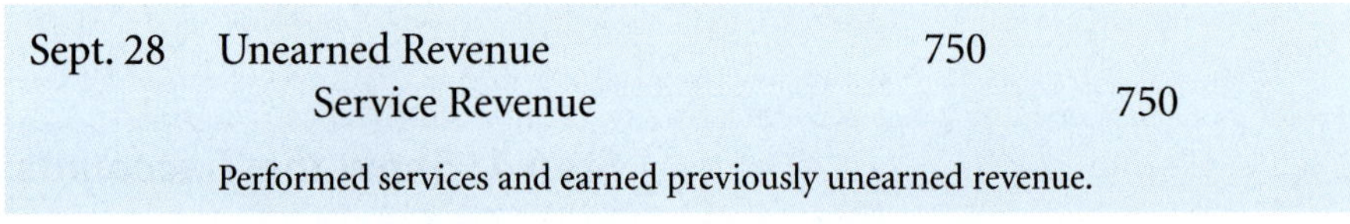

Sept. 28	Unearned Revenue	750	
	Service Revenue		750
	Performed services and earned previously unearned revenue.		

Example #3

On June 12, Appalachian Enterprises purchased $15,000 of equipment from Penn Company by paying $7,000 cash down and signing an $8,000 promissory note for the balance.

Step 1: Show the T accounts affected (classification).

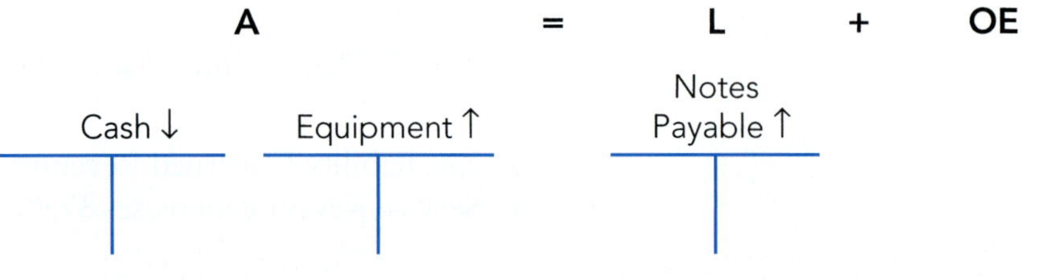

Step 2: Determine the dollar amounts of changes (valuation).

- The asset Cash decreases $7,000.
- The asset Equipment increases $15,000.
- The liability Notes Payable increases $8,000.

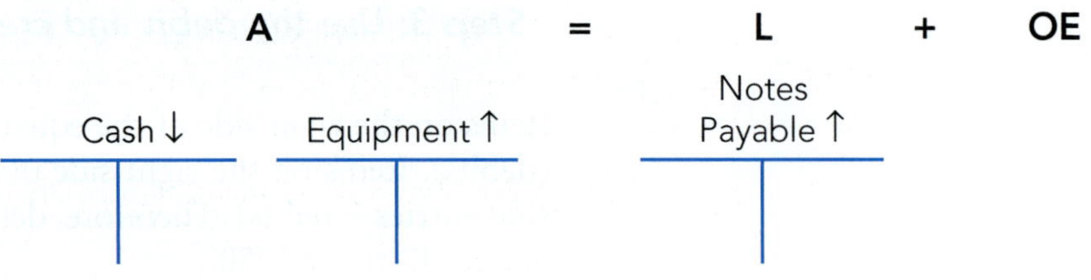

T Account Analysis, *continued*

Step 3: Use the debit and credit rules to enter the amounts.

Items on the left side of the equation are increased with left-side entries (debits) and are decreased with right-side entries (credits). Items on the right side of the equation are increased with right-side entries (credits). Therefore, debit Equipment $15,000, and credit Cash $7,000. Credit Notes Payable $8,000.

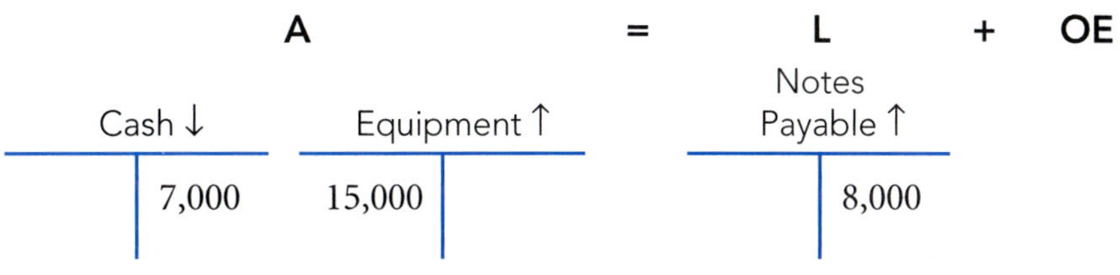

To record this transaction in the general journal, the rule is all debits first and all credits (in any order) second:

June 12	Equipment	15,000	
	Cash		7,000
	Notes Payable		8,000
	Purchased equipment from Penn Company		

Any entry with more than two accounts is called a ***compound entry***.

Example #4

On January 29, Hattiesburg Corporation made the January loan payment of $3,800 to County Bank. $2,700 of the payment was for interest on the loan, and the rest was for a payment on the loan principal.

Step 1: Show the T accounts affected (classification).

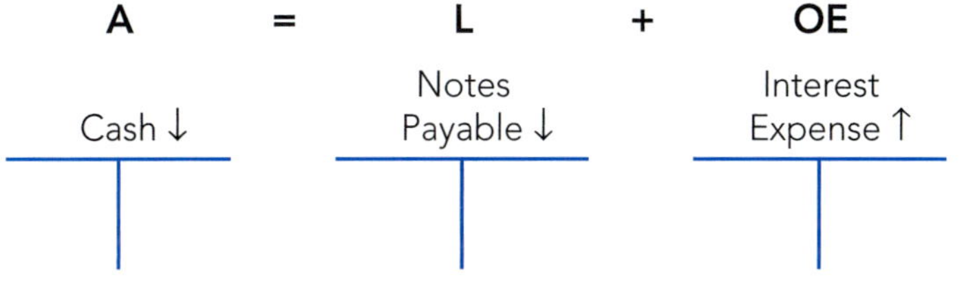

continued ▶

T Account Analysis, *continued*

Step 2: Determine the dollar amounts of changes (valuation).

- The asset Cash decreases $3,800.
- The expense Interest Expense increases $2,700. (Remember, an increase in an expense is really a reduction in the owner's equity.)
- The liability Notes Payable decreases $1,100.

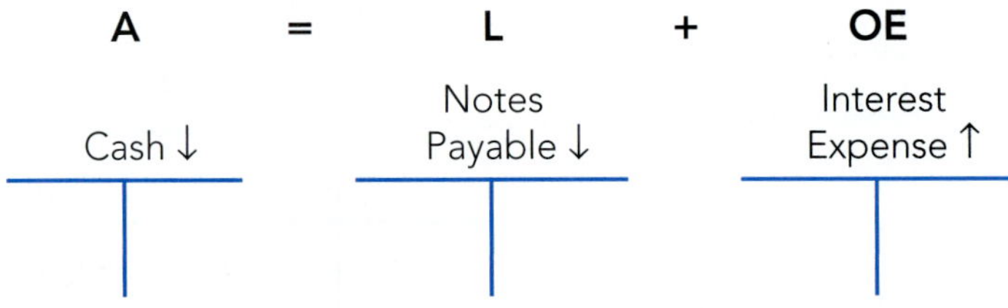

Step 3: Use the debit and credit rules to enter the amounts.

Items on the left side of the equation are decreased with right-side entries (credits). Items on the right side of the equation are decreased with left-side entries (debits). Therefore, credit Cash $3,800, debit Notes Payable $1,100, and debit Interest Expense $2,700. (The interest expense is a decrease in the owner's equity.)

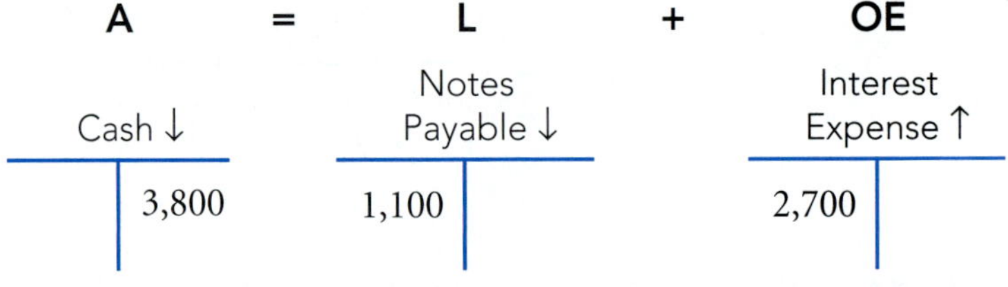

To record this transaction as a general journal entry, the rule is all debits (in any order) first and all credits second:

Jan. 29	Interest Expense	2,700	
	Notes Payable	1,100	
	Cash		3,800
	Made January loan payment to County Bank		

T Account Analysis, *continued*

Example #5

On May 8, Belhaven Company collected $3,500 from customers on account.

Step 1: Show the T accounts affected (classification).

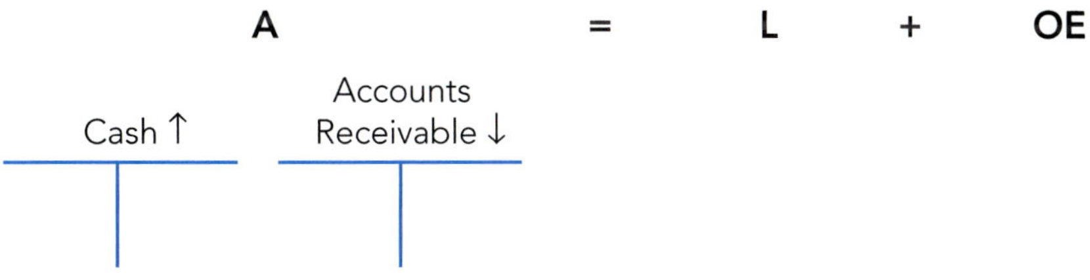

Step 2: Determine the dollar amounts of changes (valuation).

- The asset Cash increases $3,500.
- The asset Accounts Receivable decreases $3,500.

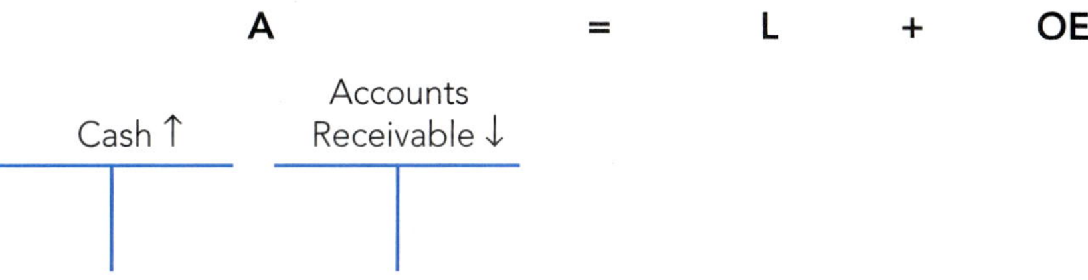

Items on the left side of the equation are increased with left-side entries (debits). Items on the left side of the equation are decreased with right-side entries (credits). Therefore, debit Cash $3,500, and credit Accounts Receivable $3,500.

Step 3: Use the debit and credit rules to enter the amounts.

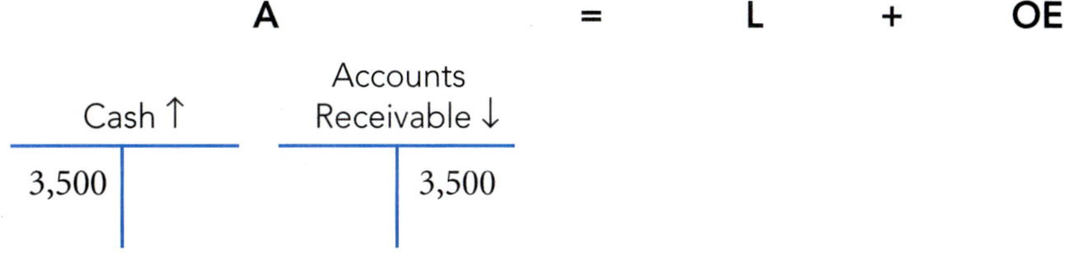

continued ▶

T Account Analysis, *continued*

To record this transaction as a general journal entry, the rule is all debits first and all credits second:

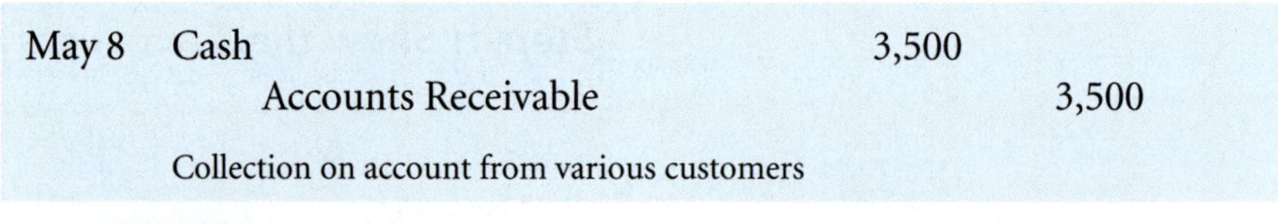

May 8	Cash	3,500	
	Accounts Receivable		3,500
	Collection on account from various customers		

Example #6

On August 11, San Marcos Company received a $700 telephone service bill that the company will pay later.

Step 1: Show the T accounts affected (classification).

Step 2: Determine the dollar amounts of changes (valuation).

- The liability Accounts Payable increases $700.
- The expense Telephone Expense increases $700. (Remember, an expense is really a decrease in owner's equity.)

T Account Analysis, *continued*

Step 3: Use the debit and credit rules to enter the amounts.

Items on the right side of the equation are increased with right-side entries (credits). Items on the right side of the equation are decreased with left-side entries (debits). Therefore, credit Accounts Payable $700, and debit Telephone Expense $700. (The Telephone Expense is a decrease in the owner's equity.)

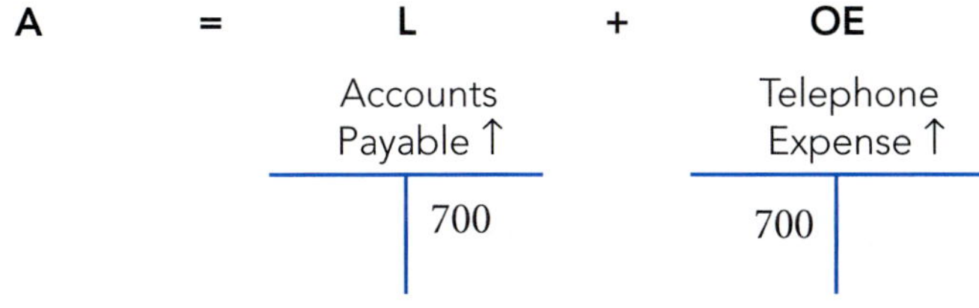

To record this transaction as a general journal entry, the rule is all debits first and all credits second:

August 11	Telephone Expense	700	
	Accounts Payable		700
	Received monthly bill from telephone company.		

QUICK REVIEW

A journal . . .	
meets these three information requirements . . .	*arranges data by . . .*
▪ find a transaction by date. ▪ see all parts of a transaction. ▪ see if the equation stays in balance.	▪ transaction.

- Analyze transactions by using T accounts. Focus on classification and valuation.

VOCABULARY

Book of original entry: a journal (page 450)

Compound entry: an entry containing three or more accounts (page 461)

General journal: an all-purpose journal that can record all types of transactions (page 451)

Journal: a chronological record of transactions (page 450)

Journalizing: recording information into a journal (page 451)

Do You Want More Examples?

Most problems in this book have detailed solutions. To use them as additional examples, do this: 1) Select the type of problem you want 2) Open the solution on your computer or mobile device screen (from the disc or worthyjames.com) 3) Read one item at a time and look at its answer. Take notes if needed. 4) Close the solution and work as much of the problem as you can. 5) Repeat as needed.

"Stranger, did you mean 'journal' or did you mean 'ledger'?"

PRACTICE Learning Goal 24

Solutions are in the disk at the back of the book and at: www.worthyjames.com

Learning Goal 24 is about learning to use the general journal. Use these questions and problems to practice what you have just read.

Multiple Choice

Select the best answer.

1. When using the general journal
   a. the name of the account used must be exactly the same as the name used in the chart of accounts.
   b. account numbers must always be entered immediately.
   c. credits are recorded before debits.
   d. both (a) and (b).
2. When using the general journal, it is good form to
   a. skip a line between transactions.
   b. always place the name of the debit account on the left margin and indent the credit account name.
   c. always place the name of the credit account on the left margin and indent the debit account name.
   d. both (a) and (b).
3. If the San Mateo Sales Company purchased $100 of supplies for cash, and the bookkeeper debited Prepaid Insurance and credited Cash in the journal, then
   a. total assets are not affected.
   b. total assets are understated.
   c. total assets are overstated.
   d. prepaid insurance is understated.
4. Which of the following functions does a journal *not* do?
   a. The journal shows all the parts of each transaction in one place.
   b. The journal provides a chronological record of all the transactions as they occurred.
   c. The journal is a way of calculating the balance in any account.
   d. The journal provides a single, convenient location to first enter transaction data into the accounting system.
5. Which of the following accounts should be entered first in a correct journal entry?
   a. Cash, when it is decreased
   b. Accounts Payable, when it is increased
   c. Expense, when it is increased
   d. Revenue, when it is increased
6. If you saw a journal entry that was a debit to Cash and a credit to Unearned Revenue, you would conclude that
   a. cash was received when revenue was earned.
   b. cash was borrowed.
   c. cash was advanced by a customer before services were completed.
   d. none of the above.
7. A journal entry that contains three or more accounts is called a
   a. compound entry.
   b. complex entry.
   c. multiple-account entry.
   d. combined entry.

PRACTICE Learning Goal 24, continued

Solutions are in the disk at the back of the book and at: www.worthyjames.com

8. Which of the following statements about journal entries is true?
   a. Assets should always be recorded before liabilities.
   b. A line must be skipped between each debit and credit.
   c. The date must always show when the entry was recorded.
   d. Credits should be indented.
9. The proper procedure for recording a journal entry is
   a. debit accounts should always be entered last and written next to the left margin.
   b. debit accounts should always be entered first and indented.
   c. the exact name of accounts must always be used, with no exceptions.
   d. always check the balance of each account that is debited or credited.
10. Which of the following statements about a journal is true?
   a. Accounts that are increased should be entered first.
   b. Explanations in the journal are seldom done.
   c. Transactions should never cause the accounting equation to be out of balance.
   d. Explanations must always be written under each individual debit and credit.
11. The proper sequence for recording transaction information is
   a. analyze, record in ledger, journalize.
   b. journalize, analyze, record in ledger.
   c. analyze, journalize, record in ledger.
   d. analyze and journalize.
12. The journal entry to record a cash receipt from a customer on account includes a
   a. debit to Accounts Receivable.
   b. credit to Cash.
   c. credit to Revenue.
   d. credit to Accounts Receivable.
13. The journal entry to record a purchase of supplies on account includes a
   a. debit to Accounts Payable.
   b. debit to Cash.
   c. debit to an expense.
   d. credit to Accounts Payable.
14. The Pelissippi Company wants to record a cash payment for repairs expense and rent expense. Which of the following entries is correct?

	Account	Debit	Credit
a.	Cash	500	
	Rent Expense	275	
	Repairs Expense		325
b.	Rent Expense	275	
	Repairs Expense	325	
	Cash		500
c.	Rent Expense	275	
	Repairs Expense		325
	Cash	500	

   d. None of the above.
15. The journal entry to record the purchase of equipment by signing a note payable and making a cash down payment includes a
   a. debit to Cash and credit to Equipment.
   b. credit to Notes Payable and a credit to Cash.
   c. credit to Equipment and a debit to Cash.
   d. debit to Equipment and a debit to Notes Payable.

PRACTICE Learning Goal 24, continued

Solutions are in the disk at the back of the book and at: www.worthyjames.com

Reinforcement Problems

LG 24-1. Analyze transactions with T accounts—Record in a journal

1. Prepare a T account analysis of each individual transaction.
2. Record the general journal entry for each transaction. (Make copies of blank journal paper from the disk at the back of this book or at the "student info." link at www.worthyjames.com.) Explanations are not necessary.

Transactions:

a. John Wilson, owner of Wilson Cleaning Services Company, invested $10,000 cash and $5,000 of equipment in his new business.
b. The business performed $1,800 of services on account for various clients.
c. The business prepaid 3 months rent in the amount of $2,400.
d. $500 of supplies were purchased on account.
e. Clients paid $600 of what was owing on account.
f. The business received a $300 bill for utility services, which was not immediately paid.
g. The business used up $150 of supplies.
h. The business paid the amount owing for the supplies purchase.

LG 24-2. Analyze transactions with T accounts—Record in a journal. All the events shown below are transactions.

1. Prepare a T account analysis for each individual transaction.
2. Record the general journal entry for each transaction. (Make copies of blank journal paper from the disk at the back of the book.) Explanations are not necessary.

a. The owner of the Sacramento Company, Boyce Gasoway, invests $15,000 in his business.
b. Palomar Company uses up $200 of supplies.
c. Mira Costa Enterprises collects $850 owing from customers.
d. Santa Monica Company purchases $10,000 of equipment by paying $1,000 cash and signing a $9,000 note payable.
e. Fairfield Partnership prepays three months' office rent for $12,000.
f. Sonoma Company receives a three-month advance payment from a customer in the amount of $5,000.
g. Salinas Enterprises pays a $400 account payable.
h. Fairfield Company, in (e) above, uses up one month of the prepaid office rent.
i. Riverside Enterprises performs $500 of services on account.
j. Crescent City Company receives a $450 bill for utility services. The bill will be paid later.
k. Sonoma Company, in (f) above, performs $1,200 of services.
l. Atascadero Corporation makes a $1,000 loan payment. The payment includes $200 of interest expense.

PRACTICE — Learning Goal 24, continued

Solutions are in the disk at the back of the book and at: www.worthyjames.com

LG 24-3. Prepare general journal entries. All the events shown below are transactions.

1. Record the general journal entry for each transaction. Remember that you can use T accounts to help you visualize transactions. (Make copies of blank journal paper from the disk at the back of this book or at the "studentinfo." link at www.worthyjames.com.) Explanations are not necessary.

   a. Abilene Company purchased $750 of supplies by paying cash.
   b. Pecos Enterprises purchased $600 of supplies on account.
   c. Houston Corporation used $900 of supplies in operations for the month.
   d. Dallas Partnership received a $2,250 advance payment from a customer.
   e. Austin Enterprises purchased $350,000 land and building. The cost allocated to the land is $100,000. Payment was made by signing a $225,000 note payable and paying cash for the balance.
   f. Dave Smiley, owner of Fort Worth Sales Company, withdrew $2,500 from his business.
   g. El Paso Partnership prepaid $800 of fire insurance.
   h. Dallas Partnership, in (d) above, completed $1,500 of services for the customer who paid in advance.
   i. Arlington Company received a $700 bill for repair services. The bill was not paid immediately.
   j. Beaumont Enterprises provided $3,500 of services to customers on account.
   k. Beaumont Enterprises collected $2,000 owing from customers on account.
   l. El Paso Partnership, in (g) above, used up $200 of the prepaid fire insurance.
   m. Corpus Christi Corporation purchased $2,000 of supplies and $7,500 of equipment on account as one purchase from a single supplier.
   n. In the following month, Corpus Christi Corporation paid the supplier in full.

LG 24-4. Prepare general journal entries. For each of the transactions described below, prepare a general journal entry. You may omit explanations in this exercise. Remember that you can use T accounts whenever you feel it is necessary to help you visualize a transaction. (For journal paper, you can make general journal copies from the template in the disk at the back of this book.) Omit explanations.

Nov. 1: Laurie Shelby invested $8,500 to start her new business, Macon Cove Information Technology Services.
Nov. 1: Macon Cove Information Technology Services rented office space and paid 3 months' rent in advance for $1,050.
Nov. 3: The company received a $750 advance payment from Augusta Partners.
Nov. 4: The business purchased $2,300 of office equipment and $700 of office supplies by making a $1,000 cash down payment and signing a $2,000 note payable.
Nov. 5: Paid Acme Cleaning Services $100.
Nov. 6: Purchased advertising in the month's computer magazine, $500 on account.
Nov. 7: Completed analysis services for Nashville Company, $980 on account.
Nov. 11: Paid $700 to an employee for wages.
Nov. 12: The business performed $1,500 of services on account for Chattanooga Computer Research Company.
Nov. 14: Laurie Shelby invested an additional $5,000 cash into the business plus $4,000 of office equipment.
Nov. 15: The business paid an account payable, $500.
Nov. 17: Received a $980 check from Nashville Company on account.
Nov. 19: The business paid $250 for gardening services for the owner's home, a personal expense of the owner, Laurie Mason.
Nov. 23: Completed the services for Augusta Partners (November 3).
Nov. 24: Received $2,000 cash for consulting services to Morristown Company.
Nov. 27: Laurie Shelby withdrew $500 cash from her business.
Nov. 30: A count of the supplies shows that the business used up $1,200 of supplies during the month of November.

PRACTICE Learning Goal 24, continued

Solutions are in the disk at the back of the book and at: www.worthyjames.com

LG 24-5. Analyze general journal entries, identify errors, prepare general journal entries. During the month of September the transactions shown below occurred as a result of Heath Company's activities. However, the company has hired a new bookkeeper. At the end of the month the owner of the company, Emily Heath, wants you to check the work of the new bookkeeper.

For each transaction, analyze the general journal entry and identify any incorrect entries. For each incorrect entry, explain what is wrong.

Sept. 1: Emily Heath transferred $17,000 from her personal bank account into her business bank account.
Sept. 1: Paid the insurance company $1,200 for six months' of insurance coverage beginning September 1.
Sept. 2: The business purchased $800 of office supplies and $4,000 of furniture on account.
Sept. 3: Performed services for a client and received cash of $3,100 from the client.
Sept. 4: Borrowed $20,000 from Enterprise Bank, signing a 5-year note payable.
Sept. 6: Paid the September rent, $1,800.
Sept. 7: Hired an office assistant who will be paid at the rate of $750 per week.
Sept. 7: Paid for cleaning services, $150.
Sept. 8: Purchased $10,000 of computer equipment by paying $4,000 cash and signing a note payable for the balance owed.
Sept. 10: Received a $2,000 payment from a client for services to begin on October 1.
Sept. 12: Performed $3,100 of services on account for a client
Sept. 18: Received an $800 bill for computer repair services. The bill was not paid immediately.
Sept. 21: Collected an account receivable in the amount of $750.
Sept. 26: Received a bill for Internet maintenance services, $350. The bill was not paid immediately.
Sept. 30: Emily Heath withdrew $2,500 cash from the business for her personal use.

Date	Account	Dr.	Cr.
Sept.			
1	Cash	17,000	
	Emily Heath, Capital		17,000
1	Insurance Expense	1,200	
	Cash		1,200
2	Office Supplies Expense	800	
	Office Furniture	4,000	
	Accounts Payable		4,800
3	Cash	3,100	
	Service Revenue		3,100

PRACTICE Learning Goal 24, continued

Solutions are in the disk at the back of the book and at: www.worthyjames.com

LG 24-5, *continued*

Date	Account	Dr.	Cr.
Sept.			
4	Cash	20,000	
	Accounts Payable		20,000
6	Rent Expense	1,800	
	Cash		1,800
7	Wages Expense	750	
	Wages Payable		750
7	Cleaning Service Expense	15	
	Cash		15
8	Accounts Payable	6,000	
	Cash	4,000	
	Computer		10,000
10	Cash	2,000	
	Service Revenue		2,000
12	Accounts Receivable	3,100	
	Service Revenue		3,100
21	Cash	750	
	Service Revenue		750
30	Salary Expense	2,500	
	Cash		2,500

PRACTICE **Learning Goal 24, continued**

Solutions are in the disk at the back of the book and at: www.worthyjames.com

LG 24-6. Prepare general journal entries. The general journal that you see below contains explanations but no journal entries. On a separate piece of paper, using the explanations, prepare the correct journal entries.

Date	Account	Dr.	Cr.
2017			
Feb. 8			
	Ken Peters invested $25,000 cash to begin his new business, Du Page		
	Delivery Enterprises.		
9			
	Prepaid 1 year of insurance for $1,500.		
10			
	Purchased office supplies from Jolliet Company, $250 on account.		
12			
	Paid $1,000 and signed a $2,000 note payable for an office computer.		
14			
	Ken Peters invested an additional $5,000 cash in the business, plus a van worth		
	$15,000. With the van is a note payable of $7,000.		
15			
	Billed Morraine Valley Company for services, $575 on account.		

PRACTICE Learning Goal 24, continued

Solutions are in the disk at the back of the book and at: www.worthyjames.com

LG 24-6, *continued*

Date	Account	Dr.	Cr.
17			
	Paid $200 owing to Jolliet Company from February 10.		
20			
	Used up $200 of supplies.		
24			
	Wrote $520 check to Sunshine Day Care for owner's child-care expense.		
27			
	Collected $300 from Morraine Valley Company on account.		

LG 24-7. **Write explanations to journal entries.** After you have practiced enough journal entries, you should be able to look at a journal entry and know what has happened. This exercise helps you practice this skill. The general journal below contains journal entries without explanations. On a separate piece of paper, write a brief, complete, and accurate explanation for each journal entry.

Date	Account	Dr.	Cr.
2017			
July 11	Accounts Payable, Grants Pass Company	1,000	
	Cash		1,000
12	Andrea Sheaffer, Drawing	750	
	Cash		750

PRACTICE Learning Goal 24, continued

Solutions are in the disk at the back of the book and at: www.worthyjames.com

LG 24-7, *continued*

Date	Account	Dr.	Cr.
14	Supplies Expense	190	
	Supplies		190
15	Cash	3,500	
	Accounts Receivable, Portland Enterprises		3,500
17	Accounts Receivable, Gresham Corporation	4,100	
	Fees Earned		4,100
20	Computer Equipment	10,300	
	Cash		2,500
	Notes Payable		7,800
22	Cash	850	
	Unearned Revenue		850
24	Rent Expense	1,500	
	Prepaid Rent		1,500
25	Land	145,000	
	Building	90,000	
	Cash		50,000
	Notes Payable		185,000
27	Repairs Expense	175	
	Accounts Payable		175

PRACTICE Learning Goal 24, continued

Solutions are in the disk at the back of the book and at: www.worthyjames.com

LG 24-8. Reconstruct journal entries from ledger accounts. You know that in the normal recording procedure, journal entries are always prepared first, before transferring data into the ledger accounts. However, in this exercise we will test your understanding by working backwards from ledger accounts. Using the information in the T accounts shown below, prepare the general journal entries for the month of May and include explanations. (Make copies of blank journal paper from the disk at the back of the book.)

Ledger (partial)

Cash

Date	Debit	Credit
May 5		900
6	330	
10	750	
12		450
17		1,050

Accounts Receivable

Date	Debit	Credit
May 6		330
15	500	

Supplies

Date	Debit	Credit
May 7	250	
17	250	

Prepaid Rent

Date	Debit	Credit
May 18		700

Equipment

Date	Debit	Credit
May 17	2,800	

Accounts Payable

Date	Debit	Credit
May 7		250
10		1,500
12	450	

Notes Payable

Date	Debit	Credit
May 17		2,000

Service Revenue

Date	Debit	Credit
May 10		750
15		500

Wages Expense

Date	Debit	Credit
May 5	900	

Advertising Expense

Date	Debit	Credit
May 10	1,500	

Rent Expense

Date	Debit	Credit
May 18	700	

PRACTICE **Learning Goal 24, continued**

Solutions are in the disk at the back of the book and at: www.worthyjames.com

LG 24-9. Prepare general journal entries; review classification, valuation, and timing. For the events described below for the Santa Cruz Office Locator Service in June 2017, prepare the necessary general journal entries. Before you write a journal entry, on a separate page identify the correct classification, valuation, and timing using the following format as an example:

Classification	Valuation	Timing
Cash	25,000	June 1
David Washington, Capital	25,000	

When entering values that are decreases, enter the amounts in parentheses, "( )".

You may omit explanations in this exercise. (For journal paper, you can make general journal copies from the general journal template in the disk at the back of this book.) When doing this exercise, use T account analysis whenever you feel it is necessary to help visualize the transaction.

June 1: David Washington transferred $25,000 from his personal bank account into his business bank account with the name of Santa Cruz Office Locator Service.

June 2: The business purchased $500 of office supplies and $2,700 of furniture from Aptos Office Supply Company. The purchase was on account.

June 2: Hired a secretary for the office to be paid at the rate of $14 per hour.

June 3: Borrowed $15,000 from Santa Cruz City Bank.

June 5: Performed services for a client and received $2,250 cash.

June 6: Paid for cleaning services, $150.

June 8: Purchased $7,000 of computer equipment by paying $3,000 cash and signing a note payable for the balance owing. Although the actual cost of the computer equipment was $7,000 paid by Santa Cruz Office Locator Service, the equipment is listed for sale by a different supplier for $6,800.

June 10: Received a $3,000 advance payment from Capitola Company with instructions to locate various kinds of office space meeting the Company's specifications.

June 12: Performed $2,500 of services on account for Corralitos Company by locating office space.

June 15: Paid secretary's wages, $1,120.

June 15: Paid $1,000 to Aptos Office Supply Company on account.

June 15: Paid the June rent, $1,500.

June 18: Received an $800 bill for advertising in the local paper. The bill was not paid immediately. The transaction was recorded on June 30.

June 22: Performed locating services on account for Moss Landing Internet Company, $750.

June 25: Received a partial collection from Corralitos Company, $1,000 (June 12 above).

PRACTICE Learning Goal 24, continued

Solutions are in the disk at the back of the book and at: www.worthyjames.com

LG 24-9, *continued*

June 28: Received a bill for Internet maintenance services, $500. The bill was not paid immediately.

June 29: Located the office space meeting the specifications for Capitola Company. The total bill to Capitola Company was $5,000 (see June 10).

June 30: A count of the office supplies purchased on June 2 shows that one-fourth of the supplies have been used up.

June 30: Paid $750 to Santa Cruz Bank. $500 of the payment was for interest on the loan, and the balance was applied to the amount owing on the note payable.

June 30: David Washington withdrew $2,000 cash for personal use.

July 3: Received a bill from the telephone company for June services up to June 30, $210. The bill was not paid immediately.

LG 24-10. Review: Distinguish between the journal and the ledger.

Using a separate piece of paper, complete the following table to contrast the essential features of a journal and a ledger.

	A journal . . .	A ledger . . .
meets these information needs . . .	(Reminder: Use a separate sheet of paper to complete the table.)	
and does not meet these information needs . . .		
and the data is primarily arranged by . . .		

Instructor-Assigned Problems

If you are using this book in a class, these review problems may be assigned by your instructor for homework, group assignments, class work, or other activities. Only your instructor has the solutions.

IA 24-1. Analyze transactions with T accounts—Record in a journal

1. Prepare a T account analysis of each individual transaction.
2. Record the general journal entry for each transaction. (Make copies of blank journal paper from the disk at the back of this book or from the "student info." link at www.worthyjames.com.) Explanations are not necessary.

Transactions:

a. Anne Mayer, owner of Internet Analysis Services invested $25,000 cash and $9,000 of equipment in her new business.
b. The business purchased $750 of supplies on account.
c. The business completed a job and billed the client $2,500.
d. The business prepaid 6 months of fire insurance for $1,200.
e. The business received a $1,575 bill for advertising, which was not immediately paid.
f. The client paid $2,000 of what was owing on account.
g $5,000 of computer equipment was purchased by paying $1,000 and signing a note payable for the balance.
h. The business paid the amounts owing for the supplies purchase and for the advertising.

PRACTICE **Learning Goal 24, continued**

Solutions are in the disk at the back of the book and at: www.worthyjames.com

IA 24-2. Prepare general journal entries

Record the general journal entry for each transaction. Remember that you can use T accounts to help you visualize transactions. (Make copies of blank journal paper from the disk at the back of this book or from the "student info." link at www.worthyjames.com) Explanations are not necessary.

Transactions:

a. The owner of University Travel Services, James Li, invested $20,000 cash in his business.
b. Terre Haute Company received a $3,800 advance payment from a customer.
c. Bloomington Enterprises collected $550 owing from customers.
d. Lafayette Company purchased $8,500 of equipment by paying $2,000 cash and signing a note payable for the balance.
e. Muncie Company provided $2,500 of services and sent the customer a bill.
f. Indianapolis Company paid accounts payable in the amount of $350.
g. Gary Company paid six months' of insurance in advance in the amount of $2,850.
h. Hammond Enterprises completed a job for which the customer had made full payment in advance in the amount of $1,200.
i. Fort Wayne Company received a $575 utilily bill that was not paid immediately.
j. Evansville Company used up one month of office rent in the amount of $1,500. The company had paid 3 months' of rent in advance.
k. The owner of University Travel Services, James Li, withdrew $1,000 cash from his business for personal use.

IA 24-3. Prepare general journal entries

Using the general journal, record the October transactions for Maxwell Insurance Consuting Services. Remember that you can use T accounts to help you visualize transactions. (Make copies of blank journal paper from the disk at the back of this book or from the "student info." link at www.worthyjames.com.) Explanations are not necessary.

Transactions:

Oct.

1 The owner, Susan Maxwell, invested $15,000 cash in her business.
2 Purchased $520 of supplies on account.
3 Prepaid 3 months of rent in the amount of $4,500.
5 Purchased computer equipment for $5,000 by paying $1,000 cash and signing a note for the balance.
8 Interviewed and hired a new assistant, to paid be paid $3,500 per month.
12 Borrowed $20,000 from 1st National Credit Union.
14 Performed $2,500 of services and billed the client.
18 Received an advance payment from Watson, Inc. in the amount of $5,000.
18 Received a utilities bill for $210, which was not paid immediately.
20 Completed $2,000 of services for Smith Company, which immediately paid $500.
21 Paid for cleaning services, $200.
27 Received $500 cash from a client, who paid on an account.
27 Counted the office supplies purchased on Oct. 2; 20% has been used up.
28 Completed the job for Watson, Inc., above.
31 One month of the prepaid rent (above) has been used up.

PRACTICE **Learning Goal 24, continued**

Solutions are in the disk at the back of the book and at: www.worthyjames.com

IA 24-4. Analyze errors

During the month of June, the following transactions were recorded by Silicon Company, a sole proprietorship. Unfortunately, the bookkeeper is very inexperienced, so the company has asked you to review the journal entries below.

For each transaction, analyze the journal entry and identify any incorrect entries. For each incorrect entry explain what is wrong and show the correct entry.

Transactions:
June
1 Borrowed $50,000 from Financing Bank, signing a note payable.
4 Collected $750 on an account receivable.
6 Purchased equipment for $10,000. Paid $1,000 cash and signed a note payable for the balance.
7 Paid for cleaning services, $300.
8 Purchased airline tickets for travel next month, $1800.
11 Completed a job and billed the customer $3,100.
12 The owner, Abe Cohen, withdrew $1,500 from the business.
15 Paid for advertising services for the month, $2,850.
17 Received a $500 bill for advertising services. The bill was not paid immediately.
17 Received an advance payment of $1,000 from a customer for a job to begin in July.
22 Hired a new employee at a salary of $5,500 per month.
25 Paid accounts payable totaling $1,950
26 Used up $630 of supplies.
30 Purchased $800 of office supplies and $1,900 of office furniture on account.

Date	Account	Dr.	Cr.
20XX			
June 1	Cash	50,000	
	Notes Payable		50,000
4	Cash	750	
	Service Revenue		750
6	Equipment	10,000	
	Cash		1,000
	Accounts Payable		9,000
7	Cleaning Expense	300	
	Cash		300
8	Travel Expense	1,800	
	Cash		1,800
11	Accounts Receivable	3,100	
	Service Revenue		3,100
12	Salary Expense	1,500	
	Cash		1,500

PRACTICE Learning Goal 24, continued

IA 24-4, *continued*

Date	Account	Dr.	Cr.
15	Advertising Expense	2,850	
	Cash		2,850
17	Cash	1,000	
	Service Revenue		1,000
22	Wages Expense	5,000	
	Wages Payable		5,000
25	Accounts Payable	1,950	
	Cash		1,950
26	Supplies Expense	630	
	Supplies		630
30	Accounts Payable	2,700	
	Office Supplies		800
	Office Furniture		1,900

INTERNET EXERCISES

Take a tour of the history of accounting. Do an Internet search to learn about the history of accounting. (Use bookmark/favorites to save the locations of links you use in an "Accounting References" folder.)

a. What are the earliest records of accounting activity?
b. What was the beginning of what later evolved into modern accounting? When and where did this beginning primarily take place? Why did it take place?
c. What person is often referred to as the "father of modern accounting"? Why does he get credit for this?
d. What connection do Britain and the industrial revolution have to the accounting profession as we know it today?
e. In the United States, what effect did the stock market crash of 1929 and the resulting great depression of the 1930s have on the American accounting profession and financial reporting?
f. Did the 2002 establishment of the Public Company Accounting Oversight Board (PCAOB) affect any long-standing privileges of American accountants? In what way? What happened to cause this?

Your Questions?

It is *very* important to be aware of what you need to understand better. What do you need to understand better about this learning goal? On a separate piece of paper, write the questions that you want to discuss with your classmates, instructor, or supervisor. Try to be very specific about what is bothering you, such as explanations that you do not fully understand.

LEARNING GOAL 25 Use a Basic Accounting System

In Learning Goal 25, you will find:

Practical Forms of the General Journal and the Ledger Account

A More Realistic Journal

Two Improvements

Only two improvements are needed to make our journal realistic and fully usable. The following page shows the general journal for David's tiny little Bodyguard Service for the first week of operations after all the transactions are recorded. Notice the two improvements in the journal.

Journal Page Number: Every journal has page numbers. The "J1" that you see in the upper right corner of the journal means page 1 of the general journal. (Sometimes the letters "G" or "GJ" are used instead.)

"Posting Reference" Column: The new column that is titled "Post. Ref." is only used during the posting procedure (which will be explained later). When data is transferred from the journal to a ledger account, that account's identification number is entered in the "Post. Ref." column. (Sometimes the "Posting Reference" column is titled "LP" for ledger page, or "folio.")

continued ▶

A More Realistic Journal, *continued*

GENERAL JOURNAL				J1
Date	**Account Titles and Explanation**	**Post. Ref.**	**Debit**	**Credit**
2017				
June 1	Cash		20	
	David Lilliput, Capital			20
	Owner made investment to start business			
2	Office Supplies		5	
	Office Equipment		20	
	Accounts Payable			25
	Purchase supplies and equipment from London Company			
3	Cash		7	
	Unearned Revenue			7
	Advance payment from Houyhnhnm Company			
4	Supplies Expense		3	
	Office Supplies			3
	Office supplies used up for the Swift report			
5	Accounts Receivable		5	
	Security Service Revenue			5
	Security services for Shadow Company			
6	Accounts Payable		3	
	Cash			3
	Payment on Accounts Payable—London Company			

A More Realistic Journal, *continued*

GENERAL JOURNAL, continued				J1
Date	**Account Titles and Explanation**	**Post. Ref.**	**Debit**	**Credit**
June				
7	Prepaid Insurance		10	
	Cash			10
	Prepaid Old Bailey Insurance Company—			
	liability insurance coverage until September 30			
7	Cash		15	
	Security Service Revenue			15
	Security services for T & P Company			

A More Realistic Ledger Account

We Expand the Basic "T"

The simple T accounts that we have been using in prior learning goals are very useful for analyzing the effects of transactions and for illustrations. However, in practice, a real ledger account needs more features than a simple T account that is used for analysis. Although the format of real ledger accounts vary somewhat, you can see a typical example in the illustration on page 486.

To assist you in making the connection to a T account, heavy blue lines are used in the illustration to form the basic "T" that is the essential part of every ledger account.

continued 

A More Realistic Ledger Account, *continued*

New Features

You can see that a ledger account is really just an expanded T account, with the following features added:

- **A "Date" column**—for the date the transaction occurred. It may not be the same date that the transaction is recorded into the ledger account.
- **An "Explanation" column**, for additional information. In practice, this is seldom used.
- **The "Post. Ref." column**—an important source reference. A number is placed in this column to show what *page of the journal* the dollar amount came from. In this way, the change in the account can be traced back to the transaction from which it originated.
- **A "Balance" column**—to update the balance every time there is an entry. This makes it easy to instantly see the balance instead of retotaling debits and credits with each new entry. The "Balance" column shows the "natural" ("normal") balance of the account. For example, we would know that the normal balance in this cash account should always be a debit because cash is an asset. (When a bookkeeper needs to show a temporary negative balance, the amount in the "Balance" column can be put in parentheses ( ), circled, or written in red.)

Note: This ledger account is known as a *three-column account form* ledger account because it has three money-amount columns: a debit, a credit, and a balance column. There are also other forms and variations.

	CASH		ACCOUNT NO. 101		
Date	Explanation	Post. Ref.	Debit	Credit	Balance

Posting: Information Transfer from Journal to Ledger

The Posting Procedure

Introduction

When we discussed journals and ledgers in prior learning goals, you learned that a transaction is first analyzed (use T accounts), then recorded in the general journal, and finally recorded in the ledger. This discussion shows you how the information on the journal is transferred from the journal to the ledger. This procedure is called ***posting***.

When Done

In manual accounting systems, posting is done at regular, frequent intervals (such as weekly). In computerized systems, posting is usually done daily.

Procedure

The table below shows the posting procedure. An example follows on page 485.

Step	Action
1	In the journal, locate the first account for which there is no entry in the "Post. Ref." column.
2	Open the ledger and locate the same account from Step 1.
3	In the ledger (using the journal information): ■ In the **"Date" column**, record the transaction date from the journal. ■ If the journal entry is a debit, record the dollar amount in the **"Debit" column**. If the journal entry is a credit, record the dollar amount in the **"Credit" column**. ■ In the **"Balance" column**, record the new account balance. ■ In the **"Post Ref." column**, record the page number of the general journal where the information came from.
4	Return to the journal and enter the ledger account number in the "Post. Ref." column on the same line as the account just posted.
5	■ Move to the next unposted account in the journal (Step 1). ■ Repeat actions in Steps 2–5.

continued ▶

The Posting Procedure, *continued*

Chart of Accounts for David's . . .

To demonstrate a manual posting procedure, we use the chart of accounts from David's tiny little Bodyguard Service. These are the numbers that are assigned to each ledger account.

David's tiny little Bodyguard Service
Chart of Accounts

Asset Accounts: numbers 101–199

#101	Cash
#105	Accounts Receivable
#107	Notes Receivable
#110	Office Supplies
#115	Prepaid Insurance
#140	Office Equipment

Liability Accounts: numbers 201–299

#201	Accounts Payable
#205	Wages Payable
#210	Unearned Revenue
#220	Notes Payable

Owner's Capital Accounts: numbers 301–399

#301	David Lilliput, Capital
#302	David Lilliput, Drawing

Revenue Accounts: numbers 401–499

#401	Security Service Revenue
#405	Interest Earned

Expense Accounts: numbers 501–599

#501	Advertising Expense
#505	Rent Expense
#507	Legal Expense
#510	Accounting Expense
#515	Wages Expense
#520	Insurance Expense
#525	Utilities Expense
#530	Supplies Expense

The Posting Procedure, *continued*

Example

The following example shows you the five steps and detailed posting procedures for David's tiny little Bodyguard Service. The June 1 and June 2 journal entries are shown below.

GENERAL JOURNAL				J1
Date	**Account Titles and Explanation**	**Post. Ref.**	**Debit**	**Credit**
2017				
June 1	Cash		20	
	David Lilliput, Capital			20
	Owner made investments to start business			
2	Office Supplies		5	
	Office Equipment		20	
	Accounts Payable			25
	Purchase supplies and equipment from London Company			

Step 1 **Identify account that needs to be posted.** In the journal, locate the first account for which there is no entry in the "Post. Ref." column. The first account for which there is no entry in the "Post. Ref." column is the Cash account in the June 1 transaction (see dotted circle above).

Step 2 **Locate the same account in the ledger.** Open the ledger and locate the same account. (To save space, we will only look at the part of the ledger account we need to use.) The Cash ledger account is shown next in Step 3.

continued 

The Posting Procedure, *continued*

Step 3 Transfer data from the journal to the ledger account.

- In the "Date" column, record the transaction date from the journal ("June 1").
- If the journal entry is a debit, record the dollar amount in the "Debit" column ("20"). (If a credit, record in the "Credit" column.)
- In the "Balance" column, record the new account balance. In this example, there was no prior balance, so the new balance is $20.
- In the "Post Ref." column, record the page number of the general journal where the information came from. This entry came from page J1.

CASH			ACCOUNT NO. 101		
Date	**Explanation**	**Post. Ref.**	**Debit**	**Credit**	**Balance**
2017					
June					
1		J1	20		20

Step 4 Cross-reference the journal to the ledger. Return to the journal and enter the ledger account number ("101") in the "Post. Ref." column on the same line as the account just posted. This entry serves as a reference if you need to verify later that the amount was correctly posted into the proper account.

GENERAL JOURNAL				J1
Date	**Account Titles and Explanation**	**Post. Ref.**	**Debit**	**Credit**
2017				
June 1	Cash	101	20	
	David Lilliput, Capital			20
	Owner made investments to start business			
2	Office Supplies		5	
	Office Equipment		20	
	Accounts Payable			25
	Purchase supplies and equipment from London Company			

The Posting Procedure, *continued*

Step 5 **Repeat the process.** Move to the next unposted account in the journal (Step 1), and repeat the actions in Steps 2–5.

GENERAL JOURNAL				J1
Date	**Account Titles and Explanation**	**Post. Ref.**	**Debit**	**Credit**
2017				
June 1	Cash	101	20	
	David Lilliput, Capital			20
	Owner made investment to start business			
2	Office Supplies		5	
	Office Equipment		20	
	Accounts Payable			25
	Purchase supplies and equipment from London Company			

The Completed Journal and Ledger

Completed Transactions

The following pages show the posted journal and ledger accounts for David's tiny little Bodyguard Service transactions from June 1 to June 4. The June 5, 6, 7, and 8 transactions have not yet been posted.

GENERAL JOURNAL				J1
Date	**Account Titles and Explanation**	**Post. Ref.**	**Debit**	**Credit**
2017				
June 1	Cash	101	20	
	David Lilliput, Capital	301		20
	Owner made investment to start business			
2	Office Supplies	110	5	
	Office Equipment	140	20	
	Accounts Payable	201		25
	Purchase supplies and equipment from London Company			

continued ▶

The Completed Journal and Ledger, *continued*

Date	Account Titles and Explanation	Post. Ref.	Debit	Credit
3	Cash	101	7	
	Unearned Revenue	210		7
	Advance payment from Houyhnhnm Company			
4	Supplies Expense	530	3	
	Office Supplies	110		3
	Office supplies used up for the Swift report			
5	Accounts Receivable		5	
	Security Service Revenue			5
	Security services for Shadow Company			
6	Accounts Payable		3	
	Cash			3
	Payment on Accounts Payable—London Company			
7	Prepaid Insurance		10	
	Cash			10
	Prepaid Old Bailey Insurance Company—			
	liability insurance coverage until September 30			
7	Cash		15	
	Security Service Revenue			15
	Security services for T & P Company			
8	Unearned Revenue		3	
	Security Service Revenue			3
	Performed part of the services for the customer			
	who paid in advance on June 3			

The Completed Journal and Ledger, *continued*

Ledger Accounts

CASH			ACCOUNT NO. 101		
Date	**Explanation**	**Post. Ref.**	**Debit**	**Credit**	**Balance**
2017					
June 1		J1	20		20
3		J1	7		27

ACCOUNTS RECEIVABLE			ACCOUNT NO. 105		
Date	**Explanation**	**Post. Ref.**	**Debit**	**Credit**	**Balance**
2017					

OFFICE SUPPLIES			ACCOUNT NO. 110		
Date	**Explanation**	**Post. Ref.**	**Debit**	**Credit**	**Balance**
2017					
June 2		J1	5		5
4		J1		3	2

PREPAID INSURANCE			ACCOUNT NO. 115		
Date	**Explanation**	**Post. Ref.**	**Debit**	**Credit**	**Balance**
2017					

continued ▶

The Completed Journal and Ledger, *continued*

Ledger Accounts, continued

	OFFICE EQUIPMENT		ACCOUNT NO. 140		
Date	Explanation	Post. Ref.	Debit	Credit	Balance
2017					
June 2		J1	20		20

	ACCOUNTS PAYABLE		ACCOUNT NO. 201		
Date	Explanation	Post. Ref.	Debit	Credit	Balance
2017					
June 2		J1		25	25

	UNEARNED REVENUE		ACCOUNT NO. 210		
Date	Explanation	Post. Ref.	Debit	Credit	Balance
2017					
June 3		J1		7	7

	DAVID LILLIPUT, CAPITAL		ACCOUNT NO. 301		
Date	Explanation	Post. Ref.	Debit	Credit	Balance
2017					
June 1		J1		20	20

The Completed Journal and Ledger, *continued*

Ledger Accounts, continued

	SECURITY SERVICE REVENUE		ACCOUNT NO. 401		
Date	Explanation	Post. Ref.	Debit	Credit	Balance
2017					

	SUPPLIES EXPENSE		ACCOUNT NO. 530		
Date	Explanation	Post. Ref.	Debit	Credit	Balance
2017					
June 4		J1	3		3

QUICK REVIEW

- Two added features to the journal are:
  - journal page numbers
  - a "Posting Reference" column
- Four added features to the ledger account are:
  - a "Date" column
  - an "Explanation" column
  - a "Posting Reference" column
  - an account "Balance" column
- The posting process is the transfer of information from entries on the journal into the ledger accounts. Posting occurs at regular intervals such as weekly or monthly. In computerized systems, it often occurs daily (or even more frequently).

Do You Want More Examples?

Most problems in this book have detailed solutions. To use them as additional examples, do this: 1) Select the type of problem you want 2) Open the solution on your computer or mobile device screen (from the disc or worthyjames.com) 3) Read one item at a time and look at its answer. Take notes if needed. 4) Close the solution and work as much of the problem as you can. 5) Repeat as needed.

PRACTICE Learning Goal 25

Solutions are in the disk at the back of the book and at: www.worthyjames.com

Learning Goal 25 is about using realistic journal and ledger accounts. Use these questions and problems to practice what you have just read.

Multiple Choice

Select the best answer.

1. When a journal entry is posted, which of the following is *not* true?
   a. The same information that is in the journal is recorded again in the ledger.
   b. The reference column of the ledger account will show a journal page number.
   c. The reference column of the journal will show either a "Dr." or a "Cr."
   d. Account numbers must be used as part of the posting procedure.
2. Posting is performed
   a. after the transaction but before the information is recorded in the journal.
   b. after transaction information is recorded in the journal.
   c. only when ledger accounts need updating.
   d. in the order of the numbers on the chart of accounts.
3. The "Posting Reference" column in the journal
   a. should be filled in at the same time that transaction information is journalized.
   b. is filled in immediately after a transaction is posted into the ledger.
   c. is seldom used in practice.
   d. none of the above.
4. The "Explanation" column of a ledger account
   a. should be filled in at the time transaction information is journalized.
   b. is an important part of the posting procedure.
   c. is seldom used in practice.
   d. none of the above.
5. The procedure of transferring information from the journal to ledger accounts is called
   a. posting.
   b. journalizing.
   c. balancing the books.
   d. recording.
6. After a journal entry is posted, the
   a. reference column in the journal will contain a page number of the ledger.
   b. reference column in the ledger will contain an account number of the journal.
   c. both (a) and (b).
   d. none of the above.
7. The general journal does *not* have a column with the title
   a. "Account," or sometimes "Description."
   b. "Date."
   c. "Balance."
   d. "Post. Ref."

PRACTICE Learning Goal 25, continued

Solutions are in the disk at the back of the book and at: www.worthyjames.com

Discussion Questions and Brief Exercises for Learning Goals 23–25

1. What is a ledger and what is its purpose?
2. What is a journal and what is its purpose?
3. Explain the difference between a journal and a ledger. What are the advantages of using each?
4. What is a debit and what is a credit? What is a debit balance and what is a credit balance?
5. Does the use of debits and credits change the rules for increasing and decreasing the accounts?
6. The meaning of "double entry" in an accounting system is that every transaction must be recorded twice. Correct? Explain what you think.
7. Anne Soleimani, a beginning accounting student in your study group, believes that debits are favorable and credits are unfavorable. Mark Reese, also in your study group, disagrees. He believes that debits are unfavorable and credits are favorable. Who do you agree with? Why?
8. Your friend Julia Chen is concerned about taking her first accounting test this week because she can never remember if debit means increase or decrease and if credit means increase or decrease. Can you explain this and help her relax?
9. Describe the process for entering transaction information into an accounting system.
10. Answer the following about general journal entries: (a) What date should be used? (b) What should you record first, debits or credits? (c) What do you write in the "account" column of the journal? (d) Should you make an entry in the "Post. Ref." column when you make the journal entry? (e) After you make the journal entry, what should you always check?
11. If you look in a ledger account, how can you tell where the entries in the account came from?
12. If you look in a journal, how do you know if the information was also entered in the ledger?
13. What is a chart of accounts? How is it organized and where can you usually find it?
14. Suppose that you decided not to use a journal. Instead, you record transaction information directly into the ledger accounts because this saves time. Could this be done? What would be the result?

Reinforcement Problems

LG 25-1. Complete the posting. Return to the journal (J1) beginning on page 491 in the "Completed transactions" discussion. Using the journal, and the ledger accounts following the journal, complete the posting for the June 5, 6, 7, and 8 transactions.

LG 25-2. Practice posting from a completed journal. The general journal shown below has not been posted yet. Complete the posting of the journal information into the ledger accounts. (For ledger account paper, you can print out copies from the disk at the back of the book.) Before you begin the posting, enter account numbers on the ledger accounts using the chart of accounts that you see below.

PRACTICE

Learning Goal 25, continued

Solutions are in the disk at the back of the book and at: www.worthyjames.com

LG 25-2, *continued*

Assets:
101 Cash
110 Accounts Receivable
120 Supplies
150 Furniture
160 Computer Equipment

Liabilities:
202 Accounts Payable
220 Notes Payable
230 Unearned Revenue

Owner's Equity:
302 David Washington, Capital
310 David Washington, Withdrawals

Revenue:
401 Service Revenue

Expenses:
510 Wages Expense
515 Rent Expense
525 Advertising Expense
530 Maintenance Expense
535 Cleaning Expense
550 Interest Expense

Page 8

Date	Account	Ref.	Dr.	Cr.
2017				
June				
1	Cash		25,000	
	David Washington, Capital			25,000
2	Supplies		500	
	Furniture		2,700	
	Accounts Payable			3,200
3	Cash		15,000	
	Notes Payable			15,000
5	Cash		2,250	
	Service Revenue			2,250
6	Cleaning Expense		150	
	Cash			150
8	Computer Equipment		7,000	
	Cash			3,000
	Notes Payable			4,000
10	Cash		5,000	
	Unearned Revenue			5,000

PRACTICE **Learning Goal 25, continued**

Solutions are in the disk at the back of the book and at: www.worthyjames.com

LG 25-2, *continued*

Page 9

Date	Account	Ref.	Dr.	Cr.
12	Accounts Receivable		2,500	
	Service Revenue			2,500
15	Wages Expense		1,120	
	Cash			1,120
15	Accounts Payable		1,000	
	Cash			1,000
15	Rent Expense		1,500	
	Cash			1,500
18	Advertising Expense		800	
	Accounts Payable			800
22	Accounts Receivable		750	
	Service Revenue			750
25	Cash		1,000	
	Accounts Receivable			1,000
28	Maintenance Expense		500	
	Accounts Payable			500
30	Interest Expense		500	
	Notes Payable		250	
	Cash			750
30	Withdrawals		2,000	
	Cash			2,000

PRACTICE Learning Goal 25, continued

Solutions are in the disk at the back of the book and at: www.worthyjames.com

LG 25-3. Record transactions in a general journal and post to a ledger. John Covina is an electrical contractor who opened his new business called Covina Electrical Contracting on September 2, 2017. The business installs electrical systems in both business and residential buildings. Using the information below, do the following:

1. Record the September transactions into the general journal. (Before journalizing use T account analysis whenever you feel it is necessary to visualize a transaction.)
2. Post the journal information into the ledger accounts. Before you begin the posting, enter account names and numbers on the ledger accounts using the chart of accounts that you see below.
3. When you finish recording all transactions, verify that each ledger account shows a current balance. (For journal paper and for ledger account paper, you can make copies from the general journal and ledger templates from the disk at the back of the book or or copy from worthyjames.com/info-papers-forms.html.) ("student info." page)

Covina Electrical Contracting
Chart of Accounts

Account	No.	Account	No.
Assets:		***Revenues:***	
Cash	103	Service Revenue	410
Accounts Receivable	110		
Office Supplies	120	***Expenses:***	
Electrical Supplies	125	Rent Expense	505
Prepaid Insurance	150	Wages Expense	510
Equipment: Office	170	Auto & Gas Expense	520
Tools	180	Insurance Expense	530
		Advertising Expense	535
Liabilities:		Utilities Expense	540
Accounts Payable	203	Office Supplies Expense	545
Unearned Revenue	210	Electrical Supplies Expense	550
Wages Payable	215	Legal Expense	560
Notes Payable	250	Accounting Expense	570
		Interest Expense	590
Owner's Equity:			
J. Covina, Capital	305		
J. Covina, Withdrawals	310		

PRACTICE **Learning Goal 25, continued**

Solutions are in the disk at the back of the book and at: www.worthyjames.com

LG 25-3, *continued*

Transactions:

Sept. 2: John Covina invested $100,000 cash plus office equipment valued at $10,000 to open his new business, Covina Electrical Contracting.
Sept. 2: The business paid $6,000 for one year of insurance in advance.
Sept. 3: Performed $7,500 of electrical installation services; the client immediately paid $2,000 cash.
Sept. 7: Purchased $1,000 of office supplies on account.
Sept. 12: Purchased tools for $7,800 and electrical supplies for $4,200 by paying $5,000 cash and signing note payable for the balance.
Sept. 14: Collected $3,000 on account.
Sept. 15: Installed electrical systems for computer servers and billed the customer $6,100.
Sept. 16: Received a utilities bill in the amount of $315 and a gasoline bill for $190.
Sept. 17: Paid $390 for office supplies.
Sept. 22: (Begin journal page 2.) Paid office rent, $2,200.
Sept. 23: Received an advance payment of $12,000 for 6 months of electrical maintenance services from a local business.
Sept. 24: Paid $720 owing on accounts payable.
Sept. 27: John Covina withdrew $2,000 from the business for personal use.
Sept. 29: A count of supplies showed that $175 of office supplies and $2,900 of electrical supplies had been consumed.
Sept. 30: Recorded $4,100 of wages expense as owing but unpaid.
Sept. 30: Recorded one month of the prepaid insurance being used up in the amount of $500.
Sept. 30: Performed $5,000 of services for the client in the September 23 transaction.

LG 25-4. **Record transactions in general journal and post to ledger.** Rita Markstein is an employee benefits specialist who opened her new business called Markstein Consulting on June 3, 2017. The business provides consulting services to large businesses that want to create employee benefit plans. Using the information below, do the following:

1. Record the June transactions into the general journal. (Before journalizing use T account analysis whenever you feel it is necessary to visualize a transaction.)
2. Post the journal information into the ledger accounts. Before you begin the posting, enter account names and numbers on the ledger accounts using the chart of accounts that you see below.
3. When you finish recording all transactions, verify that each ledger account shows a current balance. (For journal paper and for ledger account paper, you can make copies from the disk at the back of this book or copy from worthyjames.com/info-papers-forms.html.) ("student info." page)

PRACTICE Learning Goal 25, continued

Solutions are in the disk at the back of the book and at: www.worthyjames.com

LG 25-4, *continued*

Markstein Consulting
Chart of Accounts

Account	No.	Account	No.
Assets:		***Revenues:***	
Cash	101	Consulting Revenue	405
Accounts Receivable	108		
Office Supplies	115	***Expenses:***	
Prepaid Insurance	150	Rent Expense	502
Prepaid Travel	155	Wages Expense	508
Office Equipment	170	Auto & Gas Expense	512
Office Furniture	180	Insurance Expense	516
		Advertising Expense	520
Liabilities:		Utilities Expense	524
Accounts Payable	205	Office Supplies Expense	528
Unearned Revenue	210	Travel Expense	532
Wages Payable	220	Legal & Accounting Expense	536
Notes Payable	280	Interest Expense	540
		Internet Expense	544
Owner's Equity:			
R. Markstein, Capital	303		
R. Markstein, Withdrawals	304		

Transactions:

June 2: To open her new business, Markstein Consulting, Rita Markstein invested $25,000 cash, $800 of office supplies, and office furniture with a value of $4,000.
June 2: The business paid $3,000 in advance for one year of insurance and also paid $1,800 for airline tickets, which will be used in August.
June 3: Received a bill for legal services in the amount of $2,500.
June 3: Performed $5,200 of consulting services; the client immediately paid $1,000 cash.
June 7: Purchased $930 of office supplies on account.
June 9: Purchased computers (office equipment) for $12,000 by paying $8,000 cash and signing a note payable for the balance.
June 14: Collected $2,500 from Accounts Receivable.
June 16: Received a utilities bill in the amount of $420 and a bill for Internet Services of $700.
June 17: Paid office rent, $2,750.
June 21: (Begin journal page 2.) Received an advance payment of $4,000 for 12 months of consulting services from Argyle Corporation.
June 24: Paid $925 owing on accounts payable.
June 25: Rita Markstein withdrew $1,000 from the business for her personal use.
June 27: Completed a consulting engagement and billed Dunwoody Corporation $5,000.
June 29: A count of supplies showed that $245 of office supplies had been used.
June 30: Recorded $3,800 of wages expense as owing but unpaid.
June 30: Recorded one month of the prepaid insurance being used up in the amount of $250.
June 30: Completed $750 of services for Argyle Corporation in the June 21 transaction.

PRACTICE Learning Goal 25, continued

Solutions are in the disk at the back of the book and at: www.worthyjames.com

Instructor-Assigned Problems

If you are using this book in a class, these review problems may be assigned by your instructor for homework, group assignments, class work, or other activities. Only your instructor has the solutions.

IA25-1. **Record transactions in a general journal and post to a ledger.** On October 5, 2017, Armando Rubio, a psychologist, began his new family therapy practice called Family Therapy Resources. Using the information below, do the following:

1. Record the October transactions into the general journal. (Before journalizing use T account analysis whenever you feel it is necessary to visualize a transaction.)
2. Post the journal information into the ledger accounts. Before you begin the posting, enter account names and numbers on the ledger accounts using the chart of accounts that you see below.
3. When you finish recording all transactions, verify that each ledger account shows a current balance. (For journal paper and for ledger account paper, you can make copies from the disk at the back of the book or copy from worthyjames.com/info-papers-forms.html.) ("student info." page)

Family Therapy Resources
Chart of Accounts

Assets:		***Revenues:***	
Cash	102	Counseling Revenue	405
Accounts Receivable	106		
Office Supplies	110	***Expenses:***	
Prepaid Insurance	150	Rent Expense	503
Prepaid Subscriptions	155	Wages Expense	508
Office Equipment	175	Travel Expense	513
Office Furniture	185	Insurance Expense	521
		Professional Journals Expense	526
Liabilities:		Utilities Expense	531
Accounts Payable	202	Office Supplies Expense	536
Unearned Revenue	208	Continuing Education Expense	541
Wages Payable	210	Legal & Accounting Expense	546
Notes Payable	275	Interest Expense	590
Owner's Equity:			
A. Rubio, Capital	305		
A. Rubio, Withdrawals	310		

PRACTICE Learning Goal 25, continued

IA25-1, *continued*

Transactions:

October 5: To open his new business, Dr. Rubio invested $50,000 cash and office furniture with a value of $10,000.
October 6: The business paid $12,000 in advance for one year of insurance beginning in October and paid $1,500 for 12 months of professional journals subscriptions that will begin in November.
October 7: Received a bill for accounting services in the amount of $1,700. Immediately paid $500 of the bill.
October 9: During October 2–7 provided counseling services in the amount of $8,100, receiving $2,000 of cash payments. The balance was billed on account.
October 10: Purchased $1,175 of office supplies on account.
October 11: Purchased computers and software (office equipment) for $15,000 and office furniture for $5,000 by paying the vendor $10,000 cash and signing a note payable for the balance.
October 14: Collected $1,900 from Accounts Receivable.
October 17: Received a utilities bill in the amount of $385 and a bill for continuing education classes in the amount of $1,500.
October 18: Paid for monthly office rent, $2,750.
October 19: Received an advance payment from Sardis Corporation of $15,000 for counseling services to be provided to employees requesting such services.
October 24: Paid $1,800 owing on accounts payable.
October 25: Dr. Rubio withdrew $750 from the business for his personal use.
October 27: Made a loan payment of $800, of which $640 was interest expense, the balance being a payment on the note payable.
October 28: (Begin journal page 2.) A count of supplies showed that $445 of office supplies had been used.
October 29: Recorded $4,500 of office wages expense as owing but unpaid.
October 30: Recorded one month of the prepaid insurance being used up in the amount of $1,000.
October 30: Completed $1,950 of services for Sardis Corporation in the October 19 transaction.
October 31: During October 8–31 provided other counseling services in the amount of $14,500, receiving $5,000 of cash payments. The balance was billed on account.

IA25-2. Record transactions in a general journal and post to a ledger. On July 2, 2017, Dennis Kim, a licensed insurance agent and Certified Financial Planner, started a new insurance agency called Kim Insurance Agency. Using the information below, do the following:

1. Record the July transactions into the general journal. (Before journalizing use T account analysis whenever you feel it is necessary to visualize a transaction.)
2. Post the journal information into the ledger accounts. Before you begin the posting, enter account names and numbers on the ledger accounts using the chart of accounts that you see below.
3. When you finish recording all transactions, verify that each ledger account shows a current balance. (For journal paper and for ledger account paper, you can make copies from the disk at the back of this book.)

PRACTICE **Learning Goal 25, continued**

IA25-2, *continued*

Kim Insurance Agency
Chart of Accounts

Assets:		*Revenues:*	
Cash	105	Insurance Revenue	410
Accounts Receivable	110	Financial Planning Revenue	420
Office Supplies	120		
Prepaid Rent	140	*Expenses:*	
Prepaid Insurance	145	Rent Expense	505
Office Equipment	175	Wages Expense	508
Office Furniture	185	Advertising Expense	511
		Insurance Expense	514
Liabilities:		Internet Expense	517
Accounts Payable	210	Utilities Expense	520
Unearned Revenue	220	Office Supplies Expense	523
Wages Payable	225	Continuing Education Expense	526
Notes Payable	280	Legal & Accounting Expense	529
		Interest Expense	550
Owner's Equity:			
D. Kim, Capital	302		
D. Kim, Withdrawals	303		

Transactions:

July 2: To open his new business, Dennis Kim invested $30,000 cash.
July 6: The business paid $9,000 in advance for one year of liability insurance beginning in July.
July 7: Completed a financial plan for the client and billed the client $1,800.
July 7: Paid $1,500 for rent for the month of July plus another $3,000 for August and September.
July 10: Purchased $500 of office supplies on account.
July 11: Purchased computers and software (office equipment) for $18,000 and office furniture for $4,500 by paying the vendor $8,000 cash and signing a note payable for the balance.
July 14: Collected $1,000 from Accounts Receivable.
July 17: Received a utilities bill in the amount of $280.
July 18: Received cash commissions for insurance policies sold, $3,800.
July 18: Received an $800 bill for Internet service maintenance and a bill for continuing education classes in the amount of $2,100.
July 19: Received a $20,000 advance payment from Bellevue Corporation for financial planning services to be provided to the company employees.
July 24: Paid $1,600 owing on accounts payable.
July 25: Dennis Kim withdrew $750 from the business for his personal use.
July 27: Made a loan payment of $500, of which $430 was interest expense, the balance being a payment on the note payable.
July 28: (Begin journal page 2.) Completed $2,500 of financial planning services and billed the client, who immediately paid $1,000 and will pay the balance later.
July 30: A count of supplies showed that $210 of office supplies had been used.
July 31: Completed $2,000 of services for Bellevue Corporation from the July 19 transaction.
July 31: Recorded $750 of prepaid liability insurance being used for July.

PRACTICE

Learning Goal 25, continued

Solutions are in the disk at the back of the book and at: www.worthyjames.com

Ethics—analyze cases. Go to the Carnegie Mellon Tepper School of Business, Arthur Andersen Case Studies in Business (at web.tepper.cmu.edu/ethics/aa/arthurandersen.htm).

Select at least three mini-cases that interest you. (Use bookmark/favorites to save the location in an Accounting References folder.)

a. Read each case, then write down the name of the case and apply the ethics discussion and guidelines in Learning Goal 10 to analyze the case. (Do not look at the teaching notes yet.)
b. Make a decision or take a position. Write a paragraph to explain how you reached your decision or position.
c. Compare your answer to the teaching notes. Do you agree with the notes? Would you change them or add more?

Cumulative Problems for Comprehensive Practice

Learning Goals 24 and 25 complete your introduction to the use of the general journal and general ledger. For comprehensive practice in the use of the general journal, general ledger, and the preparation of financial statements, cumulative problems are included at the end of Learning Goal 26. These extended problems contain a variety of transactions.

Your Questions?

It is *very* important to be aware of what you need to understand better. What do you need to understand better about this learning goal? On a separate piece of paper, write the questions that you want to discuss with your classmates, instructor, or supervisor. Try to be very specific about what is bothering you, such as explanations that you do not fully understand.

LEARNING GOAL 26

The Trial Balance—Prepare It and Use It Two Ways

In Learning Goal 26, you will find:

What Is a Trial Balance?

The Trial Balance

Trial Balance Defined

A ***trial balance*** is a listing of all the ledger account names with their balances. The account names are listed in a column. Next to the name of each account is *the balance of that account* as either a debit or credit. Accounts with zero balances are not usually included. The next page shows an example.

"What is a trial balance?"

continued ►

The Trial Balance, *continued*

The East Lake Street Company
Trial Balance
June 30, 2017

Account Name	Dr.	Cr.
Cash	$ 7,580	
Accounts receivable	4,207	
Office supplies	533	
Accounts payable		$ 2,500
Wages payable		750
Cindy Walczak, capital		8,220
Cindy Walczak, drawing	500	
Fees earned		5,550
Rent expense	1,200	
Supplies expense	300	
Wages expense	2,700	
Total	**$17,020**	**$17,020**

When Is It Prepared?

A trial balance can be prepared at any time, but it is usually prepared at the end of an accounting period, just before the financial statements are prepared.

Where does the Information Come From?

The amounts listed in the trial balances are the non-zero ending balances of all the individual ledger accounts. Therefore, the source of the information is the general ledger.

The Two Functions of the Trial Balance

The trial balance:

- *tests* whether or not the total of all the debit balance accounts equals the total of all the credit balance accounts. This proves that both sides of the accounting equation are equal, which is necessary in double-entry accounting.
- is the *source of the financial statements.* If all the account balances in the trial balance are correct, we can prepare a balance sheet, income statement, and statement of owner's equity from the trial balance. All the accounts with balances are in the trial balance.

Example of Preparing a Trial Balance

Example

On page 510, you will find all the completed ledger accounts for David's tiny little Bodyguard Service for the entire month of June, as of June 30. Using these accounts, you can prepare a trial balance like this:

<table>
<tr><th>Step</th><th>Action</th><th>Example</th></tr>
<tr><td>1</td><td>Prepare the trial balance headings. Be sure the date is correct.

Note: The trial balance is a point in time, not a period of time.</td><td>David's tiny little Bodyguard Service
Trial Balance
June 30, 2017

Account Title   Dr.   Cr.</td></tr>
<tr><td>2</td><td>Beginning with the first account in the ledger, list the names of the accounts and their balances in the same order that they appear in the ledger.

Do not list any zero-balance accounts.</td><td>David's tiny little Bodyguard Service
Trial Balance
June 30, 2017

<table>
<tr><th>Account Title</th><th>Dr.</th><th>Cr.</th></tr>
<tr><td>Cash</td><td>15</td><td></td></tr>
<tr><td>Accounts receivable</td><td>7</td><td></td></tr>
<tr><td>Prepaid insurance</td><td>10</td><td></td></tr>
<tr><td>Office equipment</td><td>20</td><td></td></tr>
<tr><td>Accounts payable</td><td></td><td>25</td></tr>
<tr><td>Unearned revenue</td><td></td><td>4</td></tr>
<tr><td>David Lilliput, capital</td><td></td><td>20</td></tr>
<tr><td>David Lilliput, drawing</td><td>3</td><td></td></tr>
<tr><td>Security service revenue</td><td></td><td>30</td></tr>
<tr><td>Advertising expense</td><td>3</td><td></td></tr>
<tr><td>Rent expense</td><td>9</td><td></td></tr>
<tr><td>Accounting expense</td><td>2</td><td></td></tr>
<tr><td>Insurance expense</td><td>4</td><td></td></tr>
<tr><td>Utilities expense</td><td>1</td><td></td></tr>
<tr><td>Supplies expense</td><td>5</td><td></td></tr>
</table>
</td></tr>
</table>

continued ▶

Example of Preparing a Trial Balance, *continued*

LEDGER

CASH — ACCT. NO. 101

Date	Explan.	Post. Ref.	Debit	Credit	Balance
2017					
June 1		J1	20		20
3		J1	7		27
6		J1		3	24
7		J1		10	14
7		J1	15		29
15		J2		9	20
23		J3		2	18
25		J3		4	14
27		J3		1	13
28		J3	5		18
30		J3		3	15

ACCOUNTS RECEIVABLE — ACCT. NO. 105

Date	Explan.	Post. Ref.	Debit	Credit	Balance
2017					
June 5		J1	5		5
28		J3		5	–0–
30		J3	7		7

OFFICE SUPPLIES — ACCT. NO. 110

Date	Explan.	Post. Ref.	Debit	Credit	Balance
2017					
June 2		J1	5		5
4		J1		3	2
11		J2		2	–0–

PREPAID INSURANCE — ACCT. NO. 115

Date	Explan.	Post. Ref.	Debit	Credit	Balance
2017					
June 7		J1	10		10

OFFICE EQUIPMENT — ACCT. NO. 140

Date	Explan.	Post. Ref.	Debit	Credit	Balance
2017					
June 2		J1	20		20

ACCOUNTS PAYABLE — ACCT. NO. 201

Date	Explan.	Post. Ref.	Debit	Credit	Balance
2017					
June 2		J1		25	25
6		J1	3		22
12		J2		3	25

UNEARNED REVENUE — ACCT. NO. 210

Date	Explan.	Post. Ref.	Debit	Credit	Balance
2017					
June 3		J1		7	7
8		J1	3		4

DAVID LILLIPUT, CAPITAL — ACCT. NO. 301

Date	Explan.	Post. Ref.	Debit	Credit	Balance
2017					
June 1		J1		20	20

DAVID LILLIPUT, DRAWING — ACCT. NO. 302

Date	Explan.	Post. Ref.	Debit	Credit	Balance
2017					
June 30		J3	3		3

SECURITY SERVICE REVENUE — ACCT. NO. 401

Date	Explan.	Post. Ref.	Debit	Credit	Balance
2017					
June 5		J1		5	5
7		J1		15	20
8		J1		3	23
30		J3		7	30

ADVERTISING EXPENSE — ACCT. NO. 501

Date	Explan.	Post. Ref.	Debit	Credit	Balance
2017					
June 12		J2	3		3

RENT EXPENSE — ACCT. NO. 505

Date	Explan.	Post. Ref.	Debit	Credit	Balance
2017					
June 15		J2	9		9

ACCOUNTING EXPENSE — ACCT. NO. 510

Date	Explan.	Post. Ref.	Debit	Credit	Balance
2017					
June 23		J3	2		2

INSURANCE EXPENSE — ACCT. NO. 520

Date	Explan.	Post. Ref.	Debit	Credit	Balance
2017					
June 25		J3	4		4

UTILITIES EXPENSE — ACCT. NO. 525

Date	Explan.	Post. Ref.	Debit	Credit	Balance
2017					
June 27		J3	1		1

SUPPLIES EXPENSE — ACCT. NO. 530

Date	Explan.	Post. Ref.	Debit	Credit	Balance
2017					
June 4		J1	3		3
11		J2	2		5

Example of Preparing a Trial Balance, *continued*

<table>
<tr><th>Step</th><th>Action</th><th>Example</th></tr>
<tr><td>3</td><td>Add the trial balance columns and compare the totals.</td><td>

David's tiny little Bodyguard Service
Trial Balance
June 30, 2017

Account Title	Dr.	Cr.
Cash	$15	
Accounts receivable	7	
Prepaid insurance	10	
Office equipment	20	
Accounts payable		$25
Unearned revenue		4
David Lilliput, capital		20
David Lilliput, drawing	3	
Security service revenue		30
Advertising expense	3	
Rent expense	9	
Accounting expense	2	
Insurance expense	4	
Utilities expense	1	
Supplies expense	5	
Total	**$79**	**$79**

</td></tr>
<tr><td>4</td><td colspan="2">If the totals are equal and you know that the individual account balances are correct, you can use the trial balance to prepare the financial statements.
■ Income statement: Use the revenue and expense accounts.
■ Statement of owner's equity: Use the owner's capital account, the drawing account, and the net income (or loss) from the income statement.
■ Balance sheet: Use the asset and liability accounts and the final balance of owner's capital from the statement of owner's equity.</td></tr>
</table>

Prepare Financial Statements from the Trial Balance

Example

The financial statements below were prepared from the June 30 trial balance of David's tiny little Bodyguard Service on page 509.

David's tiny little Bodyguard Service
Income Statement
For the Month Ended June 30, 2017

Revenues		
Security service revenue		$30
Expenses		
Rent expense	$9	
Supplies expense	5	
Insurance expense	4	
Advertising expense	3	
Accounting expense	2	
Utilities expense	1	
Total expenses		24
Net income		$ 6

David's tiny little Bodyguard Service
Statement of Owner's Equity
For the Month Ended June 30, 2017

David Lilliput, capital, June 1	$ 0
Add: Owner investment	20
Net income	6
	26
Less: Drawings	(3)
David Lilliput, capital, June 30	$23

David's tiny little Bodyguard Service
Balance Sheet
June 30, 2017

Assets		**Liabilities**	
Cash	$15	Accounts payable	$25
Accounts receivable	7	Unearned revenue	4
Prepaid insurance	10	Total liabilities	29
Office equipment	20		
		Owner's Equity	
		David Lilliput, capital	23
Total assets	$52	Total liabilities and owner's equity	$52

Prepare Financial Statements from the Trial Balance, *continued*

To find out if the owner made an investment, you will need to look into the ledger account for the owner's capital. For example, by just looking at the $20 of David Lilliput, Capital on the trial balance, you cannot be sure if it includes any current investment or is the beginning balance. This makes a difference, because any owner's investments must be disclosed separately on the statement of owner's equity.

Locating Errors in the Trial Balance

How to Locate Errors

What if the totals are not equal? In a manual accounting system, locating errors in the trial balance can be a slow process. In a faulty computerized accounting system that requires a programming fix, the process of finding the source of an error in the trial balance can be even more difficult. Here is how to proceed: *work backwards from the trial balance.*

Step	Action	Possible Errors
1	Examine the trial balance.	■ Columns were added incorrectly. ■ An account balance was omitted. ■ A balance was placed into the wrong column. ■ Amounts were written down incorrectly.
	Note: Check the difference between the totals:	If the difference between the totals is evenly divisible by 9, a transposition (like 51 instead of 15) or a slide (like 10 instead of 100) may be the only problem. If the difference is evenly divisible by 2, an amount written in the wrong column may be the only problem. Look for exactly half the difference.
2	Check the individual ledger accounts.	■ The balance of an account was calculated incorrectly. ■ The balance is shown incorrectly (debit instead of credit, or credit instead of debit).
3	Check the posting.	■ Debit was posted as a credit, or credit posted as a debit. ■ The same amount was posted more than once. ■ Part of a transaction posting was omitted. ■ A wrong amount was posted.
4	Check the journalizing.	■ Debits did not equal credits when a transaction was journalized.

continued ▶

Locating Errors in the Trial Balance, *continued*

What the Trial Balance DOES NOT Detect!

A correct trial balance proves that the total debits equal the total credits. However, the trial balance does not detect these kinds of errors:

- Any transaction that was not journalized
- Any transaction that was not posted
- Journal entries that balance, but use wrong amounts or wrong accounts
- Multiple journalizing or posting of the same transaction
- In a computerized system, failing to choose the correct default settings

All of these errors can occur, and the trial balance will still balance! These errors must be corrected before the financial statements are prepared and given to investors, lenders, and other stakeholders. You will learn how to deal with some of these problems in the second book in this series (Volume 2) when we discuss adjusting and correcting entries.

NO Debits or Credits on Financial Statements

Even though the trial balance uses debits and credits, *financial statements never have debits and credits.* This is because most people who use financial statements do not understand debits and credits.

QUICK REVIEW

- The trial balance is a listing of all accounts and their ending balances. (Accounts with zero balances are not usually included.)
- A trial balance can be prepared at any time, but normally it is prepared at the end of an accounting period, just before the financial statements are prepared.
- A trial balance serves two important functions:
  - It proves that the accounting equation is in balance for all the ledger accounts. The total of all debit balances must equal the total of all credit balances.
  - It is the source of the account balances used on the income statement, statement of owner's equity, and balance sheet.
- The trial balance does not identify errors in which the accounting equation still balances.
- Never use debits or credits on financial statements.

Do You Want More Examples?

Most problems in this book have detailed solutions. To use them as additional examples, do this: 1) Select the type of problem you want 2) Open the solution on your computer or mobile device screen (from the disc or worthyjames.com) 3) Read one item at a time and look at its answer. Take notes if needed. 4) Close the solution and work as much of the problem as you can. 5) Repeat as needed.

PRACTICE Learning Goal 26

Solutions are in the disk at the back of the book and at: www.worthyjames.com

Learning Goal 26 is about learning to prepare a trial balance and the two ways of using the trial balance. Use these questions and problems to practice what you have learned.

Multiple Choice

Select the best answer.

1. A trial balance is prepared
   a. usually just before financial statements are prepared.
   b. at any time the accountant desires to verify that the books are in balance.
   c. using the ending balances in all nonzero accounts.
   d. all the above.
2. A trial balance is used
   a. to test if all the debit account balances equal the total credit account balances.
   b. as the source of information that is used to prepare financial statements.
   c. as a financial statement.
   d. both (a) and (b).
3. A trial balance would help in detecting which error?
   a. A journal entry that was not posted
   b. A journal entry that was posted twice
   c. A journal entry that was posted to the wrong accounts
   d. None of the above
4. If a trial balance does not balance, it could mean that
   a. a ledger account was added incorrectly.
   b. a journal entry was posted twice.
   c. a journal entry was posted to the wrong accounts.
   d. none of the above.
5. If a $700 credit to Accounts Receivable was posted as a $700 credit to Cash, on the trial balance
   a. total debits will exceed total credits by $700.
   b. total credits will exceed total debits by $700.
   c. the trial balance will be completely unaffected.
   d. none of the above.
6. If a $500 debit to Cash was posted as a $50 debit to Cash, on the trial balance
   a. the cash is understated by $500.
   b. total debits will exceed total credits by $450.
   c. total credits will exceed total debits by $450.
   d. the cash is overstated by $500.
7. If $250 of supplies are consumed, but this is journalized and posted as a $250 debit to Supplies Expense and a $25 credit to Supplies, on the trial balance
   a. total debits will be overstated.
   b. total debits will exceed total credits.
   c. total credits will exceed total debits.
   d. total credits will be overstated.
8. Debits and credits are
   a. used only on the balance sheet.
   b. used only on the income statement.
   c. never used on any financial statements.
   d. are optional on financial statements.

PRACTICE Learning Goal 26, continued

Solutions are in the disk at the back of the book and at: www.worthyjames.com

Reinforcement Problems

LG 26-1. Prepare a trial balance. Listed below in random order are various ledger accounts with balances for the Overland Park Company, as of December 31, 2017. On a separate piece of paper, prepare a trial balance in good form. Account numbers are in parentheses ( ).

(#150) Land: $35,780	(#201) Wages Payable: $1,500	(#215) Unearned Revenue: $1,250
(#115) Supplies: 425	(#401) Service Revenue: 8,400	(#520) Repairs Expense: 1,315
(#130) Prepaid Insurance: 800	(#510) Utility Expense: 202	(#110) Accounts Receivable: 7,227
(#101) Cash: 4,281	(#505) Rent Expense: 800	(#300) R. Wills, Capital: 54,555
(#515) Wages Expense: 3,500	(#301) R. Wills, Draw: 1,000	(#140) Equipment: 10,500
(#415) Interest Earned: 125		

LG 26-2. Prepare a trial balance. The ledger account activity of Pham Company has been condensed into the T accounts that you see below. Using the T accounts, prepare a trial balance in good form as of June 30, 2017.

Cash		Accounts Receivable		Office Supplies		Computer Supplies		Prepaid Rent	
90,000	6,000	5,500	3,000	1,000	440	4,200	2,400	6,000	500
2,000	5,000	6,100	500	390					
3,000	390	1,000							
7,000	2,200								
	720								
	2,000								

Office Equipment		Computer Equipment		Accounts Payable		Unearned Revenue		Wages Payable	
10,000		17,800		720	1,000	5,000	12,000		4,100
					505				

Notes Payable		Hoan Pham, Capital		Hoan Pham, Withdrawals		Service Revenue		Rent Expense	
	7,000		106,000	2,000			7,500	2,200	
							6,100		
							5,000		

Wages Expense		Travel Expense		Insurance Expense		Supplies Expense		Internet Expense	
4,100		190		500		440		175	
								3,040	

PRACTICE Learning Goal 26, continued

Solutions are in the disk at the back of the book and at: www.worthyjames.com

LG 26-3. **Prepare financial statements from a trial balance.** Shown below is the trial balance for Web Designs Innovation company. Using the information below, prepare an income statement for the month of May 2017, statement of owner's equity for May, and a report form balance sheet as of May 31.

Web Designs Innovation
Trial Balance
May 31, 2017

	Dr.	Cr.
Cash	$91,120	
Accounts Receivable	31,150	
Repair Supplies	560	
Prepaid Travel	3,500	
Equipment	22,750	
Building and Land	416,900	
Wages Payable		$5,900
Accounts Payable		27,600
Unearned Revenue		3,700
Notes Payable		295,440
Jamal Miles, Capital		232,330
Jamal Miles, Withdrawals	3,800	
Design Revenue		15,200
Consulting Revenue		4,150
Supplies Expense	380	
Wages Expense	6,200	
Advertising Expense	2,500	
Utilities Expense	750	
Repairs Expense	1,310	
Rent Expense	3,400	
Totals	$584,320	$584,320

Other information: Jamal Miles, the owner, invested $10,000 in cash and equipment during the month.

PRACTICE Learning Goal 26, continued

Solutions are in the disk at the back of the book and at: www.worthyjames.com

LG 26-4. You be the teacher—Grade the financial statement (report form balance sheet). You have just given a weekly quiz that requires your students to prepare financial statements from a trial balance. Shown below is a report form balance sheet prepared by one of your students. Preparation of a correct balance sheet is worth 10 points. Identify the mistakes and grade this balance sheet. How many points would you give? (Mistakes are from actual exams.)

Wayne Grey-Eagle Company
Balance Sheet

	Dr.	Cr.
Assets:		
Cash	$21,500	
Accounts receivable	7,150	
Office supplies	325	
Prepaid rent	2,800	
Equipment	15,900	
Total assets	47,675	
Liabilities and Owner's Equity		
Liabilities:		
Wages payable		3,300
Accounts payable		4,470
Notes payable		22,500
Total liabilities		30,270
Owner's Equity:		
Wayne Grey-Eagle, capital, January 1		17,925
Wayne Grey-Eagle, drawing		(5,000)
Net income		4,480
Wayne Grey-Eagle, capital, January 31		17,405
Total	$47,675	$47,675

LG 26-5. Cumulative problem: Journalize, post to ledger, prepare trial balance, prepare financial statements from trial balance Shown below is the June 30 trial balance and chart of accounts for Hi-Tech Truck Service, which specializes in heavy-duty commercial truck repair services.

a. Enter the June 30 balances in ledger accounts and write the notation "bal.".
b. Record the July 2017 transactions in a general journal. Use journal page 20 as the page number.
c. Post the transactions to ledger accounts. Open new ledger accounts if necessary.
d. After all transactions are recorded and posted, prepare a trial balance as of July 31, 2017.
e. Prepare an income statement and statement of owner's equity for July, and a report form balance sheet as of July 31, 2017.

PRACTICE Learning Goal 26, continued

Solutions are in the disk at the back of the book and at: www.worthyjames.com

LG 26-5, *continued*

Hi-Tech Truck Service
Trial Balance
June 30, 2017

Account	Dr.	Cr.
Cash	$39,350	
Accounts Receivable	48,650	
Repair Supplies	19,100	
Equipment	125,500	
Accounts Payable		$24,120
Unearned Revenue		10,500
Notes Payable		35,000
Michael Nguyen, Capital		162,980
Total	$232,600	$232,600

Hi-Tech Truck Service
Chart of Accounts

Assets		*Owner's Equity*	
Cash	102	Michael Nguyen, Capital	305
Accounts Receivable	110	Michael Nguyen, Withdrawals	310
Repair Supplies	115	*Revenue*	
Prepaid Rent	120	Service Revenue	405
Prepaid Insurance	125	*Expense*	
Equipment	150	Supplies Expense	504
Liabilities		Wages Expense	508
Accounts Payable	202	Advertising Expense	512
Unearned Revenue	210	Utilities Expense	516
Notes Payable	250	Rent Expense	520

Transactions:

July	
2	Paid 3 months' rent in advance, $7,500.
5	The owner, Michael Nguyen, withdrew $3,500 cash for personal use.
7	Collected $1,800 of accounts receivable.
11	Received an advance payment from a customer, $2,000
11	Completed a service job and billed the customer $8,470.
15	Received a $725 bill for utilities and a $350 bill for local advertising
18	Paid monthly wages, $4,900.
21	Completed a service job. Billed the customer $7,100.
25	Purchased $12,000 of equipment by paying $2,000 and signing a note payable for the balance.
30	Counted the supplies; $1,800 had been used.
31	One month's prepaid rent has been used up.

PRACTICE **Learning Goal 26, continued**

Solutions are in the disk at the back of the book and at: www.worthyjames.com

LG 26-6. Cumulative problem: Journalize, post to ledger, prepare trial balance, prepare financial statements from trial balance. Los Angeles Talent Resources is a talent agency that locates performers with specific talents for various entertainment companies, television shows, and local events. The company's December 31, 2016 trial balance and the company chart of accounts are presented below.

a. Enter the December 31 balances in ledger accounts and write the notation "bal.".
b. Record the January 2017 transactions in a general journal. Use page 15 as the beginning page number.
c. Post the transactions to ledger accounts. Open new ledger accounts if necessary.
d. After all transactions are recorded and posted, prepare a trial balance as of January 31, 2017.
e. Prepare an income statement and statement of owner's equity for January, and an account form balance sheet as of January 31, 2017.

Los Angeles Talent Resources
Trial Balance
December 31, 2016

Account	Dr.	Cr.
Cash	$44,200	
Accounts Receivable	18,650	
Office Supplies	1,300	
Office Equipment	15,500	
Accounts Payable		$18,600
Unearned Revenue		4,500
Notes Payable		10,000
Wendy Malone, Capital		46,550
Total	$79,650	$79,650

Los Angeles Talent Resources
Chart of Accounts

Assets		*Owner's Equity*	
Cash	103	Wendy Malone, Capital	302
Accounts Receivable	107	Wendy Malone, Drawing	303
Office Supplies	115	*Revenue*	
Prepaid Insurance	125	Service Revenue	410
Office Equipment	170	*Expense*	
Liabilities		Wages Expense	505
Accounts Payable	203	Supplies Expense	510
Unearned Revenue	215	Travel Expense	515
Notes Payable	240	Utilities Expense	520
		Rent Expense	525
		Advertising Expense	530

PRACTICE Learning Goal 26, continued

Solutions are in the disk at the back of the book and at: www.worthyjames.com

LG 26-6, *continued*

Transactions:

Jan.	
2	Purchased supplies on account for $450.
3	Prepaid 6 months of insurance for $900.
7	Received $1,500 from a customer on account.
12	Completed a job and billed the client $4,525.
17	Received a bill for gasoline purchased, $185.
18	Paid for monthly advertising in the amount of $1,900.
19	Paid monthly wages in the amount of $5,500.
22	Completed the job for which a client had paid $4,500 in advance.
22	Paid $7,500 owing on accounts payable.
28	Paid the current month rent, $2,700.
30	Counted supplies; $200 had been consumed in the current month.
31	Completed a job and billed the client $4,800. Client immediately paid $1,400.
31	The owner, Wendy Malone, withdrew $3,000 for personal use.

LG 26-7. Challenging question: Prepare financial statements from a trial balance; analyze the business. Your friend Frank Wade is an expert mechanical engineer. Early this year, he started a new engineering design and consulting business, Wade Engineering, in which he invested all the cash that the business needed to begin the consulting operations.

The first year of operations has just ended, and Frank meets you for lunch. During lunch, he tells you that he is looking for a partner to invest an additional $25,000 cash in the business. He would make you an equal partner for only the investment. You would not have to do any work in the business. He says that he has been quite busy with many clients and has not done any financial work himself. He did, however, hire a reliable bookkeeper who prepared the trial balance, which he lets you keep to review. Frank is hoping for an answer from you within the next 7 to 10 days.

PRACTICE Learning Goal 26, continued

Solutions are in the disk at the back of the book and at: www.worthyjames.com

LG 26-7, *continued*

Wade Engineering
Trial Balance
December 31, 2017

Account Name	Dr.	Cr.
Cash	$ 3,100	
Accounts receivable	17,100	
Office supplies	1,100	
Design supplies	1,200	
Prepaid rent	650	
Office equipment	3,500	
Design equipment	14,700	
Wages payable		$ 4,900
Accounts payable		2,900
Frank Wade, capital		25,000
Frank Wade, drawing	4,400	
Design fees		27,800
Interest earned		100
Rent expense	1,400	
Wages expense	12,500	
Utilities expense	380	
Supplies expense (Office)	140	
Supplies expense (Design)	530	
Total	**$60,700**	**$60,700**

Instructions:

- **Prepare financial statements.** On a separate piece of paper, prepare the balance sheet, the income statement, and the statement of owner's equity for the year ended December 31, 2017. Prove the amount of Frank's original investment when you prepare the financial statements.
- **Analyze the statements and make a decision.** After you have prepared the three financial statements, you realize that you would also like to have a statement of cash flows to analyze, but you have not yet learned to prepare one. Fortunately, you have a friend in a more advanced accounting class who can prepare this statement, which you see on the next page.

PRACTICE **Learning Goal 26, continued**

Solutions are in the disk at the back of the book and at: www.worthyjames.com

LG 26-7, *continued*

Wade Engineering
Statement of Cash Flows
For the Year Ending December 31, 2017

Cash flows from **operating** activities:		
Receipts:		
Cash collections from customers		$10,700
Interest earned		100
Payments:		
Rent expense	$2,050	
Utilities expense	380	
Wages expense	7,600	
Supplies expense	70	
Total cash payments		10,100
Net cash provided by operating activities		700
Cash used in **investing** activities:		
Purchase of equipment		(18,200)
Cash flows from **financing** activities:		
Owner investment	25,000	
Less: withdrawals	(4,400)	
Net cash provided by financing activities		20,600
Net increase in cash		3,100
Cash balance January 3, 2017		–0–
Cash balance December 31, 2017		$ 3,100

Now that you have all four financial statements available, answer the following questions to help you decide if you should invest.

a. The income statement shows the change in the company's wealth that resulted from operating the business. Was there an increase or decrease in total wealth as a result of operations? How much?

b. The statement of cash flows shows the sources and uses of cash for the business. Frank Wade claims he actually invested $25,000 cash to start the business. If the beginning cash balance was zero, and Frank invested $25,000, then why is the December 31 cash balance only $3,100?

c. How much cash did the business obtain from its operations?

PRACTICE **Learning Goal 26, continued**

Solutions are in the disk at the back of the book and at: www.worthyjames.com

LG 26-7, *continued*

d. Look at the fees earned on the income statement, and look at the statement of cash flows. What do you think of the ability of the business to collect cash from its customers?

e. What was the biggest use of cash during the year? Is it likely to happen again next year?

f. Take a close look at the balance sheet. What do you think about the company's ability to pay current liabilities when they come due? What are the immediate sources of cash? Why do you think Frank wants an answer from you in the next 7 to 10 days?

g. What might cause a company to show on the income statement that it increased its wealth from operations, and yet on the statement of cash flows show that it did not receive the same amount of cash from operations?

h. Every business always has **two** *abiding and overriding issues* that dictate its ability to survive. From the questions so far, can you guess what these two survival issues are?

i. So what do you think? Are you going to invest $25,000 to be an equal partner and not have to work in the business? What are your reasons?

LG 26-8. Cumulative problem: Journalize, post to ledger, prepare trial balance, prepare financial statements from trial balance. Mary Antonelli is a landscape designer who opened her new business called Antonelli Landscape Services, on May 1, 2017. The business provides both landscape design and gardening maintenance services to its customers. Using the information below, do the following:

a. Record the May transactions into the general journal. Skip a line between transactions as shown in the book. Explanations are not required. (Before journalizing use T account analysis whenever you feel it is necessary.)
b. Post the journal information into the ledger accounts. Before you begin the posting, enter account names and numbers on the ledger accounts using the chart of accounts that you see below.
c. After all transactions are recorded and posted, prepare a trial balance as of May 31, 2017.
d. Prepare an income statement and statement of owner's equity for the month ending May 31, 2017, and an account form balance sheet as of May 31, 2017.

PRACTICE **Learning Goal 26, continued**

Solutions are in the disk at the back of the book and at: www.worthyjames.com

LG 26-8, *continued*

(For journal paper and for ledger account paper, you can make copies from the disk at the back of this book, or from the 'student info.' link at www.worthyjames.com.)

Antonelli Landscape Services
Chart of Accounts

Account	No.	Account	No.
Assets:		*Revenues:*	
Cash	102	Design Revenue	405
Accounts Receivable	115	Maintenance Revenue	410
Office Supplies	125		
Gardening Supplies	135	*Expenses:*	
Prepaid Rent	150	Rent Expense	505
Equipment: Office	180	Wages Expense	510
Equipment: Automotive	185	Auto & Gas Expense	515
Equipment: Gardening	190	Insurance Expense	520
		Advertising Expense	525
Liabilities:		Utilities Expense	530
Accounts Payable	202	Office Supplies Expense	535
Unearned Revenue	230	Gardening Supplies Expense	540
Notes Payable	250	Interest Expense	570
Owner's Equity:			
M. Antonelli, Capital	302		
M. Antonelli, Withdrawals	305		

Transactions:

May 1: Mary Antonelli invested $90,000 cash plus office equipment valued at $12,000 to open her new business, Antonelli Landscape Services.
May 2: Paid $6,000 for four months' office rent in advance, as required by the leasing company.
May 3: Received a bill for current month insurance charges, $150.
May 4: Paid $250 for office supplies.
May 5: Purchased $1,100 of garden supplies on account.
May 5: Prepared landscape design plans for a new home. Billed the client $5,500.
May 8: Purchased a small truck for $35,000 by signing a $20,000 note payable; paid the balance in cash.
May 11: Paid for advertising in a local newspaper, $1,000.
May 14: Received an advance payment of $12,000 for 6 months of landscape maintenance services for the local city hall and city offices location.

PRACTICE Learning Goal 26, continued

Solutions are in the disk at the back of the book and at: www.worthyjames.com

LG 26-8, *continued*

May 15: Purchased gardening supplies for $2,800 and gardening equipment for $5,000 by signing a note payable.
May 15: Prepared landscape design services for a new company and received $7,500 cash.
May 18: (Begin journal page 2.) Paid the May 3 insurance bill in full and paid $800 of the May 5 garden supplies bill.
May 19: Received a bill for gasoline purchased, $280.
May 21: Performed landscape maintenance services and billed the client $250.
May 25: Received a utilities bill in the amount of $170.
May 26: Made a monthly payment to the bank in the amount of $1,800 of which $1,400 is interest, with the balance applied to the amount owing on the note payable.
May 27: Mary Antonelli withdrew $2,000 from the business for personal use.
May 28: Collected $3,000 on account from a customer.
May 30: Recorded one month of the prepaid rent being used up in the amount of $1,500.
May 30: A count of the supplies showed that $100 of the office supplies and $840 of the gardening supplies had been used up.
May 30: One-half month revenue in the amount of $1,000 of the unearned revenue has been earned for services provided to the city during the current month.
May 31: Paid wages for the month in the amount of $8,500.
May 31: Received a bill for advertising in the local paper, $950.

LG 26-9. Cumulative problem: Journalize, post to ledger, prepare trial balance, prepare financial statements from trial balance. Consolidated Eco-Tour Service Company is about to begin operations after the owner on June 30 made an initial investment in the business and obtained a loan. The company will provide guided tours through the desert Southwest to show the beauty of the area and to teach the importance of protecting the fragile environment for future generations. Consolidated has prepared an initial trial balance and will prepare monthly financial statements. Using the information below:

a. Enter the June 30 balances in affected ledger accounts and write "bal." in the explanation column.
b. Record the July transactions into the general journal. Skip a line between transactions as shown in the book. Explanations are not required. (Before journalizing use T account analysis as you think necessary.)
c. Post the journal information into the ledger accounts. Before you begin the posting, enter account names and numbers on the ledger accounts using the chart of accounts that you see below.
d. After all transactions are recorded and posted, prepare a trial balance as of July 31, 2017.
e. Prepare an income statement and statement of owner's equity for the month ending July 31, 2017, and a report form balance sheet as of July 31, 2017.

PRACTICE Learning Goal 26, continued

Solutions are in the disk at the back of the book and at: www.worthyjames.com

LG 26-9, *continued*

(For journal paper and for ledger account paper, you can make copies from the disk at the back of this book, or from the 'student info.' link at www.worthyjames.com.)

Consolidated Eco-Tour Service Company
Trial Balance
June 30, 2017

Account		
Cash	$280,000	
Supplies	1,200	
Office equipment	15,000	
Notes payable		$100,000
J. Dunston, capital		196,200
Totals	$296,200	$296,200

Consolidated Eco-Tour Service Company
Chart of Accounts

Assets:

Cash	101
Accounts Receivable	115
Supplies	125
Prepaid Insurance	130
Equipment: Office	150
Equipment: Automotive	160
Building	170
Land	180

Liabilities:

Accounts Payable	205
Unearned Revenue	220
Notes Payable	230

Owner's Equity:

J. Dunston, Capital	301
J. Dunston, Withdrawals	305

Revenues:

Tour Revenue	410
Snack Revenue	420

Expenses:

Wages Expense	510
Gasoline Expense	520
Maintenance Expense	525
Insurance Expense	530
Advertising Expense	535
Utilities Expense	540
Supplies Expense	550
Interest Expense	590

PRACTICE Learning Goal 26, continued

Solutions are in the disk at the back of the book and at: www.worthyjames.com

LG 26-9, *continued*

Transactions:

July 2: Purchased two vans for $85,000 paying $30,000 cash down and signing a note payable for the balance.
July 3: Prepaid six months of insurance $2,400.
July 5: Purchased $800 of supplies on account.
July 6: Received a bill for advertising services, $4,500.
July 6: Purchased land and building by paying $150,000 cash. The building is valued at $110,000.
July 7: Provided Mojave desert tour for customers and received $1,500.
July 9: Received an advance payment of $8,000 from a school for a canyon tour to be provided later.
July 12: Provided Mojave desert tour on account for local hotel. Billed the hotel $2,700.
July 13: Conducted Grand Canyon tour for Japanese tourists and received $4,200.
July 15: Paid drivers' wages of $3,800.
July 16: Paid amount owing on July 5 supplies bill.
July 18: Paid $2,000 of the amount owing on the July 6 advertising bill.
July 19: (Begin journal page 2) Provided Painted Desert tour for retired Canadian tour group on account. Billed the Canadian travel agency $3,700.
July 24: Received the gasoline credit card bill for $1,800. The bill showed the following purchases: Gasoline, $500; van maintenance, $1,200; towing insurance, $100. The total is credited to Accounts Payable.
July 27: Received a utilities bill in the amount of $210.
July 28: Made a monthly payment to the bank in the amount of $2,500 of which $1,900 is interest, with the balance applied to the amount owing on the note payable.
July 29: Conducted Bryce Canyon tour for the school that had made the advance payment on July 9.
July 30: Paid drivers' wages of $5,500.
July 30: Received payment in full from hotel for July 12 tour.
July 31: Recorded one month of the prepaid insurance being used up in the amount of $400.
July 31: A count of the supplies showed that $300 of the supplies had been used up.
July 31: J. Dunston withdrew $1,500 cash from the business for personal use.
July 31: Records indicate that the business received $700 from customers for food and snacks.

Instructor-Assigned Problems

If you are using this book in a class, these review problems may be assigned by your instructor for homework, group assignments, class work, or other activities. Only your instructor has the solutions.

PRACTICE Learning Goal 26, continued

Solutions are in the disk at the back of the book and at: www.worthyjames.com

IA 26-1. **Prepare financial statements from a trial balance.** Shown below is the trial balance for Zhang Insurance Agency. Using the information below, prepare an income statement for the month of March 2017, statement of owner's equity for March, and a report form balance sheet as of March 31.

Zhang Insurance Agency
Trial Balance
March 31, 2017

	Dr.	Cr.
Cash	$75,380	
Accounts Receivable	28,650	
Office Supplies	560	
Prepaid Subscriptions	1,510	
Office Equipment	21,570	
Land	120,500	
Wages Payable		$4,500
Accounts Payable		17,620
Unearned Revenue		7,700
Notes Payable		50,000
Daniel Zhang, Capital		168,740
Daniel Zhang, Withdrawals	3,500	
Commission Revenue		18,300
Consulting Revenue		2,150
Supplies Expense	160	
Wages Expense	7,800	
Interest Expense	2,950	
Rent Expense	3,500	
Utilities Expense	310	
Advertising Expense	2,500	
Miscellaneous Expense	120	
Totals	**$269,010**	**$269,010**

Other information: Daniel Zhang, the owner, invested $15,000 in cash and equipment during the month.

IA 26-2. **Cumulative problem: Journalize, post to ledger, prepare trial balance, prepare financial statements from trial balance** Presented below is the September 30 trial balance and chart of accounts for FantasticKayak Trips, a company that offers guided kayaking trips.

a. Enter the September 30 balances in ledger accounts and write the notation "bal.".
b. Record the October 2017 transactions in a general journal.Use journal page 14 as the page number.
c. Post the transactions to ledger accounts. Add new accounts if necessary.
d. After all transactions are recorded and posted, prepare a trial balance as of October 31, 2017.
e. Prepare an income statement and statement of owner's equity for October, and a report form balance sheet as of October 31, 2017.

PRACTICE Learning Goal 26, continued

Solutions are in the disk at the back of the book and at: www.worthyjames.com

IA 26-3, *continued*

Transactions:

May	
1	Paid three months' rent in advance for $10,500.
2	Purchased design supplies on account, $1,580.
5	Completed a design job and billed the client $3,500.
6	Paid accounts payable in the amount of $9,520.
8	Received an advance payment from a customer in the amount of $1,000.
11	Received a bill for utilities expense, $370 on account.
15	Returned $250 of defective supplies purchased on May 2, receiving full credit.
16	Completed work for a client and billed the client $9,500. The client had already paid $2,500 in advance.
19	Received bills for travel, $700 and for advertising, $2,250 both on account.
22	Paid office wages in the amount of $3,800.
24	Received $8,500 cash from clients paying on their accounts.
26	The owner, Mary Rodriguez, withdrew $4,500 cash for personal use.
29	Completed a full remodeling job and billed the client $28,000.
30	Counted the supplies and determined that $480 had been used. Recorded as office expense.
31	One month of the prepaid rent had been used at month-end.

IA 26-4. Cumulative problem: Journalize, post to ledger, prepare trial balance, prepare financial statements from trial balance Presented below is the September 30 trial balance and chart of accounts for Green and Clean Landscape Maintenance Service.

a. Enter the September 30 balances in ledger accounts and write the notation "bal.".
b. Record the October 2017 transactions in a general journal.Use journal page 22 as the page number.
c. Post the transactions to ledger accounts. Add new accounts if necessary.
d. After all transactions are recorded and posted, prepare a trial balance as of October31, 2017.
e. Prepare an income statement and statement of owner's equity for October, and an account form balance sheetas of October31, 2017.

PRACTICE **Learning Goal 26, continued**

Solutions are in the disk at the back of the book and at: www.worthyjames.com

IA 26-4, *continued*

Green and Clean Landscape Maintenance Service
Trial Balance
September 30, 2017

Account	Dr.	Cr.
Cash	$42,920	
Accounts Receivable	19,850	
Supplies	3,800	
Prepaid Insurance	5,570	
Office Equipment	2,800	
Service Equipment	174,960	
Accounts Payable		$11,320
Unearned Revenue		700
Notes Payable		54,620
Mark Andrews, Capital		183,260
Total	$249,900	$249,900

Green and Clean Landscape Maintenance Service
Chart of Accounts

Account	No.	Account	No.
Assets		*Owner's Equity*	
Cash	103	Mark Andrews, Capital	302
Accounts Receivable	108	Mark Andrews, Drawing	303
Supplies	113	*Revenue*	
Prepaid Insurance	122	ServiceRevenue	405
Office equipment	170	*Expense*	
Service Equipment	180	Office Expense	505
Liabilities		Wages Expense	510
Wages Payable	201	Advertising Expense	515
Accounts Payable	202	Utilities Expense	520
Unearned Revenue	215	Rent Expense	525
Notes Payable	280	Travel Expense	530
		Supplies Expense	535
		Insurance Expense	540
		Interest Expense	580

PRACTICE Learning Goal 26, continued

Solutions are in the disk at the back of the book and at: www.worthyjames.com

IA 26-4, *continued*

Transactions:

October

1	Paid $2,400 forsix months of liability insurance in advance, with coverage beginning October 1.
2	The owner, Mark Andrews, invested an additional $10,000 cash in the business.
3	Purchased supplies on account, $1,900.
3	Completed a corporate maintenance job and billed the customer $4,500.
4	Paid accounts payable in the amount of $7,500.
8	Paid the current month's rent, $2,900.
8	Received a bill for utilities expense, $300 on account.
12	Returned $400 of defective supplies purchased on October3, receiving full credit.
13	Completed work for a customer and billed the customer $2,700. The customer had already paid $500 in advance.
14	Received bills for gas and truck service, $3,700 and for advertising, $500 both on account.
15	Received $6,900 cash from clients paying on their accounts.
19	Paid wages in the amount of $5,700.
20	Received an advance payment from a customer in the amount of $750.
22	Made a $1,200 payment on the note payable. $1,000 of the payment is for interest and the remainder is a payment of the loan principal.
25	The owner, Mark Andrews, withdrew $4,000 cash for personal use.
29	Completed variouslandscape maintenance jobs and billed the customers $11,000.
30	Counted the supplies and determined that $1,200 had been used.
31	One month of the prepaid insurance had been used at month-end.

INTERNET EXERCISES

Use the AICPA website. Go to the homepage of the American Institute of Certified Public Accountants (search AICPA). When you are on the homepage, click on the "Students" link, and then click on the "The Classroom" link. Also check www.accountingedu.org (Use bookmark/favorites to save the location in an "Accounting References" folder.)

a. What are the recommended courses a student should take if he or she is considering becoming a CPA? Would these courses have value in a business career if someone does not plan to be a CPA? Explain your reasons.
b. What is the 150-hour requirement? Is this something your state requires?
c. What are the essential skills and competencies of a CPA?
d. Return to the AICPA homepage. Explore three other links that seem interesting ("CPA links" can take you to your own state board of accountancy.) Summarize what you found on each link.

LEARNING GOAL 27 Explain the Accounting Cycle

The Accounting Cycle

Definition

Accounting activity occurs in a recurring, sequential kind of pattern. The recurring, sequential pattern of accounting activity is known as the *accounting cycle*. The main elements of the cycle are analyzing, processing, and communicating.

What You Have Learned so Far

The parts of the cycle that you have learned to perform so far are:

Analyze: Business events are analyzed for classification, valuation, and timing to see if they have affected the accounting equation. Any event that changes the accounting equation is called a *transaction* and must be recorded.

Process: Processing refers to recording and organizing data. (Sometimes this is called *recognition*.) This consists of journalizing, posting, summarizing, adjusting, and correcting procedures. So far, you have learned:

- recording (journalizing) transactions
- posting
- preparing a trial balance

Communicate: Communication refers to the preparation of financial reports and disclosures and interpretations. So far, you have practiced preparing four reports: the income statement, the statement of owner's equity, the balance sheet, and statement of cash flows.

Remaining Steps

The remaining steps in the process involve adjusting account balances and closing temporary accounts. These steps involve detailed account calculating and book keeping techniques, and are explained in Volume 2. You can continue your study in this book without covering these topics.

Some Variations

Not every business and not every accountant is exactly the same. So, you can expect some small variations in the exact steps of the cycle. However, a useful overview of the cycle is on page 537 for you to study.

The Accounting Cycle, *continued*

Manual Accounting Compared to Computerized Accounting

The accounting cycle is essentially the same for both a computerized and manual accounting system. A computerized system automates some specific mechanical procedures and saves time. This is especially true about the way transaction data is processed in a computerized system.

However, computers can never perform the analysis part of the cycle. Analysis is your most important skill. Computers are also very poor communicators.

You need to have a clear understanding of all the steps in the accounting cycle. Just because a computer is doing much of the work, *this does not mean that you do not need to understand what is happening*. You do!

Although the practice and solutions in this book can also be applied to a computerized accounting system, it can be a good idea to initially practice with and understand how a *manual accounting system* functions. This is because:

- Often, people learn and remember better by practicing manually for the first time.
- Manual recording in journals and ledgers develops an understanding of the purpose and the effect of different transaction data arrangements. This is not as clear when using a computerized accounting system, which focuses on procedures for output.
- The detailed process knowledge learned from a manual system transfers easily and reinforces the learning in a computerized system (while the reverse is not true).
- You might actually have to do manual accounting work.

Spreadsheets in Accounting

Electronic spreadsheets are widely used in accounting. It is a good idea to learn to use one of them. However, spreadsheets do not replace an accounting system or journals and ledgers. Spreadsheets are primarily used for various kinds of financial analysis and information summaries. The financial data that go into spreadsheets are provided by an accounting system that uses journals and ledgers. An accounting system, particularly the journals and ledgers, provides the record keeping function that accumulates the data necessary for financial reporting and for the financial analysis performed with spreadsheets.

The Accounting Cycle, *continued*

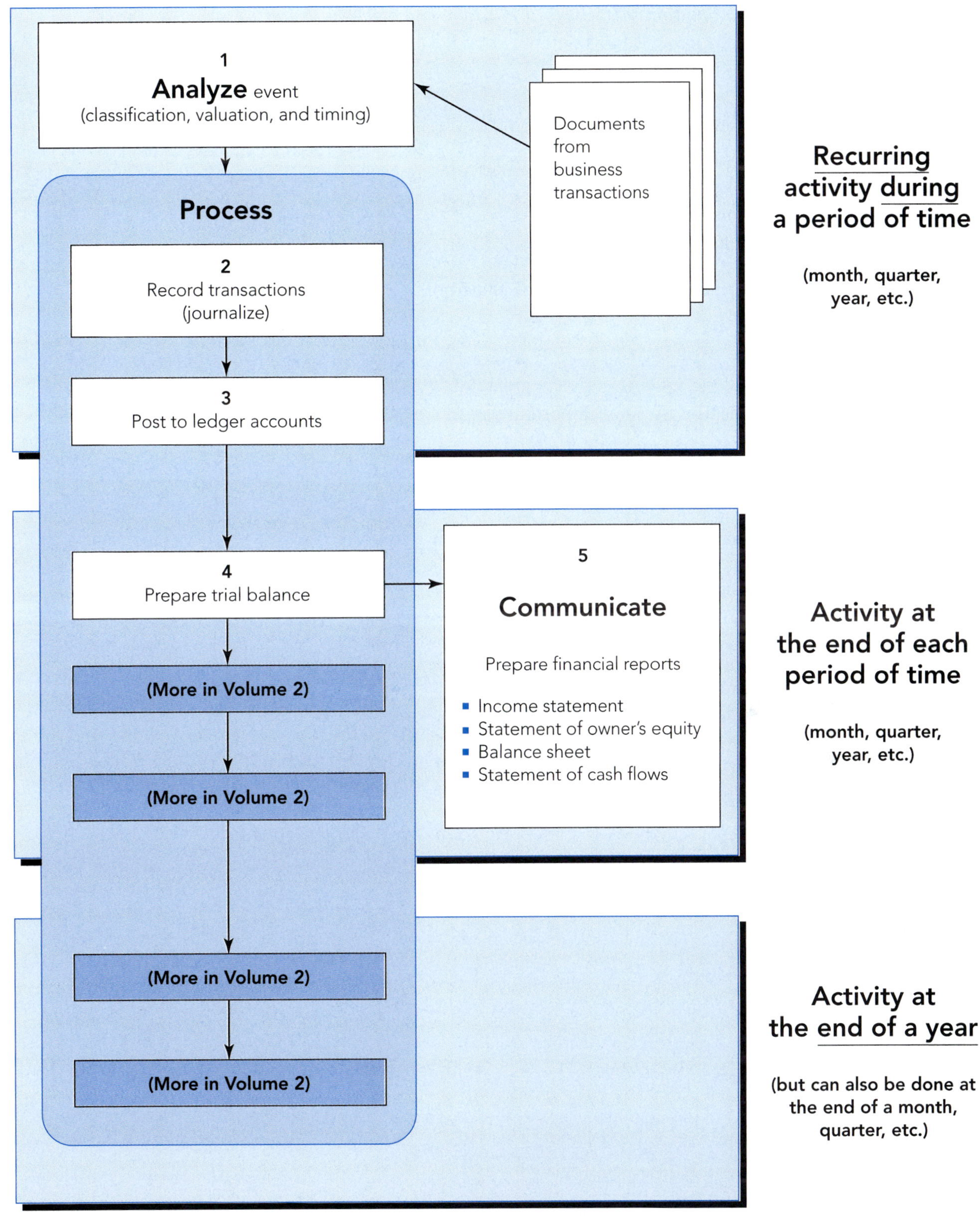

PRACTICE

Learning Goal 27

Solutions are in the disk at the back of the book and at: www.worthyjames.com

Learning Goal 27 is about the accounting cycle. Use these questions and problems to practice what you have just read.

Multiple Choice

Select the best answer.

1. The accounting cycle consists of these steps in this order:
   a. analyze, journalize, and post
   b. analyze, process, and communicate
   c. communicate, analyze, journalize, and post
   d. none of the above
2. Recording, posting, and preparing a trial balance are all part of
   a. communicating.
   b. analyzing.
   c. transactions.
   d. processing.
3. Preparing financial statements is the most important part of
   a. communicating.
   b. analyzing.
   c. transactions.
   d. processing.
4. Analyzing, journalizing, and posting are activities that happen
   a. on a recurring basis throughout a period of time.
   b. only at the end of a designated period of time.
   c. usually at the end of a year.
   d. none of the above.
5. Preparing financial statements is an activity that usually happens
   a. on a recurring basis throughout a period of time.
   b. only at the end of a designated period of time.
   c. usually at the end of a year.
   d. none of the above.

PRACTICE Learning Goal 27, continued

Solutions are in the disk at the back of the book and at: www.worthyjames.com

Reinforcement Problem

LG 27-1. The illustration below is a diagram of the five steps in the accounting cycle that you have learned up to this point. On a separate piece of paper, copy the illustration and fill in each of the five empty parts of the illustration by writing in a description for the five steps that you have learned.

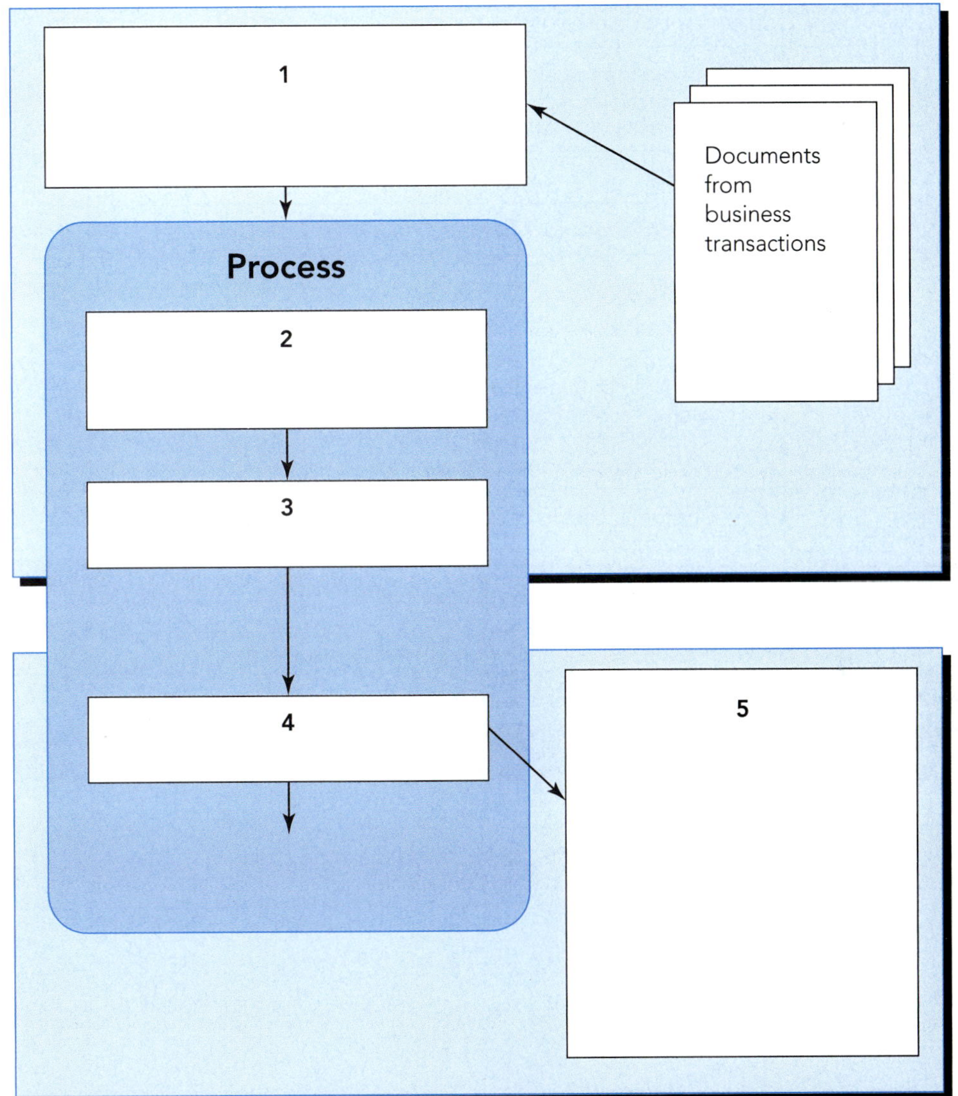

Your Questions?

It is *very* important to be aware of what you need to understand better. What do you need to understand better about this learning goal? On a separate piece of paper, write the questions that you want to discuss with your classmates, instructor, or supervisor. Try to be very specific about what is bothering you, such as explanations that you do not fully understand.

CUMULATIVE VOCABULARY REVIEW

This is a vocabulary review for Learning Goals 19 through 27. Match each description with the term that it describes. The answer for each term is in the right column. *Suggestion:* Cover the answers in the right column as you test your vocabulary.

Term	Description	Answers
1. Footing	a. A listing of all nonzero ledger account names and balances.	1h
2. Debit	b. A right-side entry or balance.	2n
3. Journalize	c. A simple form of an account used for analysis.	3l
4. Accounting cycle	d. A journal.	4j
5. Posting	e. An entry consisting of three or more accounts.	5o
6. Account	f. An abbreviation for "debit."	6k
7. Journal	g. To debit.	7m
8. Cr.	h. The balance or total of a column of numbers.	8p
9. To charge	i. A book or computer file containing all the accounts of a business.	9g
10. Dr.	j. Analyze, process, and communicate.	10f
11. General ledger	k. An historical record of all changes in an item in the accounting equation.	11i
12. Book of original entry	l. To record a transaction in a journal.	12d
13. Compound entry	m. A chronological recording of transactions, like a diary.	13e
14. Trial balance	n. A left-side entry or balance.	14a
15. Ledger account	o. Transferring information from a journal into a ledger.	15q
16. T account	p. An abbreviation for "credit."	16c
17. Credit	q. An account showing debit, credit, balance, date, explanation, and posting reference.	17b

CUMULATIVE TEST Learning Goals 19–27

Solutions are on page 546

Time Limit: 55 Minutes

Instructions

*Select the best answer to each question. Do **not** look back in the book when taking the test. (If you need to do this, you are not ready.) After you finish the test, refer to the answers and circle the number of each question that you missed. Then go to the **Help Table** (on page 533) to identify your strong and weak knowledge areas by individual learning goal.*

Multiple Choice

On the line provided, enter the letter of the best answer for each question.

1. Which one of the following is *not* one of the five basic data arrangements?
   a. seeing the balance of any item in the accounting equation
   b. seeing the audit trail posting reference of an entry in a ledger account
   c. seeing all the parts of a transaction together in one place
   d. keeping an historical record of all increases and decreases for each item in the accounting equation
2. The natural positive balance (normal balance) of an account is
   a. the minimum balance that must always be maintained in an account.
   b. always located on the side of the account used for increases.
   c. always located on the side of the account used for decreases.
   d. always calculated by excluding the beginning balance of the account.
3. Owner's equity accounts that will be increased by a debit would be
   a. revenues and expenses. c. expenses and drawing.
   b. capital and revenue. d. revenue and drawing.
4. To record a decrease in an account, use
   a. debits.
   b. credits.
   c. credits, if the normal balance is debit, and debits if the normal balance is credit.
   d. credits, if the normal balance is credit, and debits if the normal balance is debit.
5. All the accounts of a business are grouped together in a book or file called the
   a. ledger. c. trial balance.
   b. journal. d. accounting system.
6. The general journal does *not* do which of the following?
   a. provide a chronological record of all transactions
   b. show all the accounts involved in each transaction together
   c. show the balance of each account
   d. help locate recording errors by showing debits and credits together for each transaction
7. You are looking at the Accounts Payable account in the ledger, and you see an entry in the "Posting Reference" column (sometimes called the "LP" or "Folio" column). This entry
   a. refers to the account number of that account.
   b. refers to a page number in the journal.
   c. refers to the sequential number of the journal entry.
   d. refers to the date of the original transaction.
8. "Posting" means that transaction information is transferred from the
   a. journal to the trial balance. c. ledger to the journal.
   b. ledger to the trial balance. d. journal to the ledger.

CUMULATIVE TEST Learning Goals 19–27, continued

9. A trial balance is
   a. a listing of accounts and their balances, usually prepared at any point in time.
   b. a listing of the names of accounts with their account numbers, prepared before a new account is added.
   c. a listing of nonzero accounts and their balances, usually prepared at the end of an accounting period.
   d. another name for the book of accounts.
10. Which of the following account types should show a normal credit balance?
   a. asset, liability, and expense
   b. asset, revenue, and liability
   c. liability, revenue, and owner's capital
   d. liability, expense, and drawing
11. The usual sequence in the recording of transaction data is
   a. analyze the event, post into the ledger, journalize, prepare the trial balance.
   b. journalize the transaction, analyze the event, prepare a trial balance, post into the ledger.
   c. analyze the event, journalize, post into the ledger, prepare a trial balance.
   d. analyze the event, journalize, post into the ledger.
12. Use the journal entry below to answer the next question.

Date	Account Titles and Explanation	Post. Ref.	Debit	Credit
2017				
August 3	Supplies		220	
	Accounts Payable			220

   This journal entry is recording
   a. the purchase of supplies.
   b. the payment of a liability.
   c. the using up of supplies.
   d. an owner investment of personal supplies into the business.
13. A manager needs to know how much merchandise inventory the company has available. This is an example of needing to use which kind of data arrangement?
   a. a chronological record of transactions
   b. an historical record of all increases and decreases for each item in the accounting equation
   c. the balance of any item in the accounting equation
   d. all the accounts involved in each individual transaction
14. An account is
   a. an historical record of transactions, like a diary.
   b. a listing of all balances for each asset, liability, or owner's equity item in the equation.
   c. a description of recordable business events.
   d. an historical record of all changes and the balance of an asset, liability, or owner's equity item.
15. Increases in the owner's capital are usually the result of
   a. debits to revenue accounts and debits to expense accounts.
   b. credits to revenue accounts and debits to the capital account.
   c. debits to expense accounts and debits to revenue accounts.
   d. none of the above.

CUMULATIVE TEST Learning Goals 19–27, continued

16. Use the illustration to answer the next question.

Accounts Receivable	
bal. 2,000	
15,000	10,000

The best explanation of what happened in this account is
a. credits increased the account by $15,000, resulting in a $7,000 credit balance.
b. credits decreased the account by $10,000 and debits increased the account by $15,000, resulting in a $7,000 credit balance.
c. credits decreased the account by $10,000 and debits increased the account by $15,000, resulting in a $5,000 debit balance.
d. credits decreased the account by $10,000 and debits increased the account by $15,000, resulting in a $7,000 debit balance.

17. If you want to know the amount of the accounts payable owing as of today, you would look in
a. the journal. c. the book of original entry.
b. the ledger. d. the trial balance.

18. Which of the following journal entries has been recorded correctly?

		Debit	Credit
a.	Cash		500
	Wages Expense	500	
b.	Equipment	3,700	
	Cash		1,650
	Notes Payable		1,950
c.	Supplies Expense	500	
	Telephone Expense	900	
	Accounts Payable		1,400

d. None of the above.

19. Tempe Service Company shows a normal accounts payable balance of $10,500 on December 31. During December, there were payments to creditors of $11,900 and new purchases on account of $10,700. The balance of accounts payable on December 1 was a
a. credit balance of $1,200. c. credit balance of $11,700.
b. debit balance of $11,700. d. credit balance of $9,300.

20. Which error would *not* cause the total credits in a trial balance to be greater than the total debits?
a. Cash sales of $5,000 recorded in the journal is accidentally posted twice into the ledger by debiting Land $5,000 and crediting Notes Payable $5,000.
b. A journal entry recording cash collections from customers of $200 is posted as a debit to the Cash account in the ledger for $200 and as a credit to Accounts Receivable for $2,000.
c. The account balance of Accounts Receivable is a normal balance of $950, and is entered in the trial balance "Credit" column for $950.
d. None of the above.

CUMULATIVE TEST Learning Goals 19–27, continued

21. A journal entry that consists of three or more accounts is called a
    a. complex entry.
    b. simple entry.
    c. compound entry.
    d. group entry.
22. A partner of the Burlington and Champlain partnership wants to know why the Notes Payable account shows increases of $20,000 during September. This is an example of needing which kind of accounting data arrangement?
    a. a chronological record of transactions
    b. an historical record of all increases and decreases for each item in the accounting equation
    c. the balance of any item in the accounting equation
    d. all the accounts involved in each individual transaction
23. Which of the following is *not* true about the words "debit" and "credit"?
    a. Debits are increases and credits are decreases.
    b. Debits and credits can describe the balance of an account.
    c. Debits and credits can describe increases and decreases in an account.
    d. The left side of an account is called the debit side, and the right side is called the credit side.
24. The usual sequence of accounts in the ledger is
    a. assets, expenses, owner's capital, revenues, drawing.
    b. revenues, expenses, drawing, assets, liabilities.
    c. liabilities, assets, revenues, drawing, expenses.
    d. assets, liabilities, owner's capital, revenues, expenses.
25. Which of the following is *not* true?
    a. Assets are increased by credits.
    b. Liabilities are decreased by debits.
    c. Revenues are increased by credits.
    d. Expenses are increased by debits.
26. The trial balance would not detect which error?
    a. recording revenue on account by debiting Service Revenue and debiting Accounts Receivable
    b. incorrectly totaling the balance in a ledger account
    c. debiting Cash and forgetting to credit Accounts Receivable
    d. forgetting to post an entire transaction already recorded in the journal
27. The correct general journal entry to record the purchase of supplies for cash would include
    a. a debit to Cash recorded just above the credit to Supplies.
    b. a debit to Cash recorded just below the credit to Supplies.
    c. a credit to Supplies recorded just below the debit to Cash.
    d. a debit to Supplies recorded just above the credit to Cash.
28. The ending balance of any account can be calculated as
    a. the total debits, minus the total credits.
    b. the beginning balance, minus the total credits, plus the total debits.
    c. the beginning balance, plus the total increases, minus the total decreases.
    d. the beginning balance, plus the total credits, minus the total debits.
29. The Concord Company shows revenues with credit balances totaling $38,000, total debits to Accounts Receivable of $10,000, expenses with debit balances totaling $42,000, and debits to the drawing account totaling $5,000. The company had a
    a. net income of $6,000.
    b. net income of $1,000.
    c. net loss of $4,000.
    d. net loss of $9,000.
30. In October, the Supplies account of Dover Company has a normal beginning balance of $7,300, total debits of $12,950, and a normal ending balance of $14,400. What was the October Supplies Expense?
    a. $5,850
    b. $1,450
    c. $12,950
    d. none of the above

CUMULATIVE TEST Learning Goals 19–27, continued

31. If you want to find the ledger account number for Rent Expense, you would look in
a. the chart of accounts. c. the ledger.
b. the journal. d. none of the above.

32. The correct general journal entry to record fees earned on account includes
a. a debit to Cash recorded just above the credit to a revenue.
b. a credit to a revenue recorded just below the debit to Accounts Receivable.
c. a debit to a revenue recorded just below the credit to Accounts Receivable.
d. a credit to Accounts Receivable recorded just below the debit to a revenue.

33. Which of the following is correct?
a. Information is first entered in a journal, and then entered in the chart of accounts.
b. Information is first entered in a journal, which will have ledger account numbers after the information is transferred to the ledger.
c. The journal and the ledger contain exactly the same information.
d. Both (b) and (c) are correct.

34. Financial statements are prepared from the
a. general journal. c. trial balance.
b. general ledger. d. none of the above.

35. Which of these accounts is *not* a subdivision of the owner's capital?
a. revenues c. drawing
b. liabilities d. expenses

Use this table for the next two questions:

	Assets	Liabilities	Owner's Capital	Revenue	Expense	Drawing
Debit	1	2	3			
Credit			4	5	6	

36. The boxes labeled "1," "2," and "3" in the table above should contain the words
a. decrease, increase, increase. c. decrease, decrease, increase.
b. increase, decrease, increase. d. increase, decrease, decrease.

37. The boxes labeled "4," "5," and "6" in the table above should contain the words
a. increase, increase, decrease. c. decrease, decrease, decrease.
b. increase, decrease, increase. d. decrease, decrease, increase.

38. An auditor is examining the Cash ledger account. She wants to verify the account balance by locating and checking the transactions that affected the account. The auditor should:
a. use posting references in the ledger account to locate transactions in the journal.
b. scan the journal to locate relevant transactions.
c. use the posting references in the ledger account to locate accounts in the chart of accounts.
d. search documents that contain the same debit and credit amounts in the Cash account.

CUMULATIVE TEST SOLUTIONS Learning Goals 19–27

Multiple Choice

1. b **2.** b **3.** c Because expenses and drawing are reducing the owner's capital.
4. c *Remember:* decreases are simply the side opposite from increases. **5.** a **6.** c
7. b An entry in the ledger should always be traceable to the page of the journal where it originated. **8.** d **9.** c **10.** c **11.** c **12.** a **13.** c **14.** d
15. d The correct answer is credits to revenue accounts and credits to the owner's capital account.
16. d This is an asset account, so credits decrease it and debits increase it.
17. b Because the ledger contains all the accounts and their balances.
18. c (a) is wrong because the credits have been recorded before the debits. (b) is wrong for two reasons: first, the names of the accounts being credited are not indented; second, the total credits add up to 3,600 but the debit is for 3,700.
19. c When calculating a missing amount in an account, *you have two good choices:* (1) you can use the formula that applies to all accounts: **beginning balance + increases – decreases = ending balance** or (2) you can set up a T account, plug in the information that you know, and look for the missing amount. If you use the first approach, then: X + 10,700 – 11,900 = 10,500. Therefore, X = 11,700. The natural positive balance (normal balance) of accounts payable is a credit balance. Using the T account method:

Accounts Payable

Debit	Credit
	?
10,700	11,900
	10,500

20. a Even though mistakes were made in the entry (a), total debits equal total credits. In entry (b), credits will exceed debits by $1,800. In (c), a $950 debit is entered as a $950 credit, making the credits in the trial balance exceed debits by $1,900.
21. c **22.** a A journal would contain the transactions that explain the increases.
23. a **24.** d **25.** a
26. d Forgetting to post an entry does not cause total debits and credits to be unequal in the ledger accounts. All the other situations will cause the total debits and credits in the ledger to be unequal. In (a), there are two debits and no credits. In (b), the incorrect total will cause total debits and credits in the ledger to be unequal. In (c), there is a debit but no credit.
27. d *Always try to visualize the entry.* Write it down if you need to:

Supplies	xxx	
Cash		xxx

28. c Debits and credits do not mean increase or decrease, only left and right.
29. c The formula for net income (or loss) is: **Revenues – Expenses = Net Income (or loss)**. Therefore, $38,000 – $42,000 = –$4,000. The debits to the accounts receivable are already included as part of the total revenue. Drawings are not expenses and do not affect the net income.
30. a Supplies expense means the amount of supplies used up. You need to calculate the decrease in the Supplies account. So, this is like #19.
(a) You can use the formula for an account: **beginning balance + increases – decreases = ending balance**. Because Supplies is an asset account, debits are increases, therefore: 7,300 + 12,950 – X = 14,400. This gives: –X = –5,850. So, X = 5,850.
(b) *Using the T account approach:*

Supplies

Debit	Credit
7,300	
12,950	?
14,400	

31. a **32.** b *Always try to visualize the entry.* Write it down if you need to:

Accounts Receivable	xxx	
Fees Earned		xxx

33. d **34.** c **35.** b **36.** d **37.** a **38.** a

HELP TABLE Identify Your Strengths and Weaknesses

The questions in this test cover the nine learning goals of Section V. After you have circled the number of each question that you missed, look at the table below.

Go to the first learning goal category in the table: "Explain the Five Kinds of Information." The second column in the table shows which questions on the test covered this learning goal. Look on the test to see if you circled numbers 1, 13, or 22. How many did you miss? Write this number in the "How Many Missed?" column. Repeat this process for each of the remaining learning goal categories in the table.

If you *miss* ***two*** *or more questions* for any learning goal, you are too weak in that learning goal and you need to *review*. The last column shows you where to read and practice so you can improve your score.

Some learning goal categories have more questions because you need to be especially well prepared in these areas. More questions means your performance must be better.

Learning Goal	Questions	How many missed?	Material begins on . . .
Section V			
19. Explain the Five Kinds of Information	1, 13, 22		page 386
20. Explain the Use of Accounts	2, 14, 16, 19, 28, 30		page 395
21. Use the Owners Capital Accounts	3, 15, 29, 35		page 412
22. "Debits on the left, credits on the right!"	4, 10, 23, 25, 36, 37		page 428
23. Use a Ledger	5, 17, 24, 31		page 443
24. Use a Journal	6, 12, 18, 21, 27, 32		page 450
25. Use a Basic Accounting System	7, 8, 33, 38		page 483
26. The Trial Balance—Prepare It and Use It Two Ways*	9, 20, 26, 34		page 507
27. Explain the Accounting Cycle	11		page 535

* For Learning Goal 26, you should also practice preparing a balance sheet, an income statement, and a statement of owner's equity on a blank piece of paper from the information on a trial balance. Use problems in any book for which you also have a solution.

SECTION VI Corporations

OVERVIEW

What this section does

This section provides you with a comprehensive introduction to fundamental corporate concepts. Additionally, to maintain a single and unified presentation of the topic, the discussion continues beyond the basic concepts to more in-depth subjects of corporate accounting procedures and financial reporting.

How to use this section	If you want . . .	then read . . .
	. . . only an introduction to the corporate concept and form of business . . .	Learning Goal 28.
	. . . an introduction to basic corporate accounting concepts and procedures . . .	Learning Goals 28 and 29.
	. . . an in-depth introduction to corporate accounting and financial reporting, including some challenging cumulative problems . . .	all of Section VI.

Suggestion

It is not necessary to complete this section to continue to Volume 2. You can study the principles and procedures in Volume 2 and later return here as appropriate for your own goals.

LEARNING GOALS

LEARNING GOAL 28 Describe the Corporate Entity

Introduction

Because of their ability to obtain large amounts of money by selling ownership shares to the public, corporations (called ***publicly traded*** corporations) have become a successful and dominating economic force in American and international business operations. The corporation as a business entity was introduced in Learning Goal 5 when we analyzed the major types of business entities. The discussion that follows provides more detailed information about corporations.

In Learning Goal 28, you will find:

The Corporation Defined

Definition

A ***corporation*** is an entity that is created by law and has the specific qualities that are described below.

Separate Legal Person

Because a corporation is created by law, it is a "legal person," different and separate from any living "natural person." As a legal person, a corporation acts independently, in its own name. For example, a corporation buys, sells, enters into binding contracts, pays taxes, sues, and can be sued. None of these actions are legally binding on the owners (stockholders) of the corporation who purchase shares of stock. Also, as a separate legal person, a corporation has a continuous existence that is not affected by changes in ownership.

The Corporation Defined, *continued*

Stockholder Limited Liability

Because the acts of corporations do not bind the stockholders (owners), creditors can look only to corporate assets to satisfy claims. Therefore, the assets of individual stockholders are generally protected from corporate creditors, even if a corporation becomes bankrupt. The result is that a stockholder ordinarily has limited personal liability and can lose no more than the amount of the investment in a company's stock.

Note: There are a few exceptions. Especially, if an owner, officer, or director performs a fraudulent or illegal act in the name of a corporation. Such an individual may have personal liability.

Ownership

The ownership of a corporation is divided into units. These units are called shares of stock (often called capital stock), and owners are called stockholders or shareholders. Shares of capital stock are the means of identifying ownership in a corporation. There are different kinds of stock, and we will discuss this in more detail a little later.

Transfer of Ownership

Stock shares are the personal property of the owner and can be transferred by the owner. This can be done by selling the stock or by an exchange, gift, or other methods. The transfer of the stock does not require the consent of any other stockholders, and the transfer will have no effect on the activities of the business. The stock is said to be ***negotiable***. (Notice how this is different from a partnership, in which transfer of ownership usually requires approval of other partners and terminates the existing partnership.)

Note: Some limited exceptions may defer the time of transfer. This stock relates to certain employees of publicly traded companies and is called *restricted stock.*

No Mutual Agency

"Mutual agency" means that all the owners of a business can act as agents of the business. Therefore, the acts of any owner will be binding on the business and affect all the other owners. This is what happens in partnerships. There is no mutual agency for corporations. An individual can act as a corporate agent only if the corporation has approved that individual to act as an agent. Officers, directors, and employees of a corporation are generally considered to be agents.

Continuous Life

As a separate legal entity, a corporation's life is continuous and typically perpetual as set forth in its charter. Changes in ownership have no effect unless there is a sale and termination.

continued ▶

The Corporation Defined, *continued*

Centralized Management Authority

Stockholders are the owners of a corporation. Stockholders indirectly control the management of a corporation by electing a board of directors that acts as the central management authority. The ***board of directors*** is a group of responsible individuals who vote on corporate policy, supervise management, and safeguard the interests of the stockholders. In larger businesses, the board of directors delegates many management duties by hiring professional corporate officers and managers.

Often, members of the board of directors are also stockholders of the same corporation. In particular, in small corporations with just one or a few stockholders, the stockholders will also be members of the board of directors.

Double Taxation

A corporation is a separate "person" for legal purposes. Therefore, a corporation pays taxes on its income. (This is unlike a proprietorship or partnership in which an owner's share of income is reported as part of his or her personal taxable income.)

In addition to a corporation paying tax on its income, when cash from that income is distributed to stockholders in the form of dividends, the stockholders also pay tax on the dividends. For this reason, it is said that the same stream of corporate income is taxed twice—once at the corporate level and again at the individual level.

> *Exception:* Certain tax elections can eliminate double taxation for smaller corporations. One type of election creates an "S corporation", for which income is taxed similar to partnerships. A second possibility is the creation of an LLC (page 557). Professional tax advisors explain the details.

The Corporate People

Overview

Although a corporation can exist legally on paper, real people are needed to create, organize, manage, and own the corporation. The following discussion summarizes who these people are and what they do. These people are the:

- Incorporator
- Stockholders
- Directors
- Officers and managers

The Corporate People, *continued*

Incorporator

The ***incorporator*** is the person who chooses a corporate name and completes the application process to create the corporation. This application contains the articles of incorporation. The incorporator completes and signs the articles of incorporation and files the application with the official—usually the secretary of state—of the state that will approve the creation of the corporation. By law, the incorporator has a fiduciary responsibility to provide full disclosure and act independently and honestly. Incorporators are often stockholders.

Note: A *fiduciary* responsibility is one that requires honesty, trustworthiness, and competence.

Stockholders

Stockholders are the owners of a corporation. The number of shares of stock that a stockholder owns determines the stockholder's proportionate (percentage) ownership. Stockholders have the following basic rights (unless otherwise restricted):

- Share proportionately in profits and losses
- Share proportionately in voting for matters requiring stockholder approval
- Share proportionately in the remaining assets when a business liquidates (goes out of business)

Board of Directors

A director is an individual elected by stockholders to a position on the board of directors. The directors meet and vote on corporate policy and supervise the management on behalf of the stockholders. By law, directors also have a ***fiduciary duty*** to safeguard the financial condition of the corporation and the stockholders' investments and to act honestly and in good faith in the best interests of stockholders. Directors can be independent or can be company officers or employees.

Officers and Managers

Officers and managers are employees who are responsible for the day-to-day management and operations. Top officers are the president, vice president of finance, often referred to as ***chief financial officer***, or ***CFO***, other vice presidents, and corporate secretary. Frequently, a large company has a ***chief executive officer***, or ***CEO***, who is responsible for strategic planning and supervises the president (or multiple presidents) and other officers. The CEO may also be elected by the board of directors to serve as chairman of the board. Like directors, the CEO and CFO have a fiduciary duty to act honestly and in good faith. In publicly traded companies they are personally liable for the accuracy of financial statements.

Often the most powerful and influential individual in a corporation is the chairman of the board of directors.

continued ►

The Corporate People, *continued*

Organization Chart

Small Corporations

In a small corporation with one or just a few stockholders, the same individuals generally can be the incorporator, stockholder(s), directors, and officers. For example, if Jane decides to form a corporation for her new computer repair business, she can be the incorporator, the only stockholder, the only board member, and the only officer.

Organizing the Corporation

Overview

A corporation is incorporated in only one state, even if the company has operations in more than one state. Different states have different laws, so large businesses carefully review the laws of different states before deciding which state has laws that are most favorable. Some states have laws that centralize a great deal of authority and independence with officers and directors, whereas other states give more power to stockholders. A corporation does not need to have an office in the state in which it incorporates; however, corporations that have interstate activities must receive approval to operate in each state in which they do business.

The following discussion presents the fundamental steps in the process of creating a corporation.

Process

- The incorporator completes the application, which contains ***the articles of incorporation***. The articles of incorporation identify the name, address, and purpose of the corporation, and they contain the request to obtain an authorized number of shares of stock. The articles also identify the names and addresses of the incorporator(s), the initial board members, the corporate agents and make elections that are available under the laws of the state to which the application will be sent.
- When the application is approved, the company receives a ***charter*** from the state. The charter is the official document that gives "life" to the corporation. Often the charter is simply an officially approved copy of the articles of incorporation.
- The incorporator(s) selects an initial board of directors and writes the ***bylaws***. The bylaws function as a corporate constitution and establish authority, rules, and procedures for conducting the internal affairs of a corporation. The bylaws must conform to state law. When bylaws are created they include procedures for electing officers and approving the issuance of stock, as well as rules for the accounting period, bank account, and other essential matters.
- Stock is approved to be issued, and the new stockholders vote to elect a board of directors.

continued ►

Organizing the Corporation, *continued*

Summary

The table below summarizes the process of creating a new corporation.

Stage	Who Does It	What Happens
1	The incorporator	Application and articles of incorporation are filed.
2	The secretary of state or other state official	The application is approved and a charter is granted.
3	The incorporator	The bylaws are written and the initial directors are selected.
4	The initial board of directors	Shares of stock are approved to be issued.

Owners as Employees

Because a corporation is a separate legal entity, a stockholder (owner) can also be an employee of the corporation. This is unlike a proprietorship or partnership in which owners cannot be employees because there is no legal distinction between the rights and obligations of the business and those of the owner.

Classifying Corporations

Overview

Corporations may be classified in several ways based on ownership or the purpose of the corporation.

Publicly Held or Closely Held

A ***publicly held corporation*** (also called publicly traded) is the largest kind of corporation. "Publicly held" means that the stock is regularly traded on public stock exchanges, such as the New York Stock Exchange. A ***closely held corporation*** does not have stock that trades on public stock exchanges, and the stock is not available to the general public. Usually a small number of people own all the stock.

Profit or Nonprofit

When we think of a corporation, usually we think of an organization created to earn profits and potentially obtain large amounts of investor capital by selling shares of stock. This is called a ***for-profit corporation***. However, many corporations are not organized for the purpose of making a profit. These corporations are usually organized to facilitate charitable or educational goals. Such a corporation is called a ***nonprofit corporation***.

Classifying Corporations, *continued*

Limited Liability Company

A ***limited liability company*** is a business entity that has features of both a partnership and a corporation but is easier to operate. A limited liability company is often referred to as an ***LLC***. It is also sometimes called a *limited liability corporation*. The key features of an LLC are:

- Like a corporation, LLC owners have limited liability.
- Like a corporation, there is no mutual agency.
- Like a partnership, percentage ownership interests are purchased.
- Like a partnership, income and loss is allocated by agreement. LLC members can share income and losses among themselves in any way they wish. Allocated income and loss is not based on shares owned.
- Like a partnership, allocated taxable income or loss is reported directly and individually by each LLC owner, so there is no double taxation. (However, an LLC can elect to be taxed as a corporation.)
- Like a partnership, an LLC has a limited life unless the operating agreement specifies a continuous life.
- An LLC may elect to have a professional management group (like a corporation) or it may elect to be member managed.

A limited liability company is created by completing *articles of organization* for the state in which the company is formed. The operations of an LLC are governed by what is called an *operating agreement* (conforming to state law), which is similar to a partnership agreement. The owners of an LLC are referred to as "members" of the LLC.

Corporate Regulation and Management

Regulation

Corporations are independent entities in which the stockholders usually have no personal liability. Also, corporations can grow extremely large and achieve a great deal of economic power and influence. For these reasons, corporations are subject to a considerable amount of federal and state government regulation. These laws are designed to protect the stockholders of corporations as well as the general public that is affected by corporate operations. Here are some examples:

- Federal and state securities laws regulate how corporate securities sales are promoted to the public.
- Federal and state securities laws require full financial disclosure and control the accounting and auditing rules that publicly traded corporations must follow.
- State securities laws regulate corporate creation, stockholder rights, and stock issuance.
- Other laws, such as those regulating environmental pollution and working conditions, affect corporate operations.

continued ►

Corporate Regulation and Management, *continued*

Management

An advantage of a corporate entity is that the stockholders can have the benefit of professional management, hired and supervised by the board of directors. However, in larger corporations, management activity is very much separated from the stockholders. Stockholders must rely heavily on the board of directors to provide reliable supervision and guidance, to protect the stockholder interests, and to employ high-quality officers and managers. Because of its key position of authority, the board of directors must act in an independent and ethical way. An ethical and independent board combined with professional management should maximize the value of the corporation to the benefit of stockholders.

Unfortunately, the separation of ownership and management, sometimes combined with state law that is favorable to management authority, can create a problem of excessive management independence. In these cases, the board of directors may not act with sufficient independence and authority. The result can be inefficient and overpaid management that does not respond to the wishes of the stockholders and that does not maximize long-term company value for the benefit of stockholders.

Social Responsibility

Although our discussion is concerned primarily with accounting and financial matters, we should never forget that corporations are members of society. Because of the potential power of large corporations, managers and boards of directors of corporations first and foremost have an ethical responsibility (just as any good citizen) to not harm society or the communities and the environment in which the corporate businesses operate.

Financial matters must always be secondary to this social responsibility and socially ethical behavior.

Issuing Stock

Stock Issuance Procedures

Direct Issuance

A corporation may decide to promote and sell its stock directly to the public by using company resources. The approval and promotion procedure can be quite time-consuming and expensive and requires a special kind of financial marketing expertise. For this reason, direct promotion is usually done only by smaller, closely held companies on a relatively small scale.

Indirect Issuance

Larger companies usually use specialized services for advice and assistance in selling stock to the public. These services are called "investment banking" and are provided by divisions of large banks or specialized firms, both of which are called ***investment banks***.

In a typical arrangement, the investment bank makes a "best guess" estimate of the best initial selling price per share and the number of shares that can be successfully sold. Then the investment bank agrees to buy all of the shares being offered, minus a discount or commission charge. The investment bank assumes the risk of successfully selling all the shares. This process is called *underwriting*, and the investment bank that performs these functions is referred to as the ***underwriter***. A less common arrangement is that an investment bank will simply promote and advertise the stock to the public in return for receiving a percentage fee or a percentage of the shares actually sold. This is sometimes called a "best efforts" underwriting.

Initial Public Offering

The first time a corporation offers a class of stock for sale to the public is called an ***initial public offering***, often referred to as an ***IPO***.

Secondary Offering

At some time after the initial public offering, a corporation may wish to obtain additional investment capital from investors by selling more shares of stock. A sale of more stock after the initial public offering is called a ***secondary offering***. Sometimes the term secondary offering is also used to refer to the sale of stock by a small group of large investors who are liquidating their initial ownership positions.

continued ▶

Stock Issuance Procedures, *continued*

Transfer Agents

A corporation must make sure to keep very accurate records of who owns the shares of stock and when the ownership of shares of stock changes from one owner to another owner. Most large corporations employ specialized companies for this. These companies are called ***transfer agents***.

Market Value of the Stock

At the time of the IPO, the underwriter makes an estimate of the best price to offer the stock to the public. However, after the stock is sold to the public and begins to be traded on the stock exchanges the market value is strictly the result of market forces. The actual selling price of a stock changes constantly as buyers offer a ***bid price*** and sellers want a higher ***asking price***. In general, the most powerful forces that affect the price of a stock are the expected profitability ("earnings") of the company and the amount of dividends paid.

The trading of any stock on stock exchanges involves stock that is already issued. The trading is simply between investors and has no direct effect on the company.

Authorized Shares and Issued Shares

When a company receives its charter from a state, the state authorizes a specified number of shares that the company has available to sell. This is the number of ***authorized shares***. The authorization does not require any accounting entry. If all the authorized shares are issued and the company wants to issue more shares, the company must apply to the state to change its charter to allow for more authorized shares. This usually requires stockholder approval.

Issued shares are shares of authorized stock that have been sold to investors or issued for other reasons. When shares of stock are issued, an accounting entry is required. We will begin to study the accounting entries for issuing stock in the next learning goal.

We need to keep in mind that there are also non-profit corporations. These corporations do not issue stock. Therefore, the preceding discussion does not apply to these types of organizations.

QUICK REVIEW

- A corporation is an entity created by law and is treated as a separate legal "person," although not a "natural person." The ownership of a corporation is divided into units. These units are called shares of stock. The owners of stock are called stockholders or shareholders.
- Shares of stock can be freely transferred from one owner to another by sale, exchange, gift, or other methods without the consent of other stockholders. Individual stockholders of a corporation are not bound by the acts of a corporation and do not have personal liability for corporate debts. Also, there is no mutual agency between owners.
- The key people involved in the creation, ownership, and management of a corporation are the incorporators, stockholders, board of directors, and managers. The relationship of these individuals is illustrated in an organization chart.
- The process of incorporation begins with an incorporator filing an application that includes articles of incorporation. When the application is approved the company receives a charter that creates a corporation. After this, bylaws are written, corporate officers are elected, and stock is issued.
- Corporations can be classified as *publicly held* or *closely held* and as *for-profit* or *nonprofit.*
- Corporations are subject to substantial regulation, including securities laws, accounting rules, working conditions laws, and environmental laws.
- Professional and ethical corporate managers and boards of directors can increase stockholder value as well as protect the quality of life of the communities in which the businesses operate; however, due to excessive management independence combined with a weak board of directors and local law, this does not always happen.
- A corporation can sell stock directly to the public; however, corporations often use underwriters to sell the stock to the public.

PRACTICE Learning Goal 28, continued

Solutions are in the disk at the back of the book and at: www.worthyjames.com

9. If stock of a corporation can be purchased on a stock exchange by investors,
   a. the company is nonprofit.
   b. the stock is being offered by an underwriter.
   c. the company is closely held.
   d. the company is publicly held.
10. If one person owns all the shares of stock of a corporation,
   a. that person can only hold one officer's position, such as president or secretary.
   b. that person can hold all corporate officer positions.
   c. none of the above.
   d. One person cannot own all the shares of stock of a corporation.

Discussion Questions

1. Explain the process of how a corporation comes into existence.

2. Your friend is thinking about incorporating her growing advertising business. Explain to her the key features of a corporation that make it different from a proprietorship or partnership, including advantages and disadvantages of the corporate form of business.

3. Explain the authority structure of a corporation. Identify the titles and duties involved.

4. The discussion in this learning goal states that members of the board of directors as well as the officers of a corporation have a fiduciary duty to stockholders. What is this fiduciary duty? Does the fiduciary duty to stockholders supersede the corporate ethical requirement to society, community, and the environment? Can you give examples of failing to meet fiduciary responsibilities and social responsibilities?

5. Why are corporations described as "double taxed"?

6. Why do you think most large businesses are created as corporations?

7. If a company wants to issue its stock to the public, what are the possible procedures involved?

8. After an underwriter sells shares of stock to the public in an IPO, what effect does the market price of the stock have on the amount of money that is obtained from issuing those shares of stock?

9. Can a corporation sell an unlimited number of shares of stock? What is the difference between authorized shares and issued shares?

10. Explain the difference between an initial public offering and a secondary offering.

PRACTICE Learning Goal 28, continued

Solutions are in the disk at the back of the book and at: www.worthyjames.com

11. Which of the businesses listed below probably should consider operating as a corporation? Why?

- A small dress shop in a mall
- A small chemical manufacturing company
- A chain of fast food stores
- A real estate business operated as a partnership
- A biotechnology company that wants to expand

12. Can an owner (a stockholder) of a corporation also be an employee of the corporation? Is this similar to a proprietorship or a partnership?

13. Compare and contrast the key features of a corporation and an LLC.

14. Compared to a proprietorship or a partnership, which corporation features do you think investors and managers would consider to be an advantage? A disadvantage?

Your Questions?

It is *very* important to be aware of what you need to understand better. What do you need to understand better about this learning goal? On a separate piece of paper, write the questions that you want to discuss with your classmates, instructor, or supervisor. Try to be very specific about what is bothering you, such as explanations that you do not fully understand.

LEARNING GOAL 29

Explain the Owners' Equity of a Corporation

The Two Parts: Paid-in Capital and Retained Earnings

Overview

The essential difference between a corporate balance sheet and a non-corporate balance sheet is the owner's equity section. The owner's equity on a corporate balance sheet is called ***stockholders' equity*** or "shareholders' equity". Just as with owner's equity for a proprietorship, stockholders' equity for a corporation is a residual amount—it is a claim on the value of the assets that would remain if all the creditors were fully paid.

For a proprietorship, a balance sheet reports owner's equity as one combined amount—all the components of an owner's capital account. On a corporate balance sheet, stockholders' equity is divided into two basic parts that identify the sources of capital. The two parts are: 1) ***Paid-in capital***, which shows the sources of investments in the company. This part will have one or more stock accounts. 2) ***Retained earnings***, which on a balance sheet reports a combined amount of the accumulated net income (loss) minus asset withdrawals going to stockholders, which are called ***dividends.***

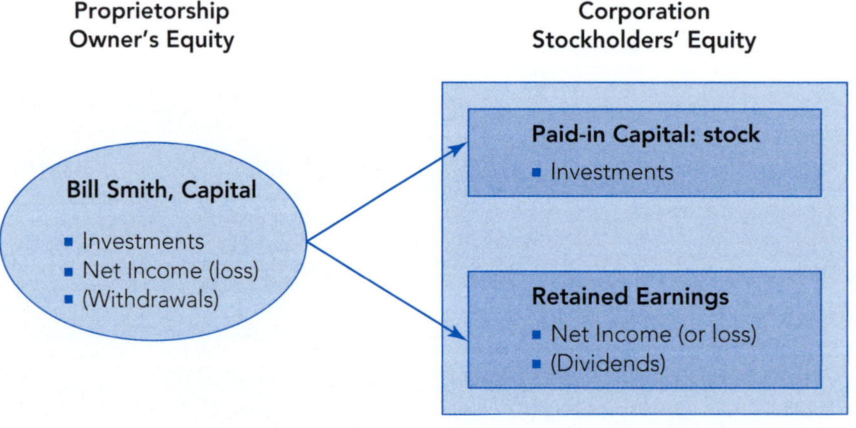

In Learning Goal 29, you will find:

The Two Parts: Paid-in Capital and Retained Earnings

Common Stock

Preferred Stock

Paid-in Capital

Definition

Paid-in capital is the part of stockholders' equity that comes from investments in the stock of a corporation. These investments usually result from the corporation selling shares of stock to investors. Each share of stock is a unit of ownership in a corporation.

Overview of Stock Types

Corporations sell two basic types of stock to investors—*common stock* and *preferred stock*. Common stock is the essential means of corporate ownership, and every corporation has common stock. Some corporations also issue a second kind of stock called preferred stock. We will carefully examine these two types of stock as we continue our study of corporations.

continued ▶

Paid-in Capital, *continued*

Different Classes of Stock

Common and preferred stock can have numerous variations. For example, there can be common Class B, common Class C, preferred Class B, and so on. Each of these different classes of stock has different features that are designed to appeal to different types of investors. There is nothing mysterious about the differences between common and preferred stock or the different classes of stock. A corporation is simply competing with other corporations in a big financial marketing game designed to attract investors. The entire idea is to attract as much investment money as possible by appealing to as many different types of investors as possible.

Other Sources of Paid-in Capital

In addition to selling stock, there are other sources of paid-in capital. These sources result from other kinds of stockholder equity transactions, such as exchanging shares of stock for property or services or converting preferred shares into common shares. We will study some of these transactions in this Learning Goal and also in Learning Goals 30 and 31.

Paid-in Capital and Creditor Protection

Overview

A fundamental and ever-present restraint placed on the formation and operation of all corporations is creditor protection. Every state that grants corporate charters also imposes legal restrictions that require a minimum paid-in capital. These restrictions prevent excessive reductions of paid-in capital caused by asset distributions to stockholders. The two basic types of restrictions are legal capital and capital maintenance.

Legal Capital

At the time stock is issued, a portion of the proceeds received is required to be treated as legal capital. ***Legal capital*** is the part of the proceeds that, by law, must be permanently retained by a corporation. By requiring this minimum amount of permanent capital, the state laws force a corporation to maintain at least an equal amount of permanent assets. This amount can only be returned to stockholders after the corporation liquidates and all creditors are fully paid. Different states have different methods for calculating legal capital.

Example

Assume that the legal capital requirement in stockholders' equity is $50,000. For the balance sheet to balance, there must also be $50,000 of assets or assets must exceed liabilities by $50,000.

Paid-in Capital and Creditor Protection, *continued*

Par Value Stock

Par value is one method of determining legal capital. ***Par value*** is the minimum amount per share that an investor is required to pay for stock. Par value also establishes the maximum personal liability for an investor. This is called ***limited liability***. Personal liability will only occur if the price paid for a stock is less than the par value; the liability will be the difference between the price paid and the par value. When common stock is issued with a par value, the charter often sets the par value at some low amount such as $.01 per share or less—which minimizes any personal liability because the stock price will be greater. Low par value is also used because some states impose an initial tax on total par value, and because low par value reduces the initial capital required by founders of a new company.

Par value is an old idea that has become obsolete, although it is still in use. Because laws allow par value to be set at any (low) level, significant creditor protection by this method has never really been achieved.

Important: Par value has no relationship to the real market value of stock. Buyers and sellers determine the market value (the price) of a stock. This value has no connection whatsoever to par value. Market value of stock is usually much greater than par value.

No-par Stock

Corporations can also issue no-par stock. ***No-par*** stock does not require a minimum investment amount per share. Different states have different rules for determining the legal capital for no-par stock. One common method is that the first issuance of no-par stock in a given time period becomes legal capital. Other states allow the board of directors to specify legal capital for no-par stock. Some states that permit no-par stock require a minimum amount called *stated value*. Stated value is essentially the same as par value.

Capital Maintenance: Expanding the Idea of Legal Capital

After a corporation is formed and begins to operate, additional laws prevent a corporation from making excessive distributions to stockholders. The purpose of these laws is to protect creditors from dishonest corporations that would remove the assets from a business by distributing them to stockholders. Doing this would leave nothing to pay to the creditors.

Capital maintenance requirements typically exceed the par-value legal requirements discussed above. Different states have different rules for calculating corporate capital maintenance. Some states have specific calculations related to stockholders' equity or retained earnings. Other states simply require that a corporation cannot make a distribution unless there will be sufficient cash to pay creditors as debts become due.

Paid-in Capital Examples

Examples of Par and No-Par Common Stock

Example #1: A corporation sold 100,000 shares of $.10 par value stock for $15 per share. The par value is recorded in an account called *Common Stock*. The amount that exceeds par value ($14.90 per share) is called ***paid-in capital in excess of par***, or ***stock premium***. The stockholders' equity section on the balance sheet would appear as follows:

Stockholders' Equity	
Paid-in capital	
Common stock, $.10 par value, 100,000 shares issued:	$ 10,000
Paid-in capital in excess of par	1,490,000
Total Paid-in Capital	$1,500,000

Example #2: 100,000 shares of no-par stock were sold for $15 per share. Because there is no par value, the entire amount is simply designated as Common Stock.

Stockholders' Equity	
Paid-in capital	
Common stock, 100,000 shares issued:	$1,500,000

Preferred Stock

Another type of stock that a corporation may issue in order to attract investors is called ***preferred stock***. Preferred stock is designed with features that appeal to a different type of investor. For example, preferred stock pays regular fixed dividends, often as a percentage of a high par value. We will discuss the features of preferred stock later in this learning goal.

Example of Common and Preferred Stock

The example below of the stockholders' equity section of the balance sheet shows both par-value preferred stock and par-value common stock that were sold above par value.

Stockholders' Equity		
Paid-in capital		
Preferred stock $100 par, 5%, 10,000 shares issued	$1,000,000	
Paid-in capital in excess of par, preferred	75,000	$1,075,000
Common stock $.10 par value, 100,000 shares issued	10,000	
Paid-in capital in excess of par, common	1,490,000	1,500,000
Total paid-in capital		2,575,000

Retained Earnings

Definition

The second part of stockholders' equity is retained earnings. ***Retained earnings*** is the part of the stockholders' equity claim that comes from the cumulative amount of net income less net losses, and less dividends paid out and certain other stockholders' equity transactions.

Retained earnings is one part of the entire stockholders' residual claim on all the assets. Retained earnings has no connection to the amount of cash or any other particular asset.

Synonyms

Retained earnings is sometimes called *earned surplus*, *retained surplus*, *accumulated earnings*, or *unappropriated profits*.

Example of Calculation

Assume that Oakland Corporation was created in 2013. The net income and net (losses) are as follows: 2013, ($25,000); 2014, ($15,000); 2015, $12,000; 2016, $22,000; and 2017, $35,000. Each period's net income or loss flows into retained earnings. At the end of 2017, the retained earnings balance is $29,000. Any dividends or distributions of assets to stockholders would reduce this amount.

Example of Total Stockholder's Equity

We now continue the example from the previous page and assume $839,000 of retained earnings. The illustration below shows that total stockholders' equity consists of both paid-in capital and retained earnings. Notice that retained earnings is shown as a single amount under the total of paid-in capital.

Stockholders' Equity

Paid-in capital		
Preferred stock $100 par, 5%, 10,000 shares issued	$1,000,000	
Paid-in capital in excess of par, preferred	75,000	$1,075,000
Common stock $.10 par value, 100,000 shares issued	10,000	
Paid-in capital in excess of par, common	1,490,000	1,500,000
Total paid-in capital		2,575,000
Retained earnings		839,000
Total stockholders' equity		$3,414,000

The calculation of exact legal capital is often more complex than the simplified par-value presentation in stockholder's equity.

continued ▶

Retained Earnings, *continued*

Summary

The example above illustrates that the value of ownership equity in a corporation consists of two basic sources. The first source is the paid-in capital that comes from the invested assets (or services) received in exchange for issuing shares of stock. This is $2,575,000. The second source is retained earnings, which comes from the accumulated wealth created by operating the business. In this example the stockholders have a total claim on the business assets in the amount of $3,414,000.

Comparing Corporation and Proprietorship Equity

Overview

From an accounting viewpoint the essential difference between a corporation and a proprietorship is how the owners' equity is recorded. The table below compares the equity of each business type:

Feature	In a proprietorship . . .	In a corporation . . .
Title of owner	▪ There is one owner, called an ***owner*** or ***proprietor***.	▪ There can be one or many owners, called ***stockholders*** or ***shareholders***.
Name of equity	▪ The equity is called ***(owner's name) capital***.	▪ The equity is called ***stockholders' equity***.
How equity is shown	▪ The combined amount of cumulative profits, losses, and investments (less withdrawals) are shown as one net amount called ***owner's capital***.	The stockholders' equity is divided into two basic sections: ▪ The paid-in capital section shows the amounts invested. ▪ Retained earnings shows the cumulative undistributed profit (or loss).
Distributions to owners (not in liquidation)	▪ Distributions of assets out of the business to the owner are called ***withdrawals*** (or ***drawing***) and reduce the owner's capital.	▪ Distributions of assets out of the business to the owner(s) are called ***dividends*** and reduce retained earnings.
Priority of claim	▪ The priority of the owner's equity claim on assets is residual—after the creditors are paid.	▪ The priority of the stockholders' equity claim on assets is residual—after the creditors are paid.
Owners' potential loss	▪ The owner can lose the amount invested, and the owner has personal liability to creditors for payment of business debts.	▪ Stockholders generally can lose no more than the amount invested. Stockholders' personal liability to creditors is limited to legal capital.

Comparing Corporation and Proprietorship Equity, *continued*

The word *capital* has different meanings, and this is often very confusing to beginners in accounting and finance. Depending on the context in which the word is used, here are the common meanings of *capital*.

- In general, wealth, especially as used for investment
- Owner's, partners', or stockholders' equity of a specific business
- A reference to an amount invested as part of stockholders' equity (paid-in capital, legal capital, capital stock, paid-in capital in excess of par)
- An asset, or an expenditure (capital expenditure) to purchase an asset

Common Stock

Common Stock Features

Overview

Common stock is the basic ownership and voting type of stock issued by every corporation. Common stock shares are authorized by a state when a charter is granted. Corporations may receive authorization to issue various classes of common stock such as Class A, Class B, Class C, and so on. Each different class has different features and limitations (for example, Class B may be non-voting but have a higher dividend). The purpose of the different classes is simply to attract different kinds of investors so the company can obtain more capital.

Voting Rights

Most of the time, there is only one class of common stock. In these situations each share of the common stock entitles the owner to one vote. Typically, common stock voting rights allow a stockholder to vote in an election for the board of directors and to vote on all actions requiring stockholder approval as set forth in the bylaws.

Share in Profits

Common stock entitles the owner of the stock to share proportionately in corporate profits by receiving dividends. Profits are normally shared based on the number of shares of stock owned.

continued ▶

Common Stock Features, *continued*

Share in Liquidation

Common stock entitles the owner to share in assets upon liquidation of the business, after the creditors are paid. This is called a ***residual claim*** and is shared proportionately among common stockholders according to the number of common shares owned.

Preemptive Rights

Sometimes common stock rights include the right to maintain the same percentage ownership. This is called ***preemptive rights***, and it guarantees the right of existing stockholders to maintain their percentage ownership by purchasing shares of stock whenever the corporation issues more shares of the same class of common stock. Preemptive rights are relatively rare.

When preemptive rights do not exist and new shares are issued and purchased by new stockholders, the existing stockholders' percentage of total issued shares is reduced. This is called ***dilution***.

Common Stock—Issuing Shares: Cash Transactions

Overview

A corporation obtains money when investors purchase shares of stock from the corporation. The way this type of transaction is usually recorded depends on whether the stock is par or no-par stock. (Stated value stock is recorded in the same way as par-value stock.)

Example: Par Value Stock

Assume that on June 5 Rodriguez Corporation sells 100,000 shares of its common stock for $12 per share in an all-cash transaction. The stock has a $.01 par value. The journal entry to record this transaction is:

Date	Account	Debit	Credit
6/5	Cash (100,000 × $12)	1,200,000	
	Common Stock (100,000 × $.01)		1,000
	Paid-in Capital in Excess of Par ($1,200,000 – $1,000)		1,199,000

Example: No Par Stock

Assume in the example above that the shares being sold are no-par stock. How much of the Common Stock account is designated as legal capital depends upon the laws of the particular state that governs the corporation.

Date	Account	Debit	Credit
6/5	Cash	1,200,000	
	Common Stock		1,200,000

Common Stock—Issuing Shares: Cash Transactions, *continued*

Stock Issue Costs

Usually when a company issues stock using an underwriter, the underwriting company (an investment bank) estimates a good selling price for the shares and then pays the issuing company this price, minus a discount, which is the underwriter's profit and a cost to the issuing company. The underwriter then owns all the stock and has the responsibility of selling the shares to the public at the estimated selling price. A company also can incur other direct stock issuance costs such as legal and accounting fees, printing costs, and so on.

The usual procedure for recording stock issue costs related to a stock issuance is to reduce paid-in capital, as a result of either less cash being received from a stock issue or cash being paid (except when part of a start-up: see 576 below).

Example of Underwriter Stock Issue Cost

On June 3, Euclid Company issues 100,000 shares of $.10 par value stock. The underwriter estimates that the stock could be sold for $20 per share, and charges a discount of 5%, buying the shares for $19 per share ($20 - $1) from Euclid.

6/3	Cash (100,000 × $19)	1,900,000	
	Common Stock (100,000 × $.10)		10,000
	Paid-in Capital in Excess of Par ($1,900,000 – $10,000)		1,890,000

The Paid-in Capital in Excess of Par has been reduced by the same amount as the $100,000 reduction in the cash proceeds for the underwriting cost.

Common Stock—Issuing Shares: Non-Cash Transactions

Overview

Sometimes a corporation will receive non-cash assets or incur services expenses in exchange for the stock that is issued. The main consideration in these situations is the determination of the value of the transaction. The general rule is to base the value of the transaction on whatever value is most accurately determinable:

1. the fair market value of the stock, or
2. the fair market value of the property or services received.

The first option is usually selected whenever a stock is regularly traded on an exchange. If no value can be reliably obtained, the board of directors of the corporation can set the value.

continued ▶

Common Stock—Issuing Shares: Non-Cash Transactions, *continued*

Example: Use Stock Value

Assume that on October 20, Miller Corporation issues 100,000 shares of its $.10 par value common stock in exchange for machine tool equipment. The stock has numerous recent trades on a stock exchange at an average price of $10.50 share.

10/20	Equipment (100,000 × $10.50)	1,050,000	
	Common Stock (100,000 × $.10)		10,000
	Paid-in Capital in Excess of Par ($1,050,000 – $10,000)		1,040,000

Example: Use Asset Value

Assume that Miller Corporation stock is privately held and does not trade on an exchange. However, the equipment is new and several reliable price quotes can be obtained from vendors. The average vendor price is $1,125,000.

10/20	Equipment	1,125,000	
	Common Stock (100,000 × $.10)		10,000
	Paid-in Capital in Excess of Par ($1,125,000 – $10,000)		1,115,000

Example: Estimated Value

Assume that no stock value or market value of the equipment can be reliably obtained. The board of directors can set the value of the transaction.

This power to determine value can potentially be used to manipulate the value of transactions for the purpose of manipulating the values that appear on a balance sheet. When a transaction is over valued, the stock is referred to as ***watered stock***. When a transaction is under valued the company is said to have ***secret reserves***.

Start-up Costs

The costs of organizing and forming a new business are called ***start-up costs***. These costs include legal and accounting fees, advertising, printing fees, and fees paid to the state of incorporation. Start-up costs are recorded as expenses when incurred, although technically they benefit the entire life of a corporation, and taxing authorities treat them as long-term intangible assets. The corporate account names used are usually ***Organization Expense*** or ***Organization Cost***.

Common Stock—Issuing Shares: Non-Cash Transactions, *continued*

Example

On June 3, Tuolumne Company incorporates a new business. Legal, accounting, and stock underwriting fees are $120,000. 100,000 common shares of $.10 par value are issued at $11 per share before fees, and the attorney and accountant are paid $20,000 cash. Because this is a new company, the $100,000 stock underwriting fees are also recorded as start-up costs. The journal entry is:

6/3	Cash	1,000,000	
	Organization Expense	100,000	
	Common Stock		10,000
	Paid-in Capital in Excess of Par – Common		1,090,000
	Organization Expense	20,000	
	Cash		20,000

Common Stock—Issuing Shares: Subscription Sales

Overview

A corporation can sell shares *on account*, collecting some of the cash when the sale is made and collecting the remainder of the cash as the balance is received from the buyer. After the final payment is received, the stock is issued to the buyer.

Example of Subscription Sale

On November 2, Leung Corporation sells 1,000 shares of $1 par value stock at a price of $15 per share. The stock is sold on a subscription basis that allows a buyer to make a 40% down payment at the time of the sale and pay the remaining 60% one month later. 20 individuals purchase the stock.

11/2	Cash	6,000	
	Subscriptions Receivable	9,000	
	Common Stock Subscribed		1,000
	Paid-in Capital in Excess of Par		14,000

Explanation

1,000 shares × $15 = $15,000. 40% down payment = $6,000 cash received. The Common Stock Subscribed account is used instead of Common Stock to indicate that the stock has not yet been fully paid.

continued ▶

Common Stock—Issuing Shares: Subscription Sales, *continued*

Example, continued

On November 23, buyers who purchased 30% of the stock pay the remaining amount in full. The stock is then issued to these buyers.

11/23	Cash	2,700	
	Subscriptions Receivable		2,700
	Common Stock Subscribed	300	
	Common Stock		300

Explanation

30% of the receivable is $9,000 × .3 = $2,700 cash received. Accordingly, 30% of the Common Stock Subscribed account is also eliminated and is replaced by Common Stock. Common Stock is used when shares are issued.

Balance Sheet Presentation

On the balance sheet a Subscriptions Receivable balance should not be shown as an asset, despite its name. It is really an offset (a minus amount) in the paid-in capital section of stockholders' equity. This is shown as a deduction amount below retained earnings. Why? State laws generally do not require buyers to pay unpaid subscriptions, so corporations cannot really count this as "reliable" equity. In the example above, on November 23, the balance of the paid-in capital after the payment would be: $15,000 total capital – $6,300 remaining balance of subscriptions receivable = $8,700.

Example of Subscribed Stock on Balance Sheet

A stockholders' equity section with subscriptions receivable is illustrated below.

Stockholders' Equity

Paid-in capital		
Common stock $1 par value 300 shares issued	$ 300	
Common stock subscribed	700	
Paid-in capital in excess of par	14,000	
Total paid-in capital		$15,000
Retained earnings		$ $ $
Less: Subscriptions receivable		(6,300)
Total stockholders' equity		$ $ $

Note: if a subscriber defaults, state law controls corporate actions, which could include: 1) keep the initial payment, 2) keep the payment but issue equivalent shares, 3) return the money.

Common Stock—Paying Cash Dividends

Overview

A cash dividend is a distribution from a successful corporation to stockholders of that corporation. Stockholders share in corporate profits by receiving dividends.

Three Steps to Pay Dividends

Before stockholders can receive dividends, three requirements must be satisfied:

- The board of directors must *vote to approve* the total amount of dividends that will be paid.
- The balance in the *Retained Earnings account must be equal to or exceed* the amount of dividends to be paid. (Dividends paid in excess of retained earnings are called ***liquidating dividends***. A liquidating dividend is essentially a return of stockholders' investments because it reduces paid-in capital. This usually happens when a company is going out of business and may require state approval.)
- The corporation must *have sufficient cash* to pay the dividend. (Remember that Retained Earnings is one part of the stockholders' equity residual claim on all the assets. Retained earnings has no relationship to the amount of cash or any other asset.)

Dividend Example

Stanislaus River Company has 100,000 shares of common stock outstanding. The board of directors, after checking the Retained Earnings and Cash account balances, decides that the company can afford to pay a $40,000 dividend. The dividend is declared on June 5 and is payable on July 15 to stockholders who own the stock on a Thursday, June 30.

Date	Account	Debit	Credit
6/5	Retained Earnings	40,000	
	Dividends Payable		40,000
7/15	Dividends Payable	40,000	
	Cash		40,000

A dividend is not an expense. It is similar to a withdrawal in a proprietorship.

continued 

Common Stock—Paying Cash Dividends, *continued*

Dividend Dates

- ***Declaration date:*** This is the date that a board of directors approves the dividend payment. The dividend becomes a *current liability* on the declaration date.
- ***Date of record:*** This is the date by which stock ownership must be formally recorded for the owner to receive a dividend. In the example above, the date of record is June 30.
- ***Ex-dividend date:*** Several days are needed from the time a stock is purchased until the buyer's name is formally recorded as an owner. Therefore the stock must be purchased *before* a cutoff date, called the ex-dividend date, for the owner to receive the dividend. Normally the ex-dividend date is two business days before the date of record; in this example, therefore, the "ex-date" is June 28.
- ***Payment date:*** This is the date the dividend is paid; here, July 15.

"So, we look to the fourth quarter as a time of healing."

Check Your Understanding

Prepare general journal entries to record each of the following independent situations.

- *Situation #1:* Sandy Hook Corporation sold 100,000 shares of $.10 par value common stock directly to investors at a price of $12 per share.
- *Situation #2:* Willow Creek, Inc., sold 100,000 shares of $.10 par value common stock by using an underwriter who did not purchase the stock, but helped sell the stock to the public and charged a 7% cash commission. The stock was sold at a price of $15 per share.
- *Situation #3:* Great Basin, Inc., issued 10,000 shares of $1 par value common stock to pay the $85,000 legal bill from the law firm that helped organize the corporation. The stock was regularly traded at a market value of $9 per share.
- *Situation #4:* Chaparral Corporation acquired equipment that had a manufacturer's suggested retail price of $150,000. The company issued 20,000 shares of its $1 par value common stock to the dealer in exchange for the equipment. At the time, the company's stock was not regularly traded and had no reliable market value.
- *Situation #5:* Assume in Situation #4 that the stock was regularly traded at $8 per share.
- *Situation #6:* The directors of Rocky Bay Corporation declared a $250,000 dividend. One month later the company paid the dividend.

Answers

Situation #1:

Cash	1,200,000	
Common Stock		10,000
Paid-in Capital in Excess of Par		1,190,000

Situation #2:

Cash	1,395,000	
Common Stock		10,000
Paid-in Capital in Excess of Par		1,385,000

Situation #3:

Organization Expense	90,000	
Common Stock		10,000
Paid-in Capital in Excess of Par		80,000

Situation #4:

Equipment	150,000	
Common Stock		20,000
Paid-in Capital in Excess of Par		130,000

Situation #5:

Equipment	160,000	
Common Stock		20,000
Paid-in Capital in Excess of Par		140,000

Situation #6:

Retained Earnings	250,000	
Dividends Payable		250,000
Dividends Payable	250,000	
Cash		250,000

Preferred Stock

Overview

As we discussed briefly, the purpose of preferred stock and its various features is simply to appeal to a different class of investors to obtain additional capital. Preferred means that preferred stock has first preference to receiving dividends and may have certain other rights superior to common stock. Preferred stock can potentially have the same basic rights as common stock; however, voting rights are often withheld from preferred stock.

Preferred Stock—Issuing Shares

Overview

The issuance of preferred stock is very similar to common stock. Preferred stock may be issued for cash, for non-cash assets, for services, and by use of subscription agreements. Preferred stock may be both par value and no-par, just as with common stock. The journal entries are very similar. The most frequent difference is that preferred stock is usually sold at a price very close to its par value.

Example: Preferred Shares Issued for Cash

Assume that Carson City Company, Inc. issues 5,000 shares of $50 par value preferred stock for $51 per share.

Cash (5,000 shares × $51)	255,000	
Preferred Stock (5,000 shares × $50)		250,000
Paid-in Capital in Excess of Par, Preferred ($255,000 – $250,000)		5,000

Preferred Stock Features

Dividend Preference: Regular Payments

A corporation promises to pay a fixed amount of dividends to preferred stockholders, before common stockholders, up to a specified annual limit as designated by the shares. The preferred dividend amount is shown either as an annual percentage of the par value or as an annual fixed dollar amount. Dividends are usually paid quarterly, and preferred stockholders expect to receive these dividends. Generally, after preferred dividends are paid up to the specified quarterly or annual limit, all other dividends go to common stockholders.

Example: $100 par value, 4% preferred stock will receive dividends of $4 per share per year. The board of directors usually votes every quarter to pay dividends, so the preferred stockholders will receive $1 per quarter, before dividends are paid to common stockholders. However, even though the dividends are preferred, they are also fixed. All other profits belong to the common shareholders.

Dividend Preference: Cumulative Payments

Preferred stock often has a ***cumulative dividend*** feature. The cumulative dividend feature means that the preferred stock must receive all prior undeclared dividends plus the current dividend before any dividends can be paid to common stockholders. Dividends not declared on cumulative preferred stock are called ***dividends in arrears.***

Example: XYZ Corporation has 10,000 outstanding shares of $50 par value 3% cumulative preferred stock. The annual dividend is $15,000 (10,000 × $50 × .03). Because of cash flow problems, the board of directors has not declared a dividend during the prior two years. Before any dividends can be paid to common stockholders for the current quarter, the preferred stockholders must receive:

- Dividends in arrears ($15,000 × 2): $30,000
- Current dividends: 3,750
- Total preferred dividends: $33,750

Preferred stock is treated as cumulative unless it is specifically identified as noncumulative stock.

Arrears Not a Liability

Dividends are not a liability until they are declared by the board of directors. Therefore, **dividends in arrears are not a liability.** However, dividends in arrears on cumulative preferred stock as well as missed dividends on noncumulative preferred stock are major financial embarrassments (the company promised to pay dividends!) and causes investors to react very negatively. The market price of such a stock usually decreases significantly.

continued ►

Preferred Stock Features, *continued*

Liquidation Preference

Preferred stock usually has a preference over common stock when a corporation is liquidated. However, the amount is limited. This means that after the creditors are paid, any remaining corporate assets can be claimed first by preferred shareholders up to a specified amount, which is usually the par value or a specified *liquidating value*, including dividends in arrears. In practice, however, the liquidating preference is usually worth little or nothing, because most liquidations occur in bankruptcy when few or no assets remain after creditors are paid.

Conversion Feature

Some types of preferred stock, called ***convertible preferred stock***, can be converted into common stock by the preferred shareholders. Each share of preferred stock can be converted into a specified number of common shares.

For example, assume that Rogue Valley, Inc. has issued 5,000 shares of $100 par value convertible preferred stock. The stock was sold at $103 per share, so the total preferred equity is $515,000. Each share of preferred stock is convertible into 4 shares of $1 par value common stock. The common stock is now selling for $35 per share, so owners of 1,000 shares of preferred stock decide to convert their shares into common stock:

Account	Debit	Credit
Preferred Stock (1,000 shares × $100)	100,000	
Paid-in Capital in Excess of Par, Preferred (1,000 × $3)	3,000	
Common Stock (4,000 shares × $1)		4,000
Paid-in Capital in Excess of Par, Common ($103,000 – $4,000)		99,000

Note the following effects:

- Some of the preferred equity is converted into common equity, but there is **no change in total stockholders' equity**.
- There is **no gain or loss**.
- The market price of the stock is not used in the journal entry calculation.
- More common shares are now outstanding, resulting in dilution of the prior common stock ownership percentages.

To check your calculations: ($515,000 preferred stock equity × 1,000/5,000) = $103,000 of preferred stock equity converted into common stock equity.

Preferred Stock Features, *continued*

Call Feature

Some preferred stocks have a call feature. ***Callable preferred stock*** allows, but does not require, the issuing corporation to buy back ("to call") the preferred stock at a fixed price any time after a specified date. The call price is usually set slightly above the par value. The call feature is always an advantage to the issuing corporation and never an advantage to the investor because the call price tends to place an upper limit on the market value of the stock.

Corporations use a call feature because it allows them to remove higher-dividend preferred stock, which can then be replaced with lower-dividend preferred, common stock or low-interest debt, which has tax-deductible interest payments. When stock is called, the stockholders are entitled to the call price, dividends in arrears, and the current dividend prorated to the call date. However, after the stock is called, no further dividends will be paid.

For example, suppose that Beaverton Corporation has issued 8,000 shares of $50 par value callable stock for $52, so the total preferred equity is $416,000. The stock has a call price of $53. After paying all dividends, the company calls the stock. All preferred stock equity will now be removed. Retained Earnings is charged for the excess of the $53 call price per share above the $52 preferred equity per share.

Preferred Stock (8,000 shares × $50)	400,000	
Paid-in Capital in Excess of Par, Preferred (8,000 × $2)	16,000	
Retained Earnings (8,000 shares × $1 excess)	8,000	
Cash (8,000 shares × $53)		424,000

Participation Feature

Participating preferred stock receives its preferential dividend and then receives an additional dividend amount, based on a formula, after common shareholders receive a designated amount of dividends. Because this feature reduces the amount of dividends that common stockholders receive, the participation feature is unpopular with common shareholders and is relatively uncommon.

continued ▶

Preferred Stock—Paying Cash Dividends

Overview

Preferred dividends are shown as either an annual percentage of par value or as a fixed dollar amount per share. This is then adjusted for frequency of payment, if paid more than once per year. Example: 6%, \$100 par value = \$6 per year or \$1.50 per quarter. Or, \$6, \$100 par value = same amounts. A key point to remember is the dividend preference of the preferred stock. The example below shows dividend payments on both preferred stock and common stock.

Example of Preferred and Common Dividends

Long Island Company, Inc. has 50,000 shares of no par, \$5 preferred stock outstanding, plus common stock outstanding. The board of directors declares a \$100,000 quarterly dividend. Because there are both preferred and common stocks outstanding, the preferred stock is paid first, and the common stockholders receive whatever is left over.

- Preferred dividends for the quarter: (50,000 × \$5)/4 = \$62,500
- Common dividends for the quarter: \$100,000 – \$62,500 = \$37,500

Example: Journal Entry

Declaration:		
Retained Earnings	100,000	
Dividends Payable, Preferred		62,500
Dividends Payable, Common		37,500
Payment:		
Dividends Payable, Preferred	62,500	
Dividends Payable, Common	37,500	
Cash		100,000

Note: If the board of directors had declared only \$62,500 of total dividends, the common stockholders would receive nothing.

Normal Stockholders' Equity Account Balances

Summary

- All Paid-in Capital accounts have normal credit balances.
- The Retained Earnings account has a normal credit balance, although it will show a debit balance if cumulative losses exceed profits (a *deficit*).
- A Subscriptions Receivable account always has a debit balance.

QUICK REVIEW

- The essential difference between a corporate balance sheet and a non-corporate balance sheet is the owners' equity section. The owners' equity of a corporation is called stockholders' equity or shareholders' equity. It consists of two fundamental parts: paid-in capital and retained earnings.
- Paid-in capital is the part of stockholders' equity that comes from investments in a corporate business. Paid-in capital consists primarily of capital obtained from issuing common stock and preferred stock. Retained earnings is the part of stockholders' equity that is the cumulative amount of net income since the business was formed, *less* net losses, dividends, and certain stockholders' equity transactions.
- Legal capital is the part of stockholders equity designed to protect creditors. A corporation cannot pay dividends that would reduce legal capital. Legal capital is often designated as par value or stated value. The exact rules and calculations for legal capital vary by state. In addition to legal capital, state laws also impose capital maintenance requirements to protect creditors.
- Common stock is the basic ownership and voting stock that every corporation is authorized to issue. Unless withheld, common stockholders normally have the right to vote, to share proportionately in profits by receiving dividends, and to share proportionately in liquidation proceeds. A company usually issues common stock for cash, but stock can also be issued for non-cash assets and for services.
- Many corporations pay dividends to their common stockholders. Dividend payments are the means of distributing profits to stockholders. For a dividend to be paid, three steps are required: the board of directors must approve the dividend, there must be a sufficient balance in retained earnings, and there must be sufficient cash. A dividend becomes a liability immediately upon declaration by the board of directors.
- Important dates relating to a dividend payment are: the date of declaration, the date of record, the ex-dividend date, and the date of payment.
- Preferred stock is a type of stock that gives its owners certain preferred rights over common stockholders. The preferred rights are usually a preference to receive fixed, regular, dividend payments and a preference in the event of corporate liquidation. Preferred stock may also be cumulative, callable, or convertible. Just as with common stock, preferred stock is usually issued for cash but may also be issued for non-cash assets and for services.
- Specific events to practice:
  - Stock issuance for cash
  - Stock issuance for other assets
  - Stock issue costs
  - Start-up costs
  - Subscription sales
  - Preferred conversion to common stock
  - Call feature
  - Cash dividends declared and paid

Do You Want More Examples?

Most problems in this book have detailed solutions. To use them as additional examples, do this: 1) Select the type of problem you want 2) Open the solution on your computer or mobile device screen (from the disc or worthyjames.com) 3) Read one item at a time and look at its answer. Take notes if needed. 4) Close the solution and work as much of the problem as you can. 5) Repeat as needed.

VOCABULARY

Callable preferred stock: preferred stock that can be purchased from stockholders by the issuing corporation at a fixed price (page 585)

Capital stock: another term for the total par or stated value of issued stock (page 573)

Convertible preferred stock: preferred stock that is convertible into common stock (page 584)

Cumulative dividend: a feature of preferred stock requiring that all dividends declared must be paid for preferred dividends in arrears plus current preferred dividend before common stockholders can receive a dividend (page 583)

Date of record: the date by which stock ownership must be officially recorded for the owner to receive a dividend (page 580)

Declaration date: the date that a board of directors approves a dividend (page 580)

Dilution: a reduction in the percentage ownership of existing stockholders in a class of stock (also a reduction in earnings per share—see Learning Goal 31) (page 574)

Dividends: non-liquidating distributions of assets from a corporation to its stockholders (page 572)

Dividends in arrears: dividends not declared on cumulative preferred stock (page 583)

Ex-dividend date: the date before which a stock must be purchased to allow enough time for the buyer's name to be officially recorded to receive a dividend—usually two business days before the date of record (page 580)

Legal capital: a minimum amount of paid-in capital that must be maintained for the protection of creditors and that can never be paid to stockholders until the corporation is liquidated and creditors are paid in full (page 568)

Limited liability: investor personal liability that is limited to the part of the investment that is legal capital (page 569)

Liquidating dividend: a dividend that exceeds the balance in retained earnings (page 579)

No-par stock: stock without a par value (page 569)

Organization Expense (also Organization Cost): the account names used to record the costs of organizing and forming a corporation (page 576)

Paid-in capital: the part of stockholders' equity that comes from investments in the corporation, primarily by stockholders (page 567)

Paid-in capital in excess of par (or excess of stated value): paid-in capital that represents non-legal capital (page 570)

Par value: a minimal amount per share that is paid in and establishes a stockholder's limit of liability (page 569)

Payment date: the date a dividend is paid (page 580)

Participating preferred stock: a preferred stock that receives additional dividends, based on a formula, after the common stockholders are paid (page 585)

Preemptive right: the right of existing stockholders to maintain the same percentage ownership in the same class of stock (page 574)

Preferred stock: a type of stock that gives its owners dividend and liquidation preferences over common stockholders (page 570)

Residual claim: the owners' right to share in assets only after the creditors are paid (page 571)

Retained earnings: the part of the stockholders' equity claim that comes from the cumulative amount of net income since the business was formed, *less* net losses, dividends, and certain stockholders' equity transactions (page 571)

Secret reserves: under-valued assets received for stock (page 576)

Start-up costs: a name that refers to the costs related to organizing and forming a corporation or any other business (page 576)

Stockholders' equity: the owners' equity of a corporation (page 566)

Stock premium: another term for paid-in capital in excess of par (page 570)

Watered stock: stock that is issued for over-valued assets (page 576)

PRACTICE Learning Goal 29

Solutions are in the disk at the back of the book and at: www.worthyjames.com

This learning goal is about owners' equity of a corporation. Use these questions and problems to practice what you have just read.

Multiple Choice

Select the best answer.

1. How is stockholders' equity categorized on a balance sheet?
   a. by claims on wealth: liabilities and capital
   b. by type of stock: preferred stock and common stock
   c. by sources of capital: paid-in capital and retained earnings
   d. by dividend preference
2. Par value and stated value
   a. provide a limited and fixed amount of protection for creditors.
   b. are the same as legal capital, which prohibits negative retained earnings.
   c. are good indicators of the true value of stock.
   d. must be used with all types of stock, by state law.
3. Stockholders' equity shows total paid-in capital of $500,000 from common stock and retained earnings of $230,000. The paid-in capital in excess of par on common stock is $450,000. What is the total par value?
   a. $50,000
   b. $450,000
   c. $500,000
   d. $730,000
4. The true amount of legal capital
   a. should always be clearly presented in stockholders' equity.
   b. may not always be able to be shown in stockholders' equity.
   c. always depends on the amount of par value.
   d. none of the above
5. The basic type of stock issued by every corporation is
   a. preferred stock.
   b. common stock.
   c. par value stock.
   d. capital stock.
6. Corporations may issue preferred stock and different classes of stock because
   a. state laws limit the number of shares of any particular class or type of stock.
   b. GAAP limits the number of shares of any particular class or type of stock.
   c. corporations are trying to obtain the most money possible by appealing to different investors.
   d. different classes of stock will provide additional protection to creditors.
7. Retained earnings
   a. cannot be negative.
   b. is part of total paid-in capital.
   c. should be included as part of legal capital.
   d. none of the above
8. Huntsville, Inc. issued 20,000 shares of $.10 par value common stock at $8 per share. The journal entry should include
   a. a debit to Cash of $160,000 and a credit to Common Stock of $160,000.
   b. a debit to Cash of $2,000 and a credit to Common Stock of $2,000.
   c. a debit to Cash of $160,000 and a credit to Common Stock of $2,000.
   d. none of the above

PRACTICE Learning Goal 29, continued

Solutions are in the disk at the back of the book and at: www.worthyjames.com

9. Montgomery Corporation has issued 10,000 shares of 4%, $50 par value preferred stock that was sold at par. The company also has issued 100,000 shares of $.01 par value common stock that has a paid-in capital in excess of par of $171,000 dollars. The retained earnings is $720,000. What is the total stockholders' equity?
   a. $720,000
   b. $891,000
   c. $1,391,000
   d. none of the above
10. Stock is issued for
    a. cash.
    b. non-cash assets, such as equipment.
    c. services.
    d. all of the above
11. Ashland Company is starting up and issued 2,000 shares of $1 par value stock to the attorney who provided legal services for the incorporation and who agreed to accept the shares instead of billing $10,000 for the value of her services. The journal entries should include
    a. a debit to Organization Expense of $2,000.
    b. a credit to Common Stock of $8,000.
    c. a debit to Organization Expense of $10,000 and a credit to paid-in capital in excess of par of $8,000.
    d. a debit to Organization Expense of $10,000 and a credit to Common Stock of $10,000.
12. To receive a dividend, stock must be purchased before the
    a. declaration date.
    b. date of record.
    c. ex-dividend date.
    d. payment date.
13. A dividend becomes a liability on the
    a. declaration date.
    b. date of record.
    c. ex-dividend date.
    d. payment date.
14. The annual amount of dividend that a corporation should pay on 20,000 shares of 6%, $100 par value preferred stock is
    a. $12,000.
    b. $120,000.
    c. $2,000,000.
    d. none of the above
15. Siskiyou Corporation has issued 5,000 shares of $5, $50 par preferred stock and 100,000 shares of $.10 par common stock. The board of directors declared a $200,000 annual dividend. How much will the common stockholders receive?
    a. $10,000
    b. $175,000
    c. $200,000
    d. none of the above
16. Klamath Falls, Inc. has issued 7,000 shares of 4%, $100 par cumulative preferred stock and 200,000 shares of $.01 stated value common stock. The preferred stock is 2 years in arrears, not including the current year. The board of directors declared a $250,000 dividend for the current year. How much will the common shareholders receive?
    a. $166,000
    b. $194,000
    c. $250,000
    d. none of the above

PRACTICE Learning Goal 29, continued

Solutions are in the disk at the back of the book and at: www.worthyjames.com

17. For which of the following rights does preferred stock generally *not* have preference over common stock?
    a. dividends
    b. preference in liquidation
    c. voting
    d. none of the above
18. No-par stock
    a. shows the legal capital as the stockholders' equity balances of "Common Stock" or "Preferred Stock."
    b. is recorded as Paid-in Capital in Excess of Par for common or preferred stock.
    c. always has a minimum stated value.
    d. none of the above
19. Which of the following does *not* correctly describe legal capital? Legal capital
    a. equals the amounts shown as "Common Stock" or "Preferred Stock" in stockholders' equity.
    b. is the minimum amount of permanent capital a corporation must maintain.
    c. is intended to provide protection to a corporation's creditors.
    d. all of the above
20. The maximum number of shares of stock that a corporation can issue is called
    a. Paid-in Capital in Excess of Par.
    b. legal capital shares.
    c. authorized shares.
    d. issued shares.
21. Organization costs of a corporation are
    a. recorded as an expense when incurred.
    b. recorded as an asset when incurred.
    c. not recorded.
    d. recorded at a value determined by the board of directors.
22. What is the correct description of the shares of stock that a corporation has sold?
    a. issued stock
    b. outstanding stock
    c. authorized stock
    d. par-value stock
23. What are the basic categories of stockholders' equity?
    a. legal capital and par value
    b. paid-in capital and retained earnings
    c. common stock and preferred stock
    d. paid-in capital, retained earnings, and legal capital
24. Capital maintenance requirements
    a. are established at the time stock is issued.
    b. are usually less than par or stated value amounts.
    c. are usually greater than par or stated value amounts.
    d. usually include the balance of retained earnings.
25. Retained earnings
    a. are part of paid-in capital.
    b. are the cumulative amount of undistributed income minus losses.
    c. do include losses incurred.
    d. cannot have a negative balance.

PRACTICE **Learning Goal 29, continued**

Solutions are in the disk at the back of the book and at: www.worthyjames.com

LG 29-8. Prepare journal entries and stockholder's equity. June 30, 2017 is the year end for Middlebury Corporation. The table below shows the stockholders' equity accounts as of year end.

a. Journalize the transactions listed below. (For journal paper, you can make general journal copies from the disk at the back of this book.)
b. Prepare the stockholders' equity section of the balance sheet as of September 30, 2017. The net income for July–September is $136,000. (*Suggestion:* After you prepare the journal entries, use T accounts to keep a record of the account balances that you will need for the stockholders' equity section.)
c. Prepare the stockholders' equity section of the balance sheet as of October 31, 2017. The net income for October is $52,000. Explain any differences between the September 30 and October 31 stockholders' equity sections.
d. Prepare tables for each type of stock to record the number of shares issued and to verify the number of common and preferred shares issued as of September 30 and October 31.

Account	Balance	Account	Balance
Common Stock, no par, 125,000 shares issued	$1,225,000	Preferred Stock, $50 par value, $2, convertible, 15,000 shares issued. . . .	$750,000
Retained earnings	710,000	Paid-in Capital in Excess of Par, Preferred	60,000

The preferred stock is cumulative and 1 year in arrears. Each share of preferred stock is convertible into 4 shares of common stock.

2017	
July 9	Middlebury Corporation sold 75,000 shares of no-par common stock for $12.00 per share. The stock was sold by subscription, which required the buyers to immediately pay 40% of the total cost and to pay the remaining 60% by October 9.
18	The company purchased land that was offered for sale at $140,000 by issuing 12,000 shares of common stock to the seller, who agreed to accept the stock for the land instead of cash. At the time the agreement was signed with the seller, the stock was actively traded on stock exchanges at $12 per share.
Aug. 24	Buyers of 30,000 shares of the stock sold on July 9 paid the remaining balance due on their stock subscriptions, and Middlebury Corporation issued the shares to the investors.
Sept. 5	Owners of 3,000 shares of preferred stock converted their shares into common stock. Preferred dividends are not payable on preferred stock that is converted to common shares.
14	Buyers of 15,000 shares of the stock sold on July 9 paid the remaining balance due on their stock subscriptions.
29	The board of directors declared a $40,000 quarterly cash dividend payable on October 17.
Oct. 3	The remaining buyers of the subscribed stock paid their balances in full.
17	The company paid the cash dividend.
23	The company sold 10,000 shares of its preferred stock by using an underwriting company that sold the stock for $55 per share and deducted a 7% underwriting commission from the sales proceeds.

PRACTICE Learning Goal 29, continued

Solutions are in the disk at the back of the book and at: www.worthyjames.com

Instructor-Assigned Problems

If you are using this book in a class, these review problems may be assigned by your instructor for homework, group assignments, class work, or other activities. Only your instructor has the solutions.

IA29-1. Prepare general journal entries; prepare stockholders' equity section of balance sheet. The December 31, 2016 Stockholders' equity section of Clovis Corporation shows the stockholders' equity accounts that you see below.

a. Journalize the transactions listed below.
b. Prepare the stockholders' equity section of the balance sheet as of March 31, 2017. The net income for the quarter ending March 31, 2017 was $210,000. Use T accounts to maintain a record of account balances for the listed transactions. Include net income in retained earnings.

Account	Balance	Account	Balance
Common Stock, $.01 par value, 200,000 shares issued	$2,000	Preferred Stock, $50 par value, 4%, 10,000 shares issued	$500,000
Paid-in Capital in Excess of Par, Common Stock	$850,000	Paid-in Capital in Excess of Par, Preferred	$45,000
		Retained Earnings	$394,000

The preferred stock is cumulative and one year in arrears.

2017	
Jan. 9	Sold 70,000 shares of common stock for $14 per share without use of underwriter.
Feb. 20	Paid Advisory Services, Inc. for legal services related to the stock issuance in the amount of $11,600.
Mar. 3	Issued 1,000 shares of stock for new computer equipment that was selling for $15,000.
Mar. 9	Sold 500 shares of preferred stock at $53 per share.
Mar. 17	The board of directors declared an annual cash dividend of $100,000.
Apr. 20	The company paid the dividend.

PRACTICE **Learning Goal 29, continued**

Solutions are in the disk at the back of the book and at: www.worthyjames.com

IA29-2. Prepare general journal entries; prepare stockholders' equity section of a balance sheet.
The June 30, 2016 Stockholders' equity section of Lewiston Corporation shows the stockholders' equity accounts that you see below:

a. Journalize the transactions listed below.
b. Prepare the stockholders' equity section of the balance sheet as of September 30, 2017. The net income for the quarter ending March 31, 2017 was $210,000. Use T accounts to maintain a record of account balances for the listed transactions. Net loss for the quarter ending September 30 was $125,000. Include net loss in retained earnings.

Account	Balance	Account	Balance
Common Stock, $1 par value, 300,000 shares issued........................	$300,000	Preferred Stock, $30 par value, 3%, 80,000 shares issued................	$2,400,000
Paid-in Capital in Excess of Par, Common Stock................................	$2,700,000	Paid-in Capital in Excess of Par, Preferred..	$140,000
		Retained Earnings................	$725,000

The preferred stock is convertible at the rate of 3 shares of common for each share of preferred.

2017	
July 11	The board of directors declared a $300,000 annual cash dividend.
July 24	Issued 50,000 new shares of common stock at a market price of $12 per share. The underwriting fee is 6% of the total issue price.
Aug. 3	Paid the dividend declared on July 11.
Aug. 27	Sold 20,000 shares of preferred stock at $32 per share.
Sept. 17	Issued 4,000 shares of common stock for land. At the time, the stock was actively traded on a public stock exchange at an average price of $12.50 per share. The seller of the land indicates that the land was recently appraised at $750,000.
Sept. 28	Some preferred shareholders exercised the preferred stock conversion feature and converted 5,000 shares of preferred stock into common stock.

PRACTICE **Learning Goal 29, continued**

IA29-3. Prepare journal entries and stockholder's equity. The June 30, 2016 balance sheet of Sycamore Corporation shows the stockholders' equity accounts that you see below.

a. Journalize the transactions listed below. (For journal paper, you can make general journal copies from the template in the disk at the back of this book or at www.worthjames.com "student info.")
b. Prepare the stockholders' equity section of the balance sheet as of September 30, 2017. The net loss for July–September is $52,300. (*Suggestion:* After you prepare the journal entries, use T accounts to keep a record of the account balances that you will need for the stockholders' equity section.)
c. Prepare the stockholders' equity section of the balance sheet as of October 31, 2017. The net income for October is $25,000. Explain any differences between the September 30 and October 31 stockholders' equity sections.
d. Prepare tables for each type of stock to record the number of shares issued and to verify the number of common and preferred shares issued as of September 30 and October 31.

Account	Balance	Account	Balance
Common Stock, $.50 par value, 250,000 shares issued.	$125,000	Preferred Stock, $25 par value, 6%, convertible, 20,000 shares issued	$500,000
Paid-in Capital in Excess of Par, Common Stock.	5,341,000	Paid-in Capital in Excess of Par, Preferred.	$12,000
		Retained earnings	862,000

The preferred stock is convertible into 1.5 shares of common stock for each share of preferred stock.

2017

July 1 The company sold 80,000 shares of common stock for $24 per share. The stock was sold by subscription agreement that required the buyers to immediately pay 40% of the total due and to pay the remaining 60% by October 31.

July 10 The company purchased computer equipment by issuing shares of common stock. The retail price of the equipment was $280,000 and the company issued 11,200 shares of common stock to the seller, who had agreed to accept the stock instead of cash. At the time of the purchase, the stock was actively traded on stock exchanges at $26 per share.

Aug. 20 Owners of 15,000 shares of preferred stock converted their shares into common stock. Preferred dividends are not payable on preferred stock that is converted to common shares.

Sept. 9 Buyers of 50,000 shares of common stock paid the remaining balance due on their stock subscriptions.

Oct. 15 The board of directors declared a $50,000 quarterly cash dividend for stockholders of record as of October 20.

28 The remaining buyers of the subscribed stock paid their balances in full.

PRACTICE **Learning Goal 29, continued**

Solutions are in the disk at the back of the book and at: www.worthyjames.com

IA29-4. Prepare journal entries and stockholder's equity. The June 30, 2017 balance sheet of Puuloa, Inc. shows the stockholders' equity accounts that you see below.

a. Journalize the transactions listed below. (For journal paper, you can make copies from the template in the disk at the back of this book.)
b. After you prepare the journal entries, use T accounts to keep a record of the account balances that you will need for the stockholders' equity section.
c. Prepare the stockholders' equity section of the balance sheet as of September 30, 2017. The net income for July–September is $374,500.
d. Prepare tables for each type of stock to record the number of shares issued and to verify the number of common and preferred shares issued as of September 30, 2017.
e. What were the dividends per share for common shareholders on July 9? On October 18?

Account	Balance	Account	Balance
Common Stock, $.05 par value, 300,000 shares issued.	$15,000	Preferred Stock, $100 par value, 6%, convertible, 7,500 shares issued	$750,000
Paid-in Capital in Excess of Par, Common Stock	9,640,000	Retained earnings	2,800,000

The preferred stock is cumulative and one year in arrears. The preferred stock is convertible into 2 shares of common stock for each share of preferred stock.

2017	
July 9	The board of directors declared a $120,000 quarterly cash dividend to stockholders of record on June 30, payable on August 15.
Aug. 5	Puuloa, Inc. sold 15,000 shares of common stock at a price of $48 per share.
12	The company issued 1,000 common shares to the underwriting company selling the stock.
15	Paid the dividends declared on July 9.
25	Owners of 6,000 shares of preferred stock converted their shares into common stock. Preferred dividends are not payable on preferred stock that is converted to common shares.
Sept. 10	Issued 10,000 shares of a new Class B $50 par, 9%, non-convertible preferred stock. The new preferred stock was sold to an underwriter at a price of $103 per share less a 7% commission.
Oct. 18	The board of directors declared a $150,000 quarterly cash dividend to stockholders of record on September 30, payable on November 5.

Your Questions?

It is *very* important to be aware of what you need to understand better. What do you need to understand better about this learning goal? On a separate piece of paper, write the questions that you want to discuss with your classmates, instructor, or supervisor. Try to be very specific about what is bothering you, such as explanations that you do not fully understand.

LEARNING GOAL 30

More Paid-in Capital and Retained Earnings Transactions

In Learning Goal 30, you will find:

Paid-in Capital Changes

Retained Earnings Changes

Treasury Stock

Definition

Treasury stock is stock that a company has issued and later purchased from investors, so that the stock is no longer outstanding. Treasury stock can be described as stock that is issued but not outstanding (no longer owned by investors).

Why It Happens

A company will purchase some of its own stock for several business reasons:

- The company hopes to purchase the stock at a low price and resell the shares at a higher price. In that way, the business can obtain more capital than it had at the time the shares were purchased without issuing any new shares.
- Reducing the outstanding shares also tends to reduce the amount by which the market price of the stock will decline, which makes investors happy.
- The company is trying to prevent another party from buying enough shares to control the company and change the management.
- The company may want additional shares of stock available for other purposes such as issuing stock to employees or using stock to purchase another company.

continued ▶

Treasury Stock, *continued*

Sale Above Cost

Greenville Company sells 500 shares of treasury stock at $30 per share.

Account	Debit	Credit
Cash	15,000	
Treasury Stock (500 × $21)		10,500
Paid-in Capital from Treasury Stock		4,500

Sale Below Cost

Greenville Company sells the remaining 400 shares at $18 per share.

Account	Debit	Credit
Cash	7,200	
Paid-in Capital from Treasury Stock	1,200	
Treasury Stock (400 × $21)		8,400

Key Points

- Gain or loss is not recorded. Sales above and below cost are just expansions and contractions of paid-in capital from investors.
- When treasury stock is sold above cost, Paid-in Capital from Treasury Stock is credited for the difference above cost. Paid-in Capital from Treasury Stock is a source of capital that is shown as part of the paid-in capital section of stockholders' equity.
- When treasury stock is sold below cost, Paid-in Capital from Treasury Stock is debited for the difference below cost. If there is not a sufficient balance in this account Retained Earnings is debited.
- Each time that treasury stock is sold there is an increase in cash and an increase in total stockholders' equity. Total stockholders' equity increases by the amount of the cash received.

Other Methods

The method illustrated here is called the *cost method*, and it is the most popular technique for recording treasury stock transactions. However, other methods are also used, some of which are required by state laws.

Multiple Purchases

If there have been multiple purchases of treasury stock, simply use the total cost divided by the total treasury shares for the average cost per share of the treasury stock. This will change as treasury shares are bought and sold.

Retirement of Stock

Overview

A corporation can also purchase shares of its stock for the purpose of permanently canceling the shares so they can never be reissued. This stock is called ***retired stock***. When stock is retired, the related stock and paid-in capital accounts are reduced. For example, if one-third of the preferred stock is retired, the journal entry includes a debit to Preferred Stock and a debit to Paid-in Capital in Excess of Par, Preferred for one-third the amount in each account. Any difference between the cash paid and the reduction of the stock accounts is debited or credited to Retained Earnings.

Example

The stockholders' equity section of Trenton Enterprises balance sheet is shown below. Assume that the company pays stockholders $9 per share to retire 100,000 shares (one-half) of its common stock.

Stockholders' Equity

Paid-in capital		
Preferred stock $100 par, 7%, 10,000 shares issued	$1,000,000	
Paid-in capital in excess of par, preferred	95,000	$1,095,000
Common stock $.10 par value, 200,000 shares issued	20,000	
Paid-in capital in excess of par, common	1,550,000	1,570,000
Total paid-in capital		2,665,000
Retained earnings		720,000
Total stockholders' equity		$3,385,000

The general journal entry is:

Common Stock ($20,000 × 100,000/200,000)	10,000	
Paid-in Capital in Excess of Par, Common ($1,550,000 × 100,000/200,000)	775,000	
Retained Earnings ($900,000 – $785,000)	115,000	
Cash (100,000 shares × $9)		900,000

Check Your Understanding

Write the completed sentences on a separate piece of paper.

Treasury Stock is a ········ ········ type of account. When treasury stock is purchased, total stockholders' equity ········ (increases/decreases). When treasury stock is sold, total stockholders' equity ········. Legal capital ········ (is/is not) affected. When treasury stock is sold, gain or loss ········ (is/is not) recorded. A purchase or sale of treasury stock changes the number of shares ········.

If 1,000 shares of treasury stock costing $12 per share were sold for $10 per share, the total increase in stockholders' equity would be $········. If 1,000 shares of treasury stock costing $12 per share were sold for $15 per share, the total increase in stockholders' equity would be $········. Prepare the correct journal entry for this transaction.

Answers

Treasury Stock is a contra equity type of account. When treasury stock is purchased, total stockholders' equity decreases (increases/decreases). When treasury stock is sold, total stockholders' equity increases. Legal capital is not (is/is not) affected. When treasury stock is sold, gain or loss is not (is/is not) recorded. A purchase or sale of treasury stock changes the number of shares outstanding.

If 1,000 shares of treasury stock costing $12 per share were sold for $10 per share, the total increase in stockholders' equity would be $10,000. If 1,000 shares of treasury stock costing $12 per share were sold for $15 per share, the total increase in stockholders' equity would be $15,000.

Cash	15,000	
Treasury Stock		12,000
Paid-in Capital from Treasury Stock Transactions		3,000

Stock Dividends

Definition

A ***stock dividend*** is a proportional distribution by a corporation of shares of its own stock to existing stockholders, with no change in par or stated value.

Example

Portland Corporation has 50,000 shares outstanding and declares a 5,000 share (10%) stock dividend. An investor who owns 500 shares will receive 50 (10%) more shares. Before the dividend the investor owned 1% of total shares (5,000/50,000 = 1%) and after the dividend the investor still owns 1% of total shares (5,500/55,000 = 1%). Each stockholder maintains the same percentage ownership as before the dividend.

Stock Dividends, *continued*

Effects of a Stock Dividend

A stock dividend has the following effects:

- The number of outstanding shares increases, but authorized shares do not.
- Some retained earnings are permanently transformed into paid-in capital.
- There is no change in total stockholders' equity.
- There is no change in par or stated value.

Why Stock Dividends Are Declared

A corporation may have several possible business reasons for stock dividends.

- Stock dividends conserve cash, yet still offer something to stockholders.
- Large stock dividends over the long term will reduce the market price of stock. This may be desirable if the stock is trading at a high price and the corporation wishes to make the stock more affordable to smaller investors.
- The corporation may wish to increase the paid-in capital by reducing retained earnings, which makes less retained earnings available for cash dividends.

Rules for Recording Stock Dividends

If . . .	**then . . .**
the dividend is less than approximately 20 to 25% of the shares outstanding prior to the declaration (small dividend) . . .	use the ***market value*** per share of the stock, multiplied by the shares outstanding.
the dividend is 25% or more than the shares outstanding prior to the declaration (large dividend) . . .	use the ***par or stated value*** per share of the stock,* multiplied by the shares outstanding.

* Values for no-par stock vary, depending on state law.

continued ▶

Stock Dividends, *continued*

Examples: Calculate Value

Assume that the board of directors of Arlington Corporation declares a stock dividend. Prior to the declaration 100,000 shares are outstanding with a par value of $.10 per share. The stock was originally issued at $5 per share. The current market value of the stock is $9 per share, and retained earnings is $200,000.

- **Example 1:** Assume that the stock dividend is 15,000 shares. The value to record is: 15,000 × $9 = $135,000 (small stock dividend).
- **Example 2:** Assume that the stock dividend is 30,000 shares. The value to record is: 30,000 × $.10 = $3,000 (large stock dividend).

Journal Entries

The journal entries for a stock dividend are recorded in two steps:

Step 1: Record the declaration.
Step 2: Record the distribution.

- **Example 1:** Assume in the first example that Arlington Corporation declared the dividend on September 15, and the stock is distributed on October 1.

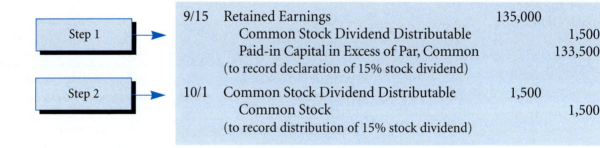

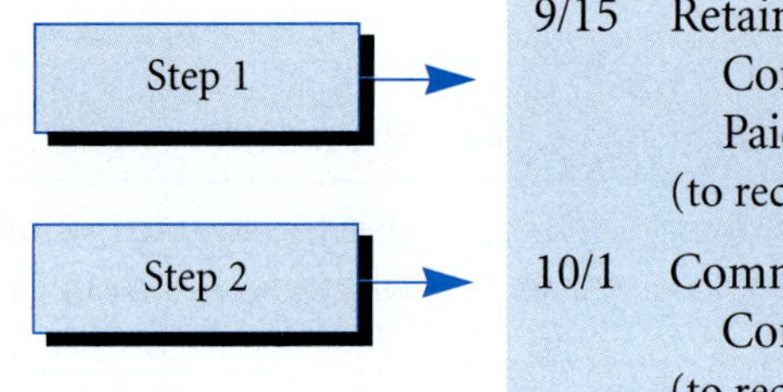

9/15	Retained Earnings	135,000	
	Common Stock Dividend Distributable		1,500
	Paid-in Capital in Excess of Par, Common		133,500
	(to record declaration of 15% stock dividend)		
10/1	Common Stock Dividend Distributable	1,500	
	Common Stock		1,500
	(to record distribution of 15% stock dividend)		

- **Example 2:** Assume the same dates in the second example.

9/15	Retained Earnings	3,000	
	Common Stock Dividend Distributable		3,000
	(to record declaration of 30% stock dividend)		
10/1	Common Stock Dividend Distributable	3,000	
	Common Stock		3,000
	(to record distribution of 30% stock dividend)		

Large stock dividends are infrequent. Instead of large stock dividends, stock splits are declared by boards of directors.

Stock Dividends, *continued*

Analysis

The ***Common Stock Distributable*** account is a stockholders' equity account; it is not a liability. The purpose of the account is to show the legal capital created when the stock dividend was declared. When the stock is actually distributed, the amount is permanently reclassified into the Common Stock account.

Using Example 1 from the prior page, the paid-in capital section on the balance sheet before the distribution of shares is:

Stockholders' Equity		
Paid-in capital		
Common stock	$ 10,000	(100,000 × $.10)
Paid-in capital in excess of par	**623,500**	(100,000 × $4.90 + $133,500)
Common Stock Distributable	**1,500**	(15,000 × $.10)
Total paid-in capital	635,000	

A stock dividend causes **no change in total stockholders' equity**. Notice that in both journal entry examples, an amount of retained earnings was simply moved into paid-in capital. This is because most state laws view additional shares issued as an increase in legal capital and paid-in capital. GAAP provides us with general rules for what values to use on financial statements, although exact amounts may vary by state law.

From Example 1: Small Stock Dividend

	Before Dividend	**After Distribution**
Stockholders' Equity		
Paid-in capital		
Common Stock, $.10 par	**$ 10,000**	**$ 11,500**
Paid-in capital in excess of par	**490,000**	**623,500**
Total paid-in capital	500,000	635,000
Retained earnings	**200,000**	**65,000**
Total stockholders' equity	$700,000	$700,000
Total outstanding shares	**100,000**	**115,000**

NO CHANGE!

No Change in Business Value

Issuing a stock dividend has no effect on the value of the business that is issuing the stock. All that has happened is that some amount has been permanently transferred out of retained earnings into paid-in capital. Retained earnings is decreased and paid-in capital accounts are increased.

continued ▶

Stock Splits

Definition

A ***stock split*** is a simultaneous increase in the number of shares issued and a decrease in the par or stated value per share.

Effects of a Stock Split

A stock split has the following effects:

- The number of shares issued increases. This includes shares held in treasury as well as outstanding shares. Total authorized shares do not change.
- The par (or stated) value per share is reduced, but total par value is unchanged.
- Stockholders receive new shares that replace all the old shares.
- The market price of the stock usually decreases because of the increased number of new shares outstanding.
- If a split exceeds the total authorized shares, the board of directors must obtain approval from shareholders and state authorities for more authorized shares.

Why Stock Splits Are Declared

- Stock splits generally involve more shares than a stock dividend and do not reduce retained earnings.
- Stock splits conserve cash for the company yet still make the stockholders feel better because they have received more shares.
- Stock splits, over the long term, will reduce the market price of stock. This may be desirable if the stock is trading at a high price and the corporation wishes to make the shares more affordable to smaller investors.

Journal Entry

A stock split has no effect on the balances of stockholders' equity accounts. Therefore, no journal entry is needed. A notation can be made indicating the change in the par value and the change in the issued and outstanding shares.

TIP

A reverse stock split? You see below an illustration of various stock split examples. One of the examples shows a *decrease* in the number of shares! Does this really happen? Yes, sometimes companies that are in trouble try to increase their stock prices by decreasing the number of outstanding shares. It rarely works for very long.

Stock Splits, *continued*

Examples

The reason that a stock split has no effect on total stockholders' equity is illustrated by the following table showing several split examples. Notice that total par value remains unchanged. Assume that a corporation has 18,000 common shares of $.10 par value stock issued.

	Par Value	×	Shares Issued	=	Total $ Par Value
Before split	$ .10		18,000		$1,800
2 for 1 split	.05		36,000		1,800
3 for 2 split	.0667		27,000		1,800
4 for 3 split	.075		24,000		1,800
1 for 2 split	.20		9,000		1,800

The last example, called a *reverse split*, increases the par value and decreases the number of issued shares. *Calculations:* Multiply the previous number of shares by the split ratio and the previous par value by the reciprocal of the split ratio. For example, (3/2) × 18,000 = 27,000 new shares, and (2/3) × $.10 = .0667 new par value.

Comparison of Effects

The table below compares the effects of stock dividends and stock splits.

Item	Stock Dividend	Stock Split
■ Total stockholders' equity	No change	No change
■ Total paid-in capital	Increase	No change
■ Total retained earnings	Decrease	No change
■ Total par or stated value	Increase	No change
■ Par or stated value per share	No change	Decrease
■ Total shares outstanding	Increase	Increase
■ Total treasury shares	No change	Increase
■ Total shares authorized	No change	No change*
■ Taxable income to stockholder	None	None

* Unless stockholders vote to authorize more shares needed

Effect on Ownership Percentages

As with a stock dividend, each investor maintains the same percentage ownership before and after a stock split. For example, assume that Vancouver Corporation has 80,000 shares outstanding and declares a 2 for 1 stock split. An investor who owned 800 shares of stock will now own 1,600 shares. Before the split, the investor owned 1% of total shares (800/80,000 = 1%), and after the split the investor still owns 1% of total shares (1,600/160,000 = 1%). Each stockholder retains the same percentage ownership as before the split.

continued ▶

Stock Splits, *continued*

Effect on Stock Price

As with a stock dividend, the decrease in the market price per share of the stock should be the reciprocal of the increase in shares. For example, if a stock is trading at $40, a 2 for 1 split should reduce the price to ($40 × 1/2) = $20. Because a stock split usually involves many more shares than a stock dividend, this price decrease per share is more likely. However, as with a stock dividend, the price change can be unpredictable. Investors usually perceive a stock split the same way they perceive a stock dividend—as something favorable, despite the fact that they have not received cash or any other asset.

As with a stock dividend, a stock split often occurs when a company wants to conserve cash—which can be the reason for a stock split instead of a cash dividend. Investors should remember that a split will reduce the rate of future share price increases compared to what would have happened if no stock split had occurred.

Retained Earnings

Definition

Retained earnings is the part of the stockholders' equity claim that is the cumulative amount of net income *minus* net losses and dividends. Retained earnings can also be affected by stockholders' equity transactions.

Features

- Retained earnings is not a claim on any particular asset, including cash. **Retained earnings has no relationship to the amount in the cash account and is not equivalent to cash.**
- The retained earnings account has a normal credit balance.
- Retained earnings can also be negative (debit balance) if the total net losses have exceeded the total of net income. This condition is sometimes called a ***deficit in retained earnings***.

Availability for Dividends

The availability of retained earnings for dividends can be limited for various reasons. A ***restriction on retained earnings*** makes an amount of retained earnings unavailable for dividends and is disclosed in footnotes.

An ***appropriation of retained earnings*** makes an amount of retained earnings unavailable for dividends and records the limitation by use of a journal entry that debits retained earnings and credits a separate "appropriated" retained earnings account. An appropriation is removed by reversing the journal entry—debit the appropriated retained earnings and credit retained earnings. Appropriations are infrequent.

Retained Earnings, *continued*

Reasons for Restricting or Appropriating Retained Earnings

Restrictions and appropriations can happen for a number of reasons. Here are some frequently occurring reasons:

- Loan agreements: A bank loan or other debt agreement may limit the amount of dividends that can be paid. This makes it more likely that the debt will be repaid.
- State laws: Many states require a retained earnings restriction for some portion of stock held as treasury stock. This is done to preserve legal capital.
- Various business reasons: The board of directors may vote to restrict retained earnings if large cash payments are anticipated, such as for business expansion.

All of the items above require disclosure in the financial statement footnotes.

Prior Period Adjustments

The net income or net loss of each accounting period flows into retained earnings when the books are closed at the end of a period. A ***prior period adjustment*** is a correction of a revenue or expense error made in a prior accounting period after the books for that period have been closed. Because the net income or net loss has flowed into retained earnings, the correction of a prior period error is made directly to retained earnings.

- *Rule:* If a material revenue or expense error from a prior period is discovered in the current period, record the retained earnings correction and show it as an adjustment to the beginning balance of retained earnings in the current period (as well as an entry to whatever other balance sheet account is also affected by the error). A prior period adjustment also requires that previous financial statements affected by the error be restated.

- *Example:* In 2017, Chicopee Corporation discovered an error from 2016 that understated 2016 revenue by $200,000 as well as understating the accounts receivable. In 2017, Chicopee Corporation should record a $200,000 increase to retained earnings (credit) and a $200,000 increase to accounts receivable. The $200,000 increase to retained earnings is shown on the statement of retained earnings as a correction to the beginning balance.

continued ►

Retained Earnings, *continued*

Change in Accounting Principle

A ***change in accounting principle*** is a change from a currently used generally accepted accounting principle to a different generally accepted accounting principle. For example, GAAP rules permit different ways to value merchandise inventory and to calculate cost of goods sold expense. In each case, a different amount of net income will be the result.

A change in accounting principle can only be made if (1) management can justify that the new principle will result in better financial reporting than the old principle or (2) if the change is required by a pronouncement from the Financial Accounting Standards Board (FASB).

- *Rule:* Determine the accumulated effect of applying the new principle for all prior accounting periods that are affected, and record this amount as a revision to the beginning balance of retained earnings (as well as an entry to whatever other balance sheet account is also affected by the change). A change in accounting principle also requires that previous financial statements affected by the change be restated.
- *Example:* In 2017, Brockton Company makes a change in the way it accounts for inventory; this qualifies as a change in accounting principle. The change in principle has a cumulative effect of decreasing the prior three years' net income by $100,000 and reduces the value of merchandise inventory by the same amount. Brockton Company should record a $100,000 decrease to retained earnings (debit) and a $100,000 decrease to the merchandise inventory asset.

What Affects the Retained Earnings Account

The table below summarizes the main categories of debit and credit items that affect the retained earnings account. Debit items reduce retained earnings and credit items increase retained earnings. The normal balance in retained earnings is a credit balance. However, if cumulative losses have exceeded income, retained earnings will have a debit balance. This is called a *deficit in retained earnings.*

Retained Earnings	
Debit items:	*Credit items:*
▪ Net loss ▪ Cash and stock dividends ▪ Prior period adjustments for errors that overstated income ▪ Accumulated prior effect of change in accounting principle (reduced income) ▪ Some sales of treasury stock below cost	▪ Net income ▪ Prior period adjustments for errors that understated income ▪ Accumulated prior effect of change in accounting principle (increased income)

Retained Earnings, *continued*

Statement of Retained Earnings

A ***statement of retained earnings*** summarizes all the current period changes in retained earnings and shows a final balance that is exactly the same amount as on the balance sheet. The primary source of the information for the statement is an analysis of the retained earnings account.

Example

The example below illustrates a statement of retained earnings that includes beginning balance revisions for a prior period adjustment and a change in accounting principle.

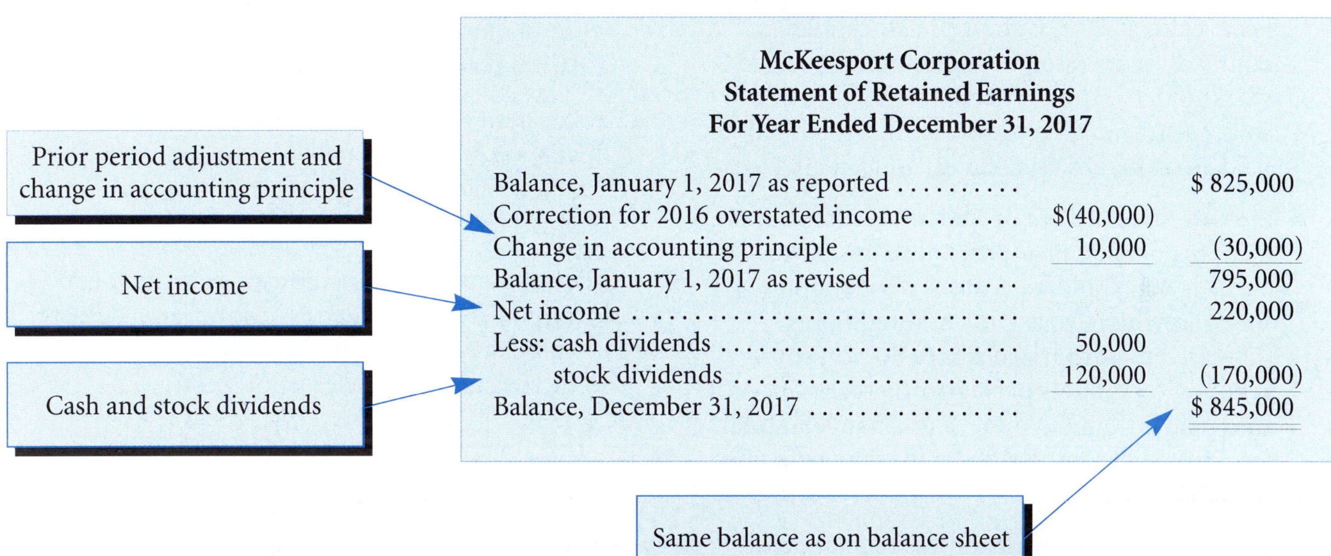

McKeesport Corporation
Statement of Retained Earnings
For Year Ended December 31, 2017

Balance, January 1, 2017 as reported		$ 825,000
Correction for 2016 overstated income	$(40,000)	
Change in accounting principle	10,000	(30,000)
Balance, January 1, 2017 as revised		795,000
Net income		220,000
Less: cash dividends	50,000	
stock dividends	120,000	(170,000)
Balance, December 31, 2017		$ 845,000

Note: If comparative statements of retained earnings are presented, the revision should be made to the beginning balance of the first period presented.

QUICK REVIEW

- Treasury stock purchases can occur for several reasons, such as: Selling the treasury stock later at a higher price to obtain more capital; reducing outstanding shares so the market price of the stock will not decline; reducing shares available to unfriendly third parties; and using the stock for other purposes such as employee stock.
- Treasury stock is recorded at cost. Treasury stock is never an asset; it is shown in stockholders' equity as a contra-equity amount that reduces stockholders' equity. When treasury stock is sold, gains and losses are never recorded; only paid-in capital or retained earnings is affected.
- A stock dividend is a proportional distribution by a corporation of additional shares of stock to existing stockholders. A stock dividend has the following effects: Outstanding shares increase but authorized shares do not; some retained earnings is permanently reclassified into paid-in capital; there is no change in total stockholders' equity; there is no change in par or stated value.
- For a small stock dividend (less than approximately 20 to 25% of outstanding shares) market value is used. For a large stock dividend (25% or more of outstanding shares) the par or stated value is used.
- A stock split is a simultaneous decrease in par or stated value and a proportional increase in the number of shares. A stock split has the following effects: The per-share par or stated value is reduced; the number of issued and outstanding shares increases in the same proportion as the change in the par or stated value; stockholders receive new shares; the market price usually decreases because of the number of new shares outstanding.
- No journal entry is required to record a stock split because the balances in stockholders' equity do not change.
- Retained earnings is the part of the stockholders' equity that represents the cumulative amount of net income that is still retained in the business, less certain transactions or adjustments. Retained earnings has no relationship to the amount in the cash account and is not equivalent to cash. Also, retained earnings is not a claim on any specific asset.
- The amount of retained earnings available for dividends can be limited by a restriction on retained earnings as well as an appropriation of retained earnings.
- Items that affect retained earnings include net income, net loss, dividends, prior period adjustments, change in accounting principle, and some treasury stock sales below cost.
- The statement of retained earnings summarizes all the current period changes in retained earnings and shows exactly the same final balance of retained earnings as on the balance sheet.

VOCABULARY

Appropriation of retained earnings: a limitation on the use of retained earnings to pay dividends, recorded by a journal entry into a separate retained earnings account (page 616)

Change in accounting principle: a change from a currently used, generally accepted accounting principle to a different generally accepted accounting principle (page 618)

Common stock distributable: an account that shows the legal capital amount of stock that has been subscribed but not yet fully paid for (page 611)

Contra equity account: an account that has a debit balance and acts as an offset against the total of the balances in other stockholder equity accounts (page 604)

Deficit in retained earnings: a debit balance in retained earnings (page 616)

Outstanding shares: shares of stock held by stockholders (page 604)

Prior period adjustment: an entry to retained earnings to correct an accounting error of a prior period (page 617)

Restriction on retained earnings: a limitation on the use of retained earnings to pay dividends, usually reported in the footnotes to financial statements (page 616)

Retained earnings: the part of the stockholders' equity claim that comes from the cumulative amount of net income since the business was formed, *minus:* net losses, dividends, and some treasury stock transactions (page 616)

Retired stock: stock that has been repurchased by a corporation, cancelled, permanently removed from paid-in capital, and never reissued (page 607)

Statement of retained earnings: a financial statement that summarizes all the current period changes in retained earnings (page 619)

Stock dividend: a proportional distribution by a corporation of shares of its own stock to existing stockholders, with no change in par or stated value (page 608)

Stock split: a simultaneous decrease in the par value or stated value of stock and a proportional increase in the number of shares (page 614)

Treasury stock: stock that a company has issued and then repurchased, so the stock is no longer outstanding (page 603)

Do You Want More Examples?

Most problems in this book have detailed solutions. To use them as additional examples, do this: 1) Select the type of problem you want 2) Open the solution on your computer or mobile device screen (from the disc or worthyjames.com) 3) Read one item at a time and look at its answer. Take notes if needed. 4) Close the solution and work as much of the problem as you can. 5) Repeat as needed.

PRACTICE Learning Goal 30

Solutions are in the disk at the back of the book and at: www.worthyjames.com

This learning goal is about paid-in capital and retained earnings transactions. Use these questions and problems to practice what you have just read.

Multiple Choice

Select the best answer.

1. Which of the following is *not* a reason for a corporation to purchase treasury stock?
   a. diminish or prevent decreases in the market price of the company's stock
   b. prevent another party from acquiring enough shares to get control of the business
   c. purchase shares at a higher price and reissue them at a lower price for paid-in capital
   d. use the shares for other purposes such as employee stock options
2. Which of the following best describes the treasury stock account?
   a. a contra equity account that reduces the amount of retained earnings shown in the stockholders' equity
   b. a contra equity account that is usually shown separately as a reduction in total stockholders' equity
   c. a type of retained earnings that increases total retained earnings when the treasury stock increases in value
   d. a paid-in capital account used when a stock dividend has been declared
3. Shares of treasury stock are
   a. increased when there is a stock split.
   b. increased when there is a stock dividend.
   c. entitled to receive all dividends.
   d. all of the above.
4. A treasury stock purchase
   a. reduces the number of outstanding shares but not the issued shares.
   b. has no effect on the legal capital.
   c. reduces the total stockholders' equity.
   d. all of the above.
5. When a company sells treasury stock, the journal entry can include a
   a. debit to Retained Earnings.
   b. a credit to Paid-in Capital in Excess of Par from Treasury Stock.
   c. credit to Treasury Stock.
   d. all of the above.
6. When stock is retired
   a. the amount retired is shown as a single reduction in total stockholders' equity.
   b. the paid-in capital accounts are permanently reduced.
   c. legal capital is permanently reduced.
   d. all of the above.
7. A stock dividend
   a. increases the number of issued and outstanding shares.
   b. increases the total stockholders' equity.
   c. reduces the par value per share of stock.
   d. all of the above.
8. A stock split
   a. increases the number of issued and outstanding shares.
   b. does not affect the total authorized shares.
   c. reduces the par value per share of stock.
   d. all of the above.

PRACTICE Learning Goal 30, continued

Solutions are in the disk at the back of the book and at: www.worthyjames.com

9. Komail Corporation had 1,000 shares of $1 par value common stock held as treasury stock and the stock had been purchased for $20 per share. The company then sold 500 of the shares for $24 per share. Because of the sale, the total stockholders' equity will
   a. increase by $500.
   b. increase by $2,000.
   c. increase by $10,000.
   d. increase by $12,000.
10. For a small stock dividend, the value to use for calculating the amount of the dividend is the
    a. par value per share.
    b. stated value per share.
    c. market value per share.
    d. book value per share.
11. How would a stock dividend and a stock split affect total stockholders' equity?

	Stock Dividend	*Stock Split*
a.	No effect	Decrease
b.	Decrease	No effect
c.	Increase	Decrease
d.	No effect	No effect

12. How would a 10% stock dividend affect retained earnings and paid-in capital?

	Retained Earnings	*Paid-in Capital*
a.	Decrease	Decrease
b.	Decrease	Increase
c.	Increase	Decrease
d.	No effect	No effect

13. How would issuing $1 par value treasury stock at a price $5 above cost affect Treasury Stock, Common Stock, and Paid-in Capital in Excess of Par From Treasury Stock?

	Treasury Stock	*Common Stock*	*Paid-in Capital in Excess of Par*
a.	Decrease	Increase	Increase
b.	Increase	Decrease	Decrease
c.	Decrease	Increase	No effect
d.	No effect	No effect	No effect

14. After a 3 for 1 stock split, the total par value amount in stockholders' equity is
    a. three times the pre-split amount.
    b. one-third the pre-split amount.
    c. twice the pre-split amount.
    d. unchanged.
15. Maxwell, Inc. declared a 3 for 2 stock split. Before the split, the company had 90,000 shares of $.15 par value common stock outstanding. After the split,
    a. the par value will be $.075 and the total shares will be 180,000.
    b. the par value will be $.10 and the total shares will be 135,000.
    c. the par value will be $.025 and the total shares will be 540,000.
    d. the par value will be $.05 and the total shares will be 450,000.
16. Which of the statements below is correct?
    a. A stock dividend increases total stockholders' equity, but a stock split does not.
    b. Neither a stock dividend nor a stock split affects the total par value in paid-in capital.
    c. Neither a stock dividend nor a stock split affects the total stockholders' equity.
    d. Both a stock dividend and a stock split require a reduction in retained earnings.

PRACTICE Learning Goal 30, continued

Solutions are in the disk at the back of the book and at: www.worthyjames.com

13. Why would a board of directors declare a stock dividend instead of a cash dividend?

14. Explain the differences between a small stock dividend and a large stock dividend. What is the effect on stockholders' equity accounts?

15. Under what circumstances do you think a board of directors would decide to declare a stock split instead of a stock dividend?

16. What kind of account is "treasury stock"?

17. Miles Corporation currently has outstanding 120,000 shares of $1 par value common stock. Show the effect on par value per share, total par value, and total outstanding shares of each the following stock splits: 2 for 1, 3 for 1, 3 for 2, 4 for 3, and a reverse split of 1 for 2.

18. Travon Fuller owns 1,000 shares of Maples Corporation stock. There are 50,000 shares of stock outstanding, and the stock is currently selling for $27 per share. The company declared a 15% stock dividend. How many shares will Travon own after the dividend? What is his percentage ownership in the company before and after the dividend? Estimate the price of the stock after the dividend.

19. What factors determine the amount of cash dividends that a board of directors can declare?

20. What is a deficit in retained earnings? What causes it?

21. On a separate piece of paper (so that you can use this exercise again), complete the following table that compares the effects of stock dividends and stock splits. Enter "no change," "increase," or "decrease" as appropriate for each item.

Item	Stock Dividend	Stock Split
a. Total stockholders' equity	....	....
b. Total paid-in capital	....	....
c. Total retained earnings	....	....
d. Total par or stated value	....	....
e. Par or stated value per share	....	....
f. Total shares issued	....	....
g. Total shares authorized	....	....
h. Taxable income to stockholder	....	....

PRACTICE Learning Goal 30, continued

Solutions are in the disk at the back of the book and at: www.worthyjames.com

Reinforcement Problems

LG 30-1. Prepare stockholders' equity section of a balance sheet. Shown below are various account balances and additional information for Crescent City Corporation for the year ended December 31, 2017. Select the necessary account balances and information and prepare the stockholders' equity section of the balance sheet at December 31, 2017.

Account	$	Account	$
Paid-in capital in excess of par-common	3,790,000	Paid-in capital in excess of par-preferred	100,000
Cash	890,000	Treasury stock	30,000
Common stock	25,000	Notes payable	1,100,000
Preferred stock	3,750,000	Retained earnings	522,300
		Paid-in capital from treasury stock transactions	27,000

Additional information:

- Common stock: $.10 par, 250,000 shares issued and 247,500 shares outstanding
- Preferred stock: $50 par, 3%, 75,000 shares issued and outstanding.
- Treasury stock: 2,500 shares at cost.

LG 30-2. Analyze stockholders' equity. The stockholders' equity section of the Gilroy Corporation balance sheet is shown below.

Gilroy Corporation
Balance Sheet (partial)
March 31, 2017

Stockholders' Equity	
Paid-in capital	
Common stock, $.05 par, 100,000 shares issued, 90,000 shares outstanding	$ 5,000
Paid-in capital in excess of par, common	872,000
Total paid-in capital	877,000
Retained earnings	985,000
Total paid-in capital and retained earnings	1,862,000
Less: Treasury stock, common (10,000 shares at cost)	(70,000)
Total stockholders equity	$1,792,000

Answer the following questions:

a. What is the total stockholders' equity after declaration of a 10% stock dividend when the market price of the stock is $8 per share?
b. What are the account balances of the accounts affected by the declaration of the above dividend?
c. How many shares are issued and how many shares are outstanding after the stock dividend is distributed?
d. After the stock dividend, Gilroy Corporation declared and distributed a 2 for 1 stock split. How many shares are issued and outstanding after the stock split?
e. What is the total stockholders' equity after the stock split?

PRACTICE — Learning Goal 30, continued

Solutions are in the disk at the back of the book and at: www.worthyjames.com

LG 30-9, *continued*

April 20	The board of directors declared a 40,000 share common stock dividend. At the time of the dividend, the common stock was selling for $30 per share.
May 17	Distributed the shares for the common stock dividend.
July 8	The board of directors declared a $350,000 semi-annual cash dividend.
Aug. 17	Paid the cash dividends.
23	Sold 2,000 shares of the treasury stock at a price of $23 per share. (There is no balance in a Paid-in Capital from Treasury Stock Transactions account.)
Sept. 19	The board of directors declared and distributed a 3 for 2 split of the common stock.
Oct. 21	Sold 1,000 shares of treasury stock at a price of $22 per share.
Nov. 30	Recorded a prior period adjustment for inventory errors that had overstated expenses and understated the net income by $352,000 during the prior five years. (The error resulted in understated inventory, so the adjustment will also increase the Inventory account.)

Other information: The January 1 Retained Earnings balance was $2,740,000. Current year operations have resulted in a net loss for the year of $284,000.

LG 30-10. Journalize transactions, prepare a statement of retained earnings, prepare stockholders' equity section of balance sheet. During 2017, Evanston, Inc. completed the stockholders' equity transactions shown below. The December 31, 2016 stockholders' equity section of the balance sheet provides additional information.

a. Prepare the general journal entries to record the listed transactions. (For journal paper, you can make general journal copies from the disk at the back of this book or from the 'student info.' link at www.worthyjames.com.)

b. Create T accounts for stockholders' equity accounts, enter the beginning balances, and post the journal entries that affect stockholders' equity into the T accounts. Also, prepare tables that record the number of shares of common stock, treasury stock, and preferred stock.

c. Using the balances from the T accounts, prepare the December 31, 2017 statement of retained earnings.

d. Using the balances from the T accounts, prepare the December 31, 2017 stockholders' equity section of the balance sheet.

e. Do you think that common stockholder dilution occurred during the year? Discuss.

Evanston, Inc.
Balance Sheet (partial)
December 31, 2016

Stockholders' Equity	
Paid-in capital	
Preferred stock, no par; $5; 130,000 shares issued and outstanding	$ 1,365,000
Common stock, no par, 200,000 shares issued and outstanding	5,400,000
Total paid-in capital	6,765,000
Retained earnings	8,210,000
Total stockholders equity	$14,975,000

PRACTICE **Learning Goal 30, continued**

Solutions are in the disk at the back of the book and at: www.worthyjames.com

LG 30-10, *continued*

Transactions:

Jan. 4	The board of directors of Evanston, Inc. declared a semi-annual cash dividend of $500,000. (Use separate Dividends Payable accounts for preferred and common dividends.)
Feb. 18	Paid the cash dividend.
March 9	Sold 50,000 new common shares at $28 per share.
April 3	Purchased 15,000 shares of common stock as treasury stock for $22 per share.
June 8	The board of directors declared a 10% stock dividend on the common stock outstanding. The stock had a market price of $30 per share.
July 7	Distributed the shares from the June 8 stock dividend declaration.
11	The board of directors of Evanston, Inc. declared a semi-annual cash dividend of $375,000.
Aug. 20	Paid the cash dividend.
Sept. 9	Sold 5,000 treasury shares for $140,000.
Oct. 15	Accountants discovered errors that overstated revenue by $250,000 for the two prior years. (Reduce the asset Short-Term Investments).
Dec. 2	Sold 8,000 treasury shares for $17 per share.

Other information: Evanston, Inc. earned $414,000 net income for the year.

LG 30-11. Cumulative problem. This problem contains transactions discussed in Learning Goals 29 and 30. During 2017, Minneapolis Corporation completed the selected transactions shown below. The December 31, 2016 stockholders' equity provides additional information.

a. Prepare the general journal entries to record the listed transactions. (For journal paper, you can make general journal copies from the disk at the back of this book or from the 'student info.' link at www.worthyjames.com.)
b. Create T accounts for stockholders' equity accounts and enter the beginning balances. Post the journal entries that affect stockholders' equity into the T accounts. Also, prepare tables to record the balance of the common shares outstanding, treasury shares, and preferred shares outstanding.
c. Using the balances from the T accounts, prepare the December 31, 2017 statement of retained earnings.
d. Using the balances from the T accounts, prepare the December 31, 2017 stockholders' equity section of the balance sheet.

PRACTICE **Learning Goal 30, continued**

Solutions are in the disk at the back of the book and at: www.worthyjames.com

LG 30-11, *continued*

Minneapolis Corporation
Balance Sheet (partial)
December 31, 2016

Stockholders' Equity		
Paid-in capital		
Preferred stock, $50 par, 9%, 40,000 shares issued and outstanding	$2,000,000	
Paid-in capital in excess of par	100,000	$ 2,100,000
Common stock, $1 par, 250,000 shares issued, 240,000 outstanding	250,000	
Paid-in capital in excess of par	8,750,000	9,000,000
Total paid-in capital		11,100,000
Retained earnings		15,980,000
Total paid-in capital and retained earnings		27,080,000
Less: treasury stock, common (10,000 shares, at cost)		(220,000)
Total stockholders' equity		$26,860,000

Transactions:

Jan. 4 The board of directors of Minneapolis Corporation declared a semi-annual cash dividend of $600,000. (Use separate Dividends Payable accounts for preferred and common dividends.)

Feb. 14 Paid the cash dividend.

March 7 Issued an additional 102,000 shares of common stock, using an underwriting company. The underwriter set the selling price at $40 per share and purchased all 102,000 shares from the company at this price, less a $280,000 underwriting fee.

May 11 Owners of 8,000 shares of preferred stock converted their shares into common shares at 4 shares of common for each preferred share. Preferred dividends are not payable on preferred stock that is converted to common shares. The stock is actively traded at $38 per share.

June 5 The company purchased some production equipment that had a dealer asking price of $500,000 by issuing 16,000 shares of common stock to the seller, who agreed to accept the stock instead of cash. At the time of the purchase, the stock was actively traded on stock exchanges at $34 per share.

July 8 The board of directors declared a semi-annual cash dividend of $600,000. (Use separate Dividends Payable accounts for preferred and common dividends.)

August 15 Paid the cash dividend.

21 The board of directors declared a 5 for 4 stock split of common stock. The stock was issued.

Nov. 20 Discovered a prior year accounting error that did not record $120,000 of commissions that are still owed to sales employees (Commissions Payable).

PRACTICE Learning Goal 30, continued

Solutions are in the disk at the back of the book and at: www.worthyjames.com

LG 30-11, *continued*

Dec. 12 The board of directors declared a 10% stock dividend on the common stock. At the time of the declaration, the stock was selling for $40 per share. Shares will be issued in January.

Dec. 29 Sold 10,000 shares of treasury stock for $38 per share.

Other information: The preferred stock is cumulative and two years in arrears. Each share of preferred stock is convertible into 4 shares of common. The net income earned for the current year was $2,970,000.

Instructor-Assigned Problems

If you are using this book in a class, these review problems may be assigned by your instructor for homework, group assignments, class work, or other activities. Only your instructor has the solutions.

IA30-1. Prepare general journal entries; review prior period adjustment. During the year, Sonora Corporation completed the stockholders' equity transactions that are listed below.

a. Prepare general journal entries to record the transactions.
b. On which financial statement would the December 9 transaction be recorded?

2017

Jan. 4 Sonora corporation sold 10,000 shares of $50 par, 5%, preferred stock at $55 per share.At the time of the sale there had been no other preferred shares issued.

Feb.14 The company declared a 20,000 share stock dividend on it's $.10 par value common stock. At the time of the declaration the stock was selling for $25 per share and there were 250,000 common shares issued and outstanding.

Mar. 30 The company issued the shares for the stock dividend.

April 9 Purchased 10,000 shares of outstanding common stock at $30 per share. There had not been any previous treasury stock transactions.

Aug. 3 The board of directors declared an annual cash dividend of $200,000.

Oct. 26 Sold 6,000 shares of treasury stock at $25 per share.

Dec. 9 The company discovered a material accounting error from the prior year. The error caused the prior year net income and prepaid insurance to be overstated by $25,000.

IA30-2. Prepare general journal entries; maintain a record stock shares. During the year, Cupertino Corporation completed the stockholders' equity transactions that are listed below.

a. Prepare general journal entries to record the transactions.
b. Maintain a record of the number of common shares, using the following table headings:

Date	Outstanding Shares Change	Total Outstanding Shares	Total Treasury Shares	Total Issued Shares

LEARNING GOAL 31

Prepare Corporate Financial Statements

Overview of Statements

Same Basic Statements

Every type of business uses the same basic financial statements. These are the *balance sheet, statement of equity, income statement,* and *statement of cash flows.* In this section we will review the stockholders' equity of the corporate balance sheet, the statement of stockholders' equity, and the corporate income statement.

In Learning Goal 31, you will find:

Balance Sheet, Statement of Stockholders' Equity, and Income Statement

Corporate Tax

Balance Sheet

Overview

The basic idea of a corporate balance sheet is the same as a proprietorship. A corporate balance sheet shows assets (wealth) and the creditors' and owners' claims on the assets. The essential difference in a corporate balance sheet is the owners' equity. As you have already seen, this part of the balance sheet is called *stockholders' equity* or *shareholders' equity* and is subdivided into various categories. Here we will focus on the stockholders' equity part of the balance sheet.

Basic Format

The basic format of stockholders' equity consists of two major sections: paid-in capital and retained earnings. Certain designated items are shown below retained earnings—for example, treasury stock.

Example

An example of the stockholders' equity section for Lahaina Corporation's balance sheet is shown on the following page. Notice the following elements:

- Name: The name of the company is followed by the word "Corporation." Instead of "Corporation," some companies use the word "Incorporated" or also "Inc."
- Sources of paid-in capital: The paid-in capital section shows the various sources of capital obtained by the company, except for net income or loss. Par value amounts (legal capital) are also disclosed as part of the paid-in capital. In the example, the total paid-in capital is $1,182,000.
- Retained earnings shows the capital that has been retained from all the net income less net losses and that was not paid out in dividends. In the example, the total of retained earnings is $998,000.
- The example shows a treasury stock amount. This indicates that the company has reduced its outstanding stock and its stockholders' equity by purchasing 3,000 shares of its own common stock at a cost of $45,000.
- The final item, "unrealized value gain in certain securities," is an accumulated other comprehensive income item. Accumulated other comprehensive income is a measure of cumulative value changes in certain asset and liability items, which are not reportable as part of net income but that affect stockholders' equity. Comprehensive income is discussed in detail later in this section.

continued ▶

Discontinued Operations: The Income Statement Special Item

Overview

A special item is a designated category that must be reported separately from the income from continuing operations. The special item category usually appears on corporate income statements, although it could appear on non-corporate statements as well. A special item is a significant activity that creates unique or non-recurring income or losses, and cannot be considered as part of regular, recurring, operations. According to current GAAP, the only activity that meets these requirements is discontinued operations.

Discontinued Operations

Many large businesses consist of a number of separate components, each having its own distinguishable operations and cash flows. These components are typically significant operating segments of a business, such as a division that provides separate products or services, or a subsidiary company. For example, if XYZ Electronics Company consists of a computer division and a printer division and if it also owns ABC Real Estate Company, each of the three activities is a component of XYZ. The discontinued activity of any one of the three components would be a *discontinued operation.*

Rules for Reporting a Discontinued Operation

Step 1: If a component of a company that represents a major part of the company's operations is either disposed of or offered for sale, then the component is defined as a ***discontinued operation***.

Step 2: The following two elements should be reported separately under the heading of "discontinued operations":

- The operating income or loss of a discontinued operation must be shown separately, ***net of tax*** expense or tax savings ("Net of" means after subtracting.)
- Any gain or loss on the disposal of a discontinued operation must be shown separately net of tax expense or tax savings.

Discontinued Operations: The Income Statement Special Item, *continued*

Example

We will now change our example by assuming that the same data includes a discontinued operation. Assume that the company sold its hotel reservation division in the current year. Up to the date of sale, the division had operating income of $40,000. Also the net assets of the division were sold at a gain of $90,000. Lahaina Corporation paid income tax at a 30% rate. Here is the part of the income statement that would show the discontinued operations:

Lahaina Corporation
Income Statement (partial)
For the Year Ended 31, 2017

Income from continuing operations before tax		90,000
Income tax expense		27,000
Income from continuing operations		63,000
Discontinued operations		
Income from hotel reservation division of $40,000 less income tax of $12,000	28,000	
Gain on disposal of hotel reservation division of $90,000 less income tax of $27,000	63,000	91,000
Net income		$154,000

Note the name changes for "income before tax" and "net income" from the prior example. Also note the clear disclosure of the discontinued operations.

Extraordinary Gains and Losses

Overview

Extraordinary gains and losses, also called extraordinary items, are events that are both: (a) unusual and (b) infrequent. Extraordinary items are rare. The idea is that such an event is very unusual and unrelated to regular business operations. This does require some judgment. For example, the occurance of floods in some geographical areas may be unusual and infrequent but floods may occur frequently in other areas.

In general, extraordinary gains and losses result from events such as fires, floods, earthquakes, property condemnations, or foreign government expropriations. Items that are *not* extraordinary are lawsuits, write-offs of asset values, and strikes.

Rule for Reporting Extraordinary Gains and Losses

Extraordinary gains or losses should be reported as a separate line item as part of continuing operations, in the "other" category. An extraordinary gain or loss should be clearly identified by name such as "fire loss". Footnotes should contain details of the event.

Note: This is a change in GAAP. The above rule became effective for fiscal periods beginning in or after December 2015. Prior to that time, an extraordinary gain or loss was presented as a special item, treated in the same net-of-tax manner as discontinued operations, and reported under income from continuing operations. You may encounter this presentation when you review prior financial statements.

Deferred Income Tax

Overview

As you know, corporations pay income tax. Unlike a proprietorship or partnership, income tax appears as an expense in the corporate income statement.

However, GAAP income before tax on an income statement and the amount of taxable income as determined by tax rules are calculated differently for certain types of revenue and expense items. When these differences occur, the income tax expense shown on an income statement will be different from the amount of tax due to taxing authorities on the ***income tax return***. For example, calculation differences can result in timing differences between recording a GAAP expense and an allowed tax deduction for the same item. Eventually, the differences reverse and the total GAAP expense and the total allowed tax deduction will be the same after a period of time. However, before that happens, the timing of the expense each year on the income statement will be different than the tax payable to taxing authorities. These are called ***temporary differences***.

The difference between income tax expense on the income statement and the tax actually payable creates a balance sheet item called ***deferred tax***. Deferred tax can either be a liability for future income tax or an asset that will benefit a company by offsetting future tax obligations.

Example 1 of Temporary Difference

(GAAP Tax Expense is More)

Because of a timing difference in how depreciation expense is calculated, the GAAP income before tax of San Benito Corporation is $100,000, but the amount allowed by tax rules results in a larger expense deduction. Thus, taxable income is only $80,000. The tax rate for the company is 30%. The journal entry to record the tax is:

Income Tax Expense ($100,000 × .3)	30,000	
Income Tax Payable ($80,000 × .3)		24,000
Deferred Income Tax Payable		6,000

Higher future tax when timing difference reverses

Example 1, continued

(Reversal: GAAP Tax Expense is Less)

Assume that in the next year all the other revenues and expenses are the same as previous year except the depreciation item. Now the depreciation expense calculations reverse; the *timing* of the methods results in a greater depreciation expense on the income statement and a lower deduction allowed by taxing authorities. The result is that income before tax is $80,000 and taxable income is $100,000. The journal entry is:

Income Tax Expense ($80,000 × .3)	24,000	
Deferred Income Tax Payable	6,000	
Income Tax Payable ($100,000 × .3)		30,000

The Deferred Income Tax Payable is eliminated as more tax is payable now. After both periods, the total tax expense on the income statement is the same as the tax actually due, but the timing of the expense and deduction is different each period.

Deferred Income Tax, *continued*

Example 2 of Temporary Difference

GAAP requires that a seller's product warranty expense and liability be recorded in the same year as the product is sold. Income tax rules allow a tax deduction only when the warranty liability is paid. The income statement of Humbolt Corporation shows income before tax of $50,000; however, the expenses include $10,000 of accrued warranty expense. The taxable income is $60,000 because the warranty expense is not deductible yet. The journal entry is:

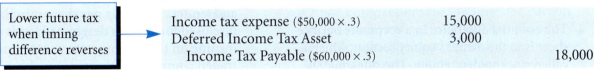

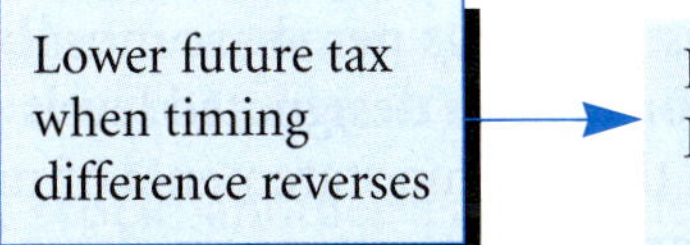

Income tax expense ($50,000 × .3)	15,000	
Deferred Income Tax Asset	3,000	
Income Tax Payable ($60,000 × .3)		18,000

A $3,000 deferred tax asset is recorded as a balance sheet item. The asset represents the benefit of a future lower tax liability. (Humbolt has incurred more taxes than the income statement indicated it "should" have.)

Example 2, continued

Assume that total revenues and expenses are the same next year except that there is no longer a GAAP warranty expense because a different product is being sold. However, in this year the company pays for repairs on the items returned from last year, and the warranty liability is paid. The journal entry to record the tax is:

Income tax expense ($60,000 × .3)	18,000	
Deferred Income Tax Asset		3,000
Income Tax Payable ($50,000 × .3)		15,000

The deferred tax asset is now realized in the form of a lower tax liability in the current period. After both periods, the tax expense on the income statement is the same as the tax actually paid, but the timing of the items was different.

Permanent Differences

Some items create differences between tax and accounting income that are not a matter of timing and do not reverse. These are called ***permanent differences***. For example, club dues paid for membership in social and athletic organizations are never deductible for income tax purposes but are an expense in determining accounting income.

Permanent differences do not create a deferred tax. The method for dealing with permanent differences is simply to apply the tax law rule for the item when calculating the tax expense on the income statement. Therefore, the tax calculation for the item will be the same for both accounting income and taxable income. In this example, club dues would be excluded as a deductible item when calculating tax expense for the income statement and tax payable for the balance sheet.

Other common permanent difference items are nontaxable municipal bond income, meals and entertainment expense limit, and penalties and fines.

PRACTICE Learning Goal 31

Solutions are in the disk at the back of the book and at: www.worthyjames.com

This learning goal is about corporate financial statements. Use these questions and problems to practice what you have just read.

Multiple Choice

Select the best answer.

1. An income statement of a proprietorship or partnership can report all the same items as on income statement of a corporation except
   a. extraordinary gains and losses.
   b. discontinued operations.
   c. income tax expense.
   d. income from continuing operations.
2. A detailed explanation in table format of all current period changes in stockholders' equity is called a(n)
   a. statement of stockholders' equity.
   b. statement of retained earnings.
   c. stockholders' equity section of the balance sheet.
   d. income statement.
3. Which of the following is *not* an example of a special item that could appear on a corporate income statement?
   a. taxes on discontinued operations
   b. comprehensive income
   c. discontinued operations
   d. gain on sale of discontinued operations
4. Restructuring charges should be reported on financial statements as
   a. an adjustment to the beginning balance of retained earnings.
   b. part of operating income on the income statement.
   c. part of discontinued operations on the income statement.
   d. either (b) or (c), depending on circumstances.
5. Hartford Corporation incurred an extraordinary flood loss of $100,000. Hartford Corporation pays tax at rate of 30%. How should the company report the flood loss?
   a. $100,000 loss as part of income from continuing operations
   b. $100,000 loss as a special item
   c. $100,000 loss less a $30,000 tax savings as a special item
   d. $100,000 loss less a $30,000 tax savings as part of income from continuing operations
6. New Haven, Inc. sold a division of its company during the year for a $400,000 gain. Prior to the date of sale, the year-to-date net loss for the division was $1,000,000. The company's tax rate is 30%. What will be reported on the income statement as a special item?
   a. $420,000 loss
   b. $1,000,000 discontinued operations loss less a $300,000 tax savings
   c. $400,000 gain less $120,000 income tax
   d. both (b) and (c)
7. On an income statement, "Income from continuing operations"
   a. would have a different name if there were no discontinued operations.
   b. must be presented by using the multiple-step format.
   c. must be presented by using the single-step format.
   d. none of the above.
8. Comprehensive income
   a. does not include net income.
   b. includes net income plus "other comprehensive income."
   c. is reported on the balance sheet as part of stockholders' equity.
   d. none of the above.

PRACTICE Learning Goal 31, continued

Solutions are in the disk at the back of the book and at: www.worthyjames.com

9. "Accumulated other comprehensive income"
   a. is reported on the balance sheet as part of stockholders' equity.
   b. is reported on the income statement.
   c. includes current period net income.
   d. none of the above.
10. An extremely important number that is widely used by investors and analysts and is part of the price-earnings ratio is
    a. net income.
    b. comprehensive income.
    c. earnings per share.
    d. total stockholders' equity.
11. Jamestown, Inc. reported $850,000 of net income for the year. During the year, the company had 50,000 shares of $100 par, 8%, preferred stock outstanding and 400,000 shares of common stock outstanding. What is the basic EPS for the year?
    a. $2.13
    b. $17
    c. $1.89
    d. $1.13
12. The Cedron Corporation balance sheet shows $3,250,000 of stockholders' equity. 175,000 shares of no par common stock are outstanding, and 25,000 of common shares are held as treasury stock. The balance of retained earnings is $2,000,000. What is the book value per share of the stock?
    a. $20.00
    b. $32.50
    c. $11.43
    d. $18.57
13. The Roxbury, Inc. balance sheet shows a stockholders' equity that consists of the following items: 200,000 shares of $.05 par value common stock issued that has a paid-in capital in excess of par balance of $3,590,000. The retained earnings balance is $800,000. Treasury Stock shows a balance of $50,000, which is the cost of 2,500 shares. What is the book value per share of the stock?
    a. $21.75
    b. $17.95
    c. $22.00
    d. some other amount
14. The stockholders' equity of Zhao corporation consists of the following: 3,000 shares of $100, 6%, preferred stock outstanding that has a call price of $105 per share and was sold at $101 per share. The stockholders' equity also shows 50,000 shares totaling $775,000 of no par common stock and $500,000 of retained earnings. The preferred stock is one year in arrears. What is the book value per share of the common stock?
    a. $24.90
    b. $25.26
    c. $31.56
    d. some other amount
15. A stock dividend is reported as a(n)
    a. adjustment to the beginning balance of retained earnings.
    b. current period reduction in retained earnings.
    c. deduction from operating income on the income statement.
    d. special item on the income statement.

PRACTICE Learning Goal 31, continued

Solutions are in the disk at the back of the book and at: www.worthyjames.com

16. What items create the difference between income from continuing operations and net income?
    a. discontinued operations, extraordinary gains/losses, and change in accounting principle
    b. extraordinary gains/losses and change in accounting principle
    c. discontinued operations and change in accounting principle
    d. discontinued operations
17. A statement of stockholders' equity
    a. shows the beginning and ending balance of stockholders' equity.
    b. shows the beginning and ending balance of retained earnings.
    c. is often prepared instead of a statement of retained earnings.
    d. all of the above.
18. Elmira, Inc. had 250,000 shares of common stock issued and 200,000 shares outstanding during the year. Operating income before tax for the year was $890,000 and net income was $630,000. What was the earnings per share (EPS) for the year?
    a. $3.56
    b. $4.45
    c. $3.15
    d. some other amount
19. On January 1, Flatbush Corporation had 500,000 shares of common stock issued and outstanding. On April 2, the company sold 300,000 additional shares. On October 31, the company purchased 150,000 shares of treasury stock. Also outstanding all year were 100,000 shares of $100, 8%, preferred stock. The company reported net income of $2,750,000 for the year. What is the earnings per share for the net income?
    a. $2.79
    b. $3.68
    c. $3.94
    d. some other amount
20. Which of the following items would be reported as part of net income?
    a. comprehensive income
    b. discontinued operations
    c. prior period adjustment
    d. accumulated prior effect of change in accounting principle
21. Which of the following items is reported as part of stockholders' equity on the balance sheet?
    a. comprehensive income
    b. other comprehensive income
    c. accumulated other comprehensive income
    d. deferred income

Discussion Questions and Brief Exercises

1. Compare and contrast the statement of retained earnings and the statement of stockholders' equity.

2. Your friend Daleesha Ames is studying for an accounting exam. She is not clear about the meaning of the following three terms: operating income, income from continuing operations, and net income. Can you explain to her what these terms mean and how they are calculated?

PRACTICE Learning Goal 31, continued

Solutions are in the disk at the back of the book and at: www.worthyjames.com

3. What is the special item that appears on an income statement? What does it mean and how is it shown?

4. Where does income tax expense appear on a corporate income statement?

5. On January 1, Shenandoah Corporation had 450,000 shares of $1 par common stock outstanding. On May 1, the company purchased 10,000 shares of treasury stock for $30 per share. On June 1, the company declared a 2 for 1 stock split. On June 2, how many shares of stock are outstanding? How many are in treasury? How many shares are issued? What is the total cost and cost per share of the treasury stock?

6. In (5) above, Shenandoah Corporation also had 150,000 shares of $100, 9%, preferred stock outstanding during the year. The net income for the year ended December 31 was $3,850,000. What are the earnings per share?

7. As an investor, does it matter to you if earnings per share are increasing or decreasing? Do you think that some earnings per share amounts on the income statement might be more important to you than others? Why?

8. Why are preferred dividends subtracted from income when calculating earnings per share?

9. Explain the concept of book value. Why is the preferred stockholders' equity claim subtracted from total stockholders' equity when calculating book value?

10. Professor Rodriguez explained the income statement presentation of earnings per share in class today with the following information, but class was over before she could complete the example. Can you complete the example by showing the proper earnings per share presentation on the income statement? Information (special item is net of tax): Income from continuing operations, $2,475,000; gain from discontinued operations, $600,000; weighted average shares outstanding during year: 800,000; annual preferred stock dividends: $680,000.

11. Fallon Corporation has stocks and other financial securities that they do not regularly trade. The value of these investments frequently changes, and at the end of the year the company had a $120,000 after-tax unrealized loss on the investments. Fallon Corporation reported $340,000 of net income. What is the amount of other comprehensive income? What is the amount of comprehensive income? Where are these items usually shown on financial statements?

12. On January 1, Zephyr Cove, Inc. had 400,000 common shares outstanding. On May 1, it issued 275,000 more shares. On August 31, 100,000 shares of treasury stock were purchased. On December 1, 75,000 of the treasury shares were sold. To calculate EPS, what is the weighted average number of shares for the year?

13. During the current year, Sparks, Inc. discontinued and sold its mining operations, which were a major component of its business. The loss on the mining operations during the current year was $1,250,000. The recorded gain on the sale was $200,000. Income from continuing operations for the year was $11,300,000. The current tax rate for Sparks, Inc. is 40%. On which financial statement would these events be shown? Show the correct presentation and discuss the reason for this method of presentation.

PRACTICE Learning Goal 31, continued

Solutions are in the disk at the back of the book and at: www.worthyjames.com

14. Which of the following items probably qualify as "extraordinary" or "infrequent or unusual"? Explain your reasons.

a. loss resulting from a lawsuit
b. loss from repairs made to a defective product
c. loss caused by a tsunami (tidal wave)
d. loss from sale of long-term investments
e. flood loss (business located next to a river)
f. loss from a labor strike
g. expropriation (takeover) of a business by a foreign government
h. business property condemned for public use a federal, state, or local agency

15. What is the difference between "net income" and "comprehensive income"?

16. Give examples of two items that would be "other comprehensive income."

17. Give examples of how a company can present misleading income statement information in its public relations and media documents.

18. What is the cause of deferred income tax?

19. The Deferred Income Tax account can be either an asset or a liability. How does this happen?

20. MacTavish Corporation reported $200,000 warranty expense on its 2017 income statement. However, income tax rules do not permit this item to be a tax-deductible expense on the income tax return until the expense is actually paid, which occurred in 2018. The company's tax rate is 40%. MacTavish Corporation had pre-tax accounting income of $2,000,000 in 2017 and $3,000,000 in 2018. Prepare the 2017 and 2018 journal entries to record the income tax expense, deferred tax, and income tax payable.

21. On a separate piece of paper (so that you can use this exercise again without seeing answers), complete the following table by checking the appropriate spaces to indicate on which financial statement an item is presented.

Item	Income Statement	Statement of Stockholders' Equity	Balance Sheet
a. Net income	_____	_____	_____
b. Sale of treasury stock	_____	_____	_____
c. Balance of treasury stock	_____	_____	_____
d. Comprehensive income	_____	_____	_____
e. Accum. other comprehensive income	_____	_____	_____
f. Prior period adjustment	_____	_____	_____
g. Cash and stock dividends	_____	_____	_____
h. Total stockholders' equity	_____	_____	_____
i. New shares of stock issued	_____	_____	_____

PRACTICE Learning Goal 31, continued

Solutions are in the disk at the back of the book and at: www.worthyjames.com

Reinforcement Problems

LG 31-1. Prepare stockholders' equity section of a balance sheet. Shown below are selected account balances of Cumberland Enterprises, Inc. as of December 31, 2017.

Prepare the stockholders' equity section of the company's balance sheet using a detailed format.

- Retained earnings: $2,820,000
- Common stock, $1 par: $450,000
- Accumulated other comprehensive income: ($410,000)
- Paid-in capital in excess of par, preferred: $220,000
- Treasury stock: $550,000
- Preferred stock, 7%, $50 par: $3,750,000
- Paid-in capital from treasury stock transactions: $180,000
- Paid-in capital in excess of par, common: $4,100,000

Other information: 500,000 shares of common stock were issued and 450,000 shares are outstanding. 75,000 shares of preferred stock are outstanding. The terms of a bank loan restricts $1,000,000 of retained earnings as unavailable for dividends.

LG 31-2. Prepare a multiple-step income statement. Shown below are selected account balances of Alexandria Corporation as of the fiscal year ended June 30, 2018. The income tax rate is 40%.

Prepare the company's multiple-step income statement for the fiscal year. (Disregard earnings per share for this problem.)

- Interest expense: $42,000
- Operating expenses: (*detailed separately*) $1,150,000
- Gain on sale of equipment: $84,000
- Net sales revenue: $3,520,000
- Interest revenue: $23,000
- Loss from discontinued operations: $125,000
- Loss on sale of discontinued operations: $450,000
- Gain on land condemnation by state: $270,000
- Cost of goods sold: $1,600,000

LG 31-3. Prepare multiple-step and single-step income statements. Shown below are selected account balances of Pasadena Corporation as of the fiscal year ended December 31, 2017. The income tax rate is 40%.

a. Prepare a multiple-step income statement for the fiscal year. (Disregard earnings per share for this problem.)
b. Prepare a single-step income statement for the fiscal year. (Disregard earnings per share for this problem.)

- Interest expense: $75,000
- Sales and marketing expenses: $310,000
- Administrative expenses: $520,000
- Other operating expenses: $540,000
- Gain on sale of equipment: $125,000
- Net sales revenue: $5,800,000
- Extraordinary loss from earthquake: $150,000
- Loss from discontinued operations: $210,000
- Gain on sale of discontinued operations: $130,000
- Restructuring charges (not part of discontinued operations): $1,120,000
- Interest revenue: $10,000
- Cost of goods sold: $2,700,000

PRACTICE

Learning Goal 31, continued

Solutions are in the disk at the back of the book and at: www.worthyjames.com

LG 31-6. Prepare a statement of stockholders' equity and the stockholders' equity section of a balance sheet. The account balances and selected transactions of Great Falls Corporation during the company's 2017 fiscal year are shown below.

a. Prepare the company's statement of stockholders' equity for the year ended December 31, 2017. (Use a single column for all preferred stock paid-in capital. Use one column for common stock and a separate "additional paid-in capital" column for all other common stock capital in excess of legal capital.)
b. Prepare the stockholders' equity section of the balance sheet as of December 31, 2017.

Selected account balances on January 1, 2017:

- Preferred Stock: $100 par, 8%; 11,000 shares outstanding; $1,100,000
- Common Stock: $.10 par value, 770,000 shares issued; $77,000
- Paid-in Capital in Excess of Par, Common: $6,250,000
- Paid-in Capital from Treasury Stock Transactions: $50,000
- Retained Earnings: $150,000
- Treasury Stock: 15,000 shares; $120,000

Events:

- Net income for the year was $240,000.
- In January, Great Falls Corporation sold 5,000 new shares of the preferred stock at a price of $103 per share.
- In April, the company issued 40,000 new shares of common stock at a price of $9 per share.
- In August, the company sold 10,000 shares of treasury stock at a price of $7.40 per share.
- During the year, the company experienced cash flow problems and had not paid any preferred dividends. In November, the company paid only a quarterly cash dividend on the preferred stock.
- In December, Great Falls Corporation declared a 40,000-share common stock dividend, with the stock to be distributed on January 3. The market price of the common stock at the time was $8.50 per share.
- Also during December, accountants discovered a prior year accounting error that understated 2016 net income by $120,000.

LG 31-7. Prepare a single-step income statement with earnings per share. Missoula Corporation has the selected account balances and information shown below for the fiscal year ending October 31, 2017.

a. Prepare a single-step income statement, including full earnings per share disclosure, for the 2017 fiscal year.
b. Calculate the price-earnings ratio for net income at October 31, 2016 and October 1, 2017. Interpret the results of your calculations.

Selected account balances on October 31, 2017:

- Net Sales: $3,440,000
- Cost of Goods Sold: 1,510,000
- Operating Expenses: 748,000
- Interest Revenue: 7,000
- Interest Expense: 69,000
- Extraordinary flood loss: 130,000
- Tax savings from flood loss: 52,000
- Rental Revenue: $36,000
- Loss on Sale of Equipment: 35,000
- Income Tax Expense: 484,000
- Discontinued Operations Loss: 97,000
- Tax savings from discontinued operations loss: 39,000
- Gain on sale from discontinued operations: 185,000
- Tax on gain on sale from discontinued operations: 74,000

PRACTICE **Learning Goal 31, continued**

Solutions are in the disk at the back of the book and at: www.worthyjames.com

LG 31-7, *continued*

Common shares outstanding during 2016 and 2017: 300,000 shares.
The market price of the stock:

- October 31, 2016: $36.75 (earnings per share for net income was $1.40)
- October 31, 2017: $45.50

No preferred stock has been issued.

LG 31-8. Record deferred tax transactions. In each of the independent situations below, on a separate piece of paper (so you can use this problem again), complete the table and record the correct journal entry for each year.

a. Amity Corporation made a $100,000 charitable contribution in 2017. This contribution is fully deductible for accounting purposes, but tax rules limit the deduction to $80,000 for calculation of the taxable income, while permitting the balance of the contribution to be used as a deduction next year.

	2017	2018
Pre-tax accounting income	$700,000	$900,000
Charitable contribution		
Taxable income		
Income tax payable @ 40%		

b. Bagwell Sales Company, Inc. uses a depreciation method for calculating income tax liability that permitted $300,000 of deductible expense more than the depreciation expense used for accounting purposes. In 2018 this difference reversed, and tax rules permitted $300,000 less than used for accounting purposes.

	2017	2018
Pre-tax accounting income	$5,000,000	$4,700,000
Depreciation difference		
Taxable income		
Income tax payable @ 40%		

c. Accelerated Corporation uses a different method for recording depreciation expense on a plant and equipment asset for accounting purposes than for tax purposes. The asset cost $100,000, and one-fourth of that amount is recorded each year as depreciation expense on the income statement. For tax purposes, the company uses a method that allows a $50,000 deduction in the first year, $25,000 in the second year, and $12,500 in each of the last two years.

	2015	2016	2017	2018
Pre-tax accounting income	$1,000,000	$1,500,000	$2,000,000	$3,000,00
Depreciation difference				
Taxable income				
Income tax payable @ 40%				

PRACTICE **Learning Goal 31, continued**

Solutions are in the disk at the back of the book and at: www.worthyjames.com

LG 31-8, *continued*

d. In 2017, the income statement of Goodtime Corporation reported $500,000 income from continuing operations before tax. As an expense item on the income statement, the company reported $30,000 of meals and entertainment expense. This expenditure is never deductible for the calculation of taxable income. The company's tax rate is 40%. Prepare the general journal entry to record the tax expense and tax liability.

LG 31-9. **Cumulative problem—journal entries, income statement, statement of stockholders' equity, and stockholders' equity on a balance sheet.** Coeur d' Alene Enterprises, Inc. completed the selected 2017 transactions that are shown below.

a. Prepare the general journal entries to record the transactions. (For journal paper, you can make general journal copies from the disk at the back of this book or from www.worthyjames.com.)
b. Enter the January 1 balances shown below as beginning balances in T accounts. Then post the transactions into the T accounts. Open new T accounts as necessary.
c. Prepare tables to record the shares of preferred and common stock outstanding and shares of treasury stock.
d. Prepare a 2017 multiple-step income statement, including earnings per share.
e. Prepare a statement of stockholders' equity for 2017.
f. Prepare the stockholders' equity section of the balance sheet as of December 31, 2017.
g. Calculate the book value per share as of December 31, 2017.

Selected January 1 account balances:

- Preferred Stock, convertible into 4 shares of common for each share of preferred; $80 par, 8%, callable at $85, 16,000 shares issued and outstanding: the preferred was sold at par.
- Common Stock, $1 par value, 450,000 shares issued and outstanding: $450,000
- Paid-in Capital in Excess of Par, Common: $7,100,000
- Paid-in Capital from Treasury Stock Transactions: $188,000
- Retained Earnings: $8,290,000
- Accumulated Other Comprehensive Income $115,000

Year-end December 31 income statement information:

- Net sales revenue: $7,450,000
- Cost of goods sold: 4,110,000
- General and administrative expense: 1,167,000
- Sales and marketing expense: 488,000
- Extraordinary loss, earthquake damage: 450,000
- Restructuring charges: $250,000
- Rental revenue (miscellaneous income): 70,000
- Interest expense: 134,000
- Loss on sale of land: 86,000
- Loss from discontinued operations: 80,000
- Loss on sale of discontinued division: 270,000

Other information:

- The tax rate for Coeur d' Alene Enterprises is 40%.
- Coeur d' Alene Enterprises changed its method of valuing inventory in 2017. This qualifies as a change in accounting principle. The accumulated prior effect of the change would have decreased prior years' net income by the $150,000.
- For the year, the company had $65,000 of after-tax unrealized losses on certain short-term investment securities.

PRACTICE Learning Goal 31, continued

Solutions are in the disk at the back of the book and at: www.worthyjames.com

LG 31-9, *continued*

Selected transactions:

Jan. 3	The board of directors issued new common shares for a 4 for 3 stock split declared in December of the prior year.
Mar. 8	Declared a semi-annual cash dividend of $200,000.
April 12	Paid the dividend.
May 2	Issued 4,000 shares of preferred stock for land to be used for future development. The asking price for the land was $345,000. The preferred stock is regularly traded, and at the time of the agreement, the stock had a market price of $85 per share.
June 1	Owners of 5,000 shares of preferred stock exercised the right to convert to common shares.
Aug. 30	The company purchased 30,000 shares of treasury common stock at $23 per share.
Sept. 7	Declared a semi-annual dividend of $250,000.
Oct. 12	Paid the dividend.
Dec. 1	Sold 25,000 shares of treasury stock for $19.40 per share.
1	Sold 40,000 new common shares at a price of $19.20 per share.

Instructor-Assigned Problems

If you are using this book in a class, these review problems may be assigned by your instructor for homework, group assignments, class work, or other activities. Only your instructor has the solutions.

IA31-1. Prepare stockholders' equity section of balance sheet; calculate book value. Shown below are various account balances and additional information for Reno Enterprises, Inc. for the fiscal year ended June 30, 2017.

a. Select the necessary account balances and information and prepare the stockholders' equity section of the balance sheet at fiscal year end June 30, 2017.
b. Calculate the book value.

Account	$	Account	$
Paid-in capital in excess of par-common	2,440,000	Paid-in capital in excess of par-preferred	55,000
Cash	550,000	Treasury stock (5,000 shares)	50,000
Common stock	20,000	Notes payable	700,000
Preferred stock	1,250,000	Retained earnings	684,000
Accumulated other comprehensive income	125,000	Paid-in capital from treasury stock transactions	19,000

Additional information:

- Common stock: $.10 par, 200,000 shares issued and 195,000 shares outstanding
- Preferred stock: $50 par, 5%, 25,000 shares issued and outstanding.
- There are no dividends in arrears and no speci•ed liquidating value for any stock.
- The terms of a bank loan has restricted the company from reducing retained earnings below $500,000.

PRACTICE Learning Goal 31, continued

Solutions are in the disk at the back of the book and at: www.worthyjames.com

IA31-2. Prepare a multiple-step income statement. Shown below are various account balances and additional information for Pleasanton Corporation for the year ended December 31, 2017. Select the necessary account balances and information and prepare a multiple-step income statement for the fiscal year ending December 31, 2017. (We omit earnings per share in this problem.)

Account	$	Account	$
Extraordinary flood loss	170,000	Net sales revenue	4,500,000
Gain on sale land	180,000	Loss on equipment sales	15,000
Cost of goods sold	2,850,000	Miscellaneous lease revenue	24,000
Interest expense	35,000	Operating expenses	920,000
Loss from discontinued operations ...	100,000	Loss from sale of discontinued operations	250,000

Additional information: Income tax rate is 30%

IA31-3. Prepare a statement of stockholders' equity. The Alexandria Corporation recorded the stockholders' equity transactions listed below during the year and reported the selected account balances below as of January 1. Prepare a statement of stockholders' equity for the company for the year ending December 31, 2017. To simplify the preparation, you can show dollar amounts in thousands (000); for example, $2,850,000 can be shown as $2,850.

Account balances on January 1, 2017:

- Common stock, $.10 par value 400,000 shares outstanding: $40,000
- Paid-in capital in excess of par: $7,240,000
- Retained Earnings: $2,850,000
- Treasury stock: 35,000 shares at cost of $420,000
- Accumulated other comprehensive income: $230,000

Stockholders' equity transactions during 2017:

- Net loss for the year was $450,000
- Issued 90,000 new shares of common stock at a price of $22.50 per share.
- Sold 10,000 shares of treasury stock at a price of $23 per share
- The company reported $50,000 of after-tax unrealized losses on certain investment securities. These losses are not reported as part of net income but are part of other comprehensive income.
- Declared a $150,000 of cash dividend
- Declared and issued a 10% stock dividend at year-end when the stock was selling at $25 per share.

IA31-4. Prepare a multiple-step income statement with earnings per share; prepare the stockholders' equity section of a balance sheet. Shown below are beginning stockholders' equity account balances, income statement account balances, and additional information for Chinook Corporation for the year ended December 31, 2017. Also listed below are all stockholders' equity transactions for 2017 other than those that affect net income.

a. Prepare a multiple-step income statement for 2017 that includes a standard earnings per share presentation and a disclosure of comprehensive income.

PRACTICE Learning Goal 31, continued

Solutions are in the disk at the back of the book and at: www.worthyjames.com

IA31-4. *continued*

b. Record journal entries for stockholders' equity transactions and prepare the stockholders' equity section of the balance sheet as of December 31, 2017.
c. Can you verify the calculation of the weighted average number of common shares outstanding for 2017?

Net sales revenue..	$2,750,000	Cost of goods sold.................................	$1,790,000
Interest revenue..	25,000	Interest expense....................................	111,000
Operating expenses (detailed separately)	575,000	Extraordinary casualty loss....................	80,000
Gain on sale of miscellaneous stock investments..	50,000	Other comprehensive income: after-tax unrealized gain on stock investment	212,000
Preferred stock, $75 par, 3%, 4,000 shares issued and outstanding..............................	300,000	Common stock, $.06 par, 500,000 shares issued, 450,000 outstanding........	30,000
Paid-in capital in excess of par, Preferred..	15,000	Paid-in capital in excess of par, common..	9,500,000
Treasury stock (50,000 shares at cost)........	780,000	Retained earnings.................................	(225,000)

Additional information:

- Income tax rate is 30%
- Weighted average common shares outstanding: 570,833 (computation based on months)

Stockholders' equity transactions:

2017

Feb. 1	Sold 100,000 shares of common stock at a price of $22 per share.
May 31	Sold 10,000 shares of treasury stock at $28 per share.
Dec.1	The board of directors declared a 3 for 2 stock split.

IA31-5. **Cumulative problem—journal entries, income statement, statement of retained earnings, and stockholders' equity on balance sheet.** Twin Falls Corporation completed the selected 2017 transactions that are shown below.

a. Prepare the general journal entries to record the transactions. (For journal paper, you can make general journal copies from the disk at the back of this book or from www.worthyjames.com.)
b. Enter the January 1 balances shown below as beginning balances in T accounts. Then post the transactions into the T accounts. Open new T accounts as necessary.
c. Prepare tables to record the shares of preferred and common stock outstanding and shares of treasury stock.
d. Prepare a 2017 single-step income statement. Be sure to record the net income amount in the Retained Earnings T account.
e. Prepare a statement of retained earnings for 2017.
f. Prepare the stockholders' equity section of the balance sheet as of December 31, 2017.
g. Calculate the book value per share as of December 31, 2017.

PRACTICE Learning Goal 31, continued

Solutions are in the disk at the back of the book and at: www.worthyjames.com

IA31-5. *continued*

Selected January 1 account balances:

- Preferred Stock, $100 par, 6%, cumulative, 25,000 shares issued and outstanding: $2,500,000
- Common Stock, $1 par value, 200,000 shares issued and outstanding: $200,000
- Paid-in Capital in Excess of Par, Common: $3,900,000
- Retained Earnings: $5,200,000

Year-end December 31 income statement information:

- Sales revenue: $4,850,000
- Cost of goods sold: 1,720,000
- General and administrative expense: 545,000
- Sales and marketing expense: 773,000
- Extraordinary gain, land condemnation: 315,000
- Organization expense: 133,000
- Restructuring charges: $524,000
- Interest revenue: 40,000
- Interest expense: 55,000
- Loss on sale of land: 90,000
- Loss from sale of discontinued operations: $100,000
- Loss from discontinued operations: $50,000

Other information:

- The tax rate for Twin Falls Corporation is 40%.
- The interest revenue is municipal bond interest revenue, which is not taxable.
- For the year, the company had $75,000 of after-tax unrealized gains on certain short-term securities.

Selected transactions:

Jan. 3	The board of directors declared a semi-annual cash dividend in the amount of $400,000. The preferred dividends are one year in arrears.
Jan. 30	Paid the dividend.
Feb. 1	Sold 100,000 shares of common stock by using an underwriting company that sold the stock for $19 per share and deducted a 7% commission from the sales proceeds.
April 12	The board of directors declared a 10% common stock dividend when the stock was selling for $18 per share.
May 1	Issued the shares for the stock dividend.
July 3	The board of directors declared a semi-annual cash dividend in the amount of $400,000.
Aug. 1	Purchased 30,000 shares of treasury stock for $12 per share.
Aug. 5	Paid the dividend.
Sept. 23	Issued 2,000 shares of preferred stock in exchange for equipment that usually sells for approximately $210,000. The preferred stock trades regularly on an exchange and had a value of $102 per share at the time it was issued for the equipment.
Oct. 19	Discovered an accounting error that overstated the prior year's income by $90,000. Service revenue was overstated and accounts receivable were overstated.
Nov. 1	Sold 10,000 shares of treasury stock for $17.50 per share.
Dec. 1	Split the common stock 5 for 4.

Your Questions?

It is *very* important to be aware of what you need to understand better. What do you need to understand better about this learning goal? On a separate piece of paper, write the questions that you want to discuss with your classmates, instructor, or supervisor. Try to be very specific about what is bothering you, such as explanations that you do not fully understand.

Financial Statement Analysis

OVERVIEW

What this section does	This section provides essential tools and procedures to analyze financial statements.
Use this section if . . .	■ you want to learn key methods for financial statement analysis. ■ you want to review major types of financial statement manipulation and fraud. ■ you want an overview of strengths and weaknesses of GAAP.
Do not use this section if . . .	■ you do not need to understand the topics listed in the index below.

LEARNING GOALS

LEARNING GOAL 32

Suggestion

It is not necessary to complete this section to continue to Volume 2. You can study the principles and procedures in Volume 2 and later return here as appropriate for your own goals.

LEARNING GOAL 32

Analyze Financial Statements

In Learning Goal 32, you will find:

Overview

Trend Analysis Using a Reference Base

MD&A

Ratio Analysis

Analysis as an Outsider

Quality of Earnings

Financial Statements Quick Review

Balance Sheet

Purpose

The balance sheet is the most basic and essential financial statement. The purpose of the balance sheet is to show the wealth of a business (assets) and the two possible claims on that wealth, which are the creditors' claims (liabilities) and the owner's claim (owner's equity, partners' equity, or stockholders' equity.) at a given point in time.

Key Issues

Two key issues concerning a balance sheet are:

1. How items are classified on the balance sheet.

   To help with analysis, a "real-world" balance sheet is normally classified into sections. On the asset side, the most common sections are current assets and long-term assets. Basically, a current asset is any asset that is or can become cash, or that can be used instead of spending cash, within a year or less, as part of normal business operations. A long-term asset (sometimes called a fixed asset) is a physical asset that will not be used up within a year. Common examples are buildings, real estate, and equipment, called "property, plant, and equipment".

   On the liability side, there are current liabilities and long-term liabilities. A current liability is any liability due within a year. A long-term liability is a liability due in more than a year.

2. How the assets and liabilities are valued, which is to say, how the dollar value is calculated.

   The dollar value is recorded initially at its original transaction value, which is usually called "historical cost." As time passes, generally accepted accounting principles (GAAP) may require valuation adjustments to the historical cost of some assets.

continued ▶

Balance Sheet, *continued*

More Balance Sheet Accounts

In addition to the balance sheet accounts previously discussed, real-world balance sheets usually contain several other commonly-used accounts, as follows:

- Merchandise inventory: (often called "inventory") is an asset account that represents the cost of the goods that are ready to be sold to customers.
- Accumulated depreciation: This applies only to long-term physical assets, and represents an estimate of the amount of the original asset cost that is considered to have been used up and become an expense (called "depreciation expense"). By convention, each long-term physical asset, such as a plant and equipment item, has its own separate accumulated depreciation account, which appears next to the asset in the ledger and acts as an offset against the asset. These totals are summarized on the long-term asset section of the balance sheet (see page 688 example).

  Every period a regular amount of depreciation expense is recorded on the income statement which also increases the balance sheet accumulated depreciation accounts. In accounting and finance, recording depreciation is about spreading an original asset cost over the asset's estimated life, and has nothing to do with what an asset might sell for.
- Intangible assets" This is a common asset category balance sheet category Intangible assets are usually legal rights, such as a patent, copyright, trademark, leasehold, or franchise right.

Income Statement

Purpose

The income statement shows the change in owner's equity (or partners' or stockholders' equity) that results from the sales made to customers (revenues) minus the resources consumed to operate the business (expenses). When revenues exceed expenses (net income) assets increase and/or debt decreases. When expenses exceed revenues (net loss) assets decrease and/or debt increases.

Key Issues

The key issues concerning the income statement are the proper classification, correct amounts, and timing of revenues and expenses. With GAAP, it is always important to remember that paying and receiving cash has nothing to do with when revenues and expenses are recorded. Revenues are recorded when they are earned and expenses are recorded when they are incurred, not paid for. This is called "accrual accounting." If you are not clear about this, review the revenue principle and matching principle in Learning Goal 18.

Statement of Stockholders' Equity

Purpose

The statement of stockholders' equity summarizes the changes to stockholders' equity for a specific period of time. This generally consists of: (1) net income or loss from the income statement (2) the stockholders' investment changes and (3) dividends (asset – usually cash – distributions). In a proprietorship or partnership, these items are usually limited and relatively easy to follow. In a corporation, they can become more involved and complex. (Example on page 642).

Statement of Cash Flows

Purpose

The statement of cash flows explains the change in cash for a specific period of time. This usually corresponds to the same period of time used for the income statement and statement of owner's equity. The change in cash is explained by three activities: operating, investing, and financing.

Key Issue

The key issue concerning the statement of cash flows is whether a transaction has been properly classified as an operating, investing, or financing activity.

Operating Activities

Operating activities relate to the cash effects of the transactions that make up net income. In effect, the cash flow from operating activities shows the income statement on a cash basis instead of an accrual basis. Cash flow from operating activities shows the cash results from the essential recurring operations of a business, and it is the most important part of the statement of cash flows.

Investing Activities

Investing activities relate to the increases and decreases in cash from transactions that involve buying and selling long-term assets and activities that involve buying and selling investments, including making and collecting loans.

Financing Activities

Financing activities relate to the cash effects of the transactions that involve obtaining and paying back sources of business capital, such as loans and investments in the business. (This does not include short-term debt related to operating activities.)

Format

The statement of cash flows presented below is shown in the most popular format. The operating activities section begins with net income and makes two types of adjustments to net income to convert it to a cash basis:

- **Add** operating items that increase cash and are not part of the net income calculation or items that reduced net income but did not reduce cash, such as collecting receivables or using supplies.

continued ▶

Statement of Cash Flows, *continued*

- **Deduct** operating items that reduce cash and are not part of the net income calculation or items that increased net income but did not increase cash, such as paying bills or sales on account.

Note: An alternative format for operating activities is sometimes used. The point here is to understand the basic elements and function of the statement. The details of preparing a statement of cash flows is a more advanced topic and is explained in depth in Volume 2.

Superior Office Supply Corporation
Statements of Cash Flows
Years Ended December 31

Cash flows from operating activities	**2017**	**2016**
Net income	$137,000	$174,600
Add: Items increasing cash or not reducing cash		
Depreciation expense	58,200	35,100
Decreases in current operating assets	1,400	17,800
Increases in current operating liabilities	25,800	12,900
Less: Items reducing cash or not increasing cash		
Increases in current operating assets	(67,400)	(165,900)
Decreases in current operating liabilities	(29,800)	(4,800)
Increase in cash from operating activities	125,200	69,700
Cash flows from investing activities		
Expenditures on plant and equipment	(45,000)	(5,000)
Expenditures on intangible assets	(10,000)	
Decrease in cash from investing activities	(55,000)	(5,000)
Cash flows from financing activities		
Increase in non-trade short-term note payable	25,500	
(Decrease) increase in long-term debt	(30,200)	10,500
Dividends	(24,500)	(40,000)
Decrease in cash from financing activities	(29,200)	(29,500)
Net increase in cash	41,000	35,200
Beginning cash balance	414,200	379,000
Ending cash balance	$455,200	$414,200

Don't be fooled. Depreciation is often incorrectly referred to as a "source of cash" because it is a well-known adjustment that is added back to net income as you see above. *Depreciation is not literally a source of cash.* It is simply a non-cash expense deduction that reduces net income but does not require the use of any cash. So, depreciation is added back to net income to cancel out the deduction for the purpose of calculating the cash flow. In fact, an add-back adjustment is made for every other non-cash expense (like using up supplies).

Trend Analysis Using a Reference Base

Overview

Introduction: Your New Business

We begin our discussion by assuming that you have just recently taken over the management of a family business. The business is a wholesale office supply store that primarily sells office supplies and office equipment on account to retail merchants. One of the first things that you need to do is to analyze the financial statements of the business to judge its condition and to decide if you need to make any changes in the operations and management.

A Reference Base

A reference base is simply a selected amount that is used to compare to other numbers. The comparison is usually done by calculating the other numbers as a percentage of the reference base amount.

Example

Suppose that you are given the following sales amounts:

	2017	2016	2015	2014
Sales	$75,000	$48,000	$55,000	$50,000

Comparing totals: If you want to compare the total sales for each year to the year 2014, then the 2014 sales of $50,000 is your reference base amount. Divide each year's sales by the base amount.

	2017	2016	2015	2014
Sales	150%	96%	110%	100%

Example: The 2015 sales compared to 2014 is: $55,000/$50,000 = 110%.

Comparing changes: If you want to compare the change for each year to the base amount, calculate the difference and divide by the base amount.

	2017	2016	2015	2014
Sales	50%	(4%)	10%	—

Example: The 2015 percent change is: ($55,000 – $50,000)/$50,000 = 10%.

continued ▶

Horizontal Analysis

Overview

Horizontal analysis is a comparison of financial statement information over a period of time. Both dollar amounts and percentage amounts are evaluated to identify changes and trends from the base year. Watching trends over an extended time period is an extremely valuable analytical procedure.

Balance Sheet Example

The example below shows a two-year horizontal analysis of comparative balance sheets (condensed stockholders' equity) for your business, with 2016 as the base year.

Superior Office Supply Corporation
Condensed Balance Sheets
December 31

			Increase or (decrease)	
	2017	**2016**	**Amount**	**Percent**
Assets				
Current assets				
Cash and cash equivalents	$ 455,200	$ 414,200	**$ 41,000**	**9.9%**
Short-term investments	35,500	36,900	**(1,400)**	**(3.8%)**
Accounts receivable, net	286,200	255,800	**30,400**	**11.9%**
Inventory	492,100	456,900	**35,200**	**7.7%**
Prepaid expenses	52,300	50,500	**1,800**	**3.6%**
Total current assets	1,321,300	1,214,300	**107,000**	**8.8%**
Property, plant, and equipment	990,500	945,500	**45,000**	**4.8%**
Less: Accumulated depreciation	365,000	306,800	**58,200**	**19.0%**
Net property, plant, and equip.	625,500	638,700	**(13,200)**	**(2.1%)**
Intangible assets	110,000	100,000	**10,000**	**10.0%**
Total assets	$2,056,800	$1,953,000	**$103,800**	**5.3%**
Liabilities and Owner's Equity				
Current liabilities				
Accounts payable	$ 414,700	$ 388,900	**$ 25,800**	**6.6%**
Short-term notes payable	50,000	24,500	**25,500**	**104.1%**
Other current liabilities	185,600	215,400	**(29,800)**	**(13.8%)**
Total current liabilities	650,300	628,800	**21,500**	**3.4%**
Long-term debt	551,400	581,600	**(30,200)**	**(5.2%)**
Total liabilities	1,201,700	1,210,400	**(8,700)**	**(0.7%)**
Stockholders' Equity	855,100	742,600	**112,500**	**15.1%**
Total liabilities and stockholders' equity	$2,056,800	$1,953,000	**$103,800**	**5.3%**

Horizontal Analysis, *continued*

Income Statement Example

The example below shows a two-year horizontal analysis of comparative income statements, with 2016 as the base year.

Superior Office Supply Corporation
Condensed Income Statements
Years Ended December 31

			Increase or (decrease)	
	2017	**2016**	**Amount**	**Percent**
Sales	$2,198,600	$2,114,100	**$ 84,500**	**4.0%**
Less: Returns and allowances	98,900	90,900	**8,000**	**8.8%**
Net sales	2,099,700	2,023,200	**76,500**	**3.8%**
Cost of goods sold	1,364,800	1,294,800	**70,000**	**5.4%**
Gross profit	734,900	728,400	**6,500**	**0.9%**
Selling expenses	252,000	222,600	**29,400**	**13.2%**
Administrative expenses	283,500	293,400	**(9,900)**	**(3.4%)**
Total operating expenses	535,500	516,000	**19,500**	**3.8%**
Operating income	199,400	212,400	**(13,000)**	**(6.1%)**
Other revenue (and expense)				
Interest expense	(2,900)	(2,100)	**800**	**38.1%**
Income tax expense	59,500	64,900	**(5,400)**	**(8.3%)**
Net income	$ 137,000	$ 145,400	**($ 8,400)**	**(5.8%)**

Analysis

- **Balance sheet:** The comparative balance sheets show that some significant changes have occurred between 2016 and 2017. Total current assets have increased by almost 9%, and Property, Plant, and Equipment increased by almost 5%. We also see that total liabilities have decreased by almost 1%, so there was no net borrowing. This means that the increase in total assets must be primarily the result of business net income unless there were owner investments.
- **Income statement:** Unfortunately, net income (although positive) has decreased by about 6%, and operating income has decreased by 6%. However, gross profit increased by almost 1%! How could this happen? It appears that gross profit has increased because sales have increased, but the company did not control the selling expenses and cost of goods sold tightly enough. These two expenses increased much faster than sales revenue. As a manager, this will require you to create a system that controls expenses more carefully. You should also investigate the increased rate of merchandise returns.

continued ▶

Vertical Analysis

Overview

Vertical analysis is a comparison of financial statement information within a single financial statement. A reference base amount is selected within the statement, and other related items in the statement are compared to this amount. So, instead of using a reference base amount to make comparisons over time, items are compared to a reference base amount within one financial statement.

Balance Sheet Example

The balance sheet below shows a vertical analysis. Can you find the reference base amounts? They are the items that are 100%—the total assets and the total liabilities and owner's equity.

Superior Office Supply Corporation
Condensed Balance Sheets
December 31

	2017	Percent	2016	Percent
Assets				
Current assets				
Cash and cash equivalents	$ 455,200	22.1%	$ 414,200	21.2%
Short-term investments	35,500	1.7%	36,900	1.9%
Accounts receivable, net	286,200	13.9%	255,800	13.1%
Inventory	492,100	23.9%	456,900	23.4%
Prepaid expenses	52,300	2.5%	50,500	2.6%
Total current assets	1,321,300	64.2%	1,214,300	62.2%
Property, plant, and equipment	990,500	48.2%	945,500	48.4%
Less: Accumulated depreciation	365,000	17.7%	306,800	15.7%
Net property, plant, and equipment	625,500	30.4%	638,700	32.7%
Intangible assets	110,000	5.3%	100,000	5.1%
Total assets	$2,056,800	100.0%	$1,953,000	100.0%
Liabilities and Owner's Equity				
Current liabilities				
Accounts payable	$ 414,700	20.2%	$ 388,900	19.9%
Short-term notes payable	50,000	2.4%	24,500	1.3%
Other current liabilities	185,600	9.0%	215,400	11.0%
Total current liabilities	650,300	31.6%	628,800	32.2%
Long-term debt	551,400	26.8%	581,600	29.8%
Total liabilities	1,201,700	58.4%	1,210,400	62.0%
Stockholders' equity	855,100	41.6%	742,600	38.0%
Total liabilities and stockholders' equity	$2,056,800	100.0%	$1,953,000	100.0%

Vertical Analysis, *continued*

Income Statement Example

The income statement below shows an example of vertical analysis for your business. When vertical analysis is done for an income statement, the net sales number is always the 100% reference base amount.

Superior Office Supply Corporation
Condensed Income Statements
Years Ended December 31

	2017	Percent	2016	Percent
Sales	$2,198,600	104.7%	$2,114,100	104.5%
Less: Returns and allowances	98,900	4.7%	90,900	4.5%
Net sales	2,099,700	100.0%	2,023,200	100.0%
Cost of goods sold	1,364,800	65.0%	1,294,800	64.0%
Gross profit	734,900	35.0%	728,400	36.0%
Selling expenses	252,000	12.0%	222,600	11.0%
Administrative expenses	283,500	13.5%	293,400	14.5%
Total operating expenses	535,500	25.5%	516,000	25.5%
Operating income	199,400	9.5%	212,400	10.5%
Other revenue (and expense)				
Interest expense	(2,900)	(0.1%)	(2,100)	(0.1%)
Income tax expense	59,500	2.8%	64,900	3.2%
Net income	$ 137,000	6.6%	$ 145,400	7.2%

Analysis

- **Balance sheet:** The balance sheet shows a significant percentage of total assets as current assets. In 2017, this is more than 64% of total assets. Cash is a high percentage of total assets. In 2017, it is more than 22%. The strong cash position indicates a high degree of short-term debt-paying ability and relative safety.
- **Income statement:** The analysis confirms that the major portion of business expense is cost of goods sold, which in 2017 was 65% of total sales. Selling and administrative expense activities combine to about equally share most of the other expenses.

continued ▶

Combined Horizontal and Vertical Analysis

Analysis

After the vertical percentages are calculated, it is very useful to compare the percentages between years to see the changes—again, remember that trend analysis is one of the most important tools of financial analysis.

- **Balance sheet:** For example, on the balance sheet, it becomes clear that current assets as a percentage of total assets have increased from about 62% to 64%. At first, this might seem to be a good thing, but notice that the percentages for Accounts Receivable and Inventory are also increasing. Does this mean that your business is having some trouble collecting receivables and also that too much inventory has been ordered and is building up?
- **Income statement:** Cost of goods sold, which is a large dollar amount, has significantly increased as a percentage of sales from 64% to 65%, thereby lowering the gross profit margin. This calls for immediate investigation. It is also interesting to note that total operating expenses remained constant at 25.5% of net sales; however, apparently you were able to decrease administrative expenses but lost some control over selling expenses, which increased from 11% to 12% of sales. Also, for some reason the percentage of returns has increased.

Common-Size Statements

Overview

A ***common-size*** financial statement is a statement that is presented as only percentages. No dollar amounts are shown.

Three Important Benefits

Three important benefits are provided by common-size statements:

- Common-size statements make it easy to see percentage trends. These clearly highlight areas that may require further management investigation.
- Common-size statements make it possible to meaningfully compare companies of different sizes. Total dollar amounts are difficult to compare, but percentages all relate to 100% and are easily compared.
- Common-size statements make it possible to compare an individual company's results against industry average percentages. Industry percentages are reported in publications such as *Annual Statement Studies* by Robert Morris Associates; *Almanac of Business and Industrial Financial Ratios* by Troy, and reports by Standard and Poors and by Dun and Bradstreet. Also, trade magazines and internet financial sites can provide industry information.

continued ▶

Common-Size Statements, *continued*

Example

The example below shows a two-year common-size income statement using only the percentage amounts from the previous income statement.

Superior Office Supply Corporation
Common-Size Income Statements
Years Ended December 31

	2017	2016
Sales	104.7%	104.5%
Less: Returns and allowances	4.7%	4.5%
Net sales	100.0%	100.0%
Cost of goods sold	65.0%	64.0%
Gross profit	35.0%	36.0%
Selling expenses	12.0%	11.0%
Administrative expenses	13.5%	14.5%
Total operating expenses	25.5%	25.5%
Operating income	9.5%	10.5%
Other revenue (and expense)		
Interest expense	(0.1%)	(0.1%)
Income tax expense	2.8%	3.2%
Net income	6.6%	7.2%

MD&A

Overview

Definition

Management discussion and analysis, usually referred to as ***MD&A***, is a required management disclosure in the annual report for a publicly held company.

Features

- MD&A must include an explanation of major financial statement items including liquidity (cash position), sources of investment and debt capital provided to the business, and operating results that includes an analysis of sales and significant expenses.
- The MD&A must include an analysis of major risks.
- The MD&A must include management's opinion about the future performance of the company. However, one must read the analysis of future performance cautiously, as it is sometimes used as an overly optimistic promotional tool.

Ratio Analysis

Overview

Introduction

Ratio analysis is a means of analyzing selected financial statement items by the use of ratios. A ratio is the comparison of one number to another by showing the numbers as a fraction, with the answer expressed as the fraction, or converted to a percentage, a rate, or a proportion. (To review these items, see the basic math reviews in the disks accompanying these volumes.)

A financial ratio is designed so that the two numbers used in the ratio are connected in a meaningful way. As a result, the ratio should provide a useful insight into some specific element of a company's condition or operations. Ratios are designed to evaluate many different elements of a business.

Business Elements Analyzed

A great deal of financial data is available that can be used for many possible ratio calculations. In this section, we look at some of the most important and useful ratios, which measure these key aspects of a business:

- **Liquidity:** The ability to pay short-term debts as they come due
- **Solvency:** The long-term survival of a business
- **Profitability:** The success of a business as measured by gross profit, operating income, and net income
- **Investment return:** Measures a company on its merit as an investment
- **Productivity:** Measures the operating efficiency

Interpreting Financial Ratios

Overview

Mechanically calculating a ratio does not tell you much—you need to be able to interpret the answer you get. Let's take a look at how to interpret the ratios we will calculate.

Research the Company

First, find out enough about a company to have an understanding of what has been happening to it. This makes the ratios more meaningful. If possible, talk to present and past managers and employees. For large companies, read financial and trade newspapers, magazines, and reports to find out about the company and its industry area. Search the Internet using the company's name, including a visit to the company's home page and links on the home page to sites that analyze the company.

Interpreting Financial Ratios, *continued*

Benchmarks

A ***benchmark*** is a norm or guideline used for the purpose of comparison. The table below shows benchmarks that are used for financial ratio analysis.

Benchmark	Advantages	Disadvantages
Company history: What are the past results for our company?	Indicates trends within our company.	Gives no point of reference outside of our company.
Main competitors: What is the performance of our competition?	Compares our company against the direct competition.	▪ The application of GAAP may be different, making comparison less useful.
Industry norms: What is the average performance for companies in the same industry?	Provides a greater scope of comparison and may encourage deeper analysis.	▪ What if norms are mediocre? (At one time American auto companies were the standard until Japan improved norms.) ▪ Data may be from operations that are not fully comparable because of size or other factors.
Independent standards: Use information from experts to help set best performance goals and best practice methods	Raises standards and shows what is possible.	There will be employee and management resistance to significantly higher standards and new processes within the company. Compensation system may have to be changed.

General Indicators and Limitations

Interpret ratios only as general indicators—ratios are more like warning lights than precise gauges. Ratios act as early warning indicators that direct you to do further analysis to clarify the exact nature of an issue. Ratios limitations are: (1) different companies can use different GAAP methods, (2) ratios are based on historical data—a "rear-view mirror," and (3) cause and effect is not always clear.

Use in Groups

Whenever possible, use several ratios together when analyzing an element of a business. Doing this provides a more reliable indication and may reveal something more subtle that a single ratio would miss.

Coming Up . . . Analysis and Comparing to Industry Data

We are now ready to continue our analysis of your business, Superior Office Supply Company. For additional help, we will also compare results to industry average benchmarks for companies of about the same level of sales or assets. The sources for industry data are Robert Morris Associates, Standard and Poors, Dun and Bradstreet, and Almanac of Business and Industrial Ratios.

continued ▶

Measures of Liquidity, *continued*

The average collection period is: $\dfrac{\textit{number of days in the period}}{\textit{accounts receivable turnover}}$

Example for Superior Office Supply Company

2017	2016	Industry Average
$\dfrac{365 \text{ days}}{7.75 \text{ times}} = 47$ days	$\dfrac{365 \text{ days}}{8.5 \text{ times}} = 43$ days	20 days

Interpretation

In 2017, Superior Office Supply required an average of 47 days to collect current receivables—more than twice the industry average. This makes the current ratio and quick ratio now look much less favorable because of the uncertainty of when the receivables will be collected and how many are bad.

Inventory Turnover—Average Days to Sell

Another important measure of operating efficiency and potential liquidity is how quickly a company has been selling its inventory. Inventory that has been slow to sell indicates potentially serious income and cash flow problems. Inventory *turnover* is a rough measure of how often inventory is purchased and sold in a given period. The turnover is calculated by dividing cost of goods sold by the average amount of inventory in the period.

A more useful calculation is to use the same information to calculate the average days needed to sell inventory, similar to our days of receivables calculation.

The inventory turnover is: $\dfrac{\textit{cost of goods sold}}{\textit{average inventory}}$

Example for Superior Office Supply Company

2017	2016	Industry Average
$\dfrac{\$1{,}364{,}800}{(\$492{,}100 + \$456{,}900)/2} = 2.88$ times	$\dfrac{\$1{,}294{,}800}{(\$456{,}900 + \$329{,}700)/2} = 3.29$ times *Note:* Inventory balance from 2015 balance sheet is $329,700.	5.4 times

Interpretation

Superior Office Supply Company is having problems with inventory buildup. The inventory has been overstocked, or for some reason it is not selling well. To clarify the turnover time, let's calculate the average days to sell.

Measures of Liquidity, *continued*

The average days to sell is: $\frac{\textit{number of days in the period}}{\textit{inventory turnover}}$

Example for Superior Office Supply Company

2017	2016	Industry Average
$\frac{365 \text{ days}}{2.88 \text{ times}} = 127 \text{ days}$	$\frac{365 \text{ days}}{3.29 \text{ times}} = 111 \text{ days}$	66 days

Interpretation

In 2017, Superior Office Supply required an average of 127 days to sell its inventory—more than twice the industry average. The "good" current ratio looks more doubtful, because there is now some question as to the time it will take to sell the inventory and the ability to sell it at normal prices. Perhaps the cause is simply buying too much inventory. As a manager, you will have to do some further investigation by checking the number of units sold, the pricing, and the inventory purchasing policy.

Caution: The inventory turnover ratio (and days to sell) gives different answers for companies using different inventory methods such as FIFO, LIFO, or average, even though the inventory is not actually moving faster or slower. The current ratio, which includes inventory, is also affected by the use of different inventory methods. This can make company comparisons more difficult. (See Volume 2.)

Sometimes, measures of liquidity are referred to as measures of the adequacy of working capital. ***Working capital*** is defined as *current* assets minus *current* liabilities. Working capital is used as an indicator of ability to pay current liabilities and to meet the needs of current operations.

The Operating Cycle

By adding the average days to sell inventory to the average days to collect accounts receivable, you can calculate the ***operating cycle,*** which is the time it takes to convert inventory into cash. For Superior Office Supply, the operating cycle in 2017 is: 47 + 127 = 174 days. Also, if vendors require payment in a period that is significantly less than the operating cycle (for example, 60 days), it may indicate potential cash flow problems.

Measures of Solvency

Overview

Solvency is the ability to remain in business for a long period of time. This mainly refers to the ability to pay all debts as they come due. It also involves the ability to raise new capital and to adapt to changing conditions. The ratios we will use to evaluate solvency are: (1) debt ratio, (2) times interest earned ratio, (3) asset turnover ratio, (4) cash flow to debt ratio, and (5) free cash flow.

Note: Profitability also affects solvency; however, we will discuss this in the next topic when we look at measures of profitability.

Debt Ratio (Leverage Ratio)

The *debt ratio* is a measure of the extent to which a company uses debt. The debt ratio compares the amount of total debt to total assets. The use of debt is often called ***financial leverage***. Although leverage can be very useful to a business, the use of leverage also involves danger. As a company incurs more debt, the danger grows, because debt requires regular fixed payments and often a large principal payment when the debt is due. Also, lenders may impose additional requirements and restrictions called ***debt covenants*** that, if violated, create the risk of the full loan becoming immediately due and payable.

The debt ratio is: $\frac{\text{total debt}}{\text{total assets}}$

Example for Superior Office Supply Company

2017	2016	Industry Average
$\frac{\$1,201,700}{\$2,056,800} = .58$	$\frac{\$1,210,400}{\$1,953,000} = .62$	.70

Interpretation

The company has both reduced its total debt and increased total assets, so the debt ratio has declined from 62% to 58%, indicating improved solvency and a reduction of risk. However, the company is still using substantial leverage, and the industry norm is also relatively high. Generally, debt exceeding one-third of total assets should be considered as substantial. (This can be seen in the bond ratings of large industrial companies. The median debt ratio at which the ratings change from "investment" grade to "speculative" grade is about 40%.)

It is especially important to know *why* a debt ratio *increases*. What was the money needed for—expansion, operations, to pay old debt? This can be a key indicator of a company's condition and strategy. The ability of a company to manage its debt depends on the size and the stability of its operating cash flow.

Measures of Solvency, *continued*

Times Interest Earned Ratio

The times interest earned ratio is a measure of a company's ability to pay interest payments. The ability to pay loan interest is very important because if the payments are not made, the lender can force a company into bankruptcy.

The times interest earned ratio is calculated by dividing operating income by interest expense.

Although this ratio is typically calculated using operating income, interest payments are not made with income. They are made with cash. Therefore, a more reliable method is to use operating cash flow instead of operating income.

The times interest earned ration is: $\frac{\text{operating income}}{\text{interest expense}}$ or $\frac{\text{operating each flow + interest paid}}{\text{interest paid}}$

Example for superior Office Supply Company

2017		2016	
Operating Income	**Operating Cash Flow**	**Operating Income**	**Operating Cash Flow**
$\frac{\$199{,}400}{\$2{,}900}$ = 68.8 times	$\frac{\$128{,}100}{\$2{,}900}$ = 44.2 times	$\frac{\$212{,}400}{\$2{,}100}$ = 101.1 times	$\frac{\$71{,}800}{\$2{,}100}$ = 34.2 times

Interpretation

If we assume that the amount of interest recorded on the income statement is typically the amount of interest actually paid, then for 2017 we would calculate: $2,900 + $125,200 (cash flow statement) = $128,100 to determine the amount of pre-interest operating cash flow. For 2016, this would be $2,100 + $69,700 = $71,800. The times interest earned ratio based on operating cash flow reveals that the coverage is much lower than is indicated by the ratio based on income. Another issue: for the amount of debt on the balance sheet (and debt ratio of .58) this coverage is very high. A typical coverage ratio for this much debt in these circumstances might be in the range of 2 to 10 times. Is interest being correctly recorded?

To get an idea of a business's coverage for **all operating fixed payment commitments** (such as debt payments + lease payments + . . . and so on), add total operating fixed payments to operating cash flow for the numerator of the fraction. Then use total operating fixed payments for the denominator.

continued ▶

Measures of Solvency, *continued*

Asset Turnover Ratio

The *asset turnover ratio* measures how many dollars of sales are created for every dollar of total assets. This has a direct effect on profitability and is also a measure of the efficiency of the use of company assets. Asset turnover ratios can vary greatly depending on the type of business. For example, an accounting firm would have a relatively low investment in assets and a much higher asset turnover ratio than an airline. Also, some analysts prefer to focus only on gross *plant and equipment* (excluding accumulated depreciation) turnover as a measure of the efficient use of "productive assets."

The asset turnover ratio is: $\dfrac{\text{net sales}}{\text{average total assets}}$

Example for superior Office Supply Company

2017	2016	Industry Average
$\dfrac{\$2{,}099{,}700}{(\$2{,}056{,}800 + \$1{,}953{,}000)/2}$ = 1.05 times	$\dfrac{\$2{,}023{,}200}{(\$1{,}953{,}000 + \$1{,}870{,}100)/2}$ = 1.06 times	3.6

Note: Total assets from 2015 balance sheet is $1,870,100.

Interpretation

Superior Office Supply is creating only about $1.05 of net sales for every dollar invested in company assets. This is clearly below the industry average of $3.60. Perhaps the company has over-invested in inventory and inproperty, plant, and equipment.

Cash Flow to Debt Ratio

The *cash flow to debt ratio* is a good measure of long-term solvency and shows the ability of a company to pay debt *using only the operating cash flow.* The ratio is calculated by dividing operating cash flow by average total debt.

The cash flow to debt ratio is: $\dfrac{\text{cash flow from operating activities}}{\text{average total liabilities}}$

Example for superior Office Supply Company

2017	2016	Industry Average
$\dfrac{\$125{,}200}{(\$1{,}201{,}700 + \$1{,}210{,}400)/2}$ = .104 times	$\dfrac{\$69{,}700}{(\$1{,}210{,}400 + \$1{,}155{,}300)/2}$ = .06 times	.3 times

Note: Total liabilities from 2015 balance sheet is $1,155,300.

Measures of Solvency, *continued*

Interpretation
In 2017, Superior Office Supply produced only $.104 of cash flow for every dollar of debt, the year 2016 was much worse, and both years are far below the industry average. This is an unfavorable long-term indication. This ratio is also useful as an estimate of how much time would be required to pay off debt using current operating cash flow. In this example, the 2017 annual operating cash flow of $125,200 would require about 9.6 years to pay off the average debt balance of $1,206,050 (calculated as 1/.104 = 9.6).

Free Cash Flow

Free cash flow is a measure of how much operating cash flow is available after paying necessary cash outlays for expansion and/or improvements. It is a good measure of financial stability. Although there is no single definition of free cash flow, a common definition is: operating cash flow less capital expenditures purchases of assets, minus dividends.

Free cash flow is: Cash flow from operating activities – capital expenditures – dividends	
Example for superior Office Supply Company	
2017	**2016**
$125,200 – $55,000 – $24,500 = $45,700	$69,700 – $5,000 – $40,000 = $24,700
Interpretation	
Free cash flow has shown an increase in 2017 of $21,000, or about 85%. This should be evaluated against past results for several years.	

continued ▶

Measures of Solvency, *continued*

EBITDA

EBITDA sounds like some kind of wild African animal, but it really means *Earnings Before Interest, Taxes, Depreciation, and Amortization*. To calculate EBITDA, start with income from continuing operations before tax and add back interest expense, depreciation, and amortization to obtain an income amount that excludes these items.

EBITDA is supposed to be an estimate of either cash flow from operations or a common unit of income measure, and is often used in financial information. This is unfortunate because it can be a very misleading estimate of both items for various reasons. It is usually best to ignore EBITDA and use cash flow from operating activities or GAAP income.

Measures of Profitability

Overview

Profitability is the essential reason for operating a business. It is also a key element in a company's success, or lack of it, in obtaining capital. Profitability information is widely used and reported to lenders, investors, and other stakeholders. Profitability ratios can be calculated at different levels of the income statement, such as net income, operating income, and gross profit.

Profit Margin Ratio

The profit margin percentage shows what percent of every dollar of net sales ends up as net income. This ratio is also sometimes called the *rate of return on net sales*. This ratio is calculated as net income divided by net sales, and is usually expressed as a percentage.

The profit margin ratio is: $\frac{\text{net income}}{\text{net sales}}$

Example for Superior Office Supply Company

2017	2016	Industry Average
$\frac{\$137,000}{\$2,099,700} = 6.6\%$	$\frac{\$145,400}{\$2,023,200} = 7.2\%$	1.5%

Interpretation

For the last two years, Superior Office Supply's profit percentage has been greatly in excess of the industry average. This could be good news or bad news. It is possible the company has some kind of very unusual advantage. *Or* it has either temporarily had an unusual amount of sales or has not been spending enough on necessary expenses. Let's explore further . . .

Measures of Profitability, *continued*

Gross Profit Ratio

The *gross profit ratio* is calculated by dividing gross profit by net sales. The gross profit ratio shows what percentage of each dollar of sales ends up as gross profit. For merchandising and manufacturing companies this is a very important ratio because it is affected by some very important things: the selling price per unit and the number of units sold (sales revenue) and the cost per unit of the merchandise and the number of units sold (cost of goods sold). These items have a very powerful effect on net income.

The gross profit ratio is: $\frac{\text{gross profit}}{\text{net sales}}$

Example for Superior Office Supply Company

2017	2016	Industry Average
$\frac{\$734,900}{\$2,099,700} = 35\%$	$\frac{\$728,400}{\$2,023,200} = 36\%$	36%

Interpretation

The gross profit ratio is about the same as the industry norm. In 2017, $.35 of every dollar remained as gross profit to cover operating expenses and provide a net income.

So, back to our question: Why is the net income percentage so high? We now know that the gross profit percentage is about normal, so that only leaves one other major area on the income statement—operating expenses. The operating expenses are unusually low. This may be good if the company is very efficient, but it will not be good if the company is avoiding necessary and important expenses, such as repairs and maintenance and the cost of high-quality management.

Caution: As discussed above with inventory turnover, FIFO, LIFO, average, and other inventory methods give different results. This can make cost of goods sold and gross profit comparisons less reliable.

Gross Profit and Market Share

Market share refers to the sales of a company as a percentage of the total sales for all companies in the same type of business. Market share is an important measure of the ability of a company to attract new customers and keep old customers. For large publicly traded companies, market share information is widely available.

Gross profit percentage is often closely related to market share. If a company's market share is growing, it means that the company is attracting new customers and/or taking customers from competing businesses. This usually means that the company will be able to maintain current prices and therefore will be able to maintain or improve the gross margin percentage. Conversely, if a company's market share is decreasing, it is often an early indicator that the gross profit percentage of the company will also decrease, as the company tries to keep customers by lowering prices.

continued ▶

Measures of Profitability, *continued*

Earnings Per Share

Earnings per share (often called *EPS*) is a calculation that is done only for a corporation. The basic EPS calculation is:

$$\frac{\text{net income} - \text{preferred dividends}}{\text{weighted average number of common shares outstanding}}$$

The EPS shows how much net income is potentially available for each share of common stock. The EPS number is important because it is a scaling method that allows the earnings of different size companies to be compared on a per-share basis. Corporations that have ***publicly traded*** stock (stock that is traded on exchanges like the New York Stock Exchange or Nasdaq exchange) are required to show earnings per share. The ratio is also important to stock investors who use it as part of a calculation called the ***price earnings ratio*** (*PE ratio*), which is the price per share divided by the earnings per share. The PE ratio is used as an indicator of relative stock value.

There is no "good or bad" EPS number; it is an amount that is watched over time and compared to the EPS of other corporations and measured against the price of the stock using the PE ratio. (Some analysts prefer to use operating cash flow or free cash flow instead of net income in the calculation.) The EPS calculation is discussed in detail on page 656.

Rate of Return on Total Assets

The rate of return on total assets is calculated by dividing net income (or sometimes income before interest expense) by average total assets. This ratio is an indicator of how much profit is being created for each dollar of assets, usually expressed as a percentage.

The rate of return on total assets is: $\frac{\text{net income}}{\text{average total assets}}$

Example for superior Office Supply Company

2017	2016	Industry Average
$\frac{\$137{,}000}{(\$2{,}056{,}800 + \$1{,}953{,}000)/2} = 6.8\%$	$\frac{\$145{,}400}{(\$1{,}953{,}000 + \$1{,}155{,}300)/2} = 9.4\%$	7.5%
	Note: Total assets from 2015 balance sheet is $1,155,300.	

Interpretation

In 2017, the business had an 6.8% return on assets That is, it had 6.8% of profit for every dollar of assets.

Measures of Investment Return

Return on Equity (Corporation)

Return on equity measures the percent profit as a return on the average amount of stockholders' equity. The investors can compare this with other businesses and also with other possible investments.

The return on equity ratio is: $\frac{\text{net income} - \text{preferred dividends}}{\text{average stockholders' equity}}$

Example for superior Office Supply Company

2017	2016	Industry Average
$\frac{\$137,000}{(\$855,100 + \$742,600)/2} = 17.2\%$	$\frac{\$145,400}{(\$742,600 + \$608,000)/2} = 21.5\%$	11%
	Note: Stockholders' equity from 2015 balance sheet is \$608,000. No preferred dividends in any year.	

Interpretation

The return on equity is much greater than the industry norm, and that is primarily because the net income percentage is so high. So again, we have to be very sure to explain the net income and investigate the low operating expenses.

Return on Equity (Proprietorship)

The rate of return for a proprietorship is simply calculated as the return on the owner's equity. The formula is:

$$\frac{\text{net income}}{\text{average owner's equity}}$$

Dividend Ratio

The *dividend ratio* is usually calculated only for the common shareholders of a corporation. The ratio measures the total common shareholder dividends as a percent of the average amount invested by the common shareholders over a designated period of time. The calculation is:

$$\frac{\text{common stock cash dividends}}{\text{average common stockholders, equity}}$$

continued ►

Measures of Investment Return, *continued*

Trading on Equity

Trading on equity refers to the effect that financial leverage (see the debt ratio discussion) has on the return on equity. The effect of trading on equity can be seen by comparing the rate of return on total assets of 6.8% in 2017 with the return on the stockholders' equity in 2017 of 17.2%. The positive difference that exceeds the return on total assets happens when a business borrows money at an interest rate that is less than the rate that the business is able to earn when it uses the borrowed money. Using borrowed funds (leverage) also means that less of the owners' money is needed to acquire assets. The borrowed money is being put to work to buy assets that create additional income and that do not require the use of owners' money. If the borrowed money more than "pays for itself," this profitabil-ity is a boost that adds directly to net income.

Trading on equity should be used cautiously. The attempt to trade on equity may result in a much worse rate of return to owners if the situation reverses and a company cannot earn a rate of return on the borrowed money that is equivalent to the interest cost. Furthermore, increased debt always means increased risk. In our discussion of the debt ratio, we saw that the median level at which debt ratings change from investment to speculative grade is about 40%. Although many companies in fact operate at a debt ratio higher than 40%, it does not lessen the increased cash flow risk and opportunity cost risk when large, sudden, and negative financial events occur.

Measures of Productivity

Overview

Measures of ***productivity*** show the level of efficiency at which a company is using and obtaining its resources. There are many measures of productivity. The measure used should relate to an important resource. Some typical examples are shown below.

Revenue (or Gross Profit) Per Unit of Resource

Revenue (or gross profit) per unit of resource shows the amount of revenue (gross profit) created per unit of scarce resource used. *Examples:*

- Revenue per square foot of floor space (used by retail stores)
- Revenue per employee or per dollar of wages expense
- Revenue per seat per mile (used by airlines)
- Asset turnover ratio. The asset turnover ratio previously discussed can also be interpreted as an overall measure of how effectively the investment in assets is used to create revenue.

Measures of Productivity, *continued*

Cost Per Unit of Resource

Cost per unit of resource shows the cost incurred to obtain or use a unit of a particular resource. *Examples:*

- Wage expense per employee or per hour worked
- Rent expense per square foot
- Cost of inventory per item

Other Good Indicators

Other indicators of productivity focus on designated activities. *Examples:*

- Plant and equipment turnover: This is an indicator of the amount of revenue created for every dollar invested in the plant and equipment (productive) assets. This is similar to total asset turnover, except that the denominator used is the average gross cost of plant and equipment.
- Inventory turnover: The inventory turnover ratio previously discussed shows how quickly a business is able to sell inventory. Also, the number of days of inventory on hand can be a good early warning of an inventory buildup.
- Accounts receivable turnover: As previously discussed, this also relates to the efficiency of collecting receivables and the management of credit policy.
- Accounts receivable compared to sales: Compare the percentage change in the age of accounts receivable to the percentage change in net sales. (The accounts receivable turnover ratio acts as a similar indicator of the ability to actually collect what is reported as revenue.)
- Percent of past-due or uncollectible receivables per sales dollar: This is an indicator of the credit policy applied and collectibility of reported sales.
- Cost of goods sold as a percentage of revenue
- Percent of returned merchandise per sales dollar
- Variances between actual costs and budgeted or standard costs

The word "earnings" can be deceptive. It usually refers to net income, but may also refer to operating income or even gross profit. You should always verify the context of the use of the word.

Analysis as an Outsider

Overview

Insider As Primary User of Financial Information

Until this point, our discussion about financial statement analysis has been from the point of view of someone who has the ability to influence or control the management—an insider. For example, we analyzed the financial statements of Superior Office Supply Company as if you were assuming management of your own family-owned business. Therefore, the financial information was primarily for your use, as an insider, to analyze and improve your business.

As an insider and primary user you want financial statements to be as accurate and as honestly representative of the real situation as possible. Your analysis of these statements *improves your understanding* of what is happening to the business and improves your decision making, which in turn results in better profits and cash flow. Your good decisions *increase the value of the business*. Moreover, if necessary, the business will be able to obtain cheaper outside capital (lower interest on loans and lower required rate of return on new investment money), because the business is secure and profitable.

Notice the priorities here for use of financial statement information: (1) create better understanding and decision making, which results in (2) an increase in real business value, and finally (3) a cheaper cost of capital.

Outsiders As Users of Financial Information

Outsiders are people who do not have authority to manage a company. The most important outsiders are providers of capital: (1) investors, (2) lenders, and (3) suppliers. For some businesses, outsiders may be a significant and regular source of capital. This is usually the situation with large corporations. Outsiders are also financial statement users and, of course, want statements that are reliable and accurate. However, outsiders must rely on the financial statements that have been prepared by the insiders—the top management.

Different Priorities

As an outsider, you naturally would like to believe that the financial information priorities of the management *are the same as yours*, which is to first create reliable financial statements that result in good decision making. Then business value increases and cost of capital decreases. Sometimes it happens this way.

Often however, when outsiders begin to provide a significant amount of capital, *the management's financial information priorities become reversed*: (1) maximize short-term business value and obtain the cheapest possible capital and (2) create better understanding and decision making.

Overview, *continued*

Be Skeptical

Maximum business value and low-cost capital happen primarily as the result of high reported profits. When high reported profits become a compelling first priority that supersedes effective management, the financial statements become a tool for reporting favorable information rather than for showing reliable and accurate information for decision making. The business begins to look more valuable—not because management has actually made it more valuable but because the financial statements are used as a shortcut to make the business *appear* more valuable.

As an outsider, it is always wise to maintain the following skeptical attitude: A company that (1) needs significant capital from outsiders and/or (2) provides significant rewards to top management based on profitability will (3) have a management that is highly motivated to create financial statements that make a business appear as profitable as possible.

Finding Information

Full Disclosure

For publicly traded companies, the law requires that information disclosures to outside parties be made available simultaneously to all outside parties. Therefore, even as an outsider, you have access to very useful information, and no other outsider legally has better access to information than you do.

SEC

Probably the single best source of detailed company information for publicly traded companies is the SEC (Securities and Exchange Commission) website at www.sec.gov. You can type in a company name (or its trading "ticker" symbol) to locate the company and its reports. The key financial information items to look for are reports 10-K (annual report) and 10-Q (quarterly report) and 8-K (disclosure of material events).

Annual Reports

Company annual reports are available at the investor relations page of a company website. Some other sites that provide annual reports are www.annualreportservice.com and www.reportgallery.com.

Conference Calls

When publicly traded companies release annual reports, top management will present a public question-and-answer session called a *conference call.* You can listen to this discussion on the Internet! Written transcripts of the call are also available on the Internet. This is often very useful information because analysts participating in the session ask very insightful questions.

Quality of Earnings

Overview

Overview

At various times, we have referred to the important topic of *event analysis*. We defined event analysis as the analytical procedure used to identify and properly record transactions. The key elements of event analysis are: (1) classification, (2) valuation, and (3) timing (recognition).

The quality of earnings issue is really a discussion about proper event analysis in the context of how the event analysis affects the income statement. Specifically, on the income statement the reported income or loss is a direct result of how revenue and gain events and expense and loss events are analyzed.

Definition

Although there is no single definition of ***quality of earnings***, the general idea is the extent to which a company's operating and net income honestly portray what has really happened. More specifically, quality of earnings refers to these issues:

1. Does income accurately measure the change in a company's wealth that has resulted from the current period operations?
2. Does income accurately represent the recurring and repeatable operations of a company so that the reported income has predictive usefulness?

Earnings Management

Whenever a company intentionally uses GAAP for the purpose of manipulating the results shown on the income statement, the company is doing ***earnings management***. This is a major cause of low quality of earnings.

Earnings Management

Example

Smith Corporation is aggressive and wants to favorably impress investors so that the price of its stock will increase. Smith uses every accounting method that it can for the express purpose of reporting higher net income. For example, it records all revenue regardless of the financial condition of its customers, it uses the straight-line depreciation method, and it uses FIFO in an industry in which prices are regularly increasing. Smith is said to have a *low quality of earnings* because there is a good chance that its selection of methods, all biased toward showing higher income, overstates the wealth actually resulting from operations. Also, outsiders are likely to be misled into believing that the favorable results come from recurring operations that will continue into future periods.

Earnings Management, *continued*

Why Is Earnings Management Possible?

Revenues should result in an increase in valuable resources, and expenses should result in a decrease in valuable resources. Thus, operating income (and net income) should be a measure of the change in valuable resources (wealth) resulting from the operations. Ideally, the methods used to analyze these events should be consistent at all times if fair, accurate, and fully comparable financial statements are to be achieved.

However, GAAP permits: (1) the use of different methods and (2) the use of estimates. Whenever transaction (event) analysis is subject to choices and estimates, the opportunity will always exist for earnings management.

Not the Same As Fraud

Earnings management is not the same as fraudulent reporting, although the ethics of earnings management is in many cases questionable. Fraud is an outright violation or ignoring of GAAP with the intent to deceive. Earnings management falls into a gray area because GAAP is not ignored or violated; rather, GAAP is "selectively" applied to create biased financial statements. The aspect of deception, however, is often still present and, if sufficiently excessive, can result in legal action by the SEC, federal prosecutors, and state attorneys general.

Revenue Management

There are many opportunities for "managing" revenue. It is also a frequent form of financial fraud. The table below shows several common methods of revenue management with descriptions. (*Remember:* Revenue either increases assets or decreases liabilities, so revenue management affects both the balance sheet and the income statement. See *revenue recognition principle.*)

Method	Description
Doubtful-credit sales	Sales knowingly made to customers who may not have the ability to pay.
Sales returns understated	Seller estimates sales returns at a low amount.
Percentage of completion manipulated	Activities occurring over a long time period such as construction projects and extended service contracts recognize revenue as the work is done based on percentage of completion. Seller manipulates this estimate.
Related-party sales	A sale is made to a division, subsidiary, or other related party who can be compelled to buy. Disclosure of the relationship is minimal.
Offsetting sales	Two companies make equivalent sales to each other really for the purpose of increasing reported revenues.
Channel stuffing	*Channel stuffing* means pressuring customers to make large purchases much sooner than they normally would. This process may involve either threats or excessive discounts. It usually happens at year end. This is not really a GAAP application; however, it is revenue management.

continued ▶

Earnings Management, *continued*

Compared to Fraud

The examples below illustrate revenue fraud. Notice that they involve clear GAAP violation or outright fictitious revenue transactions.

Method	Description
Revenue with excessive probability of return	Revenue is recorded for sales transactions with terms that will cause the merchandise to probably be returned and that allow the customer to easily return merchandise with no penalty.
Fake revenue	Revenue is recorded for sales transactions that never happened.
Wrong period	The books are held open at the end of a period to intentionally record sales from the next period into the current period.
Misclassification	Non-recurring sales of plant and equipment are recorded as sales revenue.
Shipment	Incomplete goods are shipped or goods are shipped to own warehouse and billed as revenue.
Unearned revenue mis-recorded	Advance payments from customers are recorded as revenue.

Expense Management

There are also many ways to manage expenses. The table below shows some common methods. (Remember: An expense either decreases assets or increases liabilities, so expense management affects the balance sheet as well as the income statement. Also see the *matching principle.*)

Method	Description
Uncollectible receivables underestimated	The estimate of bad receivables is intentionally understated, which reduces uncollectible account expense (and overstates assets). Different estimating methods are also available.
Control depreciation (and amortization)	■ Unrealistically long time periods are used. ■ Unrealistically large residual values are used. ■ Different depreciation methods are available.
Control cost of goods sold	■ Different inventory methods are available. ■ LIFO (Volume 2) inventory purchase decisions are made at year end. ■ Subjective inventory write-down replacement costs are used.
Accrued expenses underestimated	Examples: ■ Accrued warranty expenses ■ Accrued environmental cleanup liability ■ Employee benefits liabilities
Capitalizing expenditures instead of recording them as expenses	GAAP permits discretion in recording some expenditures as assets rather than as expenses. Examples: ■ Capitalizing software development depends upon when management decides the software is "technically feasible." ■ Oil exploration expenditures are allowed to be capitalized. ■ Manage asset write-offs: See Impairment rules, volume 2.
Expense timing	A business can decide to incur or not incur expenses in any given period, for example, repairs and maintenance. When earnings management is involved, this decision is influenced more by how the income statement will appear than by business necessities or efficient management.

Earnings Management, *continued*

Compared to Fraud

The examples below illustrate expense fraud. Notice that they all involve clear GAAP violations or outright fictitious expense transactions.

Method	Description
Capitalize operating expenses	Expenditures that are clearly operating expenses, such as payroll, repairs, maintenance, and so on, are recorded as the purchase of assets.
Misclassification	An expense is "spread around" in small amounts to various accounts.
Unrecorded accruals	Accrued expenses are intentionally ignored.
Wrong period	Expenses intentionally recorded in wrong period.

Important financial warning signs

- Decline in sales and/or income
- Collection of receivables becomes slower. The accounts receivable turnover ratio decreases and the average number of days to collect increases.
- Sales are increasing at a significantly faster rate than operating cash flow over several priods.
- Inventory is selling more slowly. The inventory turnover ratio decreases, the number of days to sell becomes greater, and the average inventory balance increases.
- Liquidity becomes a problem: continued or significant decreases in the current ratio and quick ratio, and/or in operating cash flow and the cash balance.
- Debt becomes excessive and repayment becomes more difficult. The cash flow to debt ratio begins to decline. The debt ratio begins to increase. More debt means more risk.
- The gross profit percentage is decreasing. The company is selling its goods for less—often a sign of increased competition—and also may be paying more for its inventory. This is often a reason for earnings management to begin.
- Any significant increases or decreases in gross profit percentages should be carefully investigated.
- Interim press releases use amounts that do not conform to GAAP (even though GAAP amounts are disclosed).

continued 

Earnings Management, *continued*

Other Methods

Numerous other methods for earnings management do not require showing greater revenues or smaller expenses. Here are some examples:

Method	Description
The "big bath"	After many periods of overstating net income, a company "fixes everything" by correcting the cumulative overstatement in the current year. That often involves writing off unproductive (impaired) assets and/or incurring "restructuring costs" all in a single year. This results in a very bad year, which the company knows that most investors will soon forget because the next year will look much better in comparison.
Income smoothing and the "cookie jar" (also called "secret reserves")	Companies know that investors like to see a smoothly increasing income. To achieve this, a company will overstate expenses or understate revenues in good years. Examples: ▪ In a good year, uncollectible accounts expense, sales returns, warranty expense, etc., is overstated to create an excessive balance in an allowance (or liability) account. When a bad year arrives, the excessive balance reduces the amount of expense needed. ▪ In a good year, the amount of unearned revenue earned is understated, so in a bad year, more can be recorded as earned.
Misleading press releases	Large companies sometimes publish misleading press releases using non-GAAP amounts that greatly overstate income. This usually happens at the time of quarterly earnings reports and may include misleading non-GAAP terminology such as "pro forma income" or "core income." Although these companies have reported income to the SEC on a correct GAAP basis, the press releases receive much more attention because they are widely reported by financial news services and television media. Solution: Use "Edgar" on the SEC website at www.sec.gov/ and ignore the press releases. (Or use only the GAAP data in the releases and the reconciliation of the non-GAAP data to the GAAP-based data.)
Repeated "non-recurring" losses	Companies know that most investors/lenders tend to ignore non-recurring" or "special" items and instead focus on income from continuing operations because it is perceived as a predictor of what is likely to happen next period. Some companies try hard to classify as much expense as possible as "non-recurring"(and one-time gains as part of "continuing operations").
Securities Investments	For certain types of investments in the stocks + bonds of other companies (called "marketable securities"), changes in market value are not required to be reported until management classifies them as "available for sale."

Potentially Hidden Liabilities

Overview

Importance of Knowing Liabilities

The importance of identifying all liabilities cannot be overstated. Liabilities are a claim on a company's present and future wealth. Furthermore, many liabilities are created by expenses that significantly impact the amount of income reported on the income statement and thereby affect the earnings. The analysis guidelines of classification, valuation, and timing must be applied to all liabilities.

Identifying Liabilities

Some liabilities are easy to identify because they have been recorded as the result of completed transactions such as the receipt of cash from a bank loan or by properly recording an adjusting entry for an expense accrual. These are the liabilities that regularly appear on a balance sheet. But, can there be liabilities that do not appear the balance sheet? Yes!

Liabilities Not on the Balance Sheet

Sometimes a liability has the potential to "disappear" from the balance sheet. These are called "contingent liabilities."

Contingent Liabilities

Definition

A ***contingent liability*** is a potential liability that will become an actual liability only if some other event occurs first.

This contingent liability . . .	. . . becomes an actual (recorded) liability if . . .
Product warranty	the customer wants a defective item repaired or replaced.
IRS audit	the IRS assesses a deficiency.
Activity impacting the environment	environmental damage has occurred.
Potentially dangerous product	damages are awarded or settlement is agreed.
Defendant in a lawsuit	the lawsuit results in damages awarded or settlement agreed.
Issuance of coupons	a customer uses coupons.
Guarantee a debt	the borrower does not repay the debt.
Frequent-flier miles	non-paying passengers replace paying passengers.

continued ►

Contingent Liabilities, *continued*

Contingent Liability Classifications

When you look at the list of examples, it becomes clear that not all the contingencies are equally likely to happen. For example, product warranties require some future expenditures and can be estimated from past experience. However, the outcome of a lawsuit is very unpredictable. GAAP classifies contingent liabilities into three categories:

- **Probable**
  - The amount can be reasonably estimated: *Accrue the expense and liability on the financial statements* (use the estimate to debit an expense and credit a liability).
  - The amount cannot be reasonably estimated: *Disclose in footnotes.*
- **Reasonably Possible:** *Disclose in footnotes.*
- **Remote:** *Depending on item, disclose in footnotes or no disclosure required.*

The items that are disclosed only in footnotes will be recorded on financial statements only if and when the contingency happens.

What Is the Potential Problem?

The classifications *probable, reasonably possible,* and *remote* are subjective descriptions. Only items in the probable category that can be reasonably estimated such as *warranty expenses* or *coupon expenses* will show up as accrued expenses on the financial statements.

But what should be done in the case of potential environmental damage or potentially dangerous products? These items could be very large amounts for some companies. Another example is airline frequent-flier miles, for which there is no consistent treatment.

Also, there is great variety in footnote disclosures. Sometimes disclosures are clear and easy to understand. Sometimes they are vague or quite complex and difficult to interpret.

If an aggressive management can convince auditors that an item should not appear on the financial statements or that disclosure should be vague or even eliminated by classifying an item as remote, then a contingent liability has the potential to result in a very unpleasant surprise. In a company with a high quality of earnings, contingent liabilities are fully and obviously disclosed, and expense or loss provisions are recorded as necessary, based on a conservative management attitude.

Contingent Liabilities, *continued*

Examples of Probable Liabilities That Can Be Estimated

- Warranty liabilities
- Coupons issued to customers
- Unused refundable tickets sold to customers

All of the items above (1) create probable liabilities and (2) can be estimated based on a company's past experience. Therefore a journal entry is made to record the liability and to match the related expense against current period revenue to which the liability is related. For example:

Warranty Expense	20,000	
Estimated Warranty Liability		20,000

When a customer returns and wants the product repaired:

Estimated Warranty Liability	1,000	
Parts Inventory		300
Wages Payable		700

Actual Liabilities That Must Be Estimated

There is a difference between an actual liability that must be estimated and a contingent liability that can be estimated. Remember that a contingent liability, even though it might be probable, does not exist unless some event happens.

An actual liability is one that already exists. Sometimes an actual liability needs to be estimated. *Examples:* Property taxes that have not yet been determined, estimated income taxes, and employee vacation pay.

Off-Balance Sheet Liabilities

It is possible for a business to create obligations that do not appear on a balance sheet. This is usually done by the use of contractual obligations and joint membership in another entity. Footnote disclosure is extremely important in these circumstances.

Conclusions

Financial Statement Usefulness

GAAP Does Matter

GAAP is important. GAAP provides the essential standards for maintaining the integrity of accounting information and financial reporting. Therefore, you should not conclude from our discussion that GAAP does not matter. On the contrary, GAAP is the best means presently available for communicating U.S. accounting information in American financial reporting.

High Earnings Quality Is Not Assured

However, the very flexibility and complexity of GAAP that is intended to encourage accurate reporting also enables companies to manipulate and bias the results of financial statements, creating the definite possibility of low quality of earnings. Because estimates often must be used, and because alternative methods are frequently permitted for measuring particular kinds of transactions, the meaning of financial statements can become subjective. The qualities of usefulness, reliability, and relevance can be easily compromised.

Therefore, you should retain your skepticism even when you are using GAAP-based, audited financial statements. This advice is reinforced by the fact that many investment professionals are cautious about full reliance on reported GAAP net income or income from continuing operations; instead, they base much of their analysis on the statement of cash flows, particularly operating cash flows. They also use the statement of cash flows as a tool to check against reported income. This is because the statement of cash flows is much less subject to manipulation and is much more comparable between companies. This is a rather sad commentary, considering the great efforts that have gone into developing the GAAP that measures and reports income. Nevertheless, given human nature, you should conclude that **GAAP cannot automatically be relied upon to assure high quality of earnings.**

The SEC (Securities and Exchange Commission) requires that all publicly traded companies submit the following disclosure documents according to SEC guidelines. These documents are publicly available and viewable online at the SEC website (sec.gov): 1) 10K: Annual financial report 2) 10Q: Quarterly financial report 3) 8K: Report on significant events at the time they occur 4) Proxy statement: Required disclosure to stockholders in advance of the annual stockholders' meeting. Includes executive compensation and directors' backgrounds. 5) S-1: Detailed company and financial disclosures prior to registering stock for sale to the public.

The Public Response

Sarbanes-Oxley

In 2002, Congress created the Sarbanes-Oxley Act. ***Sarbanes-Oxley*** was a response to the ever-increasing investor distrust of public company financial reporting and to the concerns that unreliable reporting would damage the American capital markets.

This distrust was later vindicated by securities and accounting fraud charges filed against numerous large public companies such as Adelphia, Health South, Sunbeam, WorldCom, Global Crossing, and Enron, all of which had published audited financial statements that aggressively reported inflated earnings and gave little or no indication of serious financial problems. The "last straw" was the sudden collapse and bankruptcy of Enron and then WorldCom, which was the largest bankruptcy ever filed. These two financial shocks were quickly followed by the license revocation and collapse of the auditor involved with both businesses, Arthur Andersen Company.

The cumulative effect of all these events was a public outcry that the accounting profession had become unable to adequately regulate its auditors because of the conflict of interest created by the large audit and consulting fees received from the clients being audited. The result was Sarbanes-Oxley.

The Sarbanes-Oxley law applies generally to publicly traded companies and has the following broad objcctives:

- Reporting: Make financial reporting fair, understandable, and independent.
- Auditing and internal control: Enforce and improve auditing standards and internal control analysis by CPA firms. Significantly improve internal control procedures used by the reporting companies.
- Corporate responsibility: Require personal accountability by top executives (chief executive officer and chief financial officer) for what is reported on financial statements of their companies. Corporate audit committees cannot be part of management and must have membership on the board of directors.
- Penalties: Enact severe criminal and civil penalties for top executives, board members, and auditors who knowingly act or fail to act in ways that cause shareholders and other stakeholders to be defrauded.

continued ▶

The Public Response, *continued*

The Public Company Accounting Oversight Board (PCAOB)

A potentially very significant development for improving the quality of earnings for public companies is the ***Public Company Accounting Oversight Board (PCAOB).*** The PCAOB is a private-sector, non-profit organization that was created by the Sarbanes-Oxley Act.

The main purpose of the PCAOB is to assure the implementation of two of the Sarbanes-Oxley goals:

- Make financial reporting fair, understandable, and independent.
- Enforce and improve high-quality auditing and internal control standards.

The Sarbanes-Oxley Act removed the final authority over audit and internal control standards and enforcement from the public accounting profession and placed this authority under the control of the PCAOB for all publicly traded companies.

The PCAOB makes proposals for auditing and reporting rule changes and submits these proposals to the Securities and Exchange Commission. In turn, the Commission must approve each proposal for it to become effective as a PCAOB rule. The PCAOB rules serve to implement existing GAAP and to create improved auditing, internal control, and reporting standards and, hopefully, to improve the quality of earnings.

To perform audits of public companies, CPA firms must register with the PCAOB. The PCAOB has broad investigative and disciplinary authority over these CPA firms. The PCAOB actively investigates potential violations and solicits information and complaints about potential violations.

The Future?

GAAP is always evolving and responding to the economic, social, and political environment. For example, the accounting profession continues to clarify the objectives of the conceptual framework of accounting. Perhaps in the future, a consensus may develop that the many rules attempting analytical precision have exceeded limits beyond which the unintended results of complexity and manipulation cancel out any subtle measurement benefits.

Perhaps the concept of single reasonable point of reference might be acknowledged as often more useful to stakeholders than current "flexibility" and the "selective accuracy" that are often the result. And for quality of earnings, hopefully the PCAOB oversight will result in continuing improvement.

However, you can at least be certain of this: In the financial world, regardless of where your future leads, a good understanding of accounting will always serve you very well. And who knows . . . in the future you may be among those who develop the new concepts and principles that will guide the rest of us.

Summary of Financial Ratios and Measurements

Ratio	Computation	Interpretation
Measures of Liquidity		
Current ratio	$\frac{\text{total current assets}}{\text{total current liabilities}}$	Shows the ability to pay current liabilities by using current assets
Quick (acid-test) ratio	$\frac{\text{cash + short term investments + current receivables (net)}}{\text{total current liabilities}}$	A more conservative measure of the ability to pay current liabilities
Receivables turnover	$\frac{\text{net credit sales}}{\text{average net receivables}}$	The number of times in a period the average level of receivables is collected—shows ability to collect
Average days to collect	$\frac{\text{number of days in the period}}{\text{accounts receivable turnover}}$	Average collection time in days
Inventory turnover	$\frac{\text{cost of goods sold}}{\text{average inventory}}$	The number of times in a period the average level of inventory is sold
Average days to sell	$\frac{\text{number of days in the period}}{\text{inventory turnover}}$	Average selling time in days
Measures of Solvency		
Debt ratio (leverage ratio)	$\frac{\text{total debt}}{\text{total assets}}$	Shows the percentage of assets that must be used to repay debt
Times-interest earned	$\frac{\text{operating income}}{\text{Interest expense}}$	How many times the operating income covers interest expense (not a measure of cash flow coverage)
	or $\frac{\text{cash flow from operating activities + interest paid}}{\text{interest expense}}$	How many times the cash flow from operations before interest covers interest expense (shows cash flow coverage)
Asset turnover ratio	$\frac{\text{net sales}}{\text{average total assets}}$	Dollars of sales generated for every dollar invested in assets
Cash flow to debt ratio	$\frac{\text{cash flow from operating activities}}{\text{average total liabilities}}$	The ability of a company to repay debt using only operating cash flow
Free cash flow	(cash flow from operating activities) – (capital expenditures)	How much operating cash flow remains after paying for capital expenditures

Summary of Financial Ratios and Measurements, continued

Ratio	Computation	Interpretation
Measures of Profitability		
Profit margin ratio	$\frac{\text{net income}}{\text{net sales}}$	Percent of sales that becomes profit
Gross profit ratio	$\frac{\text{gross profit}}{\text{net sales}}$	Percent of sales that becomes gross profit (for merchandising companies)
Earnings per share	$\frac{\text{net income} - \text{preferred dividends}}{\text{weighted average number of common shares outstanding}}$	For corporations, the net income allocable to each common share of stock
Return on total assets	$\frac{\text{net income}}{\text{average total assets}}$	The percent profit created for each dollar invested in assets
Measures of Investment Return		
Return on equity	$\frac{\text{net income}}{\text{average owner's equity}}$	The percentage net income for the average amount of owner's equity
	or	
	$\frac{\text{net income} - \text{preferred dividends}}{\text{average common stockholders' equity}}$	The percentage net income for the average amount of common stock-holder's equity in a corporation
Dividend ratio	$\frac{\text{common stock cash dividends}}{\text{average common stockholders' equity}}$	The percentage cash dividends for the average amount of common stockholder's equity in a corporation
Measures of Productivity		
Revenue (or gross profit) per unit of resource	$\frac{\text{revenue (or gross profit)}}{\text{units of important resource used}}$	Measures the ratio of revenue/gross profit that is being created for units of a scarce resource being used
Cost per unit of resource	$\frac{\text{cost}}{\text{units of important resource used}}$	Measures the ratio of cost that is incurred for units of a scarce resource used
Other measures	▪ Plant and equipment turnover ▪ Inventory turnover ▪ Receivables turnover (or average age) ▪ Percent of past-due receivables ▪ Cost of goods sold percentage ▪ Percent of merchandise returns ▪ Standard cost variances	Designed to highlight key measures that are considered important to an operation. (Note that many of these are also related to liquidity or solvency as well as productivity.) Standard cost variances measure the amount of input needed for the output produced.

QUICK REVIEW

- The essential financial statements are the balance sheet, income statement, statement of owner's (or partners' or stockholders') equity, and the statement of cash flows. The balance sheet shows financial condition as wealth and claims on wealth. The income statement shows changes in owner's equity that result from operations, the statement of owner's equity shows all changes in owner's equity, and the statement of cash flows explains the change in the cash balance as operating activities, investing activities, and financing activities.
- Horizontal analysis compares amounts over a selected time period to a reference base amount at the beginning the time period. Vertical analysis is a comparison of amounts within a financial statement to a designated amount in the statement. Vertical and horizontal analysis can be combined.
- Ratio analysis analyzes important financial relationships by use of a ratio, which is the comparison of one number to another, usually displayed as a fraction. Ratio analysis focuses on the elements of liquidity, solvency, profitability, investment return, and productivity. These ratios are summarized on pages 723 and 724.
- Analyzing a business as an outsider always requires skepticism and caution. Careful analysis of 10-K (annual financial statements), 10-Q (quarterly financial statements), and 8-K (significant event) reports filed with the SEC (Securities and Exchange Commission), of annual reports, and of conference calls is essential. All of these resources are available on the Internet.
- Quality of earnings affects the usefulness of financial reports and can be impaired by both revenue and expense management. Off-balance-sheet financing understates total obligations and makes a company's financial condition appear more secure and favorable.
- The Sarbanes-Oxley Act of 2002 was a response to increasing distrust of financial reporting by publicly traded companies. The purpose of the act is to: (1) improve the reliability and quality of financial reporting, (2) improve auditing standards and internal control, (3) increase corporate responsibility, and (4) impose significant penalties for violations. The Public Company Accounting Oversight Board (PCAOB) was created by Sarbanes-Oxley to implement the first two goals of the act.

Do You Want More Examples?

Most problems in this book have detailed solutions. To use them as additional examples, do this: 1) Select the type of problem you want 2) Open the solution on your computer or mobile device screen (from the disc or worthyjames.com) 3) Read one item at a time and look at its answer. Take notes if needed. 4) Close the solution and work as much of the problem as you can. 5) Repeat as needed.

VOCABULARY

Benchmark: a norm or guideline used for the purpose of comparison (page 695)

Common-size financial statement: a financial statement shown in percentages (page 692)

Contingent liability: a potential liability that will become an actual liability only if some other event occurs first (page 717)

Debt covenants: requirements and restrictions imposed by lenders (page 700)

Earnings management: the use of GAAP to manipulate reported income (page 712)

EBITDA: Earnings Before Interest, Taxes, Depreciation, and Amortization (page 704)

Financial leverage: the use of debt (page 700)

Free cash flow: cash flow from operating activities minus capital expenditures (page 703)

Horizontal analysis: comparing financial statement information over time (page 688)

Liquidity: the ability to pay current liabilities as they become due (page 694)

Liquid assets: assets quickly convertible into cash (page 696)

Market share: a company's sales as a percentage of total sales for all companies in the same industry or type of business (page 705)

MD&A: Management discussion and analysis (page 693)

Operating cycle: the time required to convert inventory back into cash (page 699)

PCAOB: the Public Company Accounting Oversight Board (page 722)

Price earnings ratio: stock price per share divided by earnings per share; used by investors in the stock of publicly traded companies to gauge relative value of a stock (page 706)

Productivity: the level of efficiency at which a business operates (page 708)

Publicly traded: stock that can be bought and sold on stock exchanges (page 706)

Quality of earnings: an evaluation as to whether the reported income accurately represents the true change in wealth and the recurring nature of business operations (page 712)

Quick assets: highly liquid assets (cash, short-term investments, and net short-term receivables) used to calculate the quick ratio (page 696)

Sarbanes-Oxley: a federal law that controls auditing standards for publicly traded companies and imposes personal liability on the top executives of such companies for the reliability of financial statements (page 721)

Solvency: the ability to remain in business for a long period of time (page 694)

Trading on equity: the effect on return on equity when a business incurs debt (page 708)

Vertical analysis: comparing financial statement information within a statement (page 690)

Working capital: current assets minus current liabilities (page 699)

PRACTICE Learning Goal 32

Solutions are in the disk at the back of the book and at: www.worthyjames.com

Learning Goal 32 is about the essential tools and procedures for analyzing financial statements. Use these questions and problems to practice what you have learned.

Multiple Choice

Select the best answer.

1. To evaluate the solvency of a business, which primary measurements would you select?
   a. debt ratio, accounts receivable turnover ratio, and times-interest earned
   b. gross profit ratio, return on equity ratio, and current ratio
   c. quick ratio, inventory turnover ratio and earnings per share
   d. debt ratio, asset turnover ratio, and cash flow to debt ratio.
2. To evaluate the profitability of a business, which primary measurements would you select?
   a. quick ratio, free cash flow, and asset turnover ratio
   b. current ratio, average days to sell inventory, and gross profit ratio
   c. free cash flow, return on total assets, and debt ratio
   d. earnings per share, gross profit ratio, and return on total assets ratio
3. To evaluate the liquidity of a business, which primary measurements would you select?
   a. current ratio, quick ratio, and cash flow to debt ratio
   b. current ratio, average days to sell inventory, and average days to collect receivables
   c. current ratio, average days to sell inventory, and asset turnover ratio
   d. times interest earned ratio, gross profit ratio, and return on total assets ratio
4. Earnings per share is used by investors in what important calculation?
   a. price earnings ratio
   b. profit ratio
   c. return on equity ratio
   d. dividend ratio
5. *Quality of earnings* refers to:
   a the reliability of the change in wealth indicated on the income statement.
   b. the reliability of the income statement as an indicator of recurring operations.
   c. the assurance that properly applied GAAP means unbiased financial statements.
   d. both a and b.
6. If Company X is an accounting firm and Company Y is an airline:
   a. Company X probably will have a higher gross profit ratio.
   b. Company Y probably will have a lower inventory turnover ratio.
   c. Company X probably will have a higher asset turnover ratio.
   d. Company Y probably will have a higher profit ratio.
7. A large corporation has new management that has promised to quickly stop losses and make the company profitable. Which earnings management technique would they be most tempted to immediately use?
   a. income smoothing using the "cookie jar"
   b. the "big bath"
   c. capitalizing operating expenses
   d. expense timing
8. Two ratios that can be used as measures of potential liquidity as well as operating efficiency are:
   a. gross profit and return on total assets ratios.
   b. quick and current ratios.
   c. accounts receivable turnover and inventory turnover ratios.
   d. current and cash flow to debt ratios.

PRACTICE Learning Goal 32, continued

Solutions are in the disk at the back of the book and at: www.worthyjames.com

9. If sales on account have been overstated, what calculation is most likely to detect it?
   a. inventory turnover ratio or average days to sell calculation
   b. current ratio
   c. free cash flow calculation
   d. accounts receivable turnover ratio or average days to collect receivables calculation
10. If a company changes from LIFO to FIFO in a period of rising prices, the inventory turnover ratio:
    a. will suddenly look better.
    b. will suddenly look worse.
    c. will not be affected.
    d. cannot be calculated.
11. When analyzing a change in the debt ratio:
    a. an increase is usually bad, and a decrease is usually good.
    b. an increase usually creates more risk, and a decrease usually reduces risk.
    c. When a debt ratio increases, it is essential to know the reason as this can be a good indicator of a company's condition or strategy; when the ratio decreases, it is usually an indicator of improvement in financial strength.
    d. both b and c.
12. An important audit rule-setting and compliance enforcement organization requiring registration by accountants who wish to audit publicly traded companies is the:
    a. Public Company Accounting Oversight Board (PCAOB).
    b. Securities and Exchange Commission (SEC).
    c. Financial Accounting Standards Board (FASB).
    d. American Institute of Certified Public Accountants (AICPA).
13. Which of the following does *not* represent a contingent liability?
    a. a product that has a 1-year warranty
    b. coupons issued by a grocery store
    c. an oil tanker that does not have a double hull.
    d. Unearned Revenue.
14. The greatest problem with contingent liability classification is that:
    a. contingent liabilities may be difficult to calculate.
    b. it is subjective and sometimes can be easily manipulated.
    c. it is difficult to identify a contingent liability.
    d. the classification does not apply to all types of companies.
15. If a company is using debt to acquire assets, then the business:
    a. will have a high asset turnover ratio.
    b. is said to be trading on equity.
    c. will usually increase the rate of return on owner's equity.
    d. both b and c.
16. The federal law that resulted from years of aggressive financial reporting and the sudden collapse of Enron and Worldcom is:
    a. the PCAOB.
    b. the Securities and Exchange Commission (SEC).
    c. Sarbanes-Oxley.
    d. FASB.

PRACTICE Learning Goal 32, continued

Solutions are in the disk at the back of the book and at: www.worthyjames.com

Discussion Questions and Brief Exercises

1. Explain the difference between vertical and horizontal analysis. Can they be used together or must they be used separately?
2. What is MD&A? What must it contain, and how can it be useful?
3. Explain the meanings of the following words: liquidity, solvency, profitability, investment return, and productivity.
4. What is the best way to use ratio analysis?
5. What ratios measure liquidity?
6. What ratios measure solvency?
7. What ratios measure profitability?
8. What ratios measure investment return?
9. What ratios measure productivity?
10. Explain the meaning of "quality of earnings". Why is it so important? Does the use of GAAP assure high quality of earnings?
11. What is "earnings management"? Why is it done? Is it the same as fraud?
12. There are many opportunities for earnings management. Give three examples of how a company can "manage" revenue and three examples of how a company can "manage" expenses.
13. Suppose that you are interested in investing in a company and you want to research the company before deciding to invest. After locating the financial statements, you first look for financial warning signs. Identify at least five financial warning signs.
14. What is the "big bath"? What is "income smoothing"? Why are they done?
15. What are hidden liabilities?
16. What is the Public Company Oversight Board? When and why was it created?
17. What does "financial leverage" (also called "gearing") mean?
18. What are good sources to find information about publicly traded companies?
19. What is a contingent liability? What is the rule for recording and disclosing liabilities?
20. Use the information in the table to calculate the following:
    a. Accounts receivable turnover for 2016 and 2017, rounding to one decimal place
    b. Average days to collect for 2016 and 2017
    c. Is collection time improving or worsening?

	2017	2016	2015
Net sales on account	$750,000	$800,000	$700,000
Accounts receivable at year-end	59,000	61,500	55,000

21. Use the information in the table to calculate the following:
    a. Inventory turnover for 2016 and 2017, rounding to one decimal place
    b. Average days to sell for 2016 and 2017
    c. Is inventory moving faster or slower?

	2017	2016	2015
Cost of goods sole	$750,000	$685,900	$620,000
Merchandise inventory at year-end	187,600	134,300	124,700

PRACTICE **Learning Goal 32, continued**

Solutions are in the disk at the back of the book and at: www.worthyjames.com

22. Use the financial statement information below from Able Company and Baker Company,
    a. Calculate the following for 2017:

▪ Debt ratio	▪ Times-interest earned	▪ Asset turnover
▪ Cash flow to debt ratio	▪ Free cash flow	

    b. From the information available, for 2017 which company appears to be most financially secure? Use the solvency ratios above to support your conclusion.

	Able Company		Baker Company	
	2017	**2016**	**2017**	**2016**
Cash, accts. receivable, short-term investments	$299,300	$295,900	$210,440	$122,900
Current liabilities	898,250	712,600	198,775	128,650
Interest expense	74,100	54,200	21,000	32,000
Cash flow from operating activities	215,600	325,400	202,350	355,000
Total assets	1,928,700	1,411,200	1,850,000	1,610,500
Total liabilities	1,385,900	876,500	783,800	956,200
Capital expenditures	170,200	377,000	110,000	90,000
Net sales	2,100,000	2,350,000	3,100,000	3,550,000

23. You are interested in buying the common stock of a certain company. Your first concern is determining the current financial condition of the company and your second concern is analyzing investment return, before performing additional analysis. You have obtained the information below.
    a. Calculate ratios that provide an indication of current liquidity for 2017. What are your conclusions?
    b. Calculate ratios that measure investment return and relative stock price for 2017. What are your conclusions?

	2017	2016
Net sales	$1,265,000	$1,382,000
Cost of goods sold	872,300	967,400
Net income	99,300	44,500
Cash	186,100	174,500
Short-term investments, year end	22,000	19,000
Merchandise inventory, year end	204,100	212,900
Accounts receivable, year end	122,000	97,500
Current assets	880,400	824,900
Current liabilities	431,100	331,900
Common dividends	16,000	15,000
Stockholders' equity year-end	892,800	816,500

- Common stock outstanding for 2016 and 2017: 100,000 shares.There is no preferred stock.
- Common stock price 2016: $12,and 2017: $14.50

PRACTICE

Learning Goal 32, continued

Solutions are in the disk at the back of the book and at: www.worthyjames.com

Reinforcement Problems

LG 32-1. Identifying the ratios.

Instructions: Write the name of each ratio or measure and its formula for each of the following analysis categories:

a. Liquidity b. Solvency c. Profitability d. Investment return e. Productivity

LG 32-2. Horizontal analysis.

Instructions: Prepare a horizontal analysis that shows both the dollar and percent changes in 2016 from 2015 and also in 2017 from 2016 using the income statement shown below. Why did net income increase by a higher percentage than sales in 2016? Why did net income increase by a lower percentage than sales in 2017?

Grand Forks Company
Comparative Income Statement
Years Ended December 31, 2017, 2016, 2015

	2017	2016	2015
Net sales	$605,000	$489,000	$418,000
Cost of goods sold	358,000	276,000	251,000
Gross profit	247,000	213,000	167,000
Operating expenses	165,000	140,000	126,000
Income from operations	82,000	73,000	41,000
Interest expense	2,000	1,000	2,000
Net income	$ 80,000	$ 72,000	$ 39,000

LG 32-3. Calculate ratios. Assets and liabilities and selected other financial information from the financial statements of Ketchikan Corporation are shown below.

Instructions: Compute the following for 2017:

- Current ratio
- Inventory turnover
- Rate of return on total assets
- Quick Ratio
- Accounts receivable turnover
- Debt ratio
- Rate of return on equity
- Profit margin ratio
- Average collection period
- Cash flow to debt ratio
- Earnings Per Share

PRACTICE Learning Goal 32, continued

Solutions are in the disk at the back of the book and at: www.worthyjames.com

LG 32-3, *continued*

	2017	2016
Net sales	$312,000	$285,000
Cost of goods sold	210,000	195,500
Inventories, yearend	24,300	37,800
Accounts payable	11,000	7,200
Accrued liabilities	15,500	16,900
Cash	14,000	15,200
Long-term mortgage payable	98,700	110,200
Prepaid expense	2,500	1,900
Property, plant, and equipment, net of depreciation	278,000	237,500
Accounts receivable, year end	15,700	24,800
Operating cash flow	36,300	25,200
Net cash flow	12,500	(18,600)
Total assets	355,000	325,700
Net income	37,600	31,300
Common stock shares issued and outstanding (amounts shown were outstanding all year)	210,000	150,000

LG 32-4. Calculate ratios and effect of transactions on ratios. Shown below are the condensed balance sheets and income statement of Dunsmuir Company as of December 31, 2017 and the year then ended. Also shown is a table with six ratio headings.

a. Using the financial statement data, for 2017 calculate each of the ratios shown in the table. Round answers to one decimal place if results are greater than one, otherwise show two decimal places.
b. For each of the listed events, recalculate the ratios and enter the result for any ratio that would be affected. Each event is independent.

Dunsmuir Company, Inc.
Income Statement
For the Year Ended December 31, 2017

($ in 000's)	2017
Net sales	$1,832
Cost of goods sold	1,149
Gross profit	683
Operating expenses (listed separately)	594
Operating income	89
Other revenues and expenses	2
Income before tax	87
Income tax expense	26
Net income	$61

PRACTICE Learning Goal 32, continued

Solutions are in the disk at the back of the book and at: www.worthyjames.com

LG 32-4, *continued*

Dunsmuir Company, Inc.
Comparative Balance Sheets
December 31

($ in 000's)

Assets	2017	2016	Liabilities	2017	2016
Cash	$150	$125	Current liabilities	$205	$238
Accounts receivable	182	164	Long-term liabilities	543	393
Inventory	116	89	Total liabilities	748	631
Other current assets	12	15	**Stockholders' equity**		
Total current assets	460	393	Common stock	30	25
			Paid-in capital in excess of par	422	422
			Retained earnings	181	120
Long-term assets	461	412	Total stockholders' equity	633	567
Total assets	$1,381	$1,198	Total liabilities and equity	$1,381	$1,198

Events:

#1. At year-end, as a final transaction, the company president directs the chief accountant to use $50,000 cash to pay current liabilities.

#2. Before financial statements are prepared, the chief accountant analyzes the merchandise inventory. She determines that $50,000 is damaged and cannot be sold. Shetherefore reduces theinventory balance. This is a loss that also reduces net income.

#3. At year-end, as a final transaction, the company declares a 10% stock dividend.

	Current Ratio	Quick ratio	Days sales in receivables	Inventory Turnover	Debt Ratio	Return on Equity
Before events						
Event #1						
Event #2						
Event #3						

PRACTICE Learning Goal 32, continued

Solutions are in the disk at the back of the book and at: www.worthyjames.com

LG 32-5. How transactions affect ratios.

Instructions: Consider the separate transactions shown below as they would affect the calculations in problem 3 above. What effect would each transaction have on the ratios indicated? Recompute the indicated ratios for each transaction. (*Tip:* First visualize which accounts are being debited and credited in the transaction, then visualize if the numerator and/or denominator in the ratio are affected.)

Transaction	What is the effect on the . . .?
1. Paid $10,000 of the accrued liabilities	a. current ratio b. debt ratio
2. Purchased $20,000 of inventory on account	a. current ratio b. inventory turnover ratio
3. Borrowed $50,000 using a long-term note payable.	a. debt ratio b. cash flow to debt ratio
4. Sold inventory costing $10,000 at a sales price of $19,000. The sale is on account.	a. current ratio b. accounts receivable turnover ratio c. inventory turnover ratio d. rate of return on equity
5. A $500 sales discount was taken by a customer on $7,500 of accounts receivable. (Sale was made on account.)	a. current ratio b. accounts receivable turnover ratio
6. A sales return of $10,000 was made by a customer. (Sale was made on account.) The cost of the merchandise was $6,000.	a. current ratio b. accounts receivable turnover ratio c. inventory turnover ratio
7. An adjustment to estimate and record uncollectible accounts receivable expense is $2,000. This creates an uncollectible accounts expense and reduces accounts receivable.	a. rate of return on equity b. accounts receivable turnover ratio

LG 32-6. Analysis for a loan decision. Melanie Davenport, the owner of Hilo Enterprises, has come to your bank for a $70,000 loan. Hilo Enterprises has been a long-time customer of the bank. You are a member of the loan committee reviewing the loan application. The loan officer dealing with the customer is recommending that the full $70,000 loan be made because the business has been consistently profitable, maintains a good amount of working capital, has good current and acid-test ratios, and because Melanie Davenport is a long-term customer of the bank.

Instructions: Use the measures you think are relevant to evaluate the loan application. Do you agree with the loan officer's recommendation? Do you want any other data?

Hilo Enterprises
Comparative Income Statement
Years Ended May 31

	2017	2016	2015
Net sales	$456,000	$397,000	$344,000
Cost of goods sold	214,000	188,000	158,000
Gross profit	242,000	209,000	186,000
Operating expenses:			
Selling	37,000	28,000	24,000
General and administrative	161,000	141,000	124,000
Income from operations	44,000	40,000	38,000
Loss on sale of land	2,000		
Interest expense	1,000	2,000	1,000
Net income	$ 41,000	$ 38,000	$ 37,000

PRACTICE Learning Goal 32, continued

Solutions are in the disk at the back of the book and at: www.worthyjames.com

LG 32-6, *continued*

Hilo Enterprises
Comparative Balance Sheet
May 31

	2017	2016	2015
Current assets:			
Cash	$ 37,000	$ 70,000	$ 86,000
Accounts receivable, net	119,000	62,000	49,000
Supplies	2,000	2,000	3,000
Inventory	127,000	78,000	51,000
Total current assets	285,000	212,000	189,000
Property, plant, and equipment	125,000	125,000	118,000
Less: Accumulated depreciation	44,000	28,000	12,000
Land		10,000	10,000
Total assets	$366,000	$319,000	$305,000
Total current liabilities	$123,000	$106,000	$ 97,000
Long-term notes payable	47,000	58,000	48,000
Melanie Davenport, capital	196,000	155,000	160,000
Total liabilities and owner's equity	$366,000	$319,000	$305,000

LG 32-7. **Analysis for an investment decision.** De Kalb Decor, Inc. is a small privately held home remodeling and interior-decorating company that opened in 2014 and sells to both retail and contractor customers. It is about to sell additional shares of its stock to a limited group of investors for the purpose of obtaining cash to fund an expansion of its operations and to pay off half of the short-term debt. You have the opportunity to purchase some of the shares being offered, and the company provided the audited financial statements that you see below.

Instructions:

a. Prepare a 3-year comparative common-size income statement.
b. Analyze liquidity, solvency, profitability, and investment return.
c. Is there any other important information that you would like to have?
d. Does the investment interest you?

De Kalb Decor, Inc.
Comparative Income Statement
Years Ended December 31

	2017	2016	2015
Net sales	$1,046,000	$865,000	$721,000
Cost of goods sold	607,000	519,000	481,000
Gross profit	439,000	346,000	240,000
Operating expenses:			
Selling and marketing	159,000	137,000	95,000
General and administrative	241,000	205,000	170,000
Income (loss) from operations	39,000	4,000	(25,000)
Other revenues and gains and expenses and losses:			
Other revenue	4,000	23,000	12,000
Interest expense	(24,000)	(17,000)	(5,000)
Loss on sale of short-term investments	(31,000)		
Income before income taxes	(12,000)	10,000	(18,000)
Income tax expense	–0–	2,000	–0–
Net income (loss)	($12,000)	$ 8,000	$(18,000)

PRACTICE Learning Goal 32, continued

Solutions are in the disk at the back of the book and at: www.worthyjames.com

LG 32-7, *continued*

De Kalb Decor, Inc.
Comparative Balance Sheet
December 31

	2017	2016	2015
Cash	$152,000	$105,000	$ 64,000
Short-term investments	25,000	68,000	42,000
Accounts receivable, net	107,000	111,000	84,000
Inventory	104,000	120,000	101,000
Supplies and prepaid expenses	13,000	10,000	9,000
Total current assets	401,000	414,000	300,000
Property, plant, and equipment	415,000	375,000	315,000
Less: Accumulated depreciation	95,000	54,000	20,000
Total assets	$721,000	$735,000	$595,000
Total current liabilities	$133,000	$137,000	$ 58,000
Long-term debt	164,000	128,000	75,000
Total liabilities	297,000	265,000	133,000
Stockholders' equity	424,000	470,000	462,000
Total liabilities and owner's equity	$721,000	$735,000	$595,000

De Kalb Decor, Inc.
Comparative Statement of Cash Flows
Years Ended December 31

	2017	2016	2015
Cash flows from operating activities			
Net income	($12,000)	$8,000	$(18,000)
Add: Items increasing cash or not reducing cash			
Depreciation expense	41,000	34,000	20,000
Proceeds from sale of short-term investments	12,000		
Decreases in current operating assets	20,000		15,000
Increases in current operating liabilities		79,000	10,000
Loss on sale of short-term investments	31,000		
Less: Items reducing cash or not increasing cash			
Increases in current operating assets	(3,000)	(73,000)	
Decreases in current operating liabilities	(4,000)		(17,000)
Increase in cash from operating activities	85,000	48,000	10,000
Cash flows from investing activities			
Expenditures on plant and equipment	(40,000)	(60,000)	(92,000)
Cash flows from financing activities			
Increase (decrease) in long-term debt	36,000	53,000	30,000
Dividends to shareholders	(34,000)		
Increase in cash from financing activities	2,000	53,000	30,000
Net increase (decrease) in cash	47,000	41,000	(52,000)
Beginning cash balance	105,000	64,000	116,000
Ending cash balance	$152,000	$105,000	$64,000

PRACTICE Learning Goal 32, continued

Solutions are in the disk at the back of the book and at: www.worthyjames.com

LG 32-8. Analysis for an investment decision. Financial information for Bedford and Buford companies is shown below. You are a "value investor," so you are interested in purchasing the stock of a company that has the lowest price earnings ratio and is also in good financial condition. Which company would you select?

Current year income statement information:

	Bedford, Inc.	Buford, Inc.
Net sales	$550,000	$420,000
Cost of goods sold	315,000	273,000
Gross profit	235,000	147,000
Interest income	3,000	4,000
Interest expense	35,000	15,000
Net income	95,000	72,000

Year-end balance sheet and other information:

	Bedford, Inc.	Buford, Inc.
Cash	$55,000	$44,000
Short-term investments	8,000	15,000
Accounts and short-term notes receivable, net	42,000	28,000
Inventory	110,000	75,000
Prepaid expense	5,000	4,000
Total assets	590,000	432,000
Current liabilities	131,000	77,000
Total liabilities	159,000	133,000
Common stock issued and outstanding	100,000 shares	100,000 shares
Current market price of stock	$17.20	$16.40

Beginning of the year information:

	Bedford, Inc.	Buford, Inc.
Accounts and short-term notes receivable	$51,000	$37,000
Inventory	99,000	81,000
Total assets	542,000	409,000
Stockholders' equity	336,000	227,000

Use the following ratios for each company:

- Current ratio
- Inventory turnover
- Asset turnover
- Quick ratio
- Debt ratio
- Profit margin ratio
- Receivables turnover
- Gross profit ratio
- Return on equity

PRACTICE Learning Goal 32, continued

Solutions are in the disk at the back of the book and at: www.worthyjames.com

LG 32-9. Use ratios to calculate financial statement values. The condensed income statement and balance sheet for Mystery Company are shown below. Calculate the values for items, A through R.

Mystery Company
Income Statement
Year Ended June 30, 2017

Net sales	(A)
Cost of goods sold	(B)
Gross profit	(C)
Operating expenses:	
Selling and marketing	55,000
General and administrative	238,025
Income (loss) from operations	(D)
Other revenues and gains and expenses and losses:	
Other revenue	1,500
Other expense	(11,250)
Net income (loss)	(E)

Mystery Company
Comparative Balance Sheet
June 30

	2017	2016
Current assets:		
Cash	44,000	(F)
Accounts receivable, net	63,000	67,000
Supplies	3,250	3,000
Inventory	101,000	(G)
Total current assets	211,250	(H)
Property, plant, and equipment	286,000	246,500
Less: accumulated depreciation	76,000	54,000
Land	100,000	100,000
Total assets	(N)	(I)
Total current liabilities	(O)	130,000
Long-term liabilities	278,500	(J)
Total liabilities	(P)	(K)
John Xxx, capital	(Q)	(L)
Total liabilities and owner's equity	(R)	(M)

Other information:

- The current ratio on June 30, 2017 is 2.6:1.
- The 2017 gross profit percentage is 40%
- The 2017 accounts receivable turnover ratio is 12 times.
- The 2017 inventory turnover ratio is 4.5 times.
- The debt ratio on June 30, 2016 is 65%.
- The acid-test on June 30, 2016 is .8:1.

PRACTICE Learning Goal 32, continued

Solutions are in the disk at the back of the book and at: www.worthyjames.com

LG 32-10. **Calculate various ratios.** Using the financial statement information from The El Dorado Company's condensed financial statements, calculate year-end 2017 ratios as listed below. Round answers to one decimal place if results are greater than one, otherwise show two decimal places. If you assume that this company is a large clothing retailer, for item number 1, how do you think this company's operations compare to other similar companies? (Suggestion: try an Internet search for comparative ratios.)

1. **Measures of liquidity:**
   - Current ratio
   - Quick ratio
   - Accounts receivable turnover
   - Days' sales in accounts receivable
   - Inventory turnover
   - Inventory turnover in days
   - Operating cycle
2. **Measures of solvency:**
   - Debt ratio
   - Times-interest earned
   - Asset turnover ratio
   - Cash flow to debt
   - Free cash flow
3. **Measures of profitability:**
   - Profit margin
   - Gross profit percentage
   - Earnings per share
   - Return on total assets
4. **Measures of investment return and stock valuation:**
   - Return on equity
   - Dividend ratio
   - Price-earnings (PE) ratio

Additional information:

The stock price on December 31, 2016 was $51per share and on December 31, 2017 was $58.50. Dividends were paid to both preferred and common stockholders.

El Dorado Company, Inc.
Comparative Income Statements
For the Years Ended December 31

($ in 000s)

	2017	2016
Net sales	$4,800	$3,599
Cost of goods sold	3,312	2,678
Gross profit	1,488	921
Operating expenses (listed separately)	1,078	764
Operating income	410	157
Other revenues, expenses, and losses		
Interest revenue	1	2
Interest expense	(15)	(27)
Loss on sale of equipment	-0-	(105)
Total other revenues, expenses, and losses	(14)	(130)
Income from continuing operations before tax	396	27
Income tax expense	110	8
Income from continuing operations	286	19
Loss from sale of discontinued operations of $220 less tax savings of $64	-0-	(156)
Net income (loss)	$286	($137)

PRACTICE **Learning Goal 32, continued**

Solutions are in the disk at the back of the book and at: www.worthyjames.com

LG 32-10, *continued*

El Dorado Company, Inc.
Comparative Balance Sheets
December 31

($ in 000s)

Assets	**2017**	**2016**
Cash	$992	$843
Accounts receivable	413	389
Inventory	541	746
Other current assets	24	14
Total current assets	1,970	1,992
Long-term investments	48	48
Property, plant, & equipment (net)	342	388
Total assets	$2,360	$2,428
Liabilities		
Current liabilities	$911	$1,264
Long-term liabilities	242	245
Total liabilities	1,153	1,509
Stockholders' Equity		
Preferred stock, no par, $2, 10,000 shares issued and outstanding	395	395
Common stock, $.10 par, 50,000 shares issued	50	50
Paid-in capital in excess of par – common	612	611
Total paid-in capital	1,057	1,056
Retained earnings	150	(107)
Less: treasury stock (2,000 shares at cost)	-0-	(30)
Total stockholders' equity	1,207	919
Total liabilities and stockholders' equity	$2,360	$2,428

El Dorado Company, Inc.
Comparative Statements of Cash Flows
For the Years Ended December 31

($ in 000s)

	2017	**2016**
Cash flows from operating activities		
Net income(loss)	$286	($137)
Add: depreciation expense	38	39
Net decrease (increase) in current operating assets	171	(109)
Netincrease (decrease) in current operating liabilities	(353)	214
Increase in cash from operating activities	142	7
Cash flows from investing activities		
Sale of plant and equipment	8	115
Increase in cash from investing activities	8	115
Cash flows from financing activities		
Long-term debt payment	(3)	-0-
Sale (purchase) of treasury stock	31	(10)
Cash dividends	(29)	(20)
Increase (decrease) in cash from financing activities	(1)	(30)
Net increase in cash	149	92
Beginning cash balance	843	751
Ending cash balance	$992	$843

PRACTICE Learning Goal 32, continued

Solutions are in the disk at the back of the book and at: www.worthyjames.com

Instructor-Assigned Problems

If you are using this book in a class, these review problems may be assigned by your instructor for homework, group assignments, class work, or other activities. Only your instructor has the solutions.

IA32-1. Calculate various ratios. Comparative income statements, balance sheets and other financial information of Superior Company are presented below. Compute the following for 2017 and round answers to two decimal places:

- Current ratio
- Quick ratio
- Accounts receivable turnover
- Inventory turnover
- Average collection period
- Average days to sell
- Gross profit ratio
- Profit margin ratio
- Debt ratio
- Rate of return on total assets
- Cash flow to debt ratio
- Dividend ratio

Additional information:

The statement of cash flows shows a total increase in cash for 2017 of $440,000 and a cash flow from operating activities of $334,000. Dividends were paid on both preferred stock and common stock.

Superior Company, Inc.
Comparative Income Statements
For the Years Ended December 31

($ in 000s)	2017	2016
Net sales	$2,120	$4,030
Cost of goods sold	1,470	3,100
Gross profit	650	930
Operating expenses (listed separately)	377	715
Operating income	273	215
Other revenues, expenses, and gains		
Interest revenue	2	3
Interest expense	(17)	(33)
Gain on sale of investments	-0-	5
Total other revenues, expenses, and losses	(15)	(25)
Income from continuing operations before tax	258	190
Income tax expense	85	67
Income from continuing operations	173	123
Loss from sale of discontinued operations of $300 less tax savings of $105	-0-	(195)
Net income (loss)	$173	($72)

PRACTICE Learning Goal 32, continued

Solutions are in the disk at the back of the book and at: www.worthyjames.com

IA32-1, *continued*

Superior Company, Inc.
Comparative Balance Sheets
December 31

($ in 000s)		
Assets	**2017**	**2016**
Cash	$914	$474
Accounts receivable	297	358
Inventory	244	347
Other current assets	19	12
Total current assets	1,474	1,191
Long-term investments	23	23
Property, plant, & equipment (net)	1,210	1,345
Total assets	$2,707	$2,559
Liabilities		
Current liabilities	$822	$953
Long-term liabilities	184	190
Total liabilities	1,006	1,143
Stockholders' Equity		
Preferred stock, $50 par, 6%, 5,000 shares issued and outstanding	250	250
Common stock, $01 par, 100,000 shares issued	1	1
Paid-in capital in excess of par – common	1,152	1,150
Total paid-in capital	1,403	1,401
Retained earnings	151	25
Less: treasury stock (10,000 shares at cost)	-0-	(10)
Total stockholders' equity	1,554	1,416
Total liabilities and stockholders' equity	$2,707	$2,559

IA32-2. **Horizontal analysis and common-size statement.** Using the comparative income statements presented below, complete the following, rounding all percentagesup or down to one decimal place:

a. Prepare a horizontal analysis that shows both the dollar and percentage changes for each line item from 2015 to 2016 and from 2016 to 2017.
b. Prepare a common-size income statement for each year.
c. Summarize any area of improvement you might suggest to management.

Tehachapi Company, Inc.
Comparative Income Statements
'For the Years Ended June 30

($ in 000s)	2017	2016	2015
Net sales	$2,565	$2,490	$2,350
Cost of goods sold	1,735	1,665	1,528
Gross profit	830	825	822
Operating expenses	546	535	520
Income before tax	284	290	302
Income tax	85	87	91
Net income	$199	$203	$211

PRACTICE Learning Goal 32, continued

Solutions are in the disk at the back of the book and at: www.worthyjames.com

IA32-3. **Calculate ratios and effect of transactions on ratios.** Shown below are the condensed balance sheets and income statement of Portland Company as of June 30, 2017 and the year then ended. Also shown is a table with six ratio headings.

a. Using the financial statement data, for fiscal year 2017 calculate each of the ratios shown in the table. Round answers to one decimal place if results are greater than one, otherwise show two decimal places.
b. For each of the listed events, recalculate the ratios and enter the result for any ratio that would be affected. Each event is independent.

Portland Company, Inc.
Income Statement
For the Year Ended June 30, 2017

($ in 000's)	2017
Net sales	$2,381
Cost of goods sold	1,657
Gross profit	724
Operating expenses (listed separately)	690
Operating income	34
Other revenues and expenses	(9)
Income before tax	25
Income tax expense	8
Net income	$17

Portland Company, Inc.
Comparative Balance Sheets
June 30

($ in 000's)

Assets	2017	2016	Liabilities	2017	2016
Cash	$269	$312	Current liabilities	$327	$175
Accounts receivable	169	164	Long-term liabilities	293	44
Inventory	345	94	Total liabilities	620	219
Other current assets	10	11	**Stockholders' equity**		
Total current assets	793	581	Common stock	25	15
			Paid-in capital in excess of par	412	385
			Retained earnings	137	120
Long-term assets	401	58	Total stockholders' equity	574	520
Total assets	$1,194	$739	Total liabilities and equity	$1,194	$739

Events:

#1. At year-end, as a final transaction, the company president directs the chief accountant to use $75,000 cash to pay current liabilities.

PRACTICE Learning Goal 32, continued

Solutions are in the disk at the back of the book and at: www.worthyjames.com

IA32-3, *continued*

#2. Before financial statements are prepared, the chief accountant analyzes the merchandise inventory. He determines that $70,000 is damaged and cannot be sold. He therefore reduces the inventory balance. This is a loss that also reduces net income.

#3. At year-end, as a final transaction, the company declares an 8% stock dividend.

	Current Ratio	Quick ratio	Days sales in receivables	Inventory Turnover	Debt Ratio	Return on Equity
Before events						
Event #1						
Event #2						
Event #3						

IA32-4. Calculate various ratios. Using the financial statement information from the Elmira Company's condensed financial statements, calculate 2017 ratios as listed below. Round answers to one decimal place if results are greater than one, otherwise show two decimal places. If you assume that this company is a large electronics retailer, for item number 1, how do you think this company's operations compare to other similar companies? (*Suggestion*: try an Internet search for comparative ratios.)

1. **Measures of liquidity:**
   - Current ratio
   - Quick ratio
   - Accounts receivable turnover
   - Days' sales in accounts receivable
   - Inventory turnover
   - Inventory turnover in days
   - Operating cycle
2. **Measures of solvency:**
   - Debt ratio
   - Times-interest earned
   - Asset turnover ratio
   - Cash flow to debt
   - Free cash flow
3. **Measures of profitability:**
   - Profit margin
   - Gross profit percentage
   - Earnings per share
   - Return on total assets
4. **Measures of investment return and stock valuation:**
   - Return on equity
   - Dividend ratio
   - Price-earnings (PE) ratio

Additional information:

The stock price on December 31, 2016 was $78 per share and on December 31, 2017 was $45. In 2017 the weighted average common shares outstanding was 49,500.

PRACTICE Learning Goal 32, continued

Solutions are in the disk at the back of the book and at: www.worthyjames.com

IA32-4, *continued*

Elmira Company, Inc.
Comparative Income Statements
For the Years Ended December 31

($ in 000s)

	2017	2016
Net sales	$6,251	$5,589
Cost of goods sold	4,163	3,745
Gross profit	2,088	1,844
Operating expenses (listed separately)	1,643	1,513
Operating income	445	331
Other revenues, expenses, and gains		
Interest revenue	1	2
Interest expense	(4)	(5)
Gain (loss) on sale of investments	2	(1)
Total other revenues, expenses, and losses	(1)	(4)
Income from continuing operations before tax	444	327
Income tax expense	133	98
Income before casualty loss	311	229
Extraordinary casualty loss of $11, less tax savings of $3	(8)	-0-
Net income	$303	$229

Elmira Company, Inc.
Comparative Balance Sheets
December 31

($ in 000s)

Assets	2017	2016
Cash	$248	$225
Accounts receivable	644	619
Inventory	522	514
Other current assets	13	19
Total current assets	1,427	1,377
Long-term investments	44	48
Property, plant, & equipment (net)	4,624	4,411
Total assets	$6,095	$5,836
Liabilities		
Current liabilities	$1,588	$1,612
Long-term liabilities	1,185	1,190
Total liabilities	2,773	2,802
Stockholders' Equity		
Preferred stock, no par, $1, 10,000 shares issued and outstanding	200	200
Common stock, no par, 50,000 shares issued	857	852
Total paid-in capital	1,057	1,052
Retained earnings	2,270	1,992
Less: treasury stock (1,000 and 2,000 shares at cost)	(5)	(10)
Total stockholders' equity	3,322	3,034
Total liabilities and stockholders' equity	$6,095	$5,836

PRACTICE Learning Goal 32, continued

Solutions are in the disk at the back of the book and at: www.worthyjames.com

IA32-4, *continued*

Elimira Company, Inc.
Comparative Statements of Cash Flows
For the Years Ended December 31

($ in 000s)

	2017	2016
Cash flows from operating activities		
Net income	$303	229
Add: depreciation expense	272	110
(Gain) loss on sale of investments	(2)	1
Net decrease (increase) in operating current assets	(27)	5
Net increase (decrease) in operating current liabilities	(24)	(28)
Increase in cash from operating activities	522	317
Cash flows from investing activities		
Sale of investments	6	2
Purchases and sales of plant and equipment	(485)	(110)
Decrease in cash from investing activities	(479)	(108)
Cash flows from financing activities		
Long-term debt payment	(5)	(100)
Sale (purchase) of treasury stock	10	(8)
Cash dividends	(25)	(19)
Increase (decrease) in cash from financing activities	(20)	(127)
Net increase in cash	23	81
Beginning cash balance	225	144
Ending cash balance	$248	$225

IA32-5. Financial analysis for investment decision.

Richard, one of your old school friends, opened a retail sporting goods store four years ago. Richard had lunch with you this week, explaining that his business strategy is to hire knowledgeable employees who can offer the best customer service, providing personalized one-on-one advice for whatever are their customers' sporting or outdoor interests.

Richard informs you that he wants to expand his operations and is looking for a major investor to purchase $250,000 of stock in his corporation. He also told you that sales are good, the company is in a strong financial position, cash flow is easy because most customers use credit cards that result in quick cash inflow, and that the last year had been the most profitable year on record. Richard provided you the condensed audited financial statements that you see below, and wants to know if you are interested.

For 2016 and 2017, using the information in the financial statements,

a. Analyze the liquidity of the company, particularly observing the trends in inventory and debt.
b. Analyze the long-term solvency of the company, particularly observing the trend in cash flow from operating activities and the trend in debt.
c. Analyze profitability using gross profit, profit margin, and return on assets ratios.
d. Analyze investment return using return on equity.
e. What other information would you consider important? Would you invest?

PRACTICE **Learning Goal 32, continued**

Solutions are in the disk at the back of the book and at: www.worthyjames.com

IA32-5, *continued*

Alexandria Enterprises, Inc.
Comparative Income Statements
Years Ended December 31

($ in 000s)

	2017	2016	2015
Net sales	$2,435	$2,425	$2,310
Cost of goods sold	1,775	1,625	1,550
Gross profit	660	800	760
Operating expenses	495	570	540
Operating income	165	230	220
Other revenue and expense	(15)	(3)	5
Income before tax	150	227	225
Income tax	50	79	78
Income before extraordinary gain	100	148	147
Gain from property condemnation	51	-0-	-0-
Net income	$151	$148	$147

Alexandria Enterprises, Inc.
Comparative Balance Sheets
December 31

($ in 000s)

	2017	2016	2015
Assets			
Cash	$44	$38	$105
Accounts receivable, net	20	24	26
Supplies	5	3	4
Merchandise inventory	648	412	372
Total current assets	717	477	517
Fixtures and equipment, net	444	310	106
Land	20	55	55
Total assets	$1,181	$842	$688
Liabilities and Stockholders' Equity			
Accounts payable	74	51	44
Short-term notes payable	140	-0-	-0-
Total current liabilities	214	51	44
Long-term notes payable	49	24	25
Total liabilities	263	75	69
Common stock, $10 par value 100, 000 shares issued and outstanding	10	10	10
Paid-in capital in excess of par	390	390	390
Retained earnings	518	367	219
Total stockholders' equity	918	767	619
Total liabilities and stockholders' equity	$1,181	$842	$818

PRACTICE **Learning Goal 32, continued**

Solutions are in the disk at the back of the book and at: www.worthyjames.com

IA 32-5, *continued*

Alexandria Enterprises, Inc.
Comparative Statements of Cash Flows
Years Ended December 31

($ in 000s)

	2017	2016	2015
Cash flows from operating activities			
Net income	$151	$148	$147
Add: depreciation expense	43	40	36
Gain from property condemnation	(51)	-0-	-0-
(Increase) decrease in current assets than cash	(234)	(17)	27
Increase (decrease) in current liabilities	163	7	(12)
Increase in cash from operating activities	72	178	198
Cash flows from investing activities			
Land condemnation proceeds	86	-0-	-0-
Purchases of fixtures and equipment	(177)	(244)	(116)
Decrease in cash from investing activities	(91)	(244)	(116)
Cash flows from financing activities			
Increase (decrease) in long-term notes payable	25	(1)	(1)
Increase (decrease) in cash from financing activities	25	(1)	(1)
Net increase (decrease) in cash	6	(67)	81
Beginning cash balance	38	105	24
Ending cash balance	$44	$38	$105

INTERNET EXERCISES

Accounting Scandals and Ethical Failures Go to the following websites to review some significant accounting scandals: 1) accounting-degree.org: "10 worst accounting scandals" at: www.accounting-degree.org/scandals/ 2) brighthub.com: "10 high-profile accounting scandals" at: www.brighthub.com/office/finance/articles/101200.aspx

1) For each scandal, summarize what happened and how it happened.
2) How were people injured as a result of the scandals? (Consider: those responsible, investors, employees, accountants, creditors, retirement funds, families, community)
3) Review the ethical guidelines on page 229. How might these have been applied to possibly prevent what happened?
4) What are shortcomings in auditing? To explain this, read "The Dozy Watchdogs" by searching with that name. (December 2014 Economist)"

SECTION

VIII

Partnerships

OVERVIEW

What this section does	This section provides essential tools and procedures to analyze and record partnarship transactions.
Use this section if . . .	▪ you want to the learn basic methods for partnership or limited liability company (multi-member) accounting.

LEARNING GOALS

LEARNING GOAL 33

Suggestion

It is not necessary to complete this section to continue to Volume 2. You can study the principles and procedures in Volume 2 and later return here as appropriate for your own goals.

LEARNING GOAL 33

Partnerships

In Learning Goal 33, you will find:

Overview

New Business Start-Up

Allocating Profits and Losses and Partner Drawings

Changes in Partnership Interests: Dissolutions

Overview

Partnership Defined

Definition

A ***partnership*** is an association co-owned by two or more persons, acting as partners, for the purpose of earning a profit. This description applies as well to multiple-member limited liability companies (LLC's), which often require partnership accounting.

It is easy to form a partnership. If two or more people go into business together and act as partners, a partnership automatically exists.

Characteristics of a Partnership

The Partnership Agreement

A partnership agreement, at a minimum, should address the following points:

1. Name, address, location, life, type, and business purpose of the partnership
2. Name, address, investment, and duties of each partner
3. Allocation of profits and losses among partners
4. Compliance requirements for adding new capital if needed
5. Withdrawals of partnership assets by partners
6. Procedure for admission of new partners
7. Procedure for withdrawal of partners from the partnership
8. Terminating the business and liquidating the partnership

Note: It is not necessary to have a written parntership agreement, although it would be foolish not to create one. Written agreements reduce the possibility of misunderstandings. (However, LLCs do require written agreements.)

Limited Life

Limited life means that the maximum term of a partnership is limited to the lesser of the term stated in the partnership agreement or the time that the current partners remain in the partnership. Whenever a partner withdraws from a partnership or a new partner enters a partnership, the existing partnership is terminated and a new partnership is created. The termination of a partnership is called ***dissolution.*** Unless the business also terminates, after the dissolution the business activities will continue on as before, with the new partnership.

continued ▶

Characteristics of a Partnership, *continued*

Mutual Agency

Mutual agency means that any partner who appears to be acting within the scope of the partnership's business creates a binding contract on behalf of the partnership and all the other partners. For example, suppose that Bill Anderson is a partner in the ABC accounting partnership. If Bill enters into an agreement to provide accounting services, even without the knowledge of the other partners, the partnership is obligated to fulfill that agreement. On the other hand, if the contract had been to provide car repair services, there would not be mutual agency. Mutual agency also applies to debts incurred for the purchase of goods and services.

Unlimited Liability

Unlimited liability means that each partner is personally obligated to pay partnership debts if there are not enough partnership assets to pay the debts. For example, if the liabilities of the ABC partnership exceeded its assets by $50,000 the partners would be personally obligated to pay this amount from their own assets. What would happen if partners A and B had no personal assets? Partner C would be obligated to pay the full $50,000! You can see that the combination of mutual agency and unlimited liability should make you consider your choice of partners very carefully.

Separate Financial Entity

For accounting purposes, a partnership is treated as a separate financial entity. Financial statements are prepared for the partnership. The personal assets and debts of individual partners are not part of the partnership records. The only major difference between the accounting records for a proprietorship and a partnership is that a partnership maintains a separate capital account and withdrawals account for each partner.

For the financial statements, a separate capital account balance is shown for each partner on the balance sheet. On the income statement, some accountants show the amount of net income or loss allocated to each partner directly under the net income.

Co-Ownership of Property

Partnership assets and liabilities are owned jointly by all partners. Investments by partners become partnership assets that are considered to be co-owned by all partners. The balance in each partner's capital account is the amount of that partner's claim on the total partnership assets.

No Partnership Income Tax

A partnership entity files an information tax return, but does not pay income tax. Instead, each type of partnership income, loss, or deduction is allocated among the individual partners according to their partnership ratios. Each partner receives a form that details the allocated items to that partner. The partner then includes the partnership items with all other income, loss, and deduction items in the calculation of his or her individual tax. (Note that the partnership amounts included for the tax calculation are the allocated items, not the cash or other asset withdrawals.)

Characteristics of a Partnership, *continued*

Partnership Legal Rules

Most states have adopted the rules in the ***Uniform Partnership Act***. This act provides the legal guidelines for partnership activities.

Advantages and Disadvantages

A quick summary of partnership advantages and disadvantages are compared in the summary table on page 72 in Learning Goal 5. Any type of business can be a partnership and partnerships can be any size.

Types of Partnerships

General Partnership

A ***general partnership*** is the basic and most common form of partnership. It is the type of partnership with the features discussed above.

Limited Partnership

A ***limited partnership*** is a partnership that has two types of partners: general and limited. A general partner has unlimited personal liability and the authority to manage the business operations. A limited partner's liability is limited to the amount invested, but a limited partner cannot manage business operations.

Limited Liability Company

A ***limited liability company***, often called an LLC, is a business form that has advantages of both a partnership and a corporation. The owners of an LLC can share profits and losses and ownership like a partnership; however, like a corporation, owners do not have personal liability for the business debts unless they have signed personal guarantees or in some cases of negligence. Each state has its own rules governing the formation and operation of LLCs. As well, an LLC can be formed by one person or by multiple owners. For tax purposes an LLC can elect to be treated as a corporation; otherwise, it is treated as a proprietorship (one owner) or a partnership (multiple owners).

> *Note:* There is also an entity form called a limited liability partnership (LLP) that is similar to an LLC. These are generally used for existing partnerships that wish to limit liability for all partners and to maintain the structure of a partnership.

S Corporation

An ***S corporation*** is a corporation that only for income tax purposes is treated very much like a partnership. The name 'S Corporation' is derived from the location ('subchapter S') in the Internal Revenue Code that describes this type of entity. For tax purposes an S corporation has an important advantage, because it eliminates the double taxation applied to a corporation.

New Business Start-Up

Introduction

Overview

A new partnership is formed when any of the following events occur:

- A new business is started and formed as a partnership
- A new partner is admitted to an existing partnership
- A partner withdraws from an existing partnership while other partners remain

We will begin our discussion with a new business start-up.

Accounting Procedures

Rule

At the time a new business is created, each partner's investment in the partnership should be recorded at the fair market value of the assets at that time, unless the partners negotiate a different value. If a liability accompanies an asset invested, the liability reduces the partner's investment.

Example

On July 1, John Emmans and Diane Frankel combine their individual proprietorships to form a new business called the Digital Consulting partnership. The assets and liabilities of each proprietorship are shown below at their prior recorded (book) values and current market values:

	Book Value		Market Value	
	Emmans	Frankel	Emmans	Frankel
Cash	$10,000	$5,000	$10,000	$5,000
Accounts Receivable	11,000		11,000	
Office Equipment		15,000		9,000
Allowance for bad receivables	(500)		(1,700)	
Accumulated depreciation		(4,000)		
Accounts payable	(2,000)		(2,000)	
Owner's Equity	$18,500	$16,000	$17,300	$14,000

The partners hire an appraiser to determine the market value of the equipment. The appraiser estimates a value of $9,000. Because this is a new business, any prior accumulated depreciation (depreciation is recording the using up of the cost of a long-term asset like equipment, as time passes) is not relevant because it applies only to the prior business. The partners examine the receivables together and agree that the probable amount uncollectible will be $1,700. To keep a clear record, they record this in a separate "allowance" account with a credit balance that acts as an offset to the debit balance of the accounts receivable account.

Accounting Procedures, *continued*

Journal Entry

Based on the new values, the entry below records Emmans' entry into the partnership:

July 1	Cash	10,000	
	Accounts Receivable	11,000	
	Allowance for Bad Receivables		1,700
	Accounts Payable		2,000
	Emmans, Capital		17,300

Based on the new values, the entry below records Frankel's entry into the partnership:

July 1	Cash	5,000	
	Office Equipment	9,000	
	Frankel, Capital		14,000

When a partnership is formed, all accounting methods remain exactly the same as you have learned so far. All methods of recording and all the steps in the accounting cycle are the same for proprietorships, partnerships, and corporations.

Balance Sheet

After the journal entry is recorded, the initial partnership balance sheet is prepared:

Digital Consulting Partnership
Balance Sheet
July 1, 20XX

Assets			**Liabilities and Partners' Equity**	
Cash		$15,000	Accounts Payable	$2,000
Accounts Receivable	$11,000			
Less: Allowance for			J. Emmans, Capital	17,300
Bad Receivables	(1,700)		D. Frankel, Capital	14,000
		9,300	Total Partners' Capital	31,300
Office Equipment		9,000	Total liabilities and	
Total Assets		$33,300	Partners' Capital	$33,300

Allocating Profits and Losses and Partner Drawings

Introduction

Overview of Common Methods

One of the major advantages of a partnership form of business is the great flexibility in how income statement profits and losses can be allocated among partners, into their capital accounts. Here are some examples:

1. Constant allocation based only on a fixed ratio (3:2), or a percentage (60% and 40%), or a fraction (3/5 and 2/5) as in the case of a two-person partnership
2. Allocation based on the ratio of beginning or average capital balances
3. Percentage interest on capital balances with any remainder based on a fixed ratio, percentage, or fraction
4. Specified amounts to specific partners
5. A combination of specified amounts and interest on capital with any remainder based on a fixed ratio, percentage, or fraction

The purpose of the allocation methods is to fairly represent the importance or type of contribution or personal needs of each partner. For example, some partners may work many hours in the business, others may contribute a greater investment, while others may have great experience, knowledge, or business contacts. Allocations are negotiated as part of a partnership agreement. **Finally, remember that no cash is involved in allocation**—it is simply a sharing of net income or net loss shown on the income statement among the capital accounts.

Partnership Agreement

The method of profit and loss allocation should be specified in a partnership agreement. If there is no partnership agreement, profits and losses are allocated equally. If the agreement specifies only the method of sharing profits, then losses will be allocated in the same manner as profits.

Summarizing Net Income or Loss: Quick Review

Introduction

Before we examine the most common profit and loss allocation methods, it might be helpful to quickly review how net income and loss are recorded in the accounts for any type of business. Sometimes this is called "closing the books." For a more in-depth presentation, the topic is explained in detail in Learning Goal 8, Volume 2.

Summarizing Net Income or Loss: Quick Review, *continued*

Income Summary Account

At the end of each accounting period, a single account called the income summary account is used to determine net income or net loss. The totals of all revenue account balances are transferred as a single entry to the credit side of income summary. Then the totals of the expense account balances are transferred as a single entry to the debit side of income summary. If the credit balance is greater than the debit balance, a business has net income. If the debit balance is greater than the credit balance, a business has net loss.

Examples

The accounts below show examples of income summary accounts after the total revenues and expenses have been recorded into the accounts.

Income Summary

Debit	Credit
	150,000
120,000	
	30,000

Income Summary

Debit	Credit
	129,000
145,000	
16,000	

In the example on the left, the Income Summary is a net income balance of $30,000 because the $150,000 of total revenues exceed the $120,000 of total expenses. The second example shows a net loss balance of $16,000 because total revenues of $129,000 are less than total expenses of $145,000.

Capital Accounts

A partner's allocation (share) of the net income or net loss is recorded in the partner's capital account. This is very easily done by making a journal entry that transfers the net income or loss balance out of income summary into the partners' capital accounts.

Examples

Assume that the AB partnership shares profits and losses 40% to partner A and 60% to partner B. For the $30,000 net income example the journal entry would be:

Account	Debit	Credit
Income Summary	30,000	
A, Capital ($30,000 × .4)		12,000
B, Capital ($30,000 × .6)		18,000

In the second example, the capital accounts are reduced because of the loss:

Account	Debit	Credit
A, Capital ($16,000 × .4)	6,400	
B, Capital ($16,000 × .6)	9,600	
Income Summary		16,000

continued ▶

Summarizing Net Income or Loss: Quick Review, *continued*

Asset Withdrawals (Drawing)

When a partner withdraws cash or other assets from a partnership, the asset is reduced (credit) and the amount of the withdrawal is recorded in a drawing account (debit). A separate drawing account is maintained for each partner.

Examples

The accounts below show drawing accounts for partners A and B. Partner A has made one withdrawal of $10,000 and partner B has made two with drawals; one for $3,500 and another for $7,000.

A, Drawing	
10,000	

D, Drawing	
3,500	
7,000	
10,500	

Capital Accounts

Withdrawals reduce a partner's capital. Therefore, at the same time the net income or net loss is allocated to partners' capital accounts, the capital accounts are also reduced by the amount of the asset withdrawals. This is done by simply transferring the debit balances out of the drawing accounts into the capital accounts.

Examples

The journal entry records the reduction in the capital accounts for partners A and B above.

A, Capital	10,000	
B, Capital	10,500	
A, Drawing		10,000
B, Drawing		10,500

Assuming a net income of $30,000, the final capital account balances for partner A and partner B show the increases (credits) from the net income (40% to A and 60% to B) and the decreases (debits) from the withdrawals.

A, Capital	
	12,000
10,000	
	2,000

B, Capital	
	18,000
10,500	
	7,500

Summarizing Net Income or Loss: Quick Review, *continued*

A $16,000 net loss would result in these capital balances:

A, Capital		B, Capital	
6,400		9,600	
10,000		10,500	
16,400		***20,100***	

Allocation using a constant ratio, percentage, or fraction

Introduction

The simplest method to allocate net or net loss is to use only a constant ratio, percentage, or fraction for each of the partners. In the examples below we assume that a three-person partnership called the JKL partnership shares net income and loss by using constant percentages of 30% to partner J, 20% to partner K, and 50% to partner L.

Only Constant Percentages

If the partnership uses only constant percentages, then all that is required is to prepare a journal entry that removes the balance from income summary and allocates it into the partners' capital accounts. Assume that the Income Summary account shows net income (a credit balance) of $80,000. The journal entry would be:

Income Summary	80,000	
J, Capital		24,000
K, Capital		16,000
L, Capital		40,000

Priority allocations

Overview

Priority allocations are amounts that are allocated to partners before using any constant ratios, percentages, or fractions. For example, a salary allocation is often used to allocate a fixed amount to a partner that contributes significant time and work into a business. Priority allocations based on capital balances are used to compensate partners based on the amount of capital contributed. **Caution:** the word "salary" as used in this context *does not* mean a cash payment, like a paycheck. It simply means a fixed amount that will be allocated to a partner's capital account because of that partner's service. No cash payment occurs. Also, the word "interest" on capital *does not* mean a cash payment. It is simply an allocation to capital using a calculation based on capital balances.

continued ▶

Priority allocations, *continued*

Rule

Priority allocations must always be made first, regardless of the amount of net income or loss. Any remaining balance of net income or loss is then allocated based on the constant ratios, percentages, or fractions of the partnership.

"Salary" allocation

Example

Assume that the JKL partnership agreement allocates $15,000 of salary to partner J and $10,000 of salary to partner K, with any remaining income or loss allocated 30%, 20%, and 50% respectively. Net income is $80,000.

Suggestion: when using more than one kind of allocation method, it is often helpful to use a table. The table example below shows the total amount to allocate and the amount allocated to each partner.

Item	Total	J 30%	K 20%	L 50%
Total to Allocate	$80,000			
Salaries	$25,000	$15,000	$10,000	
Balance	55,000	16,500	11,000	27,500
Total Allocated	$80,000	$31,500	$21,000	$27,500

The first line in the table shows the net income to allocate of $80,000. Because salaries are a priority allocation, the next line allocates the $25,000 of salaries to partners J and K. This leaves a remaining balance of $55,000 that is allocated to all partners based on their percentages. Finally, when the table is completed, the last line of the table is used for the amounts in the journal entry as shown below:

Date	Account	Debit	Credit
July 1	Income Summary	80,000	
	J, Capital		31,500
	K, Capital		21,000
	L, Capital		27,500

Allocation based on salary and interest on capital

Example #1

Assume that the JKL partnership agreement has two priority allocations. The agreement allocates $13,000 of salary to partner J and $22,000 of salary to partner K. The agreement also allocates 10% interest based on the beginning of the year capital balances. The beginning capital balances are: partner A: $90,000; partner B: $190,000; partner C: $120,000. Net income is $80,000.

The first line in the table shows the total net income to allocate. The two priority allocations must be done next (in any order). The total salaries are $35,000 and the total allocation based on capital is $40,000. This leaves a remaining net income balance of $5,000 to allocate. This is allocated based on the partnership percentage.

Item	Total	J 30%	K 20%	L 50%
Total to Allocate	$80,000			
Salaries	$35,000	$13,000	$22,000	
Interest on Capital	40,000	9,000	19,000	12,000
Balance	5,000	1,500	1,000	2,500
Total Allocated	$80,000	$23,500	$42,000	$14,500

After the table is completed, the last line is used for the amounts in the journal entry shown below.

		Debit	Credit
July 1	Income Summary	80,000	
	J, Capital		23,500
	K, Capital		42,000
	L, Capital		14,500

Example #2

Same facts as in example #1, except that the net income is $45,000.

Item	Total	J 30%	K 20%	L 50%
Total to Allocate	$45,000			
Salaries	$35,000	$13,000	$22,000	
Interest on Capital	40,000	9,000	19,000	12,000
Balance	(30,000)	(9,000)	(6,000)	(15,000)
Total Allocated	$45,000	$13,000	$35,000	$(3,000)

continued ▶

Allocation based on salary and interest on capital, *continued*

Example #2, continued

In this example the priority allocations exceeded the amount of net income and created a negative balance of $30,000 to allocate back to the partners. Unless the partnership agreement has a provision to suspend or reduce the priority allocations in this situation, the allocations will result in partners J and K receiving the entire $45,000 of net income, plus removing $3,000 of capital from partner L and transferring it over to partners J and K!

In this situation where most of the priority allocations go to J and K but L has the largest percentage, partner L gains significantly if the net income is high, but loses if the net income is only moderate, and loses a great deal if there are losses. (Do you think there might be some arguments between the partners?)

After the table is completed, the last line is used for the amounts in the journal entry shown below. Notice that the debit to L Capital is a reduction in partner L's capital balance.

July 1	Income Summary	45,000	
	L, Capital	3,000	
	J, Capital		13,000
	K, Capital		35,000

Allocation based on ratio of capital balances

Example

Assume that the JKL partnership has an allocation based entirely on the ratio of beginning capital balances. The beginning capital balances are: partner A: $90,000; partner B: $190,000; partner C: $120,000. Net income is $80,000.

The ratio of capital balances are

Partner	Beginning Capital	Ratio & Percentage
Partner J	$90,000	90,000/400,000 = 22.5%
Partner K	190,000	190,000/400,000 = 47.5%
Partner L	120,000	120,000/400,000 = 30%
Total	400,000	400,000/400,000 = 100%

Allocation based on ratio of capital balances, *continued*

Based on the percentages, the journal entry to allocate net income is:

July 1	Income Summary	80,000	
	J, Capital		18,000
	K, Capital		38,000
	L, Capital		24,000

Summary

Priority allocations of 'salary' or based on capital balances are allocations to capital accounts; they are not cash distributions. Priority allocations are made before any allocation based on partnership profit and loss sharing ratios, percentages, or fractions. When all allocations are completed, the total allocated must be exactly the same total as the net income or net loss in the income summary account.

Changes in Partnership Interests: Dissolutions

Overview

Introduction

As stated earlier, three events create a new partnership:

- A new business is started and formed as a partnership
- A new partner is admitted to an existing partnership
- A partner withdraws from an existing partnership while other partners remain. We previously discussed the method of recording a new partnership start-up, so we now turn our attention to the second and third items.

Dissolution

Whenever a partner is either admitted to a partnership or leaves a partnership, the old partnership ends and a new partnership is created. When a partnership ends, it is said to be "dissolved" and the process is called *dissolution* of the partnership. The partnership agreement should contain detailed procedures for conducting a dissolution and recording the change in partnership members.

continued ▶

Withdrawal of a Partner by Personal Transaction

Overview

Like the admission of a new partner, the withdrawal of a partner dissolves a partnership. A new partnership is created if two or more remaining partners carry on the business. The simplest withdrawal situation occurs when other partners use their personal funds to buy out the capital interest of the withdrawing partner or a new partner purchases the interest of the withdrawing partner. In these cases, no partnership assets or liabilities are affected. We previously looked at examples of a new partner purchasing the interest of a withdrawing partner. The example below illustrates the purchase by existing partners.

Example

Assume that the Able, Baker, and Cooper partnership capital accounts show the following balances: Able: $92,000; Baker: $105,000; Cooper: $100,000. Cooper wishes to withdraw from the partnership. Able and Baker each agree to purchase one half of Cooper's interest for $80,000 each using their personal funds. The journal entry is shown below:

Cooper, Capital	100,000	
Able, Capital		50,000
Baxter, Capital		50,000

The payment of $160,000 goes to Cooper's personal bank account and Cooper has a personal gain of $60,000, There is no change in partnership assets or liabilities, so the total capital balance is unchanged. Cooper's capital balance is now zero and the capital accounts of Able and Baker each increase by one-half of Cooper's capital balance. It does not matter how much was paid to Cooper; the journal entry would be the same, because no money goes into or out of the partnership.

Withdrawal of a Partner by Removing Assets

Overview

The second way a partner can withdraw from a partnership is by removing a share of partnership assets. A partnership agreement usually contains provisions that allow a partner to withdraw from a partnership by removing his or her share of the partnership assets.

Valuation of The Capital Account

When a partner withdraws from a partnership, that partner will expect to receive the fair market value of his or her claim (the capital account) on the partnership assets. However, in most cases the value of the assets on the balance sheet will not correspond to their actual fair market value; therefore, the capital account balance will not be at fair market value. The only way to be completely certain of the fair market asset values is to sell the assets; of course, this would liquidate the business and cannot be done for a continuing business. Therefore, the next best alternative is to hire an appraiser, who analyzes each of the assets and gives the partnership an estimated fair market value.

Withdrawal of a Partner by Removing Assets, *continued*

Accounting Method

After the partnership agrees on the total asset fair market value, two accounting methods are possible. The first method is to pay the withdrawing partner his or her share of the fair market value without actually adjusting asset values on the books. If the payment of fair market value is more than or less than the balance in the withdrawing partner's capital account, the difference is treated as a bonus either from the other partners or to the other partners, and allocated among them.

The second method is to use an adjusting entry that revalues all partnership assets to their fair market value. The revaluation of the assets will also change all the partners' capital accounts to fair market value. There will be no difference between fair market value of the withdrawing partner's capital account and payment to the partner, unless the partners negotiate otherwise. This is a common practice, so it is the method that we will illustrate and use in our examples.

Procedure

The table below shows the procedure for recording a partner's withdrawal when assets are removed from the partnership. Assume that current period net income up to the date of withdrawal is recorded in the accounts.

Step	Procedure
1	Appraise the fair market value of assets
2	Record an adjusting entry that changes assets and capital accounts to fair market value.
3	Negotiate payment amount and payment terms with partner
4	Record the payment and withdrawal.

Example Steps 1 and 2

Partner Brown wishes to retire from the Brown, Collins, Davis partnership. The condensed partnership balance sheet is prepared immediately before Brown leaves, and includes the net income up to the date of Brown's retirement. The profit and loss sharing ratios are 1:2:1 (1/4 for Brown, 2/4 for Collins, and 1/4 for Davis).

Brown, Collins, & Davis
Balance Sheet

Cash		$79,000	Total liabilities	$70,000
Supplies		21,000	Brown, Capital	82,000
Merchandise inventory		110,000	Collins, Capital	97,000
Equipment	$129,000		Davis, Capital	55,000
Less: accum. dep'n	(35,000)	94,000		
Total Assets		$304,000	Total liabilities & Partners' Capital	$304,000

continued ►

Withdrawal of a Partner by Removing Assets, *continued*

A certified appraiser provides the following asset revaluations (procedure step 1): Supplies: $24,000; Inventory: $133,000; Equipment: $84,000. The supplies and inventory have been revalued upward by a total of $26,000. The equipment has been revalued down by $10,000. The journal entries below record the revaluations (procedure step 2):

Supplies	3,000	
Merchandise Inventory	23,000	
Brown, Capital (1/4 × 26,000)		6,500
Collins, Capital (1/2 × 26,000)		13,000
Davis, Capital (1/4 × 26,000)		6,500
(To record appraisal increase and allocate gain to partners)		

Brown, Capital (1/4 × 10,000)	2,500	
Collins, Capital (1/2 × 10,000)	5,000	
Davis, Capital (1/4 × 10,000)	2,500	
Accumulated Depreciation		10,000
(To record appraisal decrease and allocate loss to partners)		

The partnership assets and capital accounts are now at the current fair market value. The balance of Brown's capital account is now $86,000: ($82,000 + $6,500 – $2,500).

Example Step 3

The partners negotiate the payment and terms of Brown's withdrawal. Because it would be a hardship for the business to pay Brown all in cash, the partnership agreement permits a cash payment of one-half of Brown's capital balance and a 5-year note payable for the balance. The partners agree that Brown will receive the $86,000 book value of his capital interest.

Payment at Book Value Example Step 4

The journal entry below records the payment and withdrawal of Brown.

Brown, Capital	86,000	
Cash		43,000
Notes Payable		43,000

Payment at More Than Book Value Example Step 4

Assume that the other partners appreciate Brown's work in the partnership, and that the partners agree that Brown will receive $5,000 more than book value, and the amount will be in cash. The journal entry below records this transaction.

Withdrawal of a Partner by Removing Assets, *continued*

Collins, Capital (2/3 × $5,000)	3,333	
Davis, Capital (1/3 × $5,000)	1,667	
Brown, Capital	86,000	
Cash		48,000
Notes Payable		43,000

Collins and Davis share the capital reduction in their profit and loss ratios relative to each other of 2:1 (2/3 and 1/3).

Payment at Less Than Book Value Example Step 4

Assume that Brown is eager to leave the partnership, so Brown agrees to accept $5,000 less than book value, and this will reduce the cash paid to Brown. The journal entry below records this transaction.

Brown, Capital	86,000	
Cash		38,000
Notes Payable		43,000
Collins, Capital (2/3 × $5,000)		3,333
Davis, Capital (1/3 × $5,000)		1,667

Death of a Partner

The death of a partner dissolves a partnership, but the business usually continues with the remaining partners. Payment is made to the heirs or estate of the deceased partner in the same manner as a withdrawing partner. Payment can be made either personally by the remaining partners or payment can be made from the assets of the partnership. Partnerships often maintain life insurance policies to provide necessary cash in the case a partner's death. This prevents the need to liquidate the business to obtain the funds to make the payment.

Liquidation of a Partnership

Overview

Liquidation of a partnership is the process of terminating business operations by selling the assets, paying all the creditors, and distributing any remaining cash or other assets to the partners. Liquidation dissolves a partnership and also ends business operations. There are a variety of possible results in a liquidation process. Here, we will follow the basic liquidation procedure and examine two of the most typical results of liquidation. These are: 1. Selling assets at a gain and having sufficient cash to pay all partners. 2. Selling assets at a loss with a resulting ***capital deficiency*** (debit balance) in a partner's capital account.

continued ▶

Liquidation of a Partnership, *continued*

Procedure

The table below shows the basic liquidation procedure. Before beginning the liquidation, the final accounting cycle should have been fully completed with the net income or loss closed into the partners' capital accounts.

Step	Procedure	
1	▪ Sell assets - convert all assets into cash ▪ Allocate gain or loss into partners' capital accounts	
2	Pay all creditors	
3	IF	THEN
	All partners have credit balances in their capital accounts	distribute remaining cash to all partners
	A partner has a deficiency in his capital account and pays cash into the partnership to eliminate the deficiency	distribute remaining cash to all other partners
	A partner has a deficiency in his capital account and does not pay cash into the partnership to eliminate the deficiency	▪ allocate deficiency loss to all other partners. ▪ distribute remaining cash to all other partners.

Step 1: the objective is to convert all assets into cash. Converting an asset into cash is called ***realization***. This is normally done by selling assets. Cash greatly simplifies creditor payments and partner distributions. Asset sales will result in a gain or loss.

Step 2: All creditors must be fully paid **before cash is distributed to partners.**

Step 3: The distribution to partners is determined by the balances in their capital accounts. Do not use profit/loss sharing ratios. These are only used for income allocation and gains and losses. A capital account balance represents a partner's claim on the business wealth.

A partner with a ***capital deficiency*** (debit balance) must eliminate the debit balance by making a payment into the partnership. If this is not done, the other partners must absorb the loss in their profit/loss sharing ratio. The remaining partners have the right to take legal action against the deficient partner to recover the loss, if feasible.

Liquidation of a Partnership, *continued*

Example #1: No Capital Deficiency

The partners of the Rossen, Smith, Travis partnership have agreed to liquidate their partnership. The profit and loss sharing percentages are Rossen: 40%, Smith 40%, and Travis 20%. The partnership liquidation summary table is shown below. The first row of the table is the accounting equation that contains all the final balance sheet account balances before liquidation begins.

Explanation	Cash	Other Assets	=	Liabilities	Rossen, Capital	Smith, Capital	Travis, Capital
Beginning Balances	$70,000	$430,000		$320,000	$115,000	$25,000	$40,000
Step 1: sell non-cash assets	480,000	(430,000)			20,000	20,000	10,000
New Balances	550,000	-0-		320,000	135,000	45,000	50,000
Step 2: pay all liabilities	(320,000)			(320,000)			
New Balances	230,000	-0-		-0-	135,000	45,000	50,000
Step 3: distribute cash to partners	(230,000)				(135,000)	(45,000)	(50,000)
Final Balances	-0-	-0-		-0-	-0-	-0-	-0-

Step 1: Non-cash assets with a cost of $430,000 are sold for $480,000. The $50,000 gain is allocated to the partners in their profit and loss sharing percentages. The following journal entries are recorded using assumed amounts for the assets:

Account	Debit	Credit
Cash	480,000	
Accumulated Deprecation - Equip.	90,000	
Equipment		275,000
Inventory		120,000
Accounts Receivable		125,000
Gain on Realization		50,000
(To record realization of non-cash assets)		
Gain on Realization	50,000	
Rossen, Capital		20,000
Smith, Capital		20,000
Travis, Capital		10,000
(To allocate gain to partners' capital accounts)		

Step 2: The partnership liabilities consist of accounts payable of $112,00 and a note payable of $208,000. The creditors are paid in full by cash payments totaling $320,000. Notice that payment of a liability has no effect on capital.

continued ▶

Liquidation of a Partnership, *continued*

Example #1: No Capital Deficiency, continued

Accounts Payable	112,000	
Notes Payable	208,000	
Cash		320,000
(To record payment of all partnership liabilities)		

Step 3: All partners have positive capital account balances; therefore, all remaining cash is distributed to partners based on the balances in their capital accounts. The journal entry below concludes the liquidation:

Rossen, Capital	135,000	
Smith, Capital	45,000	
Travis, Capital	50,000	
Cash		230,000
(To record final cash distribution to partners)		

Example #2: Capital Deficiency — Partner Pays

In this example, the facts are the same except that we assume the assets were sold for only $350,000 resulting in an $80,000 loss. The cash distribution table is shown below.

Explanation	Cash	Other Assets	=	Liabilities	Rossen, Capital	Smith, Capital	Travis, Capital
Beginning Balances	70,000	$430,000		$320,000	$115,000	$25,000	$40,000
Step 1: sell non-cash assets	350,000	(430,000)			(32,000)	(32,000)	(16,000)
New Balances	420,000	-0-		320,000	83,000	(7,000)	24,000
Step 2: pay all liabilities	(320,000)			(320,000)			
New Balances	100,000	-0-		-0-	83,000	(7,000)	24,000
Step 3: receive cash from Smith	7,000				-0-	7,000	-0-
New Balances	107,000	-0-		-0-	83,000	-0-	24,000
distribute cash to partners	(107,000)				(83,000)		(24,000)
Final Balances	-0-	-0-		-0-	-0-	-0-	-0-

Liquidation of a Partnership, *continued*

Example #2: Capital Deficiency — Partner Pays, continued

Step 1: Non-cash assets with a cost of $430,000 are sold for $350,000. The $80,000 loss is allocated to the partners in their profit and loss sharing percentages.

Cash	350,000	
Loss on Realization	80,000	
Accumulated Deprecation — Equip.	90,000	
Equipment		275,000
Inventory		120,000
Accounts Receivable		125,000
(To record realization of non-cash assets)		
Rossen, Capital (.4 × 80,000)	32,000	
Smith, Capital (.4 × 80,000)	32,000	
Travis, Capital (.2 × 80,000)	16,000	
Loss on Realization		80,000
(To allocate loss to partners' capital accounts)		

Step 2: The partnership liabilities consist of accounts payable of $112,00 and a note payable of $208,000. The creditors are paid in full by cash payments totaling $320,000.

Accounts Payable	112,000	
Notes Payable	208,000	
Cash		320,000
(To record payment of all partnership liabilities)		

Step 3: Partner Smith contributes $7,000 cash to the partnership to eliminate the $7,000 deficiency (negative capital balance). The partnership now distributes the remaining cash to the other partners, Rossen and Travis, who receive the full balances in their capital accounts.

Cash	7,000	
Smith, Capital		7,000
(To record collection from Smith to eliminate deficiency)		
Rossen, Capital	83,000	
Travis, Capital	24,000	
Cash		107,000
(To record final cash distribution to partners)		

continued ▶

Liquidation of a Partnership, *continued*

Example #3: Capital Deficiency - Partner Does Not Pay

In this example we assume that partner Smith is either unable or unwilling to contribute $7,000 into the partnership to eliminate the capital account deficiency. In this case, in Step 3 the other two partners must absorb the loss in their profit/loss ratio, relative to each other. The Rossen percentage is 40% and the Travis percentage is 20%, so this is a ratio of 4:2 (2/3 and 1/3. Note: here it is easier to use fractions rather than non-terminating percentages of 66.666.....% and 33.333....%)

Explanation	Cash	Other Assets	=	Liabilities	Rossen, Capital	Smith, Capital	Travis, Capital
Beginning Balances	70,000	$430,000		$320,000	$115,000	$25,000	$40,000
Step 1: sell non-cash assets	350,000	(430,000)			(32,000)	(32,000)	(16,000)
New Balances	420,000	-0-		320,000	83,000	(7,000)	24,000
Step 2: pay all liabilities	(320,000)			(320,000)			
New Balances	100,000	-0-		-0-	83,000	(7,000)	24,000
Step 3: deficiency adjustment					(4,667)	7,000	(2,333)
New Balances	100,000	-0-		-0-	78,333	-0-	21,667
distribute cash to partners	(100,000)				(78,333)		(21,667)
Final Balances	-0-	-0-		-0-	-0-	-0-	-0-

Steps 1 and 2: These journal entries are unchanged.

Step 3: The journal entry is shown below.

	Debit	Credit
Rossen, Capital (2/3 × 7,000)	4,667	
Travis, Capital (1/3 × 7,000)	2,333	
Smith, Capital		7,000
(To record write-off of Smith capital deficiency)		
Rossen, Capital	78,333	
Travis, Capital	21,667	
Cash		100,000
(To record final cash distribution to partners)		

QUICK REVIEW

- A partnership should be created using a written partnership agreement that controls the eight essential points of partnership operations.
- A general partnership has the six characteristics of limited life, mutual agency, unlimited liability, separate financial entity, no entity income tax, and co-ownership of property as described in the Uniform Partnership Act.
- The general partnership, limited partnership, limited liability company, and S corporation are the common entities that have partnership features and require partnership accounting.
- When a new business is formed as a partnership, use fair market value unless otherwise agreed by the partners.
- When more than one method is being used to allocate income to partners' capital accounts, create an allocation table and always record priority allocations first. Use the last line of the allocation table as the source of the journal entry that transfers income or loss from the income summary account to the capital accounts of the partners. Remember that income or loss allocation does not mean cash distribution.
- A partner can be admitted to a partnership either by purchasing an interest from a partner or investing in the partnership. An investment in a partnership can result in a bonus to new or old partners. A journal entry always records the admission of the new partner.
- A partner can withdraw from a partnership either by selling the capital interest or by removing assets from the partner-ship. Assets are appraised and adjusted to fair market value before the partner withdraws. Also, a bonus to the withdrawing partner or other partners can occur when a partner withdraws. A journal entry always entry records the withdrawal of the partner.
- A partnership is liquidated when a business is terminated, assets are sold, and partnership cash is used to pay all creditors and then is distributed to partners based on the positive balances in their capital accounts.

Do You Want More Examples?

Most problems in this book have detailed solutions. To use them as additional examples, do this: 1) Select the type of problem you want 2) Open the solution on your computer or mobile device screen (from the disc or worthyjames.com) 3) Read one item at a time and look at its answer. Take notes if needed. 4) Close the solution and work as much of the problem as you can. 5) Repeat as needed.

VOCABULARY

Capital deficiency: a debit balance in a partner's capital account. (page 772)

Dissolution: the termination of a partnership. (page 751)

General partnership: the most common type of partnership, with the features described on pages 752–753.

Limited life: the life of a partnership is limited to the lesser of the term of the partnership or the same group of partners belonging to the partnership. (page 751)

Limited liability company: a business form that has the features of a partnership but without personal liability for the owners. (page 753)

Limited partnership: a partnership form in which there are limited partners whose liability is limited to the amount invested and at least one general partner with management authority who has unlimited liability. (page 753)

LLC: limited liability company. (page 753)

Mutual agency: if a partner enters into an agreement when acting within the scope of the partnership business, the partner binds all other partners to the agreement. (page 752)

Partnership: an association co-owned by two or more persons, acting as partners, for the purpose of earning a profit. (page 751)

Realization: conversion of non-cash assets into cash, usually by a sale. (page 772)

S Corporation: a corporation that is taxed in essentially the same manner as a partnership. (page 753)

Uniform partnership act: the legal rules, adopted by most states, that govern the actions of partnerships. (page 753)

Unlimited liability: the personal responsibility of each partner to pay partnership debts if the partnership cannot pay them. (page 752)

PRACTICE Learning Goal 33

Solutions are in the disk at the back of the book and at: www.worthyjames.com

This learning goal is about partnerships. Use these questions and problems to practice what you have just read.

Multiple Choice

Select the best answer.

1. Which of the following is not true about a general partnership?
   a. The life of partnership is limited to the term stated in the partnership agreement.
   b. Profits and losses are allocated equally if not otherwise stated in the partnership agreement.
   c. Every partner can bind every other in a contract related to the partnership business activity.
   d. Partnership assets and liabilities are owned jointly by all partners.
2. Which of the following creates a partnership?
   a. The partners apply to the Internal Revenue Service.
   b. Individuals agree to be a partnership and then begin operations.
   c. Individuals obtain permission from their state of residence.
   d. All of the above.
3. Which of the following characteristics does not apply to a partnership?
   a. Limited life.
   b. Limited liability.
   c. No income tax.
   d. Mutual agency.
4. An organization in which none of the owners have personal liability is a _____
   a. general partnership.
   b. limited partnership.
   c. LLC.
   d. both b and c.
5. When a partnership is created to begin a new business, the correct values to assign to the assets is _____
   a. whatever the partners agree.
   b. fair market value.
   c. historical cost.
   d. either a or b, depending on what the partners agree.
6. The ABC partnership shares profits and losses in a ratio 4:3:2. The partnership has a net income of $81,000. How much will partner A record as her share of the income?
   a. $36,000
   b. $32,400
   c. $27,000
   d. None of the above
7. In the partnership of Mays, McCovey, and Marichal, Mays is allocated 1/4 of profits and losses. McCovey and Marichal share the remainder in a 3:2 ratio. If the partnership earned a net income of $50,000 how much was allocated to Marichal?
   a. $20,000
   b. $7,500
   c. $15,000
   d. None of the above

PRACTICE

Learning Goal 33, continued

Solutions are in the disk at the back of the book and at: www.worthyjames.com

8. The Jones and Smith partnership is admitting Green to the partnership as a new partner. Prior to Green's admission, the total partnership capital is $120,000 and Jones and Smith share profits and losses 40% to Jones and 60% to Smith. Green invests $40,000 in the partnership for a 20% interest in capital and profits and losses. Upon Green's admission the partnership should ______
   a. debit cash $40,000 and credit Green, Capital $40,000.
   b. not make any entry.
   c. debit cash $32,000 and credit Green, Capital $32,000.
   d. make some other entry
9. In question #8 above, after the admission of Green, how will Jones and Smith share profits and losses?
   a. 60% Jones and 40% Smith
   b. They share equally.
   c. 32% Jones and 48% Smith
   d. None of the above
10. Partner J is retiring from the JKL partnership. The partners share profits in a ratio of 4:4:2. Partner J's capital balance is $70,000 and she receives $80,000 upon leaving the partnership. The partnership did not revalue assets. What is the effect of the cash payment to J on partners' K and L capital accounts?
    a. No effect
    b. Each account is reduced by $5,000.
    c. Each account is reduced by $4,000.
    d. None of the above
11. In question #10 above, assume that the partnership appraised and revalued the assets immediately before J withdraws. Prior to the appraisal J's capital account was $70,000. The revaluation resulted in a $25,000 increase in total assets. What is the effect of the cash payment to J on partners' K and L capital accounts?
    a. No effect
    b. Each account is reduced by $5,000.
    c. Each account is reduced by $4,000.
    d. None of the above
12. The book value of the MNO partnership assets is $300,000 prior to liquidation. The partnership liquidates and sells the assets for $360,000. Partners share profits and losses equally. The partnership should ______
    a. debit cash for $360,000 and credit the assets for $360,000.
    b. debit cash for $360,000 and credit partners' capital accounts for a total of $360,000.
    c. debit cash $60,000 and credit partners' capital accounts for a total of $60,000.
    d. make some other entry.
13. The following events occur when a partnership is liquidated: 1) pay cash to partners 2) sell assets 3) pay liabilities 4) allocate gain or loss to partners. What is the correct order of these procedures?
    a. 1, 2, 3, 4
    b. 3, 4, 2, 1
    c. 2, 4, 1, 2
    d. 2, 4, 3, 1
14. During partnership liquidation, the payment of the liabilities ______
    a. has no effect on partner capital balances
    b. decreases partner capital balances equally
    c. decreases partner capital balances in the profit and loss sharing ratios
    d. increases partner capital balances in the profit and loss sharing ratios

PRACTICE Learning Goal 33, continued

Solutions are in the disk at the back of the book and at: www.worthyjames.com

Discussion Questions and Brief Exercises

1. Some of the essential characteristics of a partnership include: a) limited life, b) mutual agency, c) unlimited liability, and d) co-ownership of property. Explain the meaning of each of these characteristics.
2. How is partnership property owned? What is the meaning of a partner's capital account?
3. Three of your friends have a business idea and want to form a partnership. What are the advantages and disadvantages of forming a business as a partnership?
4. What are the types of partnerships? Briefly discuss each type.
5. Candice and Mabel are forming a partnership. Candice contributes the following: cash of $30,000; equipment that cost $40,000 and has $27,500 of accumulated depreciation ($12,500 book value) and land that cost $50,000. The equipment has a fair market value of $19,000 and the land has a fair market value of $82,000. What should be the balance in Candice's capital account when the partnership is formed? What would be the balance if there was a $15,000 note payable related to the land that the partnership assumed?
6. The partnership agreement of Western partnership does not specify the division of the profits and losses. The partnership agreement of Eastern partnership only specifies the division of profits. How will profits and losses be divided among the partners in each partnership?
7. Before forming a partnership, what factors should be considered to determine how profits and losses would be allocated among partners?
8. Are the financial statements of a partnership different than the financial statements of a proprietorship? Describe similarities and differences (compare and contrast).
9. The partnership of John Able and Fred Baker has a profit (net income) for the period. The partnership of Bill Cooper and Janet Dawson has a loss for the period. For each partnership, what accounts should be debited and credited to record the division of the income and loss between the partners?
10. What are common profit and loss allocation methods? What are priority allocations? Give some examples of each type of allocation and state the rule for the allocation procedure.
11. The A and B partnership has net income of $50,000. Indicate the total allocation to each partner for each of the following separate methods:

Method	Partner A	Partner B
a) A 3:2 ratio for A and B		
b) A 60:40 ratio for A and B		
c) A $10,000 salary to A, the remainder equally		
d) A $20,000 salary to B, the remainder 1/3 A and 2/3 B		

12. Record general journal entries for each of the methods a-d in 11 above.
13. Albert pays Deshawn $35,000 for 20% of his share in capital, profits and losses of the Dave-Deshawn partnership. The capital accounts are $100,000 for Dave and $112,000 for Deshawn. Profits and losses are shared equally between Dave and Deshawn. What effect does this event have on the assets of the partnership? What will be the profit and loss sharing percentage of each partner?
14. C invests $70,000 for a 40% interest in the AB partnership, which shares profits and losses 30% to A and 70% to B. Before the admission of C, A and B capital accounts total $105,000. What effect does this event have on the assets of the partnership? What will be the profit and loss sharing percentage of each partner?
15. Record general journal entries for 13 and 14 above.

PRACTICE Learning Goal 33, continued

Solutions are in the disk at the back of the book and at: www.worthyjames.com

16. The Rockford & Ramos partnership has capital balances of $105,000 and $145,000 for Max Rockford and Amy Ramos. The partners share profits and losses in a 2:3 ratio, respectively. Marsha Chen becomes a new partner by investing in the partnership. Calculate the bonus (if any) to each partner and complete the table below to show the bonus to the partners for each of the following independent situations.

Situation	Rockford	Ramos	Chen
a) Chen invests $100,000 and receives a 40% interest in capital and profits and losses			
b) Chen invests $80,000 and receives a 20% interest in capital and profits and losses			
c) Chen invests $250,000 and receives a 50% interest in capital and profits and losses			

17. Record general journal entries for each of the situations a -c in 15 above.

18. The Black, White, and Green partnership has capital balances as follows: Tom Black, $95,000; Anne White, $70,000; Janice Green, $44,000. The partners share profits and losses 5:3:2 respectively. Anne White has decided to withdraw from the partnership. Based on independent appraisal, the partnership recorded a $50,000 adjusting entry to increase asset values to fair market value.

a) How much will Anne receive?
b) The terms of payment to Anne from the partnership are 40% cash and a note payable for the balance. Record a general journal entry for the withdrawal.
c) Assume that Anne is eager to leave the partnership and accepts a 20% discount from her capital account value. The payment terms are the same. Record a general journal entry for the withdrawal.
d) Assume that Green pays White $90,000 for her partnership interest. Record a general journal entry for the withdrawal.

19. The RST partnership is going to liquidate. The accounting equation summarizes the balance sheet after completion of the last accounting period:

Cash	+	Non-cash assets	=	Liabilities	+	Partner R	Partner S	Partner T
$55,000		$276,000		$49,000		$64,000	$123,000	$95,000

The partners share profits and losses as follows: R 40%; S 30%; T 30%. Non-cash assets are sold for $376,000. Prepare a liquidation table for the partnership.

20. The Nguyen, Ramirez, Miller partnership is being liquidated. The line below shows the partners' capital balances after all assets are realized and all liabilities have been paid. The partners share profits and losses 1:2:1 respectively.

Cash	+	Non-cash assets	=	Liabilities	+	Partner Nguyen	Partner Ramirez	Partner Miller
$186,000		-0-		-0-		$75,000	$129,000	($18,000)

a) Record the journal entries to complete the liquidation assuming that Miller invests enough cash to remove his negative capital balance. b) Record the journal entries to complete the liquidation assuming that Miller refuses to invest any more cash in the partnership.

PRACTICE Learning Goal 33, continued

Solutions are in the disk at the back of the book and at: www.worthyjames.com

Reinforcement Problems

LG33-1. New business formed as a partnership On October 12, Dan Adams and Brenda Maxwell started a new business formed as a partnership. When the partnership was formed, Dan Adams contributed the following:

Item	Book Value	Market Value
Cash	$120,000	$120,000
Accounts Receivable	19,380	19,380
Allowance for Bad Receivables		(2,180)
Prepaid Rent	2,500	2,500
Office Equipment	42,750	25,000
Accumulated Deprecation	(10,100)	-0-
Notes Payable	(14,600)	(14,600)

Brenda Maxwell contributed $135,000 cash. Each partner will share equally in profits and losses.

a. Prepare a general journal entry to record the formation of the partnership.
b. Prepare the partnership balance sheet immediately upon formation of the partnership.
c. During the remainder of the year, the partnership earned net income of $24,000. As well, Adams withdrew $5,000 cash and Maxwell withdrew $7,500 of cash. Prepare journal entries to record allocation of the net income and the closing of the drawing accounts.
d. Notice that the partners have agreed to share profits and losses equally, even though they contribute different amounts of partnership capital. What do you think are the reasons for this?

LG33-2. Income and loss allocations The ABC partnership prepared the following annual information as of December 31, 200X, the end of its fiscal year's operations.

Partner	January 1 Capital Balance	Drawing
A	$20,000	-0-
B	50,000	$10,000
C	30,000	7,500

Prepare journal entries to allocate year's income or loss for each of the following independent situations:

a. Net income is $70,000 and partners A, B, & C share profits and losses 25%, 40%, and 35%.
b. Net loss is $50,000 and partners A, B, & C share profits and losses in a 3:2:1 ratio.
c. Net income is $80,000 and partners A, B, & C share profits and losses 1/4, 1/2, and 1/4. The partnership agreement specifies a $20,000 salary allocation partner C.
d. Net income is $80,000 and partners A, B, & C share profits and losses 50%, 30%, and 20%. The partnership agreement specifies an allocation to each partner as 10% of his beginning capital balance.

PRACTICE Learning Goal 33, continued

Solutions are in the disk at the back of the book and at: www.worthyjames.com

LG 33-2, *continued*

e. Net income is $100,000 and partners A, B, & C share profits and losses 50%, 30%, and 20%. The partnership agreement specifies a $40,000 allocation is to be made to partners based on the ratio of their capital balances at the beginning of the current period.
f. Net income is $30,000 and partners A, B, & C share profits and losses 50%, 30%, and 20%. The partnership agreement specifies a salary allocation to B and C in the amounts of $10,000 and $15,000. The partnership agreement also specifies 10% interest on beginning capital balances to each partner.
g The drawing account balances are closed into the partners' capital accounts.

LG33-3. Income and loss allocations At the beginning of the current fiscal year, the Nancy, Oscar, and Peter partnership beginning capital balances were: Nancy: $60,000; Oscar: $70,000; Peter: $50,000. Prepare journal entries to allocate the year's income or loss for each of the following independent situations

a. Net loss is $90,000 and the partnership agreement specifies that profits are shared in a 4:3:1 ratio for Nancy, Oscar, and Peter. The agreement does not specify how losses are to be shared.
b. Net loss is $50,000 and the partners share profits and losses equally. The partnership agreement also specifies a $10,000 salary allocation to Oscar.
c. Net income is $50,000 and Nancy, Oscar, and Peter share profits and losses 30%, 30%, 40%. The partnership agreement also specifies an allocation to each partner as 5% of his beginning capital balance.
d. Net income is $40,000 and Nancy, Oscar, and Peter share profits and losses 30%, 30%, 40%. The partnership agreement also specifies a $25,000 capital interest allocation based on the ratio of partner capital balances at the beginning of the period.
e. Net income is $20,000 and Nancy, Oscar, and Peter share profits and losses in a 2:2:3 ratio. The partnership agreement specifies a $25,000 allocation to the partners based on the ratio of the partners' capital balances at the beginning of the period, and a $5,000 salary allocation to Oscar.
f. Net income is $50,000 and Nancy, Oscar, and Peter share profits and losses 1/4, 1/4, 1/2. The partnership agreement specifies a $25,000 allocation to partners based on the ratio of the partners' capital balances at the beginning of the period, and a $5,000 salary allocation to Oscar.

LG33-4. New partner admitted to a partnership The Lee, Fisher, and Ames partnership has decided to admit a new partner, John Bloch, to the partnership. As of September 30, before admitting the new partner but after recording current period income, the partnership capital accounts and profit and loss percentages are as follows:

Partner	Sept. 30 Capital Balance	P/L %
Janine Lee	$62,000	25%
Bill Fisher	77,000	35%
Carly Ames	61,000	40%

For each independent situation below:

1. Record the admission of the new partner as of October 1
2. Calculate the new profit and loss sharing percentages of each partner.

PRACTICE Learning Goal 33, continued

Solutions are in the disk at the back of the book and at: www.worthyjames.com

LG 33-4, *continued*

a. John Bloch pays Carly Ames $90,000 to purchase all of her partnership interest.
b. John Bloch pays Carly Ames $25,000 to purchase one-half of her partnership interest.
c. John Block invests $50,000 for a one-fifth interest in the business.
d. John Block invests $50,000 for a 15% interest in the business.
e. John Block invests $30,000 for a 15% interest in the business.

LG33-5. New partner admitted to a partnership

The Jones and Smith partnership are admitting a new partner, Baxter, to their partnership as of May1. Before admitting Baxter to the partnership the capital accounts are as follows: Jones $190,000; Smith $160,000. Jones and Smith share profits and losses in a 3:2 ratio. For each independent situation below:

1. Record the admission of Baxter as of May 1
2. Calculate the new profit and loss sharing for each partner.

a. Baxter pays Smith $200,000 to purchase all of Smith's partnership interest.
b. Baxter pays $100,000 to Jones and $90,000 to Smith to purchase one-half of their partnership interests.
c. Baxter invests $150,000 for 30% interest in the partnership.
d. Baxter invests $150,000 for a 50% interest in the partnership.
e. Baxter invests $150,000 for a 20% interest in the partnership.

LG33-6. Withdrawal from a partnership The condensed balance sheet of the DEF partnership is shown below as of June 30, 20XX. Profits and losses are shared between the partners as follows: D:30%; E: 50%; F: 20%. Partner F has decided to withdraw from the partnership as of June 30, 20XX.

DEF Partnership
Balance Sheet
June 30, 20XX

Assets			Liabilities and Partners' Capital		
Cash		$185,000	Accounts payable		$127,300
Accounts receivable	$19,380				
Less: allowance for bad receivables	(2,180)		D, Capital	$160,500	
			E, Capital	105,100	
		17,200	F, Capital	146,300	
Merchandise inventory		265,000	Total partners' capital		411,900
Office equipment	92,000				
Less: accum. dep'n.	(20,000)				
		72,000	Total liabilities and partners' capital		$539,200
Total Assets		$539,200			

Record the withdrawal of partner F for each of the following independent situations:

a. As a personal transaction, F sells her partnership equity to D and E, who each pay $90,000 to F for one- half of F's equity.
b. The partnership pays partner F $40,000 and gives F a note payable for the remaining balance of the book value of her partnership equity.

PRACTICE **Learning Goal 33, continued**

Solutions are in the disk at the back of the book and at: www.worthyjames.com

LG 33-6, *continued*

c. The partnership pays partner F $30,000 and gives F a note payable for $126,300 for the book value of her partnership equity.
d. The partnership hires an appraiser, who reports that the merchandise inventory has a current market value of $280,000 and the office equipment has a current market value of $65,000. The partnership pays partner F $25,000 and gives her a note payable for the balance of her partnership equity.

LG33-7. **Withdrawal from a partnership** The condensed balance sheet of the Able, Baker, and Cooper partnership is shown below as of August 31, 20XX. Profits and losses are shared between the partners as follows: John Able:40%; Diane Baker: 35%; Linda Cooper: 25%. John Able has decided to withdraw from the partnership as of August 31, 20XX.

Able, Baker, Cooper Partnership
Balance Sheet
August 31, 20XX

Assets			Liabilities and Partners' Capital		
Cash		$75,000	Accounts payable		$64,100
Accounts receivable	$36,450				
Less: allowance for bad receivables	(2,250)		Able, Capital	$240,500	
			Baker, Capital	287,600	
		34,400	Cooper, Capital	136,700	
Merchandise inventory		125,000	Total partners' capital		664,800
Building	715,000				
Less: accum. dep'n.	(220,500)				
		494,500			
Total Assets		$728,900	Total liabilities and partners' capital		$728,900

Record the withdrawal of John Able for each of the following independent situations:

a. With the approval of Baker, Able sells his partnership equity to Cooper, who pays $210,000 to Able for his partnership equity interest.
b. The partnership pays partner Able $20,000 and gives him a note payable for the remaining balance of the book value of his partnership equity.
c. The partnership pays partner Able $10,000, gives $50,000 of merchandise inventory, and gives him a note payable for $175,000 for the book value of his partnership equity.
d. Based on appraisal, the partners agree that the merchandise inventory has a current market value of $100,000 and the building has a current market value of $825,000. The partnership adjusts the building value change in the Building account. The partnership pays Able $25,000 and gives him a note payable for the balance of his partnership equity.

LG33-8. **Partnership liquidation**

The partnership of Ramsey, Smith, and Tolliver is planning to liquidate the business and terminate operations as of June 30, the end of the current fiscal year. The partners share profits losses as follows: Ramsey 20%, Smith 30%, and Tolliver 50%. The current June 30 balance sheet account totals are shown below.

PRACTICE **Learning Goal 33, continued**

Solutions are in the disk at the back of the book and at: www.worthyjames.com

LG 33-8, *continued*

Cash	$75,000	Accounts payable	$182,000
Non-cash assets	250,000		
		Ramsey, Capital	25,700
		Smith, Capital	52,100
		Tolliver, Capital	65,200
Total Assets	$325,000	Total liabilities and partners' capital	$325,000

The non-cash assets were sold for a total of $279,000.

a. Prepare a partnership liquidation summary table.
b. Record the liquidation transactions journal entries.

LG33-9. Partnership liquidation

The partnership of Benny, Carlin, and Dangerfield is planning to liquidate the business and terminate operations as of December 31, the end of the current fiscal year. The three partners share profits and losses in a ratio of 3:2:3 The December 31 balance sheet is shown below.

Benny, Carlin, and Dangerfield
Balance Sheet
December 31, 20XX

Assets			**Liabilities and Partners' Capital**		
Cash		$92,000	Accounts payable		$ 47,000
Accounts receivable	$44,000		Notes payable		100,000
Less: allowance for			Total liabilities		147,000
bad receivables	(5,000)		Benny, Capital	$240,000	
		39,000	Carlin, Capital	187,000	
Merchandise inventory		375,000	Dangerfield, Capital	70,000	
Building	628,000		Total partners' capital		497,000
Less: accum. dep'n.	(490,000)				
		138,000			
Total Assets		$644,000	Total liabilities and partners' capital		$644,000

During the liquidation process, the accounts receivable are sold to a collection company for $25,000. The inventory is sold in a "going out of business sale" for $176,000. The building is sold for $151,000. Dangerfield advises the other partners that because he feels that his efforts have never been fully acknowledged, he will not invest any more cash in the partnership, regardless of the outcome of the asset sale.

a. Prepare a partnership liquidation summary table.
b. Record the liquidation transactions journal entries.

PRACTICE **Learning Goal 33, continued**

Solutions are in the disk at the back of the book and at: www.worthyjames.com

Instructor-Assigned Problems

If you are using this book in a class, these review problems may be assigned by your instructor for homework, group assignments, class work, or other activities. Only your instructor has the solutions.

IA33-1 Prepare general journal entries for formation; prepare a balance sheet; allocate net income. On March27, BillBaxter and JaneMiller started a new business formed as a partnership. When the partnership was formed, Bill Baxter contributed the following:

Item	Book Value	Market Value
Cash	$200,000	$200,000
Accounts Receivable	22,000	15,200
Allowance for Bad Receivables		(2,500)
Prepaid Rent	3,000	3,000
Office Equipment	52,000	20,000
Accumulated Deprecation	(24,000)	-0-
Notes Payable	(18,000)	(18,000)

Jane Miller contributed $190,000 cash. Each partner will share equally in profits and losses.

a. Prepare a general journal entry to record the formation of the partnership.
b. Prepare the partnership balance sheet immediately upon formation of the partnership.
c. During the remainder of the year, the partnership earned net income of $40,000. As well, Adams withdrew $8,000 cash and Maxwell withdrew $10,000 of cash. Prepare journal entries to record allocation of the net income and the closing of the drawing accounts.
d. Notice that the partners have agreed to share profits and losses equally, even though they contribute different amounts of partnership capital. What do you think are the reasons for this?

IA33-2 Record various profit/loss allocations. The ABC partnership prepared the following annual information as of December 31, 20XX, the end of its fiscal year's operations:

Partner	January 1 Capital Balance	Drawing
A	$50,000	$10,000
B	20,000	
C	30,000	8,000

Prepare journal entries to allocate year's income or loss for each of the following independent situations:

a. Net income is $90,000 and partners A, B, & C share profits and losses 20%, 45%, and 35%.
b. Net loss is $40,000 and partners A, B, & C share profits and losses in a 3:2:1 ratio.
c. Net income is $100,000 and partners A, B, & C share profits and losses 1/2, 1/4, and 1/4. The partnership agreement specifies a $25,000 salary allocation partner C.

PRACTICE **Learning Goal 33, continued**

Solutions are in the disk at the back of the book and at: www.worthyjames.com

IA33-2, *continued*

d. Net income is $100,000 and partners A, B, & C share profits and losses 20%, 45%, and 35%. The partnership agreement specifies an allocation to each partner as 10% of the beginning capital balance.
e. Net income is $50,000 and partners A, B, & C share profits and losses 50%, 30%, and 20%. The partnership agreement specifies a $30,000 allocation is to be made to partners based on the ratio of their capital balances at the beginning of the current period.
f. Net income is $20,000 and partners A, B, & C share profits and losses 50%, 30%, and 20%. The partnership agreement specifies a salary allocation to B and C in the amounts of $12,000 and $18,000. The partnership agreement also specifies 10% interest on beginning capital balances to each partner.
g. The drawing account balances are closed into the partners' capital accounts.

IA33-3 Record the admission of a new partner. The Davis, Enloe, and Flanagan partnership has decided to admit a new partner, Mary Ramirez, to the partnership. As of August 31, before admitting the new partner but after recording current period income, the partnership capital accounts and profit and loss percentages are as follows:

Partner	August 31 Capital Balance	P/L %
Susie Davis	$57,000	30%
Max Enloe	24,000	10%
Ian Flanagan	69,000	60%

For each independent situation below:

1. Record the admission of the new partner as of September 1
2. Calculate the new profit and loss sharing percentages of each partner.

a. Mary Ramirez pays Susie Davis $50,000 to purchase all of her partnership interest.
b. Mary Ramirez pays Susie Davis $30,000 to purchase one-half of her partnership interest.
c. Mary Ramirez invests $50,000 for a one-fourth interest in the business.
d. Mary Ramirez invests $50,000 for a 20% interest in the business.
e. Mary Ramirez invests $30,000 for a 20% interest in the business.

PRACTICE **Learning Goal 33, continued**

Solutions are in the disk at the back of the book and at: www.worthyjames.com

IA33-4 Prepare a partnership liquidation table; record journal entries. The partnership of Able, Bloom, and Chen is planning to liquidate the business and terminate operations as of June 30, the end of the current fiscal year. The partners share profits losses as follows: Able 25%, Bloom25%, and Chen 50%. The current June 30 balance sheet account totals are shown below.

Cash	$100,000	Accounts payable		$165,000
Non-cash assets	320,000			
		Able, Capital	67,000	
		Bloom, Capital	63,000	
		Chen, Capital	125,000	
Total Assets	$420,000	Total liabilities and partners' capital		$420,000

The non-cash assets were sold for a total of $350,000.

a. Prepare a partnership liquidation summary table.
b. Record the liquidation transactions journal entries

IA33-5 Record the withdrawal of a partner

The condensed balance sheet of the Jones, Knight, and Lewis partnership is shown below as of September 30, 20XX. Profits and losses are shared between the partners as follows: Max Jones:30%; Reuben Knight: 25%; Janine Lewis: 45%. Reuben Knight has decided to withdraw from the partnership as September 30, 20XX.

Jones, Knight, Lewis Partnership
Balance Sheet
September 30, 20XX

Assets			**Liabilities and Partners' Capital**		
Cash		$82,000	Accounts payable		$64,100
Accounts receivable	$24,800				
Less: allowance for bad receivables	(1,100)		Jones, Capital	$190,950	
			Knight, Capital	152,500	
		23,700	Lewis, Capital	217,250	
Merchandise inventory		108,900	Total partners' capital		560,700
Building	920,000				
Less: accum. dep'n.	(609,800)				
		410,200			
Total Assets		$624,800	Total liabilities and partners' capital		$624,800

PRACTICE Learning Goal 33, continued

Solutions are in the disk at the back of the book and at: www.worthyjames.com

IA33-5. *continued*

Record the withdrawal Reuben Knight for each of the following independent situations:

a. With the approval of Lewis, Knight sells his partnership equity to Jones, who pays $175,000 to Knight for his partnership equity interest.
b. The partnership pays partner Knight $35,000 and gives him a note payable for the remaining balance of the book value of his partnership equity.
c. The partnership pays Knight $15,000 cash, gives him $40,000 of merchandise inventory, and gives him a note payable for $87,500 for the total book value of his partnership equity.
d. Based on appraisal, the partners agree that the merchandise inventory has a current market value of $100,000 and the building has a current market value of $980,000. The partnership adjusts the building value change in the Building account. The partnership pays Knight $30,000 cash and gives him a note payable for the balance of his partnership equity.

INTERNET EXERCISES

Are you interested in starting a business? Carefully review these links so that you can access these valuable resources and consider important topics and possible issues, before you start your business:

1) www.sba.gov/starting-business (The Small Business Administration)
2) www.scu.edu/mobi/business-courses/starting-a-business/session-1-deciding-on-a-business/ (Santa Clara University, My Own Business Institute)
3) http://americassbdc.org (Small Business Development Centers)
4) www.score.org (SCORE: Service Corps of Retired Executives)
5) www.nfib.com (National Federation of Independent Business)
6) www.gsa.gov/portal/content/105344 (General Services Administration: How to sell to the U.S. government)
7) www.irs.gov/businesses/small-businesses-self-employed/checklist-for-starting-a-business (IRS checklist for starting a business)
8) www.dol.gov/oasam/programs/osdbu/sbrefa/ (Department of Labor compliance assistance)

For your own state search: "Business Start-up (name of your state)". This will not only provide additional advice, but will also help inform you of local resources available and legal and tax requirements that apply to your own state.

Glossary

Account: a detailed, historical record of all the increases and decreases of a specific item in the accounting equation. (page 396)

Account payable: a legal obligation to pay money, usually as the result of a purchase and usually requiring payment in less than 90 days. (page 154)

Account receivable: the legal right to collect an amount owed by a customer. (page 152)

Accounting: a system of activities that has the objective of providing useful financial information for decision-making. (page 217)

Accounting cycle: a recurring, sequential pattern of accounting activities usually resulting in financial reports. (page 537)

Accrual accounting: an accounting system that records a revenue when it is earned and an expense when it is incurred, rather than when cash is received or paid.; a system that applies the revenue and matching principles. (page 367)

Annual report: a document, usually prepared by a large corporation, that contains audited financial statements, footnotes, and management discussion and analysis. (page 274)

Appropriation of retained earnings: a formally recorded limitation on the use of retained earnings to dividends. (page 616)

Articles of incorporation: a formal application to a state authority for the purpose of creating a corporation. (page 555)

Asset: business property. (page 37)

Authorized shares: the number of shares a corporation is authorized to sell, as permitted by the state granting the corporate charter. (page 560)

Balance sheet: a report that shows assets and claims on assets as of a specific date. (page 294)

Board of directors: a group of responsible individuals who are elected by shareholders and who have the fiduciary duty safeguard the interests of the shareholders, as well as to supervise management. (page 553)

Bonds: long-term debt, usually unsecured and paying only interest before maturity, that are issued to investors in the general public.

Book of original entry: a journal of any kind. (page 450)

Book value: another term for stockholders' equity, usually referring to common stockholders equity; also, the undepreciated cost of a long-term asset. (page 660)

Bookkeeping: another term for the processing function of the accounting cycle, entailing recording and summarizing transactions. (page 218)

Capital: a financial term that can have several meanings including investment resources, owner equity, or business assets. (page 573)

Capitalize: to record an expenditure as an asset. (page 307)

Capital statement: another term for statement of owner's equity. (page 287)

Capital stock: another term for total par or stated value of issued stock. (page 640)

CEO: chief executive officer. (page 553)

CFO: chief financial officer. (page 553)

Charge an account: to make a debit entry. (page 429)

Chart of accounts: a listing of account names and identification numbers. (page 446)

Charter: the legal document brings a corporation into existence. (page 555)

Closely held corporation: a corporation with no publicly traded stock. (page 556)

Codification: the single source of all authoritative generally accepted accounting principles. (page 361)

Common stock: ownership shares issued by all for-profit corporations. (page 573)

Comparability: the quality of information that makes it comparable between companies over time, and therefore useful. (page 276)

Compound entry: a journal or ledger entry containing three or more accounts. (page 461)

Comprehensive income: an amount that represents all current period changes in stockholders' equity except investments and distributions. (page 643)

Consistency: the quality of information that is prepared using the same methods and procedures from one period to the next. (page 276)

Contra equity account: an account that has a debit balance and that acts as an offset against the total of the balances of other stockholder equity accounts. (page 604)

Controller: chief accountant or manager. (page 554)

Convertible preferred stock: preferred stock that is convertible into shares of common stock at some predetermined ratio. (page 584)

Corporation: an entity created by law that is a combined legal and economic entity and is owned by one or more shareholders. (page 70)

Cost of goods sold: the cost of merchandise that was sold to customers. Sometimes also the direct cost of services provided to customers called "cost of services". (page 649)

Cr.: abbreviation for "credit". (page 428)

Credit: a right-side entry or the right side of an account. (page 428)

Cumulative dividend: a feature of preferred stock requiring that all dividends declared must be first applied to prior unpaid preferred dividends before dividends are paid to common shareholders. (page 583)

Date of record: the date by which stock ownership must be officially recorded for the owner to receive a dividend. (page 580)

Debit: a left-side entry or the left side of an account. (page 428)

Deferred revenue: another name for unearned revenue. (page 127)

Deferred tax: the difference between income tax expense shown on an income statement and actual income tax liability reported on the tax return of the same period. (page 662)

Deficit in retained earnings: a negative (debit) balance in retained earnings. (page 616)

Dilution: a reduction in percentage ownership of existing shareholders in a class of stock; also a reduction in earnings per share due to the issuance of new shares. (page 574)

Dividends: non-liquidating distributions of assets from a corporation to its stockholders. (page 572)

Dividends in arrears: Undeclared dividends of past periods on cumulative preferred stock. (page 583)

Double-entry accounting: a system of recording financial changes that requires at least two changes in the accounting equation so that it will stay in balance. (page 94)

Dr.: abbreviation for "debit". (page 428)

Earnings management: methods by which financial statements, the income statement in particular, can be manipulated or biased without technically violating GAAP. (page 361, 712)

Earnings per share (EPS): a calculation that shows the income per share of common stock. (page 656)

Economic entity: any activity or operation for which the financial condition or financial information is to be reported. (page 63)

Economic entity assumption: a fundamental assumption in accounting that it is possible to identify an economic entity for which financial reporting is to be done. (page 64)

Economic resource: a resource that can be measured in dollar value. (page 4)

Ex-dividend date: the date, prior to the date of record, by which a stock must have been purchased in order to allow sufficient time to record ownership and receive a dividend. (page 580)

Expense: a decrease in owner's equity caused by using up resources in business operations. (page 10)

Extraordinary gains and losses: gains or losses resulting from events that are both infrequent an unusual. (page 651)

Fiduciary duty: a special responsibility of trust that requires honest behavior and decision making that is in the best interests of others who rely on this duty. (page 553)

Financial Accounting Standards Board (FASB): the highest non-governmental standard-setting authority in accounting. (page 368)

Full disclosure: footnotes and other material accompanying financial statements that provide a comprehensive and understandable explanation of significant accounting procedures,policies, and conditions affecting the statements. (page 274, 367)

General journal: an all-purpose journal that can record all types of transactions. (page 451)

General ledger: a book or digital file that contains all the ledger accounts. (page 444)

General partnership: a partnership in which all partners have management authority and assume personal liability. (page 753)

Generally accepted accounting principles (GAAP): the rules and method that accountants follow. Authoritative GAAP are required rules and methods. (page 360)

Historical cost principle: the requirement that transactions be recorded at original transaction value, and the value changed only when permitted by GAAP. (page 40)

IFRS: international financial reporting standards. (page 369)

Income statement: a report consisting of revenues and expenses for a specific period that explains the operational change in owner's equity. (page 280)

Income tax return: a document that must be submitted to taxing authorities to calculate and show the amount of income tax that is payable. (page 662)

Incorporator: the person who completes the application process to create a corporation. (page 553)

Intangible assets: assets that do not have physical substance, usually consisting of legal rights. (page 154)

Investment bank: a company that advises and assists corporations in selling stock to the public. (page 559)

IPO (Initial public offering): the first time that a stock is offered for sale to the public. (page 559)

Issued shares: the total number of shares of stock sold or issued for other reasons. (To be distinguished from outstanding shares which are total shares held by stockholders, and from "float" which is the number of outstanding shares that are available to be traded.) (page 560)

Journal: a book or file which maintains a chronological record of transactions, and into which the transactions are initially recorded. (page 450)

Journalizing: recording transactions in a journal. (page 451)

Leasing: renting property. (page 40)

Ledger: a book or digital file that contains ledger accounts. (page 444)

Legal capital: a minimum amount of paid-in capital that must be maintained in stockholders' equity for the protection of creditors until the corporation is liquidated and the creditors are fully paid. (page 568)

Legal entity: the entity that has legal ownership of assets and legal responsibility for debts. (page 68)

Liability: a debt; a creditor's claim on assets. (page 48)

Limited liability company (LLC): a business entity that can have elements of both a partnership and a corporation, and for which the owner does not incur personal liability. (page 557)

Limited partnership: a partnership in which some partners do not have personal liability and management authority. (page 753)

Liquidate: to sell an asset or a business for the purpose of receiving cash; also, to eliminate an obligation. (page 223)

Managerial accounting: a kind of accounting that focuses on detailed internal information needs of a specific company for use by management rather than the general public. (page 274)

Matching principle: the requirement that expense should be recorded in the same period as the revenue that it helped to create. (page 367)

MD&A: management discussion and analysis; found in an annual report. (page 693)

Measurement: another name for the valuation analysis of a transaction; sometimes used to describe all elements of transaction analysis. (page 219)

Negotiable stock: stock that can be freely traded. (page 551)

Net assets: another term for owner's equity. (page 188)

Net cash flow: the net change in cash for a specific period of time. (page 303)

Net of tax: an amount remaining after subtracting tax. (page 650)

Net worth: another term for owner's equity. (page 188)

Non-profit corporation: a corporation that is organized for charitable, educational, or other non-profit purposes, and usually does not issue stock. (page 556)

No par stock: stock with no par value. (page 569)

Note payable: a legal obligation to pay money as the result of a borrower signing a written promise to pay, called a "promissory note". (page 155)

Objective evidence: proof or documentation demonstrating authenticity of an event. (page 40)

On account: a term that means a sale or a purchase that is made on credit. (page 152)

Operating statement: another name for income statement. (page 307)

Organization chart: an illustration that shows the levels of functional authority and titles of positions in an organization. (page 554)

Overstate: to show a number that is too high. (page 362)

Owner's equity: an owner's claim on business wealth. (page 48)

P&L statement: another name for income statement. (page 307)

Paid-in capital: the part of stockholders' equity that is created from stockholders' investments. (page 567)

Par value: an amount per share that establishes a stockholder's limit of liability. (page 569)

Partnership: a business with two or more owners acting as partners. (page 751)

Personal liability: being personally or individually responsible to pay a debt. (page 68)

Price earnings (PE) ratio: the ratio of price per share of stock to the net income per share. (page 656)

Preferred stock: a type of stock that gives its owners a preference in dividends and liquidation before common shareholders. (page 570)

Prepaid expense: an advance payment made to a provider of services before they are used. (page 153)

Prior period adjustment: an entry to the retained earnings account to correct for an error of a prior accounting period that affected net income. (page 617)

Profit and loss statement: another name for income statement. (page 307)

Property: any resource that can be owned. (page 5)

Proprietorship: a non-corporate business that is owned by one person. (page 67)

Public Company Accounting Oversight Board (PCAOB): a federal government organization that supervises and enforces accounting and auditing standards that apply to publicly traded companies. (page 722)

Publicly held (Publicly traded): a corporation whose stock is traded on a public stock exchange. (page 556)

Recognition: the recording of an event as a transaction. (page 220)

Relevance: the quality of information that makes it significant enough to record. (page 276)

Reliability: the quality of information that makes it free from material error or bias. (page 276)

Report form: a balance sheet format in which assets are placed at the top of a page and liabilities and owner's equity underneath the assets. (page 294)

Reserve: an often-misleading balance sheet term that can give the false impression of cash resources available when in fact it is simply an asset offset (contra asset) account. (page 660)

Restriction on retained earnings: a limitation on the ability to pay dividends, usually reported in footnotes. (page 616)

Retained earnings: the part of stockholders' equity that is the cumulative amount of net income or loss since the business was formed, less dividends and certain stockholders' equity transactions. (page 571)

Revenue: an increase in owner's equity resulting from the sale of goods or services. (page 15, 116)

Secondary offering: a sale of stock to the public by a corporation at some time after the first sale (initial public offering) of the stock. (page 559)

Secret reserves: undervalued assets, often in the context of being received for the sale of stock. (page 576)

Security (for a loan): the particular asset or assets that a creditor can claim if a loan is not paid. (page 50)

Service potential: the future benefits provided by an asset. (page 38)

Services: labor or the use of property. (page 5)

Shareholder: another term for stockholder. (page 226)

Single-entry accounting: an accounting system that does not apply the accounting equation to record all parts of a transaction. (page 94)

Stakeholders: people and organizations that have an interest in the financial information of an organization. (page 226)

Statement of cash flows: a report that explains the change in the cash balance for a specified period of time. (page 301)

Statement of condition: another term for balance sheet. (page 307)

Statement of financial accounting standards (SFAS): an official pronouncement of the financial accounting standards board. (page 361)

Statement of owner's equity: a report that explains all the changes in owner's equity for a specific period of time. (page 287)

Statement of retained earnings: a report that explains all the changes in stockholders' equity for a specific period of time. (page 619)

Stockholders' equity: the owners' equity of a corporation. (page 566)

T account: the simplest form of an account, in the form of a left/right T, useful for analyzing transactions. (page 397)

Transaction: any event that causes a change in the accounting equation. (page 96)

Understate: to show a number that is too low. (page 362)

Underwriter: an organization, usually an investment bank, that manages and promotes the new issuance of company stock, frequently purchasing the stock at a discount and then selling it to the general public. (page 559)

Unearned revenue: a liability created by receiving an advance payment from a customer, before goods or services are delivered. (page 127)

Unrealized gain or loss: the potential gain or loss from selling an asset if it were to be sold at its current value. (page 643)

Index

O

P

Q

R

S

T

U

V

W

Essential Math Index

A comprehensive basic math review with explanations, problems, and solutions is included on the disk in the back of this book. The index for this math review is included here for easy reference to the topics covered. The Table of Contents for the Volume 1 math review is also on the disk. The math review continues on the disk with Volume 2.

READ CAREFULLY: YOU ARE AGREEING TO THE TERMS AND CONDITIONS OF THIS LICENSE

GRANT OF LICENSE and OWNERSHIP

The enclosed computer programs and data ("Software") are licensed, not sold, to you by Worthy & James Publishing and in your purchase or adoption of the accompanying textbooks you agree to these terms. Worthy & James Publishing reserves all rights not granted to you. You own only the disk(s) but Worthy & James owns the Software itself. This license allows you to use and display your copy of the Software on a single computer (that is, with a single CPU) at a single location for academic or non-commercial use only, provided that you comply with the terms of this Agreement. You may make one copy for backup, or transfer your copy to another CPU, provided that the Software is usable on only one computer.

RESTRICTIONS

You may not transfer or distribute the Software or documentation to any other person or entity, including the use of networks for simultaneous use on more than one computer. You may not deconstruct, reverse engineer, disassemble, decompile, modify, or adapt the Software, or create derivative works directly or indirectly from the software. This Software is copyrighted.

TERMINATION

This license is effective until terminated. This license agreement terminates automatically if you fail to comply with the terms of this license agreement. Upon termination, you shall destroy the software. All provisions of this agreement in respect to limitation and disclaimer of warranties, limitation of liability, remedies and damages, and ownership rights shall survive termination.

COMPLETE AGREEMENT and GOVERNING LAW

This agreement is the complete agreement between you and Worthy & James Publishing and supersedes any and all other agreements or communications or proposals, written or oral between you and Worthy & James Publishing. This agreement shall be construed in accordance with the laws of the United States of America and the state of California. **IF YOU DO NOT AGREE TO THE TERMS OF THIS AGREEMENT DO NOT OPEN THE DISK PACKAGE.**

WARRANTY LIMITATION FOR SOFTWARE MEDIA

BY OPENING THE SEALED SOFTWARE MEDIA PACKAGE, YOU ACCEPT AND AGREE TO THE TERMS AND CONDITIONS BELOW. IF YOU DO NOT AGREE TO THESE TERMS AND CONDITIONS, **DO NOT OPEN THE PACKAGE.**

THIS SOFTWARE MEDIA IS PROVIDED TO YOU ON AN "AS IS" BASIS, WITHOUT WARRANTY. IF THE SOFTWARE MEDIA IS DEFECTIVE, YOU MAY RETURN IT FOR A REPLACEMENT WITHIN 60 DAYS FROM DATE OF PURCHASE WITH PROOF OF PURCHASE. THIS IS YOUR ONLY REMEDY AND OUR ONLY OBLIGATION. WE DO NOT WARRANT THE MEDIA FOR FITNESS FOR ANY PARTICULAR USE, THAT ITS USE WILL BE UNINTERRUPTED OR ERROR-FREE, OR AGAINST THE LOSS OF DATA. WORTHY & JAMES PUBLISHING, ITS OWNERS, EMPLOYEES, AGENTS, AUTHORS, AFFILIATES, AND PARTNERS, TO THE FULLEST EXTENT PERMITTED BY APPLICABLE LAW HEREBY DISCLAIM TO YOU AND ANY THIRD PARTY, WITH RESPECT TO THIS MEDIA AND CONTENTS HEREIN, ALL EXPRESS, IMPLIED, AND STATUTORY WARRANTIES OF ANY KIND, AND ANY REPRESENTATIONS OR WARRANTIES ARISING FROM USAGE, CUSTOM, OR TRADE PRACTICES. IN NO EVENT SHALL WORTHY & JAMES PUBLISHING, ITS OWNERS, EMPLOYEES, AGENTS, AUTHORS, AFFILIATES, AND PARTNERS BE LIABLE TO YOU OR ANYONE ELSE FOR ANY CLAIM ARISING OUT OF OR RELATING TO THIS MEDIA FOR ANY TYPE OF DAMAGES, INCLUDING BUT NOT LIMITED TO DIRECT, CONSEQUENTIAL, SPECIAL, INCIDENTAL, PUNITIVE, INDIRECT, OR ANY OTHER, EVEN IF ADVISED OF THE POSSIBILITY OF SUCH DAMAGES. ANY LIABILITY FOR US, WHETHER OR NOT IN TORT, NEGLIGENCE, OR OTHERWISE, ALSO SHALL BE LIMITED IN THE AGGREGATE TO DIRECT AND ACTUAL DAMAGES.

DISCLAIMER

The contents of the disk Software that accompanies this book is designed to provide only general educational support and is sold with the understanding that the publisher, author, and contributors do not solicit and are not providing in book and disk contents accounting, financial, tax, legal, or any other kind of professional services. If professional services are needed, then competent professional help should be sought and obtained from other sources and parties. Despite all efforts to ensure that Software media contents are as accurate and useful as possible, Software may contain errors and omissions, and publisher and author make no warranties express or implied, regarding fitness of use of this Software.